TRAVEL AGENT & TOURISM

a manual of travel agency operations

TRAVEL AGENT & TOURISM

a manual of travel agency operations

James W. Morrison

ARCO PUBLISHING, INC.
219 Park Avenue South, New York, N.Y. 10003

```
TO TRAVEL AGENTS & MUFFINS
   Beverly - Cinnamon
   Barbie  - Blueberry
   Sharon  - Blueberry
   Ellen   - Chocolate
```

ACKNOWLEDGEMENTS

We would like to gratefully acknowledge the kind assistance of the Official Steamship Guide and the staff of Transportation Guides Inc., as well as the staff of Ford's Travel Guides.

We would also like to express our appreciation to Official Airline Guides, Inc., for their permission to use the materials from the manuals Complete Instructions in the Use of the North American Edition Official Airline Guide and Complete Instructions in the Use of Worldwide Edition Official Airline Guide in this volume.

Published by Arco Publishing, Inc.
219 Park Avenue South, New York, N.Y. 10003

Copyright © 1980 by James Warner Morrison

Library of Congress Cataloging in Publication Data

Morrison, James Warner, 1940-
  Travel agent & tourism.

  1. Travel agents—Vocational guidance.
I. Title.

G154.M58   338.4'7'91023   79-16402
ISBN 0-668-04746-1

Printed in the United States of America

PREFACE

Travel is now one of the larger industries in the nation and continual growth is a certainty. The interest in travel, both domestic and international, is increasing. With deregulated air fares, international public charter flights and Super Apex fares, short duration packaged trips and low cost air-sea destinations, there is a literal boom in the travel business. The interest in recent years in cruising and the subsequent growth of the cruise line is overwhelming.

Travel agents must deal with every aspect of travel, and must be able to cope with the travelling public, assisting with every travel need. They must be able to quote proper rates, make reservations, prepare necessary documents to any destination in the world by any mode of transportation desired. They must then make recommendations and handle all the arrangements at the client's destination. This might include hotels, transfers, cruises, tours, sightseeing information, special events, and other land arrangements. In short, travel agents must demonstrate an integrated and inter-related knowledge of all travel and tourism.

For these reasons the opportunities for career positions and for advancement are endless. Men and women of every age with every conceivable background are training for and entering the travel field. Those just out of high school or perhaps with a year or two of college can easily learn the methods of ticketing and other travel information. Some have worked for years in less interesting jobs and have never held a job at all. People with experience in office work, or in dealing with people in general, those with experience in sales or handling money plus many secretaries, teachers, waitresses, flight attendants or those just interested in travel - all have the opportunity to be a travel agent. To be an agent or travel agency manager is an exciting and worthwhile job in these modern times.

This book provides an introduction to the world of travel and begins with the history of tourism. The early chapters in the book focus on the role of the travel agent and agency business operations. Other chapters include domestic air ticketing, i.e., terminology, North American OAG, codes of carriers and cities, fares and taxes, air tariffs, and ticketing; and international air-fare calculation and ticketing, i.e., Worldwide OAG, all-year and excursion fares, GIT and APEX fares, international air tariff and mileage system, worldwide ticketing, documentation; and charter and group tours. Additional chapters develop the cruise areas and terminology, major ships and cruise lines, use of steamship guides, cruise sales, freighter and Air/Sea information; as well as rail, bus travel, and related travel services, e.g., rental cars, insurance and other areas. Three special chapters give an introduction to international geography and tourism, including the people and land, tourist attractions and travel advice.

During the development of this book a vast amount of published and unpublished information concerning travel and tourism was searched out and reviewed. The writing of this volume involved a great many contacts with travel agencies, government tourist organizations, air lines, steamship companies and others in the business of travel; the author is grateful for their assistance. A particular note of thanks is given to those travel agents who talked at length with the author since air deregulation. By answering many of the problems included in this text and by offering comments about them, they have made a valuable contribution to the readability, clarity, and validity of the thoughts expressed. A special thank you to Mrs. Sharon Biron, travel agent, for her insightful reading of the text and contributions to the book. Mrs. Ellen Hauge, travel agency manager, provided much needed inspiration and encouragement needed to complete the book. This book could not have been completed without the typing assistance of Marsha Glance, Blanche Duval and Kathleen Scanlon. We are indebted to Cathryn Morrison, Kathleen Richmond and Sue Menery for their graphical assistance. Particular gratitude is extended to Jim Duval and Wendy Follansbee for their careful proof reading of the book.

JWM

CONTENTS

TRAVEL AGENT & TOURISM

a manual of travel agency operations

Chapter 1

HISTORY OF TRAVEL AND TOURISM

The impulse for the voyages and travels of history did not come without a beginning in antiquity: the Franciscan missionaries to Cathay, the seafarers and marching legions of imperial Rome, the geographers of Alexandria, and ultimately the philosophers of ancient Greece. All of these groups and others contributed to the travels of Henry the Navigator, Christopher Columbus and more recently, the voyage of Apollo II to the lunar surface. The great geographers of the ancient world were the Greeks. From their earliest times these people took an interest in their physical environment which was of a far higher order than that of the older worlds along the Nile. In Homer's day, as evidenced by the Odyssey and the legend of the Argonauts, the Hellenes sought to learn of the world around them, while their early philosophers tried to solve the problems of the earth's origin and its place in the celestial system.

THE START OF TOURISM

The ancient wonders of the world were one of the first lists of tourist attractions. The seven wonders of the world of antiquity were:

The Pyramids of Egypt

Tomb Murais - Luxor   Egyptian Tourist Photo

Some 70 pyramids remain in Egypt. The famous are the <u>Pyramids of Gizeh</u>. Of those; the largest, the <u>Great Pyramid</u>, is the tomb of Cheops, a king of the 4th Dynasty, about B.C. 4000 (480 feet in height and 755 feet in length of each base). The second Pyramid, the tomb of Chephren (also 4th Dynasty) is slightly smaller (472 feet X 706 feet); and the third tomb of Menkaura, or Mycerinus (4th Dynasty, about B.C. 3630), is much smaller (215 feet X 346 feet). Each contains entrances, with dipping passages leading to various sepulchral chambers.

The Gardens of Semiramis at Babylon

In legendary history, Queen of Assyria reigned gloriously and she is said to have built the city of Babylon and its famous hanging gardens.

The Statue of Zeus at Olympia

In Homeric mythology, Zeus is king of gods and men; the conscious embodiment of the central authority and administrative intelligence which holds states together; the supreme ruler; the fountain of justice, and final arbiter of disputes. The statue of Zeus at Olympia was the work of Phidias.

The Temple of Diana at Ephesus

The temple of Diana at Ephesus, built by Dinochares, was set on fire by Erostratus for the sake of perpetuating his name. The Ionians decreed that any one who mentioned his name should be put to death, but this very decree gave it immortality.

The Mausoleum at Halicarnassus

The tomb of Mausolus, king of Caria, was erected by Artemisia (his wife) at Halicarnassus; this was the first splendid sepulchral monument, B.C. 353. The name is now applied to any sepulchral monument of great size or architectural quality, e.g., the castle of St. Angelo at Rome.

The Colossus at Rhodes

The Colossus of Rhodes, completed probably about B.C. 280, was a representation of the sun god, Helios, and commemorated the successful defense of Rhodes against Demetrius Poliorcetes in B.C. 304; it stood 105 feet high, and is said to have been made from the warlike engines abandoned by Demetrius by the Rhodian sculptor, Chares, a pupil of Lysippus. The story is that it was built striding across the harbor and ships could pass full sail, between its legs.

The Pharos of Egypt

A lighthouse built by Ptolemy Philadelphus in the island of Pharos, off Alexandria, Egypt was 450 feet high. According to Josephus, it could be seen at the distance of 42 miles. Part was blown down in 793.

In antiquity, travel agents could have planned for their clients a land or sea voyage to Babylon, Rhodes, or Halicarnassus to see the wonders of the known world. Had there been travel agents in the "middle ages," our next stop in history, they might have planned to see these tourist destinations:

The seven wonders of the Middle Ages included these tourist attractions:

The Coliseum of Rome

The great Flavian amphitheater of ancient Rome is said to be so named for the colossal statue of Nero that stood close by in the Via Sacra. It was begun by Vespasian in A.D. 72, and for 400 years was the scene of the gladiatorial contests. The ruins remaining are still colossal and extensive, but quite two-thirds of the original building have been taken away at different times and used for building material. Byron, adapting the exclamation of the 8th century pilgrims says:

> While stands the Coliseum, Rome shall stand;
> When falls the Coliseum, Rome shall fall;
> And when Rome falls--the world.

Rome – Coliseum

Italian Tourist Photo

The Catacombs of Alexandria

A subterranean gallery for the burial of the dead. The origin of the name is unknown, but it does not appear to have been used until about the 5th century (though the catacombs themselves were in existence, and used for burial, long before).

The Porcelain Tower of Nankin

   The Porcelain Tower, a famous porcelain pagoda at Nankin(g), was destroyed by
the Taiping rebels in A.D. 1854. The whole of the brick walls and projection roof
eaves were clothed in splendid colored porcelain tiles, glazed in fire colors (deep
purplish-blue, rich green, yellow, sang de boeuf red, and turquoise blue) which were
intended to suggest the fire jewels of Budhist paradise. The pagoda was composed of
seven tiers, the top one being surmounted by an urnlike element; the entire structure
was set in the hills as part of the Imperial Summer Palace.

The Moseque of St. Sophia

   St. Sophia, Constantinople, was built (C. 335) for Justinian and is considered
a supreme monument of Byzantine architecture with the development of the dome structure. St. Sophia has provided the model for many great moseques. The interior gives
the impression of one vast dome space "as if suspended by a chain from heaven."
There are examples of the original sixth-century mosaics, which were simple decorative
patterns, including Christograms and crosses, on a plain gold ground, in the inner
narthax, and the aisles. There are some wonderful picturial mosaics, dating from the
ninth to the twelfth centuries, set up in various parts of the building. Lofty
minarets were added by the Turks after the capture of Constantinople (1453). The
building is now a museum.

   The palace of the Escurial has sometimes been called the "eighth wonder", a name
which has also been given to a number of works of great mechanical ingenuity, such as
the Palace of Cyrus, the Dome of Chosroes, in Madain, St. Peter's of Rome, the Menai
suspension bridge, the Eddystone lighthouse, the Suez Canal, the railway over Mont
Cenis, the Atlantic cable and similar achievements.

ROMAN TRAVEL AND THE CRUSADERS

   During the Roman Empire, citizens could travel extensively over the roadways.
The maintenance of a large empire necessitated roads, bridges and huge public buildings. The Appian Way was stone-paved with foundations several feet deep; Roman roads
were unsurpassed in quality until the nineteenth century. In the middle of the
Samnite War, in 312 A.D., the censor Appius had begun the Appian Way, which led across
the Pontine Marshes from Rome to Capua. This great example was followed. Seven high
roads leading from Rome, to which were attached twenty secondary roads were also
constructed.

   These grand roads started from Rome: two Appia and Latina, to the south; two
Valeria and Salaria, to the Adriatic: one, Edaminia, to the northeast; two, Cassia and
and Aurealia to the northwest: and, the Via Aemilia serves for both banks of the Po.
Parts of these roadways remain in tact today and are important tourist attractions.

   By 1096 Pope Urban II had three prime motives for calling a Christian crusade
against the Moslems: (1) he hoped to channel the destructive fighting spirit of the
Europeans into work useful to Christianity; (2) he wished to strengthen the claims of
the papacy with regard to temporal affairs; and (3) he wanted to regain the Holy Land
from the Moslems. The eight Christian crusades stimulated travel and trade. These
Crusades and pilgrimages had made men familiar with the produce of foreign countries,
and the twelfth-century man was not at all a bumpkin. The practice of going on
pilgrimages accustomed people to traveling. Considering the difficulties to be over-
come, the twelfth-century men were surprising travellers.

The Great Wall of China

This is now world famous and seen by all visitors to China; much of the wall remains today. The Great Wall of China was built south of the Gobi Desert to serve as a barrier. It was begun about 200 B.C. The wall was intended to keep invaders out of the interior of Asia where they were disturbing the settled farmers.

Stonehenge

The great prehistoric monument on Salisbury Plain, originally consisting of two concentric circles of upright stones, enclosing two rows of smaller stones, and a central block of blue marble (18 feet X 4 feet), known as the Altar Stone. Many theories as to its original purpose and original builders have been propounded. It was probably used (if not built) by the Druids, and from its plotting, which, it is certain, had an astronomical basis, it is thought to have been the temple of a sun god and to have been built about B.C. 1680.

The Leaning Tower of Pisa

The famous Leaning Tower at Pisa, in Italy; the campanile of the cathedral, is 181 feet high, 57 1/2 feet in diameter at the base, and leans about 14 feet. It was begun in 1174, and the sinking commenced during construction. "The Leaning Tower of Pisa continues to stand because the vertical line drawn through its centre of gravity passes within its base."

Takut Bai Ruins - Pakistan   Pakistan Tourist Photo

The Mosque of El Aksa on The Temple
Mount, has a silver dome, in contrast
to the golden Dome of the Rock in
Jerusalem, Israel.

Israeli Tourist Photo

Chaucer's Canterbury Tales gives us another glimpse of popular and colorful
pilgrimages in medieval England. Traveling about the country was still a difficult
matter, and most people made their journeys on horseback. All Chaucer's pilgrims
rode in this way to Canterbury. Carriages were used for ladies, while the men accompanied them on horseback. The team of five horses were necessary to pull the
cumbersome vehicle over the rough roads.

FIRST WORLD TRAVELLERS

From the early history, man has used
the rivers and the sea to transport himself, his many wives, children and herds
from place to place. Along the Euphrates
man began by mastering his equilibrium on
a floating log and then quickly learned
to fasten two logs together with vines to
make a raft.

The main deck of a 350 year-old ship.

Swedish Tourist Photo

As soon as man provided himself with a stone hatchet, he conceived the idea of scooping out a hollow log into a canoe. He probably got this idea from seeing the half of a coconut shell. It took centuries to convince man that boats should be built of iron or steel as well as wood. Then, the wooden vessel as an ocean carrier has been almost driven on the shores of oblivion.

The story of the great Deluge in the Bible affords us the first more or less authentic account of the building of the original ocean freighter. The specifications of that historic sea going menagerie are worthy of the study of every adult. The ark was to be constructed of gopher wood and divided into many rooms to accommodate all manner of living things. It was to be "pitched within and without with pitch," and this is the fashion after which it was built; in length 300 cubits, in breadth 50 cubits and in height 30 cubits. For easy reckoning, the Hebrew cubit has been accepted as 22 inches, which would indicate that Noah's ark was about 550 feet long with great width of beam and depth. Having no machinery, it was therefore of greater carrying capacity than many of our modern ocean cruise ships. The Ark was a three-decker, but was scantily furnished in the matter of windows and doors. The forty-day voyage established its sea going efficiency. As the flood receded, instead of sinking to rest in the soft mud of some fertile valley near Bagdad, it went ashore on the top of Mount Ararat, some 17,112 feet above sea level; flood had covered the earth and destroyed every living thing except those with Noah in the Ark. When the waters subsided, the Ark occupied the highest dry dock in the history of maritime adventure.

Since the days of Noah, there has been a slow evolution of water carriage by different types of raft and boats with poles, oars and sails for motor power. Tyre and Sidon, on the seacoast of Palestine, were the ports from which the trade of Western Asia sought an outlet to the cities of Europe on the Mediterranean Sea seven hundred years before Christ. It is claimed that Phoenician sailors rounded the Cape of Good Hope fully 2,000 years before Vasca de Gama sailed to India.

The story of the gradual development of transportation, including the great square-rigged ships that sailed every ocean before steam took the wind out of their sails, is one of fascinating adventure and romance.

Before the thirteenth century no European had travelled east of Bagdad. Undoubtedly the Crusaders had given many men some knowledge of Syria, Palestine, and even Asia Minor, while there had always been a certain amount of pilgrimage travel to Jerusalem. In 1245 Giovanni de Plano Carpini, a Franciscan Monk, was sent by the Pope on a mission to the Mongol ruler at Kara-Korum, in a remote district of Asia between the Gobi Desert and Lake Baikal, and was the first noteworthy European to travel the Mongol Empire. It was in this period that the Venetian Marco Polo made his famous journey to China. Polo's remarkable experience at the court of Kublai Khan in Peking and other places of the Far East may be read in his work known as The Book of Messer Marco Polo of Venice. Between the years from 1256 and 1295, Marco Polo, destined to become one of the greatest travellers of all time, travelled extensively: journeying through Persia and the Pamirs; crossing northern Tibet; and remaining in China for seventeen years. During these years Marco Polo was admitted to the diplomatic service of the Khan, and was afforded the opportunity to travel widely through Kublai's dominions. In 1292 the trip homeward, proceeding by sea along the coasts of the Malay Peninsula, Sumatra, and India reached Venice three years later. The "travels of Marco Polo" by all odds the most popular and most influential travel book ever written, being represented by at least 138 manuscripts, still is in existence.

The Renaissance (14th - 17th centuries) was a period of tremendous economic opportunity and overseas voyages played a large role. The wealth of new lands quickened the economic pace of Europe; the Portuguese and the Spaniards were the first nations

SANTO DOMINGO'S FIRST TOURIST, CHRISTOPHER COLUMBUS still stands in Parque Colon (Columbas Park) in the Colonial section of town. Santo Domingo Tourist Photo.

to undertake these voyages. The epic figure of The Renaissance was the noble and lofty-minded Prince Henry of Portugal, surnamed "the navigator;" he had the vision which launched Portugal on a century of discovery. By patient, methodical exploration, of each Portuguese expedition, Henry collected information to make the work of the next voyage easier. In Sagres, Portugal, Prince Henry and a group of cosmographers, astronomers and physicians worked with the captains and pilots. Several great improvements may be traced directly to the Sagres academy; the first in the art of chart-making, the second in the craft of ship-building, the third in the science of naviga-tions, e.g., the compass and astrolabe which permitted the mariners to chart an ac-curate course on the oceans. Portuguese mariners explored the middle Atlantic and west coast of Africa. In the Atlantic they discovered and settled the Canaries and Maderira, and discovered the Azores. On the African coast the seafarers were held back by the natural obstacles of unknown waters. By 1486, a quarter of a century after Prince Henry's death, Bartholemew Diaz became the first mariner to sail to the Indian Ocean. More than a decade passed before another Portuguese, Vasco da Gama, actually reached the Orient along the seaway that the discovery of Diaz had discovered. All mankind is indebted to maritime exploration of Prince Henry..."If Columbus gave Castile and Leon a new world in 1492, if da Gama reached India in 1498, if Diaz rounded the Cape of Tempest in 1486...their teacher and master was none the less than Henry the Navigator."

The world traveller Vasco da Gama in 1497 led his little fleet around the Cape of Good Hope, up the East African coast, and across the Indian Ocean to the Malabar Coast, the western shore of India. Cargoes came to the coast by land from the interior of India and by water from eastern India, China, Southeast Asia and Indonesia, known as the "Spice Islands." From the Malabar Coast, Arab merchants transported their goods up the Persian Gulf and over land to Syria or up the Red Sea and over land to Alexandria in Egypt where the Venetians and Genoese bought merchandise for the European trade. Despite the efforts of the Arabs to drive da Gama away, he managed to get a full cargo for his ships. Two and a half years later his fleet returned to Lisbon with a cargo worth enough to reimburse the costs of the voyage sixty times over. The Portuguese were quick to exploit the sea road to riches that da Gama had explored. Portugal had established trading garrisons in India, China and the East Indies in order to secure a trade monopoly. This undertaking was led by the first governor of India, Alfonso de Albuquerque. Under his driving force, the Portuguese settled themselves firmly at Ormuz on the Persian Gulf and at Goa on the Malabar Coast. By the middle of the sixteenth century the Portuguese had stations and trading posts all the way from Macao in China to the Moluccas, to Ceylon, and to Lisbon; and began to settle the eastward bulge of South America, Brazil; but it was the Castilians who first discovered the way to the New World. After the 1588 Spanish defeat by Drake, England and Holland had taken over much of Portugal's profitable commerce.

The second half of the fifteenth century saw more and more discovery; the quest for the Indies inspired men throughout Europe. In 1474 a young man of twenty-three living in Genoa began a very serious correspondence with Paolo Toscanelli, a celebrated Florentine scholar whose hobby was geography, about the possibility of reaching the Orient by a westward passage. Toscanelli, an exponent of the western route to the Indies, encouraged his correspondent Christopher Columbus to make such a voyage. Columbus, an experienced navigator, believed the world to be a sphere and he could sail across the Atlantic and reach the shores of Asia. Columbus took his scheme to Queen Isabella and shortly thereafter he set sail from Palos with three ships in August 1492. After a month of very fast sailing, signs of land became evident, and at two in the morning on October 12, Rodrigo de Triana, on lookout on the Pinta's forecastle, shouted, "Tierra! Tierra!"--the New World has been discovered. Christo-pher Columbus' magnificent plan of reaching the East Indies by sailing westward across the Atlantic was not realized in his lifetime. The Columbus voyage in search of

another sea route to India paved the way for the Mayflower and the countless flotillas of sailing vessels that quickly established an ocean highway between Europe and America.

Spanish explorers continued to push north and south along the eastern coast of the Americas, seeking the passage that would take them to the Indies. They discovered the way in 1520, when Ferdinand Magellan, a Portuguese navigator in employ of Spain, painfully felt his way along the coast of South America with five ships. He sailed through the perilous narrows, which still bear his name(the Straits of Magellan), and across the calm waters of the Pacific to the Philippines. After reaching the Spice Islands, the Victoria (one of the Magellan vessels), sailed around the Cape of Good Hope. This voyage constituted the first circumnavigation of the earth, three years less twelve days from departure. Magellan's voyage demonstrated that the East Indies could be reached by a Pacific crossing, but it had also revealed the immense difficulties of ocean travel.

ARTIFICIAL WATERWAYS AND CANALS

We have been considering the development of transportation over the natural waterways of the earth, of which the oceans and the seven seas rank first, followed by the great lakes, estuaries, rivers, and canals. Man quickly rebelled against the obstructions that nature interposed between his chosen waterways. So, as early as thirteen centuries before Christ, Sisostris cut canals for transporting merchandise running at right angles with the Nile as far as Memphis to the sea. Various attempts were made by Roman emperors to cut a canal across the isthmus at Corinth. China had a canal nearly 700 miles long from Hang-choo-foo to Yan-kiang River in the 13th century.

Sweden's Göta Canal winds like a blue ribbon between Gothenbur/Goteborg, the country's second largest city, and Stockholm, the capital. Leisurely 3-day trips along the canal take visitors through fascinating, scenic countryside.   Swedish Tourist Photo

In Great Britain the earliest canal was one 36 miles long, 10 feet deep and 66 feet wide, from Leeds to Toole. A canal mania struck the United Kingdom toward the close of the 18th century--the longest being a shallow ditch four feet deep from Leeds to Liverpool, a distance of 127 miles. A projected canal to join Stockton and Darlington was nipped in the bud by the survey and construction of the pioneer railway between those two historic points. Ireland had two canals six feet deep, one from Dublin to the green banks of Shannon, 89 miles, and the other from Dublin to Cloondara, both of which are wet to this day. The Cloondara canal was dug in such leisurely fashion that it took 33 years to complete it.

Throughout his life, George Washington, was an ardent believer in canals to connect the great American waterways; he was especially interested in the project of a canal to link Georgetown on the Potomac to Cumberland at the base of the Alleghenies. Among other early canal projects favored by Washington were the Potomac and Ohio, the James and Ohio and the Mohawk and Great Lakes connections.

The canal transportation did not extend to the United States until the second decade of the 19th century. The Erie Canal, begun in 1817 and opened from Albany to Buffalo, 352 miles, in 1825, was the first and most ambitious attempt to solve the growing transportation needs of the United States by an artificial waterway. Between eight and nine million dollars were spent in its construction, but, though 40 feet wide at the top, it was so shallow--only four feet deep--that it was contemptuously referred to as "the longest and most expensive gutter in the world."

It is interesting to recall that three fast-walking horses could draw a canal boat four miles an hour, and it is recorded that "at the end of the fourth day from Schenectady the jaded traveler reached Buffalo." Where it had previously cost $5 and taken 30 days to ship 100 lbs. from Philadelphia to Columbus, Ohio; after the Erie Canal was opened the time was reduced to 20 days and the cost to $2.50. During the first seven years after its completion the business of the Erie Canal doubled and the rejoicings over its prospects seemed justified. The echo of the steam whistle had not yet been heard reverberating along the banks of the mighty Mohawk. Other canals opened about this time were the:

Oswego: Oswego to Syracuse, N.Y.
Cayuga and Seneca: Geneva to Montezuma, N.Y.
Black River: Rome to Carthage
Champlain: Waterford to Whitehall, N.Y.
Delaware and Hudson: Roundout, N.Y. to Honesdale, Pa.   (108 miles)
Morris: Jersey City to Phillipsburg, N.J. (102 miles)
Lehigh: Easton to Coalport, Pa.
Lehigh Delaware Division: Easton to Bristol, Pa.
Pennsylvania: Columbia to Wilkesbarre, Pa. (144 miles)
Pennsylvania West Branch Division (35 miles)
Pennsylvania Juniata Division (14 miles)
Susquehanna & Tidewater: Susquehanna, Pa. to Havre de Grace, Md.
Chesapeake & Ohio: Georgetown to Cumberland, Md. (184 miles)
Dismal Swamp: Elizabeth River to Pasquotonk, N.C.
Ohio: Cleveland to Portsmouth, Ohio (308 miles)
Ohio Hocking Branch
Ohio Walholding Branch
Miami & Erie: Cincinnati to Toledo, Ohio (264 miles)
Illinois & Michigan: Chicago to Illinois River (97 miles)

All these canals were planned, built and opened between the years 1817 and 1849, except the Dismal Swamp (which was begun in 1787 and opened in 1794) a remarkably quick job, as canal digging went in those days. The purpose of this canal was not to drain

the Swamp, but to allow small schooners with a draft of less than five feet to pass safely from Chesapeake Bay to Albemarle Sound.

The Middlesex Canal, connecting Boston and the Concord River in 1804, was really the first canal in the United States designed to facilitate general passenger and freight business. It was 31 miles long, 24 feet wide and 4 feet deep. A packet boat plied regularly between Boston and Lowell, taking nearly a day for the journey. The first "Passenger" boat voyage to Concord, New Hampshire was in 1810; this canal, having served its purpose well, was disused in 1851.

FIRST AMERICAN TRAVELLERS

The schoolboy, who draws an outline map of the nation showing its lakes, rivers, and mountains can get a glimpse of the prospect of transportation and settlement upon which Daniel Boone and other early pioneers were faced with fearlessly. The maps of the early twenties scarcely indicated the post roads between the major cities; and today, interstate highways connect all states and their urban centers.

Colonial travellers of America followed Indian trails and turnpike roads. In early days navigable streams were unbridged, and Washington crossing the Delaware in a scow in a snow storm, as painted, illustrated the dangers that attended land transportation along the coast in those times.

Early American highways, with their variants of byways, paths, trails, roads and streets were well known to our ancestors. Passengers for centuries made their journeys on horses and mules. The evolution from primitive two-wheeled carts to imposing stage coach of the seventeenth century was gradual. In America the first stage coach operated between New York City and Boston in 1782; others ran between New York City and Philadelphia, distance of 90 miles, time three days. The express coach made the run in 12 hours, fare $5.00; the "Diligence" made it in 26 hours, fare $5.50; the accommodation charge was $4.50, stopping overnight at New Brunswick. At this time the coaches were poorly constructed for eight or ten passengers, each being allowed 14 pounds of luggage free. In later years the stage coach was improved, but was never agreeable as the roads were always bad, except in the finest weather.

This highway was a part of the road General Washington took on his memorable journey from Mount Vernon to New York, whither he went to take the oath of office as first President of the United States on April 30, 1789.

Some idea of what long distance travel in the United States of 1807 was may be gained from the account of Aaron Burr's journey on horseback under arrest from Ford Stoddard to Washington, a distance of about one thousand miles. "For days torrential rains fell; streams were swollen; the soil was a quagmire. For hundreds of miles the only road was an Indian trail; wolves filled the forest; savage Indians were all about. At night the party, drenched and chilled, slept on the sodden earth."

It was under similar conditions that earlier in the history of this continent Washington crossed the Alleghenies and with the eye of a seer surveyed the undulating valleys of the Ohio that only needed practical transportation to become the Eden of the West. But his vision of the future only comprehended the possibility of the realization of that vision by means of hard wagon roads and waterways.

Turnpikes or toll roads were first introduced into America in the late eighteenth century. Some turnpikes were surfaced with wooden planks; the first plank road in America was built in 1845 from Syracuse, N.Y. to Oneida Lake, a distance of about 14 miles. The Lancaster Turnpike, a "mechanized road" between Philadelphia and Lancaster, Pa. was built in 1794. The Scottish engineer, John L. MacAdam devised the

road surface which bears his name. These turnpikes fell into disuse by the middle 19th century as railroads proved to be a better means of travel over long distances. Canals also encouraged passenger and freight business.

In his Democracy in America published in 1834, De Tocqueville, the French philosopher, wrote of the Mississippi Valley as the most magnificent dwelling place prepared by God for man's abode and "yet at present it is but a mighty desert." The Louisiana Purchase in 1803 extended our boundaries into this wilderness far beyond the Mississippi, only to make the demand for travel greater than ever. Soon the dirt roads would be travelled by a six-horse Conestoga Wagon, the forerunner of the great "Prairie Schooner."

STEAMSHIP AND TRANSATLANTIC PASSENGER SHIPS

The use of steam power in water travel was most successful and enduring. In 1807 Robert Fulton established a successful steamboat line on the Hudson River and by the 1820's steamboats travelled the Great Lakes and the great rivers of America.

From its earliest days the Savannah Steam Ship Company stated that the SAVANNAH's purpose was the establishment of a commercial transatlantic service by steam. She underwent her trials in late February 1819 and advertisements stated that she would sail from New York for Savannah on 27 March, with ample provision for passengers and cargo. In fact, she sailed on 28 March without either and took 222 hours to complete the voyage, of which 37 1/2 were under steam. Three sailing packets left New York for Savannah on the same day as she did, and two of them got there before her.

Towards the middle of April the SAVANNAH proceeded from Savannah to Charleston, South Carolina, mainly in the hope that President James Monroe would agree to travel on her from Charleston to Savannah, but he could not be persuaded to do so. Instead, the ship carried seven farepaying passengers, which was one or two less than she had on the outward voyage. Upon return to Savannah it was decided to advertise a trip to New York during the early part of May, but only three people booked and the trip was cancelled.

THE "SAVANNAH"
First steamship to cross the Atlantic

The SAVANNAH was the first steamship to cross the Atlantic; she sailed on 20 May 1819 from Savannah, Georgia and her log records that she sighted Cork, Ireland on the 18th of June. The SAVANNAH was a hybrid, for sail and steam, 99 feet long with a 26-foot beam, and registered 350 tons; the paddle wheels were arranged with a series of joints, so that they could be easily detached and hoisted on board, in case of a storm. The eastward run was made mostly under sail; limited fuel permitted use of the engine for only 80 hours. The SAVANNAH had 32 staterooms, but the "terror of steam" kept them unoccupied on her maiden voyage. The nautical feat was significant for American ingenuity seized upon the invention of Watt to improve transportation conditions in the new world.

The SAVANNAH proceeded to Elsinore, Stockholm and St. Petersburg, where she remained a month. She returned to her home port without passengers or cargo, via Copenhagen and Arendal, Norway, and according to most reports the engines were not used until she arrived in the Savannah River. Shortly afterwards she proceeded to Washington to be sold, her engines were removed and she ran as a sailing packet between New York and Savannah until she was wrecked in 1821. Nineteen years elapsed between the SAVANNAH's transatlantic voyage and the first successful attempts by others to start a regular North Atlantic steamship service. In the long run these 1838 voyages were of much greater significance, but great credit is, nevertheless, due to the SAVANNAH and her gallant captain and crew for their pioneer transatlantic steamship crossing.

Until the early 19th century, a ship had sailed only when her captain felt he had loaded enough cargo. By 1814, a group of merchants began to operate regular service between Albany and New York City. Each Saturday one packet sailed from each city; three more lines appeared within a year.

Soon packet service was extended across the Atlantic. In 1818, there was the start of cargo service between New York City and Liverpool by Black Ball Line. In 1840, Samuel Cunard operated regular steamer service between Boston and Liverpool on the BRITANNIA. The 1,135 ton wooden paddle steamer BRITANNIA, commanded by Captain Henry Woodruff undertook the first mail sailing on 4 July 1840 from Liverpool to Halifax and Boston, her 63 passengers including Samuel Cunard himself. Across the Atlantic, which steam had come to make the great ocean highway, conditions were such that millions needed little urging to take up their belongings and travel to the land of liberty and opportunity. Steamer travel boomed between 1846 and 1849. In the wake of the Irish potato famine, Britain ended its restrictions upon grain imports, thus stimulating the United States wheat exports. After gold was discovered in California (1848), there was more travel by sea to the West Coast.

1850 HELENA SLOMAN 800 tons
First German transatlantic steamer

While most of the early steamships were driven by paddle wheels, the LA PLATA (1852) was one of the last wooden Cunarders with steam heating, a cupola over the saloon to give increased height, two libraries and a comfortable smoking room; there were two funnels and two masts.

After the 1840s the screw propeller was available; the 1,794 ton iron screw ATLAS was completed in 1860 for Liverpool and the Mediterranean service but ran extensively on the North Atlantic. There were accommodations for between 40 and 70 cabin passengers and upwards to 500 steerage. Early ocean steamers also carried sails; steam engines were more reliable at the end of the century.

While sailing packets continued to carry passengers until the late 1860's British and German companies soon dominated the transatlantic passenger trade. Inexpensive steerage accommodations in the swift steamships encouraged hundreds of thousands of people to immigrate to the shores of America. Sixty days in a sailing ship was to be two weeks in a steamer from England to America.

The Mississippi Queen steamboat is an American institution, and she is a working cruise vessel. She operates eleven months out of the year and never ties up for more than twelve hours. She is the last of her era, but carries her passengers past milelong strings of barges and ocean tankers.

A journey by paddle-steamer, which plies in the inland river routes of Bangladesh, is a matter of joy for today's tourists.   Bangladesh Tourist Photo

In the last part of the nineteenth century, young Americans, almost unnoticed, were beginning to travel to Europe. These new ocean travellers were not the elite of society, but ordinary people of modest means wanting to see London and Paris, to visit Westminster or Notre Dame, and to know the culture of the Italians and Germans. It was time when Americans in mass were beginning to travel throughout Europe. The luxury ocean liners required steerage or third class return passengers to fill available quarters. As more and more people reported their inexpensive trips to Europe (probably half the cost of first-class travel), others would travel. This was a time in America when the economy was growing and people could afford to travel modestly.

By international law, any vessel with space for more than 12 passengers is classified as a passenger ship, including freighters with passenger cabins to ocean liners built for speed and luxury. Traditionally, ocean liners are primarily passenger carriers, though they carry mail and some high-value cargo. The most outstanding ocean liner at the end of the 18th century was the first OCEANIC,the prototype of six sister ships of White Star Line. With large, grand ballroom having huge chandeliers (candle lit) and fireplaces, the OCEANIC passengers enjoyed more comforts and services (water taps, steamboat, and room services) than did any previous transatlantic traveller.

The greatest ocean liner was the MAURETANIA, burning 1,000 tons of coal a day for her turbines of 68,000 horsepower. MAURETANIA and her sister ship, the LUSITANIA, were launched in 1907; the MAURETANIA trial runs were 26 knots; in later years with oil burner and mechanical improvements she had an average speed better than 27 knots. For more than a year the LUSITANIA and MAURETANIA took it in turns to beat each other's records. Both were then fitted with propellers of improved design, the MAURETANIA subsequently proving herself to be slightly faster. In 1909-11 she averaged well over 25 knots in each direction during the course of 44 round voyages. For almost 22 years she remained the fastest liner afloat. She was a liner that introduced elevators, marble statues, private baths, genuine antique furniture and original decorative oil

paintings. The MAURETANIA was a lady of elegance and luxurious with beautiful wood-work in her public rooms and corridors and oak panels in her dining saloon. The MAURETANIA could carry 2,165 passengers and a crew of 938. She was always a lovely liner with her four enormous black-topped red funnels. After 28 years of service as a passenger liner, hospital ship and American troop transport, the MAURETANIA as the "White Queen" made her last voyage on the 2nd of July 1935. She was a ship that gained the affection of those who knew her.

1907 LUSITANIA 31,500 tons

Recaptured the 'Blue Riband' for Britain. In 1915 torpedoed and sunk with loss of 1,198 lives. Sister ship of the even more famous MAURETANIA.

1914 AQUITANIA 45,647 tons

A larger but slower version of the LUSITANIA. In service until 1949 and crossed the Atlantic nearly 600 times.

The travel business was on the move in the 19th century; anyone with 100 dollars could purchase round trips to Europe. Americans, whose parents had stood at the steerage rail were travelling on the BERENGARIA, AQUITANIA, MAURETANIA, CONTE DI SAVOIA, and ILE DE FRANCE. By June 1929, the BREMEN, a passenger ship with capabilities of a destroyer, had completed her ocean voyage from Cherbourg to Ambrose Light ship in four days, 17 hours, 42 minutes (27.83 knots) - a new transatlantic speed record.

By 1935 there was a gigantic superliner NORMANDIE, a ship without equal, had grace and beauty (with a length of 1,027 feet). The NORMANDIE, 80,000 gross tons with a clipper-type bow, reigned unchallenged on the North Atlantic until Cunard placed the gallant QUEEN MARY in service.

Ocean travel was not confined to the North Atlantic, trans-Pacific passenger liner service from West Coast ports had its beginning in 1867 when the Pacific Mail

established side-wheel steamers from San Francisco. The new transcontinental railway considerably helped the West Coast travel business and led to the establishment of mail steamer service between San Francisco and Australia. By 1882, Oceanic Steamship Company operated MARIPOSA and ALAMEDA between San Francisco and Honolulu. By the 1900's there were several lines serving the Pacific Coast and this growth has continued today. The Pacific Liners have never attained the size and speed of the highest class of the North Atlantic ocean liners, but they represent a choice of five ships. Certainly Pacific Steamers have come a long way from the creaking wooden paddle-wheelers of the 19th century Pacific Mail Line.

OUT OF SINGAPORE, BOUND FOR INDONESIA -- That's Holland America's newest luxury cruise liner, the m. s. Prinsendam, which is making a series of two week-cruises from Singapore to Penang, Belawan, Sibolga, Nias, Padang, Jakarta, Bali and Semarang. The 8,700-ton vessel has a length of 427 feet, width of 62 feet, a depth up to the Promenade Deck of 45 feet and a speed of 21 knots. Holland America Tourist Photo.

LIST OF TRANSATLANTIC PASSENGER SAILINGS
EASTBOUND, JULY 1929

DATE	STEAMER	LINE	FROM	DESTINATION
July 1	France	French	New York	Plymouth, Havre
July 2	California	Anchor	New York	Mediterranean Cruise
July 2	Edam	Holland-America	New Orleans	Havana, Vigo, La Coruna, Satander, Boulogne, Rotterdam
July 2	Edison	National Greek	New York	Patras, Piraeus, Jaffa, Beyrout
July 2	Empress of Australia	Canadian Pacific	Quebec	Cherbourg, Southampton
July 2	Laconia	Cunard	New York	Cobh (Queenstown), Liverpool
July 2	Montclare	Canadian Pacific	Montreal	Cobh, Cherbourg, Southampton, Antwerp
July 2	Providence	Fabre	New York	Ponta Delgada, Lisbon, Naples, Palermo, Piraeus, Beirut, Malta, Marseilles
July 3	Cameronia	Anchor	New York	Londonderry, Glasgow
July 3	Carmania	Cunard	New York	Plymouth, Havre, London
July 3	Columbus	North German Lloyd	New York	Plymouth, Cherbourg, Bremen
July 3	Duchess of Atholl	Canadian Pacific	Montreal	Glasgow, Liverpool
July 3	Edison	National Greek	Boston	Patras, Piraeus, Jaffa, Beyrout
July 3	Estonia	Baltic America	New York	Copenhagen, Danzig, Gdynia
July 3	Homeric	White Star	New York	Cherbourg, Southampton
July 3	Kungsholm	Swedish American	New York	Gothenburg
July 3	Laconia	Cunard	Boston	Cobh (Queenstown), Liverpool
July 3	President Harding	United States	New York	Plymouth, Cherbourg, Bremen
July 3	Providence	Fabre	Boston	Ponta Delgada, Lisbon, Naples Malta, Marseilles
July 4	Cameronia	Anchor	Boston	Londonderry, Glasgow
July 4	De Grasse	French	New York	Havre
July 4	Milwaukee	Hamburg-American	New York	Galway, Cherbourg, Hamburg
July 4	Minnedosa	Canadian Pacific	Montreal	Belfast, Glasgow
July 4	Muenchen	North German Lloyd	New York	Southampton, Boulogne, Bremen
July 4	Republic	United States	New York	Cobh (Queenstown), Plymouth, Cherbourg, Bremen
July 5	Andania	Cunard	Montreal	Glasgow, Belfast, Liverpool
July 5	Acania	Cunard	Montreal	Plymouth, Havre, London
July 5	Duchess of Bedford	Canadian Pacific	Montreal	Cherbourg, Southampton
July 5	Republic	United States	Boston	Cobh (Queenstown), Plymouth Cherbourg, Bremen
July 6	Albertic	White Star	New York	Queenstown, Liverpool
July 6	Arabic	Red Star	New York	Plymouth, Cherbourg, Antwerp
July 6	Augustus	Navigazione Gen. Italiana	New York	Gibraltar, Naples, Genoa
July 6	Deutschland	Hamburg-American	New York	Cherbourg, Southampton, Hamburg
July 6	Frederik VIII	Scandinavian-American	New York	Christiansand, Oslo, Copenhagen
July 6	Ild de France	French	New York	Plymouth, Havre
July 6	Laurentic	White Star	Montreal-Quebec	Liverpool
July 6	Minnewaska	Atlantic Transport	New York	Cherbourg, London
July 6	Stavangerfjord	Norwegian America	New York	Bergen, Stavanger, Kristianssand, Oslo
July 6	Veendam	Holland-America	New York	Plymouth, Boulogne-Sur-Mer, Rotterdam
July 7	Albertic	White Star	Boston	Queenstown, Liverpool
July 7	Aquitania	Cunard	New York	Cherbourg, Southampton
July 9	Empress of Scotland	Canadian Pacific	Quebec	Cherbourg, Southampton
July 10	Majestic	White Star	New York	Cherbourg, Southampton
July 10	Montrose	Canadian Pacific	Montreal	Plymouth, Cherbourg, Southampton, Hamburg
July 10	Tuscania	Cunard	New York	Plymouth, Havre, London
July 11	Cleveland	Hamburg-American	New York-Boston	Galway, Cherbourg, Hamburg
July 11	Megantic	White Star	Montreal-Quebec	Southampton, Havre, London
July 11	Scythia	Cunard	New York	Galway, Liverpool
July 12	Alaunia	Cunard	Montreal	Plymouth, Havre
July 12	Letitia	Anchor-Donaldson	Montreal	Belfast, Liverpool, Glasgow

The largest and fastest ocean liners were built primarily for passenger travel between the United States and Europe. Smaller liners transverse other routes; many specialize in vacation cruises. By the 1970's the world's largest liners were: France's France (66,348 gross tons, 1,035 feet long, and 111 feet in beam), and

Britain's QUEEN ELIZABETH 2 (65,863 gross tons, 963 feet long, 105 feet in beam) were used in North Atlantic only during the peak tourist seasons and were used in cooler-months as vacation ships in the Caribbean cruise service. The FRANCE relied on spaciousness, elegance, fine food and gracious service to win her share of trans-Atlantic passengers. The UNITED STATES was the fastest ocean liner in the world; she set both transatlantic speed records in 1952 (3 days, 10 hours, 40 minutes eastbound; 3 days, 12 hours, 12 minutes westbound). The record-holding UNITED STATES (53,330 gross tons, 990 feet long, and 101 1/2 feet in beam) could accommodate 2,000 passengers and her top speed exceeded 40 knots.

Cunard "QUEEN ELIZABETH 2"

Transatlantic passenger travel includes fast elevators, more deck space, full-size tennis courts, and one class service, but all of this has declined since the Second World War. Cruise passenger service in 1977 is the growing travel business with more than one million passengers on Caribbean cruise ships. The following page shows a cruise ship coming into a Caribbean port.

A cruise ship comes into a Caribbean port.

RAILROADS

It was the British who perfected the basic design of the locomotive and introduced the separate firebox, multitubular boiler, direct connection to the wheels,
blast pipe and other fundamental features that remained with the steam locomotive to
the end of its production. American improvements - mainly in running gears - were
hardly as fundamental or as far-reaching as the work of the British designers, who had
perfected their basic design by 1830. The Rocket, winner of the Rainhill Trials in
1829, was the first locomotive to incorporate all these features.

Although importing many British locomotives in early days, the Americans quickly
found that the short wheelbases and rigid-frame construction of the English basic
designs took unkindly to their own railroads. At the beginning of the railway age the
U.S.A. was largely a rural nation, with little capacity for large capital investment;
and in contrast to contemporary conditions in England, where manufacturing centres
that had grown up during the Industrial Revolution, urgently needed better communications.

The first steam locomotive to run in America made a trial trip over the tracks
of the Delaware and Hudson Canal Company in Pennsylvania in 1829. The Baltimore and
Ohio Railroad began regular operation in the summer of 1830. In December 1830, an
American-built locomotive, the "Best Friend of Charleston," hauled a train of cars on
the tracks of the South Carolina Railroad. This operation combined the essentials of

track, trains, mechanical power and common carrier services. The railroad had come
to America. These early American railways started from the six Atlantic ports and
within twenty years four rail lines had crossed the Alleghenies to reach their goal
on the "Western Waters" of the Great Lakes and the tributaries of the Mississippi.

Charles Dickens describes in his American Notes what happened when he travelled
in 1842: "We left Harrisburg on Friday. On Sunday morning we arrived at the foot
of the mountain, which is crossed by railroad. There are ten inclined planes; five
ascending, and five descending; the carriages are dragged up the former, and let
slowly down the latter, by means of stationary engines; the comparatively level spaces
between being traversed, sometimes by horse and sometimes by engine power, as the case
demands. Occasionally the rails are laid upon the extreme verge of a giddy precipice;
and looking from the carriage window the traveller gazes sheer down, without a stone
or scrap of fence between, into the mountain depths below."

Dickens tells how they "rattled down a steep pass, having no other moving power
than the weight of the carriages themselves and saw the engine released long after us
come buzzing down alone, like a great insect, its back of green and gold shining in
the sun, that if it had spread a pair of wings and soared away, no one would have had
occasion, as I fancied, for the least surprise. But it stopped short of us in a very
business-like manner when we reached the canal; and before we left the wharf, went
panting up the hill again, with the passengers who had waited our arrival for the means
of traversing the road by which we had come." From that point the novelist took a
canal packet on to Pittsburgh and continued by steamboat to Cincinnati.

Appleton's Railway Guide for October 1862 gives an authentic picture of the passenger facilities of the railways. There were no through service between two American
cities in 1862. The Central Railway of New Jersey advertised the shortest time to the
west - "Time from New York to Chicago in 36 hours." The Central operated an express
train from Jersey City to Pittsburgh without change over its own rails to Easton;
Lehigh Valley to Allentown; East Pennsylvania R.R., to Reading; Lebanon Valley R.R. to
Harrisburg, and Pennsylvania Central to Pittsburgh, in 16 hours and 5 minutes. At
Pittsburgh the traveller took the Pittsburgh, Fort Wayne and Chicago Railroad, composed
of that line, the Ohio and Pennsylvania and the Ohio and Indiana, to Chicago, a routed
467 miles.

In 1862 the great New York Central System had no Hudson River attached to its
title and its time tables began with Troy and Albany and ended at Buffalo. At that
point its trains connected "with the Lake Shore Railway to Erie, Cleveland, Sandusky,
Toledo and thence to Chicago by Michigan Southern Railway." The distance between
Chicago and Albany over this combination was 836 miles, to which has to be added the
144 miles from East Albany, reached by ferry via the Hudson River Railway to New York,
making a total of 980 miles, which is practically identical with the distance today,
if Buffalo is visited en route. The journey with all connections consumed between
38 and 39 hours.

In the time tables of 1862, scrupulous attention is paid to the difference in
time between stations, the New York Central note reading: "Standard of Time Clock in
Depot at Albany, which is 21 minutes faster than Buffalo time." On the New York &
Harlem Railway, which started at the City Hall with stops at White and Center streets,
26th, 42nd and Yorkville before it reached Harlem, the standard of time was the "Clock
in Superintendent's Office, 26th Street, New York." Frequent reference was made to
the "Time Indicator" illustrated on the following page.

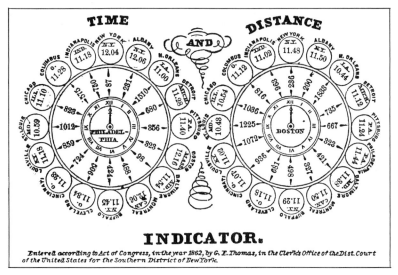

How they set their watches in 1862, before the introduction of standard time.

An interesting feature of the reading matter accompanying the time table of the Hudson River Railway, which left from the corner of Chambers Street and College Place, was the claim that "Trains of this road run with an expedition, dispatch and regularity not surpassed by any other in the country." But even more interesting, as showing the primitive measures taken to secure "the almost entire exception from accidents and collisions" claimed by the management, is the following statement: "One characteristic of this road deserves especial mention. We refer to the system of signal flags introduced to secure safety from accidents in running the trains. Flagmen are stationed upon every mile of the road, generally at the curves, or upon a slight acclivity, where a view of the track from some distance can be had. Upon the approach of a train, if all is clear ahead, the flagman displays a white signal. If there is any obstruction in sight, or a diminished speed is required, a red flag is displayed."

Through the vision, energy and organizing genius of one man, there was a departure in passenger car construction. Little had been done to relieve the long distance traveller from the tedious discomforts of the primitive passenger car. As railway lines extended their tracks farther and farther from the seaboard, these discomforts became a serious problem. Only immigrants, prospectors and persons travelling on business cared to face a night on an American railway train. The luxuries of seeing America were not to be found on the trains. The steamers on the Hudson and up the Sound from New York were literally floating palaces, with generous staterooms for those who could afford the price.

The railway sleeper of the early '50s had not advanced far from the makeshifts of the '30s and '40s. Their builders apparently took canal bunks or shelves for their models. Sometimes narrow mattresses, hardened into something resembling granite from frequent usage, were provided; more seldom an unaired blanket or unlaundered sheet was thrown in and the sleeper used his old-fashioned carpetbag for a pillow. When he was about to retire his eye fell on the necessary warning, "Passengers will please remove their boots before getting into the berths." Under such conditions George M. Pullman took a night train from Buffalo to Westfield. The distance was not great, but the discomforts were many and the conveniences were none. Possibly out of the nightmare of the experience he saw visions of the palace sleeping cars and hotels on wheels that were to herald his name to the ends of the earth. It was by 1858 Mr. Pullman had already acquired the knowledge, experience and organizing ability that was to redound to his fame and the comfort of American railway travel.

The railroad is no longer a major means of passenger transportation in the United States, though railroad passenger service thrives in much of the rest of the world. As recently as the early 1940's there was more than 20,000 daily intercity passenger trains; by the early 1970's there were only 200. In 1971, the National Railroad Passenger Corporation, a Federal agency known as AMTRAK, took over most of the intercity railroad passenger service. AMTRAK trains operate in the Northeast corridor between Boston and Washington, DC, and a large part of the New York-Washington service is by high-speed electric trains called Metroliners. AMTRAK now offers additional service throughout the nation.

AIR TRAVEL

The first successes in the history of aviation met with a durable skepticism that is in many ways attributable to the intensity of the human desire to fly. The first powered flight in history took place at 10:35 on the morning of December 17, 1903 when Orville Wright remained aloft for twelve seconds and covered a distance of 120 feet. It is not very often in history that an achievement can be precisely credited, but there is no doubt that Wilbur and Orville Wright were the first to fly a powered heavier-than-air craft. It was not until Kitty Hawk that Man was finally able to imitate the birds. Twenty four years later Charles Lindbergh flew alone across the Atlantic. And less than 45 years after the success of the Wright Brothers, airlines would fly faster than the speed of sound.

Commercial aviation started in 1909 when the Count Ferdinand von Zeppelin formed an airship passenger service. In the next five years, commercial Zeppelins carried more than 35,000 passengers over 170,000 miles between German cities without a single injury. The first airship crossing of the Atlantic was made in 1919 by a British crew; German passenger flights to North and South America followed not long after. These flights were smooth and the accommodations were luxurious; the 1937 fare was $700 round-trip between America and Germany. The age of Zeppelin passenger service abruptly ended on the 6th of May 1937 with the Zeppelin Hindenburg disaster at Lakehurst, New Jersey.

American Airlines DC-3 in Flight

American Airlines Photo.

Commercial air transportation in the United States begins with air mail service. As early as 1912 the Post Office Department requested Congressional authority to begin regular airmail service; by 1925 the Kelly Air Mail Act provided mail-carrying contracts with the airlines. The first carrier to fly under contract (1926) was Varney Speed Lines, a former runner of United Airlines; Western Air Express (Western) provided scheduled mail service between Los Angeles and Salt Lake City; and Pitcairn Aviation (Eastern) flew the mail between New York and Atlanta. This mail service gave way in the 1930's to passenger service. The first airplane passenger service in the world was offered in 1914 by the St. Petersburg Tampa Airboat Line which operated two flights a day. Some 1200 passengers took the twenty minute flight at a cost of $5.00 a ticket.

Most certainly early commercial aviation was looking forward to the jet age with these few words from "The Aircraft Year Book of 1930" (Aeronautical Chamber of Commerce of America: "...the safety, comfort and conveniences of the passenger became paramount considerations...The chairs had been studied and changed so that the passenger rode more easily...full course dinners on long flights...Hot and cold running water brought added comfort...Motion pictures were introduced as an experiment to entertain passengers on long flights...").

The airline industry developed at a time when foreign travel was restricted primarily to individuals of wealth with time to travel. Travel by steamship took a week from New York to Southampton, England, and also twenty days to Rio de Janeiro; nineteen days from San Francisco to Japan. This was an age when the average worker with limited funds and two weeks of vacation a year lived his entire life without ever leaving his homeland. A trip to Europe, South America or the Orient was out-of-the question. Early air carriers like Pan American and American Airlines provided new opportunities for the traveller.

By October 28, 1927, a Pan American Fokker trimotor airplane flew from Key West, Florida, across a narrow stretch of water to Havana, Cuba. It was a first flight and the first scheduled international flight by an American airline.

Pan Am was soon carrying passengers, mail and cargo on a regular schedule throughout the Caribbean and into Mexico and Central America. Pan Am was a major international airline with a 12,000-mile route system linking the United States with 23 Latin American countries.

In the early 30's Pan Am's Sikorsky S-40 flying boats, the world's first commercial 4-engine aircraft, started flying the length of South America. In November, 1935, the China Clipper (built by Martin to Pan Am's specifications and the largest air transport constructed) inaugurated transpacific service between the West Coast and Manila. Less than four years later, in May, 1939, the Boeing Pan Am flying boat, Yankee Clipper, made the first scheduled flight across the Atlantic.

By 1958 Pan Am led the world into the jet age. On Oct. 26, Pan Am's Jet Clipper America, a Boeing 707, inaugurated U.S.-flag jet service to Europe and to destinations all over the world. The impact of the new jets was significant. The flying times were reduced by fifty percent. For the first time in history, a traveller could go from anywhere to anywhere in the world - in just hours. Lack of time was no longer a reason not to travel.

Pan Am started operations with a fleet of two trimotor airplanes, 24 employees and one 90-mile route. During their first year they carried 1,184 passengers. Today they have a fleet of 95 jet aircraft, 27,000 employees and they serve an 88,000 mile network connecting 71 cities on six continents. In 1968 Pan Am carried more than 10 million passengers.

In the early 1930's there were several small and struggling airlines operating in the East, Midwest and Southwest. One group was Colonial Air Transport, parent company of the airlines that had inaugurated Boston-New York, New York-Montreal and Albany-Cleveland service. Another was Universal Aviation Corporation, one of whose predecessors, with Charles A. Lindbergh as chief pilot, inaugurated scheduled St. Louis-Chicago flights. Still another was Southern Air Transport, a Texas-based system. These airlines whose routes became American Highways, then became American Airlines in 1934.

In 1936 American introduced the famous DC-3 airplane. By 1949, American had nearly completed a program to replace its DC-3s and DC-4s with modern, pressurized DC-6s and Convairs. The longer-range DC-7s came along in late 1953 and by 1954 they were providing nonstop transcontinental service in both westbound and eastbound directions.

January, 1959, American inaugurated the country's first transcontinental jet service with its Boeing 707s. By 1964, American installed Sabre, then the largest electronic data processing system designed for business use and has continued in useful service for travel agents.

A major event in American commercial aviation did not happen until 1929 when Transcontinental Air Transport, the company that eventually became Trans World Airlines, was established. By 1930 there were 43 "scheduled" airlines. The principal source of revenue for all the companies was the government mail subsidy, which was lucrative enough to permit the gradual expansion of passenger service.

Several companies were building the tri-motor transport planes. The tri-motors made an important contribution to the civil aircraft industry because of their reliability. The aircraft was not considered safe enough to carry paying passengers. The "Boeing Monomail" was a low-wing monoplane built in 1931 especially for postal service; it was the first American transport aircraft with retractable landing gear. A year later the Boeing 247, a twin-engined low-wing monoplane with retractable landing gear, was the first really modern passenger airliner. Exclusively available to United Airlines, it made a success of that company, and forced Transcontinental Air Transport to commission a similar airplane from Douglas. The result was the DC-1 and eventually 200 DC-2 were built. Its succession, the DC-3, first flew in late 1935, and became one of the most prestigious aircraft in the world. More than 13,000 were built. The DC-3 became the standard for the world's passenger airlines; many hundreds of them are still in service around the world. This aircraft increased public confidence in commerical aviation and greatly expanded passenger air travel.

The Congress encouraged passenger service and in the early 1930's as routes were established (and fleets were expanded with Boeing 247's and Douglas DC-3s) dozens of small companies merged to form the operation that eventually became the largest airlines today: Transworld, Pan American, Eastern, United, and American Airlines. By 1936 Pan American World Airways inaugurated transpacific service: San Francisco to Hawaii and Manila, with China Clipper flying boats. Three years later Pan American offered regular transatlantic service.

Commercial air transportation on a world scale saw a tremendous expansion following World War II with new aeronautical facilities, i.e., landing strips, terminals, meteorological services, communications and other technical equipment. Atlantic and Pacific flights became commonplace and the foundation of today's networks of world commercial air transportation was firmly established.

Trans World 747   Trans World Airlines Photo

After 1958 Boeing 707 jets were carrying 150 passengers on intercontinental
passenger service. Ten years later the Boeing 747 "Jumbo Jet", the largest commercial
aircraft, went into world service. With thousands of air terminals scattered over
the world, air routes can be regulated, changed or discontinued without major difficulty. Proven as economically feasible, the major air routes tend to remain relatively
stable year after year.

Chapter 2

THE TRAVEL AGENT

One sporting definition with some truth about the travel agent comes from an anonymous English poem. Good travel agents certainly search the unusual as well as the usual, in order to serve their clients' travel needs.

ODE TO A TRAVEL AGENT

"Salute to the agents that travel the earth,
Seeking and searching to find you a berth.
Taking nothing for granted and looking instead,
At the lobby, the loo, and under the bed.
Off in pursuit of their tireless rounds,
Of restaurants and ships, like little bloodhounds.
Their elegant nostrils twitching with pleasure,
At the thought of pursuing a trail for your leisure.
With eyes on your welcome, wallet, and purse,
They'll see that you cheer rather than curse.
Since you've worked hard for each dollar you spend,
A word to your agent saves pounds in the end.
So don't give your plans a chance to unravel,
Ring up these dears, the agents of travel."

AN EARLY TRAVEL AGENT

An Englishman, Thomas Cook, arranged his first tour in 1841, a one-day train excursion for 570 temperance leaguers journeying from Leicester to Loughboro. This Midland Countries Railway Company tour had a five percent commission. In 1851 he provided ocean liner travel and accommodations for 150,000 visitors to the World Exposition (Fair) in London. Thomas Cook, with steamship agents, began to see the business in travel and to establish themselves on both sides of the Atlantic. Foreign travel in the beginning was limited to aristocrats. By 1856 there were grand tours of Europe, i.e., "Cook's Tour of Europe". He pioneered winter travel to the Holy Land and Egypt, built hotel, operated his own Nile Steamer, started the Bermuda Honeymoon, and sent English families to America to see Niagara Falls and Yellowstone.

Thomas Cook wanted to share his love affair with travelling by making it almost as easy to take a trip around the world as a walk around the block. He started the world's first travel agency because he believed travel should be free of care. He published the first travel magazine because he believed people should know about where they were going and what to expect when they got there.

An imaginative and adventurous fellow, Cook believed travel was one of life's unique pleasures. And that, above all, it was meant to be enjoyed - every moment - so the memories would last a lifetime.

In time, travel changed - steamships, rail and airlines became the popular mode of public transportation and made mass travel a reality. Tourism has flourished on the seas, land, and in the air.

TRAVEL AND TOURISM

Travel and tourism is the third largest retail industry in the United States in terms of consumer sales. In 1978 travel accounted for about $120 billion in domestic spending (some six percent of the gross national product) and was exceeded only by the food and automotive market.

Travel directly employs 4.4 million people at every level of skills, and indirectly produces another 2 million supporting jobs. Travel provides large numbers of entry-level positions and is preeminent in the employment of women, youths and members of minority groups. At a time when the service sector accounts for most employment growth, travel is visibly the world's leading labor-intensive service industry. Travel is a highly diversified industry with some 1.4 million component companies ranging from small travel agencies to large airlines and hotel chains.

Over 16,000 retail agencies book almost $12 billion for the public's travel by plane, and for hotel space and related travel services. The agencies receive about $1 billion, from this amount of revenues, most in the form of commissions. After paying expenses, life office equipment, office space, and salaries of employees, the net profit produced is approximately $60 million.

The travel and tourism industry, with its many diverse components, has become an increasingly important element in the national economy. It is vital at this time that we as a nation grant the tourism and travel industry the attention it deserves. Its importance affects not only the economic stability of the nation but also strengthens the hope of better communications and understanding between all the nations of the world. Its importance as an economic educational, cultural and diplomatic tool has long been underestimated. Very often it provides a bridge for better communications and understanding between the different countries of the world.

Travel has become essential to the way people carry out their business. You just cannot imagine a modern economy without business travel. But travel's importance is more than economic. It is an extraordinary industry that confers a unique array of social and intangible benefits on the people of the world. It is at the heart of this nation's value system, which supports the free flow of people and ideas. It enables tens of millions of families to fulfill some of their dreams, and to return to their daily lives rested in body and enlarged in spirit. Last year, more than 100 million Americans left their homes on overnight personal, pleasure or business trips.

SMILINE SERVICE - Passengers begin boarding a PSA smiling Boeing 727 on one of more than 180 daily flights between 13 California cities. During 1977, PSA carried more than 7.2 million passengers, making it the largest intrastate airline in the world.

Pacific Southwest Airline

TRAVEL AGENTS

Beginning with North Atlantic steamships and continuing with jet-age aircraft, the business of tourism has become a major growth industry. The number of travellers in Europe in 1978 was over four million Americans, despite stories of rising costs, fuel and energy crisis, inflationary problems, and airport delays.

Some 20 million foreigners visited America in 1978; they came partly because the drop in the value of the dollar makes the U. S. a travel bargain for sightseers financed by Japanese yen, German marks, and Swiss francs. The biggest increase in recent years has come in travel from Britain, due to lower airfares (Apex) between London and New York.

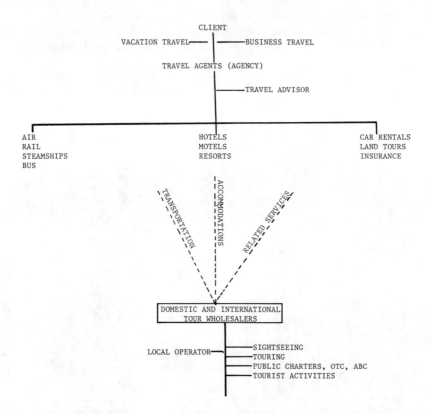

Transportation of all kinds are abundant. at affordable prices. World travellers are everywhere, and many arrange their trip through a travel agent. The travel agent is a trained professional whose experience enables him or her to counsel a client on how to travel wisely and within the confines of a budget. The job of the agent is based on specialized knowledge and skill in obtaining reliable travel information for each customer. The agent is not an order taker, The travel agent arranges transportation such as air, steamship, cruises, bus, rail, car rentals, and other related services; prepares individual itineraries, personally escorted and group tours, and travel packages; and arranges for accommodations including hotels, motels and resorts. Travel agents handle and advise clients on the many details of modern travel, and use professional knowledge and experience to interpret train schedules, hotel rates, and airline schedules.

Beirut, the capital of the Lebanese Republic.   Lebanon Tourist Photo

The agent is a genuine bargain in today's inflationary world. Hotels, packages, airlines, car rental services and tours pay a commission to the agency for the business it sends their way. Airlines pay agents commissions of eight percent of the fare for travel in the United States, 8 to 10 percent for international passage. Hotels usually pay agents 10 percent; so do steamship companies for cruise trips; and so do airlines for air tours. For regular steamship travel the agent's fee ranges 10 percent of the fare. Railroads pay 10 percent commission to agents for organized trips. Sometimes commissions are higher depending on the promotion and kind of travel service.

The traveller cannot save the cost of these commissions by avoiding the travel agent. The fare is the same for all and commissions are usually paid to the agent after the trip, and then only if the agent is recognized by the trade associations to which the carriers and hotels are members. Recognition is based on the agent's experience and financial stability, and is not given lightly by any association of airlines or steamship companies. Clients are not usually charged a fee for the agent services; charges are assessed for special services when the commission does not cover the actual expenses.

Travel agents are interested in their clients' needs and where they want to travel. A reputable agent does not hustle his customer into certain tours or push certain places. The agent is in business-like retail environment; anticipates a returning customer; and hopes to be recommended to others interested in travel.

A good agent spends a part of the working year taking what are known as familiarization ("fam") trips. The wholesale tour operators (people who organize packages including transportation, hotel and sightseeing travel), airlines, and hotels invite travel agents, after one year of full-time working experience, to evaluate their offerings. It is sometimes possible for an agent to personally recommend a particular tour, for example, because of a "fam" trip. Generally the travel agent has had enough experience to know the various elements (destination, hotel, carrier, tour operator) of any trip and will be able to judge the worth of particular tours for his client.

It is the responsibility of the travel agent to protect his client from unreliable packages (who frequently go bankrupt without warning): a client on arrival in London, discovers the luxury hotel is "overbooked" and must stay in a rooming house; cancellation of an advertised tour and no refund; excessively high penalties when a client

cancels; or last-minute price increase on packages. A well-established, professional travel service can prevent these disappointments. The agency knows that delivery of good service, no matter what the cost of the trip, means a satisfied client will become a regular customer. Responsible travel counselors must always be knowledgeable, friendly, helpful and inspiring to the traveller.

The agent saves the customer trouble, time and even money when compared to the cost of making his own arrangements. As the result of one call, in person or on the telephone, the agent makes reservations which can involve a number of kinds of transportation and several stopovers in different cities. The agent makes the reservations, pays the bills (i.e., steamer tickets, hotels, special tours) no matter how many different ones there may be on the itinerary.

A legitimate travel agent is willing to listen to the client, to help with advice based on his or her own experience and to make any or all arrangements for the trip, whether you are planning a week's cruise trip from New York to Nassau for two (at a total cost of about $450.) or a six-week air trip around the world for two (around $5,000.) or a week-long vacation by air from Los Angeles to Hawaii (around $950.).

It is difficult to find a vacation trip for two persons for less than $300 a week, but the travel agent probably knows of one or two. A recognized travel agent receives literature, brochures, and other information from carriers, hotels and government tourist bureaus all over the world. The agent knows the rates and accommodations available in the national parks and at resorts.

The travel agent can explain the difference between first and second-class sleeping accommodations on Europe trains (first class has luxury beds, second class has narrow upper and lower bunks). The agent can inform the client on exactly what services will be received when travelling, first, second, or third class, no matter what names are used to describe the classes. The travel counselor knows about tipping and can advise about the services and charges of hotels and other housing where the daily rate includes two or three meals and lodging. Agents can advise on an American plan (meals included) or European plan (room only); and book sight-seeing tours, and find insurance protection. A travel agent is prepared to do almost anything that is legal.

AGENCY APPOINTMENT REQUIREMENTS

Nearly everybody knows that the travel agent has a professional responsibility to the business of travel. The travel agent serves the client on a personal basis and is able to provide more varied and individual services than the airline representative. Air carriers do not have the locations nor the offices in many cities; consequently travellers contact the airlines by telephone (and maybe Ticketron in near future). The travel agency acts as the "agent" for all airlines, steamships, railroads, car rentals, buses, hotels, tour operators, and sightseeing companies. It is important that a travel agent be able to operate effectively and efficiently within these service areas.

Pioneering Eras of commercial aviation progress are represented by these aircraft which have served during the five decades of TWA's history.   Trans World Photo

AIR TRAFFIC CONFERENCE OF AMERICA

In 1936 the Air Transport Association of America (ATA) was formed by the domestic air carriers in order to establish regulations and procedures which all the member airlines could agree. The Air Traffic Conference of America (ATC) deals with the traffic and sales problems of airlines, the solution of which is of the greatest mutual benefit of all members. ATC, organizationally part of ATA, is composed of several working committees:procedures and methods of airline reservations, ticketing, baggage handling, air cargo, rules and fares.

The Air Traffic Conference of America (ATC) establishes standards and working agreements covering the way domestic airlines deal with each other, and the way they deal with the international carriers (IATA) and other segments of the travel industry, including travel agents. Other major conferences are maintained, such as the Atlantic and Pacific steamship lines (IPSA, and TPPC, i.e., Trans-Pacific Passenger Conference). Travel agents also secure trains (AMTRAK) and bus appointments.

The ATC appointment requirements for travel agency are reasonable and enable the travel agent to represent the domestic carriers. The agency must have a qualified manager, maintain minimum bond of $10,000. and proper location. All travel agencies have to be bonded in the event their agency should be robbed or an agent should leave with some ticket stock. This bond will cover their losses. Without this bond, an agency cannot be appointed by ATC or IATA. The travel manager must have a minimum of two or more years experience in a retail travel business, including the sale of air transportation, experience in ticketing, and training in agency management. The

travel agency's financial statement should demonstrate at least fifteen thousand dollars and sufficient working capital to meet the operating expenses (sales, rent, and overhead costs) for at least one year without any income from the agency. When an agency opens, the airline tickets are obtained from the carriers on a cash basis. If an agency obtains its appointment, commissions are received retroactively from the date of filing with ATC.

The Air Traffic Conference's "Sales Agency Agreement" states in part:

"During the term of this Agreement, the Agent shall represent the Carrier for the purpose of promoting and selling air passenger transportation offered by the Carrier: Provided, That, the Agent shall not represent any Carrier who has notified the Agent by certified or registered mail that the Agent shall not represent the Carrier; Provided, Further, That, the Agent may elect to limit such representation to certain specific product lines of the Carriers (e.g. Advertised Air Tours, Convention Air Tours, Incentive Air Tours, Independent Air Tours, Family Travel, "Discover America" fares, charters, or point-to-point domestic air passenger transportation not included in any of the foregoing categories) if the Agent limits its representation of all carriers' services alike and so notifies the Executive Secretary in writing,...In selling air passenger transportation, the Agent shall conform to and observe the tariffs, rules, regulations and instructions issued by the Carrier, and the applicable terms and conditions of tickets and exchange orders of the Carrier issued or used by the Agent. The Agent shall furnish information to its clients and the public concerning the Carrier's air passenger transportation services in conference with current authorized forms, folders, advertising, schedules, tariffs, rules, regulations and instructions issued by the Carrier.

In selling air passenger transportation on the lines of the Carrier, the Agent shall issue only Standard Agent's Tickets or exchange orders supplied pursuant to this Agreement, except to the extent the Carrier (1) authorizes the Agent, in writing, to draw its own exchange orders on the Carrier, (2) supplies the Agent with, and instructs the Agent to use, envelope-type exchange orders, (3) the Carrier authorizes the Agent in writing to receive standard teletype tickets in accordance with the terms and conditions of the ATC/IATA Teletype Ticketing Agreement Agents. The Agent shall deliver to its clients the proper forms of tickets or exchange orders as authorized from time to time by the Carrier; and routing information, et cetera, shown on any such documents shall be in accordance with the applicable rules, regulations and instructions furnished to the Agent by the Carrier.

The Agent may submit to the designated area bank in connection with the sales report hereafter provided, a settlement limitation amount authorization in the format and in accordance with the instructions prescribed by the Executive Secretary, which sets forth the maximum amount the designated area bank is authorized to draw against the Agent's trust account or other bank account.

The Agent shall report once each week for all air transportation and ancillary services sold hereunder for which the

Agent has issued Standard Agent's Ticket or exchange orders, or drawn exchange orders on the Carrier. Each such report shall include all such sales during the 7-day period, Monday through Sunday inclusive, ending midnight Sunday of that week. The report shall be in a form specified by the Executive Secretary. All tickets and other accountable documents and remittances therefor must be reported on, and be included with, the sales reports for the reporting period in which they are validated."

Other Air Traffic Conference agreements include maintenance of bond requirements, rates of commission for airline ticket sales, minimum requirements for the security of ATC standard tickets and other items, travel agent tour advertising code and other supplemental agreements, such as Schedule D - Supplement I, Resolution 80.15, Standard Travel Agent Finance Statement and Form U.C.C. - I which deals with airline ticket sales as accounts receivable in the event of agency bankruptcy.

INTERNATIONAL AIR TRANSPORT ASSOCIATION

On an international level, International Air Transport Association (IATA) performs a function similar to ATA. IATA has divided the world into three primary traffic conferences: (1) the Western Hemisphere, including Greenland and Hawaii; (2) Europe, Africa and the Middle East; and (3) Asia, Australia, and the Pacific.

IATA Carrier SWISSAIR   SWISSAIR Tourist Photo

IATA significant accomplishments include fares and tariffs between airlines operating with different currencies and connecting the routes of the international carriers so that interline transfers take place smoothly and effectively. Uniform policies and procedures have also been developed regarding schedules, airlines operations, navigational aids, safety measures, communications and other technical matters. In order to aid in the collection of interline accounts, IATA has established the IATA Clearing House in London. This enables member airlines to settle their monthly debts in one cash payment in a single currency.

IATA Passenger Sales Agency Agreement includes, for example:

"The Agent shall be responsible for all acts and omissions in respect of sales of international air passenger transportation effected under the provisions of this Agreement.

All transportation sold by the Agent under the provisions of this Agreement shall be sold in accordance with the conditions of carriage of the Carrier concerned applicable to such transportation and in accordance with the tariffs, rules, regulations and instructions governing the sale and use of such transportation in force from time to time as published in the Carrier's tariffs, timetables, notices and elsewhere. The Agent shall transmit to the Carrier such specific instructions, requests or particulars in connection with each client as may be proper to enable the Carrier to render efficient service to its clients.

All reservations for a specific itinerary and changes thereto shall be requested through one carrier whenever possible. Where this is not practical, each carrier with whom reservations have been made shall be informed that the reservation is in connection with an itinerary. The Agent shall refrain from making duplicate reservations for the same passenger except in those circumstances where the Agent is unable to secure confirmation of space on the carrier or flight of the client's choice in which case a 'protective reservation' may be made.

The Agent shall be responsible for the safe custody of such documents while in its possession; and shall be liable to the carrier for the value of any such documents except that liability for standard ticket stock issued to an Agent under the Air Traffic Conference Area Settlement Plan and fraudently issued with the identification plate of an IATA Carrier, may be limited as provided under ATC Resolution.

The Carrier and the Agent agree that in the performance of this Agreement they will observe and be bound by the Passenger Sales Agency Rules and other applicable resolutions of IATA, which may be examined by the Agent at the General Offices of the Carrier or of any IATA Member or which will be sent to the Agent at its request. The Agent recognizes that the Carrier is a Member of IATA and as such is precluded from paying commission on sales of international air transportation to agents who are not approved by IATA. Any action required by said Passenger Sales Agency Rules may be taken by the Carrier or IATA without the Carrier or IATA having to justify such action. The Agent hereby renounces for himself, his successors, and assigns, all rights of recourse against the Carrier, IATA or any of its Members, their officers, employees, agents or servants, for any loss, injury or damage suffered as a result of any action taken in good faith with regard to or in connection with the said Passenger Sales Agency Rules, or the suspension or cancellation of this Agreement."

NATIONAL RAILROAD PASSENGER CORPORATION

A retail travel agent is also an agent for AMTRAK (National Railroad Passenger Corporation); train travel is commissionable and tickets sold by travel agents can be a source of income. AMTRAK appoints the travel agency, after a review of credit and financial ability, and requires a passenger sales agreement. Some of the areas include:

1. The Agent shall abide by the terms, representations and conditions in any application or undertaking made by the Agent to AMTRAK for the purpose of causing AMTRAK to list and maintain it on the official AMTRAK Agency List. All such applications or undertakings are and shall be deemed to be incorporated herein and made a part thereof.

2. All transportation sold by the Agent under the provisions of this Agreement shall be sold subject to the conditions of carriage of AMTRAK concerned applicable to such transportation and instructions governing the sale and use of such transportation in force from time to time as published in AMTRAK's tariffs, timetables, notices and elsewhere. The Agent shall transmit to AMTRAK such specific instructions, requests or particulars in connection with each client as may be proper to enable AMTRAK to render efficient service to its clients.

3. The rate of commission for sale of all one-way transportation, any class, including reserved seat accommodation or extra fare charges, is 5%. The rate of commission for sale of all round trip transportation, any class, including reserved accommodation or extra fare charges, is 10%. Where the passenger is one-way but continuing by cruise or to an overseas destination by sea or air the rate of commission is 7% based on any class including reserved accommodations or extra fares.

INTERNATIONAL PASSENGER STEAMSHIP ASSOCIATION

Steamship appointments, such as the International Passenger Steamship Association (Conference), are important components in a travel business; steamship companies appoint sub-agents because the final ticketing is completed by the steamship line. The travel agent requirements include: experienced staff in the sale of steamship travel, adequate exterior and interior agency appearance, and a proper financial statement (good credit rating). IPSA, like the ATC, require travel agencies to adequately staff and maintain normal business hours for public convenience.

The appointment by the International Passenger Ship Association means that a travel agent would represent:

Baltic Shipping Company
Chandris America Line
C.C.N. - The Portuguese Line
Cunard Line Limited
French Line
Gdynia America Line
German Atlantic Line
Greek Line
Hapag-Lloyd A.G.
Hellenic Mediterranean Line
Holland America Cruises
Home Lines Inc.
Incres Line
Italian Line
Norwegian America Line
Paquet Lines
P & O
Royal Viking Line
Swedish American Line

The activities and functions of the Trans-Atlantic Passenger Steamship Conference and of the Caribbean Cruise Association were undertaken by IPSA, which has included under its jurisdiction virtually all of the Member Lines' trans-atlantic and cruise services.

BOHEME

Commodore Cruise Line Photo

Some of the "Minimum Standards of Eligibility and Submission of an IPSA Application" include: All applications for sub-agency appointment must include and/or be supported by documentary evidence of compliance with Standards specified hereunder. All applications and accompanying documentation shall be transmitted to the Secretary General with a covering letter enumerating all the forms and material being transmitted. Such covering letter shall be signed by the applying owner(s) (or an officer, if the applicant is a corporation) and shall include a notarized statement attesting to the authenticity and accuracy of all statements or claims made in any accompanying documentation and/or material.

Location

"The premises must be open to the general public during normal business hours for the purpose of travel business and properly staffed for that purpose.

The premises shall not be that of a private residence which is also used for residential purposes unless this specific prohibition is waived by the Agency Committee.

The premises shall be physically and distinctly separated from the office space or premises utilized by any other travel bureau whether or not authorized to represent the Member Lines.

The application shall be accompanied by at least one interior and one exterior photograph of the premises."

Experience

"If the applicant operates from only one location, the owner(s) of the applicant or one or more of its officers, if a corporation shall present evidence of:

> One year experience in the sale of general passenger transportation.
>
> One year employment in a general sales capacity by an authorized sub-agency of the Member Lines, or
>
> One year employment in a steamship sales capacity by either a Member Line or an authorized sub-agency of the Member Lines.
>
> At the option of the applicant, evidence of a compliance with the above can be met by a salaried office manager in which instance a time requirement of two years (in lieu of one year) will then prevail."

Commissions

"The sub-agency alone is entitled to the full amount of commission allowed by the Member Line upon each sale. It must not promise or hold out any improper inducements, expressed or implied, of paying any portion of the commission allowed to purchasers or prospective purchasers of tickets, orders or similar documents, or to passengers or to any other persons, by letter, circular, newspaper advertisement or otherwise.

All rebates, drawbacks, discounts, credits, commissions, presents, prizes, or allowances of any description whatsoever made or offered to be made to a purchaser, prospective purchaser, passenger, or to any other person, with a view to influencing the sale of a ticket, order or similar document are strictly prohibited."

The IPSA sub-agency agreement includes some of the following:

> "The Sub-Agent shall hold in trust for the Line any of its steamship passage tickets and order, or other documents and forms, supplied to the Sub-Agent for sale, and shall sell the same only at the rates quoted by the Line, and when any of such documents or forms are sold the Sub-Agent shall keep and hold the proceeds of sale and also any deposits made on account of any sales and any other funds received or collected for the account of the Line, whether or not the same have been deposited in a bank, in trust and entirely separate and apart from any and all other funds and moneys in the Sub-Agent's hands, and shall remit such proceeds of sale to the Line immediately after each sale, and

all deposits and other funds immediately after their receipt; and the Sub-Agent shall return to the Line or the Secretary General upon demand all unsold tickets, orders and other documents and forms and also any certificates, notice or other written authorization of sub-agency appointment issued to the Sub-Agent. The Sub-Agency must keep appropriate accounts of all transactions relating to the Sub-Agency, currently to date. Its office premises may be visited at any time and all the books, records and documents in relation to the Sub-Agency representation shall be open to inspection by the Line or by a duly authorized representative of the Association.

The relationship hereby set up between the Sub-Agent and the Line is not that of debtor and creditor but of trustee and beneficiary, and all funds derived from the sale of the Line's tickets, orders and other documents or forms, and also any deposits and any other funds received or collected for the account of the Line and any tickets, orders or other documents or forms received from the Line, are the Line's property and do not belong to the Sub-Agent.

In consideration of the granting of this Sub-Agency Appointment Agreement, it is not only represented and warranted that the Sub-Agent shall at all times safeguard and protect the property and money of the Line in the manner aforesaid, but the Sub-Agent shall add its personal indemnity to the Line for any loss which may be sustained by it for any of the causes hereinafter mentioned in this paragraph, apart from and in addition to any and all rights and remedies hereunder which the Line has by virtue of the creation of the aforesaid trust relationships, and to that end the Sub-Agent shall accept responsibility and liability for each steamship passage ticket and order, or other document or form delivered to the Sub-Agent and for all funds and moneys received by the Sub-Agent as proceeds of sale of any such documents or forms, or as deposits or for the account of the Line and agrees to indemnify and save such Line harmless from any and all loss of such documents and forms and of such proceeds of sale, deposits and funds, whether or not the same have been deposited in a bank and whether such loss is occasioned by forgery, burglary or theft or by the insolvency of either a purchaser of such documents or forms or of a bank in which such proceeds of sale, deposits or funds were deposited (notwithstanding the fact that under the terms of this trust relationship such bank deposits are the property of the Line and not the Sub-Agent's property), or by any other act, condition or omission whatsoever."

TRAVEL AGENT TRADE ASSOCIATIONS

There are several professional organizations offering membership to all appointed travel agents: the American Society of Travel Agents (ASTA), the Association of Retail Travel Agents (ARTA), Discover America Travel Organizations (DATO), and the Association of Bank Travel Bureaus (ABTB). Other major trade associations include the United States Tour Operators Association (USTOA), National Tours Brokers Association (NTBA), and Air Charter Tour Operators of America (ACTOA).

The American Society of Travel Agents, Inc. is the world's largest professional travel trade organization. The society is comprised of more than 16,000 members from over 120 countries representing all facets of the travel and tourism industry. ASTA's fundamental purpose is the promotion and advancement of the interests of the travel agency industry and the safeguarding of the travelling public against fraud, misrepresentation and other unethical practices. In the United States, ASTA members are located in more than 8,000 travel agencies.

ASTA membership services include: education, public relations, legal, consumer, and industry affairs. ASTA began in April 1931 (New York City) as the American Steamship and Tourist Association to promote programs for the advancement of the travel industry. By 1933 ASTA had members in Bermuda, England, France, Gibraltar, Greece, Mexico and Palestine. In 1945 ASTA's new name was the American Society of Travel Agents, and actively established ethical and financial requirements for membership. The society still demands that all members adhere to its principles of professional behavior and ethics. By 1949 ASTA had one thousand members and a full-time staff. In 1951 the professional development meeting was in Paris; now known as the World Travel Congress, a major tourism happening each year. ASTA has become a major leader of professionalism and respectibility of the travel agent. It is the responsibility of the ASTA member

> "to protect the public against any fraud, misrepresentation, or unethical practices in the travel agency industry. He should endeavor to eliminate any practices that could be damaging to the public or to the dignity and integrity of the travel agent's profession.

> The ASTA member should ascertain all pertinent facts concerning every tour, transportation, accommodation, or other travel service offered to the public...so that he may fulfill his obligation to inform his clients accurately about the services he sells and the costs involved.

> At the time initial payment is made for any booking, ASTA members must advise their clients in writing whether the client will be required to pay a cancellation fee or charge in the event the booking is changed or cancelled. "

ASTA has legal representation in Washington, D.C. in order to interface with Federal authorities and regulatory agencies in travel and transportation, and to protect the legitimate interest of travel agents. ASTA is concerned about survival of the small independent travel agent and questions of automation, deregulation, and travel agent's commissions. In answer to current problems ASTA sponsors frequent conferences on travel involving airlines, steamship companies, agents, government officials, and others.

The general membership requirements provide an understanding of the ASTA is concern; some of the major requirements are:

> "Hold two carrier conference approvals for two years each."

> "The ownership or effective control of the applicant shall be vested in citizens of the United States or Canada or an alien who is a permanent resident legally residing in the United States or Canada, and maintain its principal place of business in the United States, its territories and possessions, or Canada."

"Be in business under its present ownership and control for a minimum of three years prior to the time of its election to membership."

"Have derived more than 50 percent of its earned business income from the operation of its travel agency or shall have gross receipts from its travel business of $500,000 or more."

"Be of character and financial responsibility satisfactory to the society and shall conform to the society's principles of professional conduct and ethics."

The Governor General of Jamaica personally shows travel agents around King's House, the official residence as part of the Jamaican Tourist Board's "People Program."

Another major trade association is the Association of Retail Travel Agents, established in the early 1960's; ARTA has dedicated itself to providing the working travel agent with an opportunity to make his opinions, ideas, and hopes known to those who guide the travel industry - the voice of the travel agent. ARTA's membership is comprised of retail travel agencies, more than 750, and is growing. ARTA's policies are established by a board of directors, elected by the membership and there is a paid staff. ARTA established a chapter covering 13 Western States, and added a category for individual memberships, making it possible for staff members to join a trade association. Another chapter has been forwarded covering New York, New Jersey, and Connecticut. Agency membership in ARTA can be obtained after two industry appointments; individual membership requests at least three year's experience as a full-time employee of an agency. ARTA takes a stand on the issues, such as Federal licensing of travel agencies, in order to promote the survival of the retail agent. ARTA has established forms, on computers and automation of the industry. ARTA has recently supported open commissions, industry standards based on objective competency measurement, industry cooperatives and reasonable regulatory reform.

Other trade organizations for travel agents include those located in Europe. The World Association of Travel Agents (WATA) membership is restricted to one individual representative per nation or major urban area; WATA is a referral network and prints their own tariff. The Universal Federation of Travel Agents (UFTA) is a consortium of existing trade associations. Additional associations are: Pacific Area Travel Association (PATA), South American Travel Organization (SATO), and the African Travel Association (ATS).

There are a number of more specialized associations. The Association of Bank Travel Bureaus (ABTB), the Association of Caribbean Tour Operators (ACTO), the Association of Group Travel Executives (AGTE), the Discover America Travel Organization (DATO), and the Society of Polish-American Travel Agents (SPATA).

The Association of Bank Travel Bureaus (ABTB) was founded in 1962 by a group of representatives of bank travel bureaus. While ABTB members, as appointed travel agents, are also subject to internal auditors, federal and state examiners and controllers, they continue to seek solutions to travel industry problems and those agency problems related to working within the banking world. The purposes of ABTA are: to study, evaluate and interpret the various rules and regulations issued and administered by the air, steamship and other carrier conferences, and to discuss with the proper authorities all unfavorable proposals toward the protection of the interests of travel agencies owned and/or operated banks or bank affiliates, and to take every step to maintain the status and position of bank travel bureaus in the travel industry.

Discover America Travel Organization, Inc. (DATO) is the national organization of the U. S. travel industry. Its policies and programs reflect the common interest and concern of the travel industry's major components, and are supported by them. Its membership consists of individuals from more than 1,200 organizations: state and territorial travel offices; local convention and visitors bureaus; travel related associations; and individual companies connected with the travel and tourism industry.

DATO promotes and facilitates travel to and within the United States; encourages a wider understanding of travel which contributes substantially to the economic and social growth of the nation; and develops programs beneficial to the travel supplier and consumer. Over 40 years, DATO has been a central advocate for the travel industry and publishes with Travel Trade the DISCOVER AMERICA MAGAZINE which is devoted exclusively to domestic travel. DATO continues to bring cohesion to the travel industry and to increase its recognition by seeking and presenting unified positions on matters of essential interest.

The National Tour Brokers Association (NTBA) was organized in 1951; the formation of the association was developed by a need among brokers to join in a cooperative effort in dealing with the legal and regulatory issues facing the industry. Tour brokers today are recognized as professional groups who specialize in one type of business, e.g., the arranging and operating of escorted motorcoach tours. NTBA has had a steady growth over the years with an Active (tour broker) membership of 198 and an Allied membership of 1,287.

The United States Tour Operators Association (USTOA) originated in 1972 in California and by 1975 was a national association of independent wholesale tour operators. USTOA has faced the tour problems of uncertainty and diminishing confidence from the public and retailers. Active membership qualifications in USTOA include established standards of continuity, experience, business volume, financial responsibility and other requirements, including ethical principles and practices in wholesale tour operations. USTOA promotes forums for exchange of ideas and information through meetings, seminars and annual "Integrity in Tourism" Conference.

The Air Charter Tour Operators of America (ACTOA) has been organized since 1972 and its active membership is composed entirely of charter tour operators. ACTOA has been actively involved in the issues effecting charter operators, e.g., retention of affinity charters, liberalization of charter rules and prevention of minimum charter rates on the transatlantic market.

Hong Kong Funicular Railway

Hong Kong Tourist Photo

INSTITUTE OF CERTIFIED TRAVEL AGENTS

As travel has grown to its present world role, there is a vital need for - professionalism on the part of the key individual in the industry - the travel agent. To assist - and to designate - those travel agents who voluntarily give of their time and efforts to improve their proficiency, reliability, knowledge of the industry and travel agency management, the Institute Of Certified Travel Agents was established to fulfill these purposes.

Through its academic course and criteria for certification, the Institute sets the standards for travel agent professionalism. To designate the individual who earns this status, the Institute created and the industry recognizes the CTC - the Certified Travel Counselor.

While the gains of professionalism are of great value to the industry itself - through increased efficiency, trustworthiness, customer satisfaction - the benefits to the individual travel agent are noteworthy.

There will be an improvement in performance and judgement gained through an expanded expertise in management, marketing and perception of the pertinent developments which affect travel and travel services. Since clients often deal with travel agents in a relationship of trust, this knowledgeability serves to strengthen the travel agent's candor and understanding.

Chartered in 1964, the main purpose of the Institute is to increase the prestige of travel agency personnel by establishing higher educational and professional standards through a formal training program to raise the level of competency. The Institute recognizes those individuals who meet these rigorous standards by conferring the CTC designation. And, the Institute encourages the maintenance of the highest professionalism through continuing education.

To become a CTC, a travel agent must complete a college-level executive management course of four units in administration, management, marketing/sales and international travel-tourism; then prepare a research paper judged for its value to travel and to expanding the competency of other CTCs along with meeting other requirements

of expertise. While pursued on an individual basis - the CTC is attained only by the person who completes its requisites - group study is often conducted under the direction of an Institute coordinator. The CTC course usually takes two and one-half years to complete. Since the educational process for both the CTC and the CTC candidate is continuous the Institute annually sponsors, at leading universities across the country, a number of seminars on current concepts.

While many travel school programs offer courses, they are generally for entry-level personnel; the Institute's program is designed for the seasoned owner, manager or potential owner.

The Executive Management Travel Education Course covers management specifically for the travel agency.

The course is divided into four sections, self-contained yet interrelated. They cover:

ICTA Business Management for Travel Agents - enhances planning communications and personnel training along with fiscal, legal and insurance concepts.

ICTA Sales Management for Travel Agents - presents both governmental statutes and boards overseeing industry and agency operations. It attacks structuring, pricing and selling travel and travel services.

ICTA Marketing Management for Travel Agents - provides content on marketing, promotion and advertising techniques. Emphasis is on identity and methods used to reach new markets.

ICTA Domestic and International Tourism - concentrates on geographic, economic, social and cultural forces behind destination development and the part played by the retailer.

After completing the academic sections, candidates must demonstrate a working understanding of the course in one of two ways, by writing a research paper or submitting a written evaluation on any one of the Institute's seminars.

Final certification is granted to those who complete the academic requirements and who have met the experience standards.

For the CTC, a candidate must have at least five years full time employment in a travel agency including at least two years of travel agency management and/or travel agency sales. Full time employment is defined as working a minimum of 35 hours a week according to Wage and Hour standards in the United States. A combination of three years travel agency experience as described above and two years of travel sales in a travel-related activity will also fulfill the experience requirements for CTC.

For the CTA, a candidate must have five years travel-related experience within the industry, preferably with two years in travel sales.

Although some candidates earn their certification within three years, for most it requires two. The time factor depends upon the individual and the method in which the course is challenged. All requirements must be completed within three years of enrollment.

The studies for professional accreditation are not easy - earnest, disciplined study is a necessity and some candidates may repeat a section along the way.

Study groups – Although candidate enrollment doubled last year, enrollment in study groups grew at an even faster pace. Ideally groups consist of not more than 15 candidates coordinated by a volunteer. The costs to candidates in a group is generally the same as that of independent study.

Individual study – For numerous reasons, others prefer independent study which is the correspondence type of approach to the program.

The ICTA Seminar Series (or courses) – In keeping with the Institute's goal to constantly present innovative ideas in the rapidly changing field of travel management, an annual seminar series is sponsored. Industry leaders and outstanding educators present topics which expand the practical day-to-day operations with concepts to improve judgement. These three-day weekends, geographically dispersed throughout the country, are near major cities for the convenience of the participants, all of which are candidates, members or others from within the industry with both an interest and competency to comprehend the content of a particular seminar. Realistically priced, costs vary slightly with accommodation charges. Travel expenses are minimal since air and rail transportation has been authorized by CAB and Amtrak. A recent ICTA seminar (courses) include: Effective Management Communications, Management by Objectives, Management Style Development, Personal Management Development, Financial Management.

By attending a seminar, candidates expand their horizons in management, seasoned CTCs and CTAs are able to update their knowledge with current information and candidates and members alike are able to explore new areas in management with which they may not have previously been involved.

TRAVEL AGENCY MANAGER

The travel agency manager is accountable for the daily operations in the firm. Travel agencies today offer a wide variety of travel services: arranging basic transportation, i.e., air, steamship, cruises, rail, bus, car rentals, and other related services; preparing individual itineraries, personally escorted and group tours; arranging for accommodations (hotels, motels and resorts); handling and advising on the many details of modern travel including baggage roles, insurance, language study material, travelers checks, auto garaging, foreign currency exchange, documentary requirements (passport and visa), and health regulations (immunizations); and using professional knowledge and experience to interpreting train schedules, airline tariffs, and hotel rates. A manager is responsible for the quality of services and the making of a perfect trip from beginning to end.

Conversation leads to decisions.

Modern travel agency problems encompass increasing airfares, tour operators failure, low commissions and high overhead costs, consumer legal complaints, and re- liability of public charters. There are more than 16,000 travel agencies throughout the nation. Some employ a very small staff, others are much larger and still others are part of a chain of agencies. The work in these agencies is increasing as more Americans travel with budget and special fares. Staff members of travel agencies re- quire continuing inservice training in the complexities of airline scheduling and fares (which are impossible to keep current), familiarize themselves with the latest European tours, understand the newest cruise schedules, and maintain AMTRAK and ATC airline reports on a regular basis.

About three-quarters of the managers in travel agencies are women and the work is very demanding, e.g., typing, accounting, long hours of dialing 800 numbers, sell- ing to 8:00 PM on Thursdays and Saturdays, and additional time after office hours for writing tickets and organizing tours. The salary potential is limited by the agency profits which are tied to airline and other travel industry commissions.

A good manager knows that a travel agency is a service organization. Its value is not based on inventory or machinery, but is instead based on the volume of business that the travel agency generates.

The travel agency does have an intrinsic and substantial value as a going, money- making business. It has a value based on client contact, past performance, and pre- dictable future business.

The profit and loss statements of a travel agency are often dismal, and frequently do not reflect the fact that the travel agency may be surprisingly profitable. Using a profit and loss statement to evaluate a travel agency will usually give an erroneous and low idea of the worth of the business.

There is a single factor in every travel agency that can be readily established, and can be used as a basis for evaluation of the worth of the business. That is gross commissions earned. Gross commissions will vary from agency to agency depending on the type of travel sold, and will range from a low of 7% to a high of almost 12% (includ- ing overrides in some larger agencies and in chains). The average travel agency to- day earns approximately 9% commissions on total sales made. A $1 million agency would therefore produce an average of about $90,000 in gross annual commissions.

The agency manager shares the product responsibility with tour operators and the supplier (carriers). Managers are increasingly concerned with the reliability of public charters and the tendency of clients to pay post-tour visits to their lawyers. Customers frequently know about a wholesaler's cancellation policy or the possibility that a land operator may not operate a certain tour and usually have written notice of tour responsibilities. All "let the buyer beware" announcements do not seem to resolve legal actions. The legal situation can be viewed in the tour brochure state- ment on cancellations and refunds:

Cancellations must be submitted in writing to the Public Travel Company. On cancellations received by the Tour Operator at least 60 days prior to the flight departure the participant will get a full refund of monies re- ceived. Cancellations received by the Tour Operator between 60 and 45 days prior to flight departure, are subject to a $100.00 per person service charge; the remainder of monies received will be refunded. On cancella- tions received within 45 days of flight departure, a full refund of monies received can only be made in the event that the space is resold in ac- cordance with the substitution regulations of the CAB, as explained under

"Eligibility" and "Booking Requirements". If the space remains unsold on cancellations received within 45 days of departure, a full forfeiture of the entire cost of the tour including the air and land portions will occur. If cancellation of a tour is forced upon the Tour Operator due to inadequate participation or circumstances beyond its control such as strikes, riots, war, acts of God or similar circumstances, a full refund of all monies deposited will be made directly by Citibank. This refund constitutes the only liability on the part of the Tour Operator in connection with such cancellations. However, the Tour Operator shall not have the right to cancel due to inadequate participation once the passenger list for the flight is filed with the CAB. No reductions in the price paid and/or partial refunds can be granted to passengers for any changes or deviations from the itinerary of the tour. For more information on cancellations, see the "Responsibility" section.

Trip Protector Insurance is available and is strongly recommended. Further details are available upon request from the Tour Operator.

The legal responsibility of travel can be observed on these levels:

1. Air carriers, hotels, tour bus companies, cruise ships and rail carriers.
2. Wholesalers and tour operators.
3. Retail travel agents.
4. Consumers of travel services.

When travel complaints arise and nobody accepts the specific responsibility, the courts ultimately have to decide who has liability.

FAMILIARIZATION TRIPS

One of the many fringe benefits of a travel job include a certain amount of travel at greatly reduced prices. The carriers, for example, want to help travel agencies further increase air sales by familiarizating (FAM) trips for agents to their various vacation destination(s). To qualify for a FAM trip, the participating travel agent must be a fulltime employee, have been continuously employed at the agency for at least one year, have had at least six months' tariff/ticketing experience, and devoted all agency time to the promotion and sale of air transportation and related services.

Every travel agent has opportunities for free (or at a very modest cost) trips in the U. S. and overseas.

Travel agencies are inundated with offers of "Fam Trips" or perhaps cruises for just a very small percentage of the regular fare. Airline management and tour operators now realize that the more a travel agent knows about their airline or tours, the more likely that agent is to favor and recommend that particular airline or suggest a particular tour or cruise.

An Eastern 727 over Florida   Eastern Airline Photo

<u>Tampa/Orlando Tour (FAM)</u>   October 5 - 8

Cost: $35.00
Host Property: Don Cesar Beach Resort Hotel - Tampa
                Ramada Inn - Southwest - Orlando

ITINERARY HIGHLIGHTS

    Thursday: Afternoon arrival at Tampa International Airport and transfer
                via Greyline Tours to Don Cesar Beach Resort Hotel; welcome
                reception and dinner at resort. Balance of the evening free.

    Friday: Breakfast seminar at host property; check-out and depart Don
                Cesar for Busch Gardens; lunch on your own in Gardens; depart
                Busch Gardens for Circus World; tour of Circus World; arrive and
                check-in at Ramada Inn - Southwest; Welcome reception and dinner
                at Ramada Inn - Southwest ; balance of the evening free.

    Saturday: Breakfast seminar at host property; tour of Wet 'N Wild; arrive
                Florida Walt Disney World; lunch on your own in the park; return
                to Ramada Inn - Southwest; dinner at Travelodge - International
                Drive; evening entertainment at Rosie O'Grady's; return to
                Ramada Inn - Southwest.

    Sunday: Breakfast at leisure; check-out of hotel and depart for tour of
                Sea World; transfer to Orlando Airport for return flights home.

    Cut-off Date: September 21.

    Note: Air fare paid by carrier

Gap of Dunloe, Killarney   Irish Tourist Board Photo

Ireland Tour (FAM)   March 26 - April 2

"We are pleased to welcome you on the March 26 familiarization tour of Ireland. The details are as follows:

    March 26:   Flight IN/116; depart Boston 8.45 pm
                                    arrive Dublin 8.40 am
                     Check-in Logan Airport   7.45 pm

    March 27:   Dublin - Burlington Hotel - 2 nights

    March 29:   Killarney - Great Southern Hotel - 2 nights

    March 31   Galway - Corrib Great Southern Hotel - 1 night

    April 01   Limerick - Fitzpatrick's Shannon Shamrock - 1 night

    April 02   Flight IN/117; depart Shannon 3.50 pm
                                    arrive Boston   4.25 pm

Travelling with you will be Senior Sales Representative Anne Flynn. Anne is looking forward to meeting you at Logan Airport on March 26th, at which time she will present you with your air ticket and other travel documents. Please ensure that you are in possession of a valid passport."

ITINERARY HIGHLIGHTS

Saturday, March 26	Depart Boston for Dublin on Aer Lingus Boeing Shamrock Jet. Dinner and refreshments enroute.
Sunday, March 27	Arrive Dublin Airport. Aer Lingus Irish Coffee reception upon arrival. Transfer to Dublin hotel. Balance of day is free. Dinner at Dublin hotel. (Burlington Hotel)
Monday, March 28	Breakfast at Burlington Hotel, tour Dublin and environs, visit Fitzpatrick's Castle hotel etc. Lunch at hotel. Reception and dinner, sponsored by Aer Lingus at Abbey Tavern.
Tuesday, March 29	Breakfast at hotel. Transfer to rail station. Rail from Dublin to Killarney. Lunch on train. Arrive Killarney and transfer to the Great Southern Hotel. Dinner at Hotel.
Wednesday, March 30	Breakfast at hotel. Tour Killarney, Ring of Kerry and area. Lunch at the Towers or Falcon Inn, Glenbeigh. Reception and dinner in evening at Great Southern Hotel, Killarney, hosted by Irish Tourist Board.
Thursday, March 31	Breakfast at Hotel. Transfer to Tarbert, board Shannon ferry to Killimore. Seminar enroute. Lunch at Old Ground Hotel, Ennis. Transfer to Corrib Great Southern Hotel, Galway. Reception and dinner at the Gt. Southern Hotel, Eyre Square, Galway.
Friday, April 1	Breakfast at Hotel. Journey from Galway to Shannonside, visiting Limerick etc. Transfer to Fitzpatrick's Shannon Shamrock Hotel. In evening, attend Medieval Banquet.
Saturday, April 2	Breakfast at Hotel. Transfer to Shannon Airport in time for duty free shopping. Return to Boston on Boeing Shamrock Jet.

"Siamsa" at Tralee, County Kerry   Irish Tourist Board Photo

Israel Tour (FAM)   February 25 - March 3

"Dear Travel Agent:

This is to welcome you upon your arrival, and with you a hearty and pleasant stay in Israel. During your visit in Israel, you will be staying at the following hotels:

February 25 - 28	Hilton, Jerusalem.
February 28 -	Kibbutz
March 1	Hagoshrim
	Guest House.
March 1 - 3	Hilton, Tel Aviv.

It is indeed our hope that your Fam. Trip will be crowned with success and leave you with lasting impressions.

Ministry of Tourism"

ITINERARY HIGHLIGHTS

Sunday, February 25
Arrival at Ben Gurion International Airport. Welcome by a representative of Tourism Administration. Transfer to your hotel in Jerusalem, Eternal Capital of the State of Israel. Briefing by the representative of the Tourism Administration and informal dinner at your hotel.

Monday, February 26
08.15 a.m. - Tour of Jerusalem: Visit the Old City of Jerusalem, via the Dung Gate to the Western Wall, sole remnant of the Temple, Continue to the Temple Mount and visit its mosques. Proceed to the Via Dolorosa (way of the Cross) to the Church of the Holy Sepulchre and drive to Bethlehem, birthplace of King David and Jesus, and visit the Church of the Nativity. Lunch at the Israel Museum Cafeteria. Following lunch, visit the Shrine of the Book where the Dead Sea Scrolls are on exhibit and the Billy Rose Sculptures Garden on the Museum Grounds. Continue to Yad Vashem-National Memorial to the Holocaust. Visit the Model of Jerusalem from the 2nd Temple period, at the Holyland Hotel.

08.00 p.m. - Dinner at the Diplomat Hotel, Jerusalem.

Tuesday, February 27
08.00 a.m. - Tour of the Dead Sea Region: Via Ein Gedi, the site where David hid from King Saul, ascend by cable car to Massada, last stronghold of Jewish Resistance against the Romans (73 C.E.).

12.00 - Lunch at the 5:5 Cafeteria - Massada.

05.00 p.m. - Review of hotels in Jerusalem.

07.00 p.m. - Reception offered by the Jerusalem Hotels Association at the C.P. Plaza Hotel.

08.00 p.m. - Cocktails offered by the Hilton Hotel Management followed by dinner.

BETHLEHEM, Judea: A Catholic friar details the history of Bethlehem to a tourist group in the courtyard of the Church of Nativity. Israel Tourist Board Photo.

JERUSALEM, Israel: The Dome of the Rock/Mosque of Omar is one of the most beautiful examples of Islamic architecture in the world, covered with blue, green and white tile mosaics, and topped by its dome of Gold leaf. Israel Tourist Board Photo.

Wednesday, February 28	08.00 a.m. - Depart with your luggage for a tour to the Galilee along the Jordan Valley and Jericho, one of the oldest cities of the world. Visit Nazareth, childhood town of Jesus, and the Church of Annunciation. Proceed to Tiberias. Visit the new SPA installations of Hamei Tveria. Lunch at the SPA. After lunch visit the Holy Places around the Sea of Galilee:

- Tabgha - traditional site of the Miracle of Loaves and Fish.

- Capernaum - the site where Jesus gained his first disciples. Remains of ancient synagogue and St. Peter's House.

- Mount of the Beatitude - traditional site of the Sermon on the Mount.

Proceed to the Kibbutz Hagoshrim and Guest-House.

Thursday, March 1	08.00 a.m. - Visit the kibbutz.
	09.00 a.m. - Leave for the coastal plain of the Mediterranean: Visit Haifa, Israel's main port and an important industrial centre. Lunch at hotel Shulamit on Mt. Carmel. After lunch drive to Caesarea, former Roman Capital and harbour and visit the reconstructed Roman Theatre and the remains of the Crusader town, today a resort centre with Golf course. Via Herzeliya (review of the Dan Accadia Hotel), proceed to Tel Aviv and check-in at the hotel.
	07.00 p.m. - Professional Seminar held by a panel of representatives of the Tourist Trade (at the Hilton Hotel).
	08.00 p.m. - Farewell dinner hosted by the Tourism Administration, shared by the Association for Tourism Tel-Aviv-Yafo at the Hilton Hotel.
Friday, March 2	Morning free.
	01.00 p.m. - Reception offered by the Association for Tourism Tel-Aviv-Yafo at the Park Hotel followed by Sightseeing of the City, including a review of various hotels, conducted by the Association.
	07.30 p.m. - Dinner at the Sinai Hotel, Tel-Aviv. After dinner visit Old Yafo, including a visit to Yaffa Yarkoni's Aladin Nightclub for Israeli entertainment.
Saturday, March 3	Depart for Ben Gurion Airport for your homebound flight.

Bermuda Briefing
FAM PROGRAM

THE **BERMUDA**

DEPARTMENT OF TOURISM

FRONT STREET,
HAMILTON. 5 23
BERMUDA

THE HON. C. V. WOOLRIDGE, M.P.
MINISTER OF TOURISM

July 1st, 1978.

Dear Travel Agent:

I would like to invite you or one of your employees to file an application for our
September travel agent familiarization programme — the Bermuda Briefing '78.

This year we will again give agents an on-the-spot look at Bermuda's hotels, beaches,
entertainment and other facilities. The working programme will begin with a
Wednesday arrival and end on a Sunday.

Dates for Bermuda Briefing '78 are Sept. 6–10, Sept. 13–17, Sept.20-24 and
Sept.27-Oct.1st. Every week participating hotels will host a group of 30 agents ... an
average total of about 300 a week for the four week period.

Air Canada and United States airlines serving Bermuda are offering complimentary
transportation to the island. Domestic interline travel from selected cities will also be
available on a complimentary basis.

If you or an employee of yours have NOT participated in any of the three most recent
Briefings ('75, '76, '77) we would like you to consider filing the enclosed application
form. In five working days, you will learn about the island's facilities and
accommodation; you will meet hotel people, airline people, sightseeing people,
government people and many of the just plain Bermudian people who have given
Bermuda a reputation as one of the world's friendliest resorts.

I promise a warm Bermuda welcome.

Sincerely,

C. V. "Jim" Woolridge
Minister of Tourism

630 Fifth Avenue,   44 School Street, Suite 1010   Room 1422   2 Bloor Street West   9/10 Savile Row
New York, N.Y. 10020   Boston, Massachusetts 02108   401 N. Michigan Avenue   Toronto, Ontario,   London W1X 2BL
U.S.A.   U.S.A.   Chicago, Illinois 60611, U.S.A. Canada M4W 3E2

Wednesday – 6th, 13th, 20th, 27th September

Arrival on all scheduled flights during the day, register at briefing desk
at Bermuda Airport and transfer to host hotel.

P.M. – Cocktails and dinner at host hotel. Introduction to Bermudian host.
Visit cruise ships in port.

Thursday – 7th, 14th, 21st, 28th September

A.M. – Bus leaves host hotel for the City Hall, Hamilton. Welcome by
Minister of Tourism in the City Hall Theatre. 'Introduction to Bermuda'
an audio-visual presentation. Bus leaves for hotel tour, including lunch.

P.M. – Cocktails dinner and entertainment at another hotel.

Friday – 8th, 15th, 22nd, 29th September

A.M. – Meeting with management of host hotel. Tour of hotels and places
of interest.

P.M. – Lunch cruise on board 'Canima'. AFTERNOON FREE for relaxing, shopping
or sport. Cocktails, Dinner and Entertainment at another hotel.

Saturday – 9th, 16th, 23rd, 30th September

A.M. – Tour of hotels and places of interest. Lunch.

P.M. – Hotel tour continues. Cocktails at a Bermudian home. Farewell dinner
at Host Hotel.

Sunday – 10th, 17th, 24th September, 1st October

A.M./P.M. – Departure on scheduled flights.

```
┌────────────────────────────────────────────────────────────────────────────────────┐
│  [Bermuda Briefing '78 logo]         APPLICATION        Forward application to:      │
│                                                                                      │
│  Bermuda Briefing                                       Bermuda Briefing Tour '78    │
│        '78                                              44 School Street,            │
│                                                         Suite 1010,                  │
│  Please Type:        □ MISS  □ MRS.  □ MR.              Boston Mass. 02108           │
│                                                         U.S.A.                       │
│         Name _____           Your Age Bracket (For Rooming Purposes) │
│                                                         Under                  Over  │
│         Agency _____           30    30-40   40-50   50     │
│                                                         □      □       □       □     │
│         Address _____           SMOKER □      NON-SMOKER □   │
│                                                                                      │
│         City _____ State _____ Zip _____        Position in                  │
│                                                         Agency: _____│
│                                                         Area Code and                │
│  DATES: (List in order of preference 1, 2, 3, 4)        Telephone No. _____│
│     □ WEEK 1:     □ WEEK 2:      □ WEEK 3:     □ WEEK 4:                              │
│     Sept. 6-10    Sept. 13-17    Sept. 20-24  Sept. 27 — Oct. 1                       │
│                                                                                      │
│  AIRLINES: (List in order of preference 1, 2, 3, 4)                                  │
│     □ Air Canada    □ American       □ Delta       □ Eastern                         │
│                                                                                      │
│  GATEWAY DEPARTURE/RETURN CITY: (Check in order of preference 1, 2, 3, 4, 5, etc.)   │
│   □ Atlanta  □ Baltimore  □ Boston  □ Chicago  □ Hartford  □ New York  □ Newark  □ Philadelphia  □ Toronto │
│                                                                                      │
│  INTERLINE TRANSPORTATION REQUESTED: □ Yes  □ No    INTERLINE DEPARTURE/RETURN CITY: _____ │
│                                                                                      │
│  HOTEL PREFERENCE: (List in order of preference 1, 2, 3, 4, 5, 6, 7, 8, 9 for the weeks you have selected) │
└────────────────────────────────────────────────────────────────────────────────────┘
```

Week 1 September 6-10	Week 2 September 13-17	Week 3 September 20-24	Week 4 September 27-October 1
□ Sonesta	□ Newstead	□ Rosedon	□ Belmont
□ Southampton Princess	□ Belmont	□ Hamilton Princess	□ Hamilton Princess
□ Inverurie	□ Southampton Princess	□ Inverurie	□ Elbow Beach
□ Elbow Beach	□ Inverurie	□ Castle Harbour	□ Inverurie
□ Castle Harbour	□ Elbow Beach	□ Grotto Bay	□ Harmony Hall
□ Harmony Hall	□ Castle Harbour	□ Holiday Inn	□ Holiday Inn
□ Grotto Bay	□ Bermudiana	□ White Sands	□ Sonesta
□ Bermudiana	□ Mermaid	□ Bermudiana	□ Southampton Princess
		□ Rosemont	□ Mermaid

```
                              DO NOT WRITE IN THIS SPACE
  YOU ARE CONFIRMED AS FOLLOWS:

  Week: _____    Hotel: _____

  Date: _____    Airline: _____   Flight: _____  Departure Time: _____  From To _____

  Date: _____    Airline: _____   Flight: _____  Departure Time: _____  From To _____
```

IMPORTANT NOTE
DO NOT DETACH ANY PART OF THIS APPLICATION. RETURN ALL COPIES.

All applications are to be received by the Bermuda Briefing Tour '78, c/o Bermuda Department of Tourism office, indicated above, with check for $65.00, made payable to BERMUDA BRIEFING TOUR, together with photostat copy of IATA list (Resolution 203), postmarked no later than July 31, 1978. Applications received without these or after that date will not be honored.

Bermuda Briefing Information and Instructions

The Bermuda carrier assigned will contact you regarding your interline ticketing after confirmation. Note: The same interline carrier for both departure and return must be used. Please consult your OAG to ensure that connections can be made and are feasible. Last minute changes are extremely difficult if not impossible.

The hotel should be listed in order of preference for each week you marked in your choice of dates. We will attempt to offer you your first preference whenever possible. This will be handled on a first-come-first served basis. In all, about 1,000 travel agents will attend the Bermuda Briefing '78. A limited number of agents can be accommodated on any given weekend from any given geographic area. Each week's average of about 300 agents will be accommodated in groups of 30 at each participating hotel.

A check in the amount of $65 must accompany the application form. No telephone reservations will be accepted. Application must be postmarked no later than July 31, and check should be made payable to BERMUDA BRIEFING TOUR. Full refund will be made only in the event your cancellation is received at least two weeks prior to departure. Refunds will not be made for NO-SHOWS and/or cancellations received after the two week's deadline. Full and prompt refunds will of course be made when application must be returned due to over-subscription.

This will be a WORKING, EDUCATIONAL PROGRAM. Activities will include an industry exhibition, hotel visitations and an audio-visual program. All participants will be expected to attend all scheduled activities. There will, however, be free time for

shopping, sports, etc. Much walking is involved. Please bring comfortable shoes.
We have not planned a formal function. Suits or sport coats and ties will be required
most evenings. Ladies will want to bring cocktail dresses and/or pant suits. Dress
for all activities during the day is casual sportswear. Average maximum temperature
in September is 84 and average minimum is 73. For detailed information and travel
tips, please consult our folder 'Bermuda Travel Tips'.

Only one person per agency. Applicant must be on IATA list. Once confirmation
is given, reservation is not transferable. Agents who participated in the Bermuda
Briefing '75, '76 and '77 are not eligible.

THE TRAVEL AGENT'S RETAIL SELLING APPROACH

In the multi-billion dollar travel industry, the carriers (the trade names for
the airlines, the shipping companies, trains, and the bus companies) obviously cannot afford to maintain offices in every community, and they depend on retail travel
agencies to sell their tickets and fill their available spaces for them.

This architectural
masterpiece is the
Tzu Eng Pagoda at
the Sun Moon Lake
in central Taiwan.

Taiwan Tourist Photo

Selling superfares and dealing with the public can be an especially self-fulfill-
ing activity or a shattering experience. It is a mistaken notion in some minds that
working with clients is a hard job. Selling travel, houses, or anything is mostly what
one makes it. Generally, if a travel agent treats the public courteously, people will
respond in equal manner. The few exceptions should be quickly forgotten. A travel
agent begins with a positive attitude and a genuine desire to do a good job for the
agency. Good travel counseling starts with good intentions on the part of the staff.

The agent's job is to help the client buy travel. Success in travel sales is based on meeting the customer's needs. When a customer comes into the office with an inclination to travel, the travel agent can perform a valuable, professional service. The travel agents should be warned against only thinking of themselves as counselors rather than as salespersons for the transportation industry. Many agents are not comfortable with themselves as salespeople and feel that giving advice and counsel is far more important (similar to psychiatric social worker in a United Fund agency). If agents do not sell travel, the agency cannot earn commissions and ceases to exist.

The agent's attitude is first essential consideration of the job. When an agent feels personally responsible for the customer's travel, the sales relationship has a good beginning. It is in the office that personal contact begins when the agent and the travelling public are face to face, perhaps for the first time. If customers have never contacted a travel agent before, they will obviously judge the entire travel industry by the agent's manner and approach; therefore, it is important that the agent be business-like and friendly in order to encourage the sale of travel. It is at this moment, just as the customer approaches the desk that the counselor becomes the most important person in the organization and has been entrusted to represent the agency. The attitude, job knowledge, and sales ability of the counselor will determine to a large degree the success of the agency.

HOW TO SELL TRAVEL

You will be the cause of your own success. What do you do to improve your chances of successful travel sales? Effective travel sales begins with good health. The way you feel has a definite effect upon the way you look, the way you think, and the way you behave.

A sales oriented travel agent uses the basic steps of good salesmanship; qualifying the prospect, listening effectively, controlling the travel part of the conversation, translating trip features into instant benefits, overcoming objections of price, schedule or other problems, closing the sale, and follow-up with telephone selling. Qualifying, for example, means finding out the specific reason why a person has come to an agency. The usual agency transaction involves a person's asking a fare to a destination (which is not easily answered) but can end in a no sale, unless the agent takes steps to begin the qualifying process. Creative sales techniques are more than handing out brochures; objections must be answered and the information must be specific. Closing a travel sale is sometimes awkward and many agents don't want to ask for a firm order: "can I write the ticket?" The selling of travel and counselling travellers requires a professional, caring, human being.

An oasis in the Sinai brings refreshment to desert travellers.

MEETING THE CUSTOMER

The way in which you meet the prospective client has an effect on your agency's reputation as a travel service organization. You know that you must greet the customer as he approaches you, but sometimes agents fail to realize the effect of a well-planned greeting.

Your greeting is the beginning of the actual sale. Be cordial. Make an effort to learn each customer's name and use it in conversation. Be nice to your customers and, more than likely, they will be nice to you. Every successful sales agent smiles and acts pleasantly, no matter how one actually feels, because a smile will sell. All customers should receive the same courteous treatment, no matter who they are.

Remember that customers expect quick service in this computer reservation age, so be prepared to offer it. Some ways to give prompt service are: say "hello" to the customer first with a "Good Morning" or "Good Afternoon", don't wait for the customer to get your attention; use the customer's name if you know it; if you are busy with another customer get the new customer's attention and say something like, "Good morning; I'll be with you in a few seconds!" It is important to acknowledge the presence of a waiting customer. Be courteous in your retail selling approach. Following are a few tried and tested phrases considered to be personalized, friendly and courteous service: "Good morning, may I help you?" "Glad to see you again." Avoid using short, curt greetings such as: "Next", "Yes?", "Well?", or "You, Sir?"

Listen to your client's questions. Be attentive to the customer's questions because we are all apt to ask foolish questions about unfamiliar things like "super-saver" air fares. Remember the question is not foolish to the customer or he would not have asked it. Never be short, impatient, or superior. It may take you five minutes to explain a new Super Apex vs. Apex fare. Give clear, careful answers and in a way that the customer can understand. If you are selling travel, you should always be in control of the conversation, and one clear sign that you are losing control is when you answer several questions in a row. Your questions should assist you in preparing the reservation card; a completed card means a completed sale.

When giving information to a passenger, don't be ashamed to look him in the eye so that he will have more confidence in the words you say. Be sure to address the customer by name at least once during your conversation. People are flattered when they hear their name's spoken. Attempt to remember names and faces of frequent travellers. Always make it a point to speak to them. If conditions permit, carry on a short friendly conversation. They will be flattered by your recognition. Ask them about the family - how are the children? Ask them about their last trip.

PROVIDING COUNSELING

Part of your travel sales job is to help customers obtain a vacation tour, business trip or some other related travel service. A client seldom buys merely a service; the purchase is for the expected benefit or pleasure to be derived. The customer wants to know what the product or service will do for his or her needs. A really helpful travel agent has to do more than merely answer questions correctly. The travel agent must communicate, show as well as illustrate the many features which the agency offers to travellers, including the highlights of a forthcoming trip.

Selling travel means that you as the agent must take a "special" interest in the client's travel problems. Every normal human likes to feel that he or she is considered important. One of the best ways to let a customer know that he is important is to take a genuine and sincere interest in his travel problem. The undivided attention which you give to a customer will pay dividends in the end, because he will sense the keen

interest and attention that he is being shown. A sales counselor who has cultivated the art of talking with the customer about a trip and makes a sale is always an asset to the agency.

Do these things in order to take an interest in your client's travel needs:

Try to answer the questions in a way that the customer can understand.
Word your reply in a way that will correct any misunderstanding that might exist.
Be patient with the inexperienced traveller.
Give the passenger more of what he likes and less of what he dislikes.
Place yourself in the customer's environment and treat him as you would like to be treated.
Explain carefully restrictions, rules and other regulations affecting the traveller.
Know how to deal with the experienced traveller.

The travel agent should always give correct and complete information; this may not be so easy to do! Agents should "ration" information because the agent who simply gives away travel brochures (or reads them to clients) frequently loses the sale and the customer. Customers can read. Other reasons to limit the information available include confusion with too many facts and everybody's time (yours and your clients) is a precious commodity in today's busy world.

Remember that the travelling public looks upon you as an "expert" in the field. It is of fundamental importance that what you say is accurate and reasonably complete in every detail.

Expression such as "I believe" or "I think" and "It is my understanding" and the like, indicate either indifference or lack of knowledge. You must create the impression that you know what you are talking about or that you can and will find the correct answers, e.g., "I will verify this with the airline rate desk," or "the tour desk reports".

EXPLAINING TRAVEL

You must explain your agency's travel services in such a way that your customer will truly feel that you are helping and not "high pressuring" into something not desired.

When explaining your services you should always be mindful of these two sales factors: travel features and benefits. Customers are primarily interested in the benefits they will receive.   Sales techniques must explain the features as well as benefits of the proposed trip.

The language in travel brochures is candid. This helps you understand exactly what you're selling. Read the brochure, study the fine print, ask questions of the tour operator, understand the conditions, and know about the refunds or cancellations. Look for the following in a tour brochure:

Name of tour.
Name of operator.
Destination, length of tour, price.
Quoted round-trip air fare.
Rates and dates for each departure
  in bold type.
Number of nights in each hotel in
  each city.

Name and location of hotel in each city.
Photos of public rooms as well as bed-
  rooms in hotel brochures.
Map of itinerary.
Name and registry of ship.
Definition of hotel classification.
Detailed descriptions of sightseeing ex-
  cursions.

Number of meals covered by the tour price.

Optional costs spelled out.

Day-by-day itinerary.

Information on tipping policy, admission fees, single supplement charge.

Suggestions for use of free time.

Car rental costs, description of car.

Description of transport service used on tour.

Amount of time a guide or escort will be present.

Pace of tour and size of group.

Shots, passport and visa information.

Warranty.

Refund and cancellation information.

Deposit and payment schedule.

Your agency has many travel items to offer in the way of satisfying the customer's needs. Items that the average person does not know exists, for example, are certain tariff rules, special fares, or non-stop service which may be exactly what the passenger is looking for but he won't know about it until you suggest it. "Suggestive selling" in your agency is merely showing and/or telling about related services, i.e., "our new, low $45 (a Y23 fare) from New York to Miami on a regularly scheduled Braniff DC-8 Jet with full meal service, lower than the published $69.50 advertised by National Airline in today's newspaper leaving at the exact same time - would you like a round-trip reservation?"

Clients should know not only about the new schedules but also equipment, new stops, flying time, arrival and departure times, as well as other services.

Fares are important to most people in these times of high inflation. Customers want to know about the "special rate" or the economy coach fare, Family Plan Fares (children go free), Discount Fares (Super Savers), Round-trip Fares and all other special fares in effect now or in the future when they plan to travel. It is the travel agent's obligation to explain the lowest possible tariff and any accompanying restrictions. To illustrate this point, if a passenger is purchasing several coach tickets, you can suggest the Family Fare by saying "Have you heard about Family Plan Fares with children who can fly free if under a certain age, but only in February and March?" The intent is to acquaint the client with the Family Fares which may be advantageous. All special fares have certain advantages and limitations, so you owe it to each customer to suggest any fares which you feel will benefit him. Routings and

various ways to travel can be important. This would include all travel: trips to special events, conventions, and resort areas, vacation or business travel.

Selling cruises can be profitable.   Photo courtesy of Princess Cruises.

As a travel counselor you will advise and recommend the most economical and convenient airfare available at time of departure. Consider that probably the most confusing aspect of travel to Europe are the airfares across the Atlantic. Because most major international airlines belong to IATA (International Air Transport Association), airfares must be approved by all members and applicable governments before they can be instituted and this process is not only time consuming, but also restrictive. For example, the GIT fare might require groups of five or more passengers travelling together for at least 14 days, but not more than 21 days. GIT add-ons to New York (usually the "assembly" city) are applicable for travel from home city to and from assembly point. A fourteen day advance ticketing restriction may apply. Cancellations received after ticket has been written can be subject to a 25% cancellation fee unless cancellation is a result of death or serious illness. Apex fares are based on individual travel on scheduled service, and requires reservations be made and tickets issued 45, 21, or 7 days prior to departure. Cancellation charges of 10% or $50 (which ever is greater) are applicable once ticket has been issued.

Domestic Airline Tariff

from		BALTIMORE		BINGHAMTON				BOSTON			
FARE CLASS	to	ST. LOUIS	WASHINGTON	BOSTON	CHICAGO	NEW YORK/ NEWARK	PITTSBURGH	ALBANY, N.Y.	ALLENTOWN	BALTIMORE	BINGHAMTON
S	OW	87.00	22.00	52.00	87.00	41.00	53.00	43.00	53.00	57.00	52.00
SCH	OW	58.00	15.00	35.00	58.00	27.00	35.00	29.00	35.00	38.00	35.00
SN	OW	70.00	. . .	. . .	. . .	. . .	. . .	. . .	. . .	46.00	. . .
YM	OW	65.00	16.00	39.00	65.00	31.00	40.00	32.00	40.00	43.00	39.00
SCD	OW	58.00	15.00	35.00	58.00	27.00	35.00	29.00	35.00	38.00	35.00
SCL	OW	58.00	15.00	35.00	58.00	27.00	35.00	29.00	35.00	38.00	35.00
SE6	RT	104.00	26.00	62.00	104.00	49.00	64.00	52.00	64.00	68.00	62.00
SWE88	RT	87.00	22.00	52.00	87.00	41.00	53.00	43.00	53.00	57.00	52.00
SE46	RT	139.00	35.00	83.00	139.00	66.00	85.00	69.00	85.00	91.00	83.00
SE54	RT	122.00	31.00	73.00	122.00	57.00	74.00	60.00	74.00	80.00	73.00
SCHE46	RT	87.00	22.00	52.00	87.00	41.00	53.00	43.00	53.00	57.00	52.00
SCHE6	RT	87.00	22.00	52.00	87.00	41.00	53.00	43.00	53.00	57.00	52.00
SG10	OW	74.00	19.00	44.00	74.00	35.00	45.00	37.00	45.00	48.00	44.00
SG10	RT	139.00	35.00	83.00	139.00	66.00	85.00	69.00	85.00	91.00	83.00

from		BOSTON									
FARE CLASS	to	BUFFALO	CHICAGO	CINCINNATI	CLEVELAND	DAYTON	DETROIT	ELMIRA	ERIE	HARRISBURG	HOUSTON
S	OW	61.00	99.00	90.00	75.00	86.00	80.00	57.00	71.00	63.00	156.00
S1	OW	. . .	69.00	. . .	. . .	. . .	. . .	. . .	. . .	. . .	. . .
SCH	OW	41.00	66.00	60.00	50.00	57.00	53.00	38.00	47.00	42.00	104.00
SN	OW	49.00	79.00	. . .	60.00	. . .	. . .	. . .	. . .	. . .	. . .
YM	OW	46.00	74.00	67.00	56.00	65.00	60.00	43.00	53.00	47.00	117.00
SCD	OW	41.00	66.00	60.00	50.00	57.00	53.00	38.00	47.00	42.00	104.00
SCL	OW	41.00	66.00	60.00	50.C0	57.00	53.00	38.00	47.00	42.00	104.00
SE6	RT	73.00	119.00	108.00	90.00	103.00	96.00	68.00	85.00	76.00	187.00
SWE88	RT	61.00	99.00	90.00	75.00	86.00	80.00	57.00	71.00	63.00	156.00
SE46	RT	98.00	158.00	144.00	120.00	138.00	128.00	91.00	114.00	101.00	250.00
SE54	RT	85.00	139.00	126.00	105.00	120.00	112.00	80.00	99.00	88.00	218.00
SE87	RT	. . .	. . .	. . .	. . .	. . .	. . .	. . .	. . .	. . .	156.00
SCHE46	RT	61.00	99.00	90.00	75.00	86.00	80.00	57.00	71.00	63.00	156.00
SCHE6	RT	61.00	99.00	90.00	75.00	86.00	80.00	57.00	71.00	63.00	156.00
SG10	OW	52.00	84.00	76.00	64.00	73.00	68.00	48.00	60.00	54.00	133.00
SG10	RT	98.00	158.00	144.00	120.00	138.00	128.00	91.00	114.00	101.00	250.00

CLOSING THE SALE

If you are going to increase sales and obtain the results of your helpful attitude, then you must ask for the reservation and/or sell the ticket. Using positive sales phrases and words will do wonders to clinch the sale. For example:

"In what name shall we hold the reservations?"

"Which of these two would you prefer?"

These are phrases which require more than a yes or no answer.

You must assure people by your courteous approach and the information you offer, that they are being treated as individuals and not just as a part of the crowd. A client who is unfamiliar with the travel details of the trip, will be grateful if you volunteer a few statements concerning his flight and what he should do. It reassures him of the routine and safe air travel procedure.

Recap all pertinent information; put in writing.

People like to know their patronage is appreciated, and when you say "Thank you," mean it! The customer is the only reason for your present position and your agency existence. Take good care of your customer and your customer will take good care of you.

CREATIVE TRAVEL SALES

Travel sales require that you provide:

A courteous sales approach.
Attention to the passenger's travel requirements.
Presenting the service that fits the needs.
Anticipating and answering the questions in the client's mind.
Suggesting related or allied service.
Selling and recording the trip.

The following are twenty points for creative sales that you should remember in selling travel:

1.   Proper physical preparation and appearance before you sell any travel. You have to sell yourself. Your physical appearance is important, e.g., dress, makeup, chewing gum, good posture, happy smile, and a good attitude.

2.   Smile when you smile; the other person feels the warmth. Make your client comfortable; the joy of travel should be in the planning as well as the making of the trip.

3.   Sales communications is important. You are hired to produce; productive salesmanship provides a continuing business climate.

4.   Knowing what you are selling, i.e., travel; you are selling an experience, the anticipation and planning of travel, the realization of the trip itself, and the lasting memories of a good vacation. You are competing with other travel agents but also car rentals, tour guides, hotels, and the airlines.

5.   Your sales material is crucial; the reference books are needed as sales aids. The tools of your trade should be well organized - not all over the place. Your trade papers should not be on the floor; your travel brochures should be well organized; and information handouts readily available.

6.   Let the prospect talk, be sure your client has a chance "to get a word in edgewise." Do not confuse your enthusiasm; don't do all the talking. If you let them talk you'll know what they have in mind for their trip. Do not overpower the sales opportunity with your conversation; your customer is looking for things in his mind that he will develop if he can talk. Do not read from directories or brochures. Be sure to give the client in writing the itinerary and the prices.

7.   Inform; do not tell your prospect about the travel plans. Nobody likes to be told what should be done with their own vacation and money. Because many selections are available, the client wants and needs counseling. Organize the travel options carefully.

8.   Early in the discussion establish a reason why a client should buy from you: maybe personal preference, special service other agents do not give, member of same club or organization, friendship, long established agency, convenient location, or attentive personal service. When talking try to develop reason for dealing with you and the agency. Remember that travellers have always needed the services of a travel agent.

9.   Sell the benefits of travel; not the lowest travel price. Benefits mean sound sales and are based on performance of carrier, the economy of one plan versus the others, parts of the package, prestige significance of travel, comforts carried

by first hotels, your services and the advantages which are beneficial to the client. You might say that a "...travel business built on selling lowest price is built on sand; whereas, travel business built on selling benefits is built on concrete foundation."

10. Never discredit competitors; those other agents in town. Few people like to hear others run down. Establish the benefits of your own service and do not become critical of competitors. Point out your own services. Criticism of others may bring on negative reaction. Remember that business should be confidential and requires a discrete relationship with customers.

11. Sincere enthusiasm sells; show enthusiasm in product and in selling it to your prospect. Exciting travel products sell well. Enthusiasm is contagious. Show through friendliness, keen personal interest, a thorough knowledge of the pleasures of travel and the value your travel agency services.

12. Loyalty commands respect; be true to yourself and employer. Do not be false to anyone, including your client. You are obligated to employer as long as we accept the salary and your client pays the agency. Venting job unhappiness to clients result in loss of confidence and respect toward selves. This can destroy your personality. Your good mental health is the beginning of every successful travel sale.

13. Remember that when you radiate self-confidence, you instill confidence in your client for your sale and the agency. To acquire confidence you need preparation in travel knowledge, the basis of customer advice. You don't have to know all - just where to find it.

14. The informed sales person makes a sale. Good sales person must know what's happening; anything new and upcoming in the airlines, hotels, tours and the like must be immediate information i.e., latest travel packages advertised in the Sunday newspapers or new airfare on television news. You should read the trade magazines and papers regularly. Be informed about the latest travel opportunities, should your client request clarification. Know what's happening on new fares, i.e., "in three weeks we will have the new pay fare to Paris."

15. Service is an essential part of selling in a travel agency: mailing brochures, passing out information, answering questions and explaining every detail of a trip. Service and sales functions are the best insurance for future sales; remember that a satisfied customer will come back for the next trip. Do your best to provide "service with a smile."

16. Make the complete sale; you are a travel counselor, not an order taker or a ticket printer. Plan for optional stopovers, complete land packages, car rentals - all travel components are commissionable. Sell benefits of a professionally organized and planned travel. For most people vacation travel climaxes years of preparation, gathering information like things to do and see, and saving enough money to afford the trip. You are their "dream merchant."

17. Never argue a point and lose the sale with a customer. Self control and patience; admit to understanding his opinion, and then explain your side again - maintain your composure. You have to sell your client an economy cruise vacation because that is all he can afford, although you know that he would enjoy a luxury cruise.

18. Give your office warmth and friendliness. Everyone enjoys cheery people. Do you contribute to warmth or gloom? If you keep the office friendly, the sales climate will be favorable. Leave your problems at home. Offer a holiday; help people "get-away" from their problems.

19.   When you use the telephone, be sure that your voice and sales personality "sparkles" with confidence. You should always try to convey a mood of cheerfulness and friendliness to the caller. Move your lips and smile as if the customer were in the office. Speak with enthusiasm; put expression into your words that sound friendly. Avoid a monotone and vary your voice (pitch and loudness). Speak at normal pitch; for some people a lower voice pitch is better on the phone. Speak slowly and repeat information if your client is taking notes. Remember that more than half of all travel sales probably occur over the telephone; busy clients do not have time to come to the office when they have a professional travel service available.

20.   Communicate well with other co-workers; in-house communications are essential. When you become a manager make sure everyone understands what you expect of them and what you think of the job he or she is doing. All travel staff must be responsible and productive in sales. Eliminate the communication barriers and office confusion in order to improve client relations.

Chapter 3

TRAVEL AGENCY BUSINESS

AGENCY MANAGEMENT

Management can be defined as that process by which a travel agency creates, directs, maintains, and operates a purposive organization through systematic, coordinated, cooperative human effort. The management process is a complex social activity. Travel agency management is rooted in the interactions of people at work; the manager's responsibility is to guide, direct, influence and control the actions of others in the attainment of planned company objectives.

The practice of travel agency management is a world wide problem and good management is required for agencies to survive. Management organization reflects a growing professionalism in the field; increased body of knowledge and growth of special skills and techniques, better formal training and higher level of management education, and growth of special skills and techniques, better formal training and higher level of management education, and growth of specialized trade and professional associations.

The travel agent managers know the importance of good management. Agency management should be viewed as an organized set of activities for coordinating and integrating the use of resources to accomplish the organizational purpose of selling travel. The central focus of managerial activities with their related organizational elements include:

> PLANNING - corporation purpose
> OPERATING - organizational techniques and structure
> COORDINATING - sales people require direction
> CONTROLLING - information and budget reports

PLANNING

With the owners of the travel agency objectives determined, the means necessary to achieve these stated objectives can be presented in the form of plans. Plans are developed for activities that may be short-term or require many years to complete, i.e., travel customer development is long-term planning activity. Planning precedes all human endeavors and attempts to anticipate future contingencies. Travel business planning is a way of thinking about corporate objectives and of determining in advance what is to be accomplished. In the marketplace of tomorrow, more planning is required to meet the increasing complexities of travel. The travel agency must survive in a world of great uncertainty. Most agencies see themselves a full-service operation serving the corporate business executives and the vacation traveller, but those with good planning capabilities will calculate how to sell more of what pays the best and reduce, particularly, those time consuming activities which do not contribute significantly in the overall profit level.

OPERATING

To implement any planning, there is a requirement to have an agency organization. It is a responsibility of management to determine the type of agency required to carry out the stated plans. The kind of organization that is developed determines in real measure, whether or not the plans are realized, since the objectives of an enterprise and the plans required to meet these objectives have a direct relation to the characteristics and structure of the organization. The organization principal defines the number of agents reporting to a single manager. The delegation of authority is understood by both manager and agents, i.e., what is to be accomplished, what the subordinate is to report, and how the work will be evaluated. The organizing practices should be complete in order that every activity necessary to achieve the organization's objectives is easily undertaken by the staff. In the agency, the line of authority must be equal to the level of responsibility so that each individual has sufficient and appropriate authority to perform the work assigned for which the agent is held accountable. The manager may delegate activities; authority assigned by the owner but this delegation does not relieve manager responsibility for how well the activity is performed.

The operating management in a travel agency deals with salaries, staffing, training and increasing technology:

Some agencies use salary base plus incentives for sales that surpass a specified figure which can mean that the travel counselor should be of more value to themselves and the agency. Incentive sales causes agents to hustle more and be more creative.

Larger agencies have full-time in-house staff members, supplemented by part-time outside sales persons.

A manager may use office funds to send employees to industry functions; provide familiarization trips for those counselors who come back with information that is useful in sales. Travel agents can go on cruises or other destinations on company time that will improve their sales knowledge on those products which pay the highest commissions.

Several managers concerned with the difficulties in reaching the carriers, tours, and hotels are reaching the 800 telephone numbers with a Touch-a-Matic telephone which allows the user to push one button for each of several frequently used numbers. This installation can be worth the value of one employee during busy times in the office.

Some managers with more than $600,000 in sales are using a Teleticketing machine; others are operating the more sophisticated reservations and ticketing systems offered by the airlines.

COORDINATING

The third function of management is a term coordinating the people resource, i.e., motivating, leading, guiding, stimulating, and actuating, and is concerned with the human factor of an organization. It is as a result of the efforts of each agency that goals are attained; hence, a major function of the management process is to direct the organization so that objections will be achieved.

Travel agency management requires leadership and good human relations. Leadership in the travel business depends upon the characteristics of the manager: attitudes,

needs and personal characteristic of employees, characteristics of the organization and social and economic conditions. The leadership role reflects the extent behavior has in influencing agents. Leadership is defined as the capacity to guide, direct or influence the behavior of others toward a set of goals. Agents have an intense need for effective leadership in which they can place their confidence. Leadership is a continuing requirement in all travel agencies, and substantial organizational resources are always devoted to developing and maintaining the quality of leadership. The need for leadership is apparent in the various professional trade associations.

Good human relations is the practice of utilizing human resources through knowledge as well as understanding of the activities, attitudes, and interrelationships of people at work. The human relations movement in business started in the 1940's and nearly forty years has filled many gaps in knowledge about business organizations and contributed to present day management theory.

Human factors of organization plays a significant role in the behavioral climate in a small business. Travel organizations promote face-to-face contacts. The concept of informal organization may be thought of as any human interaction which occurs spontaneously and naturally over extended periods of time. Informal groups in the office environment develop from the cultural focus, customs, morals, and habits of a social group.

CONTROLLING

Controlling, the final management function, refers to managerial activities which measure the performance of agents and guides the agency toward some predetermined goals. An agency may keep track of sales on large booking sheets showing a chronological listing of advance sales by the date of departure for an instant review of advance bookings. Another agency after each trip is completed may prepare a product line breakdown report, showing the total trip price, the commission parcel and the cost of the various components of the trip. Monthly summaries show the totals from all completed trips and indicate the real source of business and earnings; this management mechanism records agent sales accurately for the month in the areas of domestic air, international air, hotels, package tours, steamship, FIT's, and agency tours as well as other travel related services.

MARKETING

Travel marketing is a major responsibility of the travel agency, and holds a strategic place in the business world. Marketing requires that all decisions reflect the market orientation and the special needs of the travelling consumers. Frequently all decisions are integrated in terms of what is best for the agency in the competitive market place. Marketing is defined as that business activity which directs the flow of goods and services from the agency (producer) to the consumer and includes selling, purchasing, financing and risk-taking. A marketing program is a "plan" for guiding the agency's marketing activities toward specific objectives, and defines what happens, when, and who is responsible for the implementation of activities. A marketing program's objectives are usually established by the owner(s) and covers a definite time period, i.e., five years. Marketing policies involve product pricing, advertising, service, warranty, credit, product-line, branding, terms of sale, sales services, distribution channels and market coverage. Activities which are part of the agency's marketing program are generally recognizable in these units:

Pricing reflects nature and extent of consumer demands, costs of the product or service, the competitive response, promotional strategy and marketplace factors, i.e., when to sell Caribbean cruises or European tours to beat high inflation costs.

Product includes product differentiation, market segmentation and planned obsolescence. An attractive tour package should protect the package, inform the consumer, advertise and stimulate sales, lower marketing costs and facilities.

Promotion refers to the selling activities of the firm, involving advertising, personnel selling and direct sales promotion.

Channels of distribution is the way that the products move, i.e., general or intensive distribution, outside sales personnel.

Market-research involves the systematic gathering, recording and analyzing of data about the problems relating to the sale of travel, e.g., consumer surveys and advertising studies.

Price, promotion, product, channel of distribution and market research are elements of the responsibility of the travel agency manager.

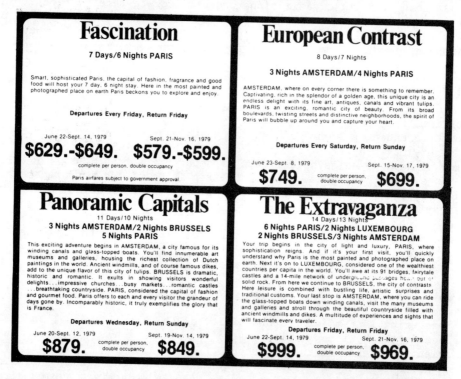

One specialty area of marketing is advertising; each year a travel agency will spend thousands of dollars promoting travel. Some travel is advertised in Sunday newspapers in the travel section or other local newspapers. A small travel agency will want to allocate up to 10 percent of the annual budget on all forms of advertising.

The foremost kind of local advertising is in the yellow pages, "...a business in the black is in the yellow pages". A quarter page of advertising in the Yellow Pages (under travel) is an absolute priority for most agencies in the advertising budget. People turn to the Yellow Pages in order to get answers to their travel questions, telephone users get their questions answered before they call the agency. An ad in the Yellow Pages tells the customer who the agency is; the business name and phone number, company slogans or emblems, e.g., "a full service agency," "complete travel service," "we pamper our clients with personalized service," free counseling service," "never a charge for our services," and "tickets and reservations everywhere."

The Yellow Pages explains <u>what</u> the agency's full line of travel products and services are: "airline tickets, hotel and resorts, bus tours, cruises, rail, package and escorted tours, car rentals, seasonably priced tours, group and executive travel, and travel insurance." In the Yellow Pages the question of <u>when</u> is the travel agency open, i.e., "six days a week, 8 am to 6 pm, open to 9 pm Thursday, and after hours call..." The Yellow Pages answer <u>why</u> your travel agency is special. Your reliability; years in the travel business; endorsements; brand names you carry; which credit cards you honor; emergency service; whether you're bonded, licensed, insured; types of service and guarantees offered; parking facilities; delivery service; completeness of inventory, selection of merchandise; and size of agency. The potential client can see that you are an ASTA or ARTA member; you have American Express, VISA and Master Charge. There may also be pictures of airplanes, ships, trains, beach scenes or castles to represent travel. The <u>where</u> is also found in the Yellow Pages, i.e., your address and location, area served, plus directions or map, if required. Additional offices located in the area are also listed for your clients convenience.

Look in your own Yellow Page Directory and see how well travel agencies are advertised. The telephone company states that "4 out of 5 adults (over 112 million people) use the Yellow Pages to locate a product or service in a 12 month period, and 84 percent of these references were followed up by a phone call, visit or letter." The Yellow Pages are for the prospect who is ready to buy. Because every telephone subscriber receives a Yellow Pages Directory, circulation is enormous - and because of circulation, your cost per prospect is minimal. The value of other advertising you may use may last one day in newspapers, or one minute in broadcast media. Your Yellow Pages ad stays in a home or place of business, 24 hours a day - 365 days a year. Whenever a person uses the Yellow Pages and looks under travel, he usually wants to take a trip and plans to contact a travel agent.

Newspapers are probably the next place for the advertising budget spending. Newspapers frequently have Sunday sections devoted to travel interests, including travel highlights on seasonal travel programs. As soon as the IATA air fares are known in the late winter months, the New York Times, like other papers, will have a "special" Sunday travel section on European travel in the summer ahead. Newspapers and other community interest magazines publish regular articles on travel and provides a perfect opportunity for effective advertising.

Generally speaking radio and direct mail are other ways to reach potential clients. Frequently travel agents will use special events or public presentations as opportunities to "sell" travel. Usually television advertising is very expensive, but occasionally there are travel agents on television talking about trips and other special travel topics. Travel agents can be found at country fairs, home and travel shows, mall or shopping center festivals and at civil group lunches.

TRAVEL AGENCY BUDGET

Accounting in a travel agency as in other businesses is founded upon the cost evaluation principle. The amount of money actually exchanged in ticket sales is the amount used as a basis for the recognition of travel services acquired. A travel agency works within the commission income structure established by the airlines, rail, steamships, tours, hotels and other transportation companies and under restrictions imposed by ATC, IATA, AMTRAK and other agencies. Due to these limitations, skillful management of the office budget is essential. Travel managers should have a budget to operate the agency in order to plan for a profit. The agency can't pay for familiarization trips for employees if the budget is out of balance, or schedule an effective promotional campaign when the funds aren't really available. Frequent financial reports reflect increases or decreases in income and expense categories, and can provide valuable information for the travel agency manager.

The annual budget in a travel agency is a plan of operation for the coming year. The budget reflects anticipated sales, expenditures (salaries and wages), and other control factors, such as advertising and telephone costs. Strict budget controls are very important for a small agency. Budgets should be reviewed monthly; ticket sales summaries, accounts receivable, and all expenditures should be studied for financial control.

Once a budget is in balance or in whatever relationship between revenues and expenses which an agency shall determine is an acceptable basis (for whatever reason) upon which to operate the business for ensuing fiscal year, the budget should be declared to be "locked," so that no expenditure can be made without first encumbering the appropriate budget line allocation. The principle is no different from making the proper deduction from the balance in a checkbook to determine that adequate funds are available to cover each check as it is written and before the check is released.

The technique for this routine is simple regardless of the size or complexity of the travel agency. The procedure may range from a simple manual method in a small agency to a completely computerized method in larger agency with sophisticated computers and the required skilled programmers. The essential instrument for control is a formal requisition form which must be presented (several types of forms for various purposes are used concurrently) in support of any and all expenditures. Since only those requisitions for which funds are available will be approved, no over expenditure in any budget line can be made.

The budget is undeniably a primary instrument of fiscal control, and demonstrates the efficiency (or lack thereof) with which a travel agency is combining its available resources to achieve sales results. The budget exhibits the flow of funds between income and expenditure, and shows the extent to which present activities contribute to the long-range goals.

AGENCY ACCOUNTING

Accounting services can help the owner-manager of a travel agency keep the business on a sound basis. Among these services are setting up recordkeeping procedures, interpreting a firm's records, and providing financial advice based on such an interpretation. Sample profit and loss statements are used in this section to illustrate how accounting services can help reveal and correct trouble spots.

Many small travel agencies seem to have the potential for success. The owner-managers are good travel counselors and offer services which attract customers. And in many cases, ticket sales are good.

Yet, because of poor financial management, some small service agencies fail. Others struggle to keep out of the red. Still others stay in the black only because the owner-managers are willing to work for low pay.

In some cases, the poor results are caused by inadequate financial records. In other firms, the records may be good, but the owner-manager lacks the ability or experience to use them.

In achieving effective financial management, the services of a public accountant are helpful. He can design records, set up ways for maintaining them, draw off vital information, and help relate it to a profitable operation.

Daily ticket sales provide a valuable source of information flow into a small service agency. As customers are served, pieces of information are generated about sales; cash; payroll; accounts payable; and, if credit is offered to customers, accounts receivable.

To capture these facts and figures, a system is necessary. The accountant can help design one for recording the information which the owner-manager needs if he is to control finances and make profitable decisions.

Such a system usually consists of bookkeeping records which may be set up in journals, ledgers, or other records. The accountant, with the following basic records, sets up a system according to your particular need.

Cash Receipts - used to record the cash which the business receives.

Cash Disbursements - Used to record the firm's expenditures.

Sales - Used to record and summarize weekly income.

Purchases - Used to record the purchases of merchandise bought for processing or resale.

Payroll - Used to record the wages of employees and their deductions, such as those for income and Social Security taxes.

Equipment - Used to record the firm's capital assets, such as equipment, office furniture, and motor vehicles.

Inventory - Used to record the firm's investments in stock which is needed for arriving at a true profit or financial statements and for income tax purposes.

Accounts Receivable - Used to record the balances which customers owe to the firm.

Accounts Payable - Used to record what the firm owes its creditors and suppliers.

DRAWING THE PICTURE

A set of books is like a roll of exposed film. The latter must be developed before you can see the picture.

Similarly, your books contain facts and figures which make up a picture of your business. They have to be arranged into an order before you see the picture.

The accountant draws such a picture by preparing financial statements, such as a profit and loss statement. The P and L statement shows what profit or loss your business had in a certain time period. A sample - "Profit and Loss Statement for Travel Agency" is shown below.

PROFIT AND LOSS STATEMENT
FOR TRAVEL AGENCY COMPANY

Gross Sales	Last Year	Percent	This Year	Percent
Airline Sales	$375,000	% 62.50	$ 880,000	% 58.67
Tours and Hotels	178,000	29.67	475,000	31.67
Cruises	21,000	3.50	72,000	4.80
Rail Sales	20,000	3.33	60,000	4.00
Other Sales (Car rental, travel ins., etc.)	6,000	1.00	13,000	.86
	$600,000	%100.00	$1,500,000	%100.00

OPERATING EXPENSES				
Salaries (Payroll Taxes)	$ 26,300	% 48.70	$ 68,500	% 50.74
Rent	2,700	5.00	6,750	5.00
Utilities	4,300	7.96	10,750	7.96
Office Supplies	1,000	1.85	2,500	1.85
Cleaning & Maintenance	1,000	1.85	2,600	1.93
Fees & Subscriptions	800	1.48	1,900	1.41
Insurance & Taxes	700	1.31	1,750	1.30
Employee Familiarization Trips	800	1.48	2,000	1.48
Advertising	3,600	6.67	9,000	6.67
Good Will	1,000	1.85	2,300	1.70
Miscellaneous	800	1.48	2,200	1.63
Total	$ 43,000	% 79.63	$ 110,250	% 81.67

SALES ALLOCATIONS				
Gross Sales	$600,000	100.00	$1,500,000	100.00
Commission 9%	54,000		135,000	
Operating Expenses	-43,000	-79.63	- 110,250	-81.67
Net Profit*	$ 11,000	%20.37	$ 24,750	% 18.33

*Before owner's salary.

Some aspects of the finanical picture of a small travel service may be a disappointing, although true, example. In the P and L statement the net profit of $24,000 does not warrant the time and effort which the owner-manager puts into a $1,500,000 business operation. Why is the profit so low?

The reason begins to appear when the accountant analyzes the agency's financial picture. The profit and loss statement shows how the operating expenditures are allocated to each category. Such information is easy to accumulate when your ticket sales records are set up to capture the breakdown at the time of the sale. In addition, it is possible to use percentages to show the part of each sales dollar used by each of the various expenses. This method is especially good for comparing current year financial statements with those of prior years to determine the trend of the business. It is also valuable in comparing your figures with those of other agencies in the travel business.

Two trouble areas in the budget stand out when the expenses figure of the Travel Agency Company are analyzed: increased sales with no substantial increase in net profit and the excessive payroll. Staff salaries could be reduced and a Teleticketing machine might be introduced to improve the efficiency of the office operations are two possible recommendations; other ways to cut operating expenses may focus on advertising, good will and other costs. It certainly does not make business sense to increase gross sales by 150 percent or $900,000 and earn a lesser percentage (-2.04%) in profits.

The increased gross sales were not from airline sales but tours and hotels which pay a higher commission. An airline sales breakdown would indicate if domestic and international revenues as well as an analysis of business and vacation travel during the year.

Now look at the other trouble area - payroll, where more than 51 percent of the commission income is spent for salaries and wages, a further study is required. It is even more serious when you recall that this percentage does not include the owner-manager's salary. Automation may be one way to make more efficient use of staffing resources.

The reasons for a large payroll cost are difficult to pinpoint in a service business. The accountant analyzes the situation by looking for answers to the following kinds of questions: (1) Is an accurate record maintained of time spent on travel services? (2) Is the 8-hour day of each agent accounted for? (3) When employees are paid overtime, is the additional expense justified? (4) Can employees do their work with minimum wasted effort and time? (Would a new automatic telephone system save time?) and (7) Is the percentage spent for payroll appropriate for travel service activities? These are some of the ways to use a P and L statement in a travel agency.

ADVICE AND ASSISTANCE

In addition to analyzing the profit and loss statement and pointing out areas which need control, your accountant can advise on financial management. He can advise on cash requirements, budget forecast, borrowing, business organization, and taxes.

On cash requirements, the accountant can help you work out the amount of cash needed to operate your firm during a certain period - for example, 3 months, 6 months, a year. He considers how much cash you will need for the following: to carry customer accounts receivable, to add to inventory, to pay current bills, to buy equipment, and to repay loans. In addition, he can determine how much of the cash will come from collections of accounts receivable and how much will have to be borrowed.

While working out the cash requirements, the accountant may notice and call to your attention danger spots such as accounts that are in arrears. One travel agency, for example, allowed a customer to fall behind in his payments until he owed approximately $18,000 in airline tickets. When he went bankrupt, the agency lost $16,000 - almost as much as a year's profit.

When you borrow, the accountant can assemble financial information such as a profit and loss statement and a balance sheet. The purpose of such data is to show the lender the financial position of your business and its ability to repay the loan. Using these data, the accountant can advise on whether you need a short-term or a long-term loan. The financial data which he compiles may include: the assets you will offer for collateral, your present debt obligations, a summary of how you will use the borrowed money, and a schedule of how you intend to repay. In addition, if the owner-manager has never borrowed before, the accountant may help by introducing him to a banker who knows and respects the accountant's reputation.

You, your accountant, and your attorney should work together to decide the type of organization that best fits your need. The accountant can point out the tax advantages and disadvantages of the various types of business organization - proprietorship, partnership, and corporation.

Taxes are another area in which the accountant can provide advice and assistance. Normally, a bookkeeping system which provides the information you need for making profitable decisions will suffice for tax purposes. However, if additional facts are needed because of your type of business, your accountant can bring them to your attention and suggest a method for recording them.

"We better weigh everything before we make a decision."

Lufthansa Photo

KEEPING TRAVEL AGENCY RECORDS

Adequate records are necessary to prepare various tax returns as well as ATC and AMTRAK reports. Business records are required by banks and other financial institutions. Many times financial records and reports are required by suppliers or other creditors.

A good recordkeeping system in a travel agency must be (1) simple to use, (2) easy to understand, (3) reliable, (4) accurate, (5) consistent, and (6) designed to provide information on a timely basis in order to complete the ATC, AMTRAK, and other required reports.

MINIMUM RECORDS REQUIRED

You will need four basic records:

1. Sales records (ticket sales)
2. Cash receipts
3. Cash disbursements (payments to ATC, wholesalers)
4. Accounts receivable

A travel business can enter each item in the Sales (ticket) and Cash Receipts register showing date, name, invoice number, and amount.

All receipts for the day should be deposited in the bank in a night depository. Deposit the exact amount received. Instead of paying out small amounts from receipts, use a Petty Cash Fund. By depositing the exact amount of receipts, the bank statement enables you to balance your Cash Receipts book readily.

Just as all receipts are deposited, all disbursements should be made by check, using the Petty Cash Fund for payment of small items, and purpose of expenditure in checkbook. Enter date, name, check number, and amount for each item. A bank charge is entered in the same manner as a check except that there is no check number.

Columns should be provided for common expense items for distribution of expenses. The amount disbursed is entered in the appropriate column, and a separate column is provided for miscellaneous charges.

BALANCING—BANK RECONCILIATIONS

Each page of sales, cash receipts, and disbursements should be balanced. A balance is also taken at the end of each month.

As soon as bank statements are received, balance them with your checkbook. Usually a form is provided on the back of the statements from the bank, substantially as follows:

Bank balance	$_____
Add deposits not recorded by the bank	$_____
Less outstanding checks	$_____
Balance as per books	$_____

PETTY CASH FUND

A Petty Cash Fund should be set up to be used for payment of small amounts not covered by invoices. A check should be drawn for, say, $25.00. The check is cashed and the fund placed in a box or drawer. When payments are made for such items as postage, freight, and bus fares, the times are listed on a printed form or even on a blank sheet. When the fund is nearly exhausted, the items are summarized and a check drawn to cover the exact amount expended. The check is cashed and the fund replenished. At all times the cash in the draw plus listed expenditures will equal the amount of the fund.

LIST EQUIPMENT

Keep a careful list of permanent equipment used in the business. Keep track of items useful for a year or longer and of appreciable value. Show date purchased, name of supplier, description of item, check number by which paid, and amount. If you own quite a number of items, prepare separate lists for automotive equipment, tools and manufacturing equipment, and furniture and fixtures. These lists provide the basis for calculating depreciation and provide supporting data for fixed asset accounts.

INSURANCE RECORD

Most travel businesses will have several types of insurance. Each policy should be listed showing type of insurance, coverage, name of insurer, dates effective (expiration date), and annual premiums. Be sure that all necessary types of coverage are obtained. Ask your insurance agent or broker to check your coverage.

ACCRUAL BASIS FOR RECORDS

The travel agency will use the accrual basis in order to account for the credit which is granted to customers. Accrual basis is defined as "a method of recording income and expenses, in which each item is reported as earned or incurred, without regard as to when actual payments are received or made." Charge sales are credited at once to Sales and charged to Accounts Receivable. When the bills are collected, the credit is to Accounts Receivable. Accruals should also be made for expense items payable in the future, such as yearly or semi-annual interest on loans. Such accruals are made by Journal entries.

DEPRECIATION

A charge to expenses should be made to cover depreciation of fixed assets, other than land. The corresponding credits are to Reserves for Depreciation. Fixed assets may be defined as items normally in use for one year or longer, such as buildings, automotive equipment, computers, equipment, furniture, and fixtures. Smaller agencies will usually charge depreciation at the end of their fiscal year, but a business with very substantial fixed assets will probably calculate depreciation monthly. Typically small businesses will use straight line depreciation based on the expected life of the items for book purposes. Buildings perhaps may have an estimated life of 20 years, with depreciation of 5% a year. Automobiles will have estimated lives of four or five years and should be depreciated at 20% or 25% per year.

BOOKKEEPING SYSTEMS

There are several copyrighted systems providing simplified records, usually in a simple record book. These systems cover the basic records with complete instructions

for their use. You can examine some of these systems at most office supply stores, or there are other systems available in the travel trade which are better suited for a travel agency.

FINANCIAL STATEMENTS

Use an outside accountant to prepare financial statements for your travel business. The principal financial statements, the Balance Sheet and Profit and Loss Statement, can easily be prepared from the basic records which also are the basis for keeping general books as described further on. The Balance Sheet is a picture of the business at a given moment, usually at the close of business at the end of a fiscal year, or at the end of a month or a quarter. It lists Assets, Liabilities, and Capital which is obtained by subtracting Liabilities from Assets. The Profit and Loss Statement pictures what has happened during a month or a longer period. Basically, it states the amount of sales from which is subtracted Expenses and Taxes, the balance being Profit or perhaps Loss. Up-to-date Balance Sheets and Profit and Loss Statements which follow will enable man to know the amount of his investment, how much he owes, his net worth, and indicates how profitable his business is this year compared with prior years.

GENERAL BOOKS

In addition to basic records a business will need a book for Journal entries. A Journal entry is used to record business transactions not involving cash, such as accruals for depreciation, expenses due at later dates, and so on. The following is a typical entry.

		Debit	Credit
Jan. 31	Interest Expense	$58.33	
	Accrued Interest Payable		$58.33

To record January share of
interest due on First National
Bank loan. Principal Amount
$10,000 @ 7% = $700.00
January share $58.33

A General Ledger is also kept to record balances of Assets, Liabilities, and Capital and to accumulate Sales and Expense items. A typical Classification of Accounts, all of which are recorded in the General Ledger, follows. At the end of each fiscal year, accounts are balanced and closed. Sales (income) and Expense Account balances are transferred to the Profit and Loss Account. The remaining Asset, Liability, and Capital accounts provide the figures for the Balance Sheet.

GENERAL CLASSIFICATION OF ACCOUNTS (Sample)

Assets (Debit)

100 - Cash in Banks
101 - Petty Cash Fund
102 - Accounts Receivable

105 - Materials and Supplies

107 - Prepaid Expenses
108 - Deposits

120 - Land
121 - Buildings
122 - Reserve for Depreciation - Buildings (Credit)
123 - Tools and Equipment
124 - Reserve for Depreciation - Equipment (Credit)
125 - Automotive Equipment
126 - Reserve for Depreciation - Automotive Equipment (Credit)
127 - Furniture and Fixtures
128 - Reserve for Depreciation - Furniture and Fixtures (Credit)

130 - Organization Expenses (to be amortized)

Liabilities (Credit)

200 - Accounts Payable
201 - Notes Payable

205 - Sales Taxes - Payable
206 - FICA Taxes - Payable
207 - Federal Withholding Taxes
208 - State Withholding Taxes
209 - Unemployment Taxes

220 - Long-Term Debt - Mortgages Payable
221 - Long-Term Debt - Other

225 - Miscellaneous Accruals

Capital Accounts (Credit)

300 - Common Capital Stock   } for Corporations
301 - Preferred Capital Stock
        or
300 - Proprietorship Account   } for Proprietorship
301 - Proprietor's Withdrawals

305 - Retained Earnings

Sales Accounts (Credit)

400 - Retail Ticket Sales and Commissions
401 - Domestic Airline Ticket Sales
402 - International Airline Ticket Sales
403 - Rail Ticket Sales
404 - Hotel Packages
405 - Bus Tours
406 - Tour Programs
407 - Rental Car Sales
408 - Insurance Sales

410 - Miscellaneous Income

Expenses (Debit)

500 - Salaries and Wages
501 - Contract Labor
502 - Payroll Taxes
503 - Utilities
504 - Telephone
505 - Rent
506 - Office Supplies

507 - Postage
508 - Maintenance Expense
509 - Insurance
510 - Interest
511 - Depreciation
512 - Travel Expense ("FAM" Trips)
513 - Entertainment
514 - Advertising
515 - Dues and Contributions

520 - Miscellaneous Expenses

The use of too many accounts should be avoided. Break down sales into enough categories to show a clear picture of the business. Use different expense accounts covering frequent or substantial expenditures but avoid minute distinctions which will tend to confuse rather than clarify. Use Miscellaneous Expense for small unrelated expense items.

ACCOUNTS RECEIVABLE CONTROL

A few rules should be followed to keep Accounts Receivable current. First, be sure bills are prepared when goods are shipped or service is rendered and mailed to correct addresses. Keep a close watch on larger accounts. At the end of each month, "age" your Accounts Receivable. List accounts and enter amounts that are current, unpaid for 30 days, and those 60 days and over. Find out exactly why all accounts 60 days and over are unpaid. Your system should help you collect these accounts.

Pay close attention to customers' complaints about bills. If a complaint is justified, propose an adjustment and reach an agreement with the customer. Do this promptly. If a customer is delinquent, try to obtain a promise of payment on a definite date. If payment is not received on the date promised, ask the customer to explain why and obtain a new promise. If you don't know a customer who asks for credit, use a simple form listing name, address, telephone number, place of employment, bank and credit references. Make sure that credit is warranted before you grant it.

PAYROLL RECORDS

Yearly and quarterly reports of individual payroll payments must be made to State and Federal Governments. Each individual employee receives a W-2 form at the yearend showing total withholding payments made for the employee during the calendar year. An employment card should be kept for each employee showing, among other things, social security number, name, address, telephone number, and name of next of kin and his address. Indicate whether the employee is married and the number of exemptions claimed. A W-4 form should also be on record.

A summary payroll should be made each payday showing names, employee number, rate of pay, hours worked, overtime hours, total pay and amount of deductions for FICA, withholding taxes and deductions for insurance, pension and/or savings plans. Also a separate sheet should be kept for each employee. On this individual Payroll Record, list rate of pay, social security number, and so on. Enter amounts for each pay period, covering hours worked, gross pay and the various deductions. At the end of each quarter add the amounts and balance. These forms provide the data you need for quarterly and annual reports.

EASY FILING

An easy filing method for a small business is to use a large manilla envelope for each month's paid invoices, tax returns, etc. Staple paid returned checks to paid invoices or tax returns. The cash disbursement record, which shows dates of payment and check numbers, makes it easy to locate paid invoices. It is good policy to keep records up to date. The best way to do it is by seeing that your recordkeeping is done daily.

SMALL BUSINESS FINANCIAL STATUS SUMMARY
(What a Travel Owner-Manager Should Know)

Daily
1. Cash on hand.
2. Bank balance (keep business and personal funds separate).
3. Daily Summary of sales and cash receipts (see attached).
4. That all errors in recording collections on accounts are corrected.
5. That a record of all monies paid out, by cash or check, is maintained.

Weekly
1. Accounts Receivable (take action on slow payers).
2. Accounts Payable (take advantage of discounts).
3. Payroll (records should include name and address of employee, social security number, number of exemptions, date ending the pay period, hours worked, rate of pay, total wages, deductions, net pay, check number).
4. Taxes and reports to State and Federal Government (sales, withholding, social security, etc.).
5. ATC Reports on Airline Ticket Sales (complete Summary of Invoices and Receipts of Travel Sales).

Monthly
1. That all Journal entries are classified according to like elements (these should be generally accepted and standardized for both income and expense) and posted to General Ledger.

2. That a Profit and Loss Statement for the month is available within a reasonable time, usually 10 to 15 days following the close of the month. This shows the income of the business for the month, the expense incurred in obtaining the income, and the profit or loss resulting. From this, take action to eliminate loss (adjust mark-up? reduce overhead expense? pilferage? incorrect tax reporting? incorrect buying procedures? failure to take advantage of cash discounts?).

3. That a Balance Sheet accompanies the Profit and Loss Statement. This shows assets (what the business has), liabilities (what the business owes), and the investment of the owner.

4. The Bank Statement is reconciled. (That is, the owner's books are in agreement with the bank's record of the cash balance.)

5. The Petty Cash Account is in balance. (The actual cash in the Petty Cash Box plus the total of the paid-out slips that have not been charged to expense total the amount set aside as petty cash.)

6. That all Federal Tax Deposits, Withheld Income and FICA Taxes (Form 501) and State Taxes are made.

AIR LINE REGISTER

AGENCY NAME Welcome Broads
STREET ADDRESS 1271 Ellen St
CITY AND STATE Sharon, NH
AGENCY NUMBER 3679-0
PAGE 1 of 1 PAGES
PERIOD COVERED 10/12– 10/18

DATE	NAME	DEBIT	CREDIT (CASH)	DISCOUNT TRAN. NO.	CREDIT (CHECK)	BALANCE	OLD BALANCE	COMM	AIRLINE CODE	TICKET FORM AND NUMBER	REMITTANCE NET AMOUNT
10-12-76	Ms. Nellie Byrne	146 00				146.00	(1) -0-	VOID	220	8436-201-340	VOID
10-12-76	Mr. G. Ouellette 2351	168 00				173 00	(2) 5 00 [168 00]	10 89	001	341	157 11
10-12-76	Mr. John Graf 2351	244 00				417 00	(3) 143 00 [244 00]	15 82	001	342	228 18
10-12-76	Mrs. Phyllis Knowlton	348 00				298 00	(4) (50 00)	27 60	015	343	320 40
10-12-75	Mr. Tony Truax	712 00				712 00	(5) (60 00)	56 72	026	344	655 28
	VOID	VOID				VOID	(6) --	VCID	001	345	VOID
10-13-76	Mrs. Barbara Roff	282 00				428 00	(7) 146 00	20 89	001	346	261 11
10-13-76	Mr. R. Buckley 2352	178 00				178 00	(8) -0- [178 00]	11 54	016	347	166 46
10-13-76	Ms. Joan Ferraro 2352	208 00				386 00	(9) 178 00 [208 00]	13 48	016	348	194 52
10-14-76	Linda Paradis	--				--	(10)		001	349-353	Exchange
10-14-76	Florence Magnuson	186 00				186 00	(11) -0-	13 78	016	354	172 22
10-14-76	Catherine Dumont	124 03				310 03	(12) 186 00	9 19	016	355	114 84
10-14-76	Liz Labelle	307 50				617 53	(13) 310 03	22 78	001	356	284 72
10-14-76	Mary Labelle	194 16				811 69	(14) 617 53	14 38	001	357	179 78
10-15-76	Mr. T. Hall	61 56				388 69	(15) 327 13	3 99	006	358	57 57
10-15-76	Mr. D. Demers	423 00				811 69	(16) 388 69	28 79	014	359/60	394 21
10-18 76	R. LaBonte 2353	71 00				20320	(17) 132 20 [71 00]	4 60	006	364	66 40 out of seq.
10-17-76	Mr. A. Senecal	338 00				676 00	(18) (1014 00)	28 48	015	361	309 52
10-18-76	Mrs. D. Senecal	338 00				338 00	(19) (676 00)	28 48	015	362	309 52
10-18-76	Miss J. Senecal	338 00				-0-	(20) (338 00)	28 48	015	363	309 52
10-18-76	E. Cohen	53 00				53 00	(21) -0-	3 43	006	365	49 57
10-18-76	W. Desmond	53 00				106 00	(22) 53 00	3 43	006	366	49 57
10-18-76	K. Cormier	53 00				159 00	(23) 106 00	3 43	006	367	49 57
10-18-76	Cassie Vanasse	367 00			-30 94	354 06	(24) 18 00 [367 00]	30 94	085	368	336 06
10-18-76	F. Krauzer	37 00				274 86	(25) 237 86	2 40	037	369	34 60
10-14-76	Ms. M. Fletcher	316 00				316 00	(26) 316 00	32 18	001	8642-385-284	283 82
10-14-76	Mr. A. Jamrog	316 00					(27)	32 18	001	285	283 82
10-12-76	J. Cassidy	376 00					(28)	37 60	007	8050-025-917	338 40
10-18-76	E. Riveria	234 20					(29)	18 50	007	8010-067-586 8010-067-587	215 70 3 42
		6 326 45					(T) 1,236 00	G 42 89			5825 89

EACH ENTRY IN REMITTANCE NET AMOUNT COLUMN MUST BE SUPPORTED WITH A DOCUMENT AUDITOR'S COUPON REFUND FLIGHT COUPON DEBIT MEMO OR CREDIT MEMO

April 6, 1979
DATE PREPARED
SIGNATURE

7. That Accounts Receivable are aged, i.e., 30, 60, 90 days, etc., past due. (Work all bad and slow accounts.)

8. That Inventory Control is worked to remove dead stock and order new stock. (What moves slowly? Reduce. What moves fast? Increase.)

9. Rail (AMTRAK Ticket Sales).

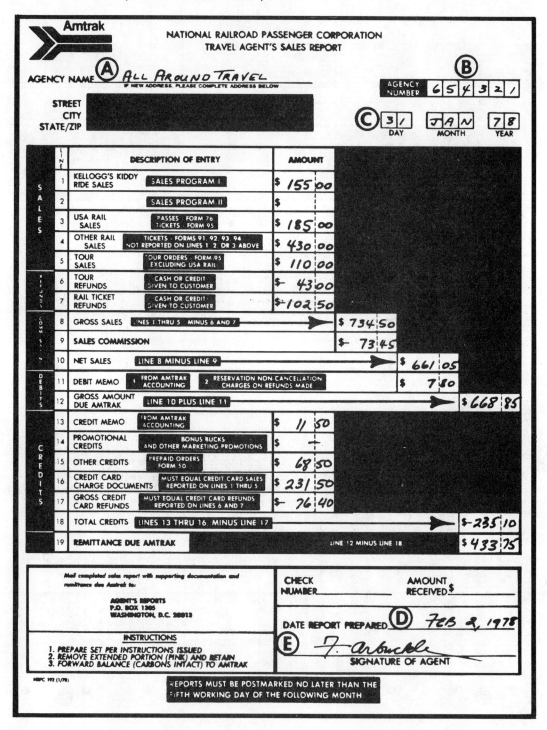

Chapter 4

TRAVEL AGENCY MANUALS

Knowing travelers call their travel agent indispensable, and unknowing travelers may not even call an agent at all. When an agent does answer questions, the major travel industry manuals are consulted. Agency manuals (guides and schedules) cover all areas of travel and are an important part of any travel training program. The major travel agency reference manuals are:

TRAVEL AGENTS HANDBOOK

NORTH AMERICAN EDITION of the OFFICIAL AIRLINE GUIDE (NAOAG)

WORLDWIDE EDITION OFFICIAL AIRLINE GUIDE (WEOAG)

THE TRAVEL PLANNER AND HOTEL/MOTEL GUIDE

CONSOLIDATED AIRTOUR MANUAL (CATM)

THE WORLDWIDE TOUR GUIDE

JAX FAX - THE TRAVEL MARKETING MAGAZINE

OFFICIAL STEAMSHIP GUIDE

OAG THE WORLDWIDE CRUISE AND STEAMSHIP GUIDE

THE OFFICIAL RAILWAY GUIDE

Since all of these publications provide "how to use" sections and later chapters in this text discuss portions of these guides and others, the focus in this chapter will be to provide an overview of the travel industry manuals available today. It is a skillful and experienced travel agent who uses these guides along with the telephone toll free numbers, and even the on-line computer reservation system to find the answers. In order to write a ticket for a client, the agent must know where to find a vast amount of information and must have available the flight itineraries of all scheduled airlines (including departure and arrival times, airline flight numbers and classes of service available) and the fares charged between any points. Travel agents should learn to use the OAG and other "quick, easy to use guides" in their daily work.

TRAVEL AGENT'S HANDBOOK

The OFFICIAL TRAVEL AGENTS HANDBOOK has been developed by the certified air carriers and is published by the Air Traffic Conference of America (ATC). All of the

25

trade practices are developed in this handbook and have been approved by the Civil Aeronautics Board (CAB). This ATC handbook is for the agent and includes these general operation procedures:

Standard Agent's Ticket and Area Settlement Plan which requires the travel agent to be responsible for the ticket stock.

Reservation procedures are established.

Ticketing instructions explain how to write all forms of tickets. The TRAVEL AGENTS HANDBOOK keeps agents informed on changes in ticketing procedures with an up-to-date filing.

U. S. Transportation and Tax Regulations are explained. Agents are obligated, as a participant in Interstate and International Travel, to collect the 8% domestic tax and U. S. International departure tax of $3.00. The HANDBOOK states the exact laws which govern the collection of these taxes by an authorized travel agent.

Commercial Credit Card Instruction states collection standard credit cards as well as Universal Air Travel Plan Card (UATP) payment procedures.

Free and Reduced Rate Travel are privileges of reduced rate transportation for the travel agent. After a continuous year of employment in an agency, the agent qualifies for reduced rate travel both Domestically and Internationally, i.e., FAM trips. The travel agent may qualify for as little as 25% of the regular international fare for vacations; many agents may also be able to secure land arrangements for as little as 10% to 25% of their actual value.

ATC Bond Requirement means that all travel agencies have to be bonded in the event their agency should be robbed or an agent should leave with some of their ticket stock. This bond will then cover their losses. All agencies must be bonded for at least $10,000 per agent. This section of the handbook explains the procedures in securing a bond and the requirements for an office. Without this bond an agency cannot be appointed by ATC or IATA.

Procedures to Change Name and/or Location and/or Ownership of a Travel Agency means that an agency has satisfied the experience requirements of two years in active promotion of the ATC and IATA carriers, and have had at least one of those years experience at an appointed agency or airline in ticketing and reservations. In addition to the experience requirements, the agency must furnish satisfactory personal references, and business references, as well as, a financial statement. The agency location must meet the necessary requirements of exposure to the general public. An appointed member of the Air Traffic Conference is assigned an identification number, similar to a checking account number. If for any reason the agency should fault on your agreement with the conference(s), the agency would forfeit ATC approval.

OFFICIAL AIRLINE GUIDE

The OFFICIAL AIRLINE GUIDE, the "OAG", contains the information schedules needed to provide your client with an itinerary anywhere in the world. The OAG contains useful travel information and should be used quickly and efficiently. The OAG comes

in two editions: NORTH AMERICAN EDITION OAG, which is published twice monthly and includes the United States, Canada and Mexico. WORLDWIDE EDITION OAG, which is published monthly, includes all international schedules.

The NAOAG shows both Direct and Connecting flights and fares of all scheduled airlines in U. S., Mexico, Canada and the Caribbean and shows departure/arrival times, type of aircraft, meal service, stops en route and a great deal more. Each issue is updated to include over 125,000 changes.

The WEOAG has complete city-by-city listings of worldwide scheduled airline flights to and between points outside the U. S., Canada, Mexico and the Caribbean. WEOAG includes a special carrier information section with timetable format, fares, reservation phone numbers and more. Each issue is updated to include over 100,000 changes.

Each OAG is divided into three parts. By far the largest is the middle section which contains flight schedules and includes point to point fares for the schedules shown. The front and back sections of the book contain supplementary information and regulations combined into what can best be termed "Passenger Service Information."

Front Section: abbreviations and reference marks; flight itineraries; U. S. Government and State Transportation taxes; stop press (last minute revisions); money and exchange rates; special fares; city/airport codes; minimum connecting times.

Flight Schedules: the largest and most frequently used section of the OAG is the part devoted to flight schedules. To find what flights are available between any two cities, you would look in this section under the heading for the "to", or destination city. All of the cities served by regularly scheduled airlines are listed in alphabetical order.

Back Section: interline ticketing and baggage agreements; free baggage allowance and excess baggage charges; indices of air carriers appearing in the publication; carrier acceptance of credit cards; how to use the OAG; U. S. and Canadian Domestic Airline Mileages; car rental agencies Worldwide Directories.

OAG TRAVEL PLANNER AND HOTEL/MOTEL GUIDE

The OAG TRAVEL PLANNER is a resource guide designed to answer "How can I get to Manchester, New Hampshire?"; "Is there a rental car on St. Simion Island, Georgia?"; "What is the nearest airport to the University of Southern New Mexico?"; or "What hotel is the nearest to the Tahsis, British Columbia (Canada) airport?" The OAG TRAVEL PLANNER is a convenient reference guide designed to answer the most difficult travel questions accurately and quickly. In the OAG TRAVEL PLANNER these are some travel facts an agent can locate:

Aircraft Landing Facilities	International Airline Route Maps
Airline Ticket/Sales Offices	Island Maps
Airline Ticket Reservation Phone Numbers	Limousine Fares, travel time and pick-up points
Airport Diagrams	Limousine Operators and the Areas served
Airport Facilities for Handicapped and Elderly	Local International Taxes
Airport Hotels/Motels	Major Attractions in Resort Areas
Airport Names, Codes and Distance	Metropolitan Area Maps

Area Codes
Bus Service
Calendar of Events (U.S. & Intern)
Carrier Gate and Ticket Counter
    Positions
Car Rental
Charter Air Taxi Fares
Charter Air Taxi Ticket Offices
Climate
Colleges and Universities
Commuter Air Carrier Ticket Offices
    & Reservation Phone Numbers
Consulate Offices in the U. S.
    and Canada
Convention Board Locations - U. S.
Credit Cards Accepted by Hotel/
    Motel Systems
Documents Accepted in Lieu of
    Passport
Documentary Requirements for U. S.
    and Canadian citizens
Free Limousine Pick-up Service
General Travel Information
Ground Transportation
Hotels/Motels
Hotel/Motel Locator Maps
Hotel/Motel Reservation Services
Hotel/Motel Systems

Mileage between off-line points and
    the airport
Military Installations
Mobil Quality Ratings (Hotel/Motel)
National Parks
Off-line Cities
On-line Cities
Parking Rates at the Airport
Passports
Photo requirements for visas
Postal Codes
Rail Service
Resort Areas
Scheduled off-line limousine service
Ski Areas
Tobacco Allowances
Toll-Free Reservation Numbers
Tourist Board locations
United States Airline Route Map
United States Foreign Service Offices
United States Passport Information
Vaccination Certificates Required
Visa Costs and validity period

The OAG TRAVEL PLANNER contains these major sections: Hotel/Motel Systems
Directory, Hotel/Motel Representatives, Destination Index, major airport diagrams,
metropolitan area maps, college and universities (U. S. and Canada), domestic non-
stop air mileages, military installations, directory of travel-related 800 numbers,
aircraft statistics, international airline route maps, international listing of
local taxes, and how to obtain a passport.

The European edition of the OAG TRAVEL PLANNER HOTEL/MOTEL GUIDE provides a
hotel/motel directory with classifications, weather and custom information, airport
diagrams, driving time and mileage between major European cities, local currency,
how to reach destinations without scheduled air service, car rental directory, hotel
reservation directory, a directory of European railroads, hotel reservation directory,
city and hotel locator maps, general travel and passport information, cities with
over 5,000 population, and a directory of travel-related toll free numbers. The
European Edition of the OAG TRAVEL PLANNER & HOTEL/MOTEL GUIDE is a complete guide
to destination and reference information in Europe. It features well over 85 city
center locator maps, country maps and airport diagrams. Alphabetical city listing
data includes how to reach destinations without scheduled air service; hotel information complete with classification; local airline numbers; and available Car Rental,
Rail and Airport Transportation services.

The European North American Editions of the OAG TRAVEL PLANNER are published
four times yearly.

CONSOLIDATED AIR TOUR MANUAL

The CONSOLIDATED AIR TOUR MANUAL (CATM) is a reference guide published by the

air carriers on tours offered in the United States, Canada, Bermuda, and the Caribbean. Any tour package printed in the CATM has a tour code (IT #) which means that the wholesaler has the approval of the carrier(s) and ATC, and thereby, any airline ticket sold in conjunction with one of these tours automatically qualified for a higher rate of commission (11%). The CATM is printed in 3 editions: the ALL YEAR manual--the packages in this book do not change according to seasons. They are the same all year; the SEASONAL manual--this manual is published twice a year (winter and summer); and the SPECIAL manual--printed for winter months that has skiing packages in U. S. and Canada.

OAG WORLDWIDE TOUR GUIDE

The OAG WORLDWIDE TOUR GUIDE is a comprehensive, easy-to-use catalogue of over 5,000 tours, each listed by destination, operator, duration, cost, itinerary and specific departure dates. There is a section of Special Interest Tours and the latest Inclusive Tour Charters. Every section offers a selection of escorted, independent, fly/drive and air/sea programs available for each destination. Each issue updated to include over 25,000 changes. The WORLDWIDE TOUR GUIDE is published three times a year.

OAG WORLDWIDE CRUISE AND SHIPLINE GUIDE

OAG CRUISE & SHIPLINE GUIDE contains booking procedures, steamship companies and reservation offices, detailed ship profiles, port terminal diagrams, quick reference cruise list organized on a "To" and "From" basis, shipline cross-reference tables, port-to-port sailings, as well as passenger/freighter service. This guide is published every two months.

JAX FAX TRAVEL MARKETING MAGAZINE

JAX FAX provides an official reference directory of public charters and inclusive tour schedules; all listings are grouped by destination. This TRAVEL MARKETING MAGAZINE offers a directory of ground operators, and tour operators, wholesalers and carriers; special reports are in each monthly issue. Each JAX FAX schedule gives the destination, "To" and "From" cities, departure and return dates, number of days, price, type of charter, e.g., public, airline operator, operator/wholesaler, hotel information, and additional information. JAX FAX also provides monthly features and "department" reports of interest to the travel agent.

OFFICIAL STEAMSHIP GUIDE

The OFFICIAL STEAMSHIP GUIDE provides shipline schedules and fares and extensive cruise lists for the Bahamas/Bermuda, Caribbean (West Indies),Mexico (South America), Alaska, Australia, Canada, World Cruises, South Pacific/South America/Far East, Scandinavia, Europe/Mediterranean/Dalmation/Africa, and the Greek Islands (Eastern Mediterranean). The GUIDE also contains: consolidated schedules of Atlantic passenger liners; port-to-port passenger index; port-to-port passenger freighter index; vessel tonnages; and alphabetical index of ship lines.

The "cruise list" in the OFFICIAL STEAMSHIP GUIDE is updated monthly and is arranged by departure dates. Each cruise listing shows the name and the Table Number of the operator for easy reference to the Schedule/Fare listings which appear in the order of their Table Nos. in the Schedules/Fares section immediately following the Cruise List. In "schedules/fares" each ship line supplied detailed data essential to your booking procedures. Ship lines are listed, not necessarily alphabetically, but by their Table Nos. which appear in bold type at the top corner of each page. The GUIDE also contains a "late news digest" which is useful for the travel agent.

THE OFFICIAL RAILWAY GUIDE

The OFFICIAL RAILWAY GUIDE (ORG) offers a monthly resource of North American and Worldwide rail information. AMTRAK, CONRAIL, SOUTHERN, to name only three, have schedules (names of trains) by metropolitan and/or suburban areas of service, e.g., Newark/New York City. The ORG provides a convenient reference for the AMTRAK tariff. The carriers and their schedules in Canada are given the ORG. There is also a Mexican railway passenger service schedule, names of trains and areas served. The ORG "international schedules" are representative of the major rail services used by North Americans who travel in other parts of the world. ORG schedules are condensed, showing only major points along particular routes fror Australia, Western Europe, Germany, and Great Britain, Japan and South Africa. The ORG also provides rail tour and operator information for the convenience of the travel agent.

Additional industry reference guides which provide accurate, authoritative schedules and useful travel information are:

ABC TRAVEL GUIDES: RAIL AND SHIPPING (UNITED KINGDOM)

AMERICAN SIGHTSEEING INTERNATIONAL WORLD TARIFF

AMTRAK TIMETABLE, TARIFF, AND TOUR MANUAL

EURAIL GUIDE

FORD'S FREIGHTER TRAVEL GUIDE/DECK PLANS

HOTEL AND TRAVEL INDEX

OFFICIAL HOTEL AND RESORT GUIDE

RUSSELL'S BUS GUIDE

THE GRAYLINE TARIFF

THE RED BOOK

THOMAS COOK'S CONTINENTAL TIMETABLE (BUS)

THOMAS COOK INTERNATIONAL TIMETABLE (RAIL)

WORLD HOTEL GUIDE

Chapter 5

AIRLINES AND AIR TARIFFS

DOMESTIC CARRIERS

Several hundred airlines serve the world today. In the United States there are some fifty large corporations providing air transportation. No one air carrier serves every city in our nation. The major airlines, domestic trunk carriers, have permanent operating rights within the continental United States; these airlines are hired by the public and operate on a fixed schedule. There are currently ten major trunk carriers serving medium and high density traffic routes, i.e., the "golden triangle" of New York, Washington, and Chicago. The domestic trunk carriers operating between the larger United States cities include: American, Braniff, Continental, Delta, Eastern, National, Northwest, Trans World, United and Western. As a travel agent, it is frequently necessary to use several airlines to complete a trip and since no one airline services every city, it becomes essential for you to know the major route structure and remember the general geographic regions served. In this time of de-regulation air routes are frequently being changed.

AMERICAN AIRLINES	AA serves the east and west coasts of the United States via cities in the central portion of the nation. AA also provides international service to the Caribbean, Mexico, and the South Pacific.
BRANIFF AIRLINES	BN flies the east coast, the northwest and central portions of the United States, Hawaii, South America, and Europe; the headquarters for Braniff is Dallas.
CONTINENTAL AIRLINES	CO serves Chicago and cities west of the Mississippi River, Hawaii and the South Pacific.
DELTA AIRLINES	DL serves the United States coast to coast and with a concentration of service in the Eastern portion, with routes to Canada and the Caribbean.
EASTERN AIRLINES	EA offers direct service to most east coast cities; also serves the West Coast, Mexico, Canada and the Caribbean.
NATIONAL AIRLINES	NA serves the east and west coasts and international service from Miami to London, England.

NORTHWEST ORIENT AIRLINES
NW serves the United States coast to coast, Florida, Hawaii, Alaska, Canada, the Orient and Scotland.

TRANS WORLD AIRLINES
TW serves the United States coast to coast through the mid-section of the nation; TW has trans global service.

UNITED AIRLINES
UA serves the United States coast to coast, including Hawaii.

WESTERN AIRLINES
WA serves the western states, including flights to Hawaii, Alaska, Canada, and Mexico

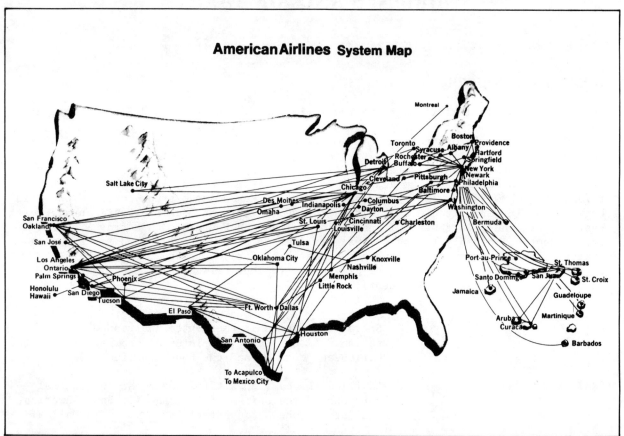

American Airlines System Map

Regional airlines, domestic local service carriers, were granted Certificates of Convenience and Necessity on an experimental basis in 1945; in 1958, the airlines still in operation were granted permanent certificates. There are currently eight domestic local service carriers operating on routes of lesser traffic density.

ALLEGHENY
AL serves the Northeast and the Ohio River Valley region with western limits of Chicago, St. Louis, and Memphis, and recent service to Florida and other southern cities.

FRONTIER AIRLINES
FL provides service to the Midwest and Rocky Mountain states.

HUGHES AIRWEST

RW serves the west coast region, including Canada and Mexico.

NORTH CENTRAL AIRLINES

NC serves the North Central portion of the nation with scheduled service to Denver and New York City.

OZARK AIRLINES

OZ services the Midwest with routes to Denver, Dallas/Ft. Worth, Washington, and New York.

PIEDMONT AIRLINES

PI serves the Southeastern region and states of Virginia, Tennessee, Carolina (North and South) and Georgia. Additional service to New York City, Boston and Chicago is also provided.

SOUTHERN AIRWAYS

SO provides the Southeast with additional service to St. Louis, Chicago, Washington, DC and New York.

TEXAS INTERNATIONAL AIRLINES

TI serves the Southwestern portion with routes into California, Utah, Colorado, Tennessee and Mississippi; it also provides air service to Mexico.

International and territorial air carriers serve the United States and a US territory or foreign country with the exception of Canada include: Alaska, American, Braniff, Delta, Eastern, National, Northwest, Pan American, Trans World, United and Western.

The US Flag Carriers operating around the world:

Airline	Code	Region
PAN AMERICAN	PA	Africa, Asia, Middle East
TRANS WORLD	TW	
AMERICAN	AA	Australia/New Zealand
PAN AMERICAN	PA	
AMERICAN	AA	
DELTA	DL	
NORTHWEST	NW	
PAN AMERICAN	PA	Canada
UNITED	UA	
WESTERN	WA	
BRANIFF	BN	London and Paris only
NATIONAL	NA	London only
NORTHWEST	NW	Scotland
PAN AMERICAN	PA	Europe
TRANS WORLD	TW	
NORTHWEST	NW	
PAN AMERICAN	PA	Far East (Asia)
TRANS WORLD	TW	

AMERICAN	AA		
BRANIFF	BN		
EASTERN	EA		
AIR WEST	RW	Mexico	
PAN AMERICAN	PA		
TEXAS INTERNATIONAL	TI		
WESTERN	WA		
AMERICAN	AA		
CONTINENTAL	CO		
DELTA	DL		
NORTHWEST	NW	Pacific Islands	
PAN AMERICAN	PA		
TRANS WORLD	TW		
BRANIFF	BN	South America	
PAN AMERICAN	PA		

Frequently air carriers offer only or primarily intra-state airline service, such as Pacific Southwest Airlines (PSA); routes that do not cross state lines are not under Federal control (CAB). Intra-state air carriers operate under the control of the state transportation departments.

There are two intra-Hawaiian Air carriers: Aloha Airlines (TS) and Hawaiian Airlines (HA) operating exclusively with the Islands. Similar to the intra-Hawaiian carriers, the Intra-Alaskan air service includes: Kodiak, Western Alaska, Wien Consolidated and Reeve Aleutian carriers.

Helicopter carriers provide both mail and passenger service between large urban centers; presently certified helicopter air carriers are: New York Airways, Los Angeles Airways, Chicago Helicopter Airways, and San Francisco-Oakland Helicopter Airlines.

There are more than a dozen supplemental air carriers on charter airlines in existence; business comes from government contracts and charters. All cargo air carriers which operate on a scheduled basis are restricted to the transport of livestock, freight and mail; the main cargo air carriers are: Airlift International, Flying Tiger, and Seaboard World.

Non-certified air carriers include Air Taxi companies and Air Freight Forwarders. Air Taxis are light aircraft up to a gross weight of 12,500 lbs., and operate a short haul transport of passengers and cargo.

INTERNATIONAL CARRIERS

International airlines or "Flag Carriers" represent their country and normally have the country's flag painted on the airplane. The majority of international carriers are owned and sponsored by the government of that country. The international airlines and routes require agreements between the various governments based on socio-economic considerations as well as the frequency of flights from one nation to another. The International Air Transport Association (IATA) attempts to resolve policies and fares applicable to the participating international air carriers. The largest of the US Flag Carriers are: Trans World (TW), Pan American (PA), Northwest Orient (NW), and Braniff International (BN). TW and PA have around the world service; PA also provides air service to South America. BN operates from the US to Mexico and South America; and more recently to London. NW operates from the US to Alaska, Hawaii, the Orient, the United Kingdom, and Scandanavia.

IATA CARRIER

Yesterday's Junker G 31 delivered to Lufthansa was baptized "Hermann Kohl" in recognition of his pioneer-crossing of the North Atlantic from East to West. When it put this three-engine Junker G 31 into service, Lufthansa was the world's first airline to serve food and beverage on board.   Lufthansa Photo

Lufthansa Boeing 747   Lufthansa Photo

International airline name, code and country are listed for review; an appendix listing provides a description of the routes and other pertinent information.

AIRLINE	CODE	COUNTRY
AER LINGUS	EI	IRELAND
AEROFLOT	SU	U.S.S.R. (Soviet Union)
AEROLINEAS ARGENTINAS	AR	ARGENTINA
AERO MEXICO	AM	MEXICO
AIR AFRIQUE	RK	IVORY COAST, (West Africa)
AIR CANADA	AC	CANADA
AIR FRANCE	AF	FRANCE
AIR INDIA	AI	INDIA
AIR JAMAICA	JM	JAMAICA
AIR NEW ZEALAND	TE	NEW ZEALAND
ALITALIA	AZ	ITALY
AMERICAN AIRLINES	AA	U.S.A.
ANSETT AIRLINES	AN	AUSTRALIA
AUSTRIAN	OS	AUSTRIA
AVIANCA	AV	COLUMBIA, SOUTH AMERICA
BRANIFF	BN	U.S.A
BRITISH	BA	UNITED KINGDOM
BRITISH WEST INDIAN AIRWAYS	BW	TRINIDAD, WEST INDIES
CHINA AIR LINES, LTD	CI	TAIWAN, REPUBLIC OF CHINA
CZECHOSLOVAK-CSA	OK	CZECHOSLOVAKIA
CUBANA	CU	CUBA
DELTA	DL	U.S.A.
EAST AFRICAN AIRWAYS	EC	KENYA
EGYPTAIR	MS	ARAB REPUBLIC OF EGYPT
ETHIOPIAN	ET	ETHIOPIA
FINNAIR	AY	FINLAND
IBERIA	IB	SPAIN
JAPAN AIR LINES	JL	JAPAN
KLM-ROYAL DUTCH AIRLINES	KL	NETHERLANDS
KOREAN	KE	KOREA
KUWAIT AIRWAYS	KU	KUWAIT
LOT	LO	POLAND
LUFTHANSA	LH	GERMANY
MAS-MALAYSIAN AIRLINE SYSTEM	MH	MALAYSIA

AIRLINE	CODE	COUNTRY
MEXICANA	MX	MEXICO
MEA—MIDDLE EAST AIRLINES	ME	LEBANON
NATIONAL	NA	U.S.A.
NORTHWEST ORIENT	NW	U.S.A.
OLYMPIC AIRWAYS	OA	GREECE
PAKISTAN INTERNATIONAL	PK	PAKISTAN
PAN AMERICAN WORLD AIRWAYS	PA	U.S.A.
PHILIPPINE	PR	PHILLIPINES
QANTAS AIRWAYS, LTD	QF	AUSTRALIA
SABENA	SN	BELGIUM
SCANDINAVIAN	SK	SWEDEN
SINGAPORE	SQ	SINGAPORE
SOUTH AFRICAN AIRWAYS	SA	REPUBLIC OF SOUTH AFRICA
SWISSAIR	SR	SWITZERLAND
TAP	TP	PORTUGAL
THAI	TG	THAILAND
TWA	TW	U.S.A.
UTA	UT	FRANCE
VARIG	RG	BRAZIL
VIASA	VA	VENEZUELA

AIRLINE REGULATION AND DEREGULATION

The United States has had forty years of airline regulations. Before 1938 there were no legal regulations in the United States for determining airline fares, and each carrier charged whatever fares it believed necessary and treated passengers by whatever rules it thought necessary. In December 1978 deregulation of the airlines took place in the United States. Does this mean that in the future there will be a complete lack of uniformity among the carriers, and passengers will not be sure what fare they are going to be charged?

Recent decisions by the CAB have avoided the awarding of routes that require some protection from new competitors. The CAB claims that the best way to guarantee a sustained price competition for the public is to allow all qualified carriers to compete freely in the marketplace, with a minimum of government interference. The future, like the early 1930's, may be full of surprises for the air traveler.

The Civil Aeronautics Act of 1938 was the organizing principle of modern aviation or the Federal regulation of fares and services of scheduled airlines operating in the United States. The Congress established that airlines should be regulated so that travellers would not be charged unreasonable rates and the methods of handling passengers be safe and uniform. The Congress did not want the scheduled airlines to engage in price wars, and thereby, competition which could curb or eliminate the growth of smaller airlines in the marketplace.

AIRLINE TARIFF PUBLISHING COMPANY, AGENT

JOINT PASSENGER FARES TARIFF No. EJ-17

CONTAINING

JOINT ONE WAY AND ROUND TRIP FARES AND RULES

Governing The Transportation of

PASSENGERS

and Baggage

APPLICABLE

BETWEEN POINTS IN

ALASKA AND POINTS IN THE UNITED STATES

BETWEEN POINTS IN CANADA

BETWEEN POINTS IN

CANADA AND POINTS IN THE UNITED STATES

BETWEEN POINTS IN

HAWAII AND POINTS IN THE UNITED STATES

For List of Participating Air Carriers See Page 1

FOR REFERENCE TO GOVERNING TARIFFS, SEE RULE NO. 1, AS AMENDED

Departure from the terms of Section 221.165 of its Economic Regulations authorized by the Civil Aeronautics Board (5934).

FOR EXPLANATION OF ABBREVIATIONS, SYMBOLS AND REFERENCE MARKS, SEE PAGES 2 - 9.

| ISSUED:
AUGUST 1, 1978 | Issued by
C. C. SQUIRE,
President
AIRLINE TARIFF PUBLISHING COMPANY, AGENT
DULLES INTERNATIONAL AIRPORT
P. O. BOX 17415
WASHINGTON, D. C. 20041 | EFFECTIVE:
SEPTEMBER 15, 1978 |

Between 1938 and 1978, all fares which an air carrier charges its travellers for transportation between any two points in the nation were approved by the Civil Aeronautics Board (CAB). The CAB is an independent agency, responsible only to the President and has certain judicial powers delegated by the Congress; and consists of five members, including a Chairman and Vice-Chairman. The primary purpose of the Civil Aeronautics Board has been as an economic regulatory agency for the airlines industry. The CAB would authorize reasonable competition to develop the quality of air service, and would control the number of airlines allowed to operate over each available route.

Before a carrier could provide interstate scheduled air service, it would have to obtain a Certificate of Public Convenience and Necessity. Each airlines had to demonstrate to the CAB that it was capable of performing the transportation properly and that the services would be a public convenience and necessity. After an airline has been certificated, it remains under the constant surveillance of the CAB. While the airline must comply with a long list of service requirements, it is important to realize that a scheduled airliner, CAB approved, must provide regular service to all points designated on its certificate according to a complete system flight schedule filed with the agency. The carrier cannot suspend service at any uneconomic point without CAB authorization. Airlines were required to file all fares with the CAB, which can reject them if not justified in the public interest. Further regularly scheduled airlines must maintain records open to CAB inspection at any time and file quarterly full service, traffic and financial reports. Air carriers cannot merge, consolidate or acquire another airline without CAB approval.

The 1938 Act provided for a "Tariff" structure or guideline to establish passenger rules and fares, and once a fare was approved between two cities, that became the only legal fare the airliner could charge. Airline tariffs include air costs for transportation and the rules covering such passage. Air tariffs are a compardium of regulations and fares that public carriers are authorized to charge. All rules and fares are binding on both travelers and carriers. Travel agents in the United States (and Canada) are required to use two sets of tariffs; domestic fares and rules and international regulations and fares.

All scheduled domestic airlines publish their fares in one official publication, the AIRLINERS CONSOLIDATED PASSENGER TARIFF (ACTP). Airline tariffs include the fares and routes points in the United States and Canada.

The passenger tariff is generally divided into several categories which include: the LOCAL AND JOINT PASSENGER RULES TARIFF; the LOCAL PASSENGER FARES TARIFF; and the JOINT PASSENGER FARES TARIFF. The tariff is kept current through revisions which occur frequently and is used widely by travel agents and airline offices. With more than 375,000 joint and over 200,000 local passenger fares, the tariff is a complex publication. The tariffs do not include fares of intrastate carriers or nonscheduled airlines unless specific exceptions are stated, e.g., Aloha Airlines.

Airlines and travel agencies must have a complete copy of all tariffs at all offices where air tickets are being sold in order to obtain the correct fares. Revisions are received at least monthly, sometimes weekly, and it is essential to review and revise all tariffs promptly. To maintain a tariff properly, the agent should compare each revision transmittal number with the list on the cover sheet to be sure that each revision is in sequence and complete. It is important to check the correction numbers on the correction number pages published in the front of each tariff. The agent should note each effective date and any information on the transmittal that is specially important, and then collate and insert in the tariff all effective pages.

Be sure to keep all transmittal pages and any pages not yet effective in a separate three-ring binder; keep this binder available at all times for future booking information.

DELTA AIR LINES, INC.

Fares include U.S. Government Transportation Tax

The rules and conditions applicable to the listed fares are shown in the Table following the listing of fares and are cross-referenced by the fare class codes which are explained in that Table.

from BALTIMORE

FARE CLASS		ATLANTA	BOSTON	COLUMBIA, S.C.	FT.LAUDER-DALE	HOUSTON	MIAMI	NEW ORLEANS	NEW YORK/NEWARK	ORLANDO	TAMPA
F	OW	96.00	74.00	79.00	134.00	164.00	134.00	139.00	48.00	118.00	123.00
Y	OW	74.00	57.00	61.00	103.00	126.00	103.00	107.00	37.00	91.00	95.00
FN	OW	74.00	57.00	61.00	103.00	126.00	103.00	107.00	37.00	91.00	95.00
YN	OW	59.00	46.00	49.00	82.00	101.00	82.00	86.00	30.00	73.00	76.00
YM	OW	56.00	43.00	46.00	77.00	95.00	77.00	80.00	28.00	68.00	71.00
YNWE6	RT	89.00	68.00	73.00	124.00	151.00	124.00	128.00	44.00	109.00	114.00
YNXE6	RT	74.00	57.00	61.00	103.00	126.00	103.00	107.00	37.00	91.00	95.00
YCD	OW	49.00	38.00	41.00	69.00	84.00	69.00	71.00	25.00	61.00	63.00
YWE6	RT	104.00	80.00	85.00	144.00	176.00	144.00	150.00	52.00	127.00	133.00
YXE6	RT	89.00	68.00	73.00	124.00	151.00	124.00	128.00	44.00	109.00	114.00
YCHE6	RT	74.00	57.00	61.00	103.00	126.00	103.00	107.00	37.00	91.00	95.00
YE78	RT	...	...	...	144.00	...	144.00	...	...	127.00	133.00
YWE46	RT	126.00	97.00	104.00	175.00	214.00	175.00	182.00	63.00	155.00	161.00
YXE46	RT	118.00	91.00	98.00	165.00	202.00	165.00	171.00	59.00	146.00	152.00
YNWE46	RT	111.00	86.00	91.00	154.00	189.00	154.00	160.00	56.00	137.00	142.00
YNXE46	RT	104.00	80.00	85.00	144.00	176.00	144.00	150.00	52.00	127.00	133.00
YCHE46	RT	74.00	57.00	61.00	103.00	126.00	103.00	107.00	37.00	91.00	95.00
YWE88	RT	...	57.00	...	...	...	...	...	41.00	...	...
YG3	OW	...	48.00	...	...	...	...	...	31.00	...	...
YG3	RT	...	91.00	...	...	...	...	...	59.00	...	...
YG18	RT	...	80.00	...	...	176.00	...	...	...	...	...
YG49	RT	...	...	...	137.00	...	137.00	143.00	...	121.00	127.00
YCHG49	RT	...	...	...	103.00	...	103.00	107.00	...	91.00	95.00
YG77	RT	...	...	...	...	164.00	...	...	48.00	...	...
YV28	RT	...	...	...	...	...	...	...	171.00	...	...
YHV17	RT	...	...	...	144.00	...	144.00	...	...	...	...
YHV28	RT	...	...	...	177.00	...	177.00	...	...	...	...
YLV17	RT	...	...	...	134.00	...	134.00	...	...	...	...
YLV28	RT	...	...	...	163.00	...	163.00	...	...	...	...

from WASHINGTON

FARE CLASS		ATLANTA	BANGOR	BIRMINGHAM	BOSTON	HOUSTON	JACKSON, MISS.	MONTGOMERY	NEW ORLEANS	ORLANDO	PORTLAND, ME.
F	OW	96.00	100.00	107.00	78.00	164.00	129.00	110.00	139.00	118.00	90.00
Y	OW	74.00	77.00	82.00	60.00	126.00	99.00	85.00	107.00	91.00	69.00
FN	OW	74.00	...	82.00	60.00	126.00	99.00	85.00	107.00	91.00	...
YN	OW	59.00	...	66.00	48.00	101.00	79.00	68.00	86.00	73.00	...
YM	OW	56.00	58.00	62.00	45.00	95.00	74.00	64.00	80.00	68.00	52.00
YNWE6	RT	89.00	...	98.00	72.00	151.00	119.00	102.00	128.00	109.00	...
YNXE6	RT	74.00	...	82.00	60.00	126.00	99.00	85.00	107.00	91.00	...
YCD	OW	49.00	51.00	55.00	40.00	84.00	66.00	57.00	71.00	61.00	46.00
YWE6	RT	104.00	108.00	115.00	84.00	176.00	139.00	119.00	150.00	127.00	97.00
YXE6	RT	89.00	92.00	98.00	72.00	151.00	119.00	102.00	128.00	109.00	83.00
YCHE6	RT	74.00	77.00	82.00	60.00	126.00	99.00	85.00	107.00	91.00	69.00
YHE8	RT	111.00	...	123.00	...	...	149.00	127.00	...	...	...
YLE8	RT	89.00	...	98.00	...	...	119.00	102.00	...	...	...
YE78	RT	...	...	...	...	...	...	...	...	127.00	...
YWE46	RT	126.00	131.00	139.00	102.00	214.00	168.00	144.00	182.00	155.00	117.00
YXE46	RT	118.00	123.00	131.00	96.00	202.00	158.00	136.00	171.00	146.00	110.00
YNWE46	RT	111.00	...	123.00	90.00	189.00	149.00	127.00	160.00	137.00	...
YNXE46	RT	104.00	...	115.00	84.00	176.00	139.00	119.00	150.00	127.00	...
YCHE46	RT	74.00	77.00	82.00	60.00	126.00	99.00	85.00	107.00	91.00	69.00
YWE88	RT	...	...	...	60.00	...	...	...	...	...	...
YG3	OW	...	...	...	51.00	...	...	...	...	...	...
YG3	RT	...	...	...	96.00	...	...	...	...	...	...
YG18	RT	...	...	...	84.00	176.00	...	...	...	...	...
YG49	RT	...	...	...	...	...	...	...	...	...	...
YCHG49	RT	...	...	...	...	...	...	...	143.00	121.00	...
YG77	RT	...	...	...	...	164.00	...	...	107.00	91.00	...
YV28	RT	...	...	...	...	...	...	...	171.00	...	...

OW-ONE WAY   RT-ROUND TRIP

BALTIMORE - NEWARK

DELTA AIR LINES, INC.

FARE	FARE CLASS CODE		FARE DESCRIPTION	FARE APPLIES	MINIMUM/ MAXIMUM STAY	RESERVATIONS AND TICKETING	APPROXIMATE CHILDREN'S DISCOUNT (2-11 YEARS - ACCOMPANIED).	SPECIAL CONDITIONS
48.	F	OW	First Class	Any Day	None	Any time prior to departure.	1/3	None
37.	Y	OW	Day Coach	Any Day	None	Any time prior to departure.	1/3	None
37.	PN	OW	Deluxe Night Coach	Any day on specified flights departing between 9:00 p.m. and 6:59 a.m.	None	Any time prior to departure.	1/3	None
30.	YN	OW	Night Coach					
28.	YM	OW	Military Reservation	Any Day	None	Any time prior to departure.	None	Passenger must be on furlough, leave, or pass and have valid military identifica- tion.
25.	YCD	OW	Senior Citizens Coach	Any Day	None	Reservations may not be made prior to one day before departure. Tickets may be purchased up to one hour prior to departure.	None	Passenger must be at least 65 years of age and have proof of age in possession at all times. Fares are not available on all flights.
	YHE8	RT	Peak Season Coach Excursion	From May 25, 1979 through Aug. 31, 1979. On Saturday for the outbound portion and return on the first Monday or Tuesday following departure or on any other Saturday within 30 days. Fares are not available on certain days during holiday and peak travel periods. EXCEPTIONS: Fares to/from Miami/ Ft. Lauderdale apply Dec. 16, 1978 through Apr. 14, 1979.	2-Day Min. 30-Day Max.	Reservations must be confirmed and tickets purchased for the entire trip prior to departure.	None	None
41.	YLE8	RT	Off-Peak Season Coach Excursion	Through May 24, 1979. On Saturday for the outbound portion and return on the first Monday or Tuesday following departure or any other Saturday within 30 days. Fares are not available on certain days during holiday and peak travel periods. EXCEPTIONS: Fares to/from Miami/ Ft. Lauderdale apply through Dec. 15, 1978 and Apr. 15, 1979 through Aug. 31, 1979.				
	YWE88	RT	Saturday Flight Sale Coach	Between 12:01 a.m. Saturday and 12:01 p.m. Sunday.	No Min. 2-Day Max. Including day of departure.	Reservations must be confirmed and tickets purchased for the entire trip prior to departure on the outbound portion.	None	All travel must be completed within the same weekend.
52.	YWE6	RT	Peak Coach Advance Purchase Excursion	Friday, Saturday, Sunday EXCEPTIONS: From Noon Friday through Midnight Sunday between Los Angeles/San Diego/San Francisco and Ft. Lauderdale/Miami/Tampa. Travel to/from Florida is not available on certain days during holiday and peak travel periods.	7-Day Min. Except to/ from Florida cities (not including Jackson- ville) minimum stay is 12:01 a.m. of 1st Sunday after departure. 45-Day Max.	Reservations must be confirmed and tickets purchased 30 days prior to departure. To/from Florida cities, except Jacksonville, reservations must be confirmed and tickets purchased 7 days prior to departure.	See YCHE6 Fares.	Fares are not available on all flights.
44.	YXE6	RT	Off-Peak Coach Advance Purchase Excursion	Monday, Tuesday, Wednesday, Thursday EXCEPTIONS: From 12:01 a.m. Monday through 11:59 a.m. Friday between Los Angeles/San Diego/San Francisco and Ft. Lauderdale/Miami/Tampa. Travel to/from Florida is not available on certain days during holiday and peak travel periods.				
37.	YCHE6	RT	Children's Coach Advance Purchase Excursion	Any Day EXCEPTIONS: Travel to/from Florida is not available on certain days during holiday and peak travel periods.				
44.	YNWE6	RT	Peak Night Coach Advance Purchase Excursion	Friday, Saturday, Sunday on Night Coach flights generally departing between 9:00 p.m. and 6:59 a.m. EXCEPTIONS: Travel to/from Florida is not available on certain days during holiday and peak travel periods.			See YCHE6 Fares.	
37.	YNXE6	RT	Off-Peak Night Coach Advance Purchase Excursion	Monday, Tuesday, Wednesday, Thursday on Night Coach flights generally departing between 9:00 p.m. and 6:59 a.m. EXCEPTIONS: Travel to/from Florida is not available on certain days during holiday and peak travel periods.				

OW - One Way Fares.   RT - Round Trip Ticket Required.

BAL-003

DELTA AIR LINES, INC.

	FARE CLASS CODE		FARE DESCRIPTION	FARE APPLIES	MINIMUM/ MAXIMUM STAY	RESERVATIONS AND TICKETING	APPROXIMATE CHILDREN'S DISCOUNT (2-11 YEARS - ACCOMPANIED).	SPECIAL CONDITIONS
63.	YWE46	RT	Weekend Advance Purchase Excursion Coach	Friday, Saturday, Sunday	12:01 a.m. of the 1st Sunday after departure- Min. 45-Day Max.	Must be completed 7 days prior to departure.	See YCHE46 Fares.	Fares are not available on all flights.
59.	YXE46	RT	Midweek Advance Purchase Excursion Coach	Monday, Tuesday, Wednesday, Thursday				
56.	YNWE46	RT	Weekend Night Coach Advance Purchase Excursion	Friday, Saturday, Sunday on Night Coach service generally departing between 9:00 p.m. and 6:59 a.m.				
57.	YNXE46	RT	Midweek Night Coach Advance Purchase Excursion	Monday, Tuesday, Wednesday, Thursday on Night Coach service generally departing between 9:00 p.m. and 6:59 a.m.				
37.	YCHE46	RT	Advance Purchase Excursion Children's Coach	Any Day				
	YHV28 (Peak Season)	RT	15- Passenger Air/Sea Group Inclusive Tour-Coach	Any day from Dec. 1 through Apr. 30. Fares are not available on certain days during holiday and peak travel periods.	3-Day Min. 17-Day Max.	Reservations for the outbound portion of the trip must be confirmed and tickets must be purchased 14 days prior to departure.	None	Group must travel together on outbound portion of trip. In addition to air fare, each passenger must purchase a prepaid Air/Sea Tour of $95.
	YLV28 (Off- Peak Season)	RT		Any day from May 1 through Nov. 30. Fares are not available on certain days during holiday and peak travel periods.				
	YV28	RT		Any day from Dec. 1, 1978 through May 31, 1979.				

	FARE CLASS CODE		FARE DESCRIPTION	FARE APPLIES	MINIMUM/ MAXIMUM STAY	RESERVATIONS AND TICKETING	APPROXIMATE CHILDREN'S DISCOUNT (2-11 YEARS - ACCOMPANIED).	SPECIAL CONDITIONS
	YE78	RT	Florida Individual Inclusive Tour-Coach	Any day except fares are not available on certain days during holiday and peak travel periods.	Not earlier than the 1st Monday following departure- Min. 14-Day Max.	Must be completed 7 days prior to departure.	1/3	In addition to air fare, passenger must purchase an Advertised Air Tour of $45 plus $10 for each day after the third.
	YHV17 (Peak Season)	RT	50- Passenger Air/Sea Group Inclusive Tour-Coach	Any day from Dec. 16 through Apr. 30 except certain days during holidays and peak travel periods.	3-Day Min. 17-Day Max.	Reservations must be confirmed and tickets purchased 7 days prior to departure.	None	Group must travel together on outbound portion of trip. In addition to air fare, each passenger must purchase a prepaid Air/Sea Tour of $135.
	YLV17 (Off- Peak Season)	RT		Any day from May 1 through Dec. 15 except certain days during holidays and peak travel periods.				
31.	YG3	OW or RT	10- Passenger Group-Coach	Any Day	None	Reservations must be confirmed 7 days prior to departure. Tickets must be purchased 5 days prior to departure.	None	Group must travel together.
	YG18	RT	20- Passenger Group Coach	Any day after Sept. 25, 1978.	12:01 a.m. of the day following departure- Min. 14-Day Max.	Must be completed 7 days prior to departure.	None	Written application required at least 7 days prior to departure.
	YG49	RT	40- Passenger Single Entity Group-Coach	Any day except fares are not available on certain days during holiday and peak travel periods.	3-Day Min. 30-Day Max.	Must be completed 21 days prior to departure.	See YCHG49 Fares.	Group must travel together. Written application required at least 30 days prior to departure.
	YCHG49	RT	Children's 40- Passenger Single Entity Group-Coach					
48.	YG77	RT	40- Passenger Group-Coach	Any Day	1-Day Min. 14-Day Max.	Must be completed 21 days prior to departure.	None	Group must travel together. Written application required at least 21 days prior to departure.

OW - One Way Fares.   RT - Round Trip Ticket Required.

The LOCAL AND JOINT PASSENGER RULES TARIFF provides the individual and group airline policies governing the transportation of passengers and their baggage. There are airline rules for handicapped passengers, children under five years of age traveling alone, carrying firearms aboard a commercial flight, food service aboard flight, excess baggage charges and hundreds of more regulations in the Rules Tariff governing all aspects of airline and passenger relations. The Rules Tariff are approved by the CAB and become official guidelines for passenger handling. If a travel agent and an airline employee follow the rules published in the tariff, they will be correct, and to give advice or perform an act contrary to these rules would render the agent or the company liable. The LOCAL PASSENGER FARES TARIFF contains hundred of pages of the regular fares of each participating carrier. The Local Fares Tariff lists each participating airline's fares in alphabetical sequence. After some study, reading the fares is not a difficult task although this may not be so at first glance.

The JOINT ONE-WAY AND ROUND TRIP FARES AND RULES are published to cover transportation on two different airlines, i.e., a joint fare becomes one fare covering transportation over two different carriers with the stipulation that the passenger must change airplanes in a certain specified city.

Because the joint fare is available as a single amount to cover transportation over two different airlines, it becomes a lesser amount than the sum of the two one-way fares would be over the same route.

AIR FARE CHANGES

In 1929 the United States Air Transport (11 West 42 Street, New York) flew from Logan Field, Baltimore to Newark Airport one way for $30.00 (including R.R. Fare, Penn. Station, N.Y. to Newark and taxicab to Newark Airport); the schedule was:

New York			Baltimore		
2:00 p.m.	Lv	New York	Ar	11:45 a.m.	
3:50 p.m.	Ar	Baltimore	Lv	9:50 a.m.	

This was a time when airline fares were simple and easily understood by the average traveller. Until 1978 most passengers knew only first-class or tourist, round trip or one-way fares. Deregulation has opened up the previous rigid fare regulations and created a ferocious competition among the airlines giving the customer lower fares and a variety of service. A look at the Delta Air Lines service from Baltimore to Newark/ New York in September 1978 illustrates the varied fares, rules, and conditions. (See table.)

This is one way to demonstrate the possible permutations available from a sample trip, i.e., Baltimore to Newark. As you can see in this simple round trip from Baltimore to Newark, the fare can be as high as $96. and as low as $41.

One problem resulting from the new, relaxed fare regulations is that ticket prices are constantly changing as the airlines come up with new offerings.

INTERNATIONAL AIR TRANSPORT ASSOCIATION

The International Air Transport Association (IATA), a voluntary trade association of the world's major airlines, has unified fares and tariffs between airlines operations with different currencies and in connecting the routes of the international carriers so that interline transfers take place smoothly and conveniently. All agreements involving travel to or from the United States require CAB approval. Uniform policies

and procedures have been developed regarding airline operations, navigational aids, safety measures and communications. IATA cooperation makes it possible for passengers with a single airline ticket purchased in a single currency at a published price to go from any point in the world to any other point over the routes of several airlines and across the boundaries of several nations.

In 1978 the 108-member International Air Transport Association abandoned its 33-year-old role as the industry's fare-fixing cartel. It also gave up its authority to regulate in-flight meals, drinks and entertainment, and will henceforth confine itself to such noncompetitive matters as safety standards, security and ticket exchange arrangments. The end of administered fares will heat up competition in the briskly growing air-travel market, and without IATA to coordinate international fare agreements, many airlines and their governments will probably become entangled in complicated bilateral and multilateral negotiations to fix prices and frills.

Through the IATA, the airlines have organized a system of fares published in several tariff listings. Most American travel agents work with the AIR TARIFF, published by the American international carriers. The various tariffs publications cover the same information and use basically the same format. The AIR TARIFF is a compendium covering:

1. General Rules
2. Mileage Fares within IATA Area 2
3. Within IATA Area 3 and between Areas 2 and 3
4. Within Europe (including Cyprus)
5. Transatlantic
6. Transpacific and
7. Within the Western Hemisphere.

Rules cover the various conditions and limitations that apply to the carriers and are published in the tariff as they relate to the IATA Traffic Conference areas.

Area 1 includes all of the North and South American continents and the adjacent islands: Greenland, Bermuda, the islands of the Caribbean Sea and Hawaii.

Area 2 includes Europe, Africa, and adjacent islands, as well as Ascension Island and Asia west of and including Iran.

Area 3 includes the rest of Asia and adjacent islands, the East Indies, Australia, New Zealand, and the Pacific Islands not included in Area 1.

The tariff listings contains the normal/all-year fares, usually those fares that allow a passenger to travel at any time on any flight and that have few, if any, restrictions (they are always published as one-way fares); and special fares, ones that have special provisions and requirements, such as age restrictions, group restrictions, restrictions on time of travel, hours, weeks, or seasons (excursion fares are always published as round-trip fares). If a fare, charge, or rule has been agreed upon by the carriers but not yet approved by the governments, all publications and tickets issued pending consent are published and advertised with the notation, "subject to government approval".

SIMPLE WAYS OF FINDING AND READING INTERNATIONAL TARIFF RULES

1. Make sure that the latest edition of Air Tariff is available, including the most recent supplements.
2. Check the airline tariff fare schedule for the applicable rule.
3. Consult the tariff index for the rule numbers; don't try to remember the rule numbers.
4. Check the rule for the conditions governing normal and special fares. Analyze your question and identify the section of the rules most applicable. Make sure there are no recent fare changes.
5. Know the subject headings and their general interpretation of the rules. Conditions governing normal and special fares are described under the subject headings listed below. These headings always follow the same sequence.

   (1) APPLICATION
   F/Y OW, RT or CT fares

   (2) PERIOD OF APPLICATION
   Fares apply all year

   (3) FARES
   The applicable fare is that quoted against the rule number.

   (4) VALIDITY
   a. <u>Maximum Stay</u>: One Year
   b. <u>Minimum Stay</u>: No minimum stay requirement
   c. <u>Extension of Ticket Validity</u>

   (5) GROUP SIZE
   The number stated in the rule is the minimum number of passengers required to make up a group. An entry under this heading will only be found in a group fares rule.

   (6) STOPOVERS
   "Stopover" means a stop at an intermediate point from which the passenger is not scheduled to depart on the day of arrival. If there is no scheduled connecting departure on the date of arrival, departure on the next day within 24 hours will not constitute a stopover.

   (7) ADVERTISING AND SALES
   Advertising and sales (including but not limited to issuance of MCO's and XO's and PTS's) are permitted worldwide.

   (8) AFFINITY AND OWN USE PROVISIONS

   (9) BAGGAGE

   (10) CANCELLATIONS AND REFUNDS
   Group Inclusive Tour Fares: See Governing Rule X900.
   Affinity/Own Use Group Fares: See Governing Rule Z900.
   Other Fares: See General Rule R.01.

   (11) COMBINATIONS
   Combinations with international and domestic fares are permitted subject to Fare Construction Rules.

(12) COMMISSION
      Normal procedures apply

(13) DISCOUNTS
      Available for:
      a. Children, Infants
      b. Tour Conductors
      c. Sales Agents

(14) DOCUMENTATION
      Normal provisions apply--e.g., passports, visas required, etc.

(15) ELIGIBILITY
      Unrestricted--e.g., not restricted to a particular type of passenger
      such as military personnel, etc.

(16) MINIMUM TOUR PRICE
      See Governing Rule X900

(17) MODIFICATION OF INCLUSIVE TOURS
      See Governing Rule X900

(18) NAME CHANGES AND ADDITIONS
      Rule Z900 will apply if the fare involved is governed by Rule Z900.
      Otherwise, no name changes and additions are permitted.

(19) PASSENGER EXPENSES

(20) PAYMENT

(21) RESERVATIONS
      See General Rule T.03

(22) REROUTING
      Inclusive Tour Fares: See Governing Rule X900
      Affinity Group Fares: See Governing Rule Z900
      Other Fares: See General Rule R.02

(23) ROUTING
      Normal Fare Construction Rules apply, unless a routing map number is
      indicated opposite the fare shown in the yellow pages.

(24) TICKETING

(25) TOUR FEATURES

(26) TOUR LITERATURE

(27) TRAVEL TOGETHER
      Group Inclusive Tour Fares: See Governing Rule X900
      Affinity/Own Use Group Fares: See Governing Rule Z900

6. Find and read the rule very carefully. Read the entire rule in order to
    answer your question completely.

7. Read carefully the first paragraph or paragraphs of the rule, which are
    applicable to all carriers.

8. Check the rules for the one carriers with which you are concerned.

9. Study the paragraphs which begin, "Not applicable to..." and "Applicable to..." to see if the carrier is mentioned.

10. Look for NOTE or EXCEPTION statements to see if the carrier is mentioned.

FARE CONSTRUCTION RULES IN BRIEF

"ITINERARY" means all portions of the passenger's reservation to include surface transportation, if any, from origin to final destination. In general, the types of itineraries include: one-way trips, round-trips (return journeys), circle trips, around the world trips, and open jaw trips. A one-way trip is considered to be any journey which, for fare calculation purposes, is not a complete round or circle trip entirely by air.

"ROUTING" consists of carriers, class of service and cities served. Example:

```
        BOS
        JFK      AA-F
```

The term "ROUND TRIP" means travel from one point to another and return to the point of origin by the same air route as that used for the outbound portion. This definition will still apply when the fare used for the outbound portion is different from that used for the inbound.

"ROUND TRIP" means a point of origin to point of destination and return to point of origin. Example:

```
        LAX
        JFK      AA-F
        LAX      AA-F
```

The term "ROUND TRIP" also means travel from one point to another and return to the same point of origin by an air route different from that used for the outbound portion. This definition will only apply when the same one-way fare is applicable to both the outbound and inbound portion.

The term "CIRCLE TRIP" means travel, other than a round trip, from one point and return to the same point by a continuous, circuitous air route, including around the world trips.

"CIRCLE TRIP" can be to any number of cities using any routing and return to point of origin as long as all transportation is made by commercial scheduled airlines. Example:

```
        BOS
        JFK      AA-F
        LAX      AA-F
        BOS      AA-F
```

Around the world trips are circle trips and apply to continuous eastbound or westbound travel commencing from and returning to the same point via both the Atlantic and Pacific Oceans.

The fare for an around the world trip is constructed in the same manner as a circle trip.

Some other elementary tariff definitions that will be useful in fare construction include:

"SURFACE" refers to a portion of the complete itinerary of the passenger not transited by air, i.e., ARUNK--arrival unknown; or VOID, i.e., no air provided on that segment.

"ONLINE SERVICE" means the segments of same airline (i.e., EA to EA).

"OFFLINE SERVICE" means the segments of differing carriers (i.e., DL to EA).

"INTERLINE SERVICE" means the segments of two or more differing carriers.

"LOCAL FARE" means a fare for online transportation.

"JOINT FARE" means a fare for offline or interline transportation.

"CONNECTION" means a required aircraft change at an intermediate point between point of departure and the point of destination. In order for a passenger to connect, he must depart the connection city on a flight scheduled to depart within four (4) hours of arrival; or on the first flight on which space is available; or on a flight that will provide for an earlier arrival.

"STOPOVER" refers to a deliberate interruption of a travel by the passenger in agreement with the carrier, at a point between the place of origin and the place of destination equal to a break in the trip.

"INTERMEDIATE STOP" means a point of landing between the passengers' original place of departure and final destination which does not require deplaning by the passenger.

"NONSTOP" means a boarding point to a deplaning point with NO intermediate stop(s).

"DIRECT" means a boarding point to a deplaning point with any number of intermediate stops.

"OPEN JAW" is an itinerary which is essentially of a round trip or circle trip nature but has a segment not transited by air. Example:

SFO

JFK   OPEN JAW

LAX

An open jaw trip consists of travel which is essentially of a round trip nature with the exception that either the outward point of arrival and inward point of departure are not the same.

LOT Photo

Passengers arriving Lisbon on Pan American's Inaugural Transatlantic Passenger Flight which left Port Washington, N.Y. June 28, 1939. Route was via Horta, Azores, then Lisbon and Marseilles. Pan American World Airways Photo.

The IATA Basic fare construction principles state that when no through fare is specifically published for a desired itinerary, it must be constructed. Such a constructed fare must not be less than the lowest amount obtained by any of the following principles: lowest combination of fares principle; mileage system; more distant point principle. Detailed explanations of these fare construction principles will appear in the text which follows. Note that fares constructed by the use of add-ons are considered THROUGH fares.

A published direct fare always takes precedence over any combination of fares, of the same type, which may exist between the same points for the same class of service, e.g., for the direct journey, NYC-MAD-TUN, the published fare NYC-TUN must be used even in the sum of NYC-MAD plus MAD-TUN is lower.

A published direct fare takes precedence when such a fare is used as a component part of a constructed fare to a further point, e.g., for the direct journey NYC-MAD-TUN-DJE, when no through fare is published, the correct construction to be used is NYC-TUN plus TUN-DJE, even though the result is higher.

Special domestic fares (e.g., Super Saver, ITX's, etc.) within the U.S. and Canada may be combined with international fares, even though such a combination undercuts a published through international fare.

The applicable fare will be the published or constructed through fare in effect at the time travel begins on the first flight coupon.

Lowest Combination of Fares Method:

When a required fare between two points is not published, it may be constructed by the particular combination of two or more sectional fares along the desired routing which produces the lowest fare.

Given the itinerary, BOM-NYC-SFO-BKK, there are two possible combinations of fares:

A. BOM-NYC   593   B. BOM-NYC-SFO   738
    NYC-SFO-BKK   639   SFO-BKK   520

    Total Fare: 1,232   Total Fare: 1,258

In this particular case, the lowest combination of fares constructs over New York. A desired itinerary may be constructed over fictitious construction points to which the passenger is not, in reality, travelling, if such a construction produces a lower fare.

Mileage System:

The mileage system should be used whenever a desired itinerary between two points is not included in an applicable diagrammatic or linear routing published in connection with a fare. There are three basic elements involved in the application of the mileage system. They are as follows: maximum permitted mileages; non-stop sector mileages; and, excess mileage surcharges.

In addition to these three basic elements, other factors must be taken into consideration when the mileage system is used. The most frequent considerations include: extra mileage allowances and special mileage provisions; stopovers; limitation on indirect travel; higher rated intermediate fares; special provisions for one way journeys (or one way backhaul rule); fictitious ("Hidden") construction points; and, the "more distant point" principle.

The maximum permitted mileage (MPM) published in connection with a fare governs the maximum distance a passenger is allowed to travel en route between two particular points at the direct fare. When a through fare is constructed by combination of sector fares, through maximum mileage (if available) from the origin to the destination of such constructed fare may be used unless prohibited by rules applicable to one of the sector fares.

Non-stop sector mileages for all sectors of a routing are used to compute the total mileage of the journey flown. Only non-stop sector mileages published in the latest list of non-stop sector mileages, as amended may be used.

Application of Mileage System:

In order to determine whether a desired routing between two points is permissible at the through fare, the following basic steps should be taken:

1. Look up the applicable MPM between the two particular points.
2. Add up the non-stop sector mileages between ALL the points of the routing. The computation must be made according to the actual route of travel, including all scheduled stopovers, intermediate transit points and connecting points.
3. Compare the total of the non-stop sector mileages to the applicable MPM permitted at the direct fare between the two points. If the total of non-stop sector mileages is equal to or less than the MPM, the itinerary is allowed at the published direct fare, except as provided for in the following rules of this section.

Example: Itinerary: NYC-LON-AMS-MUC-ROM-NCE-LIS-TER-NYC

Fare Construction Point: Rome
MPM NYC-ROM: 5,136

NYC-LON	3,456
LON-AMS	230
AMS-MUC	420
MUC-ROM	440
	4,546

ROM-NCE	294
NCE-LIS	913
LIS-TER	967
TER-BOS (Connecting point)	2,293
BOS-NYC	191
	4,658

Since the total sector mileage of each half of the itinerary is less than the MPM, the above routing is allowed at the through published fare.

Excess Mileage Surchages:

If the total sector mileage for a desired routing exceeds the MPM published in connection with a fare, a surchage becomes necessary. The excess mileage percentage table must be used to determine the applicable amount.

EXCESS MILEAGE

PUBLISHED MILEAGE	MILEAGE PERMITTED WHEN PUBLISHED FARE IS INCREASED BY					PUBLISHED MILEAGE	MILEAGE PERMITTED WHEN PUBLISHED FARE IS INCREASED BY				
	5%	10%	15%	20%	25%		5%	10%	15%	20%	25%
90	93	97	101	105	112	6000	6250	6500	6750	7000	7500
91	95	98	102	106	114	6100	6355	6609	6863	7117	7626
92	96	100	103	107	115	6200	6458	6717	6975	7233	7750
93	97	101	105	109	117	6300	6562	6825	7087	7350	7875
94	98	102	106	110	118	6400	6667	6934	7200	7467	8001
95	98	102	106	110	118	6500	6771	7042	7312	7583	8125
96	100	104	108	112	120	6600	6875	7150	7425	7700	8250
97	101	105	109	113	121	6700	6980	7259	7538	7817	8376
98	102	106	110	114	123	6800	7083	7367	7650	7933	8500
99	103	107	112	116	124	6900	7187	7475	7762	8050	8625

The direct fare becomes subject to a surcharge in amounts varying from five to twenty-five percent depending upon the amount of mileage in excess of that published in connection with the fare. To use the Excess Mileage Percentage Table, you should refer to the first column of the table headed "Published Mileage," and the figures in the column which cover every number up to 100, (after which the series progress in groups of 100 up to 24,900) in order to obtain the exact mileage. These figures present the normal MPM published in connection with a fare.

Example: Itinerary: BOS-LIS-MAD-LON-AMS-FRA-MIL-ROM
MPM BOS-ROM: 4,950

Sector Mileage Computation:

BOS-LIS	3,185
LIS-MAD	319
MAD-LON	765
LON-AMS	230

AMS-FRA	228
FRA-MIL	311
MIL-ROM	311
	5,249

Since the sum total of sector mileages of 5,249 for the above itinerary exceeds the MPM of 4,950 allowed between Boston and Rome, a surcharge becomes necessary. This surcharge is calculated by using the Excess Mileage Percentage Table; when the MPM of 4,950 is increased to the ten percent surcharge level, the figure arrived at is 5,363. This figure of 5,363 is the only figure which exceeds the sum total of sector mileages of 5,249. Therefore, the appropriate excess mileage surcharge for the above itinerary is ten percent of the direct fare.

How to Surcharge a Fare:

The surcharge for the itinerary in the above example is calculated as follows:

Direct Fare BOS-ROM:	453.00
10% Fare Surcharge:	45.00
Total Fare:	498.00

If the sum total of non-stop sector mileages exceeds the adjusted MPM shown in the 25% column of the Excess Mileage Percentage Table, the applicable fare will be the combination of two or more fares along the desired routing which produces the lowest fare (including, for example, the use of such fare construction methods as "The More Distant Point" Principle). In certain areas of the world, extra mileage allowances are permitted in addition to the MPM's published in connection with fares.

Polskie Linine Lotnieze Iliushin 62   LOT Photo

TWA — TRANSATLANTIC FARE GUIDE · EFFECTIVE APRIL 1, 1978

FROM NEW YORK TO / TYPE OF FARE / ROUND TRIP IN US $	SEASONS	SNN	DUB	LON	LIS	PAR	MAD AGP	CAS	BCN	FRA	GVA	MIL	NCE	ROM	ATH	CAI	TLV	BAH	FREE STOPOVERS PERMITTED	WEEKEND SURCHG (h)	MINIMUM/ MAXIMUM VALIDITY	DISCOUNTS PERMITTED	APPLICATION/PAYMENT/TICKETING REQUIREMENTS	MIN GROUP SIZE	MIN LAND PACKAGE REQUIRED	CANCELLATIONS/ REFUNDS	TICKETING CODES
**FIRST CLASS ** #	All Year	1298	1322	1378	1378	1436	1436	1436	1488	1434	1434	1592	1592	1674	1776	1974	2030	2356	Yes (Unlimited on mileage)		0—1 year	Children/ Agents/ Tour Conductors	Normal TWA Time Limits	NONE	NONE	Normal cancellation and refund procedures apply	F
ECONOMY * #	Basic 1	558	568	626	626	—	650	650	660	694	694	764	764	832	978	—	1194	1432	Yes ▲ (Unlimited based on mileage) (s)	No	0—1 year	Children/ Agents/ Tour Conductors	Normal TWA Time Limits	NONE	(I.T. Commission will be paid if used in connection with Inclusive Tours.)	Normal cancellation and refund procedures apply	YL / YL2 / YL / YH2 / YH
	Basic 2	—	—	—	—	—	—	—	—	672▲	672▲	720▲	720▲	720▲	902▲	—	—	—									
	Basic 3	—	—	—	—	—	—	—	—	—	—	—	—	—	—	—	—	1586									
	Peak 1	694	706	764	720▲/764	822	822	822	848	878	878	916	916	970	1132	1330	1330	1586									
	Peak 2	—	—	—	764	—	—	—	—	744▲	744▲	916	916	890▲	1000▲	—	—	—									
EXCURSIONS 14-21 Day *	Basic 3	509	519	541	—	567	567	587	618	634	634	666	666	717	769	913(m)	939	1095	2 in each direction plus POT(k)	Yes	14—21 Days (14—45 to SNN/DUB)		Must purchase tickets before departure.				YLE21 / YHE21
	Peak 1	599	610	631	—	681	681	681	711	725	725	758	758	807	875	994(m)	1023	1176									
14-45 Day * (h)	Basic 1	—	—	—	—	299(l) / 360(l)	—	—	—	340▲/398▲	350▲/440▲	432/512	499(l)/560(l)	460/550	—	—	—	—	No	No	14—45 Days (h)	Children Agents Only (None to France)	To Italy—Normal Time Limits 45 days before departure. (L) To France—Reservations/ticketing required at same time. RT must be confirmed.			No change in routing allowed. If booking cancelled, 10% of fare paid or $50 whichever is more will be withheld as a penalty.	YLE2/45 / YHE2/45
14-60 Day *	Basic 2	—	—	424▲/498▲	424▲/498▲	—	—	—	—	—	—	—	—	—	535▲/595▲	—	—	—		LIS—yes ATH—no	14—60 Days		To Portugal—Tickets must be purchased before departure.				YLE2/60 / YHE2/60
22-45 Day *	Basic 1	—	—	467	290/343	511	487	487	502	511	511	561	561	561	—	788	860	1130	No(n)	Yes	22—45 Days	Children/ Agents Only	Must purchase tickets before departure.				YLE45 / YHE45
	Peak 1	—	—	587	343	631	601	601	617	628	628	676	676	—	—	891	965	1223									
APEX (Advance Purchase Excursion) 14-45 Day *	Basic 3	—	—	429	—	435	435	—	—	340▲	—	422	487	449	473	545	545	—	No	Yes (xcpt not to DUB/ SNN)	14—45 Days (7—60 LON)	Children pay 66% of Apex fare (No Discounts to LON)	Reservations/payments/ticketing must be made at least 30 days before departure. (L) (Eff. June 1—30 days before departure SGA, except to Germany—45 days and LON—21 days)			No change or refund.	YLAP45 / YHAP45 / YLAP45 / YHAP45 / YLAP45 / YHAP45
	Peak 3	—	—	320	—	345	423	—	—	398▲	—	487	487	540	622	655	655	—									
	Winter 1	—	335	360	—	390	400	—	—	—	—	436	436	—	—	—	(aa)	—									
	Peak 4	325/379	335/389				406/444																				
7-90 Day *	Basic 5	—	—	290	290	435	295	295	313	340▲	—	422	533	541	635	657(u)	657(u)	1001	No(l)	No	7—60 Days (14—60 LIS)	None	Reservations/payment/ticketing must be made at least 30 days before departure. (30 days to LIS/LON)			Normal cancellation and refund procedures apply	YL2 / YH2
	Peak 5	—	—	345	343	345	345	345	363	—	—	487	588	597	719	693(u)	693(u)	1046									
	Winter 1	—	—	309+ / 349+	—	—	—	—	—	—	—	—	—	—	—	—	—	—									
	Shoulder 1	—	—	309+ / 399+	—	—	—	—	—	—	—	—	—	—	—	—	—	—									
	Peak 3	—	—																								
YOUTH * (12 thru 21 Years)	Basic 3	484	491	473	496	514	490	490	510	499	499	533	533	541	635	657	657(u)	—	No(l)	No	0—1 Year	None	Reservations not accepted until 5 days before each Transatlantic flight. Tickets must be purchased before departure. (u)		None (u)	No change in routing allowed. If booking cancelled before departure a charge of $50 will be assessed the passenger for one way or round trip travel.	YL2 / YH2
	Peak 1	554	560	536	563	573	546	546	568	552	552	588	588	597	719	693	693(u)	—									
BUDGET ▲ ▲	Basic 3	—	—	256(g)/299(g)	—	—	—	—	—	398(g)	398(g)	398(g)	398(g)	398(g)	—	586(g)	—	—	No ▲	No	0—1 Year	Infants only	Reservations/payment/ticketing must be made at least 21 days before departure at LHR. (g)	None (u)	No I.T. commission will be paid.	Normal procedures apply. (except to TLV cancellation penalty is $100).	YLAP8 / YHAP8
	Peak 3	—	—	256(g)/299(g)	—	—	—	—	—	442(g)	442(g)	442(g)	442(g)	442(g)	—	—	—	—									
NO RESERVATION (Standby) ▲ ▲	Basic 3 (l)	—	—	256(g)/299(g)	—	—	—	—	—	—	—	—	—	—	—	—	575/675 (l)	—	No ▲	No	0—1 Year	Infants Only	Reservations may not be made. Tickets must be purchased no later than 3 hours before departure at JFK and TLV and 2 hours before departure at LHR. (g)				YLU / YHU
GROUP INCLUSIVE TOURS 7-8/10 Day * (c)	Winter 4	373	375	382	—	395	381	387	—	405	405	435	435	463	—	586(g)	—	—	No but one at a $10 charge	Winter No Shldr Yes	7—8 Days	Children only	Written application/payment/ticketing must be made at least 15 days before departure (f)	5	$70 Winter/ $90 shldr(i).	25% of fare paid will be withheld as a penalty in case of cancellation after tickets have been issued (exceptions exist for death and/or illness, contact TWA).	YLE8/10 GV5 / YHE8/10 GV5 / YLE8/10 GV5 / YHE8/10 GV5 / YOE8/10 GV5
	Shoulder 4	416	418	424	—	438	423	429	—	447	447	477	477	506	587	657(z) / 689(z)	734(z) / 817(z)	—						$140 Basic			
	Winter 4	392	394	401	—	416	400	406	—	425	425	457	457	487	—	—	—	—						$200 Peak			
	Shoulder 1	437	439	445	—	460	444	451	—	470	470	501	501	531	632	—	—	—									
7-14 Day ▲ / 18/21 Day ▲		—	—	—	—	—	—	—	—	—	—	—	—	—	—	—	—	—			Bs 7—14 Days Pk 10—21 Days				$70 (e)		YLE14 GV5 / YHE14 GV5
7-21 Day	Winter 4	—	320	445	—	479	—	438	—	491	491	554	554	622	495	727	812	837	No	No	7—21 Days	Children only	Written application/payment/ticketing at least 7 days before departure.				YLE21 GV10 / YLE21 GV5 / YOE21 GV5 / YHE21 GV5
	Basic 5	—	374	—	—	595	—	544	—	601	601	671	671	739	—	835	925	947									
	Shoulder 2	—	427																								
	Peak 1																										
14-21 Day *	Basic 1	428	435	—	460(a) / 585(a)	487	438	438	467	—	—	—	—	—	753	—	—	—	1 in each direction plus POT(k)	Yes	14—21 Days	Children	Written application/payment/ticketing must be made at least 15 days before departure. (w)	5	$120 for 14 days plus $10 per day after (e)		YLE21 GV5 / YHE21 GV5
	Peak 1	519	525	562		595	544	544	576	601	601	671	671	739	868	—	—	—									
4-9 Day ▲	Winter 2	—	—	—	—	—	—	—	—	—	—	—	—	—	—	—	628(q)	—	No(q)	No(z)	4—9 Days	Children only	Written application at least 5 days in advance. Payment/ticketing any time before departure.	10	$45		YE9/2 GV10
NON-AFFINITY GROUP	Basic 3	480	485	467	290	487	295	295	313	511	511	561	561	526(w) / 633(w)	657(z) / 623(w)	586(w)	734(z) / 817(z)	—	No(z)	No(z)	Variable (w, z)	Children/ Agents	5/10/15 days in advance (See notes w,z)		None		YL/GM(w,z) / YH/GM(w,z)
AFFINITY GROUP	Peak 1	—	—	—	343	601	345	345	363	628	628	—	644	516(w) / 623(w)	—	—	570(q)	—	Yes (not to TLV)	No(a)	0—1 Year	Children only	Written application/payment/ticketing must be made at least 15 days before departure. (w)	40(w) (from LIS-20)	Must have a ground pkg in the travel program.		YL/GA(q) / YH/GA(q)
INCENTIVE GROUP	Basic 5 / Peak 5 / Peak 1 / Winter 2	—	—	—	—	—	—	—	—	—	—	—	—	—	623	—	—	—	Yes (xcpt not to TLV)	No(v)	5—14 Days (except 4—9 TLV, 4—13 CAS, LIS/Spain)	Agents only	Written application/payment/ticketing must be made at least 15 days before departure (21 days to Spain/CAS/LIS) (p)	40 (xcpt 80-TLV, 20-CAS, 4—13-CAS MAD/ AGP/ BCN)			YL13 GV20 / YL14 GV40 / YL18 GV20 / YE8 GV60

*Single open jaw permitted. Terminal points of an open jaw count as a single stopover or single point of turnaround. The fare to charge for an open jaw trip is the sum of the applicable RT fares for each leg, divided by 2.

■ Commissions: TWA pays 10% on all fares, with 3 percent additional for inclusive tours, provided the Eastbound transatlantic leg is on TWA and ticketed with a TWA pass. Otherwise the rates are 8 and 3.

◆ One way fare is ½ the round trip fare shown.

POT—Point of turnaround   EB—Eastbound   WB—Westbound

* For Super APEX/Budget No Reservation fares from interior points to LON, see preceding page where applicable.

▲ To be used for construction to/from interior U.S. points.

▲ A Transportation must be on TWA direct service without change of flight number. No enroute stopovers allowed. No stopovers allowed to/from interior U.S. points when domestic routing is totally on the services of TWA and/or one other domestic carrier.

AIR FARE BARGAINS

There was a time in air travel when all air fare to the same places were similar and expensive. No longer. Deregulation of the airlines and liberalized air carriers agreements with other nations, there are new airlines, new routes and new promotional fares offering bargains and confusion. It all began with first-class and economy fares; now there is no end to the number of fares: 14-27 excursion, 22-45 day excursion, mid-week, weekend, APEX, Super APEX, standby, budget, youth and group fares. These are some of the fares being used for trans-atlantic service. The scheduled domestic carriers have developed their own, special fares: Discover America, Super Saver, Freedom, No Frills, Super Jackpot, Chicken Feed, Small Potatoes, Peanuts, Senior Saver, Super Coach, night, weekend, and midweek fare permutations. The flurry of competition has produced special conditions and reading the fine print has become an absolute necessity for the passenger and travel agent alike:

> Any changes must be made at least seven days prior to the
> new flight and tickets must be issued at least seven days
> in advance or within 10 days of confirmation--whichever
> is sooner, except that when there is no change in origin,
> stopover or destination cities, and reservations are con-
> firmed seven days prior to the new flight, tickets may be
> reissued up to 30 minutes prior to departure.

With so many fares and new rules, travel counselors and ticketing agents must answer "I can't give you fares; there are all kinds of different regulations." It seems like a simple matter to fly from New York to London and five days later on to Brussels and then surface to Rome and then return to New York at the end of the month. Because the trip is six months away and not today, the airline clerk and travel agents alike have great difficulty knowing the rules and fares that will be in effect and answers like this should be anticipated:

First Agent: "Those fares have not been established but the current one-way APEX fare to London of $155.00, and a one-way APEX fare back from Rome of $230.00; a separate one-way ticket can be issued for London to Brussels ($190.00); a total of $475.00."

Second Agent: "You should take a public charter flight; that will be the cheapest way: $410.00 plus $80.00 for London to Brussels for a total of $490.00."

Third Agent: "The total fare using TWA is based on a budget fare ($148.00) ticket to London instead of $155.00. In three or four months each carrier will have their own fare. Nobody has the answer now."

Fourth Agent: "The best way is 14-21 day, which may become 7-60 day, excursion ticket to Rome for $700.00 including the two stopovers or you could for $460.00 take APEX to London, $150.00; London to Brussels $77.00; APEX from Rome $275.00 plus a $17.00 'surcharge'".

Until the full impact of the Airline Deregulation Act of 1978 is known, American agents will have to call the rate desk and inquire about the latest fares and route changes. The confusing and fluctuating multitudes of fares will probably continue over the short term; in time the airline fare structure will be differentiated by schedules, equipment and amenities in order to smooth out peak loads and increase off-hour load factors.

To most Europeans, train travel has been a way of life. It is fast, efficient and cheap. European air travel, on the other hand, has been fast, efficient and expensive. National air carriers divide up the market and, lacking stiff competition, charge pretty much what they think the tariff should be; and the results are an extraordinary high cost of flying point-to-point within Europe. To fly from Frankfurt to Geneva costs 337 Deutchmark ($175.24) for 65 minute first-class ticket in 1978.

Comparison of EUROPE/USA Air Fares:

	Frankfurt/Geneva	NYC/Buffalo
Mileage:	287 miles	292 miles
First Class Fare:	$175	$59
Rate per mile:	60.9¢	20.2¢
Coach/Economy Fare:	$124	$49
Rate per mile	43.4¢	16.7¢
Equipment:	DC -9/727	DC -9/727
Airlines:	SR & LH	AA & AL

Similarly a 213-mile Paris-London flight cost twice as much as a 205-mile New York-Washington trip.

In a move to attract more nonbusiness customers and to fill half-empty, off-peak-hour flights, European air executives are starting to realize what their American counterparts learned: lower fares lead to more customers and greater profits. Recently British Airways reduced prices as much as 40%, pegging the London-Paris round trip at $92.50, vs. $154.00. Now Lufthansa, Alitalia and KLM have reduced fares 15% to 25% on some flights between Germany, Italy and The Netherlands. Air France is also getting into the act with a 40% reduction on some of its round trip Paris-London excursions. Other European carriers are expected to follow suit. Such news may well bring air travel within the budgets of more Europeans, many of whom have never flown.

Travel agents should advise their vacationing clients that scheduled air travel within Europe can cost about three times as much as a flight covering the same distance in the U.S.A. Advise them to seek alternate means of transportation such as rail or motorcoach. If several people or a family are travelling together, a rental car is the better buy.

Pacific Southwest Airline Captain

Chapter 6

AIRLINE TICKETING

RESERVATION SHEET

Basic airline ticketing begins with the proper completion of a reservation sheet; booking the desired travel with the appropriate carrier(s); writing the airline ticket; and invoicing the sale. A travel agency must account to ATC weekly for all ticket stock and any funds received for tickets must be reported. An invoice system is usually employed to account for the ticket stock issued and payment (credit cards) received for the sale.

Airline ticketing requires the completion of a Reservation Sheet for several reasons: (1) to prepare and organize the trip prior to telephoning the airlines for the actual reservation, (2) to establish a permanent agency record of the customer's travel intentions, and (3) to make it possible for any individual agent in an office to complete the transaction in the absence of the original agent.

NAMES		NO. PARTY	TEL. HOME 345-9282 OFFICE 345-5289 OTHER				BILLING INFORMATION	
Mr. + Mrs. William Constable		2					Constable Supply	
Beaver Lane, Utopia, Ill. 33065							15 Industrial Drive - Rome, Ill. 33466	

FROM TO	AIR FLT	CLASS	DATE	DEP	ARR	STATUS	TX & SKD CHANGE	FORM OF PAYMENT CASH ___ CHECK X CHARGE
Chicago	NC 309	F	5/2	11:00 am	12:07 pm	OK	4/29 NC 309 11:12 am - 12:17 pm	CREDIT CARD VISA
Madison	NC 308	F	5/6	1:02 pm	2:20 pm	OK		OTHER
Chicago								OTHER INFO Confirmed By Suzi - North Central 4/10

FARE		DEPOSITS	AMOUNT	DATE	AUTO				AMOUNT Unlimited Mileage
	200.00		220.00	4/15	AJAX CAR RENTAL - CAT. C $20.00 Day				
TAX	16.00		202.00	6/10	HOTEL HOLIDAY INN - DOWNTOWN $35.00 Day DBL				
TOTAL-AIR	216.00	TOTAL-ALL			OTHER				
COMM.	14.00	60% 8.40	40% 5.60		PAID	DATE 4/16	AMOUNT 80.00	LESS COMM 8.00	PAID TO ESTAB. 72.00 - AJAX
NET REMIT	202.00				PAID	4/16	140.00	14.00	126.00 - HOLIDAY INN
					PAID				

Reservation sheets or cards will differ from one agency to another, but some of the basic information includes: date, name(s), home address(es) including zip code, telephone (home and/or business), ages of children, billing information, i.e, credit card, cash, etc., travel plan (From-To), carrier, flight number, day of week, date, departure and arrival time of each flight, the flight number and type of service, the fare and taxes of each flight, and other reservation information such as status (O.K. or standby), name and date of airline representative making reservation. The reservation sheet may also contain information for hotel, tour, rail, rental car bookings or other pertinent information necessary for the customer's trip.

The reservation sheet contains a shorthand of travel information, i.e, Airline Codes, Airport Codes, flight numbers and types of service. All of the information on the reservation sheet is important, for example, the status designation of a flight means:

O.K. - in the status box means that this particular segment has been confirmed by the airline.

OK/F - in the status box means that this particular segment has been confirmed
WL/Y   FIRST CLASS and is WAIT LISTED On the Y/COACH CLASS.

RQ - in the status box means that this particular segment has been placed on request from another airline.

NO-OP - in the status box means that this particular leg (segment) does not operate as you have requested it.

UK - in the status box means that this particular leg is unable to confirm either class of service (often times, during peak travel periods, a flight can be waitlisted both classes of service).

Other details about the reservation sheet and its relationship to airline ticketing will be explained in this chapter.

AIRLINE TICKETS

Learning how to write an airline ticket is usually an on-the-job activity and can be both exciting and interesting work. Writing airline tickets can be likened to a child who learns for the first time about writing bank checks; the ticket you write can be for a $1.01 or more, and only requires a validation stamp in order to be a negotiable instrument. All ticket stock is accountable as unused, issued, voided or refunded. The interesting part of ticket writing is the very activity represents the totality of a travel agent's work, i.e., counseling, reservations work and customer satisfaction.

The following is an example of a passenger's coupon from a standard interline ticket. The first two digits of the form serial number indicate that it is an agency ticket (8) with four coupons (4), and the rest of the digits are the serial number. The ticket examples start on the following page.

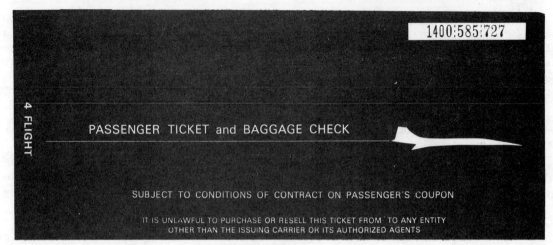

1400 585 727

4 FLIGHT

PASSENGER TICKET and BAGGAGE CHECK

SUBJECT TO CONDITIONS OF CONTRACT ON PASSENGER'S COUPON

IT IS UNLAWFUL TO PURCHASE OR RESELL THIS TICKET FROM TO ANY ENTITY
OTHER THAN THE ISSUING CARRIER OR ITS AUTHORIZED AGENTS

Front Cover

ADVICE TO INTERNATIONAL PASSENGERS ON LIMITATION OF LIABILITY

Passengers on a journey involving an ultimate destination or a stop in a country other than the country of origin are advised that the provisions of a treaty known as the Warsaw Convention may be applicable to the entire journey, including any portion entirely within the country of origin or destination. For such passengers on a journey to, from, or with an agreed stopping place in the United States of America, the Convention and special contracts of carriage embodied in applicable tariffs provide that the liability of certain carriers, parties to such special contracts, for death of or personal injury to passengers is limited in most cases to proven damages not to exceed U. S. $75,000 per passenger, and that this liability up to such limit shall not depend on negligence on the part of the carrier. The limit of liability of U. S. $75,000 above is inclusive of legal fees and costs except that in case of a claim brought in a state where provision is made for separate award of legal fees and costs, the limit shall be the sum of U. S. $58,000 exclusive of legal fees and costs. For such passengers traveling by a carrier not a party to such special contracts or on a journey not to, from, or having an agreed stopping place in the United States of America, liability of the carrier for death or personal injury to passengers is limited in most cases to approximately U. S. $10,000 or U. S. $20,000.

The names of carriers, parties to such special contracts, are available at all ticket offices of such carriers and may be examined on request.

Additional protection can usually be obtained by purchasing insurance from a private company. Such insurance is not affected by any limitation of the carrier's liability under the Warsaw Convention or such special contracts of carriage. For further information please consult your airline or insurance company representative.

REV. 1-74

Inside Cover with Limitation of Liability

NOTICE OF BAGGAGE LIABILITY LIMITATIONS

Liability for loss, delay, or damage to baggage is limited as follows unless a higher value is declared in advance and additional charges are paid: (1) For most international travel (including domestic portions of international journeys) to approximately $9.07 per pound ($20.00 per kilo) for checked baggage and $400 per passenger for unchecked baggage; (2) For travel wholly between U.S. points, to $750 per passenger on most carriers (a few have lower limits). Excess valuation may not be declared on certain types of valuable articles. Carriers assume no liability for fragile or perishable articles. Further information may be obtained from the carrier.

IMPORTANT RECONFIRMATION NOTICES

INTERNATIONAL JOURNEYS

If you break your journey for more than 72 hours at any point, please reconfirm your intention of using your continuing or return reservation. To do so, please inform the airline office at the point where you intend to resume your journey at least 72 hours before departure of your flight. Failure to reconfirm will result in the cancellation of your reservation.

If your journey is wholly within Europe, this notice does not apply to you.

JOURNEYS WITHIN CANADA/U.S.A. AND TO OR FROM MEXICO.

Contact the carrying airline for the applicable requirements.

Insert with baggage liability limitations notice
and reconfirmation requirements.

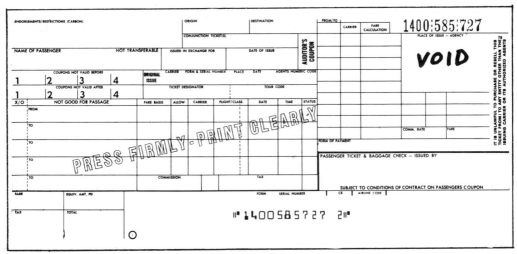

Auditor's Coupon

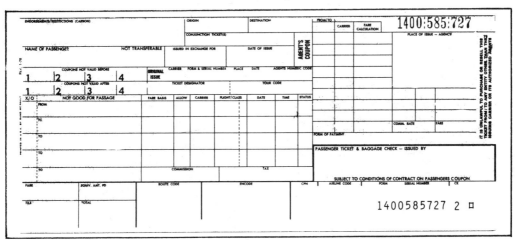

Agent's Coupon

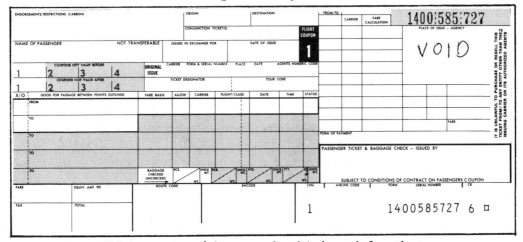

First flight coupon (the second, third, and fourth coupons
are identical except for the coupon number).

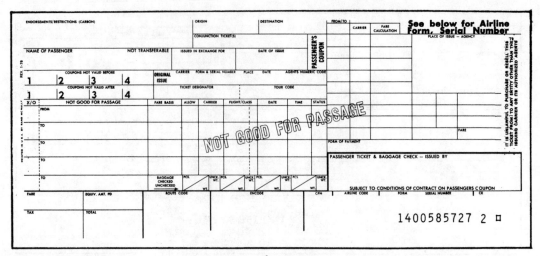

Passenger's Coupon

NOTICE

If the passenger's journey involves an ultimate destination or stop in a country other than the country of departure the Warsaw Convention may be applicable and the Convention governs and in most cases limits the liability of carriers for death or personal injury and in respect of loss of or damage to baggage. See also notice headed "Advice to International Passengers on Limitation of Liability."

CONDITIONS OF CONTRACT

1. As used in this contract "ticket" means this passenger ticket and baggage check, of which these conditions and the notices form part, "carriage" is equivalent to "transportation", "carrier" means all air carriers that carry or undertake to carry the passenger or his baggage hereunder or perform any other service incidental to such air carriage, "WARSAW CONVENTION" means the Convention for the Unification of Certain Rules Relating to International Carriage by Air signed at Warsaw, 12th October 1929, or that Convention as amended at The Hague, 28th September 1955, whichever may be applicable.

2. Carriage hereunder is subject to the rules and limitations relating to liability established by the Warsaw Convention unless such carriage is not "international carriage" as defined by that Convention.

3. To the extent not in conflict with the foregoing carriage and other services performed by each carrier are subject to: (I) provisions contained in this ticket, (II) applicable tariffs, (III) carrier's conditions of carriage and related regulations which are made part hereof (and are available on application at the offices of carrier), except in transportation between a place in the United States or Canada and any place outside thereof to which tariffs in force in those countries apply.

4. Carrier's name may be abbreviated in the ticket, the full name and its abbreviation being set forth in carrier's tariffs, conditions of carriage, regulations or timetables; carrier's address shall be the airport of departure shown opposite the first abbreviation of carrier's name in the ticket; the agreed stopping places are those places set forth in this ticket or as shown in carrier's timetables as scheduled stopping places on the passenger's route; carriage to be performed hereunder by several successive carriers is regarded as a single operation.

5. An air carrier issuing a ticket for carriage over the lines of another air carrier does so only as its agent.

6. Any exclusion or limitation of liability of carrier shall apply to and be for the benefit of agents, servants and representatives of carrier and any person whose aircraft is used by carrier for carriage and its agents, servants and representatives.

7. Checked baggage will be delivered to bearer of the baggage check. In case of damage to baggage moving in international transportation complaint must be made in writing to carrier forthwith after discovery of damage and, at the latest, within 7 days from receipt; in case of delay, complaint must be made within 21 days from date the baggage was delivered. See tariffs or conditions of carriage regarding non-international transportation.

8. This ticket is good for carriage for one year from date of issue, except as otherwise provided in this ticket, in carrier's tariffs, conditions of carriage, or related regulations. The fare for carriage hereunder is subject to change prior to commencement of carriage. Carrier may refuse transportation if the applicable fare has not been paid.

9. Carrier undertakes to use its best efforts to carry the passenger and baggage with reasonable dispatch. Times shown in timetable or elsewhere are not guaranteed and form no part of this contract. Carrier may without notice substitute alternate carriers or aircraft, and may alter or omit stopping places shown on the ticket in case of necessity. Schedules are subject to change without notice. Carrier assumes no responsibility for making connections.

10. Passenger shall comply with Government travel requirements, present exit, entry and other required documents and arrive at airport by time fixed by carrier or, if no time is fixed, early enough to complete departure procedures.

11. No agent, servant or representative of carrier has authority to alter, modify or waive any provision of this contract.

CARRIER RESERVES THE RIGHT TO REFUSE CARRIAGE TO ANY PERSON WHO HAS ACQUIRED A TICKET IN VIOLATION OF APPLICABLE LAW OR CARRIER'S TARIFFS, RULES OR REGULATIONS
Issued by the Carrier whose name is in the "Issued By" section on the face of the Passenger Ticket and Baggage Check.   SUBJECT TO TARIFF REGULATIONS

Back cover with condition of contract of passenger's travel.

NOTICE — OVERBOOKING OF FLIGHTS

Airline flights may be overbooked, and there is a slight chance that a seat will not be available on a flight for which a person has a confirmed reservation. If the flight is overbooked, no one will be denied a seat until airline personnel first ask for volunteers willing to give up their reservation in exchange for a payment of the airline's choosing. If there are not enough volunteers the airline will deny boarding to other persons in accordance with its particular boarding priority. With few exceptions, persons denied boarding involuntarily are entitled to compensation. The complete rules for the payment of compensation and each airline's boarding priorities are available at all airport ticket counters and boarding locations.

Supplemental Notice of overbooking of flights.

The travel agency is responsible for the ticket stock received, collection of the correct amounts written on the issued tickets and remittance of all funds collected in trust for the air carriers. Since 1964 travel agents have used the above common ticket coupons for both ATC/IATA carriers. This standard ticket permits a uniform accounting and remittance procedure under the area settlement plan. Air passenger tickets are usually issued in sequence by serial number and reported in the same way; the tickets sold also are reported by dollar value (or monetary amount in a foreign currency). The auditor's coupon contains all information: the passenger's name, all flight segments of the passage, fare calculation, and form of payment collected. The auditor's coupon, included with sales report, is mailed weekly to the central accounting office. The fares calculated by travel agents is checked by central accounting; discrepancies are reported; and agents are liable for undercollections of fares.

In review, it is essential that the travel agent knows the function of each flight coupon. The coupon authorizes passage between the points shown on the light area of the coupon, and serves as evidence that the fare shown on the coupon has been paid. The coupon is an agreement between the airline and the passenger for reserved seat on the flight specified. The coupon contains all information necessary to insure expeditious handling of the passenger and his luggage. In other words, it helps airline agents to guide the passenger on the correct flights. The coupon establishes all the conditions which must be known to a ticket agent should he have to re-issue or refund the coupon. The coupon contains all the necessary information which enables the carrying airline to bill the issuing airline for the fare between the two points shown on it, if the issuing airline and carrying airline are not the same. Flight coupons can not be honored individually. The passenger must present the coupon to the carrier to which it is made out, in the order in which it is issued and only if all unused coupons are presented together.

AIRLINE RESERVATIONS

All scheduled airlines have established standard reservations procedures. It is important to realize that each airline has its own method of controlling seats on an airplane. Carriers operate on the principle of centralized space control on a first come, first served basis, and each system is designed to give the public an immediate yes or no answer in regard to available airplane seats. When the general public, travel agent, with another carrier, or between their own offices, every airline must have certain basic information in order to make a reservation.

The first contact between travel agent, his client, and airline reservations agent, is the telephone call. (Some 2000 travel agency reservations are using computer terminals.) If the travel agent knows in advance what the client desires, he can prepare his information prior to the call and thereby efficiently relaying this information to the airline reservations agent. The travel agent should know the items needed by the reservations agent in order to conclude a reservations transaction so that the telephone conversation can be expedited.

The majority of airlines use similar procedures in their telephone handling with prospective passengers. The information that a reservations agent requires is generally the same regardless of the carrier contacted.

The reservations agent will need to know the following items (with example in parenthesis) for each flight segment with regard to a planned reservation:

1. The flight number: (AA 701)
2. Class of service: (F)
3. Date of departure: (3-29)

4. The originating point: (BOS)
5. The destination: (DCA)
6. The desired number of seats: (1)
7. The passenger's family name and first initial(s), and residence and/or business telephone(s) contact: (Mr. Smith, A: 603-784-0621, business telephone)
8. Time as given by which the passenger must secure the confirmed ticket or else suffer loss of the reservation: (3-21, 5:00 PM)
9. Travel agent's name and name of individual handling itinerary (Windson Travel, Dwight)

When issuing, reissuing or revalidating the passenger's ticket: it's necessary to check with the airline reservations office that cleared the space in order to verify the reservations claimed for the passenger and to remove the time limit.

All space must be obtained by contacting the (nearest) reservations office of the originating airline. This will simplify the ticketing when more than one airline is involved, protect the passenger travelling via connecting flights by providing the receiving carrier with proper arrival information, and insure proper execution of reconfirmation rules when applicable.

The airlines recognize that under unusual circumstances the travel agent may be required by the passenger to obtain continuing space from the individual airlines concerned. If so, the travel agent must give originating airline the passenger's complete itinerary, including the current reservation status of each flight. The agent must give each other airline the passenger's means of arrival and originating. flight at the time of the original request.

When the travel agent prepares itineraries for his customers, it is important, as a service to the passenger and a requirement of the airline, that sufficient time be allowed for the passenger and his baggage to move from one airline to the other. It is the travel agent's responsibility to determine and adhere to the minimum connecting times published in the airline guides.

The airline reservations agent must know the passenger's telephone number, the travel agency's name, and telephone number, and the name of the particular travel agent handling the reservation. The reservations agent must have the passenger's contact in the event there are any operational difficulties and it is either too late or inconvenient to call the travel agent.

If the reservation is for more than one passenger, and if names are different, each name should be given to the airline reservations agent. If the itinerary of the passenger begins at a point other than where the reservation is being made, the reservations agent will desire to know how the passenger will be arriving at his first boarding point. If it is possible, the passenger's contact at the city where he will board his first flight should be given to the reservations agent. This will enable the reservations office at the passenger's boarding point to be able to contact the passenger if the occasion arises.

As indicated in the governing tariff rule, certain member airlines require ticketed passengers, under certain given circumstances, to reconfirm, i.e., advise the airline at the boarding point of their intentions to use their reservations no later than the time set forth in the tariff rule. Upon failure to reconfirm, the concerned passenger's reservations are cancelled, including their complete remaining itineraries. When ticketing a passenger, the travel agent must inform the passenger of his responsibility to reconfirm each segment of his itinerary subject to the reconfirmation rule.

AIRLINE TICKETING PROCEDURES

Standard Bank Settlement Plan Ticket

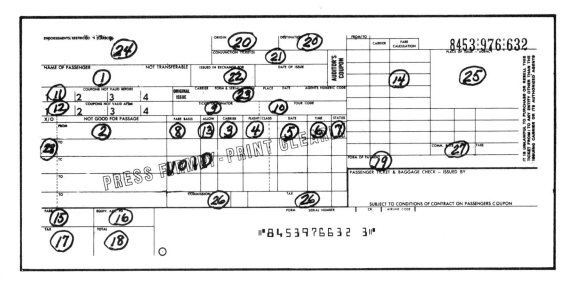

1.   Enter the passengers surname followed by a slash, first initial and then title. EXAMPLE: Jones/T. Mr. If the passenger is an unaccompanied minor, enter UM followed by the age in brackets. EXAMPLE: WILSON/L. Master (UM 8)

2.   Enter the passengers complete itinerary using block letters starting with the city of origin and listing each connection, city, stopover city, and destination. When a city is served by more than one airport, enter both the city name and the air-port name. EXAMPLE:

From:
NEW YORK/KENNEDY
To:
LONDON/HEATHROW

3.   Enter the two-letter code of the airline involved. EXAMPLE: AA

4.   Enter the passengers flight number followed by the class of service. The class of service determines in which compartment of the aircraft the passenger will be seated. EXAMPLE: 501Y

5.   Enter the date using a 3-letter abbreviation for the month and a 2-digit for the day. EXAMPLE: 07 FEB

6.   Enter the time that the flight departs. On domestic tickets use A or am, P or PM, and N for noon. EXAMPLE: 715A   On international tickets show the time in the 24-hour clock style. EXAMPLE: 2145

7.   Enter the status of the reservation (OK) for confirmed, (WL) for waitlisted, or (RQ) for requested. EXAMPLE: WL

8.   Enter the fare basis code. This code consists of three parts--the prime code, secondary code, and discount code. All tickets must have the prime code, which

indicates the class of service. If applicable use the secondary and discount codes.
EXAMPLE: YLE 45   (Y) is the primary code, which shows that this is for coach seating (L) is the secondary code indicated the low season, (E 45) is the discount code
which indicates the passenger is travelling on a 45-day excursion.

9.   Enter the type of discount if it applies to the entire ticket. EXAMPLE:
CH (child)

10.   Enter the official tour code number if issuing the ticket for an international
journey. On a domestic ticket involving a tour, use a tour ticket.

11.   If the passenger is travelling on an excursion or restricted fare, enter the
earliest return date for each segment.

12.   Enter the date by which all travel must be completed.

13.   On international travel only enter the free baggage weight allowance when
applicable. Domestic travel and most of the major international routes are now using
a per-piece allowance.

14.   Complete the fare calculation box. This is required only for conjunction
tickets, reissued tickets, when a city not shown on the itinerary is used to construct
the fare, to show a surcharge, a differential, a stopover charge, or a mileage charge.

15.   Enter the fare (without tax) and currency code if writing an international
ticket.

16.   Enter the amount of currency collected from the passenger and currency code.
This box does not have to be completed when the passenger pays in U.S. dollars.

17.   Enter the tax. If a ticket involves both international and domestic tax,
show them separately.

18.   Enter the sum of the fare and tax.

19.   Enter the form of payment, when payment is other than cash or travellers
check. When issuing an exchange ticket, enter form of payment shown on the original
ticket. When a credit card sales is involved enter the 2-letter code of the credit
card company and the credit card number.

MAJOR CREDIT CARDS AND THEIR CODES

Access Credit Card - XS
Air Canada - AC
Air Travel Card (UATP) - TP
Air West Credit Card - RW
Alaska Airlines Credit Card - AS
Aloha Airlines Credit Card - TS
American Express - AX
American Airlines Vacation Credit
  Card - AA
Bank of Hawaii - BH
Barclaycard - BB
Braniff Fastcharge - BI
Canadian Pacific Credit Card - CP
Carte Blanche - CB
China Airlines Dynasty Travel Card - DT
Citizens and Southern National Bank - CS
Club des 2000 Air France - AF
Connecticut Bank & Trust Co. - CU
Continental Airlines System Travel
  Card - CO
Diamond Credit - MD
Diners Club/American Torch Club - DC
Eastern Airlines Charge-a-Trip Card - EA
Empire Card - MT
Federated Credit Card - FC

Hawaiian Airlines Credit Card - HA
Master Charge - CA
Million Credit Service - MC
National Airlines Sun King Travel
  Card - NA
North Central Airlines On-Line Card - NC
Northwest Airlines Air Credit Card - NW
Ozark Airlines Tic-a-Trip Card OZ
Pan American Airways Take-Off Card - PA
Piedmont Airlines Air Travel Credit
  Card - PI
Select Credit - SR
Shoppers Charge - SC
Southern Airways Air Travel Credit
  Card - SO
Texas International Airlines On-Line
  Travel Card - TI
Trans World Airlines Getaway Credit
  Card - TW
Trust Card - TC
United Airlines Personal Credit Card - UC
Uni-Serve (UNI-Card) - US
Visa (BankAmericard) - BA
Western Airlines Travelcard - WA
Western International Hotels - WH

20. Enter the city names in full showing where the transportation will commence and terminate.

21. When more than one ticket is needed to complete a passenger itinerary, you have to issue conjunction tickets. In this box enter the complete form and serial number of all other tickets being issued to complete the passenger's itinerary.

22. Complete this box when you are issuing a ticket in exchange for another ticket. Enter the complete form and serial number of the original ticket.

23. Enter the number of the original tickets, the place and date of original issue, and the agents numeric code.

24. This box can be used to show any special restrictions or information or to show a requested or waitlisted flight.

25. This box is complete with the validator and shows the agency name, location, and numeric code.

26. Enter the appropriate commission and tax. If these figures are a straight percentage such as 8% for domestic tax, put 8 in the tax box. If not a straight percentage, such as a $3.00 international tax, write in the actual dollar amount.

27. Enter the commission codes applicable to the ticket. EXAMPLE: FT-8. This indicates an 8% commission based on family travel.

28. On domestic tickets use an (X) to indicate a connection, no stopover permitted or a (0) to indicate a stopover next to all cities except origin and destination.

DOMESTIC AIRLINE TICKET

On November 20, Mr. Derek Cronin comes into your office to purchase a trip to Honolulu. He would like to depart on November 23, but wants to stop over in Los Angeles for two nights. He prefers to travel first class. You would now refer to the North American Official Airline Guide (NAOAG) and look up to Los Angeles from Boston. See schedule A on the following page.

Mr. Cronin has asked for a mid-afternoon departure. You select TWA flight 65, which departs Boston at 3:00 PM and arrives Los Angeles at 5:45 PM. Your client wishes to proceed to Honolulu from Los Angeles on November 25. You again refer to the NAOAG and look up to Honolulu from Los Angeles. See schedule B on the following page.

Pan American's "China Clipper" San Francisco, Honolulu

Schedule A   Schedule B

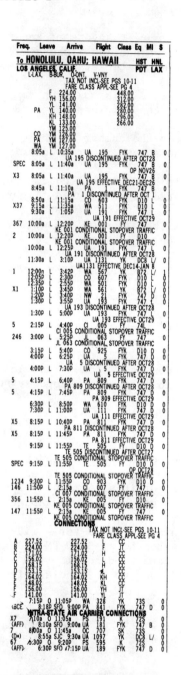

Your client wants a mid-day departure, so you choose Western #501 which departs Los Angeles at 12:35 PM and arrives in Honolulu at 2:55 PM.

On his return from Honolulu, Mr. Cronin would like to stop over in San Francisco for three nights. He wants to leave Honolulu on December 14. In the NAOAG to San Francisco from Honolulu, you select a late afternoon departure from Honolulu on Western Airlines flight #530 departing at 4:10 PM and arriving in San Francisco at 11:59 PM. See schedule C on the following page.

Your client wants to return from San Francisco to Boston on December 17, first thing in the morning. You again refer to the NAOAG and look up to Boston from San Francisco. You select TWA flight 32 departing San Francisco at 8:30 AM and arriving at 4:40 PM. See schedule D below.

Schedule C   Schedule D

Trans World Airline's 727

Your next step is to enter the flights you have chosen on your reservation sheet and call the airlines to book the flights. After the airline reservationist has confirmed the flight, you should ask her for the air fare. She has current fare information in her computer. In the example below we have your completed reservation sheet.

Name: Mr. Derek Cronin	Home Phone 345-6789	Order Rec'd 11-20	Pick Up Date 11-22	Fare	898.00
194 Lowell Street	Office Phone 345-5432	Call Client	Advised Client OK unless we call – X	Tax	
Manchester, New Hampshire				Total	
				Passport	

DATE	DAY	ITINERARY	FL.NO.	CLASS	STATUS	LEAVE	ARRIVE		
								Small Pox	
								Option Date	
11/23	M T W TH F SA SU	BOS	TW 65	F A T Y K R	OK Req. List	AM 3:00PM	5:54 AM PM	Ticket No.	By
11/25	M T W TH F SA SU	LAX	WA 501	F A T Y K R	OK Req. List	AM 12:35PM	AM 2:55 PM		
12/14	M T W TH F SA SU	HNL	WA 530	F A T Y K R	OK Req. List	AM 4:10 PM	AM 11:59 PM		
12/17	M T W TH F SA SU	SFO	TW 32	F A T Y K R	OK Req. List	8:30 AM PM	4:40 AM PM		
	M T W TH F SA SU	BOS		F A T Y K R	OK Req. List	AM PM	AM PM		
	M T W TH F SA SU			F A T Y K R	OK Req. List	AM PM	AM PM		
	M T W TH F SA SU			F A T Y K R	OK Req. List	AM PM	AM PM		
	M T W TH F SA SU			F A T Y K R	OK Req. List	AM PM	AM PM		
	M T W TH F SA SU			F A T Y K R	OK Req. List	AM PM	AM PM		

At this time you are ready to compute the air fare. You should refer to the <u>Squire's Tariff Joint Fares</u> and look up between Boston and Honolulu. See sample below:

FOR THE APPLICATION OF FARES, SEE RULE 3

MARKET	FARE CLASS	FARE	ROUTING	ROUTING	ROUTING
between BOSTON and					
Hono-lulu	F OW	449.00	AL CHI CO AA/DL/EA DFW BN TW LAS WA TW LAX CO/NW/PA/UA/WA NA/TW/UA NYC NW UA PDX NW/PA UA SFO PA/WA UA YVR CP	AA/TW CHI CO/NW TW DEN CO/WA AA LAX CO/NW/PA/UA/WA UA LAX PA/WA AA/TW PHX WA AA SAN UA/WA EA SEA CO/PA	UA CHI NW UA DEN WA EA LAX CO/NW/PA/UA/WA DL/EA NYC NW/UA EA PDX CO/PA AA/TW SFO NW/PA/UA/WA UA SEA NW/PA

We first look under Honolulu. The client is travelling First Class and his outbound routing is via Los Angeles using Trans World Airlines from Boston to Los Angeles
and Western from Los Angeles to Honolulu. The time which verifies that your routing
is allowed at the joint one-way fare of $449.00 is as follows:

TW LAX CO/NW/PA/VA/WA

The line which verifies your return routing is as follows:

AA/TW SFO NW/PA/VA/WA

We now double the one-way fare of $449.00 to arrive at a round-trip first-class
fare of $898.00. Hawaii fares are shown in the tariff without tax. To compute the
tax you refer to the Hawaiian tax tables in the OAG. Note that for Boston we must
figure the tax from Column 25 of Hawaiian Tax Table II.

HAWAIIAN TAX TABLE I

When the city is: CITY	CODE	Figure the Tax from: COLUMN	When the city is: CITY	CODE	Figure the Tax from: COLUMN	When the city is: CITY	CODE	Figure the Tax from: COLUMN	When the city is: CITY	CODE	Figure the Tax from: COLUMN
Akron	CAK	18	Elmira	ELM	22	Lamar, Colo	LAA	12	Pueblo	PUB	9
Albany, GA	ABY	15	El Paso	ELP	8	Lansing	LAN	17	Quebec, QUE	YQB	25
Albany, NY	ALB	24	Ely	ELY	7	Las Vegas	LAS	7	Quincy	UIN	11
Albuquerque	ABQ	8	Erie	ERI	19	Laurel/Hattiesburg	PIB	13	Raleigh	RDU	22
Alexandria	ESF	11	Eugene	EUG	4	Lawton	LAW	9	Rapid City	RAP	9
Allentown	ABE	23	Eureka	ACV	3	Lexington	LEX	15	Red Bluff	RBL	4
Amarillo	AMA	9	Evansville	EVV	15	Lincoln	LNK	12	Redding	RDD	4
Anchorage	ANC	6	Fairbanks	FAI	6	Little Rock	LIT	11	Regina, SASK	YQR	14
Asheville	AVL	18	Fairmont	FRM	14	London, ONT	YXU	20	Reno	RNO	7
Astoria	AST	4	Fargo	FAR	14	Long Beach	LGB	2	Rhinelander	RHI	16
Atlanta	ATL	15	Fayetteville, AR	FYV	14	Los Angeles	LAX	2	Richmond	RIC	22
Augusta	AGS	18	Fayetteville, NC	FAY	18	Louisville	SDF	15	Roanoke	ROA	21
Austin	AUS	9	Flint	FNT	17	Lubbock	LBB	9	Rochester, MN	RST	14
Bakersfield	BFL	2	Florence, SC	FLO	18	Lynchburg	LYH	21	Rochester, NY	ROC	22
Baltimore	BAL	22	Fort Lauderdale	FLL	18	Macon	MCN	17	Rockville, IL	RFD	16
Bangor	BGR	25	Fort Leonard Wood	TBN	11	Madison	MSN	16	Sacramento	SMF	2
Baton Rouge	BTR	13	Fort Meyers	FMY	18	Manitowoc	MTW	17	Saginaw	MBS	17
Beloit	JVL	16	Fort Polk	POE	11	Mankato	MKT	14	St. Louis	STL	11
Benton Harbor, MI	BEH	16	Ft. Smith, AR	FSM	11	Marion	MWA	16	Salem	SLE	4
Billings	BIL	8	Ft. Wayne	FWA	17	Mattoon	MTO	16	Salina	SLN	12
Binghamton	BGM	23	Fresno	FAT	2	Medford	MFR	4	Salt Lake City	SLC	8
Birmingham	BHM	15	Gainsville, Fla	GNV	15	Melbourne	MLB	18	San Antonio	SAT	10
Bismarck	BIS	12	Galveston	GLS	10	Memphis	MEM	15	San Diego	SAN	2
Bloomington, IL	BMI	16	Garden City, Kan	GCK	12	Merced	MCE	2	San Francisco	SFO	3
Boise	BOI	7	Goldsboro, NC	GSB	22	Meridian	MEI	16	San Jose	SJC	3
Boston	BOS	25	Goodland, Kan	GLD	12	Miami	MIA	18	Santa Barbara	SBA	2
Bozeman	BZN	8	Grand Canyon	GCN	7	Midland, TX	MAF	9	Santa Maria	SMX	2
Bradford	BFD	22	Grand Forks	GFK	12	Milwaukee	MKE	16	Sarasota	SRQ	18
Bristol	TRI	19	Grand Junction	GJT	8	Minneapolis	MSP	14	Saskatoon, SASK	YXE	14
Brownsville	BRO	9	Grand Rapids	GRR	17	Missoula	MSO	8	Savannah	SAV	18
Brownwood	BWD	9	Great Bend, Kan	GBD	12	Mobile	MOB	15	Scotts Bluff	BFF	12
Buffalo	BUF	21	Great Falls	GTF	8	Modesto	MOD	2	Scranton	AVP	23
Burlington, IA	BRL	16	Green Bay	GRB	16	Moline	MLI	16	Seattle	SEA	5
Butte	BTM	8	Greensboro	GSO	20	Monroe	MLU	11	Shreveport	SHV	14
Calgary	YYC	7	Greenville, MS	GLH	11	Monterey	MRY	3	Sheridan	SHR	8
Cape Girardeau	CGI	11	Greenville, SC	GSP	18	Montgomery	MGM	15	Sioux City	SUX	12
Casper	CPR	8	Gulfport	GPT	13	Montreal	YUL	25	Sioux Falls	FSD	12
Castlegar, BC	YCG	5	Harlingen	HRL	9	Mt. Vernon	MVN	16	South Bend	SBN	17
Cedar Rapids	CID	16	Harrisburg	HAR	23	Muskegon	MKG	17	Spokane	GEG	7
Champaign	CMI	16	Hartford	BDL	25	Muscle Shoals	MSL	20	Springfield, IL	SPI	16
Charleston, SC	CHS	18	Hays, Kan	HYS	12	Myrtle Beach	CRE	22	Springfield, MO	SGF	11
Charleston, WV	CRW	18	Helena	HLN	8	Nashville	BNA	15	Stockton	SCK	2
Charlotte	CLT	18	Homer	HOM	6	Newark	EWR	24	Syracuse	SYR	23
Chattanooga	CHA	15	Hot Springs	HOT	11	New Bern	EWN	22	Tallahassee	TLH	15
	CYS	8	Houston	IAH	10	New Orleans	MSY	13	Tampa	TPA	18
		.6		..TS	19	Newport News	PHF	23	Temple	TPI	
						Ne...	...C	24			

First look at Hawaiian Tax Table I. Look up the Continental U. S. city of departure to determine which column of Hawaiian Tax Table II to use. (Table II is on
the following page.) Our total joint fare BOS-NHL is $898.00. In Tax Table II you
look under the Column amount. The amount goes up to only $500.00. So to compute the
tax for $898.00, we will use the $00. column first and double the amount. Then use
the $90.00 amount and the $8.00 amount.

HAWAIIAN TAX TABLE II

Column Amount	1	2	3	4	5	6	7	8	9	10	11	12	13
$ .50	.00	.00	.00	.00	.00	.00	.01	.01	.01	.01	.02	.02	.02
1.00	.00	.00	.00	.00	.00	.00	.01	.02	.03	.03	.03	.03	.03
2.00	.00	.00	.00	.00	.00	.01	.02	.05	.05	.06	.06	.06	.06
3.00	.00	.00	.00	.01	.01	.01	.03	.07	.08	.08	.09	.09	.09
4.00	.00	.00	.00	.01	.01	.02	.04	.09	.10	.11	.12	.12	.13
5.00	.00	.00	.00	.01	.02	.02	.05	.12	.13	.14	.15	.16	.16
6.00	.00	.00	.00	.01	.02	.02	.06	.14	.16	.17	.18	.18	.19
7.00	.00	.00	.00	.02	.02	.03	.07	.16	.18	.20	.21	.22	.22
8.00	.00	.00	.00	.02	.03	.03	.08	.19	.21	.22	.24	.25	.25
9.00	.00	.00	.00	.02	.03	.04	.09	.21	.23	.25	.26	.26	.28
10.00	.00	.00	.00	.02	.03	.04	.10	.23	.26	.28	.31	.31	.32
20.00	.00	.00	.01	.05	.06	.08	.20	.46	.52	.56	.62	.62	.64
30.00	.00	.01	.01	.07	.10	.12	.31	.70	.78	.84	.93	.94	.95
40.00	.00	.01	.02	.09	.13	.16	.41	.93	1.04	1.12	1.22	1.25	1.26
50.00	.01	.02	.02	.12	.16	.20	.51	1.16	1.30	1.41	1.53	1.56	1.58
60.00	.01	.02	.02	.14	.19	.23	.61	1.39	1.56	1.69	1.84	1.87	1.90
70.00	.01	.02	.03	.16	.22	.27	.71	1.62	1.82	2.07	2.14	2.18	2.21
80.00	.02	.02	.03	.19	.26	.31	.82	1.86	2.08	2.25	2.45	2.50	2.53
90.00	.02	.03	.04	.21	.29	.35	.92	2.09	2.34	2.53	2.75	2.81	2.84
100.00	.02	.03	.04	.23	.32	.39	1.02	2.32	2.60	2.81	3.06	3.12	3.16
200.00	.04	.06	.08	.46	.64	.78	2.04	4.64	5.20	5.62	6.12	6.24	6.32
300.00	.06	.09	.12	.69	.96	1.17	3.06	6.96	7.80	8.43	9.18	9.36	9.48
400.00	.08	.12	.16	.92	1.28	1.56	4.08	9.28	10.40	11.24	12.24	12.48	12.64
500.00	.10	.15	.20	1.15	1.60	1.95	5.10	11.60	13.00	14.05	15.30	15.60	15.80

Column Amount	14	15	16	17	18	19	20	21	22	23	24	25
$ .50	.02	.02	.02	.02	.02	.02	.02	.02	.02	.02	.02	.02
1.00	.03	.03	.04	.04	.04	.04	.04	.04	.04	.04	.04	.04
2.00	.06	.07	.07	.08	.08	.08	.08	.08	.08	.08	.08	.09
3.00	.10	.10	.11	.11	.11	.12	.12	.12	.12	.12	.13	.13
4.00	.13	.14	.14	.15	.15	.16	.16	.16	.16	.17	.17	.17
5.00	.16	.17	.18	.19	.19	.20	.20	.20	.20	.21	.21	.21
6.00	.19	.21	.21	.23	.23	.23	.23	.24	.24	.25	.25	.26
7.00	.23	.24	.25	.26	.27	.27	.27	.28	.28	.29	.29	.30
8.00	.26	.28	.28	.30	.31	.31	.31	.32	.32	.33	.33	.34
9.00	.29	.31	.32	.34	.34	.35	.35	.36	.37	.37	.38	.38
10.00	.32	.35	.35	.38	.38	.39	.39	.40	.41	.41	.42	.43
20.00	.64	.69	.70	.75	.76	.78	.78	.79	.81	.83	.84	.85
30.00	.97	1.04	1.05	1.13	1.15	1.17	1.17	1.19	1.22	1.24	1.25	1.28
40.00	1.29	1.38	1.40	1.50	1.53	1.56	1.56	1.58	1.62	1.65	1.67	1.71
50.00	1.61	1.73	1.76	1.88	1.91	1.95	1.96	1.98	2.03	2.07	2.09	2.14
60.00	1.93	2.07	2.11	2.25	2.29	2.34	2.35	2.37	2.44	2.48	2.51	2.56
70.00	2.25	2.42	2.46	2.63	2.67	2.73	2.74	2.77	2.84	2.89	2.93	2.99
80.00	2.58	2.76	2.81	3.00	3.06	3.12	3.13	3.16	3.25	3.30	3.34	3.42
90.00	2.90	3.11	3.16	3.38	3.44	3.51	3.52	3.56	3.65	3.72	3.76	3.84
100.00	3.22	3.45	3.51	3.75	3.82	3.90	3.91	3.95	4.06	4.13	4.18	4.27
200.00	6.44	6.90	7.02	7.50	7.64	7.80	7.82	7.90	8.12	8.26	8.36	8.54
300.00	9.66	10.35	10.53	11.25	11.46	11.70	11.73	11.85	12.18	12.39	12.54	12.81
400.00	12.88	13.80	14.04	15.00	15.28	15.60	15.64	15.80	16.24	16.52	16.72	17.08
500.00	16.10	17.25	17.55	18.75	19.10	19.50	19.55	19.75	20.30	20.65	20.90	21.35

Column Amount	Column 25
$400.	$17.08
400.	17.08
90.	3.84
8.	.34
$898.	$38.34

We must now add International Tax of $3.00 for a one-way or $6.00 for round trip to the tax we just computed. Our total fare is as follows:

Base Fare	$898.00
Tax from Column 25	38.34
International Tax	6.00
TOTAL	$942.34

We are now ready to write the ticket; review the example on the following page.

ENDORSEMENTS/RESTRICTIONS (CARBON)

ORIGIN *Boston* DESTINATION *Boston* *Bos*

NAME OF PASSENGER   NOT TRANSFERABLE   ISSUED IN EXCHANGE FOR   DATE OF ISSUE

Cronin / D. Mr.

FROM/TO | CARRIER | FARE CALCULATION
Lax | *TW* |
HNL | *WA* | *449.00*
SFO | *WA* |
Bos | *TW* | *449.00*

8453:976:630

PLACE OF ISSUE — AGENCY

COUPONS NOT VALID BEFORE 1 2 3 4

ORIGINAL ISSUE

CARRIER FORM & SERIAL NUMBER PLACE DATE AGENTS NUMERIC CODE

COUPONS NOT VALID AFTER 1 2 3 4

TICKET DESIGNATOR TOUR CODE

VOID

X/O	NOT GOOD FOR PASSAGE	FARE BASIS	ALLOW	CARRIER	FLIGHT/CLASS	DATE	TIME	STATUS
	FROM *Boston*	F		TW	65 F	*Nov. 23*		OK
O	TO *Los Angeles*	F				*25*		OK
O	TO *Honolulu*			WA	530 F	*Dec. 14*		
O	TO *San Francisco*	F		TW	35 F	*Dec. 17*	*8:30 AM*	OK
O	TO *Boston*							

COMM. RATE *7*   FARE *898.00*

FORM OF PAYMENT

COMMISSION

TAX *44 34*

PASSENGER TICKET & BAGGAGE CHECK — ISSUED BY

TRANS WORLD AIRLINES

SUBJECT TO CONDITIONS OF CONTRACT ON PASSENGERS COUPON

FARE *898.00*   EQUIV. AMT. PD

TAX *38.34*
6.00   TOTAL *942.34*

FORM SERIAL NUMBER   CK AIRLINE CODE

⑈845397 6630 ⑈

INTERNATIONAL AIRLINE TICKET

Tina McCarthy comes into the office. She wants to book a round-trip flight from Boston to Paris. She will depart Boston on December 16 and return on December 20.

Procedure

1. The agent refers to the Worldwide Edition (December) of the OAG, and looks up to Paris from Boston. See sample page of the OAG below.

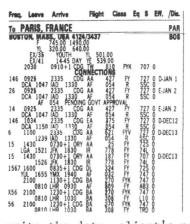

2. On a reservation pad write the data, client's name, and home telephone contact. Then write in the flight you have selected and date for customer's flight.

3. Once again refer to the Worldwide Edition of the OAG to select her return flight. Look up to Boston from Paris (December 1978 edition, Pg. 299). Her return date is December 20. Transfer this information to the itinerary pad.

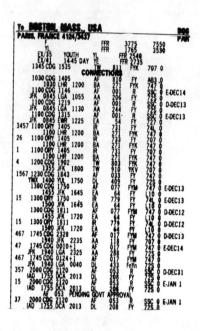

4. Call the airline and book the flights. Assuming the flights are available, circle OK and make a note of the airline reservationist's name and the date the booking was made. Give the airline reservationist the passenger's name, home phone contact, and the travel agency's phone number. Check the fare with the airline. They should have the information in their computer. She gives us a fare of YL (coach, low season) $320.00 one way. Double the fare for round trip and add the $3.00 international tax. Review completed sample of itinerary sheet below.

Name: Ms. Tina McCarthy			Home Phone (617) 343-0000	Order Rec'd 11-28	Pick Up Date 11-30	Fare	640.00
4 Dwight Lane			Office Phone (603) 342-4121	Call Client	Advised Client OK unless we call –	Tax	3.00
Boston, Mass.						Total	643.00
						Passport	
DATE	DAY	ITINERARY	FL.NO.	CLASS	STATUS	LEAVE	ARRIVE	Small Pox	
								Option Date	
12/16	M T W TH F SA SU	BOS	TW 810	F A T Y K R	OK Req. List	2030 AM PM	0910 AM PM	Ticket No.	By
12/20	M T W TH F SA SU	PAR	TW 811	F A T Y K R	OK Req. List Maria	1345 AM PM	1535 AM PM		
	M T W TH F SA SU	BOS		F A T Y K R	OK Req. 11-28 List	AM PM	AM PM	YL 320.00 O.W.	

5. Re-verify the fare. Refer to the <u>Air Tariff-Worldwide</u>, Book 1 (latest edition, yellow pages). Look up the fare from Boston to Paris. Note the YL one way fare which is $320.00 in the headline city currency (USD) and $302.00 in FCU's. (See the example below.)

FROM/TO	FARE TYPE	HEADLINE CITY CURRENCY	FCU	RULES	MAP RTE REF	GI/MPM ——— VIA PT.
BOSTON (BOS) Mas., U.S.A.		U.S. $ (USD)				
PARIS	F	675.00	636.00			4124
	YL	320.00	302.00			4124
	YH	406.00	383.00			4124
	YLE21	580.00	547.00	N201		4124
	YHE21	674.00	635.00	N202		4124
	YLE45	482.00	454.00	N226		4124
	YHE45	596.00	562.00	N228		4124
	YLZ	477.00	449.00	N151		4124
	YHZ	533.00	502.00	N153		4124
	YLGA	482.00	454.00	N515		4124
	YHGA	596.00	562.00	N517		4124
	YGC	482.00	454.00	N530		4124
	YGV	390.00	368.00	G225		4124
	YLGV	451.00	425.00	G206		4124
	YHGV	561.00	529.00	G207		4124

The fare given by the airline is correct and now this reservation would be ready for ticketing. The above itinerary we have used was a very simple, basic itinerary. Now let's suppose Ms. McCarthy has decided to stopover in London for a day enroute to Paris. Her itinerary is now BOS–LON–PAR–BOS. We must now check the mileage on the one way BOS–LON–PAR. In the tariff listing the maximum permitted mileage for the YL Boston to Paris fare is 4124. We will now refer to the "Routing--non-stop sector mileages" section of the tariff to check the non-stop sector mileages.

Sector Mileages

LONDON	U K	LON
Birmingham	U K	100
Bombay	India	4477
Bordeaux	Fra	449
Boston Mas	USA	3265
Bremen	Ger	405
Brussels	Bel	211
Bucharest	Rom	1302
Budapest	Hung	917
Cairo	Egypt	2185
Newquay	U K	213
New York NY	USA	3456
Nice	Fra	635
Norwich	U K	117
Oporto	Port	801
Oslo	Nor	730
Palma Majorca	Spain	826
Paris	Fra	209
Perpignan	Fra	612

By looking up the mileage under London, we have the sector mileage listings for both BOS-LON and LON-PAR. We now compute the sector mileage as follows:

```
        BOS
        LON    3265
        PAR     209
              _____
               3474
```

Since the allowed mileage is 4124 we are well within the mileage and it is not necessary to increase the fare. More complicated fare itineraries should always be verified with the airline's rate desk. They will give you a rate number, and the rate number should be written on the fare construction portion of the ticket.

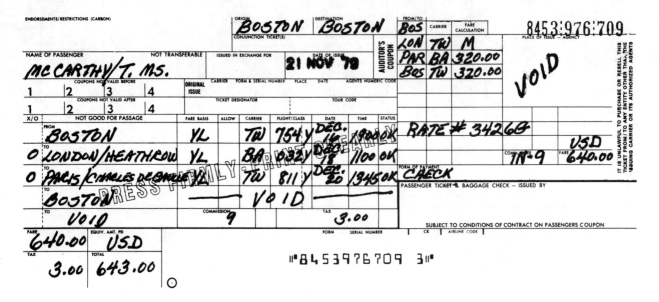

AIRLINE TICKET-RELATED DOCUMENTS

A miscellaneous charges order (MCO) is a prepaid order form used when a client pays in advance for travel services and accommodations that are not included in a ticket. An MCO may include:

Air transportation (only when it cannot be included in a ticket). Note that if a carrier does not have a ticket agreement, it will not have an MCO agreement and will not accept an MCO for ticket payment.

Refundable balances

Land arrangments (other than those included in a tour package)

Collections for PTAs (Prepaid Ticket Advices)

Surface transportation

Additional collections

Steamship transportation (air/sea tours, for example)

Deposits (initial payments with balance due)

Car rental or hotel accommodations (other than those included in a tour package)

Taxes (only when they cannot be included on a ticket - usually foreign)

Upgrading or undercollections

An MCO has an auditor's coupon, an agent's coupon, and a passenger's coupon. The value of an MCO must not exceed certain limits. Specified transportation and land arrangements must not exceed the value of the MCO.

A Tour Order is used for the sale of advertised air tours. The standard tour order contains several coupons, i.e., auditor's, agent's, ground transportation, accommodations, and passenger's. When ticketing an air tour package, a standard air ticket (air) and tour order (land portion) is required. The use of a Tour Order assures the travel agent that over-ride air commissions are being claimed from IT-approved air tours.

Standard Tour Order for Travel Agents

BILL TO: NAME OF TOUR OPERATOR 2		TOUR CODE IT 3	AUDITOR'S COUPON	805 0:000:001
TOUR NAME 4		DATE OF ISSUE 1-B	TOTAL TOUR COST 21	PLACE OF ISSUE – AGENCY
PASSENGER NAME 5	NOT TRANSFERABLE PTY OF 6		LESS DEPOSIT 22	1-A

CPN	PRESENT TO	AT	VALUE		
1	7		8	FINAL PAYMENT 23	
2	9		10	EQUIV AMT PAID 24	AIR TICKET NUMBER(S) 26
3	11		12	COMM RATE 10	ISSUED IN EXCHANGE FOR 27
4	11		12	FORM OF PAYMENT 25	DATE AND PLACE OF ORIG ISSUE 28

TOUR FEATURES
13

ISSUED BY
1

HOTEL DETAILS	COMMISSION 19	NET REMITTANCE-TAX 20
☐ SINGLE ☐ DOUBLE 14 ☐ TWIN		
NUMBER OF NIGHTS 15 ☐ OTHER IN DATE 16		
OUT DATE		
ARRIVAL FLIGHT/DATE 17	DEPARTURE FLIGHT/DATE 18	O

⑂ 805 0000001 0 ⑂

Item:

1. 1A Date of Issue/Issued by—Validate with same carrier ID plate used to issue passenger(s) air ticket(s); the agent's validation plate; and the current date.
2. Bill to Tour Operator—Enter name of tour operator.
3. Tour Code—Enter approved tour code as shown in Manual.
4. Tour Name—Enter name of tour.
5. Passenger's Name—Enter passenger's first initial and last name.
6. Party of—Enter total number in party.

COUPON 1

7. Present to—Enter name of airport transfer company or rental car company and name of city where service will commence.
8. Value—Enter value of services rendered only when required by specific ticketing instructions.

COUPON 2

9. Present to—Enter name of tour operator or hotel as specified in ticketing instructions and name of city where tour commences.
10. Value—Enter value of services rendered only when required by specific ticketing instructions.

COUPON 3 & 4

11. Present to—Enter name and location of airport transfer company or additional services provided in the tour.
12. Value—Enter value of services rendered only when required by specific ticketing instructions.
13. Tour Features—Enter services included in the package as specified in tour.
14. Hotel Details—Check the type of hotel occupancy purchased.
15. Number of nights—Enter number of nights purchased at hotel.
16. In/Out Date—Enter check-in and check-out dates at hotel.
17. Arrival Flight/Date—Enter the arrival airline flight number and date.
18. Departure Flight/Date—Enter the departure airline flight number and date.
19. Commission—Enter applicable commission code (maximum allowable commission is 10% of final payment).
20. Net Remittance—Enter dollar amount to be remitted on travel agency sales report.
21. Total Tour Cost—Enter total value of tour (this amount should equal total coupon values if coupon values are required by specific ticketing instructions).
22. Less Deposit—When prior deposit has been made, enter total amount of deposit, and insert MCO number in "Form of Payment" box (see item 25).
23. Final Payment—Enter total value of tour (less deposit when applicable).
24. Equivalent Amount Paid—If payment is made with other than U.S. dollars, enter equivalent amount of currency presented and the three-letter ALPHA currency code.
25. Form of Payment—Enter form of payment used to purchase tour, e.g., cash, check, credit card number, etc. Also enter deposit MCO number if applicable.
26. Air Ticket(s) Issued—Enter air ticket(s) issued in connection with tour order.
27. Issued in Exchange for—Enter appropriate number only when issued in exchange for another tour order or miscellaneous charges order (MCO).
28. Date and Place of Original Issue—Show date and place of original issue of tour order or MCO. (Used only when tour order is issued in exchange for another tour order or MCO).

American Airlines DC-10 Luxury Liner Take-off

OFFICIAL AIRLINE GUIDE REVIEW

Directions: Answer all of the following questions about the Worldwide and North American OAG Editions. The questions are reprinted with permission from The Worldwide and North American Editions of the Official Airline Guides.

1. In the Worldwide Edition, schedules to Milan are presented _____
    (before/after)
    schedules to Prague.

2. Schedules to Berlin are found toward the _____ of the book.
    (front/rear)

3. The Carrier Code AZ stands for _____Airlines.

4. A CVL is a _____ Jet.

5. The Frequency Code 2 represents _____.

6. SK Flight 607 originates in _____. After _____ stops, it
    (code)   (number)
    terminates in _____.
    (code)

7. The three-letter City Code STO represents _____.

    SVO represents _____.

    BNE represents _____.

8. In the North American Edition, schedules to Phoenix are presented _____
    (before/after)
    schedules to Rochester, N.Y.

9. Schedules to Boston (NAOAG) are found toward the _____of the book.
    (front/back)

10. The Carrier Code SO stands for _____Airways.

11. A B11 is a _____Jet.

12. The Frequency Code 2 represents _____.

13. FL Flight 27 originates in _____. After _____stops, it terminates
    (code)   (number)
    in _____.
    (code)

14. The three-letter City Code MRY stands for _____.

    YYZ stands for _____.

    BFL represents _____.

USE THIS SCHEDULE INFORMATION FOR THE FOLLOWING QUESTIONS.

To CHICAGO, ILL.   CDT CHI
C-CGX (MEIGS FIELD) O-ORD (O'HARE)
M-MDW (MIDWAY)

Freq.	Leave	Arrive		Flight	Class	Eq	MI	S
From SPRINGFIELD, ILL.							**CDT SPI**	
	A	25.93	2.07	28.00	56.00			
QX 1	A	25.93	2.07	28.00	56.00			
I	INTRASTATE							
	S	27.78	2.22	30.00	60.00			
UX	YM	19.00						
OZ	YM	22.00						
UX	YZ	19.00						
	QX+YM 19.00							
*	INTRASTATE							
	QX+YZ 19.00							
*	INTRASTATE							
	6.27a	7.40a	O	OZ 920	SB	D9S		1
X67	9.35a	11.00a	O	OZ 816	SB	FH7		1
	11.05a	12.15p	O	OZ 956	SB	D9S		1
X67	1.00p	2.00p	O	OZ 820	SB	FH7		0
67	2.20p	3.45p	O	OZ 890	SB	FH7		1
X6	3.05p	4.30p	O	OZ 826	SB	FH7		1
X6	4.47p	5.47p	O	OZ 842	SB	FH7		1
	5.25p	6.25p	O	OZ 848	SB	FH7		0
X6	7.03p	8.30p	O	OZ 854	SB	FH7		1
INTRA-STATE								
X67	7.00a	7.45a	C	QX 701	A	748		0
X67	9.00a	9.45a	C	QX 703	A	748		0
X67	1.45p	2.30p	C	QX 705	A	748		0
X67	3.45p	4.30p	C	QX 707	A	748		0
X67	5.45p	6.30p	C	QX 709	A	748		0
COMMUTER AIR CARRIERS								
X67	7.20a	8.20a	C	UX 212	A	DTO		0
67	1.30p	2.30p	C	UX 422	A	DTO		0
X67	4.30p	5.30p	C	UX 152	A	DTO		0

To CINCINNATI, OHIO   EDT CVG

Freq.	Leave	Arrive		Flight	Class	Eq	MI	S
From EL PASO, TEXAS							**MDT ELP**	
CONNECTIONS								
A	132.41	10.59	143.00	F	JT/THRU			
B	126.85	10.15	137.00	F	((SDF))			
C	101.85	8.15	110.00	FnY	((SDF))			
D	98.15	7.85	106.00	Y	((ABQ))((IND))			
E	90.74	7.26	98.00	Y	THRU			
F	81.48	6.52	88.00	YN				
6	3.15a	9.15a	AA 206	FnYnB	72S		0	
(CF@)	5.40a DFW 6.15a	AA 70	FnYnB 707	B	0			
X6	3.15p	9.15a	AA 206	FnYnB	72S		0	
(CF@)	5.40a DFW 6.15a	AA 70	FnYnB 727	B	0			
	3.15a	12.01p	AA 206	FnYnB	72S	SB	1	
(BD@)	8.54a ORD 10.05a	DL 759	FYB D9S	0				
	7.00a	2.42p	AA 332	FYB	707	B	1	
(AC@)	11.54a ORD 12.45p	AA 282	FYB 727	S	0			
	7.00a	2.56p	AA 332	FYB	727	S	1	
(AC@)	11.54a ORD 1.00p	DL 643	FYB D9S	S	0			
	8.40a	3.55p	CO 204	FYKB	72S	B	0	
(ACE@)	11.04a DFW 12.55p	AA 342	FYB 707	L	1			
	8.45a	3.55p	AA 98	FYB	72S	L	0	
(AC@)	11.10a DFW 12.55p	AA 342	FYB 707	L	0			
	12.13p	8.23p	AA 116	FYB	727	L	0	
(AC@)	3.59p ORD 6.30p	DL 337	FYB 72S	S	0			
6	2.20p	9.20p	AA 128	FYB	D10		0	
(AC@)	4.45p DFW 6.20p	AA 394	FYB 727	D	0			
X6	2.20p	9.20p	AA 128	FYB	D10		0	
(AC@)	4.45p DFW 6.20p	AA 394	FYB 707	D	0			
X6	2.50p	11.24p	AA 336	*	707	D	0	
(*)	8.01p ORD 9.25p	AA 216	FYB 727	0				
	AA 336 FYKB-SAT- FYB							

To GRAND JUNCTION, COLO.   MDT GJT

Freq.	Leave	Arrive		Flight	Class	Eq	MI	S
From SALT LAKE CITY, UTAH							**MDT SLC**	
	A	27.78	2.22	30.00	60.00			
FS	A	36.11	2.89	39.00	78.00			
	S	27.78	2.22	30.00	60.00			
FL	YM	22.00						
6	1:50p	2:42p	FL 578	S	CV5		0	
	FL 578 EFFECTIVE DEC 7							
	6:28p	7:20p	FL 515	S	CV5	S	0	
CONNECTIONS								
A	77.78	6.22	84.00	CC				
B	73.15	5.85	79.00	CC				
C	62.67	5.01	67.68	S	CC-T			
D	60.82	4.87	65.69	CC-T				
E	42.59	3.41	46.00	S	((GUC))			
	7:25a	10:45a	TT 989	SB	DC9	B	0	
(C@)	8:30a DEN 10:00a	FL 63	SB 73S	B	0			
	7:35a	10:45a	FL 14	SB	73S	B	0	
(E@)	8:40a DEN 10:00a	FL 63	SB 73S	0				
	7:40a	10:45a	UA 166	SB	73S	B	0	
(AC@)	8:45a DEN 10:00a	FL 63	SB 73S	L	0			
	12:00n	2:39p	FL 62	SB	73S	L	0	
(BD@)	1:03p DEN 1:55p	UA 303	FYB 727	0				
X6	3:30p	6:47p	TT 987	SB	DC9		0	
(C@)	4:35p DEN 5:50p	FL 677	SB CV5	S	0			
X6	5:00p	8:44p	FL 66	SB	73S	S	0	
(E@)	6:03p DEN 7:47p	FL 675	SB CV5	0				
6	5:00p	9:04p	FL 66	SB	73S	S	0	
(E@)	6:03p DEN 7:47p	FL 875	SB CV5	1				
X6	6:25p	9:27p	WA 492	Y	737	D	0	
(C@)	7:30p DEN 8:30p	FL 671	SB CV5	0				
COMMUTER AIR CARRIERS								
	5:30a	7:10a	FS 362	A	PNV		2	
X7	12:15p	1:25p	WE 103	A	PRP		0	
X7	5:30p	6:40p	WE 170	A	PRP		0	
	6:00p	7:40p	FS 366	A	PNV		2	

To GRAND RAPIDS, MICH.   EDT GRR
13.0 MI SE 30 MIN T RA

Freq.	Leave	Arrive		Flight	Class	Eq	MI	S
CHICAGO, ILL.							**CDT CHI**	
M-MDW, O-ORD, C-CGX								
	F	27.78	2.22	30.00	60.00			
	S	21.30	1.70	23.00	46.00			
	Y	21.30	1.70	23.00	46.00			
YM	17.00							
7	5:55a	7:38a	O	UA 572	FYB	737	0	
X67	8:00a	10:09a	O	NC 911	SB	CV5	1	
	8:44a	10:27a	O	UA 642	FYB	737	0	
	12:00n	1:46p	O	UA 650	FYB	737	0	
	12:30p	2:36p	O	NC 915	SB	CV5	1	
	1:15p	3:00p	O	UA 628	FYB	737	0	
	3:25p	5:10p	O	UA 628	FYB	737	0	
	4:50p	6:56p	O	NC 919	SB	CV5	1	
X6	7:20p	8:57p	O	NC 106	SB	D9S	0	
	7:40p	9:28p	O	UA 626	FYB	737	0	
	9:30p	11:07p	O	NC 927	SB	D9S	0	

To MIAMI, FLA.   EDT MIA

Freq.	Leave	Arrive		Flight	Class	Eq	MI	S
From PITTSBURGH, PA.							**EDT PIT**	
P-PIT. A-AGC								
	F	108.33	8.67	117.00	234.00			
	Y	83.33	6.67	90.00	180.00			
	FN	83.33	6.67	90.00	180.00			
	YN	65.74	5.26	71.00	142.00			
	YM	68.00						
	EX/4 Y 7-21 DAY 139.00							
9:00a	P	11:19a	EA 303	FYB	D9S	B	0	
	EA 303 DISCONTINUED AFTER DEC 2							
9:00a	P	11:19a	EA 303	FYB	72S	B	0	
	EA 303 EFFECTIVE DEC 3							
9:10a	P	2:04p	EA 731	FYB	D9S	L	3	
9:55a	P	12:15p	UA 563	FYB	727	L	1	
12:05p	P	3:26p	EA 305	FYB	727	L	1	
5:50p	P	9:37p	EA 315	FYB	727	D	0	
6:30p	P	8:50p	UA 315	FYB	727	D	0	
6 6:55p	P	10:07p	EA 309	FYB	72S	D	1	
10:35p	P	12:56a	EA 483	FnYnB	D9S	S	0	
	EA 483 EFFECTIVE DEC16							

To PHILADELPHIA, PA.   EDT PHL

Freq.	Leave	Arrive		Flight	Class	Eq	MI	S
From NEW YORK, N.Y.							**EDT NYC**	
J-JFK, L-LGA, S-WKW, E-EWR								
	F	21.30	1.70	23.00	46.00			
NA	A	22.22	1.78	24.00	48.00			
NW	A	22.22	1.78	24.00	48.00			
	A	19.44	1.56	21.00	42.00			
DR	A	25.00	2.00	27.00	54.00			
	Y	16.67	1.33	18.00	36.00			
NA	Y	17.59	1.41	19.00	38.00			
NW	Y	17.59	1.41	19.00	38.00			
	FN	16.67	1.33	18.00	36.00			
	YN	12.96	1.04	14.00	28.00			
	YM	15.00						
NA	YM	15.00						
NW	YM	15.00						
2:10a	E	2:44a	P	DL 689	FnYnB	D8S	0	
7:10a	L	7:55a	P	EA 519	FYB	727	0	
7:50a	E	8:30a	P	EA 507	FYB	72S	0	
9:00a	E	9:32a	P	DL 257	FYB	72S	0	
X6 10:30a	E	11:06a	P	NW 537	FYB	727	0	
1:45p	E	2:22p	P	NA 411	FYB	72S	0	
3:07p	J	3:53p	P	NA 415	FYB	72S	0	
X6 4:15p	E	4:52p	P	NW 223	FYB	727	0	
6:55p	E	7:32p	P	NA 417	FYB	72S	0	
9:00p	E	9:40p	P	EA 481	FnYnB	D9S	0	
	EA 481 EFFECTIVE DEC16							
COMMUTER AIR CARRIERS								
X67	9:00a	9:30a	S	DR 9	A	DTO	0	
X67	9:30a	10:15a	P	WQ 161	A	HRN	0	
X67	11:00a	11:30a	S	DR 11	A	DTO	0	
X67	1:00p	1:30p	S	DR 1	A	DTO	0	
X67	2:15p	3:00p	P	WQ 163	A	HRN	0	
X67	3:00p	3:30p	S	DR 3	A	DTO	0	
	4:45p	5:30p	J	WQ 165	A	HRN	0	
X67	5:00p	5:30p	S	DR 5	A	DTO	0	
X67	6:15p	6:45p	S	DR 7	A	DTO	0	
	7:15p	8:00p	P	WQ 167	A	HRN	0	
	9:45p	10:30p	J	WQ 169	A	HRN	0	

15. The first morning non-stop flight from Pittsburgh to Miami on December 23 is _____ Airlines flight number _____ leaving at _____ and arriving at _____. The type of aircraft is a _____. The class/es of service is/are _____. Do both First Class and Coach passengers receive the same type of meal service? _____.

16. What is the one-way fare, including tax, on a Sun Valley Key (Commuter Air Carrier) flight from Salt Lake City to Grand Junction? _____.

17. What is the 7-21 day excursion fare published between Pittsburgh and Miami? _____. Does this include tax? _____.

18. The Military Reservation fare one-way, including tax, between Grand Rapids and Chicago is _____.

19. From what airport does the 7:10 a.m. flight from New York to Philadelphia depart? _____.

20. What is the latest time on Saturday a passenger could depart El Paso, Texas to fly to Cincinnati, Ohio? _____. The connecting city for this flight is _____. From ELP to the connecting city, the passenger would fly on _____Airlines flight number_____. This flight arrives at _____. Is there any meal service? _____. From connecting city to CVG, the passenger uses _____Airlines flight number _____, departing at _____ and arriving at _____. How many stops does this flight make? _____. Is there any meal service? _____. What is the total fare (including tax) for a Jet Coach passenger on this connection? _____.

21. What is the latest time on a Saturday that a passenger could depart New York's JFK Airport to fly to Philadelphia? _____.

22. A passenger wants to fly from Springfield, Ill. to Grand Rapids, Mich., leaving as early in the day as possible. Determine the best possible schedule.

    Connecting city _____.

    Springfield to connecting city _____.
    (carrier and flight number)

    Connecting city to Grand Rapids _____.
    (carrier and flight number)

23. How many miles and in what direction is the Grand Rapids airport from the city? _____. What type of ground transportation is available? _____.

OFFICIAL AIRLINE GUIDE REVIEW ANSWERS

1. before
2. front
3. Alitalia
4. Caravelle
5. Tuesday
6. ARN (Stockholm, Sweden-Arlanda Arpt.)
   GVA (Geneva, Switzerland)
7. Stockholm, Sweden
   Moscow, U.S.S.R.
   Brisbane, Australia
8. before
9. front
10. Southern
11. BAC 111 (General Designator)
12. Tuesday
13. STL (St. Louis, Mo.)
    PHX (Phoenix, Ariz.)
14. Monterey, Calif.
    Toronto, Ontario, Canada
    Bakersfield, Calif.
15. Eastern
    303
    9:00 a.m.
    11:19 a.m.
    Boeing 727-200
    Jet First Class/Jet Coach/Controlled Inventory-Coach
    Yes
16. $39.00
17. $139.00
    Yes
18. $17.00
19. LGA (La Guardia)
20. 2:20 p.m.
    DFW (Dallas/Ft. Worth)
    American
    128
    4:45 p.m.
    No
    American
    394
    6:20 p.m.
    9:20 p.m.
    0
    Yes (Dinner)
    $110.00
21. 9:45 p.m.
22. Chicago
    OZ 920
    UA 643
    (The passenger could not use QX 701 which leaves SPI later than OZ 920, which seems to have enough Minimum Connecting Time, because QX 701 arrives at Meigs Field (C) and not O'Hare (O). Additional traveling time is required between airports at the connecting city.)
23. 13.0 miles southeast
    taxi, rental car

Chapter 7

CHARTER AND GROUP TRAVEL

Charters, which used to be available only on an affinity and organizational basis, are now offered to the general public. This enables clients to take advantage of the benefits of group travel at substantially reduced fares. Charter flights remain attractive bargains in the world of travel. All the major airlines (Pan Am, TWA, United, American, Air France, and other carriers) have planes for charter. The airline acts as a wholesaler, selling blocks of tickets on one flight to a charter operator, who retails the seats directly or through a travel agent. Charter operators are allowed to set their own prices and compete with each other, so there are bargains. The scheduled airlines do not usually get into price wars and all have the same rates, except when wholesaling a planeful of tickets to a charter operator. This may change in the future because of deregulations of the airlines.

Scheduled and supplemental airlines offer the charter flight programs. Supplemental airlines are certificated by the CAB and offer the same equipment and service as scheduled airlines. The only difference is that supplemental airlines are by law, not permitted to operate on regular schedules and to serve on an individual basis to the public.

Traditionally charter vacations are sold on a roundtrip basis and operate on fixed schedules, i.e., the dates are fixed and the departure time may not be known at the moment of booking. Travellers cannot extend their stays and must choose well in advance their trip packages based on schedules which are offered with deviations.

The client receives immediate confirmations of flight and hotel arrangements which otherwise might be difficult or impossible to secure. Included in these tour packages are such items as transfers, porterage, gratuities, and taxes.

The arrangements have been made and confirmed in advance, usually with large financial obligations by the tour operator. Experience shows that reliability of departures of charters is similar to scheduled flights.

Hotel room assignments are based on general availability in the hotels at the time of arrival, and it is impossible to designate specific locations of rooms. Brochures carefully stipulate all ingredients as well as conditions included in attractive charter programs, and must be read very carefully particularly those regulations which apply to booking procedures, cancellations and deviations. Travelers should be encouraged to purchase the available low-cost insurance coverage to guard against loss of baggage and unexpected health emergencies, and purchase airfare protector insurance coverage which provides protection against unexpected cancellations or postponements of your trip due to medical reasons. The actual policy specifies the details of the coverage.

Major developments always seem to be taking place in the travel industry and today's changes appear to be reducing air travel costs for millions of Americans (at least domestically) and to be making travel arrangements more convenient as well as increasing agency commissions. Recent laws, since 1976, have permitted the United States travel industry to simplify and lower the costs of what were once expensive, time-consuming ways to visit far places in the world. Tour operator, Arthur Frommer, after liberalized rules established the charter revolution in 1976, said "the future of vacation travel rests primarily, if not exclusively, with charter travel." The supplemental airlines and tour operators who fought for lower air fares have a "Pyrrhic victory" with the lower air fares, but it's the scheduled carriers that have the Super Apexes and increased their passenger revenue miles.

A first step in the mass travel age, and one of the most significant, was the "ABC" regulations which became effective in October 1976, and in short time, more than 3,000 new charters were approved by CAB. "Advanced Booking Charters" permitted competition in the air travel market, including no minimum charges and important regulations to increase the public's protection against unscrupulous charter operators. ABC's were only sold by travel agencies, not by airlines. There were distinct requirements for advance bookings, i.e., Europe, United States, anywhere else in the world; length of stay regulation (seven-day time requirements for Europe) and "affinity groups" requirements. There is no longer the need to be a member of an affinity group or purchase advance hotel or other ground arrangements. The "affinity charter" meant the rental of an airplane on an exclusive basis for the carriage of a common group (affinity) with the renter (tour operator) paying a flat over-all rental for the entire vehicle. Changes in the air charter regulations which formerly specified that agents as well as wholesalers could not offer publicly (through advertising in mass media) charter tours for sale. The group was required to seek the agent's or carrier's assistance spontaneously and have to have a common affinity, such as a club, association, or commercial organization. Non-affinity charters are now marketable publicly.

Public charters permit the sale of charters up to departure time, one way charter travel, virtually no time limits on minimum or maximum stays, and no mandatory purchase of unwanted hotel or ground packages at destination. Public charters, discarding the restrictive charter rules, allows price discounting on seats and tours up to the last minute on flights where demand is weak at the full rate, but travellers are available for "specially priced" tours. The positive effect of these charter regulations for the travel agents and clients is that more charters will be operating as planned and organized.

TYPES OF TOURS

Some of the more established types of flights or charter tours have been available to the traveller:

ABC "Advance Booking Charter" refers to airfare only, but may include land arrangements.
AFF "Affinity Group on Charter Flight" are available only to bonafide affinity groups with a minimum of 20-40 passengers.
APX "Apex or Super Apex" (Advance Purchase Excursion) fares offered only on scheduled carriers for trips includes restrictions, i.e., 14-15 days; full payment must be made in advance, and there is a cancellation penalty.
GIT "Group Inclusive Tours" are available on scheduled flights; minimum group sizes vary with destinations, generally 10-15 passengers. Wholesalers and carriers make up the minimum groups.
GRP "Group Fares" are available through tour operators of airlines. Some group fares require purchase of land packages.

ITC "Inclusive Tour Charters" include air fare, land packages and minimum of three destinations per program.

ITX "Inclusive Tour Excursion Fare" which is available on scheduled flights only. Price usually includes airfare and ground/hotel packages.

NAG "Non Affinity Group Fare" which is operated on scheduled services.

OTC "One Stop Inclusive Tour Charter" includes air fare and land package to one destination. May include more than one destination.

PUB "Public Charters" refer to charter flights open to all with no affinity or group size requirements. Advance purchase not required. One-way flights usually available. Optional return dates may be offered by charter operation.

SVR "Super-Saver Fare" or similar discounted fare on scheduled airline service. Advance booking and payment required. Minimum/maximum stay requirements. Available on most U.S. domestic airlines. Check with airline regarding restrictions and limitations.

AIRLINE TOUR PACKAGE

Caribbean Individual Inclusive Tour

		ROUND-TRIP FARE		
FROM	TO	YLX1T14	YLW1T14	YHX1T14
BOS	FDF/PTP	272.	304.	304.
BDL	FDF/PTP	272.	304.	304.
PVD	FDF/PTP	272.	304.	304.

Add departure tax

Ticketing Code:
    YHXE14/YLXE14/YHWE14/YLXE14
Dates Applicable:
    YHW1T14/YHX1T14 - Applies January 6 through April 14 each year.
    YLX1T14/YLW1T14 - Applies April 15 through December 15 each year.
Conditions of Travel:
    Class of Service: Y
    Days/Hours of Travel
    - YHX1T/YLXIT - Mon/Tue/Wed/Thu/Fri at all times
      YHWiT/YIWIT - Sat/Sun at all times
    Blackout Dates/Periods:
    - December 16 through January 5 each year.
    Minimum/Maximum Stay:
    - Minimum - 3 days plus day of departure
    - Maximum - 14 days plus day of departure
    Minimum Tour Price:
    - $45.00 for the first three days
    Reservations Requirements:
    - None
    Ticketing Requirements:
    - Must be purchased prior to departure
    Stopovers:
    - One additional stopover permitted
    Agent/Tour Conductor Discounts:
    - Not applicable
    Other:
    - No children discount.
    - One-half of the weekend fare may be combined with one-half of the midweek fare.

Source: CAB 74 Rule 231

BARGAINS AND CHARTERS

By 1979 some of the largest tour organizers went out of business, i.e. Overseas National Airlines, one of the early champions of cheap seats, folded its wings for good; Pan American and United, the two scheduled airlines that offered charter-seat suppliers, have reduced availability; at least four tour operators have cancelled all their charter programs and others have reduced operations. The two of the leading supplemental airlines, World and Capital, have authority to operate scheduled cheap-fare flights to several points in Europe and Asia, and will be dividing their attentions.

Charters to Frankfurt from 11 U.S. cities, are now operating and a traveller can get to London from both the East and West Coasts. There are charters to the Cayman Islands from Houston, to Israel from Chicago and Cleveland, as well as New York, Washington and Philadelphia; to Greece from Miami; to Mazatlan from New York, Chicago and Detroit. Public charters can be found to these gateways:

Europe - United Kingdom, Italy, Germany, Spain, Portugal, the Soviet Union, Switzerland, Austria, France, and Greece.
Caribbean - Bahamas, Aruba, Antigua, Barbados, Cayman Islands, Cuba, Curacao, the Dominican Republic, Guadeloupe, Jamaica, Martinique, Puerto Rico, St. Kitts, St. Lucia, St. Maarten, Trinidad.
South America - Brazil, Peru.
Africa and the Middle East - Morocco, Egypt, Israel, the Canary Islands.
Far East - Hong Kong, Philippines, Tahiti, Bali.
North America - Denver, Idaho Falls, Los Angeles, Reno, Sun Valley, Honolulu, Miami, Las Vegas, Canada, Mexico, Guatemala.

It is the job of the travel agent to know and to sell these new "bargains" in travel: your client must schedule the vacation when the charter goes; competitive air and tour prices are offered on scheduled flights operating far more frequently; and a charter may not be the best travel program.

Charters occasionally develop defects, such as substantial delays and changes of days or departure points, and many travel agents are not interested in selling them. Notwithstanding, a few retail travel agencies will still arrange individual trips step by step for clients, but today that's a complex, time-consuming proposition that doesn't pay the agents unless it's a no-cost-spared deluxe trip. The great majority of agents reach for already-assembled package tours that can be joined like building blocks. Almost all packages these days contain transportation and lodging, sightseeing, meals, entertainment, transfers between hotels and airports; any or all of these and other items may be part of the arrangements.

The package tours look just like what the customer asked for; some buyers don't even realize that what they've bought is a package tour rather than a little handmade something run up on the agency's premises. Ethical agents will of course explain and customers had better listen carefully, since buying a tour amounts to signing a contract, often one with penalties for later "changes of mind" or cancellation.

The great majority of charters make the purchase of a tour package mandatory. Most, though, are simple packages involving little more than air fares and hotels. Tour operators are the ones who buy all these things from suppliers on the scene, normally paying "discount" rates for buying in volume. Then they "package" them all together as a "tour," with the price marked back up to cover their work, selling costs and as much profit as the traffic will bear. Some tour operators offer less expensive tours than others when both are selling the same ingredients because they

buy in larger quantities. Others sell virtually the same thing for less because they organize a cheaper air fare.

Determining what differences there are in similar tour packages and telling the "old reliable" from the questionable operators often calls for considerable expertise. The travel agent's experience becomes an invaluable asset for the customer.

Although some charters are advertised as "tours," the transportation only is sold because new "public charter" rules allow charter operators to sell the same public charters both with and without tour packages. The OTCs of the past have become public charters; all charters except affinity charters are public charters.

Affinity charters continue to do well. Travellers supposedly have to be a member for six or more months in the sponsoring organization, because affinities are still virtually the only types of charters allowed into such countries as Australia, Japan, Denmark, Sweden, and Norway.

TYPICAL AFFINITY/CHARTER TOUR

On behalf of DWIGHT TRAVEL of Boston, "Benvenuti a Roma," the Eternal City.

Let us introduce ourselves. We are "ALL SEASONS TRAVEL" representatives here in Rome. Our names are Carlo, Roberto and Domenico.

It is our purpose and pleasure to answer any questions you may have or solve any problems that may arise and do everything possible to make your vacation a most happy and memorable one.

"ITALIAN TRAVEL" will coordinate your included tours, and has also arranged many delightful optional excursions for your enjoyment.

Whenever possible, there will be a Hospitality Desk in the lobby of the hotel and one of us will be there at specific times. Ask us, we will find the answer!

Rome is a magnificant city, with a history that has no equals. Its monuments and all other historic points of interest are of a uniqueness that you will never forget.

So, come along and as the saying goes, "WHEN IN ROME, DO AS THE ROMANS DO." Relax, and let Rome guide you through the centuries.

Naples and surroundings are also very fascinating places for their history as well as for the natural glowing beauty; Enchanting! You will love the people. Just fantastic!

Well, once again we wish to say: Please, do not hestitate to ask for our assistance in any way.

MONDAY, 27 Dec.

Arrival in ROME at "Leondardo da Vinci's Airport."
Assistance, porterage and transfer by private motor-
coach to the HOTEL CLARIDGE - Viale Liegi, 62-tel. 868-556.
Afternoon at leisure.

TUESDAY, 28 Dec.

8:00 AM. Breakfast at the hotel.
9:00 AM. Departure for morning sightseeing tour visiting <u>Via Veneto</u> (the enchanting avenue of the "dolce vita"), <u>St. Peter's in Chains</u> (with the famous statue of Moses by Michelangelo), Piazza della Repubblica, Via Nazionale (the Fifth Avenue of Rome), <u>Venice Square</u>, the monument to Victor Emanuel II and the tomb to the Unknown Soldier, <u>the Roman Forum</u>, <u>the Colosseum</u>, <u>the Fountain of Trevi</u> (time to throw a coin in the fountain and make a wish), and <u>the Pantheon</u>. Lunch at the "Re degli Amici's Restaurant"-Via-della Croce. Afternoon at leisure. OPTIONAL-"<u>Excursion to Tivoli's Gardens</u>". Price $7.50

WEDNESDAY, 29 Dec.

8:00 AM. Breakfast at the hotel.
Morning at leisure.
<u>Have your luggage ready by 11:00 AM.</u>
12:00 AM. Meet in the lobby of the hotel and departure by motor-coach for "Leonardo da Vinci's Airport"
3:05 PM. Departure for Athens on OLYMPIC AIRWAYS FLT. 236
3:50 PM. Arrival in ATHENS. Assistance, porterage and transfer by motor-coach to the <u>HOTEL CHRISTINA-Petmeza 15 & Kallirrois-tel. 921-5353</u>
Rest of day at lesiure.

THURSDAY, 30 Dec.

8:00 AM. Breakfast at the hotel.
9:00 AM. Sightseeing tour of ATHENS. We will visit the <u>ACROPOLIS</u>, the Parthenon, the Areios Pagos (the Supreme Court), the Ancient Agora, the Herodion, the Temple of Olympian Zeus.
Lunch in a restaurant.
Afternoon at leisure.

FRIDAY, 31 Dec.

8:00 AM. Breakfast at the hotel.
FULL DAY AT LEISURE.

SATURDAY, 1 Jan.

8:00 AM. Breakfast at the hotel.
FULL DAY AT LEISURE.

SUNDAY, 2 Jan.

6:30 AM. HAVE YOUR LUGGAGE READY
7:00 AM. Breakfast at the hotel.
8:00 AM. Departure for Athens Airport.
9:50 AM. Departure on OLYMPIC AIRWAYS FLT. 233 for Rome
10:35 AM. Arrival in ROME and from the airport proceed to Naples by motor-coach.

Accommodations in NAPLES at the HOTEL MEDITERRANEO—Via Nuova Ponte di Tappia, 25—tel. 312—240 in double rooms with private bath.

MONDAY, 3 Jan.

8:00 AM. Breakfast at the hotel.
FULL DAY AT LEISURE. OPTIONAL—"Full day excursion to Pompei, Amalfi e Sorrento" with lunch in a restaurant. Price $11.50

TUESDAY, 4 Jan.

8:00 AM. Breakfast at the hotel.
FULL DAY AT LEISURE. OPTIONAL—"Excursion to Capri and, weather permitting, visit of the Blue Grotto," with lunch in a restaurant. Price $13.00.

WEDNESDAY, 5 Jan.

8:00 AM. Breakfast at the hotel.
9:00 AM. Departure by motor-coach on the way to Rome. Arrival around noon. Accommodations at the HOTEL CLARIDGE Viale Liegi, 62—tel. 868—556
AFTERNOON AT LEISURE. OPTIONAL—"ILLUMINATIONS OF ROME" in the evening. Price $6.00

THURSDAY, 6 Jan.

8:00 AM. Breakfast at the hotel.
Further instructions will be given at a later date.

Lufthansa shuttle-busses carried tour passengers to the city (around 1928).

Lufthansa Photo

HOW THE MONTE CARLO PUBLIC CHARTER WORKS

Glittering Monte Carlo is a world-renowned symbol of glamour. Once the playground of European royalty and the likes of Mata Hari, Sarah Bernhardt, King Farouk and Aly Khan, Monte Carlo and the surrounding principality of Monaco offer outstanding diversity. You'll enjoy the scenic splendor of terraced hills, dotted with white plaster villas and red tiled roofs, azure waters and architectural masterpieces.

The Monte Carlo Casino remains a fascinating and extravagant example of period architecture - an opulent setting for trying your luck at a wide variety of games. The oldest part was designed by Charles Garnier, architect of the Paris Opera. The Salle Garnier in the Casino is the setting for outstanding opera, concerts, theatre and ballet from October through April.

Other points of interest are readily accessible: the palace of Prince Rainier and Princess Grace, with its Napoleon Museum, the Oceanographic Museum with its remarkable aquarium, and a Wax Museum, tracing figures of the Grimaldi family who have reigned over Monaco since 1297.

ITINERARY FOR THE MONTE CARLO TOUR

Day of Departure

Passenger arrives at the airport approximately 120 minutes prior to departure and checks in for the flight. At this time, he/she will receive tickets, seat assignment, and dine-around coupons, if applicable. Bags will be tagged with airline tags and taken to the aircraft. Purchases can be made at the duty-free shops at this time. The plane will be boarded approximately 20 minutes prior to departure. Meal and beverage service will begin approximately 45 minutes after take-off.

Day of Arrival

Upon deplaning, passengers will clear through immigration and then will be escorted to the buses for transfer to the hotel. (Approximately 60 minutes.) Upon arrival, passengers will receive room keys at the hospitality desk and will most likely go to their rooms to freshen up and relax. Baggage will be delivered to the individual rooms approximately 1 hour later. At 5:00 PM there will be a briefing held in one of the hotel's large function rooms, appoximately one hour.

Following the briefing, there will be a Welcome Aboard to Monte Carlo Party, (probably a "rum swizzle" party) with wine, soda, and snacks. Optional land tours may be purchased at this time. Evening at leisure or to gamble.

Second Day

Monte Carlo City Sightseeing Tour: included feature; half day tour; afternoon of swimming and evening at leisure (a "breakage" item)

Third Day

Italy and the Italian Rivera: full day tour; evening at leisure.

---

*The information presented in this section has been organized for instructional purposes; should not be used as official travel booking purposes, or representative of existing charters.

Fourth Day

St. Paul de Vence: full-day tour; evening at leisure.

Fifth Day

Cannes and Vallauris: full-day tour; evening at leisure.

Sixth Day

Grasse and the Gorges du Loup; full-day tour; evening at leisure.

Seventh Day

Nice: half day tour; afternoon at leisure; Pere Vignon evening tour.

Eighth Day

Bags outside the door approximately 2 hours prior to departure for the airport. All incidental bills must be settled prior to departure from the hotel. Transfer to the airport. Check-in at the airport and proceed through immigration into departure area to await boarding of flight. Duty-free shopping is available in the departure area. Passengers will begin boarding the aircraft 20 minutes prior to departure. Meal and beverage service will begin approximately 45 minutes after take-off. Upon deplaning in the U.S., passengers will have to clear immigration and customs.

Included Features

Complete travel and tourist information, including bag tags and itineraries mailed to each passenger (bag tags, optional tours, traveller tips, hotel brochure, and itineraries).

Check-in facilities at the major airport nearest to you, supervised by a staff member (at the time of check-in, passengers will receive tickets and seat assignments and check their luggage).

Round trip jet transportation via Global International Airlines with deluxe in-flight dining and soft drink service.

All flight reservations and tickets.

Pre-registration at the fabulous hotel.

Delightful deluxe hotel accommodations at the Loews Monte Carlo Hotel or comparable for seven nights.

All transfer and baggage handling between the airport and the hotel.

A "Welcome to Monte Carlo" Party.

All taxes and tipping for services included in the program (hotel taxes, U.S. airport departure taxes, Monte Carlo airport departure taxes, bellboys, chambermaids, baggage handling, general hotel staff).

Half day sightseeing tour of the highlights of Monte Carlo.

A hospitality desk in the hotel lobby manned by a tour staff member.
Optional comprehensive travel insurance (Cost: $23.25).
A variety of optional tours available for purchase.
A special meal option available for purchase which includes a choice of five Continental breakfasts and five dinners for $69.00.
The cost at Monte Carlo, guaranteed O.T.C. (8 days/7 nights) is $509.00. Over 25 tours scheduled for the winter season; telephone for availability dates.

RESERVATION POLICY

Reservations will be confirmed upon receipt of $100.00 deposit per person. The price per person is based on double or triple occupancy. Reservation deposits may be paid for with major credit card.

PAYMENT POLICY

Payment of the final balance is due sixty (60) days in advance of final departure. Credit cards <u>are not accepted</u> for final payments. Payments must be made by cash, personal check, or money order.

CANCELLATION POLICY

Reservations may only be cancelled by written notice sent by registered mail, return receipt requested, to the tour operator.

Up to sixty (60) days prior to departure, cancellations will be accepted and refunds made, less $25.00 per person administrative processing charge.

From sixty to thirty days prior to departure, cancellations will be accepted and refunds made only if eligible substitute(s) can be found. If a substitute(s) cannot be found, the deposit amount of $100.00 per person is forfeited.

From thirty days prior to departure to the day of departure the cancellation fee will be the cost of the airfare, in the event an eligible substitute(s) cannot be found. (approximate airfare $200.00)

TOUR OPERATION CANCELLATION POLICY

In the case of cancellation by the tour operator for any reason including, but not limited to strikes, government action, fuel shortage, and acts of God, the operators liability shall only include a full refund for the money paid by the passenger.

BRIEF HISTORY

Monte Carlo is the enchanting capital of the Principality of Monaco, ruled by the Grimaldi Family, one of the oldest ruling families of Europe, who, for centuries, have carried out a proud tradition of peaceful co-existence with their neighbors. Today, governed by Prince Rainier III beside his lovely American wife, Princess Grace, Monaco is one of the most beautiful places in the world. Fabulous gardens, exquisite palaces, and breathtaking villas, all reflect an age of elegance and glitter of the centuries past. Yet Monte Carlo retains the air of this glorious era, while Time has created another dimension - that of an international crossroad. The combination creates a wonderland of luxury, excitement, and tradition.

This is the European Riviera at its best - where the society is multilingual, and people sit at sidewalk cafes for hours. Things to see and do are endless, and Monte Carlo's year-round mild climate is perfect for sightseeing. Open-air fruit markets

and street vendors line the narrow side streets of the old city, while the famous Monte Carlo Casino and ornate Opera House decorate the fashionable boulevards. Stroll through Monaco's incomparable exotic garden, built high on a cliff overlooking the Mediterranean, which boasts a rare display of nature's most unusual plants. The museums and art exhibits rate among the best in the world. Spend a day "in the deep" at the Jacques Cousteau Oceanographic Museum! For the more actively inclined, Monte Carolo offers year-round tennis, golf, and fishing.

The Principality is an ideal location from which to experience the flavor of many worlds. Visit Cannes, home of the International Film Festival; or Nice, the luxurious city on the Cote d'Azur, famous for its exciting night life. Visit Italy, only a short distance away, and see the celebrated marketplace of Ventemiglio. Even make an excursion into the majestic French Alps - a breathtaking world where one truly feels "on top of the world". The influence of these surrounding lands has made its mark in Monte Carlo - best seen in the French, Italian, American, Oriental, and even African restaurants which line the streets. The options are boundless and it is easy to see why, in this wonderland called Monte Carlo, anything is possible!

Palace of Monaco.   Monaco Tourist Photo.

LOCATION OF MONTE CARLO AND THE LOEWS MONTE CARLO HOTEL

Monte Carlo, the capital city of the Principality of Monaco, is located on the European Riviera on the French/Italian border. It consists of 453 acres at the foot of the Southern Alps, approximately 302 air miles (40 minutes) from Rome, 420 air miles (50 minutes) from Paris, and 155 air miles (less than 1/2 hour) from Milan. The Loews Monte Carlo Hotel is directly behind the famous Monte Carlo Casino in the heart of the Principality, overlooking the sparkling Mediterranean and within easy access to all areas of Monte Carlo.

CLIMATE

Monte Carlo is famous for its year round mild climate. Its streets are studded with palm trees and rooftops are dotted with tropical gardens. Average temperatures in the months of January to March range from fifty-five to sixty-five degrees. From April to the summer, the temperatures range from sixty to seventy-five degrees.

LANGUAGE

The official language of Monaco is French but due to its international atmosphere, English is widely spoken in all restaurants, shops, and hotels.

PEOPLE

The Monégasques are extremely friendly and helpful with respect to tourists, always willing to lend a helping hand. They are a very polite and respectful people who take great pride in their small Principality and its dignified tradition.

TIME

Monaco is six hours ahead of the East Coast of the U.S.

CURRENCY AND EXCHANGE

The unit of currency in Monaco is the French Franc which consists of 100 centimes.

The approximate rate of exchange is 4.9 French Francs to the U.S. dollar. Money can be exchanged at either the front desk or at a local exchange bureau or bank. It is likely that the bank will give a better rate of exchange although there will be a small service charge. Passengers are advised to check both locations as to the better rate.

It is also advised that pasengers carry and cash only large denomination travel-ler's cheques to avoid numerous service charges.

DRESS CODE

The dress code during the day is basically casual and comfortable. In the eve-ning, restaurants, casinos and theaters require a sportcoat of men and similarly appro-priate dress for women.

---

*All the information presented in this report on the hotel has been assembled from reliable sources and deemed to be reasonably correct at the time of printing. However, it is possible, that upon arrival in Monte Carlo, some of the information contained herein may vary slightly.

YOUR DECLARATION

ALL articles acquired abroad and in possession at the time of your return must be declared. The price actually paid for each article must be stated on the declaration in U.S. currency or its equivalent in country of acquisition. If the article was not purchased, obtain its fair retail value in the country in which it was acquired. The wearing or use of any article acquired abroad does not exempt it from duty. It must be declared at the price paid for it. The customs officer will make an appropriate reduction in its value for wear and use.

ORAL DECLARATION

Customs declaration forms are distributed on vessels and planes and should be prepared in advance of arrival for presentation to the immigration and customs inspectors. Fill out the identification portion of the declaration form. Travellers can declare orally to the customs inspector the articles acquired abroad, if not exceeded the duty-free exemption allowed. A customs officer may require a written list.

WRITTEN DECLARATION

A written declaration will be necessary when:
   The total fair retail value of articles acquired abroad exceeds $300.
   More than one quart of alcoholic beverages or more than 100 cigars are included.
   A customs duty or internal revenue tax is collectible on any article.

DUTY TAXES

Should the figures exceed the limits, the government will tax only 10 percent duty on the next $600 worth, or from U.S. Possessions, only 5 percent. The new law also increases duty free limit for people who have been out of the country for less than 48 hours; and bring back $25 worth of goods without tax. Gifts sent from foreign lands have had their duty free limit increased to $25; from U.S. Possessions the figure is $40. Save even more tax money when the land visited is considered a developing nation; in these lands, e.g., Egypt, items made in that country call for no duty tax.

REGISTRATION OF VALUABLE ARTICLES

It is advised that anyone travelling abroad register their valuable articles at the U.S. Customs Office at the airport from which they are departing. This is to prevent any problems concerning where it was purchased and possible duty charges. (Some items to Register: cameras, jewelry, radios, recording equipment, furs, etc.)

AIRLINE AND SEATING

Global International Airlines
DC-8   252 seating configuration

Global International Airlines, founded in 1945, has flown charters over every continent and ocean in the world with an outstanding record, including over 21 billion passenger miles flown. The pilots of Global's charter jet-aircraft are among the most highly trained specialists in the world, as are their crew and flight attendants, who are graduates of Global's own training school where the specialty is charter service.

INFLIGHT SERVICE

Inflight there will be a complimentary meal and soft drink service.

To Monaco: If the plane departs prior to 10:00 p.m., meal service will consist of a delicious hot dinner, followed by a Continental breakfast (rolls, coffee, juice) before arrival. If the plane departs after 10:00 p.m., meal service will consist of a snack (sandwich) followed by a hot breakfast before arrival (generally eggs).

To U.S.A. Between Monaco and the U.S., a hot lunch will be served.

NOTE: Depending on the weight of the aircraft (loaded), the departure city, and the flight plan, there may be a fuel stop on the eastbound leg (to Europe) in Gander, Newfoundland, or Shannon, Ireland. Westbound flights, there may also be a fuel stop in Gander, Newfoundland, or Shannon, Ireland depending upon the above criteria.

FLIGHT TIMES

Eastbound to Europe		Wesbound to U.S.	
from: NY	8:00 hours	NY	9:00 hours
PHL	8:15 hours	PHL	9:15 hours
BALT	8:30 hours	BALT	9:30 hours
RALEIGH	9:30 hours	RALEIGH	10:30 hours
PITTS	8:15 hours	PITTS	9:15 hours
DETR	8:30 hours	DETR	9:30 hours
CHIC	9:00 hours	CHIC	10:00 hours
WASH	8:30 hours	WASH	9:30 hours
BOS	7:30 hours	BOS	8:30 hours

THE ABOVE TIMES ARE APPROXIMATE AND REFER ONLY TO FLYING TIMES AND DO NOT REFLECT GROUND TIME FOR FUEL STOPS, APPROXIMATELY 1.3 HOURS.

AIRLINE PASSENGER CONTACT NUMBERS

Telephone numbers at which flight times can be checked :

ATLANTA	404 671-4891
BOSTON	617 334-8946
CHICAGO	312 888-9120
CLEVELAND	216 456-7777
DALLAS	214 478-9040
DETROIT	313 231-3333
HOUSTON	713 834-2323
NEW YORK	212 889-3783
PHILADELPHIA	215 291-3858
WASHINGTON, D.C.	301 222-8958

LUGGAGE ALLOWANCE

Each passenger is allowed 2 pieces of checked luggage, not to exceed 44 lbs. Carry on bags are permitted, provided they fit under the seat.

TRANSFER TO HOTEL

After airport formalities, passengers will be directed to the buses and transferred to the hotel, approximately 45 minutes from the airport. Luggage will be loaded onto trucks, and taken, carefully, to the hotel.

HOTEL

Registration: everyone at the hotel should be pre-registered and need only pick up their room key envelopes upon arrival at the hotel. (The location of the pick up will be designated upon arrival.)

LOEWS MONTE CARLO HOTEL

Avenue des Speluges
Monte-Carlo
Principality of Monaco
Tel: 50-65-00

Your home during your Monte Carlo holiday will be the fabulous Loews Hotel, newest and largest resort complex on the Riviera. You'll enjoy a magnificently terraced guest room, with refrigerator and fully stocked bar.

Within the hotel, there is an American-style gaming room – with Black Jack, Roulette, and Slot Machines for your pleasure – along with an array of bars and restaurants, a supper club featuring international stars and spectacular review, plus a rooftop year-round swimming pool. Other sports facilities are available nearby.

Harbor view of Monaco.   Monaco Tourist Photo.

The Loews Monte Carlo is a dazzling springboard to a superb Riviera experience. For your stay in Monte Carlo, choose from a variety of exciting cultural, gourmet and sports-oriented holidays, or just enjoy the Monte Carlo Magnifique program which gives you six unforgettable nights at the Loews Hotel, a half-day sightseeing tour of the principality and a car for a day to explore the Riviera.

```
SIZE - 637 ROOMS:  TRIPLES AND QUADS AVAILABLE
ALL ROOMS HAVE PRIVATE BALCONIES.
ALL ROOMS ARE IDENTICAL WITH TWIN-BEDDED ACCOMMODATIONS.
FACILITIES:  RESTAURANTS, COCKTAIL LOUNGES, AND CASINO
```

Cafe Jardin

An informal, colorful and attractive restaurant with continuous service from 7:00 AM until 9:30 PM. Brasserie-style serving breakfast, lunch, and dinner.

Le Pistou

A typical inn of our region with a marvelous view of the sea and surrounding areas. Specializes in local dishes. Serves breakfast, lunch, and dinner. Opens at 8:00 AM daily to 11:00 PM. Dial 87135 for reservations.

L'Argentin

A recreated Argentinean steak house serving only the finest of European aged beef, broiled or roasted as well as a fine selection of fish and other specialities. Typical strolling musicians will entertain you during dinner which is served from 8:00 PM to 5:00 AM. Dinner only, and reservations required.

Folie Russe

In authentic Russian setting, this supper club has an exciting program of music, dancing and entertainment. Dinner is served from 8:00 PM. Closed for lunch. State show and revue at 10:30 PM (Approximate cost $20.).

Marlowe's

Discoteque, cocktails, and dancing from 10:00 PM - 4:00 AM.

CASINO

For the first time in Europe, a gaming room is available within the premises of a hotel. For the first time also, a gaming room is now available, on this side of the Ocean which dedicates itself to American games of chance. A small booklet is placed in the bedroom which is called "Casino Guide" to give you all pertinent information as to the type of games operating as well as a general rundown of the basic forms of play. For additional information or to establish credit, please contact our Casino Manager. The gaming tables are operated daily from 1:00 PM until at least 4:00 AM.

OTHER FACILITIES

Banking and exchange: La Societe Generale in shopping arcade: 10:30 AM. - 6:30 PM. Closed Saturday and Sunday.

J. Dupre Men & Women's Clothing (Cardin-Leonard): 9:00 AM. - 1:00 PM. & 3:00 PM. - 8:00 PM.

Fred Jewels: 10:00 AM. - 1:00 PM. & 3:00 PM. - 8:00 PM. Sunday: 4:00 PM. - 8:00 PM.

Perfume Shop: 10:30 AM. - 1:00 PM. & 2:30 PM. - 8:00 PM.

Finkel Dior: scarves, furs, boots, bags: 9:30 AM. - 1:00 PM. & 2:30 PM. - 8:00 PM.; Sunday: 10:45 AM. - 1:00 PM. & 4:00 PM. - 7:30 PM.

Emir Carpets: 10:00 AM. - 1:00 PM. & 3:00 PM. - 8:00 PM.; Closed Monday and Sunday morning.

Candy Store: 10:00 AM. - 1:00 PM. & 4:00 PM. - 8:00 PM.

Newsstand: magazines, newspapers, cigarettes, etc. 8:00 AM. - 10:00 PM. daily.

Hairdresser: men & women: 9:00 AM. - 12:00 PM. & 2:00 PM. - 6:00 PM.; Closed Sunday & Monday morning.

Sauna: men & women: 10:00 AM. - 9:00 PM. Sunday: 3:00 PM. - 9:00 PM.

Thermic Sidonia Institute: 10:00 AM. - 12:00 PM. & 2:00 PM. - 6:00 PM.; Closed Sunday.

Car Rental Service: available at the Travel Desk:

Car Group	Per Day	Per KM	Weekly Unlimited
Renault 5	$9.05	$.077	$145.60
Ford			
Simca 1100	$9.95	$.102	$175.00
Renault 5GTL			
Peugeot 104			
Simca 1307			
Renault 14TL	$11.70	$.126	$209.70
Peugeot 504	$13.15	$.134	$225.60
Renault 30 TS	$18.95	$.182	$311.85
Peugeot 504			
Station Wagon	$15.55	$.163	$276.30

Tax: rates subject to 17.6% tax.
Collision Damage Waiver: Daily $2.80: Weekly $16.70.
Personal Accident Insurance: Daily and per car $1.15.
Gasoline: not included in rates.
Age Requirement: 21 years minimum except for Mercedes, Group E, where the minimum age is 25.
Drivers License: Must be valid from country of residence at least one year old or international license.

HOTEL SERVICES

Voltage: 220 volts. Converter & adaptor should be purchased prior to departure.

Valet service is available.

Physician, nurse, emergency health care: Please call Information Desk. Should an emergency occur dial the Operator who will alert our special unit.

Room service is available.

Safety deposit boxes are available.

Postage stamps: sold at the Newsstand. Whenever the Newsstand is closed, these can be purchased at the Information Desk.

Babysitting services available. Contact: Housekeeping Department. Rates: 15 FF/hour before midnight; 20 FF/hour after midnight. These rates are approximate and subject to change.

Shoeshine service: Please place your shoes in front of your bedroom door prior to retiring.

Telegrams: The Information Desk handles telegrams and cables. Please fill out the form placed in your bedroom stationery kit for this purpose.

Tennis: Twenty courts are available at the Monte-Carlo Country Club.

All rooms are centrally air-conditioned.

All rooms have mini-refrigerators, stocked with mini-bar.

All rooms have radios.

All major credit cards accepted. The cards excepted are American Express, Bankamericard, Carte Blanche, Carte Bleue, Diner's and Eurocard/Inter Bank.

Drugstore: Drugs in France and in the Principality can only be sold by a chemist. Shaving cream, toothpaste, lotions and other grooming aids are available at "La Parfumerie".

Every room has a private telephone: Telephoning: Guests may make local or international calls directly from their rooms (dialing codes may be obtained from the hotel operator), Note: It is advised that guests make only collect international calls. (Approx. cost of person-person collect call to U.S.A. is $12.00 for the first three minutes and $4.00 for each additional minute. These prices are without hotel taxes.)

Concierge or Hall Porter: located in the main lobby. The Concierge is a walking encyclopedia of information and can help guests with many of their questions.

HOSPITALITY DESK

The tour will maintain a hospitality desk in the main lobby, staffed by their local representatives. They are there to serve the passengers in any way possible (problems, questions, etc.). As an added convenience, our representatives will aid the passengers in acquiring reservations at any of the local restaurants.

Desk Hours: 8:00 AM. - 11:00 AM. (These times are tentative and approximate
4:00 PM. - 7:00 PM.   and subject to change.)

BRIEFING

At approximately 5:00 PM. on the afternoon of arrival, there will be a briefing held in one of the large function rooms. (The room is to be designated later.) During the briefing, our local representatives will tell the passengers absolutely everything they will need to know about their visit to Monte Carlo. During the briefing ,there will also be a colorful and informative slide presentation on the optional tours that we have made available to the passengers.

NOTE: It is strongly advised that all passengers attend the briefing, as its primary function is to give the passengers enough information to make their vacation as carefree as it should be.

Optional tours will be sold after the slide show during the Welcome to Monte Carlo Party.

WELCOME PARTY

Immediately following the briefing there will be a Welcome to Monte Carlo Party for all the travellers. There will be wine, soft drinks, and snacks served. It is a great time for the passengers to get to know one another, and most of all, begin to relax. These parties usually continue in one of the local restaurants.

DINING

Monte Carlo is a gourmet's delight with a wide variety of restaurants and cuisines to satisfy any whim. Italian and French fare is the specialty, but due to such diverse international influences, Monte Carlo offers an array of cuisines from Oriental or Greek to British and even American.

The Dine-Around program includes five Continental Breakfasts at the Hotel, and five dinners at a choice of Monte Carlo's finest restaurants. (cost: $69.00 per person)

NOTE: A complete list of Dine-Around restaurants will be available to the passengers at the briefing upon arrival.

TIPPING

Tips are included for bellboys, chambermaids, luggage handling, and any other service included in the program. For any special services passengers may require, a tip is left up to their discretion.

Most restaurants and bars include a service charge of from 10 to 15% in the bill. However, where service charge is not included it is customary to divide 10 - 15% among the staff who provided the service. For service that was particularly excellent, it is not unusual to leave a little extra.

Tips for taxi drivers are again 10 - 15% of the fare. Tips are not included for local guides and representatives and are left up to the individual.

PUBLIC HOLIDAYS

Monaco celebrates all the same religious holidays as the United States (such as Easter, Christmas, New Years, etc.). The week of April 29 is the famous Grand Prix week in Monte Carlo when race cars make the renown speed competition through the streets of Monaco - passing right underneath the windows of the Loews Monte Carlo Hotel.

At the end of February, Nice celebrates the Mardi Gras - a celebration that the whole Riviera partakes in. A colorful, exciting spectacle not to be missed!!

MAIL

Postcard to U.S. : 1.70 FF, airmail
Letter to U.S.　 : 2.90 FF, one ounce letter

RELIGIOUS SERVICES

Catholic: Cathedrale de Monaco
10:00 AM.; 11:30 AM.; 6:00 PM.

Anglican: St. Paul's Church
avenue de Grande Bretagne
8:00 AM.; 11:00 AM.; 12:00 AM.

Israelite: Synagogue
15 Avenue de la Costa

Protestant: Eglise Reformee
9 rue de la Poste

Antoinist: Chapelle des Antoinistes
Boulevard du Jardin Exotique

SHOPPING

Shopping in Monte Carlo is diverse and international. All the latest fashions and styles dot Monte Carlo's fine boutiques, and specialties range from French perfume to Italian leather goods.

Duty-Free Shopping: Duty-free shopping is available upon departure from international U.S. airports, and the Nice Cote d'Azur airport, before returning to the States. Duty-free shopping also available if a fuel stop is made in either Gander, Newfoundland, or Shannon, Ireland.

VALUE ADDED TAX

The standard rate of tax on goods bought in Monte Carlo is anywhere from 10% – 20% depending upon the article bought, and where the goods are purchased. However, visitors are able to obtain relief from the Value Added Tax.

Goods sent directly by the store to an address in the U.S. are free of VAT.

Goods purchased by visitors may be delivered free of VAT to the airport for pick-up by the passengers for exportation as baggage. Such purchases should be made a few days before departure to allow time for delivery.

When making purchases free of VAT, passengers will have to present their passports.

BANKING

Currency may be exchanged at banks and change bureaus throughout the Principality of Monaco:
Banking Hours: 9:00 AM. – 2:00 PM.   (Every day except Saturdays, Sundays, and
                 2:00 PM. – 4:00 PM.   Holidays.)

TRANSPORTATION

Car Rental: information is available from the Hospitality Desk, or the car rental office in each hotel.

Bus Service: There is a year-round bus service that runs approximately every 12 minutes throughout the Principality of Monaco. Price is approximately 2FF/ticket or a book of 8 tickets for 8 FF.

To Nice: Seaside route with buses approximately every 30 minutes.
(Approximate cost 70¢ one way)

To Menton: Seaside route with buses approximately every 30 minutes.
(Approximate cost 70¢ one way)

There are also buses to La Turbie, Roquebrune-Village, and into Italy.

Train Service: For longer excursions, the efficient SNCF runs an extensive train service from the Principality to all neighboring towns.

Helicopter Service: Heli-Air-Monaco links Monaco with Nice Cote d'Azur Airport, golf clubs, and all points along the Cote d'Azure and to Italy.

Taxi Service: Stands: Allee des Boulingrins
                          Monaco-Monte-Carlo Railway Station

Basic Rates: Approximately 5 FF drop charge.   (1st charge on meter; 1FF per additional kilometre (1.50 FF at night); Minimum charge: 7 FF (8 FF at night)
The doorman at the hotels can arrange for taxi service.

All rates listed above are tentative and approximate and subject to change.

EXPLORING THE COTE D'AZUR

One of the joys of vacationing on the Cote d'Azur is the almost inexhaustible variety of sightseeing and excursions within an easy driving distance. Monte Carlo holiday offers a glorious opportunity to find beaches and bays with isolated inlets all along the coast. Inland are the fascinating hilltowns. And throughout the country-side are extraordinary landmarks - ancient ruins, fortified villages dating back to the Phoenicians, Ancient Greeks and Romans.

And if Italy strikes a fancy, the Italian border is only a short drive from Monte Carlo. Crossing it, there is the charming town of Ventimiglia, and 9 miles further, San Remo, on the Italian Riviera. It's a perfect opportunity to include a taste of Italy in the holiday, and take advantage of shopping for merchandise made by fine Italian craftsmen.

Here are a few suggestions for touring on the Riviera:

Antibes - Quiet charm, perhaps unequaled along the French Riviera. Site of the Grimaldi Museum housing one of the greatest single Picasso collections in the world. Nearby is celebrated Cap d'Antibes, a peninsula studded with villas of the wealthy.

Biot - Local artisans specialize in glass blowing, ceramics and woodworking. Visit the local factory and shop for the unusual and decorative designs.

Cagnes-sur-Mer - site of the famous Riviera racetrack - the foremost meeting place of the European horse-set. Village of painters and the setting for Renoir's country house. His studio, complete with paintings, sculpture and sketches, may be visited.

Cannes - King Edward VII was a devoted visitor. The chic and beautiful have maintained its popularity. Two casinos, bountiful shopping, excursions by boat to Ides des Lerins. Nearby Nougins is an ancient Roman village, offering fantastic views of the entire Riviera coastline.

Cap Ferra - Grand villas secluded behind high gates and hedges - a backdrop for one of the most beautiful promenades in the world. A beautiful hideaway for many of the world's top film stars.

Eze-Village - Authentic village dating from the Middle Ages, perched on top of a hill, with a fantastic view of the blue Mediterranean.

Grasse - The perfume capital of the Riviera, since the 16th Century. Hillsides of jasmine and wild flowers plus hot houses serve the town's thirty-five perfume factories, some of which are open to visitors.

Menton - A delightful seaside resort, combining old and new - from picturesque narrow streets to wide avenues; fishermen living in typically Mediterranean style buildings to luxury modern hotels. Menton is the frontier to Italy.

St. Paul de Vence - Probably the best-known of all the perched villages of the Riviera. 16th Century houses on narrow cobblestoned streets.

Vence - Site of the world-famous Matisse Chapel. Charming Vieille Ville (Old Town) with picturesque fountain which has been a setting for numerous movies. Other highlights: The 15th Century Square Tower and a Cathedral dating to the 10th Century.

Villefranche - Steep, layered streets characterize this charming village between Nice and Cap Ferrat. The Jean Cocteau Chapel located here was designed by the French poet for the local fishermen.

Monte Carlo - The hub of this fairy tale principality. Enjoy games in one of the world's most glittering casinos. Visit the Royal Palace with its Napoleonic Museum, and the Oceanographic Museum. Not to be missed.

San Remo - In a wide bay of the Italian Riviera of Flowers, San Remo is the tourist center for the Ligurian Riviera. Majestic palm trees grace the streets and a wide promenade along the sea front. Great shopping in smart shops and boutiques. Many restaurants.

Ventimiglia - A colorful and warm encounter with Italy - sun, art, sea, history archeology, folklore. 11th Century churches, a Roman theatre in the center of the large excavations of the ancient Albintimilium, and the most important of Ligurian archeological museums. The well-known Hansbury of Mortala gardens are near the French/ Italian border.

OPTIONAL TOUR ITINERARY

Monday	9:00 AM.	Monte Carlo City Sightseeing Tour (included feature)
Tuesday	9:00 AM.	Italy and the Italian Riviera
Wednesday	9:00 AM.	St. Paul de Vence
Thursday	9:00 AM.	Cannes and Vallauris
Friday	9:00 AM.	Grasse and the Gorges du Loup
Saturday	9:00 AM. 6:00 PM.	Nice City Sightseeing Tour Pere Vignon Evening Tour

The above itinerary is approximate, tentative, and subject to change.

OPTIONAL TOURS

Monte Carlo City Sightseeing Tour (included feature): Monte Carlo is a lovely city, full of color, sights, and sounds. This tour will encompass many sights of interest in this charming city. The Prince's Palace resembles the castles from fairy tale books, and the Casino is as awe-inspiring as imagined. Less famous but no less beautiful is the Monte Carlo Opera House, frequented by royalty from the world over. We'll also try to take this opportunity to introduce you to the many great museums

that are found in Monaco; for example, the Jacques Cousteau Oceanographic Museum; a fascinating Puppet Museum; or the famous Exotic Garden - the only one of its kind in Europe. It's a great tour of a great city!

St. Paul De Vence (full day tour) Approx. $28.00: St. Paul de Vence, a 16th century walled city north of Monte Carlo, has long been famous as a haven for artists, writers, and movie stars. Picasso, Matisse, and Chagall have all lived and created there, while numerous European stars and starlets call it their home. But its notoreity has not detracted from its simple beauty and charm. People come to pay homage to its majestic Gothic Cathedral which houses countless art treasures, and its narrow, side streets are quiet and clean. Craftsmen such as olive-wood carvers, rope makers, hand weavers, and silk painters sit working on doorsteps or in little shops. Needless to say, the shopping is varied, and it is not unusual to walk out unknowingly with an art piece that may some day be very valuable.

Italy and the Italian Riviera (full day tour) Approx. $26.00: The land of pizza, spaghetti, and pasta is only a short distance away along the Riviera, and the ride itself is almost as great as the destination! On the way to Italy, we'll pass Menton - famous for its orange and lemon trees; a jagged and breathtaking coastline; and villas and mansions that belong to nobility from all over the world. We'll visit Ventimiglia and shop at its celebrated flea market. Our desintation is San Remo, a very typical Italian town where we'll be able to shop in the old or new sections; and wine and dine "italiano". All the sights and sounds of Italy are close at hand, and not to be missed on our European Riviera Adventure.

Pere Vignon Evening Tour (evening tour) Approx. $25.00: It will be an unforgettable evening at the Auberge du Pere Vignon - a typical European farm nestled in the countryside outside of Nice. Dress casually for this evening's tour - wine and food are unlimited, and the entertainment consists of a live orchestra and local attractions. It's an informal evening of great food, relaxation, and great company, and one that will be remembered for years.

Cannes and Vallauris (full day tour) Approx. $29.00: Cannes, the gala center of Europe, is the home of the International Film Festival. Its port is alive with transatlantic liners and luxury yachts. It is one of the most sought-after of all the Riviera resorts due to its marvelous weather, international clientele, great nightlife, and fascinating museums. We'll continue to Vallauris, a quaint town frequented by potters and famous for its ceramics since Greek and Roman times. Time has not tarnished its reputation, for the pottery is still unique and beautiful. A great place for shopping!

Grasse and The Gorges du Loup (full day tour) Approx. $27.00: A short drive will take us to Grasse, the capital of the perfume trade, where four million pounds of roses, and five million pounds of jasmine are grown yearly in the surrounding countryside. We'll continue on to the famous Gorges du Loup - Europe's answer to the Grand Canyon. The famous gorges, whose precipitous cliffs and sparkling waterfalls create an extraordinary picture, plunge to depths of over 3,250 feet! One of the most unusual natural curiosities in Europe.

Nice (half day tour) Approx. $12.00: Nice's famous seaside streets are lined with oleanders, palm trees, and palatial hotels. The old part of the town still keeps its narrow streets and typical Mediterranean atmosphere where slatted window shutters are kept closed or half-ajar to keep out the mid-day sun. Its carefree, colorful atmosphere is interspersed with the very new and the very cosmopolitan. Yet it retains its open-air markets of flowers and vegetables which overflow with a colorful variety of products which offer an endless series of prismatic scenes to the delighted

painter or photographer. A beautiful, clean city and one that many people will doubt-less return to during their week on the European Riviera.

THINGS TO SEE AND DO

<u>Sightseeing</u>

1. The Prince's Palace: residence of Prince Rainier III and Princess Grace.

2. The Palace Grand Apartments: the beautifully decorated interior of the royal palace.

3. Fort Antoine: 15th century fortress named after Antoine I, son of Rainier I.

4. The Old City: Narrow, ancient streets full of outdoor markets selling hot peanuts, steaming pizza, and colorful fresh vegetables and fruits.

5. The Opera House: Gold-leaf trimmed Opera House inaugurated in 1879. Some of the most famous ballerinas, choreographers, and singers have performed in this elegant Opera House - among them Enrico Caruso!

6. The famous Monte Carlo Casino: Finished in 1865, in pure Liberty style, the Casino of Monte Carlo is a meeting spot for the most beautiful people of the world. Set in an elegant decor, black jack, roulette, and all sorts of gam-bling take place till the wee hours of the morning.

7. The Zoological Gardens: Created in 1954 by Prince Rainier III, the zoo is a centre of acclimitization for different species of tropical fauna, particularly from Africa. The constant temperature permits the different species of exotic fauna and animals to reproduce and grow in the best possible manner.

8. The Changing of the Guard at the Prince's Palace: Pomp and pageantry at its best.

9. The European Riviera: From St. Tropez, a quaint town in France, to large Genoa, located in the heart of the Italian Riviera. See the optional tours.

10. The Cathedral of Monaco: Finished in 1884, the Cathedral was created by Charles LeNormand and today overlooks the sea at the extreme point of the rock of Monaco.

<u>Sports</u>

1. Tennis: Available at only a short distance from the hotels: 20 clay courts: 2 squash courts. Racquets may be rented. Open daily.

2. Golf: Approximately 10 minutes away from the hotel. 18 holes: Par 70. Carts and clubs may be rented. Open year-round.

3. Horseback Riding

4. Physical Fitness Center: Centre d'Esthetique Corporelle Stade Nautique Rainier III, quai Albert 1er. Tel: 30 23 35. Open all year-round.

5. Sailing School: Yacht Club de Monaco, quai Antoine 1er. Tel: 30 23 96. Open all year round except Wednesdays and Saturdays.

6. Skiing: Available two hours away in the Alps. Check at the Hospitality Desk upon arrival.

7. Sun-bathing: Sun bathing is possible almost year-round in Monaco.

Museums

1. Waxwork Museum (Monte Carlo): An interesting collection of life-like wax figures.

2. National Museum of Monaco: Automatons and Dolls: A fabulous display of man-made mechanical puppets and dolls. A fascinating museum and one not to miss.

3. Jacques Cousteau Oceanographic Museum and Aquarium (Monaco): A collection of exotic sea-life from all over the world. The museum is located in a beautiful, elegant building as rich in design as the displays are in exotic fish.

4. Exotic Garden of Monaco: Unique in the world, this exotic garden built high on a cliff overlooking the Mediterranean boasts a rare display of plants from all over the world. Only Monaco's mild year-round climate makes this garden a reality.

5. The Anthropological Museum: Founded by Prince Albert I in 1902, the museum retains the remains of man's ancestors that were discovered in the Monaco region. An interesting journey back into time.

6. Chagall Museum (Nice): See the museum designed by Chagall himself to house his own works. Paintings range from early Chagall to very modern. Inside is even a chapel with stained glass windows done by the artist.

7. Matisse Museum (Nice): A great collection of the works of Matisse.

8. Cocteau Museum (Menton): A wild display of Cocteau's and other works.

Museums along the European Riviera are countless, and for any particular interest it is best to ask in your hotel for a list of the various museums in the area.

Nightlife

1. Loews Casino: American style gambling Casino right in the Loews Monte Carlo Hotel.

2. Folies Russes at the Loews: An exciting nightclub entertainment also in the Loews Hotel.

3. Theatres- Operas, ballets, concerts, and plays, are popular in Monaco and the surrounding region.

4. Nightclubs: Nightclubs are very popular in Monaco, and especially in Nice. See the Nice Negresso and its world-famous floorshow....one of the most celebrated in Europe.

5. Restaurants: The cuisine of this area is greatly mixed, due to the international influence. The fare is excellent anywhere - from the luxury hotel restaurants along the Riviera, to the street vendor in the Old Town. Superb cuisine to tantilize any palate.

DEPARTURE INFORMATION

Baggage will be placed outside the individual hotel room doors for pick up and delivery to the aircraft (the time is designated by group, but it is generally 2 hours prior to departure for the airport). Passengers must settle all incidental accounts prior to departure for the airport. If a late departure is scheduled, hospitality rooms will be provided for the use of the passengers from the time they are required to vacate their rooms. The reason people have to vacate their rooms prior to departure for the airport is because the chambermaids need a certain amount of time to prepare the rooms for the incoming passengers. Upon arrival at the airport, passengers will check-in at the designated counter and then proceed through passport control to the departure area to await boarding and subsequent departure. (duty-free shops are located in the departure area) One of the tour's representatives will be at the airport to make sure everything goes smoothly, and to see the plane off.

Years ago the airlines would weigh the passengers before flying home due to a small payload capacity of early commercial airplanes.

Lufthansa Photo

Chapter 8

HOTELS, RESORTS AND MOTELS

EUROPEAN HOTELS

"The cost of a tour in Switzerland depends of course upon the habits and tastes of the traveller. The traveller, who prefers driving and riding to walking, who always goes to the best hotels, and never makes an ascent without a guide, must be prepared to spend whatever the cost. Switzerland is famous for its hotels. The large modern establishments at Geneva, Montreux, Vevey, Zurich, Lucerne, and Interlaken, are models of organization; the smaller hotels are often equally well conducted, and indeed a really bad inn is rarely met with in French or German Switzerland. The ordinary charges at the first-class hotels are: bedroom, light, and attendance 3 1/3-5 fr.; breakfast (tea or coffee, bread, butter, and honey) 1 1/2 fr. in the public dining room, 2 fr. in the traveller's apartment; luncheon 3-4 fr.; table-d'hote dinner 4-6 fr.; supper generally a la carte. The traveller should at once ascertain at the office the charge for the rooms. Absence from table-d'hote is apt to be looked at askance. At the large hotels the best accommodation is generally reserved for families and parties, while the solitary traveller is consigned to the inferior rooms at equally high charges.

'Pension' generally includes room, full board, service, and lights. Boarding-houses or pensions abound at Lucerne, Geneva, Interlaken, and in many other parts of Switzerland; and most of the hotels also make pension arrangments with guests who stay for 4-5 days and upwards. The charge for board and lodging varies; at some of the most famous health-resorts and watering places sometimes amounts to 20 fr. per day. As the word pension is sometimes used to signify board only, the traveller should ascertain whether rooms are included in the charge or not. It is always advantageous, when possible, to make arrangements for pension in advance by writing to the landlord.

At the second-class inns the average charges are: bedroom 1 1/2-2 fr., breakfast 1-1 1/4 fr., table-d'hote 2-3 fr., service discretionary, and no charge for 'bougies'. In many of the more remote mountain-inns, however, the prices are higher owing to the difficulty and cost of the transport of supplies. The sensible traveller will easily make allowance for this; and he will generally find the entertainment remarkably good under the circumstances. Previous enquiry as to charges is quite customary.

The Hirschen in Oberstammheim with
three-storey oriel is one of the finest
timber-framed houses in Eastern Switzerland and has been an inn since 1786.

Opinions regarding hotels often differ; but travellers will rarely
have much cause to complain if they try to comply with the customs of
the country, restrict their luggage to a moderate quantity and learn
enough of the language to make themselves intelligible.

If a prolonged stay is made at a hotel the bill should be asked
for every three or four days, in order that errors, whether accidental
or designed, may more easily be detected. When an early departure is
contemplated the bill should be obtained over-night. It sometimes
happens that the bill is withheld till the last moment, when the hurry
and confusion of starting render overcharges less liable to discovery.

Hotel-keepers who wish to commend their houses to British and
American travellers are reminded of the desirability of providing the
bedrooms with <u>large</u> basins, foot-baths, plenty of water, and an adequate supply of towels. Great care should be taken to ensure that
the sanitary arrangements are in proper order, including a strong
flush of water and proper toilette-paper; and no house that is defi-
cient in this respect can rank as first-class or receive a star of
commendation, whatever may be its excellencies in other departments."

<u>Switzerland</u>:
<u>Handbook for Travellers</u>
Karl Baeder, 1907

Hotels and resorts continue to play a significant role in the world of travel.
It is important to remember that air travel arrangements are a mere fraction of total
travel planning. The land arrangements (transfers, hotel and tours) constitute a
major portion of travel cost and require a specialist to organize these accommodations.
In the last twenty years the hotel industry has recognized the motel as a permanent
fixture on the travel scene and entered into the business, further expanding the operation. By 1962, 62,000 motels were available in America.Today, motels are often indis-
tinguishable from hotels; the two industries have effectively merged, symbolized by
the merging of their respective trade associations in the early 1960's.

Bucharest's Hotel Continental
Romania
Romanian National Tourist
Office

The classification of hotels are generally understood in Europe and throughout the world by general definitions but is frequently difficult to understand whether the hotel is being described accurately and reliably or misleadingly by a promoter. Unfortunately, there is neither an official nor generally accepted rating system for American hotels; various directories will provide their own definitions and sometimes evaluation of accommodations.

Many governments frequently rate their hotels, e.g., France, according to the international five-star system under which a five-star hotel is the best accommodation. Some European countries are meticulous and up-to-date with their ratings; many are not current. Correspondently, MICHELIN travel directories, for example, refer to hotels in these terms:

> Luxury
> Top Class
> Very Comfortable
> Comfortable
> Good average
> Plain but adequate
> Other recommended accomodations, at moderate prices

The hotels are also described according to available facilities, e.g., television in room, external phone in room, or garage available. Hotels also are rated by their amenties, i.e., "a stay in certain hotels can be pleasant or restful, and a welcoming atmosphere and service.":

```
Pleasant hotel
Pleasant restaurant
Particularly attractive feature
Very quiet, secluded hall
Quiet hotel
Exceptional view
Interesting view
```

TEL AVIV, Israel's largest city was founded on sand dunes in 1909. The city's beach front is lined with luxury hotels including (right to left) the Dan Hotel, Astor Hotel, the new skyscraper Sheraton Hotel, the Ramada Continental and the Plaza.

Israel Tourist Photo.

HOTEL TERMS

American Plan (AP) - A hotel rate that includes a room and three meals a day.

Bermuda Plan (BP) - A hotel rate that includes a room and full American Breakfast.

Check-In Time - The time established by the hotel when arriving guests may occupy the room. Usually this is not until after the established check-out time.

Check-Out Time - The time established by the hotel when guests must vacate their rooms.

Commercial Rate - Means a rate agreed upon by a company and a hotel.

Connecting Rooms - Two or more rooms that are side by side and have a private door that opens from one to the other.

Adjoining Rooms - Two or more rooms that are side by side but have no connecting door. Must be reached by use of hotel corridor.

Day-Rate - A special rate for using the hotel room for the day. Not good for over-night stay.

Government Rate - A rate agreed upon by the Federal and/or State and hotel.

Guaranteed Reservation - A hotel reservation secured by the guest's agreement to pay for the room whether he uses it or not.

Hospitality Suite - A hotel suite used for entertaining those attending a convention or business meeting.

Hostel - Inexpensive, supervised lodging, usually for young people.

Lana - A room with a balcony overlooking the water or a garden.

No Show - A reservation that is made but neither used or cancelled.

Rack-Rate - A hotel's official tariff rate as posted, e.g., regular rate.

Run of the House Rate - When a hotel agrees to offer any of its rooms to a group at a flat rate.

Service Charge - A percentage of a hotel bill (usually 10% or 15%) automatically charged to the guest in lieu of tipping.

Room Accommodations include:

Single Room - 1 person
Double Room - 2 people (can have 1 bed)
Twin Room - 2 persons - must have two beds
Triple Room - 3 people
Quad Room - 4 people

Children's Rates - While most hotels and motels welcome children, there is no standard pattern of acceptance or rates. Children's rates will always be on request basis. Request such rates giving full information - number of adults in the party, number and ages of children, and accommodations required (extra bed or cribs). Rates for children over six will often be the triple or full adult rate, unless otherwise indicated.

Travel agents must know where to find accurate information for travellers destinations, i.e., hotels, resorts and motel properties. The agent can quickly locate a hotel listing by using the TRAVEL PLANNER and HOTEL/MOTEL GUIDE (North American or European Edition). The NAOAG TRAVEL PLANNER lists room rates, phone numbers and addresses for more than 17,000 hotels and motels, over 15,000 which are Quality Rated by the Mobil Travel Guide. Over 150,000 other travel facts arranged in easy-to-use fashion: how to get to cities without scheduled air service; ground transportation information; toll-free reservation numbers; major airport diagrams and metro area maps; hotel locator maps for major resort areas; international travel information and much more. Published 4 times yearly. Each issue is updated to include over 50,000 changes.

The NAOAG TRAVEL PLANNER specifically includes:

Hotel/Motel Locator Maps:

Acapulco	Montego Bay
Alaska	Nassau
Antigua	Ocho Rios
Bermuda	St. Croix
Freeport	St. John
Jamaica	St. Thomas
Kingston	San Juan
Mexico City	Waikiki

Hotel/Motel Representatives and Reservation Services Directory: A Listing of Hotel/Motel Representatives including office locations and local/toll free reservation numbers. Also includes codes used throughout the Index & Resort Sections to indicate through which Representatives reservations at the individual properties can be made.

Hotel/Motel Systems & Referral Groups: An alphabetical listing of Hotel/Motel Systems including Headquarter Office locations, a roster of Executive personnel, credit cards accepted and local/toll-free reservation numbers. Also includes codes used in individual property listings throughout the Index & Resort Section to indicate the availability of System toll-free reservation numbers.

The Mobil quality ratings in the North American Edition of the OAG TRAVEL PLANNER have listings of all hotels and motels located within the 48 contiguous United States, certain cities in Canada and borderline cities in Mexico are rated as to relative quality by the MOBIL TRAVEL GUIDE Rating Service. All motels, hotels, resorts and restaurants listed in these guides are inspected yearly by trained, experienced representatives. In hotels and motels, the quality of the facilities and services offered the guests are the prime factors in determining the number of stars. Each type of establishment is rated in comparison with others of the same type, not with those of a different type. The following categories are used in rating hotels, motels and resorts as stated above. These ratings are available only for properties in the 48 contiguous United States, certain cities in Canada and borderline cities in Mexico.

Good, better than average (one star)
Very Good (two stars)
Excellent (three stars)
Outstanding - worth a special trip (four stars)
One of the best in the country (five stars)

EUROPEAN TRAVEL PLANNER

The European OAG Travel Planner is also a comprehensive guide, organized by country, for travel to and through Europe. Features well over 100 city center locator maps, country maps and airport diagrams. Alphabetical city listings data includes how to reach destinations without scheduled air service; hotel information complete with classification; local airline numbers; and available Car Rental, Rail and Airport Transportation services. First issue summer '78-will be published 4 times yearly.

AMHA'S THE RED BOOK

The American Hotel and Motel Association (AHMA) publishes THE RED BOOK which includes hotels, motels, and resorts in the United States and other countries. AHMA is a federation of state and regional lodging industry trade associations covering the United States, Canada, Mexico, and Central and South America. THE RED BOOK contains information about European or American Plans, winter and summer rates, location in relation to airport and/or downtown, number of rooms and average room rate.

HOTEL AND TRAVEL INDEX

The HOTEL AND TRAVEL INDEX has a listing and current information of 25,000 outstanding hotels, resorts, motels, guest ranches and lodges all over the world. The INDEX contains:

Hotel & Motel Systems - Headquarters and branch addresses, telephone and cable/telex information and officials of some 400 domestic and foreign hotel and motel organizations.

Hotel Representatives & Reservation Services - A worldwide directory of hotel representatives and reservations systems arranged alphabetically by Hotel & Travel Index's codes. Includes toll-free and other reservations telephone numbers, headquarters addresses with telephone and cable/telex information.

Hotel Representatives Quick Reference - A worldwide directory of hotels served by representatives and reservations systems. Geo-alphabetical sequence instantly spots readily booked hotels in all cities worldwide.

Air Carriers (North America) - An airline reservations telephone directory of air carriers and commuter/intrastate airlines represented in North America. Includes worldwide headquarters addresses, routes, executive telephone numbers and area-by-area lists of reservations telephone numbers.

Auto Rental Systems (North America) - Includes the equivalent information offered for air carriers.

Railroad Systems (North America) - Includes railroad reservations telephone directory, cities served and regional offices.

United States Hotel-Motel Listings - Lists states and cities alphabetically within each city.

International Hotel-Motel Listings - Lists hotels alphabetically under their cities in: Canada; Mexico; Bahamas; Bermuda; Caribbean; Central America; South America; Europe; Middle East; Africa; Asia; Australia and Pacific.

The following symbols and abbreviations are used in hotel listings throughout the general pages of the Index:

Properties that pay commission to Travel Agents are coded from 8% to 15%.

Credit cards - The following letters placed on second line of listing following phone/telex data indicate acceptable credit cards: AE American Express, VS Visa (Bank-Americard), DC Diners Club, BC Barclays, CB Carte Blanche, EC Eurocard, MC Master Charge, AC Access.

Other Hotel Codes:

100 R	Number of Rooms
100 U	Number of Units
100 B	Number of Beds
100 G	Number of Guests
$\boxed{W}$	Winter Rates
$\boxed{S}$	Summer Rates
$\boxed{A}$	American Plan Rates (3 meals)
$\boxed{M}$	Modified American Plan (2 meals)
$\boxed{E}$	European Plan (no meals)
$\boxed{B}$	Rates include Bed & Breakfast
$\boxed{C}$	Rates include Continental Breakfast
SWB	Single Room with Private Bath
DWB	Double Room with Private Bath
DDWB	2 Double Beds with Private Bath
TWB	Twin Beds with Private Bath

The HOTEL AND TRAVEL INDEX is an excellent guide; is issued four times a year; and is considered the largest hotel industry directory.

Agents may also use the WORLD HOTEL GUIDE, jointly published by six European intercontinental airlines: Alitalia, KLM, Lufthansa, Sabena, SAS and Swissair. This guide is backed up by the pooled reservation systems of the participating carriers and allows for the selection, requested accommodation and received confirmation with convenience and speed. All hotels are listed in accordance with local standards: Delux, First Class, Standard Class, and Tourist. The six carriers guarantee full instant commission: at the percentage indicated for each hotel on their respective Service Order validated by an IATA Travel Agent, or by a carrier on behalf of agent not holding stock. Offices of the six carriers may issue and validate Service Orders on behalf of agents not holding own stock. The full name and address of such an agent shall be entered in the appropriate box of the Service Order in accordance with the rules of the issuing carrier. The commission may be deducted when the amount of the Service Order is settled with the carrier, no loss than foreign hotel commissions.

THE STAR SERVICE

The Sloane Travel Agency Reports are one of the better evaluations of hotels: THE STAR SERVICE, a bi-monthly issue separated by country or state. All reports in each issue are arranged alphabetically by city and hotel name. The reports are concise and review in an orderly fashion the hotel accommodations. The evaluations include review of facilities, service, management, cuisine, atmosphere, type of clients, value offered, rate information and other useful information for the travel agent.

A TYPICAL STAR SERVICE LISTING

The STAR Service   No. 108 September — October 1978

SUGAR BIRD BEACH AND TENNIS CLUB, Water Island, in Charlotte Amalie harbour 15 minutes and
$2.00 (except for guests) from downtown pier by hourly ferry, is the former WATER ISLE COL-
ONY CLUB, an attractive modern Maltese-Spanish-Mediterranean-Italian style resort on the order of St. Croix's Jockey Club on the Cay, has undergone many incarnations and never done as
well as it deserves, but seems to be faring well under new imaginative ownership and management that has provided much more personal attention, service and improved cuisine. Though
seemingly handicapped by its captive location, it currently emphsizes seclusion and most
guests seem to enjoy the novelty of it. Facilities include full activities program, complimentary tennis (6 courts by year's end), fine sheltered beach (snorkeling, sailboats extra),
large saltwater pool with spacious sundeck, weekend entertainment year round, nightly music
in season. Handsome arcaded architecture effectively mixes European styles; plant is built
around a central tiled court with a big upper level bar-lounge-dining area overlooking ele-
vated pool and patio amid tropical landscaping with panoramic view of coastline. Atmosphere
is designed to please a wide range of clients from sports enthusiasts and honeymooners to
older people. Rooms have colorful West Indian decor, bright fabrics, two double beds, balconies with good sea and harbor views, standard size tile showers, large open closets; all
were recently remodeled, are cool, clean and quiet. Seven 2- and 3-bedroom villas on property have full kitchens, standard combination baths, air conditioned bedrooms with twin beds,
ceiling fans in other rooms, large furnished balconies or patios, carpeting, comfortable if
slightly worn commercial furnishings, are best suited for families or small groups. Hotel
launch leaves hourly from 7 a.m. to 11:30 p.m. with one morning and afternoon trip directly
to town center; though isolated, it is not all that remote, actually takes less time to reach
town than from many outlying resorts on island. Attentive owner-manager, dedicated staff,
excellent meals, redecoration of public areas as well as rooms have served to elevate this
one time white elephant considerably. 66 rooms, 7 villas, $60.00 to $75.00 single, $80.00 to
$110.00 double MAP, 12% service, tax, highest Dec. 16 to April 15, higher in villas. Ms.
Gayle Wirtz, mgr. (C) (Warner.)

OFFICIAL HOTEL AND RESORT GUIDE

Another important agency manual for the travel counselor is the OFFICIAL HOTEL
AND RESORT GUIDE (OHRG). This travel agency guide is a worldwide directory of hotels
and resorts, and is designated exclusively for travel agents, airlines, motor clubs,
tour operators, corporated traffic departments and other booking hotel accommodations.
The Guide does not rate the hotels that are described in their general pages, but in
a classified edition printed periodically and OHRG does give a cross section and a
general rating of the hotels represented in their pages. The OFFICIAL HOTEL AND RE-
SORT GUIDE is organized according to five sections: (1) United States of America;
(2) Europe; (3) Canada; (4) Caribbean,
Bahamas, Bermuda and Latin America;
and (5) Africa, Asia, Australia,
New Zealand and the Pacific.

Prime examples of the Danish
Colonial architecture are seen in
Charlotte Amalie, St. Thomas, U.S.,
V.I. In the left foreground is the
recently restored Grand Hotel.

F. Henle Photo

Hotels are classified by Deluxe, First-Class, and Tourist Class and in the OHRG, hotels are further "cross-divided" by these additional categories: (1) superior; (2) average; and (3) moderate. The OHRG, in effect, states that "superior deluxe" hotels are the best in the world; "average, first-class" hotels are mid-range facilities; and all other hotels may not be up to Western Standards for travellers. Some definitions may be of assistance in booking hotel accommodations:

Deluxe - Luxury hotels offering a high standard of service and accommodations. This category includes: the exclusive and expensive "Superior deluxe" hotels with elegant and luxurious public rooms, a prestige address and higher personalized service. Outstanding deluxe or superior deluxe means a top-grade hotel; a high standard of decor and services is observed; all rooms have private bath; and all the usual public rooms and services are provided. Maybe "moderate deluxe or a delux hotel with qualifications."

First Class - Hotels offering comfortable accommodations and good service, i.e., the excellent "superior first class" hotels and the "moderate first class" hotels with attractive, simple accommodations. A first class establishment is a medium-range hotel; some of the rooms have private baths; and most of the services, as well as public rooms, are available to guests. In short, comfortable accommodations, good service and simple surroundings could best describe a first class hotel.

Tourist Class - Comfortable hotels with modest accommodations providing minimal facilities. "Superior tourist class" hotels in this category may have some first class accommodations. A budget operation (economy or second class) with modest accommodations would be a tourist class hotel; few or no private baths available; and services very limited or non-existent. Tourist class hotels may also be "moderate tourist: (old, low budget operations and not well maintained); or "second and third class" hotels, i.e., ratings used by some governments to designate properties that range between moderate first class and modern tourist class hotel accommodations.

For the most part, hotels rate their rooms in much the same way as the OHRG rates the complete facility. Obviously, a room located on the ocean front with a living room and two bedrooms would cost the client more than a double accommodation with relatively no view, i.e., a suite would be rated as superior or deluxe. The service given to these clients will also vary.

Deluxe (or Superior) - Can be either a suite or an oversized room usually located on the top of the building for the "quiet comfort" of the guest and has a view.

Standard - Accommodations located in the middle part of the hotel; the rooms which constitute the vast majority of rooms available at the hotel; and the facilities in the room are more than adequate.

Minimum - These economy rooms are located on the lower levels (more noise and no view) of the hotel.

In the OFFICIAL HOTEL AND RESORT GUIDE, the accommodation listing has the amount of rooms in the hotel; the manager's name; the hotel address; the hotel phone number and a telex number if available. The physical description usually includes room characteristics, e.g., air conditioning, electric blankets, private balcony; also hotel services and other accommodations are listed, e.g., swimming pool, gourmet restaurants. The hotel's location, as well as any special features, are included in the description. Sometimes a photograph of the hotel is included in the description.

In each OHRG listing RATE CODES are included, and the numbers following each code are the rates for the various accommodations described by the codes. These codes and the accommodations they describe are as follows:

EP   (European Plan) means no meals are included in the rates listed after this code.

CP   (Continental Plan) means only rolls and coffee are included in this rate; this service is typical in Europe.

MAP   (Modified American Plan) means full American breakfast and dinner are included in this rate.

AP   (American Plan) means full three meals a day are included in the rate of the hotel.

SWB   (Single with bath) means a single accommodation, one person, with a bathroom facility.

DWB   (Double with bath) means a room comfortable for two persons, with a bath.

TWB   (Twin room with a bathroom facility) means the room is actually outfitted with 2 single beds.

SUITE   (Suite for 2 persons) means this may only have a bedroom and sitting room
2/P   facility.

EAP   (Each additional person) means the rate following EAP denotes the additional charge each person would pay in the appropriate accommodation. EAP12 would mean that the person would pay $12.00 for each additional individual in the room.

Hotels, in resort locations especially, have seasonal rates; i.e., high on on-season and low on off-season. These rates usually have specific dates.

Travel agents usually work with "hotel Rep" or Representatives who offer hotel reservations to agents, wholesalers, and public and is paid by the hotels represented on a fee basis.

On the bottom line of the OHRG listing, the name of a Hotel Representative, as well as the commission rate paid by this hotel to the Travel Agent is given. The "Hotel Rep" typically offers more coverage to an individual hotel or a chain of hotels because they can concentrate on the total sale of the individual properties. In many cases these various Hotel Reps have a "free sell" on a particular property, i.e., an open availability on rooms given by a specified Hotel to a Hotel Representative for the "automatic confirmed" sale. This can aid the agency in that the accommodations requested can be confirmed immediately.

The pool at the Laromme Elat Hotel on the Red Sea.

HOTEL RESERVATIONS

A travel agent typically makes a reservation for the client giving complete information concerning date and time of arrival, rate, and plan of accommodation, and length of stay. Agents should try to use the "standard reservation and confirmation forms" whenever possible. Hotels will answer all requests for reservations or information within the shortest time possible, by telephone, by fastest mail or by telegram. Overseas hotels may require that funds should be sent in advance. Reservations, when confirmed by the hotel, are usually considered firm without re-confirmation by the agency, unless otherwise specified by the hotel at time of confirmation. Reservation will be held usually without deposit until 6 p.m. (or some specified time) on

date of arrival. If the agent makes reservation by telephone or direct conversation, he should re-confirm this reservation in writing with specific reference to conversation and name of employee who took reservation.

Hotels

To assist you, we have arrangements with five large chains of hotels throughout the U.S.A. and Canada, who offer special rates for visitors. We can reserve accommodation, subject to availability, and arrange prepaid vouchers to enable settlement to be made prior to departure.

RAMADA INN

Single: £13.15 Twin: £15.75 Includes local taxes.
Single based on one adult; twin based on two adults.
Children 18 years and under, occupying same room (single or twin) are free.

HOLIDAY INN

Single: 14.60 Twin: £16.60 **U.S.A.**
Includes local taxes.
Single: £17.75 Twin: £20.60 **Canada**.

TRAVELODGE

Twin U.S.A./Canada: £19.45 Includes local taxes.
Rates are based on 1-4 persons occupying same room.

SHERATON

Twin U.S.A./Canada: from £17.00. Rates are based on one to four persons of the same family occupying same room.

Please note that some of the hotels of the above groups, except Travelodge, charge a supplement for the room per night dependent upon location.

HILTON HOTELS

HILTONPASS I

No advance payment is required – you must take along a Hiltonpass I folder and on production of this you are automatically entitled to this special rate. Hiltonpass I folders can be obtained free of charge from Laker Air Travel Ltd. before you leave Britain.

First class single or twin rooms £16.00
Superior class single or twin rooms £21.75
De-Luxe class single or twin rooms £27.45
Local taxes NOT included.

HILTONPASS II

You can purchase in advance Hilton accommodation vouchers that are valid at virtually all Hilton Hotels throughout the U.S.A.

First class single or twin rooms £17.20
Superior class single or twin rooms £23.35
De-Luxe class single or twin rooms £29.50
Local taxes included.

APARTMENT

Subject to availability, it may be possible to rent an apartment in San Francisco. Further information on request.

SPECIAL NOTE

If it is necessary for you to stop overnight in New York and your onward connection departs from La Guardia Airport the following day, Laker can offer a special arrangement at the Midway Motor Hotel. This hotel is situated near to La Guardia and the prices quoted are inclusive of room, taxes and transfers between hotel/JFK/La Guardia Airports.
Single £18.40. Twin £22.20

Laker Air, Gatwick Airport

The hotel reservation information should be provided when booking a room accommodation by the agent:

1.   Names of customers and their address.

2.   Date of arrival and specific arrival time, i.e., most hotels will hold a room until 6 P.M. without deposit.

3.   Method of arrival for complimentary transportation arrangements.

4.   Number in party.

5.   Specific type of hotel room.

6.   Type of service, e.g., European, American or Continental plan.

7.   Rate confirmation.

8.   Duration of stay; number of days (nights) between "check-in" and "check-out".

9.   Method of payment.

10.   Special arrangements; request special requirements for clients, e.g., flowers.

Travel agents will not usually make long distance telephone calls to make a hotel reservation. Hotels, resorts and motels have reservation systems which use central computer reservation banks. Western International, Sheraton, Howard Johnson, Ramada, Hilton, Hyatt, Holiday Inns, Quality Inns and almost all other chain hotels have nationwide toll-free (800) telephone numbers for reservations. The airline computer systems, e.g., Apollo One (United), Salne (American) systems provide hotel reservations as part of a one-step reservation system.

Commission will be paid on only the room portion of the client's account, unless reservation is made on the American Plan. Commission will be paid generally on a sojourn not to exceed sixty days, unless specified by the hotel at the time of confirmation. If client extends his stay beyond period for which reservation was made, commission for full length of stay should be paid by the hotel. Commissions paid usually without billing from the agency; preferably as soon as client checks out but no later than the 10th of the month following. In a market increasingly dependent on the travel agent business, alienation of the travel agent by non-payment of commissions is surely self-defeating policy for any responsible hotel. Overseas hotels, however, will pay periodically when and as arrangements are made with currency control officials. Hotels should notify agencies promptly of "no-shows," cancellation by clients, or non-payment of hotel bill by client.

"Am Platzl" - downtown - at the "Hofbrauhaus" in Munich.

German National Tourist Office Photo.

HOTEL VOUCHER

A travel agent earns a commission for booking a hotel accommodation. This rate may vary according to the hotel but the standard commission is 10% taken from the base hotel rate before tax. A few hotels do not commission agents; others commission the agent 15% and 20%. These higher rates of commissions are usually earned as an override or on a group sales.

The time involved and the percentage of yield on each sale of a hotel room is so small in comparison to the time involved in the booking and vouchering, the travel agency is wise to collect from the client for the accommodation in advance of the trip and send the appropriate hotel the collected amount less the commission earned. This is particularly true for European and other non-U.S. hotels and resorts, many agencies never receive their commissions from foreign hotels.

The hotel voucher is the travel agent's record of the sale and protection for the client when they arrive at the hotel. The standard voucher is printed on a paper which cannot be erased, much like the type of paper which our money is printed on. This is done to eliminate any alterations that could be made to a rate or a coupon. This voucher serves not only as a reservation confirmation, but also as a receipt for the monies collected by the agent which has been sent ahead to the hotel. This voucher states in detail, what accommodations have been confirmed in the reservations, at what rate they have been confirmed, what special instructions have been given the hotel in advance of the guest arrival, who confirmed the reservations, on what date the reservations were confirmed, and the date of arrival of the passenger. Vouchers can have a face value, as a money order because it's guaranteed by the travel agency. A "Travel Agent Guarantee" is used when a party will be arriving after the hour of 6:00 P.M., and the agent wishes the accommodation to be held for this late arrival. Since some form of guarantee must be given as prepayment for the room, the agent places his name and address as the "Guarantee." In the event the guest does not arrive, the hotel then has the authority to bill the Travel Agent for that particular night's accommodations.

A voucher can encourage the hotel Front Desk to think twice before "walking" a client who has a confirmed reservation. The hotel voucher is generally used only for hotel bookings, in the absence of land tour or sightseeing arrangements. The hotel voucher serves as a reservation confirmation; a receipt for money collected by the travel agent which has been sent ahead to the hotel.

The agency can send three types of payment to the hotel:

A.   A deposit which is one night room rate and no commission is deducted.
B.   A partial payment which is more than the one nights room rate but not the total number of nights staying. No commission is deducted.
C.   The full payment (prepayment) which covers all the nights staying. This is the only time when it is possible to deduct the commission. The hotel tax must be included with full payment.

Information on the hotel voucher should include:

What accommodations have been confirmed.
How may days and nights.
What rate of tax.
Date of arrival and departure date of passenger.
Value of coupon based on the money being sent by the agency for the client.
Travel agent guarantee used only when you know your client and under the following circumstances:

> Used for the guest arriving after midnight.
> In event the guest does not arrive until after 6:00 P.M. - the room will be held all night.
> The travel agent is BILLED for the room if the client is a NO-SHOW.

The top part of the voucher is for the clients use, and the bottom part is for the hotels use and sent with the payment from the agency. The following is a sample completed hotel voucher.

Welcome Aboard
VACATION CENTER

SERVICE VOUCHER	

SERVICES TO BE PROVIDED:

One double-bedded room for 7 nights, MAP, at the rate of $80.00 per night plus 5% tax. Confirmed by Jane Host Reservations, June 1, 1979.

Prepaid in Full: $588.00

DATE: June 2, 1979

PLEASE PROVIDE OUR CLIENTS: Mr. & Mrs. Peter Glance

WITH THE SERVICES SHOWN

SERVICE TO BE RENDERED BY
Host Farm & Corral
2300 Lincoln Highway East
Lancaster, Pennsylvania 17602

IF CHECKED HERE ADDITIONAL DETAILS ARE ON REVERSE ☐

ARRIVAL DATE: 30 June 1979
DEPARTURE DATE: 07 July 1979

ISSUED AS AGENTS ONLY AND SUBJECT TO THE TERMS AND CONDITIONS AS INDICATED BY THE SUPPLIER(S) OF SERVICES.

WELCOME ABOARD VACATION CENTER

BY: Beverly

ORIGINAL COUPON HELD BY CLIENT SHOULD BE SURRENDERED IN EXCHANGE FOR SERVICES.

☐ PLEASE RESERVE AS ABOVE
☐ DEPOSIT CHECK ATTACHED
☒ FULL PAYMENT ATTACHED
☒ PREVIOUSLY RESERVED. YOUR CONFIRMATION DATE:
☐ BILL US FOR PAYMENT
6/1/79 by Jane
☐ COLLECT FROM CLIENT
☐ COMMISSION DUE US $

V A L U A T I O N	
RATE	$ 560.00
TAX	28.00
TOTAL	588.00
DEPOSIT	–0–
COMMISSION	56.00
NET	532.00

CLIENT FOLDER

HOTEL, RESORT AND MOTEL

As more Americans travel in the deregulated air travel industry, more rooms will be required. More airlines are serving more markets more often, so the client has more choice. U.S. properties will benefit from the increasing domestic travel and the record numbers of foreign tourists. Travel agents will also be booking more rooms in the future by computer terminal systems which will replace telephone dialing (800 numbers) hotel representatives.

A successful travel agent understands the needs of individual clients, e.g., commerical and vacation travellers. Hotel, resort, and motel literature (brochure) is the selling tool that tells you and your client the "Who, What, Where, When, Why, and How much" about a particular travel desintation. THE OHRE, STAR, HOTEL AND TRAVEL INDEX are necessary and convenient guides but it is important for the travel agent to visit properties and personally evaluate the accommodations; the following FAM trip of HOST Resorts provides illustrations of how travel agents learn more about new destinations for clients.

TYPICAL ITINERARY

HOST FARM & CORRAL: A PENNSYLVANIA DUTCH HEXTRAVAGANZA

Friday, November 17:

    10:30 a.m. - Depart Boston on Allegheny's Flight #117
                     non-stop service to Harrisburg Airport.

    11:42 a.m. - Arrive in Harrisburg.

    12:00 noon - Depart airport via luxury coach bound for the beautiful
                     HOST TOWN in Lancaster, Pa.

    12:45 p.m. - Arrive at the HOST TOWN in Lancaster where you will
                     be officially welcomed at a buffet luncheon.

    2:30 p.m. - Depart for a tour of the Brunswick Hotel, HOST's newest property.

    4:00 p.m. - After the tour, we will proceed to the HOST FARM & CORRAL for
                   check-in.

    6:30 p.m. - You are cordially invited to attend a dinner theatre per-
                   formance at the HOST CORRAL - "Mary, Mary" (A comedy).

    10:00 p.m. - After the theatre, more nightclub excitement begins at the
                     HOST FARM Cabaret.

Saturday, November 18

    8:00 a.m. - Breakfast will be served in the Heritage Room.

    9:30 a.m. - You will depart for a first-hand look at Pennsylvania Dutch
                   Country, via deluxe motor coach, hosted by Conestoga Tours.
                   This tour will include a luncheon at the Dutch Haven Family
                   Style Restaurant in the very hub of the Pennsylvania Dutch
                   Community.

    2:30 a.m. - Arrive back at HOST FARM & CORRAL.

    6:30 p.m. - Cocktail reception.

    7:45 p.m. - Dinner will be served in the Heritage Room. After dinner,
                   the excitement begins in the Cabaret.

Sunday, November 19:

    8:30 a.m. - Breakfast will be served in the Heritage Room.

    10:15 a.m. - Depart for Harrisburg International Airport.

    11:33 a.m. - Depart on Allegheny Airlines for Boston on Flight #207.

    12:35 a.m. - Arrive in Boston.

Chapter 9

STEAMSHIP TRAVEL AND CRUISES

World-wide steamship services continue and are an important part of the travel business. Trans-Atlantic travel to Ireland, France, England and the rest of Europe from the U.S. (New York) and Canada (Montreal) can be found on these ships: the KUNGSHOLM (Flagship), STEFAN BATORY (Polish Ocean), ROYAL VIKING STAR (Royal Viking), ALEXANDER PUSHKIN (Baltic) and QUEEN ELIZABETH 2 (Cunard).

The 22,000 ton-ROYAL VIKING STAR, first of the three Royal Viking Line sisterships to enter worldwide cruise service, sails resplendently in open waters. The vessel offers all-first-class accommodations for approximately 500 passengers, providing 94 percent with an outside view from their staterooms.   Royal Viking Line Photo.

The Pacific cruises include Honolulu, Yokohama, Hong Kong, Bali, Cairns, Sydney, Picton, Wellington, Auckland, Papeetee Morrea and return to San Francisco. Trans-Pacific travel for 70 days on CIRCLE PACIFIC (Royal Viking Line) starts at $9000. A 45-day cruise from Los Angeles to the same places can cost $13,000 for first class travel on the SOUTH SEAS (Royal Viking Line); this, of course, would have superb international cuisine and be a deluxe trip. Ships like SANTA MARIANA and SANTA MERCEDES leave from the west coast ports to Manzanillo, Balboa, Panama Canal (transit), Cartagena, Puerto Cabello, La Guaira, Rio de Janeiro, Sanatos, Parangua/Rio Grande (optional), Buenos Aires, Strait of Magellan, Valparaiso, Callao, Guayaquil, Buenaventura. Passengers can board vessel at Vancouver or Tacoma. Others leave from east coast ports to South America.

A cruise ship in The Geiranger fjord in Norway's Fjord Country, seen from the famous Flydal canyon.

Norwegian National Tourist Office Photo.

Not all ships leave from America, there are many outstanding cruises from Europe to the Orient, Europe to Australasia, and Europe to Africa, and these lists can be found in the Official Steamship Guide. And, there are "Round-the-World" steamship travel, such as the QUEEN ELIZABETH 2 which begins in Port Everglades, Barbados, Caracas, Salvador, Rio de Janeiro, Montevideo, Tristan da Cunha, Cape Town, Durban, Seychelles (Mahe), Bombay, Colombo, Singapore, Manila, Hong Kong, Kagoshima, Yokohama, Honolulu, Los Angeles, Acapulco, Panama Canal, Cristobal, Caracas, St. Thomas, Port Everglades. The world of steamship travel also includes the local steamboats and ferry services, European river and canal cruises, New England and Virgin Island (Caribbean) schooner cruises, and passenger/freighter travel. A cruise to Martinique, steamship to Cartagena, a barque bound for Barbadoes, a freighter to Istanbul, ferry to Juneau, or a liner to Bergen are all commissionable sales for the travel agent, and cruise travel is steaming ahead at full speed after years of concern by steamship lines. Many cruise

liners have been sold out six months ahead of their sailings though a client can usually secure a cabin or two open on short notice because of cancellations.

The 25,300-ton s/s DORIC on a 7-day "Linger Linger" cruises which dock on Hamilton's Front Street, the heart of Bermuda, for the entire stay from Monday to Thursday. The ship, which many consider to be "The Best to Bermuda" is convenient to everything the fabulous island has to offer, including golf and tennis that can be reserved aboard.

Home Line Photo.

SEA TERMS

Travel agents should be aware of some of the common nautical terminology in the steamship industry. Many travel agents have never been to sea nor had an opportunity to board a ship to investigate the facilities and to know the bow from the stern of a cruise ship. The vessel your client will be boarding is a ship, not a boat. The floor on a ship is a deck; the stairs are ladders, and ladders take clients topside or below. The wall of a ship is the bulkhead, and the ceiling is the overhead. When you look to the front of the ship you are looking to the bow; your right side is starboard, your left is port; and when you look to the rear, you look aft to stern. Cruise travel is not in miles-per-hour, but knots. Knots means nautical miles per hour. A nautical mile is roughly one-seventh longer than a land mile. The length of a nautical mile is 6,080 feet. Embarkation means the process of boarding a ship to begin the cruise, and debarkation is the process of leaving the ship from voyage. The following list includes a brief glossary that have been used with customers in selling steamship transportation.

GLOSSARY OF TERMS

AFT - Near, toward or in the stern (rear) of a vessel.

ALLEYWAY - A passageway of the ship.

AMIDSHIPS (or Midships) - In or toward the middle of a vessel, between bow and stern.

BEAM - The breadth of a vessel at its widest part.

BERTH - A bunk (bed) in a cabin, or the ship's place at anchor or dock.

BOARD - To go aboard or on the ship.

BOLLARD - An upright metal post on a wharf to which a ship's mooring line may be secured.

BOW - The forward (front) part of a vessel.

BREAKWATER - A structure for breaking the force of waves so as to protect a harbor.

BRIDGE - The ship's command center.

BULKHEAD - Any of the partition walls used to separate various interior areas of a ship such as rooms, holds, etc.

CHART - A nautical map of seas.

COMPANIONWAY - A set of steps leading from the deck to a cabin or saloon below; also the space occupied by these steps.

DISEMBARK - To land; to put or to go ashore from a ship.

DOCK - The water area occupied by a ship alongside a wharf. A wharf, often called a dock in common usage, is the structure usually supported upon piling to which the ship's lines are made fast and upon which cargoes are deposited.

DOCKAGE - The charge assessed a vessel for berthing at a wharf, pier or bulkhead. The charge varies with the size of the vessel.

DRAFT (or Draught) - The depth of water a ship draws.

EMBARK - To go aboard a ship to begin a journey.

FATHOM - A measure of length, containing six feet, used chiefly in measuring cordage, cable, and depth of water by soundings.

FORE (Forward) - In or towards the bow (front) of a vessel.

FREEPORT - A restricted zone at a seaport, where duty-free goods are sold.

GALLEY - A ship's kitchen.

GANGWAY - The aperture in a ship's side for the accommodations of persons entering and leaving.

GROSS REGISTER TON - This is a measure, not of weight, but of the cubical content of the enclosed spaces on a ship, and is the measurement used in giving the size of passenger vessels. 100 cubic feet is equal to one gross register ton.

HELM - A generic term for a ship's steering apparatus.

HOUSE FLAG - The official flag of a shipping line. Usually flown by their vessels when in port and over offices and transit sheds used by them.

KEEL - The chief and lowest support of a vessel. The frame extending along the longitudinal center of the bottom of a ship from bow to stern.

KNOT - A unit of speed, equivalent to one nautical mile (6,080 feet) per hour.

LEE, LEEWARD - The direction away from the wind.

LOG - A daily record of a ship's speed, progress. Also, a device for measuring the speed of a ship.

NAUTICAL MILE - A nautical mile is 6,080 feet, compared to a land, or "statute" mile, which is only 5,280 feet.

PIER - A structure built out into the water for use as landing places for vessels.

PORT - The left side of a ship, looking forward.

PORTHOLE - An opening in a ship's side (window).

PROW - The bow of the ship above water.

REGISTRY - The country in which the ship is registered (official nationality of the ship).

SALOON - The main lounge on a passenger ship.

STABILIZER - A retractable fin extended from either side of the ship for smoother sailing.

STARBOARD - The right side of a ship looking forward.

STERN - The after or rear end of a ship.

TRAMP SHIP - A cargo ship operating under no regular schedule and connected with no particular trade route. The term is often misconstrued to mean an old ship but it can be a new ship and the terminology has nothing to do with the age or condition of the ship.

WEIGH ANCHOR - To raise anchor.

STEAMSHIP ABBREVIATIONS

Travel agents should know the frequently used abbreviations used by the steamship lines when offering and booking accommodations. The name of an ocean liner is generally prefixed with several initial letters ("S.S." or M/V). A list of ship prefixes, berthing and ticketing abbreviations follows:

Bibby	"L" Shaped Cabin with porthole	Pos.	Positive
Bth.	With Bath	P.T.	Port Tax
Conf.	Confirmed	Q.S.S.	Quadruple Screw Steamship
Dbl.	Double Cabin (Two beds or berths)	R.M.S.	Royal Mailship
D/R	Deposit Receipt	R/T	Round Trip
E/B	Eastbound	S.S.	Steamship
F.	First Class	S & T	With Shower and Toilet
Guar.	Guarantee	TBA	To Be Assigned (Advised)
I/S	Inside Cabin	Tkt.	Ticket
K.I.P. or K.A.I.P.	Keep Alone if Possible	T, Toil.	With Toilet
		Trip.	Triple Cabin (Three beds or berths)
M/M	Mr. & Mrs.	T.S.	Turbine Ship
M.S.	Motor Ship	T.S.S.	Turbine Steamship
M.V.	Motor Vessel	T.V.	Turbo-Vessel
NRS	No Rate Specified	Tour	Tourist Class
Opt.	Option	W/B	Westbound
O/S	Outside Cabin	W/C Fac.	Without Facilities
O/W	One Way	W/Fac.	With Facilities
		W/Shw.	With Private Shower
		W.L.	Wait List

Aquarius - Hellenic Mediterranean Lines

MAKING A CRUISE RESERVATION

    The first step in making a reservation for a cruise is to place a telephone call to the cruise line. Usually a toll free number is available. Give the reservationist the name of the ship, sailing date, whether it is an air/sea booking, and the departure gateway city. Then request a specific cabin. If the first choice is not available, ask for a similar cabin in the same rate category or request a guaranteed cabin in that rate category. A guarantee assures the customer of a cabin in a specific category, and a cabin assignment is given as soon as a cabin becomes available. If the cruise line is unable to assign a cabin in that category, the customer will be upgraded to a higher category at no additional charge.

    Once you are satisfied with the accommodations offered, you will be asked to take an option. This means that your reservation will be confirmed pending receipt of a deposit. Usually you are given a seven day option period.

    The final date is established by the cruise line. Generally this is six to eight weeks prior to departure. Documents for the cruise are mailed to the agency after receipt of final payment.

Blossom time cruise in Norway's fjord country. Courtesy of Norwegian Tourist Office.

m/s ANGELINA LAURO

LOUNGE DECK

BOAT DECK
SPORTS DECK
UPPER DECK
LOUNGE DECK
MAIN DECK
"A" DECK
"B" DECK
"C" DECK
"D" DECK

AMERICAN BAR
TOUR READING LOUNGE
BAR
PROMENADE
PROMENADE
CARD ROOM
READING AND WRITING ROOM
PROMENADE
PROMENADE
"CARPET" LOUNGE
CINEMA
CHILDREN'S ROOM
TAVERN

MAIN DECK
HOSPITAL
INFORMATION
NAVIGATOR'S HALL
LOBBY
MAITRE HOTEL
PURSER'S OFFICE
CHIEF STEWARD
CRUISE OFFICE
EXCHANGE
SALOON CLUB
GYM
VERANDAH

"A" DECK
HOSPITAL
HOSPITAL
INFORMATION
NAVIGATOR'S HALL
PHOTO
COLOM
BARBER SHOP
BEAUTY SALON
CURIO SHOP

"B" DECK
CONTINENTAL DINING ROOM
GALLEY
BAKERY
PHOTO SHOP
CURIO SHOP
PASTRY SHOP
MEDITERRANEAN DINING ROOM
RIVIERA DINING ROOM

"C" DECK

BOAT DECK
OFFICERS QUARTERS
PROMENADE
PROMENADE

SPORTS DECK
ENGINEER QUARTERS
RADIO STATION
SWIMMING POOL
GYMNASIUM
BAR
AQUARIUS NIGHT CLUB
CHILDREN'S SWIMMING POOL

UPPER DECK
SWIMMING POOL
BAR
CHILDREN'S SWIMMING POOL

OFFICIAL STEAMSHIP GUIDE

EUROPE - MEDITERRANEAN - DALMATIAN - AFRICA CRUISES

Leave Return	No. of Days	Air-Sea	Ship	Table No. Min. Rate Operator
July 15-July 29 Genoa *Naples, Alexandria, Port Said, Haifa, Kusadasi, Istanbul, Piraeus, Capri*	(14)		**Daphne**	267 $1,070.00 Lauro Line
July 16-July 23 Barcelona *Malta, Istanbul, Yalta, Odessa (terminates)*	(7)		**Belorussia**	160 $391.00 Black Sea
July 21-Aug. 4 Southampton *Trieste, Itea, Messina, Lisbon*	(14)		**Oriana**	100 $667.00 P&O
July 21-July 31 Genoa *Cannes, Malaga, Funchal, Santa Cruz de Tenerife, Casablanca*	(10)		**Enrico C**	041 $750.00 Costa
July 22-July 29 Genoa *Cannes, Barcelona, Palma de Mallorca, Bizerte (Tunis), Malta, Catania, Naples*	(7)		**Galileo**	041 $455.00 Costa
July 22-July 29 Venice *Dubrovnik, Corfu, Piraeus, Rhodes*	(7)		**Flavia**	041 $425.00 Costa
July 22-July 29 Venice *Dubrovnik, Corfu, Malta, Tunis, Costa Smeralda, Elba, Portofino, Nice (terminates)*	(7)		**Stella Maris**	130 $455.00 Sun Line
July 22-July 29 Genoa *Barcelona, Palma De Majorca, Tunis, Palermo, Capri or Naples*	(7)		**Irpinia**	320 $220.00 Siosa
July 23-Aug. 6 Odessa *Piraeus, Naples, Genoa, Marseilles, Barcelona, Malta, Istanbul, Yalta*	(14)		**Belorussia**	160 $715.00 Black Sea
July 23-July 30 Odessa *Piraeus, Naples, Genoa, Marseilles, Barcelona (terminates)*	(7)		**Belorussia**	160 $391.00 Black Sea
July 24-Aug. 5 Venice *Piraeus, Delos, Mykonos, Istanbul, Kusadasi, Rhodes, Santorini, Corfu, Dubrovnik*	(12)		**Andrea C**	041 $725.00 Costa
July 29-Aug. 11 Toulon *Katakolon, Piraeus, Kusadasi, Rhodes, Alexandria, Haifa, Piraeus, Messina, Capri*	(13)		**Azur**	095 $780.00 Paquet
July 29-Aug. 12 Genoa *Naples, Alexandria, Haifa, Kusadasi, Istanbul, Piraeus*	(14)		**Ausonia**	041 $920.00 Costa
July 29-Aug. 5 Genoa *Cannes, Barcelona, Palma de Mallorca, Bizerte (Tunis), Malta, Catania, Naples*	(7)		**Galileo**	041 $455.00 Costa
July 29-Aug. 5 Venice *Dubrovnik, Corfu, Piraeus, Rhodes*	(7)		**Flavia**	041 $425.00 Costa
July 29-Aug. 12 Genoa *Naples, Alexandria, Port Said, Haifa, Kusadasi, Istanbul, Piraeus, Capri*	(14)		**Daphne**	267 $1,070.00 Lauro Line
July 29-Aug. 12 Southampton *Las Palmas, Teneriffe, Madeira, Horta, Ponta Delgada Vigo*	(14)		**Canberra**	100 $667.00 P&O
July 30-Aug. 6 Barcelona *Malta, Istanbul, Yalta, Odessa (terminates)*	(7)		**Belorussia**	160 $391.00 Black Sea
July 31-Aug. 10 Genoa *Cannes, Malaga, Funchal, Santa Cruz de Tenerife, Casablanca*	(10)		**Enrico C**	041 $750.00 Costa

AUGUST

Leave Return	No. of Days	Air-Sea	Ship	Table No. Min. Rate Operator
Aug. 2-Aug. 18 Calais *Stavanger, Lerwick, Thorshavn, Reykjavik, Dublin, Cork, La Coruna, Vigo, Palma, Toulon (terminates)*	(16)		**Mermoz**	095 $890.00 Paquet
Aug. 5-Aug. 12 Venice *Dubrovnik, Corfu, Malta, Tunis, Costa Smeralda, Elba, Portofino, Nice (terminates)*	(7)		**Stella Maris**	130 $455.00 Sun Line
Aug. 5-Aug. 12 Venice *Dubrovnik, Corfu, Piraeus, Rhodes*	(7)		**Flavia**	041 $425.00 Costa
Aug. 5-Aug. 12 Genoa *Cannes, Barcelona, Palma de Mallorca, Bizerte (Tunis), Malta Catania, Naples*	(7)		**Galileo**	041 $455.00 Costa
Aug. 5-Aug. 12 Genoa *Barcelona, Palma De Majorca, Tunis, Palermo, Capri or Naples*	(7)		**Irpinia**	320 $220.00 Siosa
Aug. 5-Aug. 17 Venice *Piraeus, Delos, Mykonos, Istanbul, Kusadasi, Rhodes, Santorini, Corfu, Dubrovnik*	(12)		**Andrea C**	041 $725.00 Costa
Aug. 6-Aug. 20 Bremerhaven *Tilbury, Jersey, Glengariff, Dublin, Helensburgh, Torshavn, Kikwall, Edinburgh*	(14)		**Europa**	245 DM 3090 Hapag-Lloyd
Aug. 6-Aug. 20 Odessa *Piraeus, Naples, Genoa, Marseilles, Barcelona, Malta, Istanbul, Yalta*	(14)		**Belorussia**	160 $715.00 Black Sea
Aug. 6-Aug. 13 Odessa *Piraeus, Naples, Genoa, Marseilles, Barcelona (terminates)*	(7)		**Belorussia**	160 $391.00 Black Sea

A summer ferry excursion in Europe.   Norwegian Tourist Photo.

While there are several publications available for the travel agent's convenience in planning and booking "sailing vessels," the most widely used manual is the OFFICIAL STEAMSHIP GUIDE. This publication is a listing directory for all of the steamships throughout the world, and is corrected and revised from the latest available resources.

The OFFICIAL STEAMSHIP GUIDE offers a "Cruise List" (shown on the previous page) which is updated monthly and is arranged by departure dates. Each cruise listing shows the name and the Table Number of the operator for easy reference to the Schedule/Fare listings which appear in the order of their Table Nos. in the Schedules/Fares section immediately following the Cruise List. The Cruise listings give the name of the port which one departs from, the date it departs and the date it returns, the length of the cruise, the destination of the ship, the name of the ship, and the minimum rate available on that particular sailing. At a glance the agent is able to give a capsule of information to anyone who desires the bare facts. Of course, when clients have decided on the ship of their choice, the travel counselor would then go directly to the Brochure of the particular ship for more explicit details and booking information.

Rates: ss ROTTERDAM
Fall Entertainment Festival at Sea

Cate-gory	DESCRIPTION	U.S. $ PER PERSON — FALL (Sept. 2 thru Nov. 4)
A	OUTSIDE DOUBLE CABINS DELUXE: Extra large, extra comfortable cabins with sitting room alcove, separate wardrobe room. Possibly the most deluxe cabins on any cruise ship anywhere.	$820
B	OUTSIDE DOUBLE ONE ROOM SUITES: Luxurious staterooms with twin beds and sitting area.	770
C	OUTSIDE DOUBLE ROOMS: Beautiful staterooms with twin beds and space for entertaining.	750
D	OUTSIDE DOUBLE ROOMS: Beautiful staterooms with twin beds and space for entertaining.	715
E	OUTSIDE DOUBLE ROOMS: Beautiful staterooms with twin beds and space for entertaining.	690
F	OUTSIDE DOUBLE ROOMS: Staterooms with twin beds.	670
G	INSIDE DOUBLE ROOMS: Comfortable rooms with twin lower beds.	635
H	INSIDE DOUBLE ROOMS: Comfortable rooms with twin lower beds.	605
I	ECONOMY OUTSIDE DOUBLE ROOMS: Upper and lower beds, with sea view.	570
J	ECONOMY INSIDE DOUBLE ROOMS: Upper and lower beds.	545
K	ECONOMY INSIDE DOUBLE ROOMS: Upper and lower beds.	510
L	ECONOMY INSIDE DOUBLE ROOMS: Upper and lower beds.	460
M*	OUTSIDE SINGLE ROOMS: Charming sea view staterooms with lower bed.	820 & 745
N*	INSIDE SINGLE ROOMS: Lower bed.	675 & 645

*Prices vary according to cabin number.

Rates: ss STATENDAM
Fall Entertainment Festival at Sea

Cate-gory	DESCRIPTION	U.S. $ PER PERSON — FALL (Sept. 2 thru Nov. 11)
A	DELUXE OUTSIDE DOUBLE ONE-ROOM SUITES: Elegant, extra large, extra comfortable bedrooms with sitting room alcove, bath and shower.	$815
B	OUTSIDE DOUBLE DELUXE ROOMS: Luxurious extra-large rooms with twin beds, vanity and closets, full bathroom; table and chairs allow you to entertain friends in comfort.	795
C	LUXURY OUTSIDE DOUBLE ROOMS: Superb, spacious staterooms with twin beds. Private shower and bath.	745
D	LUXURY OUTSIDE DOUBLE ROOMS: Superb, spacious staterooms with twin beds. Shower and/or bath.	725
E	LUXURY OUTSIDE DOUBLE ROOMS: Superb, spacious staterooms with twin beds and shower.	700
F	SUPERIOR OUTSIDE DOUBLE ROOMS: Luxurious staterooms with twin beds, shower and/or bath, and space for entertaining.	675
G	OUTSIDE DOUBLE ROOMS: Luxurious staterooms with twin beds, shower and/or bath, and space for entertaining.	655
H	OUTSIDE DOUBLE ROOMS: Sofa converts to comfortable double bed.	640
I	INSIDE DOUBLE ROOMS: Twin beds, shower and/or bath.	625
J	ECONOMY OUTSIDE DOUBLE ROOMS: Two-porthole rooms with upper and lower beds, shower and/or bath.	615
K	INSIDE DOUBLE ROOMS: Sofa converts to double bed, shower.	580
L	ECONOMY INSIDE DOUBLE ROOMS: Upper and lower beds, shower.	550
M	ECONOMY INSIDE DOUBLE ROOMS: Upper and lower beds, shower.	510
N	ECONOMY INSIDE DOUBLE ROOMS: Upper and lower beds, shower.	460
O*	OUTSIDE SINGLE ROOMS: Two-porthole rooms with lower bed, shower and/or bath.	820 & 745
P*	INSIDE SINGLE ROOMS: Lower bed, shower.	675 & 645

*Prices vary according to cabin number.

The Cruise List makes reference to the "Schedules/Fares" section which each ship line supplies detailed data essential to an agent's booking procedures. Ship lines are listed, not necessarily alphabetically, but by their Table Numbers which appear in bold type at the top corner of each page (and cross reference in the Cruise List). The Schedules/Fares includes: Passenger Lines, Local and Ferry Services, European River and Canal Cruises, New England Schooner Cruises, and Passenger/Freighters. In the passenger line listings, the steamship companies describe their cruises: a port to

port itinerary and special instructions for passengers, fares according to categories, and special notes and exceptions for the sale of this cruise. Passenger fares include, for example, "per person according to the number of persons intending to occupy each stateroom suite are in U.S. dollars and include stateroom, ocean transportation, all meals, ship as hotel throughout, social features, and entertainment."

HOLLAND AMERICA'S 25,000-ton SS STATENDAM cruises into the harbor at Bermuda.

The OFFICIAL STEAMSHIP GUIDE provides a useful Port-to-Port index for the passenger liners, Port-to-Port Index for the Passenger freighters, Consolidated Schedules of the Trans Atlantic and Trans Pacific Vessels, a list of every cruise leaving from a U.S. port, a pier directory, schedules and fares of passenger lines, schedules and fares of passenger freighter lines, and the size (vessel tonnages) of the different ships. This book gives the travel agent a quick look at what is available. An

important cross reference is the "Consolidated Schedules of the Atlantic and Pacific Passenger Liners" because in the table agents can find the vessels listed, the cruise ship line they belong to, the date they sail and the date they arrive at their destination. For the most part these ships listed in this fashion are not the cruise ships but are the ships used for transportation.

Consolidated Schedules (Westbound) 1978

Atlantic Coast U.S. & Canada from Poland—Sweden—Denmark—Norway—Germany—Holland—Spain—Italy—England—France—Ireland

VESSEL	LINE	TABLE	FROM	TO CANADA		TO U.S.A.	
ROYAL VIKING STAR	RVL	120	Malaga (Mar. 29); Tangier (Mar. 30); Funchal (Apr. 1)			Apr. 9	Ft. Laud.
QUEEN ELIZABETH 2	Cunard	042	Southampton (Apr. 25); Cherbourg (Apr. 25)			Apr. 30	New York
STEFAN BATORY	Polish Ocean	105	Gdynia (Apr. 28); Rotterdam (May 1); London (May 2)	May 11	Montreal		
QUEEN ELIZABETH 2	Cunard	042	Southampton (May 15); Cherbourg (May 15)			May 20	New York
ROYAL VIKING STAR	RVL	120	Malaga (May 15); Gibraltar (May 15); Tangier (May 16); Horta (May 19)			May 24	New York
QUEEN ELIZABETH 2	Cunard	042	Southampton (June 4); Cherbourg (June 4)			June 9	New York
STEFAN BATORY	Polish Ocean	105	Gdynia (May 30); Rotterdam (June 2); London (June 3)	June 12	Montreal		
QUEEN ELIZABETH 2	Cunard	042	Southampton (June 16); Cherbourg (June 16)			June 21	New York
QUEEN ELIZABETH 2	Cunard	042	Southampton (June 28); Cherbourg (June 28)			July 3	New York
STEFAN BATORY	Polish Ocean	105	Gdynia (July 1); Rotterdam (July 4); London (July 5)	July 14	Montreal		
QUEEN ELIZABETH 2	Cunard	042	Southampton (July 10); Cherbourg (July 10)			July 15	New York
QUEEN ELIZABETH 2	Cunard	042	Southampton (July 22); Cherbourg (July 22)			July 27	New York
QUEEN ELIZABETH 2	Cunard	042	Southampton (Aug. 4); Cherbourg (Aug. 4)			Aug. 9	New York
QUEEN ELIZABETH 2	Cunard	042	Southampton (Aug. 15); Cherbourg (Aug. 15)			Aug. 20	New York
STEFAN BATORY	Polish Ocean	105	Gdynia (Aug. 8); Rotterdam (Aug. 11); London (Aug. 12)	Aug. 21	Montreal		
QUEEN ELIZABETH 2	Cunard	042	Southampton (Aug. 27); Cherbourg (Aug. 27);			Sept. 1	New York
ROYAL VIKING STAR	RVL	120	Southampton (Sept. 9)			Sept. 17	New York
						Sept. 20	Ft. Laud.
STEFAN BATORY	Polish Ocean	105	Gdynia (Sept. 8); Rotterdam (Sept. 11); London (Sept. 12)	Sept. 21	Montreal		
QUEEN ELIZABETH 2	Cunard	042	Southampton (Sept. 20); Cherbourg (Sept. 20)			Sept. 25	New York
QUEEN ELIZABETH 2	Cunard	042	Southampton (Oct. 2); Cherbourg (Oct. 2)			Oct. 7	New York
STEFAN BATORY	Polish Ocean	105	Gdynia (Oct. 10); Rotterdam (Oct. 13); London (Oct. 14)	Oct. 23	Montreal		
QUEEN ELIZABETH 2	Cunard	042	Southampton (Oct. 30); Cherbourg (Oct. 30)			Nov. 4	New York
ROYAL VIKING SEA	RVL	120	Piraeus (Nov. 4); Malaga (Nov. 7); Gibraltar (Nov. 8); Funchal (Nov. 10)			Nov. 18	Ft. Laud.
ORIANA	P&O	100	Southampton (Nov. 10); Bermuda (Nov. 16); Port Everglades (Nov. 18); Nassau (Nov. 19); Cristobal (Nov. 21/22); Acapulco (Nov. 25)	Dec. 2	Vancouver	Nov. 28 Los Angeles Nov. 29/30 San Francisco	
QUEEN ELIZABETH 2	Cunard	042	Southampton (Nov. 27); Cherbourg (Nov. 27)			Dec. 2	Boston

OFFICIAL STEAMSHIP GUIDE INTERNATIONAL — FEBRUARY 1978

SELECTING A CRUISE

As steamship travellers become experienced, they will discriminate in their selection of ships. No two ships are the same. Cruise companies want first-time passengers but they want you to come back. The weekend cruise from Miami to Nassau is very different from a week long Caribbean Cruise trip. A more comprehensive trip is an around-the-world cruise in 87 days, 19 countries, 22 ports from Port Everglades to Oranjestad, Cartagena, Cristobal, Balboa, Acapulco, Los Angeles, Bombay, Djibouti, Suez, Alexandria, Haifa, Istanbul, Yalta, Odessa, Piraeus, Naples, Villefranche, Lisbon, with arrival back in Port Everglades, four months later.

When passengers return from a cruise they might say a number of things about their voyage. This will give you, as the travel agent, a greater understanding of the merits and problems of particular cruises, for example:

"Food is good but commercial, portions small, and there are no midnight buffets; coffee ship is available for purchasing snacks."

"Lower decks provide best ride but lesser views; other decks have views but experience more motion and sometimes noise, especially near disco."

"Lido deck and pool are usually busy with breakfast, lunch and lounging; two dining rooms easily hold full complement of passengers, and the menus are identical in both dining rooms and non-listed items often are available."

"Top deck lounge is done in beautiful Scandinavian modern style and a favorite gathering place. Expensive, good for sophisticated travelers looking for something different."

"Ship is smooth riding, beautifully decorated in public rooms, has excellent children's play area, fine plumbing, large baths; deluxe cabins and suites have Italian tile floors. Cuisine is excellent and varied, international, features daily Lido Deck lunch buffet and usual midnight buffet."

"Short cruises are a bit hectic with their multiple stops and short stay in Istanbul, and some of the offbeat islands have relatively littly interest for shore excursions."

"All cabins have lower beds and insides are larger than outsides. All cabins have ample closets but those above and below lounges may be noisy."

"Staff comes from 30 nationalities and service can range from excellent on down, depending on language and other uncertainties."

"Cabins are roomy, well appointed, but best in higher priced upper decks; lower-rated passengers must dine in former tourist class dining room."

On board ship relaxing.   Royal Viking Line Photo.

Sun Line Tourist Photo.

As a travel agent you will have some or all of the answers to your client's questions because you know that each ship has a special personality (and atmosphere) and it is your job to match your customer with the proper ship.

The cost of a cruise may start at $200.00 for a short one or buy an around-the-world cruise for as much as $150,000.00 per person. Passengers require assistance from travel agents in order to choose from 140 cruise ships world wide. As a travel agent you are expected to take familiarization trips aboard these ships so you can advise your clients. You need answers to questions about large ships with lots of passengers, a ship of certain nationality, ports of calls, cabin arrangements and more. As a travel agent you will have diagrams of the ships showing facilities and cabins; and all the literature (information) you require.

As a travel agent you will have dozens of brochures to give the clients about cruises. Steamship travel literature is attractive, colorful, hyper-descriptive and can be misleading. Cruise brochures sell "Ship Board Excitement". It is important not to mis-read the materials, including cancellations and refunds information. A cruise brochure typically contains a deck plan in order to designate the exact location of any given cabin on the ship. The cabins on the lower decks are the cabins which are generally economy. The higher up on the ship a passenger goes for his accommodation the higher the cost. Although the cabins on the upper decks are the highest in cost they are not always the ones with the smoothest ride. Due to the stabilizing unit that most ships have in their hull, the cabins located on the lower decks give the smoothest ride. Cabins are also provided inside and outside. Remember that all

cruises are one class travel so that a client can buy the least expensive cabin and yet live it up on an equal basis with the penthouse crowd.

The Atlantic Coast stretches for miles of pure white sand and crystal sea for cruise line passengers. Willie Alleyne Associates Photo Ltd., Bridgetown, Barbados, W.I.

Brochures give essentially general information on embarkation, travel documents, sightseeing tours and other passage contract information.

Do not try to sell the client one ship as the only one. As a good travel agent you should offer a couple of suggestions and explain differences between ships. You will have reports from your customers on their cruises; other agents in the office will make suggestions about ship travel; The Star Service (Sloane Travel Agency Reports) provide a report on the "Florida-Based Cruise Ships;" your own FAM (cruise) trips; trade publication reports on cruise travel will be of assistance in discussing the merits of a particular cruise with a customer.

AIR/SEA PACKAGES

For years the airlines and shiplines were seeking the same passengers traveling the oceans. Steamships lost the trans-Atlantic travel when people could reach far destinations in a few hours by air. Since steamships were no longer required for transportation, the idea of vacationing at sea became a new travel opportunity. More than one million Americans are cruising in the Caribbean. Most cruise lines are experiencing high occupancy rates and are finding it increasingly difficult to meet consumer demands. Things are so busy that the cruise lines are looking for new ships and the Port of Miami has become the biggest cruise port in the world. Miami is

building a ninth passenger terminal and has launched a $40 million port expansion. The "new" Port of Miami is located in tranquil Biscanyne Bay facing the heart of Miami. This cruise capital is only a few minutes from the famous resort hotels and motels in Miami and Miami Beach and from the Miami International Airport.

The 39,241-ton s/s OCEANIC, whose number of repeaters are the largest of any ship in modern cruise annals, will again offer passengers a choice of 2 days and nights in Nassau or a day in Bermuda in addition to a day and night in Nassau. While the Spring and Summer sailings feature either the one-port and two-port itineraries, all Autumn cruises call at both ports. While there are many reasons for the consistent popularity of the OCEANIC among one-week vacationers, travel experts attribute Home Lines' reputation for high cruise standards as the major factor. This is especially apparent in the quality of cuisine and in the dedicated service of the well-trained Italian personnel. Worth noting, too, is the fact that all double cabins have 2 lower beds.

Home Line Photo.

Cruise marketing has flourished with nationwide air/sea programs. As a result, travel agents located outside port cities today sell cruises almost as easily as those doing business in New York, Miami/Ft. Lauderdale, Los Angeles, or San Francisco. The "Windy City", Chicago, far from any passenger port, is one of the most important marketing areas for major cruise lines, a significant change from just a few years ago. And with the air/sea package so complete, the agent's total commission has increased and, hopefully, agency's profit picture brightened.

Steamship lines have successfully generated a market using more than 130 cities with air/sea packages. Generally the total vacation price of cruise fares and round-trip airfares from central and mid-western population centers to port cities is offered for substantially reduced air fares to act as the catalyst to encourage more land-locked Americans to cruise. This marketing package worked. By combining the advantages of the then-available group discounted airfares and subsidizing a portion of the airfare, steamship lines are able to offer to the cruise prospect in Denver an air/sea vacation for essentially the same package price paid by his counterpart in Los Angeles.

Confirmation/Deposit Receipt

To

Mr.& Mrs. J. Strnad

Cruise Data

Date: April 8th, 1978

To: Caribbean

Departing From Ft. Lauderdale

Vessel: Fairwind

Cabin: To be assigned

Passengers:

We are pleased to confirm these services:

Flight Data

Seats reserved on following flights
Outbound: WILL ADVISE

Inbound:

Costs

Cost of Cruise $	1339.50
Port Taxes $	26.50
Cost of Air $	120.00
Airport Taxes $	
Cost of Land $	
Misc. $	
Misc. $	
Total $	1486.00

No receipt will be sent for the balance; tickets will be forwarded approximately two weeks prior to departure.

Information on travel insurance is enclosed. You may use the self-addressed envelope for returning the balance due; one check may be used for final payment and for insurance premiums, if desired.

Thank you for your patronage.

Nancy Vollec

☑ Proof of citizenship is required (Passport, Birth Certificate, or voter's registration).
International Certificate of Vaccination is required for:
☐ Small Pox
☐ Other _____

Received/Due

Total $ 1486.00

Deposit Received $ Paid in Full

Balance $ NONE

Date Balance Due _____

Please remit with attached form.

Thank you!

The typical air supplement for roundtrip air transportation from Baltimore to Miami (Ft. Lauderdale) is $60 and no matter where the client lives in the United States, Canada or Mexico, steamship lines have made it easy for them. Clients fly aboard regularly scheduled airlines and are met on arrival by a uniformed steamship line representative who escorts the passengers by private motor coach directly to the ship. The Air/Sea Caribbean package price may require an "add-on" of $60 for a client from Quebec or free from Savannah. The steamship line writes the tickets (air and sea tickets) for the client.

AIR/SEA CRUISE ADD-ON AIR FARE COST

	Mexico	Canada & Alaska	Caribbean	Trans-Panama & 14 Day Caribbean
Ottawa, Ont.	$190	$190	$110	Free
Palm Springs, Calif.	Free	Free	*110	Free
Paso Robles, Calif.	Free	Free	*110	Free
Pensacola, Fla.	150	165	Free	Free
Philadelphia, Pa.	150	165	60	Free
Phoenix, Ariz.	Free	50	150	Free
Pittsburgh, Pa.	150	150	60	Free
Portland, Ore.	25	Free	250	Free
Prince George, B.C.	190	150	**125	Free
Providence, R.I.	150	165	60	Free
Quebec, Que.	225	250	175	Free
Raleigh, N.C.	150	190	50	Free
Regina, Sask.	190	90	190	Free
Reno, Nev.	Free	Free	**125	Free
Richmond, Va.	150	190	60	Free
Roanoke, Va.	190	190	90	Free
Rochester, N.Y.	150	165	90	Free
Sacramento, Calif.	Free	Free	**125	Free
St. Louis, Mo.	90	125	60	Free
Salt Lake City, Utah	25	25	190	Free
San Antonio, Texas	60	125	60	Free
San Diego, Calif.	Free	Free	110	Free
San Francisco, Calif.	Free	–	125	Free
San Jose, Calif.	Free	–	**125	Free
San Juan, P.R.	290	290	60	Free
San Luis Obispo, Calif.	Free	Free	*110	Free
Santa Ana, Calif.	–	Free	*110	Free
Santa Barbara, Calif.	Free	Free	175	Free
Santa Maria, Calif.	Free	Free	*110	Free
Sarasota, Fla.	150	165	Free	Free
Saskatoon, Sask.	190	90	190	Free
Savannah, Ga.	150	165	Free	Free
Seattle, Wash.	25	Free	250	Free

*From Los Angeles Airport } Transportation to and from Los Angeles or San Francisco
**From San Francisco Airport   airports not included.

1. These rates represent supplementary charges for computing Air/Sea package prices. They are not air fares.
2. The Air/Sea program is applicable to all cabin categories from cities for which the air supplement is shown as "Free." The Air/Sea program is not otherwise acceptable to categories M, N & P.
3. Only full-fare, complete cruise passengers are eligible for the Air/Sea program.

Air/Sea Program on Queen Elizabeth 2

Over and back for the price of over. Passengers in both First Class and Tourist Class on the QUEEN can sail to or from Europe and fly the opposite way on British Airways all for no more than their one-way sea cost.

Thus, for the cost of the regular one-way sea fare, your clients receive the following:

(1) One-way sea ticket for grade chosen between New York and Europe.

(2) Air allowance up to an amount equal to the one-way economy airfare at the time of printing between London and their home town for First Class passengers and an air allowance up to a limit of $450 for those in Tourist Class. There are some restrictions based on the total length of their vacation and if travel on the QE2 is Tourist Class.

In advising your clients about the offer and to calculate their fare, you can follow these six simple steps:

1. **Determine Duration of European Trip,** that is, total period starting the day of departure for Europe and to the day of arrival back in the U.S./Canada.

   A. **For maximum Air Allowance (equal to the lowest one-way economy airfare between London and home town as of 1/1/78).**
      (1) First Class—Travel must be completed within 40 days.
      (2) Tourist Class—Travel must be completed within 20 days.
   B. **For Air Allowance (equal to 50% of the lowest one-way economy airfare between London and home town as of 1/1/78).**
      (1) First class—Travel over 40 days and completed by December 31, 1978.
      (2) Tourist Class—Travel over 20 days and completed by December 31, 1978.

2. **Determine the Appropriate QE2 Season, grade and one-way fare your clients wish** (see Chart in consumer brochure Q268 on pages 20 and 25.)

3. **Determine the amount of Allowance for Air Travel to be deducted from the one-way sea fare**

   (Air Allowances are listed in the Chart in the consumer brochure Q268 on page 20.)

   The Air Allowance is the amount Cunard will credit towards your client's air fare between London and your client's home town within the continental USA/Canada. Hometown is to mean the airport closest to where your clients reside and where your clients will either begin or end their European trip.

NOTE: The amount of air allowance in Chart is based on the approved airfares as of January 1, 1978. The air allowance chart will be in effect unless changed by Cunard, regardless of the direction of the air flight and/or any changes in airfares by the airline. **The air allowance remains the same, regardless of the final air routing. The transatlantic air crossing must be on British Airways.**

4. **Calculate your client's total amount**

   A. If the actual airfare is higher than the air allowance in the chart, your client merely pays the difference plus the cost of the sea fare.

   B. Add in applicable departure tax and the port and handling charges as shown in consumer brochure Q268 on page 24. Other charges for pets, automobiles etc. (shown in Q268 page 30) should be included in this total.

5. **Reservations Procedures**

   A. Ship reservations are made in the normal manner and we ask you to indicate at that time that this is an air/sea booking. It is also important to indicate the date and client hometown/airport departure city your clients plan to use. **This information will be the basis for calculating the adjusted sea fare** and help us process your reservations in a more efficient manner.

   B. Air reservations are made in your normal manner with British Airways.

6. **Accounting and Ticketing**

   A. The adjusted sea fare is the balance after subtracting the amount of the air allowance (Step 4) from the appropriate one-way sea fare selected.

   B. **Deposit.** An initial deposit of $150 for each Tourist Class passenger and $300 First Class is required within seven working days.

   C. **Final Payment.** Final Payment is equivalent to the net balance after subtracting your commission (7% of the adjusted sea fare), plus the applicable port and handling charges. This amount is due to Cunard within 60 days prior to departure.

   D. **Air Ticket Payment.** The air ticket issued is paid by you to British Airways in the normal manner. **A copy of the air ticket listing the British Airways transatlantic flight must accompany your final payment to Cunard before any sea tickets can be issued.**

Air Sea Fare Calculation Examples.

An Example on Using the Five Easy Steps for an Air/Sea Booking

Situation—Client living in Evanston, Illinois, sailing QE2 from New York to Southampton on May 28th (shown on the tariff sheet as "Intermediate Season") and flying back to Chicago from Paris, France.

		EXAMPLE			
		1	2	3	4
1.	**Duration of Trip**				
	A. Date of Return	June 28	June 16	July 28	Oct. 28
	B. Length in Days	32	20	62	154
2.	**Seasonality/Rate Basis**				
	A. Ship Season	Inter.	Inter.	Inter.	Inter.
	B. Class of Accommodations	First	Tourist	First	Tourist
	C. Air	Peak	Peak	Peak	Basic
3.	**Amount of Air Allowance***				
	A. From Cunard Air Allowance Chart	$459	$450	$230	$195
4.	**Total Amount to be Paid by Passenger**				
	A. Ship Cabin Grade	H	M	H	M
	B. One-Way Sea Fare (Intermediate)	$1350	$ 800	$1350	$ 800
	C. Cunard Air Allowance	−459	−450	−230	−195
	D. Adjusted Gross Sea Fare (B–C)	$ 891	$ 350	$1120	$ 605
	E. Add Actual Air Fare (Paris—Chicago)	536	536	536	+ 449
	F. Add QE2 Port and Handling Charges	$ 35	+ 30	+ 35	+ 30
	G. Add Air Taxes (Eastbound Only)	—	—	—	—
	H. Add QE2 Misc. Charges (Autos, Pets etc.)	—	—	—	—
	I. Total to be Paid by Passenger D+E+F+G+H	$1462	$ 916	$1691	$1084
5.	**Payment Schedule—Air Segment**				
	A. Actual Air Fare (Paris—Chicago) (From Airline Rates Desk)	$ 536.00	$ 536.00	$ 536.00	$ 449.00
	B. Agent Commission from Airline (pay 10%)	53.60	53.60	53.60	44.90
	C. Net Balance (A–B)	$ 482.40	$ 482.40	$ 482.40	$ 404.10
	D. Air Taxes (Eastbound only)	—	—	—	—
	E. Final Payment to Airline (C–D)	$ 482.40	$ 482.40	$ 482.40	$ 404.10
6.	**Payment Schedule—Sea Segment**				
	A. Adjusted Gross Sea Fare (from 4D)	$ 891	$ 350	$1120	$ 605
	B. Agent Commission of 7% of Adjusted Gross Sea Fare	−62.37	−24.50	−78.40	42.35
	C. Balance (A–B)	$ 828.63	$ 325.50	$1041.60	$ 562.65
	D. Add QE2 Port and Handling Charges	+ 35.00	+ 30.00	+ 35.00	+ 30.00
	E. Add QE2 Misc Charges (Autos, Pets etc.)	—	—	—	—
	F. Total to be Paid to Cunard Line (C+D+E)	$ 863.63	$ 355.50	$1076.60	$ 592.65
	G. Less Deposit Paid Cunard Line	−300.00	−150.00	−300.00	−150.00
	H. Final Payment to Cunard Line (F–G)	$ 563.63	$ 205.50	$ 776.60	$ 442.65

Notes: °Allowances are based on airline fares in effect as of January 1, 1978 and will remain in effect unless changed by Cunard regardless of the direction of the flight and/or any changes in airfare by the airline.
A copy of the air ticket listing the British Airways transatlantic flight must accompany the final sea payment in order that passage contracts may be issued.

Composition of Ticket:
When a ticket has been issued, the various parts should be detached in following manner:

1. Revenue Coupon
2. Reservations Coupon
3. Accounts Coupon

} To be detached by the issuing agent at the time of booking and sent to us on the day of sale with covering payment, to: Att. Cashiers.

4. Embarkation Coupon

} To be given to passenger as contract ticket for

5. Sailing Coupon
6. Passenger's Coupon

} detachment at embarkation time. To be retained by the passenger together with the conditions of contract.

7. Issuing Office Coupon

} To be detached and retained by agent in his files.

Fare Basis:
The information to be shown is the type of booking; i.e., Air/Sea.

ALL COUNTERFOILS are pre-carbonized on the reverse side with "patch carbonizing" subsequent to the first two counterfoils to ensure that details of commission appear only on the Advice Portion, Accounts Copy, and Agent's Record Counterfoil.

°Fare Basis.

TIME OF EMBARKATION: This panel must show the time of embarkation as advertised in our timetable.

CUNARD PASSAGE CONTRACT TICKET

CUNARD LINE LIMITED. ISSUED SUBJECT TO THE TERMS AND CONDITIONS PRINTED ON THE INSIDE OF THE COVER AND SUCCEEDING PAGES OF THIS CONTRACT TICKET WHICH FORM PART THEREOF

REVENUE COUPON 41 **161210**
(NOT GOOD FOR PASSAGE) NOT TRANSFERABLE

| CLASS First | SHIP QE 2 | BRITISH REGISTRY | DATE OF EMBARKATION 28 May | TIME OF EMBARKATION 5:00-6:30 PM |

| FROM JFK Airport, New York | TO Southampton | FARE BASIS Air/Sea |

FULL NAMES OF PASSENGERS	FARE	AGE	ROOM	BED/BERTH	FACILITIES	NATIONALITY
Brown, Mr. William	$ 1350.	A	1106	All		U.S.A.
Brown, Mrs. Millie	$ 1350.	A	1106			U.S.A.
	$					
Less Air Allowance	$ 764.					
	$					

PRINTED IN U.S.A.

ISSUED IN CONNECTION WITH

FLIGHT	DATE	TICKET NO.	FARE	CLASS
BA 501	28 June	125 440568700 701	382.00 382.00	Y Y

IF WEST BOUND, PASSENGERS EUROPEAN ADDRESS

TOTAL FARE(S)	$ 1936.00
TAX(ES)	$ 70.00
	$
TOTAL	$ 2006.00
ISSUED IN EXCHANGE FOR PPR NO 36-112233	
VALUE	$ 600.00
BALANCE COLLECTED	$ 1406.00

DATE AND PLACE OF ISSUE ABC TUL NYC

FOR COMPANY'S USE ONLY	ACCOUNTS USE
1100	

| COMMISSION 7% | 135.52 |

AGENT **1** AGENTS CODE 33-6-9999

ROUND TRIP DETAILS:
Air/Sea—When issuing sea ticket in conjunction with a flight, you must show the British Airways flight number, date, ticket number, fare, and class.

CREDIT CARD NUMBER: When payment is made by credit card, type of card and account number must be shown here.

PART PAYMENT RECEIPTS: Value of Part Payment Receipts should be deducted here. Remember to enclose the receipt with your remittance.

CODE NUMBER: It is essential that your IATA Code Number be shown in this panel.

IMPORTANT—How to Receive Tickets and Documentation Long Before Your Client Leaves the U.S.

1. Send final payment and necessary documents including the British Airways counterfoil to Cunard 60 days before your client either sails or flies from the U.S. or Canada.
2. Keep a copy of all documents sent.
3. If your client books too late for this procedure, you must send payment by special delivery or a moneygram to Cunard, New York.

CANCELLED TICKETS: If any tickets are spoiled they must be clearly marked "voided" and returned to us.
ISSUANCE OF TICKETS: Tickets must be issued in strict numerical order and should be completed by printing with ball point pen or indelible pencil.

QUEEN ELIZABETH 2
the Greatest Ship In The World

Queen Elizabeth Suite
Queen Mary Suite

Tables Of The World Restaurant

Satellite Navigation
Promenade

Synagogue

Launderette

Wine Cellar

Gymnasium

Children's Playroom

Queen's Grill Restaurant
Terraced Deluxe Suites
Club Atlantic Bar
Princess Grill

Pool/Sauna

Hospital

530-seat Theater/Lecture Hall

Columbia Restaurant
Casino
Kennels
Theater Bar

Midships Bar

Card Room

Library

Stabilizers

Bureau

Bank

Double Room

Queen's Room

Pool/Turkish Bath

Shopping Arcade

Florist

Barbershop
Beauty Salon

Garage

Q4 Room

Jogging Track

Miniature Golf Course

Lido Bar

Launderette

Crew's Quarters

Outdoor Pool

Staterooms

AIR/SEA PROGRAM CONDITIONS

Air/Sea Tour: In addition to the services and facilities included in the cruise fare, any Air/Sea tour includes roundtrip, coach air transportation between the originating air/sea city and the port of embarkation, and ground transfers to and from the ship. Passengers are required to use flight schedules and routings specified by the cruise line if they wish to utilize the ground transfers arranged by cruise line. The airlines are independent contractors and the line is not responsible for their conduct. The cruise line will not be responsible for any expenses or other consequences resulting from a change or delay in the vessel's schedule, or a change or delay in schedule or routing made by a passenger, travel agent or airline.

Air Transportation: Civil Aeronautics Board certificated scheduled and charter airline services will be used. In the case of charter flights, no stopovers will be permitted. The cruise line reserves the right to substitute charter flights for scheduled flights and scheduled flights for charter flights, without prior notice. Changes in airline routings will be at cruise line's discretion and the line reserves the right to change them to facilitate consolidation of groups of passengers, or for any other reason. If due to airline schedules, the cruise line is unable to provide same-day service to or from a cruise with an Air/Sea package flight, the cruise line assumes no responsibility for additional expenses incurred by the passenger.

The Air/Sea packages have been so well received that today approximately 85% of the passengers arrive at the embarkation city by way of the air/sea package. In many respects, the popularity of air/sea packages now being offered by the steamship lines is responsible for the current boom in the cruise industry. The packages offered cruises to Americans who otherwise might never have considered a vacation at sea. Americans seem to be enjoying the "new vacation option," because statistics show cruise lines enjoy one of the highest repeat passenger factors in the travel industry. Passengers have passed the word to neighbors, friends and relatives so that now demand for cruises is increasing.

With more and more people cruising and enjoying it, travel agents can benefit not only by offering the complete package which includes the airfare and cruise fare as well as all the meals, entertainment, and activities aboard ship, plus transfers between the airport and pier, but also from a usually satisfied client who's likely to bring his future vacation bookings back to the agent.

For the travel agent, the really significant advantage of selling an air/sea cruise is the ease with which the booking is obtained. Usually one tollfree phone call to the steamship company will book the client's air transportation, cruise accommodations, transfers - even his dining room and sitting preference. All this takes less than five minutes. For a couple travelling together on a Caribbean vacation, this one call results in a commission averaging $250.

Consider the time and expense involved in booking a vacation for the same couple where a number of hotels, flights, sightseeing tours, and car rentals are involved. The steamship line writes all of the tickets. Each element of this vacation requires a separate telephone call and each element must be coordinated. When you consider the simplicity of an air/sea vacation, you begin to see the real beauty of selling a cruise.

Since most steamship lines use only scheduled air carriers for passengers, the lines can offer the same stopover privileges available to any air passenger using the same tariff. The cruise lines have combined these stopover privileges with two-night sightseeing tours, e.g., West Coast passengers returning from a Caribbean cruise stopover in New Orleans.

Ferryboats connect the colorful harbor in downtown Fort-de-France, capital of Martinique; cruise line customers enjoy local hospitality. French West Indies Photo.

What has happened is that cruising suddenly has seized the public's imagination. The television series "Love Boat," in particular, has turned on younger people and those from the landlocked midwestern states who were little acquainted with cruising. While the new converts to cruising lost their hearts to "Love Boat," just as many have come to realize that cruising is good travel value.

Miami and Port Everglades, Florida aren't the only cruise ports in the world, and clients can wander elsewhere to board steamships. Clients can sail down the Nile River, visiting the ruins of Egypt's glorious past, call at ports in China, and take a tour of this giant nation so long closed to westerners, explore the Antarctic or the primeval Galapagos Islands, watch glaciers from the deck on a ship in Alaska, and visit the storied South Seas. Other customers will want to remain closer to home and sail off the New England coast on a schooner, travel on the Delta Queen on the Mississippi River or cruise along the East Coast of Canada.

With cruise business so active, ship companies are searching the world for new ships to put their passengers into, and they are few to be had. Carnival Cruise Lines bought the former Vaal of the Castle Line last year, took it apart, added a couple of decks, refurbished and redecorated for $20 million, and re-christened it the Festivale.

The Italian Line did a major resprucing job on its Marconi and brought it to New York to make Caribbean cruises.

Royal Caribbean, unable to find a ship to its liking, sawed the Song of Norway in half and inserted a new 85-foot-long section into it, adding almost 300 more passenger capacity.

All cruise lines have been considering building entirely new ships, but the cost has been prohibitive; Carnival Cruise has ordered a new 28,000-ton ship to be delivered in late 1981.

In short, few vacations offer as much pleasure and relaxation as a cruise.

CRUISE SHIP TICKETING

Most of the ISPA steamship lines continue to do their own ticketing. Sometimes short cruise travel agents can hold ticket stock and issue the tickets. Most of the Caribbean cruises are commissionable at 10% per person. A travel agent's commission is derived on the base air/sea amount, not on the total amount of the ticket(s) which include the port tax.

The attention of the passenger is specifically directed to the Conditions for Carriage of Passengers as set forth in the Passage Contract Ticket. The acceptance of the ticket constitutes acceptance of those terms and conditions. Among other rights reserved, the line may choose not to accept or retain any person as a passenger. The steamship line's responsibility does not extend beyond their own vessels and before passengers board or whenever passengers leave it, any arrangements made by or for them are at their own risk.

The following are samples of tickets for recent Caribbean cruise as well as selected materials from the voyages.

Sample One

SITMAR CRUISES	PASSAGE CONTRACT TICKET NOT TRANSFERABLE	PASSENGER'S COUPON not good for passage	COUPON 7	SC/ № 501768

SHIP LIBERIAN REGISTRY	VOYAGE Nr.	FROM	TO	SAILING DATE	LOCAL TIME	PIER AND LOCATION
T.S.S. FAIRWIND	PE/204	PEV	PEV	APR08'78	7 PM	2 FT. EVERGLADES

NAME OF PASSENGERS	AGE	NATIONALITY	DECK	ROOM	BED	FARE BASIS	CURRENCY	FARE
STRNAD, MR. J.	A		ACAPULCO	193		I/7		$ 705.00
MRS.	A		ACAPULCO	193		I/7		$ 705.00
			FINAL SITTING					

HOME ADDRESS CRUISES UNLIMITED GROUP AIR/SEA/DCA IT SIT CAR 78	AGENT VALIDATION AGENT CRUISES UNLIMITED TRAVEL CHEVY CHASE, MD. ADDRESS	TOTAL FARE(S) $1410.00
ISSUED IN CONNECTION WITH SHIP - FLIGHT DATE TICKET No. FARE	DATE OF ISSUE	TAXES AND PORT FEES 26.30 GRAND TOTAL $1436.30
ENDORSED TO: DATE: SIGNATURE: VALUE:	SIGNATURE: For SITMAR CRUISES Inc. AS AGENTS ONLY NW	AGENT'S CODE GR-5

IMPORTANT: Passengers should read the terms of this Passage Contract which are incorporated into, and form part of, this Contract which is binding upon the parties by acceptance of same by the Passenger. The terms of this Passage Contract supersede all representations which may have been made by anyone on behalf of the Carrier.

Sitmar Cruise Ticket - FAIRWIND

SITMAR CRUISES, INC.
Passage Contract Ticket Conditions

In these conditions, unless the context otherwise requires, the words « the passenger » or « the passengers » include all persons named on the face hereof or travelling on this ticket and the words « the vessel » include any ship or vessel substituted for the vessel named on the face hereof or to which the passenger may be transhipped; the word « carrier » shall include the vessel, her owner, operator, demise charterer or time charterer if bound hereby.

By acceptance of this Passage Contract Ticket, whether or not signed by him or on his behalf the passenger agrees that in consideration of the passage money paid, the transportation provided for under this contract and the relations between the carrier and the passenger, are subject to the following terms in every possible contingency whenever occurring and even in the event of unseaworthiness of the vessel existing at the inception of the voyage or subsequently.

1) The passenger to whom or to whose agent this ticket is delivered and/or whose agent has paid the fare set out on the face hereof warrants that he has the authority of any other passenger or passengers named on this ticket to accept and does accept on their behalf as well as for himself all the conditions contained in this ticket and agrees to indemnify the carrier against any liability or expense whatsoever the carrier may incur or sustain by reason of any breach of the warranty aforesaid.

2) The fare paid includes the meals on board but no wines and spirits, which may be purchased at moderate prices. Passengers are not allowed to take on board wines, spirits and other liquors for use during the voyage. All government taxes and stamp duties for tickets to be paid by passengers.

3) No passenger who in judgment of the Master or any official of the carrier is or becomes by reason of disease, infirmity (mental or otherwise), or any other cause whatsoever unfit to travel, or is or becomes in need of an attendant but is not accompanied by one, or is or becomes or is likely to be or becomes dangerous or obnoxious to other passengers, shall be entitled to transportation hereunder. Any such passengers may be refused embarkation or be landed or left at any port or place at which the vessel calls without any liability upon the carrier, and without any right of such passenger to a refund of the fare paid or any part thereof.

4) Physician, surgeon or stewardess are not provided on every vessel, but if they are carried their ordinary services are included in the passage money. Passengers who by reason of illness or through any other cause require special attendance or accommodation will be charged extra therefor. Laundry or hairdresser are not provided on every vessel, but if they are carried, their services are not included in the passage money.

5) If by reason of war, strikes, riots or civil commotions, quarantine, ice, orders of any Government or Government Authority or any other cause whatsoever the vessel is unable or the Master or the carrier or in his or their discretion it is considered unsafe or liable to delay the vessel to enter the port of destination or to land the passenger and his baggage there, the passenger and his baggage may be landed at any port or place (before or after the port of destination) at which the vessel calls and thereupon this contract shall be deemed to be fully performed and the carrier's responsibility shall wholly cease. Should the vessel be prevented from sailing at the appointed time, or be delayed for any cause, accidental or otherwise, the carrier shall not be responsibie for the maintenance of the passenger, and the passenger shall in such case, or in the event of the vessel being detained in quarantine, defray his own expenses during such delay or detention, and shall pay to the Master daily US $ 5.- per day for his maintenance on board during the period of such delay or detention.

6) The carrier has liberty without previous notice:

(a) to cancel the contract herein contained at the port of embarkation or at any port returning to the passenger, if the contract is cancelled at the port of embarkation, the fare paid or if the contract is cancelled later a proportionate part thereof;

(b) to delay or cancel any sailing;

(c) to substitute at the port of embarkation for the vessel named on the face hereof any vessel, whether belonging to the carrier of the same class or size or not;

(d) to tranship or land at the port of embarkation or at any stage of the voyage and forward the passenger and/or his baggage at the expense of the carrier but at the sole risk of the passenger to the port of destination by any other vessel, craft or conveyance whatsoever and whether by land, water or air and whether belonging to the carrier or not and by any route direct or indirect.

7) The vessel has liberty to tow and assist vessels in all situations although deviating from the voyage, to proceed by any route whatsoever, to call, stay and return to any port whatsoever (including the port of embarkation), whether in, out or beyond the customary or advertised route to the port of destination, in any order of rotation, once or oftener, for any purpose whatsoever, whether in connection with this, a preceding or subsequent voyage, to sail with or without pilots, to make trial trips, to adjust compasses, to repair or drydock, to sail armed or unarmed in convoy or out of convoy, all as part of the contract voyage and with or without notice and to carry cargo of all descriptions dangerous or otherwise, all as part of the contract voyage.

8) The carrier shall not be liable in any capacity for any loss, damage, delay or injury to any passenger or to his baggage, personal effects or other property, or for the death of any passenger, whether occurring before, during or after embarkation, transit, transfer, discharge, delivery or debarkation arising from any of the following causes, wheresoever and howsoever occurring: The acts of God, perils or accidents of the sea or other waters and of navigation, causes beyond the carrier's control, collision, stranding, jettison or wreck; fire from any cause, barratry of the Master or crew, enemies, pirates, robbers; theft or pilferage by any person, and whether in the employ of the carrier or not; faults or errors in the navigation or management of the vessel; arrest or restraint, capture, seizure, detention, interference of any sort, or any act of princes, rulers, governments or people, or any power, legal process or stoppage in transit; epidemics, pestilence, quarantine, wars, rebellions, hostilities, riots, strikes, lockouts, stoppage of labour troubles of the carrier's employees, or others; shortage or lack of fuel or facilities of any sort; explosions; bursting of boilers, breakage, accidents or derangements of machinery or appurtenances; unseaworthiness whensoever existing, provided the carrier has exercised due diligence to make the vessel seaworthy before sailing; salt or fresh-water, heat, frost, ice, floods, freshets, smell, taint or leakage from other cargo or baggage or damage from stowage or contact therewith; temperature, refrigeration, fumigation, disinfection, moisture; sweat, rain or spray, stains, breakage, chafage, vermin, insufficiency, or absence of marks numbers, addresses or description; transhipment to or from and risk of craft and storage thereon; prolongation of the voyage; giving way, falling or destruction of wharf, shed or warehouse. In addition to but not in substitution for the provisions of this clause, the carrier shall not be liable with respect to any claim whatsoever unless the circumstances giving rise to the claim are due to the negligence of the carrier, and the burden of proving negligence shall be on the party asserting the claim. The carrier shall also be entitled to any exemptions from or limitations of liability provided by the law of the port of discharge or any other state or country, including Sections 4281-4286, inclusive of the Revised Statutes of the United States of America, as circumstances may warrant. Nothing in this contract shall operate to limit or deprive the carrier of any statutory protection or limitation of liability which would have been applicable in the absence of the terms hereinabove set forth.

9) If for any reason whatsoever the passenger is refused permission to land at the port of destination or such port or place as is provided in this contract, the passenger and his baggage may be carried to and landed at any port or place at which the ship calls, or carried back to and landed at the port of embarkation, and shall pay the carrier full fare according to the tariff in use at the time for such further carriage. Such further carriage shall be upon the terms herein contained.

10) If a passenger is landed or lands at any port or place, and the carrier or the vessel, under the law in force there, become liable to pay any sum or sums whatsoever in respect of such passenger or his baggage to the Government having jurisdiction over that port, or Minister of any Department thereof or any Authority, he shall upon demand pay the carrier the amount thereof.

11) Passengers will not be liable to pay, nor entitled to receive any general average contribution in respect of property taken with them on the vessel.

12) This ticket is not transferable and is valid only for the passengers named on the face hereof. In no case whatsoever other than as provided in clause 6 (a) is the carrier liable to make any refund of the fare, whether the vessel or passenger be lost or not or the carriage begun or not. If the passenger does not use this ticket for the ship and date mentioned on the face of it or other vessel

Continued over leaf on page 2

Sitmar Passage Contract Ticket Conditions

substituted or if this ticket is lost or mislaid it is to be considered cancelled and the passage money will be forefeited The carrier retains the right to let unoccupied berths at intermediate ports at which the ship calls.

13) Each adult and half fare paying passenger is allowed, without any extra charge, at carrier's option, baggage restricted to clothing and personal effects. The baggage allowance is that printed in the carrier's tariff. Passengers must plainly label their baggage with names and the port of destination; otherwise the carrier shall not be responsible for any miscarriage or misdelivery thereof.

14) All luggage for which there is no room in the cabin and all luggage in excess carried in the hold, also motor cars, household furniture, animals or birds can be refused by the carrier and only be carried if accepted as cargo on a bill of lading and/or if only a receipt is given according to the conditions of the usual bill of lading against an extra charge to be agreed upon. All arrangements must be made with the carrier or the company or their authorized agents, in writing, prior to shipment.

15) The carrier shall not be liable in any capacity whatsoever for any loss or damage to money, jewelry, precious stones, securities and other valuables, and the articles mentioned in Section 4281 of the Revised Statutes of the United States of America, or mentioned in similar statutes of other states or countries, howsoever and wheresoever occurring, which have not been delivered to and accepted by the carrier for transportation under a bill of lading or which have not been deposited with the Master or ship's officers assigned to that duty for safekeeping and covered by a receipt issued by the Master or such officers. Unless a higher total value and a true description of articles shall be declared in writing to the Master or such officers by a passenger at the time of deposit of such articles, the value thereof shall be taken to be not more than US $ 100.- and any liability of the carrier shall not exceed such sum or the actual value if it be less; any liability for partial loss or damage shall be computed pro rata on such valuation or on the actual total value if it be less. If the actual value of such articles exceeds US $ 100. and is so declared by the passenger and a charge of 1% on such value paid to the carrier, the total value of such articles shall be taken to be the value so declared and any liability of the carrier whatsoever shall not exceed such valuation. Any liability for partial loss or damage shall be computed on such basis or a less actual value if it be less. In no event shall the carrier be liable for more than the damage actually sustained nor for any consequential or special damage and shall have the option of replacing any lost articles or effects and/or replacing or repairing any damaged articles or effects. If the vessel is equipped with boxes or receptacles, which are available, without charge, to passengers for their convenience, it is agreed that whatever effects, property or valuables of whatever description a passenger places in such a box or boxes shall not be deemed delivered to or put in possession of the carrier or deposited with the Master or the vessel's officers as referred to in this contract. It is agreed that the carrier shall not be under any liability whatsoever for loss, conversion of, or damage to such effects, property or valuables from any cause whatsoever even though resulting from the negligence of the carrier, its agents or servants, or any independent contractor or resulting from unseaworthiness of the vessel or because of or during any deviation of the vessel. The passenger represents and warrants and it is agreed that the total value of the effects, property or valuables placed in such box or boxes does not exceed a value of US $ 500.-

16) The fare for transportation under this contract ticket is based partly upon the valuation of the baggage provided for herein. Unless a higher value shall be declared as hereinafter provided, the value of the baggage of a passenger paying full fare, shall be agreed at and taken to be not more than US $ 75. The agreed value of the baggage of a passenger paying less than full fare shall be proportionately less. If the value of the passenger's baggage for any class exceeds the valuation above agreed to and provided for that class and is so declared in writing by the passenger to the carrier and written upon the contract ticket before embarking, and a charge of 1% on such excess value is paid to the carrier, the value of such baggage shall be taken to be not more than the value so declared. An increased valuation will be effective only from the time the payment is made by a passenger. The valuations provided in the second sentence of this clause or such higher value as may have been declared by the passenger or the actual value, if it be less, shall constitute the measure of damage with respect to any loss of, damage to or other claims in connection with the passenger's baggage wheresoever occurring for which the carrier may be liable. Any liability of the carrier for partial loss or damage to the baggage of any passenger shall be computed by taking that percentage of the valuation in the second sentence of this clause, or such higher value as may have been declared and paid for by the passenger, or of the actual value, if it be less, obtained by a comparison of the value of the lost or damaged baggage with the value of the passenger's entire baggage if it all had been delivered undamaged.

17) In the event of any claim for loss of life or bodily injury or of any claim whatsoever except as to those matters covered in clauses 15 and 16 hereof arising from any cause whatsoever for which the carrier may be liable, the damage recoverable by the passenger or by his executors, or legal representatives, or heirs, shall not exceed the sum of US $ 2500.- The carrier shall not be liable in any event whatsoever for more than the actual amount of damages legally proved to have been sustained.

18) The carrier shall not be liable for any claim whatsoever of the passenger, his legal representatives, heirs and howsoever and wheresoever occurring unless written notice thereof with full particulars shall be lodged in writing with the carrier or his agents as follows:

(a) within six (6) months from the day when the death or injury occurred in respect of any claim for loss of life or bodily injury in any case where Section 4283 A of the Revised Statutes of the United States of America shall apply;

(b) within two (2) months after death of the passenger when occurring before landing or when occuring within fifteen (15) days after landing or the abandonment or breaking up of the voyage in respect of any claim for loss of life, except where said Section 4283 A shall apply;

(c) within fifteen (15) days after the passenger shall be landed or the voyage is abandoned or broken up, in respect of any claim whatsoever unless such claim is included within one of the two categories mentioned.

Suit to recover on any claim shall not be maintainable unless commenced and process served as follows: 1. Within one (1) year from the day when the death or injury occurred in respect of any claim for loss of life or bodily injury in any case where said Section 4283 A shall apply; 2. Within six (6) months after the passenger shall be landed from the ship or the voyage shall be abandoned or broken up or after the death of the passenger when occurring before landing, whichever may be the case, in respect of any claim whatsoever unless such claim is included within category 1., just mentioned. Any action by the carrier or its agents or attorneys in considering or dealing with claims shall not be considered a waiver of such requirements.

19) The liability of the carrier is limited to the time the passenger and/or his baggage has been on board of the carrier's steamer or auxiliary vessels. Booking on connecting routes is for the convenience of the passengers, and all money received hereon for transportation on such routes is accepted solely for the accommodation of the passengers, no responsibility of any kind being assumed thereby by the carrier, for any damage in connection with, or incidental to transportation of the passenger, his baggage or property over such connecting route. Passengers booked for transhipment on a connecting line, who cancel their passage on the connecting line or whose transhipment proves to be impracticable, will be paid the amount refunded by such connecting line deducting the expenses incurred. The carrier will not assume any further liabilities in any case.

20) By accepting or receiving this ticket each passenger agrees without prejudice to its other provisions and both on his and her behalf and on the behalf of any person or child travelling with him or her or in his or her care that all rights, exemptions from liability, defences and immunities of whatsoever nature referred to in this ticket applicable to the carrier (which term shall for the purpose of this clause include the Ship-owners, the Line, Charterers, Managers, Operators and the Ship, as the case may be) shall in all respects enure also for the benefit of any servants or agents of the carrier acting in the course of or in connection with their employment so that in no circumstances shall any such servant or agent as the result of so acting be under any liability to any such passenger or to any such person or child greater than or different from that of the carrier. For the purpose of the agreement contained in this clause, the carrier is or shall be deemed to be acting on behalf and for the benefit of all persons who are or may be its servants or agents from time to time, and all such persons shall to this extent be or be deemed to be parties to the contract contained in or evidenced by this ticket.

21) It has been agreed that in case of a lawsuit the courts of London shall be considered competent.

In all cases not expressly otherwise agreed upon in this contract, the English law shall apply. Sitmar Cruises, Inc. vessels are of Liberian registry. If for some reason any of the stipulations of this contract should be inapplicable or of no effect, the validity of all other regulations remain in force.

SITMAR CRUISES INC.

Passage Contract Ticket Conditions (Continuation)

Things You Should Know

Accommodations: You may be interested in knowing why there are differences in fares. A ship's staterooms are rated according to type and location of accommodation. Fares are based on two to a room per person basis. The color brochure describes each type of stateroom.

Alcoholic Beverages: If you wish to have a Bon Voyage party in your stateroom, we can supply alcoholic beverages, ice, glasses, and soft drinks if we are advised one week in advance of sailing. This is a Customs regulation. If we do not have a week's notice, you may bring your own alcoholic beverages aboard. Your room steward will make ice, soft drinks and glasses available to you at nominal prices.

Baby-sitter Service: Arrangements can sometimes be made with your Cabin Steward or through the Purser for this service.

Drain pipe Obstruction: Please do not throw any extraneous objects into wash basins or toilet bowls. It is impossible to repair outboard outlets at sea or in foreign ports.

Electrical Outlets: The ONLY item which you may plug in is an electric razor. Please do NOT use hair dryers, irons, etc.

Foreign Cameras, Jewelry, etc.: If you are bringing with you foreign-purchased items, it is wise to declare these with U.S. Customs prior to boarding. Otherwise, have your sales slips with you as proof of prior purchase.

Rendezvous Lounge/Casino: Casino open ONLY at sea. Roulette, Blackjack, "21" and other games of chance.

Rainbow Lounge: This is the slot machine room...nickel, dime and quarter slot machines are available. This room is open ONLY at sea.

Gift Shop: The fit and duty-free shops aboard ship offer, for sale, alcoholic beverages, cigarettes and many gift items from around the world. There are also sundries for sale. The gift shop is open ONLY at sea. Times are posted for ordering cigarettes and liquor which are then delivered to your stateroom during the last night of your cruise.

Personal Monies: Aboard ship, we accept Travelers Checks and cash. We regret that it is impossible to cash personal checks.

Photographs: PRIOR to sailing, the ships photographer is available to take pictures in black-and-white for your hometown paper at no charge. Simultaneously, he will photograph in color...a nice "bon voyage" momento which you may purchase. For your hometown paper, please fill in the form specifying to which paper you would like the photo sent. We suggest the smaller weeklies, as large metropolitan newspapers very seldom use these photographs. Throughout the trip, the photographer will be taking color pictures which you may purchase. Be sure to get those you want before returning to Miami. Once your cruise is over, the negatives are destroyed.

Safety Precautions: Be sure you do not have fireworks, matches, gunpowder, gasoline, cartridges in your baggage. Do not smoke in bed. Do not throw lighted cigarettes, cigar butts or matches overboard because they may fly into an open window or porthole. Please use ashtrays located throughout the ship. Do not use hair dryers, blowers, irons or other electrical appliances. The only exception is an ELECTRIC RAZOR which may be plugged into the plate indicated in your stateroom.

Ship's Doctor: There is always a qualified physician aboard. For any illness not originating aboard ship, there is a nominal fee for service.

Shore Excursions: Shore excursions are sold aboard ship by the Cruise Director for sightseeing...shopping, and nightclubbing, as agent for the tour operator.

Valet Service: We have limited valet service; ask your room steward or the purser if you wish to have something pressed. We do NOT have cleaning facilities aboard ship.

Valuables: Please give any items of value to the purser for safe keeping. With the many visitors who come aboard, the steamship company cannot be responsible for loss of valuables left in your stateroom.

What to Pack: Dress for most of your cruise aboard or ashore, is casual. You may wear sports clothes throughout the day and for breakfast and luncheon with the exception of bathing suits. For dinner every evening on the s/s Steamship, jacket is requested for the gentlemen. Ladies wear pantsuits or dressy dresses. For the Captain's "Welcome Aboard" cocktail party, jackets are requested for gentlemen and ladies do enjoy dressing in long or short cocktail gowns. The same dress is in order for the Farewell Dinner. We suggest that you do not wear short shorts ashore. Bring walking shoes for comfortable shore excursions and shopping. Wear beach robes over bathing suits when going to the pool or to the beach. The tropical sun is strong and sometimes deceiving because of cool, tropical breezes. Take the sun a little at a time for a smooth, tropical tan.

Food...And More Food...

If you have hurried to arrive at the ship and have skipped luncheon, we serve sandwiches, coffee, tea and cookies prior to sailing. This will tide you over until dinner.

Tss. F A I R W I N D
Captain RODOLFO POTENZONI, Commanding

Welcome Dinner

Sunday, April 9, 1978

IRANIAN CAVIAR ON ICE THRONE

MELBA TOAST   AMERICAN DRESSING

FLAKES CRAB MEAT COCKTAIL

FRESH TROPICAL FRUIT CUP WITH LIME SHERBET

CELERY AND VEGETABLE RELISH TRAY

JELLIED CONSOMME MADRILENA

HOT BEEF TEA PRINCE OF GALLES   CREAM VELOUTE, AGNES SOREL

HOME MADE RAVIOLINI THE BLUE COVE

OCEAN SOLE FILLETS IN CHAMPAGNE SAUCE, FLEURONS

ISLAND ROCK LOBSTER , CARDINALE, RICE PILAW

ROAST CORNISH HEN, MONTMORENCY   GLAZED CALF'S SWEET BREAD, SOUVAROFF

PRIME BEEF TENDERLOIN, DUKE OF WELLINGTON

STEAMED BROCCOLI   BUTTERED GARDEN PEAS   CRETAN POTATOES

WALDORF SALAD

GRAND GATEAUX ST. HONORE   COUPE SULTANE   ITALIAN ASSORTED PASTRIES

W I N E   S U G G E S T I O N

White : Pouilly-Fuisse
         Capri-Scala
         Riesling P. Masson

Red   : Clos de Vougeot '71
         Medoc
         Rubion P. Masson
         Rose' Antinori

Tss. F A I R W I N D
Captain RODOLFO POTENZONI, Commanding

Farewell Dinner

Thursday, April 13, 1978

BELUGA MALOSSOL CAVIAR ON ICE THRONE

AMERICAN DRESSING   MELBA TOAST

HOT BUTTERFLY DEEP FRIED SHRIMPS TARTAR SAUCE

PINEAPPLE RINGS   ST. HUMBERT VENISON PATTY

RELISH TRAY

JELLIED CONSOMME WITH CELERY

DOUBLE ESSENCE OF BEEF, SHERRY FLAVOURED

CHICKEN VELOUTE, QUEEN MARGOT   IMPERIAL OX-TAIL SOUP

COLD WATER BROILED FRESH STURGEON STEAK . LEMON SAUCE

ROCK LOBESTER, ARMORICAINE, PATNA RICE

MILK FED VEAL CHOP, LA BELLE EPOQUE   FRIED CHICKEN SUPREME A LA KIEV

ROAST PRIME RIBS OF BEEF NATURAL GRAVY, YORKSHIRE PUDDING

CORN ON THE COB   BAKED IDAHO POTATOES   STEAMED BROCCOLI

BELLE HELENE SALAD

FLAMING BAKED ALASKA   DELICATE PATISSERIE DES DAMES

SPARKLING WINE

COFFEE

Daily Schedules for Food: Early morning coffee, rolls - pre-breakfast for early risers.

 Full-course breakfast - order as much as you wish.
First sitting: 7:00 AM, Second sitting: 8:15 AM.
Mid-morning bouillon or coffee with crackers.
Full-course luncheon - Hot...cold buffet...a combination.
First sitting: 12:00 noon, Second sitting: 1:30 PM.
You may order from the hot menu, go directly to the cold buffet table and help
 yourself, or combine the two with (as a suggestion) a hot soup, side dishes
 from the cold buffet and a hot main dish...or the reverse.
Afternoon tea - Mid afternoon, coffee, tea and cookies or cake.
Full-course dinner with a different menu nightly.
First sitting:6:00 PM, Second sitting: 8:15 PM.
Late night buffet - 11:30 PM. You may help yourself to anything from just coffee
 to a full course buffet.

Wines and Champagnes: We have a fine list of imported wines and champagnes. To be sure these are properly chilled, we suggest you place your order in advance of dinner with the Wine Steward. He will be available during luncheon to take your requests.

Speical Personal Events: For birthdays, honeymoons and anniversaries, you may want to order a special cake, champagne or wine. These are special events to us, too. Please advise your travel agent or call Passenger Services, prior to your cruise.

Tipping

Tipping is always a personal matter. However, many first-time cruisers are unfamiliar with shipboard tipping. We are, therefore, offering suggested guide-lines.

1. Room Steward - Keeps your stateroom clean; supplies clean towels, soap, ice; turns your bed down at night; takes care of your personal requests for special room service. We suggest $1.00 to $1.50 per day per person.

2. Dining Room Waiter - You will have the same waiter for the entire voyage. He will be serving you three times a day. We suggest $1.50 per day per person.

3. Busboy - Sets and clears your table; keeps you supplied with beverages, dressings, butter, rolls and assists the waiter in serving. We suggest from 75¢ to $1.00 per day per person.

4. Wine Steward - Bartenders, Lounge Waiters - Tip a percentage, just as you would ashore. We regret that we cannot run stateroom tabs as the voyages are too short. We submit charges per drink ordered.

5. Maitre d' - The Maitre d' is there to see that the dining room runs smoothly. If you require special service, he will be happy to take care of your requests. Your tip is your personal thank you for his extra service.

Tipping is usually taken care of the last night to avoid confusion on your morning arrival in Miami.

Debarkation or Going Ashore in Miami

On arrival in Miami the ship must be cleared first by U.S. Immigration. No one may debark the ship until ALL baggage is ashore in the U.S. Customs area. Until the ship is cleared and all baggage put ashore, we suggest you relax in one of the ship's

lounges. Crowding into the lobbies will be uncomfortable for you and will not help you to get ashore any faster. When it is time to leave the ship, an announcement will be made. We regret that we have to ask you to leave your stateroom following break- fast. The stewards must have time to change linens and clean all rooms for the pas- sengers coming aboard at 1 PM. Be sure you have your "Landing Card" available to sur- render to the officer at the head of the gangway.

Proceed to the customs area and to the section where your baggage has been placed. Have your Customs Declaration form filled out and handy for the Customs officer. Be ready to open any and all of your baggage as requested for inspection. When you have been cleared by the Customs officer, be sure you take only your luggage or personal belongings. Many problems arise when passengers accidentally take another person's luggage. Porters are available to assist you in getting your luggage to your trans- portation.

Stella Oceanis - Sun Line Cruises

YOUR FIRST CRUISE

Before Embarking

Immigration Forms, Passports and Visas: Completely fill and SIGN the white U.S. Immigration forms forwarded with your ticket. EACH passenger must submit this form with ticket prior to boarding. United States and Canadian citizens do not need passports or visas. It is recommended that you carry identification such as your driver's license or voter's registration card. Aliens residing in the United States as permanent residents are requested to have their alien registration receipt card, Form 1-151. Non United States and Non Canadian citizens must have their proper passport and visas, plus multiple entry card. Vaccination certificates are not required for re-entry to the United States from the Bahamas

Luggage: Each passenger is permitted 200 lbs. of personal baggage. Please be sure your baggage tags (sent with tickets) are properly marked with your name and stateroom number and affixed to each piece of baggage. Port porters will put your baggage aboard the ship. Ship stewards will place your luggage in your stateroom.

What To Do At Embarkation

Time: Embarkation hours are important; don't miss the sailing of your ship.

Checking Aboard: After giving properly tagged baggage to porters, go to check-in counter in the terminal. Give ticket and immigration forms to steamship line personnel. Now go to your stateroom if your wish.

First night at sea on a Sun Line Cruise.

Dining Room Reservations: only one person in a party need make dining room reservations. There are two seatings for each meal. The seating chosen and the table assigned are for the complete voyage, three meals daily. Reservation tables for the dining room are located on B deck. This lounge is one deck above the Purser's Lobby (where you enter ship in Miami). You may take the stairs one deck up or use the elevator. Please be sure to make dining room reservations. After returning to your room and unpacking or relaxing, it is a good time to familiarize yourself with the ship.

Visitors: Visitors are welcome and boarding passes are available upon request at the check-in counter. We suggest going on a tour of the ship particularly with your guests. For relaxation prior to sailing, the lounges are open and the bars will serve your favorite beverage. Complimentary coffee and finger sandwiches are served. Visitors are requested to leave the ship one hour prior to sailing.

At Sea

Life Boat Drill: Immediately on leaving port, U.S. Coast Guard regulations require that all passengers participate in the Life Boat Drill. You will receive instructions over the Public Address System. The basis for the Drill is to be sure you know how to don a life jacket and to know the location of your boat station. Please read your posted instructions carefully...don your life jacket...and proceed to your station. If you are accompanied by a child, request a child's jacket from your room steward or through the Purser's office.

Landing Card and Immigration Card: Your boarding pass, received at "check-in" is your pass to go from and to the ship. This Card MUST be surrendered when debarking in Miami. You will also receive a Willemstad, Curacao Immigration card aboard ship. This card must be filled out and turned over to your waiter or the ship's Purser before arriving in port.

Shipboard Friends: Friends are made very quickly aboard a cruise ship. If you are travelling alone, you will become part of the action at once. First night out, you have table companions in the dining room. The cruise director has "get-acquainted" programs in which you may participate...or which you may just want to watch. Either way, you will enjoy these sessions which "break the ice." Passengers gather round the swimming pool; deck chairs are complimentary and are not assigned...another spot to make friends.

On board ship relaxing.

Highlights of Main Activities During the Cruise

SUNDAY, APRIL 9, 1978 – AT SEA

Dance Class
Welcome Talk and Port Information
Bingo
Muster Drill for all Passengers
Dance Music and Movie
Captain's Welcome Cocktail Party and Dinner
Showtime and Late Cabaret
Dress: FORMAL

MONDAY, APRIL 10, 1978 – CAP HAITIEN
Arrival: 8.00 a.m. – Departure: 3.00 p.m.

Tours Ashore
Horse Races
Singles Party
Dance Music and Movies
Showtime and Late Cabaret
Ladies Night
Dress: INFORMAL

TUESDAY, APRIL 11, 1978 – SAN JUAN
Arrival: 2.00 p.m. – Departure: 2.00 a.m. (after midnight)

Tours Ashore
Visit to the ship's bridge
Travel talk on Ports
Dance Music and Movies
Dress: INFORMAL

WEDNESDAY, APRIL 12, 1978 - St. THOMAS
Arrival: 8.00 a.m. – Departure: 4.00 p.m.

Tours Ashore
Service Clubs Meeting
Bingo
Masquerade Carnival
Late Cabaret
Dress: INFORMAL or COSTUME

THURSDAY, APRIL 13, 1978 - AT SEA

Bridge Tournament
Ship's tournaments on deck
Visit to the ship's bridge
Gala Kentucky Derby
Showtime and Late Cabaret
Dress: FORMAL

FRIDAY, APRIL 14, 1978 - NASSAU
Arrival: 1.00 p.m. – Departure: 7.30 p.m.

Disembarkation talk and briefing on tipping etc.
Tours ashore
Snowball Bingo
Showtime
Dress: CASUAL

SATURDAY, APRIL 15, 1978
Arrival at Port Everglades, Florida

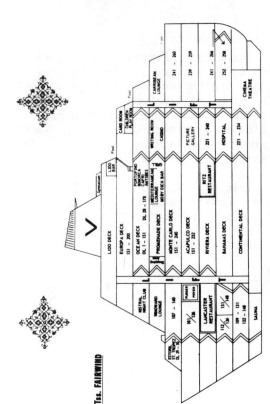

Tss. FAIRWIND

The above advanced program is for general information only and is subject to last minute changes. For detailed events.
Please see "The New on The Wind" which will placed in your cabin every night – Thank You.

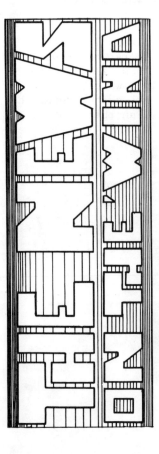

WELCOME ABOARD

Widely known as the "Happy Ship", the FAIRWIND is your floating hotel for the enjoyable days and nights as she sails into balmy tropical waters. Everything about her is designed for carefree vacation living and you are invited to make the most of her spacious decks, pool areas and the beautifully appointed lounges.
Of course the sun and the sea are yours to enjoy during the cruise, just stretch out in your deck chair and let the sun and the seabreezes chase your cares away.

Please feel free to make use of all the facilities made available for your comfort, pleasure and convenience.

Above everything else, it is the "People" who man the "FAIRWIND" who make your dream vacation come true. Attentive cabin stewards and stewardesses to cater to your needs, the gracious restaurant staff who serve in a manner which makes dining a delight, with tempting dishes prepared by master chefs. Also, the friendly personnel in attendance in the public rooms and at the bars will cater to your wishes.

An experienced cruise staff will conduct indoor and outdoor activities inviting your participation and supply top flight entertainment.

On board "FAIRWIND" the emphasis is on ease and comfort, so completely relaxing and unwinding that everything is easy to get used to in no time at all.

Captain Rodolfo POTENZONI, Chief Purser Angelo GHIGGINI, Cruise Director Tony NOICE and his Staff, and the Hospitable Italian Officers and Crew extend sincere wishes for a wonderful Cruise vacation and promise to make this a most memorable vacation.

Today's Activities

SUNDAY, APRIL 9, 1978
Sunrise 5.51 * Sunset 6.12

8.00 a.m.	THE GOLF RANGE OPENS. Come and practice your swing.
9.00 a.m.	CATHOLIC MASS will be celebrated in the Cinema by Rev. Thomas Butler.
9.30 a.m.	MORNING EXCERCISES — Promenade Deck.
9.55 a.m.	HIGHLIGHTS OF THE DAY — Broadcast over P.A. System and on Radio Channel 4.
10.00 a.m.	INTERDENOMINATIONAL DIVINE SERVICE with Rev. Thomas Butler — Cinema.
10.00 a.m.	COMPLIMENTARY DANCE CLASS with Jamie and Jackie — Windward Lounge.
10.00 a.m.	SCRABBLE, CHESS AND CHECKERS TOURNAMENTS in the Mediterranean Lounge.
10.15 a.m.	COMPLIMENTARY GOLF CLINIC with Rick — Promenade Deck, Fwd.
11.00 a.m.	INFORMAL TRAVEL TALK ON OUR APPROACHING PORTS OF CALL. By the Cruise Director, Tony NOICE, plus details on the shore excursions and latest U.S. Customs Information. This will take place in the Windward Lounge and also projected on TV and broadcast on radio channel 4.
2.30 p.m.	ITALIAN LESSON with Georgiana in the Mediterranean Lounge.
2.30 p.m.	PING PONG TOURNAMENT — Meet at the table on the Promenade Deck, Fwd.
2.45 p.m.	BRIDGE MEETING — Interested passengers are invited to join our Bridge Experts, Col. and Mrs Sommers in the Card Room, on Riviera Deck, Fwd.
3.45 p.m.	GENERAL MUSTER OF PASSENGERS FOR EMERGENCY DRILL — In accordance with the International Convention of the Safety of Life at sea, all passengers are obliged to attend this important and compulsory Muster. **Please follow the instruction given by P.A. System.**
4.15 p.m.	AFTERNOON MUSICAL TEA with Dan Lanning at the Piano — Mediterranean Lounge.
4.15 p.m.	B I N G O — Windward Lounge.
4.30 p.m.	SHUFFLEBOARD TOURNAMENT — Meet on Lido Deck.
5.00 p.m. - 8.00 p.m.	TUNE IN ON RADIO CHANNEL 2 FOR SIX HALF HOUR NOSTALGIC MUSIC.
5.00 p.m. - 6.00 p.m.	CALYPSO MELODIES with ''The Calypso Quartet'' in the Caribbean Lounge.
6.00 p.m. - 6.45 p.m.	MUSICAL COCKTAIL TIME
7.45 p.m. - 8.30 p.m.	with ''The Roger James Trio'' in the Caribbean Lounge.
6.00 p.m. Main Sitting 7.45 p.m. Final Sitting	C A P T A I N ' S C O C K T A I L P A R T Y The Master of the vessel, Captain Rodolfo POTENZONI, cordially invites all passengers for Welcome Aboard Cocktails in the Windward Lounge.
7.45 p.m. - 8.45 p.m.	MUSICAL COCKTAIL TIME with Dan Lanning at the Piano in the Mediterranean lounge.
9.00 p.m. - 12.00 Mid.	MUSIC FOR YOUR DANCING with ''The Quintet'' in the Windward Lounge.
9.00 p.m. & 10.45 p.m.	G A L A W E L C O M E S H O W

Starring: DAVID MASTERS ''The Funnyman from Fiddler on the Roof''
JEAN BONARD ''An Enchanting Song-Stylist''
BERNIE FIELDS ''Virtuoso of the Harmonica''
Accompanied by ''The Quintet'' in the Windward Lounge (2nd show also on TV)

10.00 p.m. - 1.30 a.m.	MUSIC FOR DANCING with ''The Roger James Trio'' interludes by ''The Calypso Quartet'' in the Caribbean Lounge.
10.00 p.m. - 12.00 Mid.	PIANO MELODIES with Dan Lanning in the Mediterranean Lounge.
11.00 p.m. - 3.00 a.m.	THE MISTRAL NIGHT CLUB opens. Music by ''The Fair-Ones''
12.30 a.m.	LATE SHOW CABARET Starring: RON MARRIOTT ''A new fashioned song & dance man'' — Music by ''The Fair-Ones''

THE SUGGESTED ATTIRE FOR THIS EVENING IS: F O R M A L
(This applies in all lounges until the wee hours)

TODAY'S MOVIE: The Cinema is situated on the Continental Deck, Aft. Please use aft elevators.

8.30 p.m. & 10.30 p.m. ''THE ONE & ONLY'' Rated: PG Duration: 98 minutes
Starring: Henry Winkler and Kim Darby. (Shown also on TV)

N O T E : There will be a meeting of the NRTA / AARP Group with your escort, Anita, this morning at 10 o'clock in the Mistral Lounge, Ocean Deck, Fwd.

MEDICAL
SERVICE OFFICE : Bahamas Deck, Aft. From: 9.00 a.m. to 11.00 a.m. and from 3.30 p.m. to 5.30 p.m.
CALL ANY TIME — DIAL 700 — NIGHT TIME: ONLY EMERGENCY

N O T E : Our golf range can ONLY be reached by taking the stairway up from Monte Carlo and Acapulco Decks, all the way forward

---

MEAL HOURS

COFFEE FOR EARLY BIRDS will be served on Promenade Deck	6.30 a.m. - 7.30 a.m.
BREAKFAST will be served in both Restaurants	7.30 a.m. - 9.30 a.m.
CONTINENTAL BREAKFAST served in your cabin - Contact your cabin steward	7.30 a.m. - 10.30 a.m.
BOUILLON will be served on Promenade Deck	11.00 a.m.
POOLSIDE SNACK FOR SUN LOVERS with Calypso Quartet - Prom. Deck aft	12.00 noon - 1.30 p.m.
LUNCHEON - MAIN SITTING - will be served in both Retsaurants	12.00 noon
NEAPOLITAN PIZZA will be served in the Grill Promenade Deck, midship	
LUNCHEON - FINAL SITTING - will be served in both Restaurants	2.00 p.m.
AFTERNOON TEA - will be served in the Mediterranean Lounge	1.30 p.m.
WELCOME GALA DINNER MAIN SITTING	4.15 p.m.
WELCOME GALA DINNER FINAL SITTING will be served in both Restaurants	6.45 p.m.
PIZZA - The Grill, Prom. Deck, midship (sorry, pizza is NOTSERVED in the cabin)	8.30 p.m.
MIDNIGHT BUFFET will be served in the Ritz Restaurant, Riviera Deck aft	11.00 p.m. - 2.00 a.m.
SNACKS FOR THE NIGHT OWLS will be served in the Mistral Night Club	12.00 mid - 1.00 a.m.
	1.30 a.m.

ACTIVITIES FOR JUNIORS ''YOUTH CENTRE'' EUROPA DECK AFT - Centre Hours : 9.00 a.m. to 12.00 Midnight

CHILDREN'S PROGRAM :

9.00 a.m.	Meet the counselors and explore the ship
10.00 a.m.	Cartoons
11.00 a.m.	Arts and Crafts- Making Yarn Animals
1.30 p.m.	Supervised Swimming
4.00 p.m.	Ice Cream
4.30 p.m.	Bingo-Win a Prize!
8.30 p.m.	Paper Design
9.30 p.m.	Story Time

TEENAGER'S PROGRAM :

9.00 a.m.	Soda a Go-Go opens
10.00 a.m.	Teen meeting to learn about the ship
11.00 a.m.	Teenage Ping Pong Tournament
1.30 p.m.	Swimming and Pool Games Lido Pool
4.00 p.m.	Ice Cream
4.30 p.m.	Music and Games
8.30 p.m.	Dancing and More!
10.30 p.m.	Late Feature Movie

T.S.S. FAIRWIND

MASTER
Captain RODOLFO POTENZONI C.S.L.C.

S H I P ' S   S T A F F

Staff Captain
DOMENICO TRINGALE

Chief Purser
ANGELO GHIGGINI

Chief Engineer
GIORGIO DORIGO

Staff Engineer
ANTONIO VAUDO

Chief Surgeon
FILIBERTO ZADINI M.D.

H O T E L   D E P A R T M E N T

Chief Steward
UGO BENEDETTI

Chief Cabin Stewards
FRANCO ROSSINI
ROBERTO PORCELLA

Maitre d'Hotel
MARIO ANSELMI

C R U I S E   S T A F F

Cruise Director
TONY NOICE

Social Directress/Director
GEORGIANA MAGOLIE
JUDI BARLOWE
RICK ADAMS
BERNIE FIELD

Children's Co-ordinator
MAUREEN RICKER

Asst. Cruise Director
RON MARRIOTT

Children's Counselors
ALICE WELCH
CYNTHIA RUTKOWSKI
PENNY CRADDOCK
PAULINE PAPLAS

Dance Team
HENRY & MARIA HOFFMAN

Piano Vocalist
NICK MESSINA

Entertainers
DAVID MASTERS
JEAN BONARD
KAY CAROLE
JAMIE & JACKIE McVICAR

Bridge Lecture
COL. AND MRS SOMMERS

Catholic Chaplain
BUTLER Rev. THOMAS

Ship's Orchestras
''THE QUINTET''
THE FAIR-ONES
ROGER JAMES TRIO
CALYPSO QUARTET

SHORE TOURS

T.S.S. FAIRWIND — **SITMAR CRUISES**

CAP HAITIEN, Haiti

CITADELLE ADVENTURE TOUR

Departure: 8.30 a.m.
Duration: 6 hours
Price: Mule Only $17.00
Car/Mule $25.00

Tour begins with 30 minute scenic drive through the town of Cap Haitien and into the picturesque countryside. First stop is the village of Milot and the ruins of Regal Sans Souci Palace, built by King Henri Cristophe. You then proceed to the Citadelle, one of the greatest fortresses built in the Western Hemisphere. To get to the top of the 3,000 foot-high-peak where the fortress is located, you can ride on horse/mule back from Milot or you can travel partway by station wagon or jeep and then finish the journey by horse or mule. The Citadelle is a fantastic feat of engineering. Built in the early 1800's at a cost of 20,000 lives, the fortress was Cristophe's safeguard against an attack by Napoleon. Included in the tour are transportation, a picnic lunch and guide service. Participation Limited

SAN SOUCI PALACE TOUR

Departure: 8.30 a.m.
Duration: 3½ hours
Price: $10.50

This tour takes you on a delightful journey into the past. The first step is a drive past ruins of a French-built rampart, Pauline Bonaparte's Castle and Fort Magny. Next is the Iron Market, the native "Shopping Center". Then a scenic drive to milot, and the ruins of King Henri Cristophe's Sans Souci Palace. The Return route includes the Vertieres battlefield, where the French were finally ousted by the natives: Toussaint-Louverture, the College of Notre Dame, with its spectacular view of the city and harbor and the Cathedral, built at the end of the 17th century and restored in 1942. The tour ends at the handicraft place, near the wharf, for shopping.

CORMIER BEACH TOUR

Departure: 8.30 a.m.
Duration: 4 hours
Price: $12.00

Colorful native "Tap-Tap" buses takes you along a dirt road through the town of Cap Haitien and past typical Haitian landscape to Cormier Beach. Here on the secluded and unspoiled sand beach you can beachcomb, go for a swim or simply lie back and enjoy a boxed picnic lunch provided by the ship. A bar, set up on the beach will serve complimentary rum punch and soft drinks. An interesting way to see a Haiti that the average tourist doesn't see. On the return trip to the ship, you can stop at the native market for shopping and browsing. Participation limited.

CITY TOUR AND FOLKLORIC SHOW

Departure: 10.00 a.m.
Duration: 4 hours
Price: $14.00

Haitian architecture, landscapes, history and folkloric arts are all wrapped up in one neat package on this tour. The architecture reflected in many of the town's buildings, is stamped with a distinct 18th century style. Land-

scape are uniquely Haitian - ranging from tropical to high desert. History is everywhere. There are ruins of French ramparts, Castle and forts, a battlefield monument at Vertieres, the Cathedral, and the College of Notre Dame. You will be treated to the folkloric arts during a rum punch Back Home for a luncheon buffet, spiced with a rumpark. Here, you will see a typically Haitian floorshow. Participation Limited.

SAN JUAN, Puerto Rico

CITY TOUR OF OLD AND NEW SAN JUAN

Departure: 2.30 p.m.
Duration: 2½ hours
Price: $7.00

A comprehensive tour of the new city and of San Juan's famous historical landmarks. Highlights include a complete tour of El Morro Fortress, key historical landmarks in the old city, University of Puerto Rico.

EL YUNQUE RAIN FOREST / LUQUILLO BEACH

Departure: 2.30 p.m.
Duration: 3½ hours
Price: $9.00

This tour begins with a fascinating drive to the central northeast part of the island. The route winds through typical towns and villages before arriving at El Yunque Rain Forest, located in the Luquillo mountain range. The Rain Forest at an elevation of 3,000 feet, features jungle-like vegetation, wild orchids, waterfalls and panoramic views. Following a stop for refreshments, the tour continues to beautiful Luquillo Beach. There are ample opportunities for photography at both the Rain Forest and Luquillo Beach. Participation limited.

NIGHT CLUB TOUR

Departure: 9.30 p.m.
Duration: 3½ hours
Price: $17.00

San Juan's Night Life is sensational, with colorful shows and star performers appearing nearly year round. This tour features an evening at one of SanJuan's exciting nightclubs. The tour includes transportation to and from the pier, admission to the club and a reserved seat for the show, two drinks of your choice, gratuites for the waiter and admission to the Club's Casino. Participation limited.

CHARLOTTE AMALIE, ST. THOMAS U.S., V.I.

City and Island Tour

Departure: 8.30 a.m.
Duration: 2 hours — Price: $6.50

Spectacular views highlight this tour through the bustling City of Charlotte Amalie, past Bluebeard's Castle Hotel to Drake's Seat, overlooking Magen's Bay. Final destination is Mountain Top Hotel for a panoramic view and a panoramic view of Freebooter's Passage and the island below. Native paintings are on sale at the Hotel. There is ample time for duty-free shopping in Charlotte Amalie at the end of the tour. Transportation: Minibuses.

Island of St. John's Land and Sea Tour

Departure: 8.30 a.m.
Duration: 4 hours
Price: $15.00

This tour begins with 20 minutes surrey ride to Red Hook and then a ferry trip to the village of Cruz Bay the main town of St. John. From there, you will be taken on a drive through beautiful National Park, past Carnel Bay Plantation, to Trunk Bay, one of the ten most beautiful beaches in the world. The beach is an ideal setting for a swim, sunbathing, swimming. Included on the tour is a delicious rum punch. There is ample time at the conclusion of the tour for duty free shopping in Charlotte Amalie. Transportation: Minibuses

Coral World Island Tour

Departure: 8.30 a.m.
Duration: 3 hours
Price: $13.50

This excursion is an indepth tour of St. Thomas with the highlight being the Coral Word Underwater Observatory and Marine Gardens. Passengers enjoy a scenic 15 mile drive with many picture-taking stops. Guides explain the sights and speak of the history, culture, and colorful traditions of the Virgin Islands. A 1½ hour visit to the Marine Park of Coral World where your visitors are again guided through this unique attraction. Return for the shopping of St. Thomas is along a picturesque mountain run including Skyline Drive overlooking the town of Charlotte Amalie

Scuba Adventure

Departure: 9.00 a.m.
Duration: 3 hours — Price: $25.00

One of the most exciting views of the "American Paradise" is from beneath the sparkling surface of the Caribbean. Expertly qualified staff members will pick-up passengers at the ship and give one hour of classroom instruction. From there, it's off to one of the spectacular coral reefs, teeming with fish for a never-to-be-forgotten adventure. Close supervision at all times, small classes and diving groups, and personal attention are part and parcel of this tour. The price includes round-trip transportation, instruction and all equipment.
Transportation: Minibuses.

Kon Tiki Raft

Departure: 9.30 a.m.
Duration: 2½ hours — Price: $13.50

Passengers are met shipside by the fabulous Kon Tiki built to accour like the original Kon Tiki Raft, this Kon Tiki was designed and constructed in the Caribbean specifically to cater for cruise ship tours. Kon Tiki leave shipside with her steelband playing. Cruising gently past Bluebeards Hill, Blackbeards Castleand the bustling town of Charlotte Amalie the Captain introduces himself over the speaker system, inform everyone of all the facilities available and points out highlights and places of interest as they pass by. Photographers take advantage of the open upper deck to get their shots. The other guests help themselves to unlimited quantities of Rum Punch from the bottomless barrels. Stopping over a reef behind Water Island, the glassbottomed

tanks are lowered and Kon Tiki drifts lazily to the Oo's and Aa's of the passengers as they watch the underwater world slide past. Nudging into a small pier on a palm fringed beach everyone disembarks to swim, laze or beachcomb for shells. Cruising back past Hassel Island Limbo is announced and passengers are treated to a display of this island speciality. An hilarious time is had from there on as the Captain gets passengers to participate. The tour usually ends with a rousing "The Saints Come Marching Home" and everyone doing the conga around the decks.

NASSAU, Bahamas

NASSAU CITY AND ARDASTRA GARDENS TOUR

Departure: 2.30 p.m.
Duration: 2½ hours
Price: $8.50

Leaving the dock area this tour proceeds via Bay Street, the shopping center of Nassau, past the famous British Colonial Hotel to Fort Montague built in 1741 and held by the U.S.A. for a few days some 35 years later. Next is the Queen's Staircase a 102 foot high limestone staircase named because its 66 steps angled steps number the years of Queen Victoria's reign. It is said that these steps were carved out of the rock by slave to provide an escape route from nearby Fort Fincastle. A stop is then made at Fort Charlotte to view its ancient dungeons. A spectacular panorama of Nassau unfolds from this point. You then will be driven to the beautiful Emerald Beach Hotel and to the flamingo show in the Ardastra Gardens, where trained pink flamingos perform Ardastra Gardens, where trained pink flamingos perform.

NASSAU CITY TOUR WITH SEAFLOOR AQUARIUM

Departure: 2.30 p.m.
Duration: 2½ hours
Price: $8.50

Your tour begins with a drive past the colorful Straw Market in Rawson Square and then along Bay Street, Nassau's main street. A sightseeing highlight in the Queen's Staircase a 102 foot high limestone staircase named because its 66 steep-angled steps number the years of Queen Victoria's reign. Next is a visit to Fort Fincastle and the Water Tower which offers a representative collection of the under-water life found in the tropical Bahamian seas. The Aquarium's Bahamian Lagoon features a replica of Columbus' ship Santa Maria. Highlight of this visit is at the show staged at the Dolphin Stadium.

HARBOR AND ISLAND CRUISE BY CATAMARAN

Departure: 2.30 p.m.
Duration: 3 hours
Price: $10.00

"Tropic Bird" a beautiful 85 foot catamaran takes you from Prince George wharf for a cruise through the picturesque harbor where private vessels and blockade runners of the past are anchored. While cruising a fascinating around and around Paradise Island, you can sunbathe on the broad deck, relax in the shade and listen to the music of the island's alias steel band. Blackbeards a stop for this lovely cruise include historic Fort Montague and the beautiful blue water of the harbor. The tour includes a scenic stop at one of the beaches in the underwater world for swimming or beachcombing. You may change to swimsuits on board the "Tropic Bird". Participation Limited

CRUISE ADVISORY

Recent years have active and sparkling periods for the cruise industry. In 1978 nine new ships entered the North American steamship market. The most spectacular arrival as well as departure was the S.S. AMERICA. On its inaugural cruise to nowhere June 30, the vessel was heavily overbooked and about 250 passengers were ferried from the ship to Staten Island in the pre-dawn hours of July 1. The second cruise, July 3, encountered bad weather and massive breakdowns of the ship's plumbing system. The U.S. Customs Service fined the owners nearly $500,000 for irregularities in the two voyages; Public Health Service gave the ship a sanitation inspection score of six; New York State's attorney general launched an investigation and intervened to make sure passengers got refunds; more than a dozen suppliers slapped liens against the ship; and crew members charged that the line had left them without money or tickets to get home.

The ship was sold back to Chandris at auction August 28 for $1,010,000. Chandris promptly brought the ship back to Piraeus, Greece for refurbishing and cruises in the Mediterranean.

Several cruise ships based and/or regularly calling in Miami (and New York) have failed to pass U.S. Public Health Service inspections. Violations include: dirty dishes in storage compartments, infestations of roaches and weevils in food areas, and improperly treated drinking water. Ships that still have not passed inspection include the Carnivale, Rotterdam, Atlas, Vera Cruz I, Istra, Renaissance, Canberra, and Queen Elizabeth II. Ships that failed previous inspections but passed this year were the Engelina Lauro, Caribe, Carla C., Eugenio C., Federico C., Leondardo da Vinci and Sun Viking. Other ships that have failed include Australis, Doric, Kungsholm and Rotterdam, with some of the lowest scores going to Australis, Atlas, Doric, Istra, Kungsholm and Rotterdam. Ships passing their most recent inspections with high or perfect scores are Angelina Lauro, Fairwind, Italia, Royal Viking Sea, Royal Viking Star, Vistafjord and Federico C. Some ship lines disagree with the importance of the inspections, which do not accurately represent the cleaniness of their ships.

MONTHLY SUMMARY OF VESSEL SANITATION INSPECTIONS PERFORMED DECEMBER 1978

Name of Vessel	Date Last Insp.	Meets Standard (85-100)	Does Not Meet Standard (0-84)	Name of Vessel	Date Last Insp.	Meets Standard (85-100)	Does Not Meet Standard (0-84)
Achille Lau.	03/06/78		X	Oceanic	10/28/78	X	
Amerikanus	03/03/78	X		Odessa	10/17/78		X
Angelina Lauro	10/20/78	X		Oriana	12/07/78		X
Aquarius	12/18/78		X	Pacific Princess	12/30/78	X	
Boheme	10/21/78	X		Princess Patricia	07/28/78	X	
Britanis	12/24/78		X	Prinsendam	07/20/78	X	
Canberra	09/15/78		X	Queen Elizabeth II	12/21/78		X
Caribe	12/30/78		X	Rotterdam	12/19/78	X	
Carla C	07/29/78		X	Royal Viking Sea	11/16/78	X	
Carnivale	12/24/78	X		Royal Viking Sky	12/06/78	X	
Cunard Countess	09/08/78	X		Royal Viking Star	10/19/78	X	
Cunard Princess	10/04/78	X		Sagafjord	11/04/78	X	
Dalmacija	12/30/78		X	Santa Magdalena	09/16/78		X
Danae	02/18/78		X	Santa Maria	10/25/78	X	
Daphne	03/09/78		X	Santa Mariana	12/06/78	X	
Doric	12/20/78		X	Santa Mercedes	12/03/78	X	
Emerald Seas	10/06/78	X		Skyward	12/23/78	X	
Enna G	11/21/78		X				
Eugenio C	11/24/78		X				
Europa	12/29/78		X				
Fairsea	12/16/78	X					
Fairwind	10/18/78	X					
Federico C	12/27/78		X				
Festivale	12/16/78		X				

FREIGHTER TRAVEL

The idea of a freighter trip to a Middle East port might be enough to spark fantasies in most minds but the possibility is remote, unless your time and funds can afford it. An around-the-world freighter is at least $7,000 per person and might require six months. A freighter is principally engaged in the transportation of goods which is licensed to carry a maximum of 12 passengers, and cruise between 16 and 23 knots. Freighters are frequently described as a quiet, restful world of travel away from stress and strain of everyday living.

Some people travel on a freighter because it is an opportunity for complete relaxation and leisure time. There are no crowds, only 12 passengers; no planned entertainment or formal attire. Passengers learn the operation of the ship and dine with (and know) the ships officers. Freighters call at off beat ports. The low cost of a freighter is an attractive feature. The accommodations are usually midship and spacious, and are smoother sailing than cruise vessels.

Freighter travel is not for passengers with health problems; or families with children. Freighter travel does not provide a luxury cruise service. Freighters are for individuals who do not require a lot of other people around them and for people who love the sea. Schedules and itineraries are not strictly adhered to. The time spent in port is contingent upon the volume of cargo to be loaded and discharged, and the ports of call themselves are dependent upon cargo bookings and subject to change without notice. The usual ports are in Mexico, Guatemala, El Salvador, Honduras, Nicaragua, Panama, Spain, Italy, Greece, Turkey, Lebanon, India, Sri Lanka, Singapore, Hong Kong and Japan.

Some travel agencies specialize in booking passengers on freighters; travel agents generally are not equipped with the information required to book freighters and do not take the time it takes to obtain a complete booking, i.e., three years in advance. Each year about 100 foreign cargo vessels are sailing from United States ports and these ships have accommodations for more than 1,300 passengers.

The United States shipping companies that continue to take passengers aboard cargo vessels from New York area are Farrell Lines, with sailings to Australia, Africa and Northern Europe; Delta Steamship Lines, with sailings to the west coast of South America, Moore-McCormack, which serves the east coast of South America and Africa, and Kerr Steamship Corporation for West Coast departure on the United Yogoslav lines. Freighter trade publications are: "Trip Log Quick Reference Freighter Guide", "Traveltips Freighter Bulletin", and "Freighter Travel News". Travel agents may want to consult the monthly edition of OFFICIAL STEAMSHIP GUIDE for freighter listings. Another source is FORDS FREIGHTER TRAVEL GUIDE which attempts to furnish reliable information about these vessels, their passenger services and trips from all ports of the world. FORDS FREIGHTER TRAVEL GUIDE includes a "Ports of Call Index" for freighter passenger services in order to find services between any 2 ports, i.e., look for the names of steamship lines that are common to both ports. FORDS also lists passenger carrying freighter services, such as, schedules, accommodations listed in geographical sections according to port of origination, and cargo passenger liner services (over 12 passengers).

Chapter 10

RAIL TRAVEL

In 1976, over 270 million people rode railroads in America and modern day rail travel is frequently as attractive as airline transportation; i.e. far less costly and can be faster than air service between cities.

Travel Mode Comparisons
WASHINGTON, D.C. TO PHILADELPHIA, PA.

AIR			RAIL		
EXPENSE		TIME	EXPENSE		TIME
TAXI TO TERMINAL	$ 4.50[1]	20 min.[1]	TAXI TO STATION	$ 1.10[1]	10 min.[1]
AIR FARE (COACH)	35.00[2]	55 min. FLIGHT TIME[2] / 30 min. IN TERMINAL	METROLINER COACH	15.50[4]	102 min. CITY TO CITY[4] / 10 min. IN STATION
TAXI TO DESTINATION	8.10[3]	30 min.[3]	TAXI TO DESTINATION	3.50[3]	10 min.[3]
	$47.60	135 min. *(2 hr. 15 min.)*		$20.10	132 min. *(2 hr. 12 min.)*

WASHINGTON, D.C. TO NEW YORK, N.Y.

AIR			RAIL		
TAXI TO TERMINAL	$ 4.50	20 min.	TAXI TO STATION	$ 1.15	10 min.
AIR FARE (SHUTTLE)	41.00	55 min. FLIGHT TIME / 10 min. IN TERMINAL	METROLINER COACH	26.00	198 min. CITY TO CITY / 10 min. IN STATION
TAXI TO DESTINATION	10.00	50 min.	TAXI TO DESTINATION	3.00	15 min.
	$55.50	135 min. *(2 hr. 15 min.)*		$30.15	233 min. *(3 hr. 53 min.)*

[1] Capitol Cab, Washington D.C.
[2] Allegheny Airlines
[3] Yellow Cab, Philadelphia, Pa.
[4] AMTRAK

Time & Taxi Fare Computations By GSA & Small Business Committee

In 1971, the Congress mandated passenger service on thirteen major railroads, joined together under the AMTRAK arrow, creating for the first time in history a single centrally-managed nationwide intercity rail system. The following railroads are providing services for the National Railroad Passenger Corporation ("Amtrak") under contract:

Atchison, Topeka and Santa Fe Railway Company;
Baltimore and Ohio Railroad Company;
Burlington Northern Inc.;
Chesapeake and Ohio Railway Company;
Chicago, Milwaukee, St. Paul & Pacific Railroad Company;
Consolidated Rail Corporation;
Illinois Central Gulf Railroad;
Louisville and Nashville Railroad Company;
Missouri Pacific Railroad Company;
Norfolk and Western Railway Company;
Richmond, Fredericksburg and Potomac Railroad Company;
Seaboard Coast Line Railroad;
Southern Pacific Transportation Company;
Union Pacific Railroad Company.

The purpose of this contract was to stop the twenty-year decreasing train ridership, and to improve and develop intercity rail travel facilities. The goal of AMTRAK is to provide the public with another option for convenient travel.

The AMTRAK corporation, established on a "for-profit" basis, is financed by revenues from the "fare box" (fare collected) and by federal credits. The staff is made up not only of experienced railroad people but also of individuals from the aerospace, airline, shipping, travel agencies, and other related fields.

AMCAFE

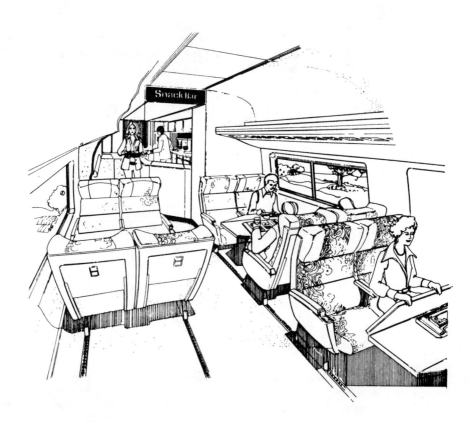

In the Amcafe and Amclub cars, seats are divided by a large food service bar in the center of the car. The food service centers contain two microwave cooking and holding ovens, refrigerators, freezers, soda dispensers, storage cabinets, cash register and other innovative features. One end of the car contains men's and women's washrooms, with special facilities and assist bars for handicapped passengers. Room has been provided in each Amcafe for wheelchairs.

AMTRAK has grown substantially since it began operations in 1971. The number of AMTRAK routes has increased from 25 to 40, the number of trains per week is up 20 percent, and the train miles per week are up 40 percent. AMTRAK carried 19.2 million passengers in 1977 compared to 16.6 million in 1972, an increase of only 15.6 percent. The bus companies carried total passengers of about 340 million, but their intercity passengers are probably around 70 million and they have been going down, so there is something to be said about this shift in passenger service, passenger preference. According to the numbers, 86 percent of all intercity passenger-miles are in an

automobile, airlines now carry about 11 percent of those passenger-miles, and the rest of them go to the buses, AMTRAK and some Waterways.

AMTRAK believes social environmental benefits such as safer intercity travel, improved and more convenient services to the public, lower fuel consumption, and lower air pollution in highly populated areas justify the economic cost of rail passenger service. These benefits depend on increased ridership. For example, a train can be fuel efficient when heavily loaded and moving over relatively long distances, but. AMTRAK is not fuel efficient because it does not carry enough passengers.

Fuel Efficiency and Safety of Major Intercity Transportation Modes

	Passenger-miles per gallon fuel*	Fatalities per 10,000,000,000 passenger-miles**
Bus	116	3
AMTRAK	56	1
Automobile	40	140
Airlines	20	6

*1976.
**3-yr average (1974-76).

The above illustrates the relative fuel efficiency of different transportation modes. AMTRAK's passenger loads are not likely to go up unless a disruption occurs in another transportation mode.

AMTRAK's 7-year experience shows conclusively that under current conditions, all but about 1 percent of intercity travellers in the United States prefer other modes of transportation. Air travel is much quicker and more convenient for time-sensitive travellers, smoother and more comfortable, especially considering the comparatively short time the traveller occupies the airplane, and, on longer trips, air travel is in the same price range as AMTRAK.

Buses go more places than AMTRAK, and bus travel is somewhat cheaper. Automobiles give travellers more control over where and when they go, are convenient to have at the destination points, and are perceived as being much cheaper than the train, particularly when more than one traveller is involved. These factors are illustrated in the following table:

AMTRAK Fares on Potential Corridor Routes Compared With Other Transportation Modes

	Fare necessary for AMTRAK to break even	AMTRAK	Bus	Air*	Automobile	
					Full cost	Incremental cost
Chicago to Milwaukee	$38.85	$ 6.25	$ 5.50	$25.00	$14.45	$ 4.25
Chicago to Detroit	29.80	20.50	**21.40	40.00	47.43	13.95
Los Angeles to San Diego	14.45	9.00	8.35	11.45	21.76	6.40

*Lowest existing day coach fare.
**Round trip ticket reduces 1-way cost by approximately 5 percent.

Under current conditions, AMTRAK cannot offer most intercity travellers a service that is as good as the available alternatives.

The exception that seems to prove the rule is the northeast corridor, where the train offers comparatively high speed, low fares, and where the major cities along the route have adequate public transportation minimizing the convenience value of the automobile.   In 1977, Northeast corridor operations accounted for 57 percent of AMTRAK's total ridership, 31 percent of AMTRAK's revenues and only 24 percent of AMTRAK's costs.

AMCOACH

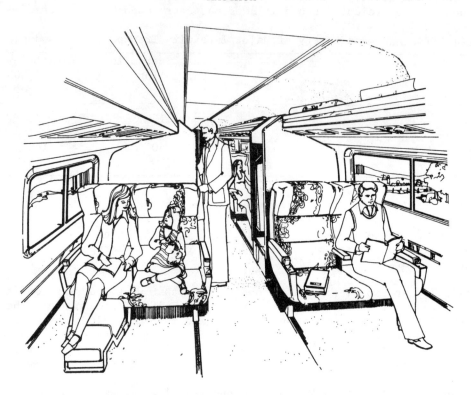

All Amfleet cars have variable interiors. Seats can be added or removed for short or long-distance travel. Amcoach seats are fully reclining, with two seats on either side of the aisle. Each seat is equipped with a center arm rest, a fold down table and individually controlled reading lights. Personal belongings may be conveniently placed in an overhead luggage rack.

Everyday over hundreds of AMTRAK trains arrive and depart from over 545 locations coast-to-coast. Travelling around the AMTRAK nationwide system you will find:

Equipment: AMTRAK owns approximately 2,000 cars and 330 locomotives. Since 1971 Amtrak has received 557 new cars with 284 more on order for delivery. With few exceptions, all rolling stock on the trains is AMTRAK owned.

New Trains: A fleet of nearly 500 Amfleet cars serves most short distance routes between major cities in the East, Midwest and West. They also have 13 modern Turboliners serving New York State and a number of lines in the Midwest. On order are double-decked Superliners for many of the long-distance western routes.

Stations: AMTRAK has constructed seventeen new stations in the past seven years; three new stations have been completed and opened for business - Miami, Flordia; Canton, Ohio; and Rochester, New York. System-wide, most of the stations are owned by operating railroads but maintained for passenger service at AMTRAK expense.

Personnel: All on-board service employees (in food service, sleeping cars and coach cars) are AMTRAK employees. Conductors and engineers are still employees of operating railroads. Many station employees in large stations work for AMTRAK but in smaller stations are operating railroad employees performing passenger duties on a part-time basis.

Operations and Track: AMTRAK operates neither freight nor commuter trains. Outside the Northeast Corridor, between Washington and Boston, AMTRAK owns virtually no mainline track and contracts with twenty operating railroads for actual movement of passenger trains. These railroads (such as the Sant Fe, Seaboard Coast Line and Illinois Central Gulf) operate no other intercity passenger service and are primarily freight railroads. They are responsible for maintenance of tracks and dispatching of trains. While AMTRAK has incentive contracts with many operating railroads to reward good on-time performance, it has no direct authority over the day-to-day operation of its passenger trains on the railroad. Auto-Train is a separate, privately-owned corporation operating between the Northeast and Florida.

Northeast Corridor: AMTRAK owns and maintains the Northeast Corridor between Washington and Boston, including branches to Springfield and Harrisburg. It is presently undergoing a $1.6 billion rehabilitation and improvement program which allow 120 MPH speeds by 1981. Over 50% of AMTRAK's passengers come from the Northeast Corridor.

Toll-free Reservations: AMTRAK has one of the world's most modern and extensive systems; phone toll-free anywhere in the nation. It provides information and reservations on a 24-hour basis for all of AMTRAK's 27,000-mile system.

The energy crisis in America will continue to divert many car passengers to this economical means of transportation. Because of this fact and the high commission percentage you can earn on each ticket, it is imperative for a Travel Agent to be able to function as an active AMTRAK agent.

FOR THE FUTURE—HIGH LEVEL CARS

Each car will have center entrance doors, with a stairway to the upper level. Passage through the train would be through the upper level in the coach cars.

TRAVELLING BY TRAIN

<u>Things You Should Know About AMTRAK</u>

Reservations are required for all club and sleeping car accommodations. Reservations are required for coach travel on all Metroliners, and on all trains indicated in this timetable as "All-Reserved" trains. Coach reservations are available on certain other trains as shown in the Services listings. A time limit for purchase of tickets will be assigned when reservations are confirmed; if not purchased within this period, reservations will be cancelled. Passengers with reservations whose travel plans change should cancel them as soon as possible. A service charge will be assessed if reservations are cancelled less than 30 minutes prior to scheduled train departure, or if not cancelled. AMTRAK trains are operated in four time zones - Eastern, Central, Mountain and Pacific. All schedules in the timetable are presented in prevailing local time.

AMTRAK encourages handicapped, elderly and other passengers who need special assistance in stations or on board trains to call the toll-free reservation number in advance of travel. Whether it's assistance with baggage, with a wheelchair, boarding a train, or special food service, we will be better able to help you if we have advance notice of your travel plans.

Coach tickets purchased at regular fares allow travellers to stop over anywhere along their route at no additional charge, so long as they reach the final destination before their ticket expires. Stopovers do not apply to Metroliner tickets. Ask your ticket or travel agent to provide separate coupons to and from the stopover point. If travelling in reserved coach, club car or sleeping car accommodations, make your initial reservation only to the point of stopover and then make separate reservations onward from that point. (In the case of club or sleeping car accommodations, this will cause charges slightly higher than for passengers travelling through, since separate charges will apply to and from stopover point.)

For the convenience of our passengers, AMTRAK timetables show many rail and motor coach services providing connections to various points not served by AMTRAK. These schedules represent the most current information available to us at the time of publication; however, they are not guaranteed and are subject to change. Also, motor coach schedules shown herein are condensed - in many cases, other trips are operated in addition to those shown, and service is available to intermediate points.

There is a 25 cents additional charge for tickets bought aboard trains when passengers board at stations where ticket offices are open at departure time. Excursion and round-trip tickets, also most discounted tickets, must be purchased before boarding at ticket offices or from your AMTRAK travel agent, unless the ticket office at your boarding stations is closed at departure time.

The Interstate Commerce Commission has issued Rules concerning the quality of intercity rail passenger service. Some of the Rules are summarized below:

Reservations (Rules 3, 4 and 5): If you hold paid reservations for accommodations which are not available, you are entitled to relief. The carrier must try to provide you with equal or better accommodations if they are available. Some other type of assistance may be required in some circumstances, such as food and shelter while you wait for a later train.

Performance of Trains (Rule 6): If a train arrives more than 30 minutes late (less for certain trains under 500 miles) where safe operation would have permitted

earlier arrival, you may be entitled to relief. If the late train causes you to miss a connecting train, plane, or bus, you should receive food and shelter until you can resume your trip.

Cancellation en route (Rule 9): If your train is terminated en route, you are entitled to alternate service, food and shelter.

Stations (Rule 12): With certain exceptions, stations must be open for a sufficient time before departure (and after arrival) of a train, and must have adequate lighting, restrooms, telephones and train information availability.

Baggage (Rules 13 and 16): On trains offering checked baggage service, the carrier must deliver checked baggage within 30 minutes after arrival. If it fails to do so, it must forward baggage to you at carrier's expense.

Food and Beverages (Rule 17): Complete meals must be available during normal meal hours. Full dining service must be available on trains which travel 12 hours or more.

Coaches (Rules 18 and 20): Coaches must have drinking water and clean restrooms. Leg or foot rests, reclining seats, and clean pillows must be provided on most overnight trains. Room temperature must be between 60 and 80 degrees F.

Smoking (Rule 21): Smoking is not permitted except in designated cars or in designated areas of cars. Pipe and cigar smoking is not permitted except in private sleeping car compartments and in cars which have been designated as smoking cars in their entirety.

The schedules, services and fares shown in this timetable are subject to change without notice. AMTRAK cannot accept liability for inconvenience, expense or damage resulting from errors in the timetable, shortages of equipment or delayed trains, except when such a delay causes a passenger to miss a reasonable connection.

Future Diner

AMTRAK ACCOMMODATIONS

Sleeping cars contain private sleeping-rooms [Roomettes (one bed), Bedrooms (two beds), and Drawing Rooms (three beds)], each room having its own beds with full bedding, and its own toilet and washbasin. Unlike in Europe and other continents, persons travelling alone are not assigned beds in rooms containing more than one bed unless they purchase the entire room.

Roomettes, Bedrooms and Drawing Rooms are described below. AMTRAK standard abbreviations are shown in parentheses.

Roomette (RM) - (One Bed) - A small, comfortable private room with a seat, a single bed, toilet and washbasin. The bed, which folds out fully made up from the wall, is designed to be lowered and raised by the passenger himself.

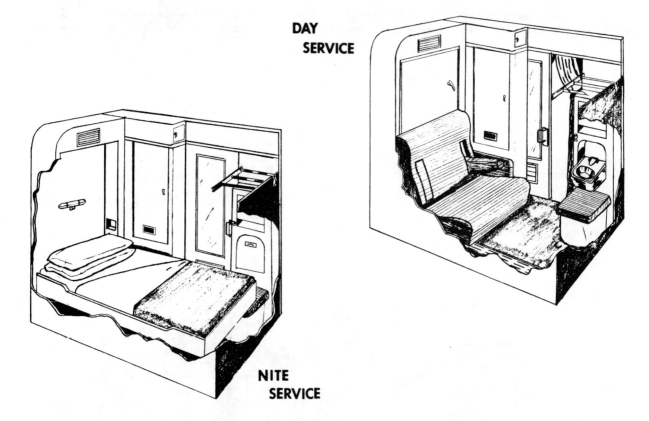

DAY SERVICE

NITE SERVICE

Bedroom (BR) - (Two Beds) - A comfortable room with two beds, generally one above the other, floor space, toilet and washbasin. These rooms are designed for two persons travelling together. The upper bed is folded back by the attendant if the passengers desire to share the lower bed, or if only one person is occupying the bedroom. In most Bedrooms, the toilet is enclosed in a separate small room within the bedroom, called an annex.

Drawing Room (DR) - (Three Beds) - A Drawing Room has two lower and one upper beds, floor space, washbasin and annex toilet. When only the lower beds are to be used, the upper bed is folded back. A Drawing Room by day seats up to 5 persons.

Generally, club cars contain large, comfortable seats (PS) which both recline and revolve, arranged singly on each side of a center aisle. However, club cars on Amfleet trains, called Amclub cars, contain large comfortable seats (PS) which recline but do not revolve. They are arranged in pairs on one side of the aisle, with a single seat on the other side of the aisle. A few club cars have Rooms (DR) in them which seat up to 5 persons travelling together.

A custom class accommodation is a reserved seat in a Turboclub or Amclub car on The Adirondack, The Blue Water Limited or The Niagara Rainbow. These cars contain large comfortable seats which recline but do not revolve. The seats are arranged in pairs on one side of the aisle with a single seat on the other side of the aisle.

Coach Seat (CS) - Coach seats are in open cars and are arranged in pairs, two on each side of a center aisle. The seats usually recline and have foot-rests. On most long-distance trains and some shorter-distance trains, the coach seats also have leg-rests, which pull out for support. Pillows are provided on overnight trains. Lavatory facilities are at the ends of each car.

Single Slumbercoach Room (SS) - A small private room with a bed, toilet and wash-basin, designed for one person. The bed is narrower than the bed in a Roomette and the mattress is thinner, but access to the toilet is not blocked when the bed is in use. Slumbercoach rooms provide private-room sleeping accommodations, with full bedding, at a cost only slightly more than that of a coach seat.

Double Slumbercoach Room (SD) - The same as a Single Slumbercoach Room, but with an upper bed as well. By day, two seats are available.

AMTRAK ACCOMMODATIONS

SLUMBERCOACHES

Economy Rooms (ES for single occupancy; ED for double occupancy) - (Two Beds) - A small private room with a lower berth and an upper berth, closet, folding wall table and mirror. The beds may be lowered without assistance of the attendant. Passengers may change clothes when beds are lowered. When only one passenger is travelling, one bed will be used and passenger will pay the single economy room rate. When two or more passengers are travelling the double economy room rate will apply. Economy rooms do <u>not</u> include a toilet or washbasin. Restrooms are located elsewhere in the car.

Economy Family Rooms (FM) - (Four Beds) - A comfortable private room which may sleep two adults and two children. Economy Family Rooms contain a wide lower berth, one upper berth, two short berts, closet, folding wall table and mirror. Passengers may change clothes when beds are lowered. The beds may be lowered without the assistance of the attendant. Economy Family Rooms do <u>not</u> include a toilet or washbasin. Restrooms are located elsewhere in the car.

Handicapped Bedroom - (Two Beds) - A comfortable private room with a lower berth, an upper berth, closet, folding wall table, annex toilet (which allows a wheelchair full turning radius) and an electrical outlet capable of powering a portable respirator. When room is occupied by a qualified disabled passenger, the single or double economy room rate will apply. When occupied by any other type of passenger, the single or double bedroom charge will apply.

Lounge cars, dining cars, observation cars and seats in rooftop glass observation domes are provided on many trains for the use of passengers. Special cars are found on various AMTRAK trains, subject to route and availability.

Hi-Level Dining Car - spacious dining rooms with magnificant views and quiet atmosphere - a menu of delicious choices, expertly served.

Coffee Shop Car - delicious thrifty meals and snacks in an informal dining atmosphere - varied selections and prompt, courteous service.

Dome Lounge Car - living-room-like comfort plus a grandstand view of the countryside - a place to relax, chat, enjoy a refreshing drink - may be combined with lounge, coach parlor or meal service. (Also called Vista Dome, Astra Dome, Great Dome.)

Hi-Level Coach - reclining stretch-out seats and windows with sweeping views - a setting of quiet relaxation - restrooms within easy reach on lower level.

Lunch Counter Car - tasty light meals and excellent beverage service in a casual, relaxed setting - passengers may return to their seats with their selections, if they wish.

AMTRAK TRAVEL AGENT

AMTRAK furnishes each appointed travel agent with all the "tools" necessary to sell transportation over its 28,000 miles of routes spanning the entire nation. These materials should be used regularly when selling and writing AMTRAK tickets. These tools consist of:

The ALL-America Train Fares Tariff
AMTRAK System Time Table
Travel Agents Manual
Brochures and Promotional Material
AMTRAK Ticket Stock, Tour Orders, and U.S.A. RAIL PASSES

The Central Reservation Offices and sales representatives are always available for assistance in any way.

Through the ARTS Automatic Reservation and Ticketing System computer, agents can immediately confirm reservations for any of the variety of accommodations available on the growing fleet of passenger trains including the famous Metroliners.

Most important, your commission is 10% and is earned immediately at the time of sale.

AMTRAK appointed Travel Agents shall represent the National Railroad Passenger Corporation in the sale of rail passenger transportation and related services over the lines of AMTRAK and other carriers with whom AMTRAK has authorized agreements.

Reservations for accommodations on AMTRAK trains must be made through an AMTRAK Central Reservation Office. Tickets must be issued under the methods described by AMTRAK. Agents must provide adequate security for AMTRAK tickets and other documents. They must submit a report of ticket sales promptly following the close of each month's business as required by accounting procedures.

To better acquaint Travel Agents with the AMTRAK product, and the various accommodations available on the Trains, AMTRAK offers Familiarization travel to authorized Travel Agents and their employees. Familiarization travel at a discount of 75% is available on all AMTRAK trains and in any type of accommodation. To obtain Familiarization discount authorization, qualified Travel Agents must complete a Familiarization Trip Request and submit it to the local AMTRAK District Sales Office ten days or more in advance of travel departure.

MAKING RESERVATIONS

A reservation is an agreement for travel between AMTRAK and a customer. As a travel agent you give AMTRAK an "order" for travel in the name of your client. As a result of your contact with an AMTRAK Reservation Agent, the "space" you have requested for your client has been set aside from further sale to anyone else.

It should be remembered that a reservation is a conditional request for space and is not a contract for travel until AMTRAK has been notified that a ticket has been issued.

Reservations are required for all sleeping car, slumbercoach, and club car accommodations. The same is true for Metroliner travel and coach reservations when required on certain long distance trains. Your AMTRAK Reservation Agent will advise you if a reservation is necessary.

Reservations can be obtained for any reserved train in the AMTRAK system by calling the appropriate Central Reservation Office designated to handle your calls. Trained R&I agents, using AMTRAK's Automatic Reservation and Ticketing System (ARTS), can immediately book and confirm reservations for any accommodation available in our inventory.

Reservations must be booked in the traveller's name. The name of your travel agency, telephone number and a personal contact will be included in our records for later use.

A thorough knowledge of AMTRAK's tariff and schedules will be helpful in a satisfactory arrangement of the customer's travel plans. Specific details of any

traveller's special requirements must also be included in the reservation record. As an example, information regarding travel of handicapped persons must be made known to AMTRAK to permit adequate preparation by on-board and station service personnel.

All reservations are subject to "Hold Limit" cancellations. Until appropriate tickets have been issued and AMTRAK Reservations has been furnished a ticket number of each reservation record, reserved accommodations will be automatically cancelled when the hold limit is passed. Space is then returned to inventory for use by other prospects.

AMTRAK Hold Limit policy, which is shown in the chart below, is automatically assigned to each reservation record.

For Reservations Confirmed	Latest Purchase Date Is
0 to 2 days before departure	30 minutes before departure
3 to 7 days before departure	2 days before departure
8 to 21 days before departure	5 days before departure
22 to 45 days before departure	15 days before departure
46 or more days before departure	30 days before departure

Agents may wish to advise the customers of the reservation hold limit, if tickets are not issued at the time of booking; however, travel agents themselves are ultimately responsible for protection of reserved space by issuing tickets and advising associated numbers to AMTRAK Reservations before the assigned limit has passed.

Reserved accommodations which have not been ticketed and are no longer desired should be cancelled promptly to make the space available to other travellers. Ticketed accommodations are subject to service charges detailed in the All-America Train Fares Tariff when not properly cancelled.

AMTRAK TICKETS

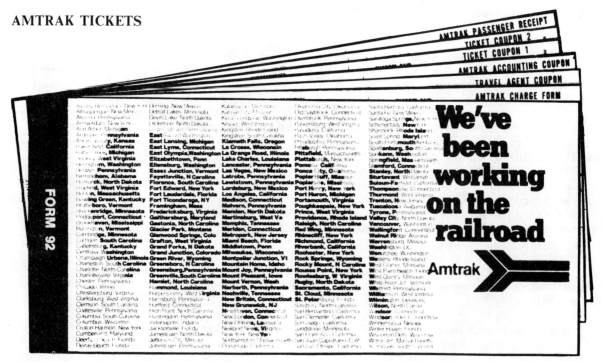

Illustrated on the previous page is the newly redesigned Travel Agent ticket showing complete arrangement of all coupons including a new Universal Charge coupon. All Travel Agent Tickets are a standard ATC size designed to be validated with the ATC imprinter or by hand validator. The required information may be entered by hand, with the aid of an imprinter or by typewriter. When completed by hand use a ball point pen working on a hard surface and press hard to insure a clear impression on all coupons.

On the following pages are some numbered illustrations with a description of the entries to be made in each block of the ticket. Agents are urged to exercise care in preparing tickets to avoid any misunderstanding by the customer who purchases the ticket or the conductor on board the train who must honor it as evidence of proper fare paid.

SUMMARY OF CONDITIONS OF CONTRACT

Valid for passage for six months from date of issue, unless otherwise noted. Reservations must be secured when required; failure to cancel unneeded reservations prior to train departure may result in a substantial service charge. This ticket is not transferable and Amtrak shall not be liable to the purchaser in the event of its loss, destruction or theft or if it is honored for transportation or refund when presented by any other person.

Carriage hereunder is subject to the Conditions of Contract and the rules and regulations of Amtrak, including those limiting liability for loss of or damage to checked baggage and such Conditions of Contract and rules and regulations are available for inspection by the passenger at any Amtrak ticket office. Amtrak shall neither be liable for loss, damage, injury or delay to baggage not placed in checked baggage service, nor in excess of prescribed limits for loss of or damage to undeclared valuable property contained in checked baggage.

Times shown on timetables or elsewhere and times quoted are not guaranteed and form no part of this contract. Time schedules and equipment are subject to change without notice. Amtrak expressly reserves the right to, without notice, substitute alternate means of transportation, and to alter or omit stopping places shown on ticket or timetable. Amtrak assumes no responsibility for inconvenience, expense or other loss, damage or injury resulting from error in schedules, delayed trains, failure to make connections, shortage of equipment or other operating deficiencies, except as required by the ICC Adequacy of Service Regulations.

Illustrated below is a numbered example of the book ticket charge coupon. Each coupon of the ticket is identical in format, with the applicable segment outlined. Not all "Blocks" are identified.

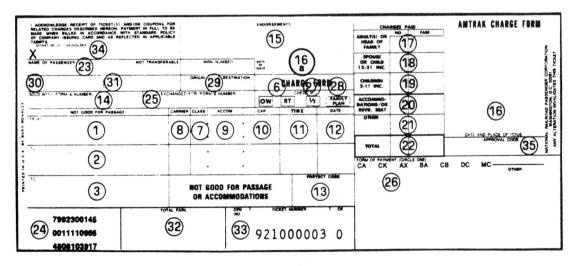

All tickets must be completed using the charge coupon as the original, observing the rules and procedures described on the following pages.

<u>Block</u>

   1. Point of origin.

   2. Destination if this were used as a one coupon ticket.

   3. Destination if two coupon one-way ticket (with one transfer or junction point) or point of origin if return portion of round-trip ticket.

   6. (√) or (x) to indicate ticket is one way (OW) or round trip (RT).

   7. The entry in block 7 will designate the type of service the ticket or coupon is issued for.

       "C" – When ticket or coupon is issued for reserved or unreserved coach travel including slumbercoach or Metrocoach accommodations.

       "F" – When ticket or coupon is issued for sleeping car, club car or Metroclub car travel.

       "C" – When open or unreserved tickets are issued which do not include specific accommodations. Refer to complete details for issuing "Open Reservation" tickets.

   8. Carrier Column – Coupons covering AMTRAK service must show 'AM' for AMTRAK. Coupons covering non-AMTRAK service MUST use the appropriate carrier abbreviation.

   9. Accommodations – The accommodation block must be completed on all manual tickets with approved abbreviation or entry. Following is a list of accommodation types available throughout the AMTRAK system with approved designation.

ACCOMMODATIONS	Designation	Example
Unreserved Coach	Unreserved**	
Guarantee Coach Seat	1 Seat, 2 Seats, etc.	
Reserved Coach Seat	S or Seat	
Single Slumbercoach Room.	SS	
Double Slumbercoach Room.	SD	
Club Car Seat	1 Seat, 2 Seats, etc.	
Drawing Room Club Car Day Room	DR	
Roomette	R or RM	
Bedroom	BR	

**Car number not required.

10, 11, & 12. The "car", "time", and "date" blocks must be completed on all tickets.

13. The associated reservation system "Protect Code" must be entered when ticket is issued for any type of reserved accommodation. A reservation "protect code" will be furnished by AMTRAK Reservation Agent upon advice that appropriate tickets have been issued. Tickets must not be issued for reserved accommodations without assignment of space by AMTRAK Central Reservations.

14. Insert form and ticket numbers if sold in connection with another ticket that is a part of the total revenue.

15. The "Tariff" endorsement must be placed in block 15 when tickets are issued at discounted Fare. Tickets must not be issued which include a combination of discount and regular fares. For example, Family Plan and Regular Fare, or Military Furlough and Regular Fare. Separate tickets must be issued for each Fare category.

16. Tickets must be validated with the agency's official stamp or imprinter showing the actual date of issue.

16a. When ticket is validated with ticket imprinter, the date of issue will appear in block 16a.

17. Regular ticket (not Family Plan). Insert number of adults and applicable fare. Family Plan Tickets - Insert 1 and adult head of family fare (not excursion) and check Family Plan block 28.

18. Used only for accompanying spouse or children ages 12-21 travelling on Family Plan. Enter total number of fares. Check Family Plan block 28.

19. Enter the number of children 2-11 years of age and applicable fare. If Family Plan, check Family Plan block 28.

20. Show the number and amount collected for reserved accommodations. When round trip tickets are issued, indicate if accommodation charges cover "one-way" (OW) or "round-trip" (RT).

21. Show total amount collected for any other charge that may apply.

22. Enter the total number of passengers and total charges covered by this ticket. NOTE: Cross out any unused "Charges Paid" blocks 17 through 21.

23. The name of the passenger, as it appears in AMTRAK's Passenger Name Record (PNR), is required on all tickets with reservations. The WRN # may also be included.

24. The numbers printed on the charge coupon are for credit card company use only. This block on all "passage" and "receipt" coupons contains baggage block which is to be punched at the time baggage is checked.

25. If exchange ticket, enter form and number of lifted exchange ticket. Enter reason for exchanging in block 15. Example: Extend ticket limit, change routing, etc.

26. The "form of payment", cash, check or credit card, must be entered in block 26. Circle the form of payment when cash or check, or the appropriate credit card company initials when payment is by credit card. A blank space is provided when another form of payment is used. When payment is by credit card, the complete credit card account number must be included. Credit Card information may be recorded in

block 26 with the ATC ticket imprinter. This provides an exact record of the required credit card information. Refer to blocks 34 and 35.

27. If child's ticket (not Family Plan), check 1/2 block, enter fare in blocks 19 and 22.

28. If ticket issued is Family Plan, check Family Plan block. Endorsement "Family Plan ticket not good for travel starting Friday or Sunday from origin or destination of ticket" must be shown in block 26 when applicable.

29. These blocks are used only when two or more conjunctive tickets are issued when the city codes of original origin and destination stations must be entered.

30 &
31. It is not necessary to use these blocks if regular six month limit ticket is sold. The blocks must be used to establish the ticket limit when special one-way or round-trip excursion ticket is sold. The advance sale of tickets, not specifically prohibited, is accomplished by entering the desired initial date of use in the "Not Valid Before" block and the expiration date in the "Not Valid After" block.

32. Enter the total charges for this ticket as shown in block 22.

33. Block 33 contains a preprinted ticket number assigned to each book of coupons for accounting purposes. When tickets are issued for reserved accommodations, AMTRAK Reservations must be advised the ticket number associated with each reservation.

34. VERY IMPORTANT. When payment is by credit card, secure the purchasers signature in block 34. Credit card sales without proper signature may be charged back to the selling agency.

35. A credit card company approval code must be entered on all credit sales over the floor limit of the referenced credit card company. NOTE: When credit card information is manually entered in block 26 an approval code must be secured from the appropriate credit card company and entered in this block.

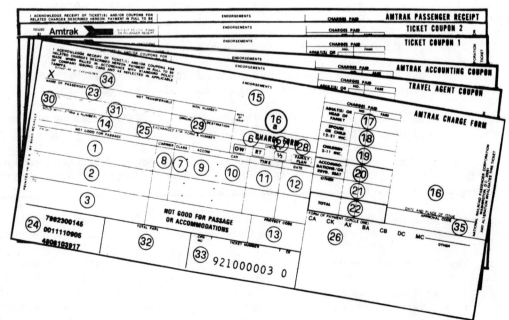

AMTRAK TICKETING

Mr. and Mrs. Bernard Cahill comes into your agency to reserve a trip from Boston to Denver by rail. After you have taken down their name, phone numbers and dates they wish to travel, you will refer to your AMTRAK National Train Timetable. In the center of the timetable booklet is a map of the continental United States. Refer to the map to find the page number for the route your clients will be taking. Then turn to the page numbers circled on the route lines you will be using. For the Boston to Chicago leg, you would refer to page 33.

How to Use the Timetable

Locating Your Schedule—Check the alphabetical list of stations on pages 5 through 8 for the page number for service to your destination. If more than one route serves this point, or if your starting point is not on the same route, use the map on pages 26-27 to trace the route(s) you will need to use. Turn to the pages indicated by the circled numbers along the route lines to find your schedules.

Reading the Tables—On many schedules, service in both directions is shown in a single table, with the cities served shown in the center. If your destination is listed *below* your starting point, use the *left-hand* column(s) and *read down*. If your destination is *above* your starting point, use the *right-hand* column(s) and *read up*.

303	21	301	Train Number	300	308	22
The State House	The Inter-American	The Ann Rutledge	Train Name	The State House	The State House	The Inter-American
Daily	Daily	Daily	Frequency of Operation	Ex. Su	Su only	Daily
✓ ⊡ ⌂	⊠ ⌂	✓ ⊡ ⌂	Type of Service	✓ ⊡ ⌂	✓ ⊡ ⌂	⊠ ⌂
			(Illinois Central Gulf)	Km Mi		
5 15 P	11 15 A	8 35 A	Dp Chicago, IL (Union Sta.) (CT) Ar	0 0	10 05 A	12 15 P	2 15 P
5 58 P	11 58 A	9 18 A	Joliet, IL	60 37	8 58 A	11 08 A	1 07 P
6 49 P			Pontiac, IL ●	148 92	8 09 A	10 19 A	
7 25 P	1 21 P	10 41 A	Bloomington, IL ●	203 126	7 38 A	9 48 A	11 50 A
7 52 P			Lincoln, IL ●	251 156	7 05 A	9 15 A	
8 25 P	2 21 P	11 41 A	Ar Springfield, IL	288 185	6 35 A	8 45 A	10 50 A

In this example, if travelling from Chicago to Springfield, read down on the left.

Distances along the way

Name of railroad contracting with Amtrak to operate trains over this route or segment of route.

If travelling from Springfield to Chicago, read up on the right.

Summary of on-board services. Symbols are explained on page 51. Details are given in the text accompanying each table.

Time Zones—through which trains operate—shown with first and last station in each zone.

What days does the train operate? Be sure to check reference marks for holiday period exceptions.

Where very frequent service is available, separate tables are printed for each direction. Cities served are listed on the left-hand side. Find the table showing your destination below your starting point, and read down in the columns to the right.

In this example, if travelling from Chicago to Milwaukee, read down in this table. Service in the opposite direction will be found in a separate table.

Km Mi		(Milwaukee Road)				
0 0	Dp Chicago, IL (Union Sta.) (CT) Dp	8 05 A	11 30 A	1 55 P	4 30 P
27 17	Glenview, IL ●	⊗ 8 28 A	⊗ 11 53 A	⊗ 2 18 P	⊗ 4 53 P
100 62	Sturtevant, WI ● ((Racine))		9 07 A		2 57 P	F 5 32 P
137 85	Milwaukee, WI Ar	9 37 A	12 59 P	3 27 P	6 02 P
137 85	Milwaukee, WI Dp		2 45 P		⊗ 8 25 P
303 188	Green Bay, WI Ar		8 05 P		⊗ 10 40 P
137 85	Milwaukee, WI Dp		1 05 P		
241 150	Columbus, WI ● ((Madison)) Ar		2 23 P		

Nearby cities and points of interest. For example, Sturtevant is the station for Racine. Where motor coach symbol appears, schedule of connecting service is shown nearby.

Shaded background indicates recommended rail or motor coach connection shown directly in same column as train to or from which connection is made.

Be sure to check the explanation of reference marks—this information could affect your travel plans!

The Lake Shore Limited

New York   Cleveland
Boston   Toledo
Albany   Chicago

READ DOWN				READ UP
49		Train Number		48
Daily		Frequency of Operation		Daily
⇌ ✕ ⌂		Type of Service		⇌ ✕ ⌂
	Km Mi	(Conrail)		
6 40 P	0 0	Dp New York, NY (ET) Ar		1 10 P
		(Grand Central Terminal)		
R 7 37 P	53 33	Dp Croton-Harmon, NY Ar		D 12 05 P
R 8 21 P	117 73	Poughkeepsie, NY (Highland)		D 11 18 A
8 37 P	142 88	Rhinecliff, NY (Kingston)		11 01 A
9 02 P	182 113	Hudson, NY		10 40 A
9 45 P	227 141	Ar Albany-Rensselaer, NY Dp		10 00 A
449				448
⊞ ⇌ ⊠		Thru Cars Boston-Chicago		⊞ ⇌ ⊠
⌂				⌂
4 15 P	0 0	Dp Boston, MA (South Sta.) Ar		3 45 P
R 4 20 P	2 1	Boston, MA (Back Bay Sta.)		D 3 40 P
F 4 50 P	34 21	Framingham, MA ●		F 2 55 P
5 20 P	71 44	Worcester, MA		2 20 P
6 25 P	158 98	Springfield, MA		1 10 P
F 7 35 P	240 148	Pittsfield, MA ●		F 12 01 P
9 40 P	351 218	Ar Albany-Rensselaer, NY Dp		10 15 A
10 00 P	227 141	Dp Albany-Rensselaer, NY Ar		9 45 A
10 30 P	257 160	Schenectady, NY ●		9 16 A
11 52 P	383 238	Utica, NY		7 51 A
12 45 A	460 286	Syracuse, NY		7 00 A
2 20 A	599 372	Rochester, NY		5 12 A
3 50 A	705 438	Ar Buffalo, NY (Central Tml.) Dp		3 45 A
4 05 A	705 438	Dp Ar		3 30 A
6 10 A	846 526	Erie, PA		1 42 A
8 02 A	996 619	Ar Cleveland, OH (Lakefront Sta.) Dp		11 49 P
8 10 A	996 619	Dp Ar		11 41 P
8 40 A	1036 644	Elyria, OH (Lorain)		11 09 P
10 35 A	1170 727	Ar Toledo, OH (Central Union Tml.) Dp		9 24 P
10 50 A	1170 727	Dp Ar		9 14 P
1 30 P	1384 860	Elkhart, IN		6 38 P
2 00 P	1410 876	South Bend, IN (ET)		6 13 P
3 05 P	1547 961	Ar Chicago, IL (Union Sta.) (CT) Dp		3 30 P

Page 33

The San Francisco Zephyr

Chicago   Ogden
Omaha   Oakland
Denver   San Francisco

READ DOWN				READ UP
5		Train Number		6
Daily		Frequency of Operation		Daily
⊞ ⇌ ✕		Type of Service		⊞ ⇌ ✕
⌂				⌂
	Km Mi	(Burlington Northern)		
6 15 P	0 0	Dp Chicago, IL (Union Sta.) (CT) Ar		1 25 P
⊗ 6 55 P	61 38	Aurora, IL		D 12 10 P
8 50 P	261 162	Galesburg, IL (S. Seminary St.)		10 15 A
9 07 P	288 179	Monmouth, IL ⊕		9 45 A
9 38 P	330 205	Burlington, IA		9 15 A
10 08 P	375 233	Mt. Pleasant, IA ⊕		8 40 A
10 53 P	451 280	Ottumwa, IA ⊕		8 00 A
12 10 A	579 360	Osceola, IA ⊕		6 40 A
12 45 A	632 393	Creston, IA		6 10 A
2 50 A	798 496	Ar Omaha, NE Dp		4 15 A
3 05 A	798 496	Dp Ar		4 05 A
4 15 A	887 551	Ar Lincoln, NE Dp		2 58 A
4 35 A	887 551	Dp Ar		2 38 A
6 25 A	1041 647	Hastings, NE		1 00 A
7 13 A	1130 702	Holdrege, NE ⊕		12 11 A
8 30 A	1254 779	McCook, NE (CT)		11 00 P
9 33 A	1484 922	Akron, CO ⊕ (MT)		8 03 P
10 06 A	1538 956	Fort Morgan, CO ⊕		7 31 P
11 35 A	1664 1034	Ar Denver, CO Dp		6 20 P
12 20 P	1664 1034	Dp Ar		5 35 P
1 10 P	1748 1086	(Union Pacific) Greeley, CO		4 15 P
2 00 P	1836 1141	Ar Cheyenne, WY Dp		3 25 P
2 25 P	1836 1141	Dp Ar		3 00 P
3 50 P	1928 1198	Laramie, WY		1 40 P
5 45 P	2115 1314	Rawlins, WY		11 45 A
7 35 P	2306 1433	Rock Springs, WY		9 50 A
8 05 P	2330 1448	Green River, WY ⊕		9 30 A
9 55 P	2491 1548	Evanston, WY ⊕		7 40 A
11 45 P	2614 1624	Ar Ogden, UT (MT) Dp		6 15 A
12 30 A	2614 1624	Dp Ar		6 00 A
	2979 1851	(Southern Pacific) Elko, NV ● (PT) 3rd and Silver Sts. (No. 6 only) 684 Railroad St. (No. 5 only)		12 01 A
3 10 A				
3 40 A	3014 1873	Carlin, NV		11 35 P
F 5 35 A	3203 1990	Winnemucca, NV ● ☑		F 9 49 P
8 17 A	3478 2161	Ar Sparks, NV ● Dp		7 12 P
8 37 A	3478 2161	Dp Ar		6 52 P
8 50 A	3483 2164	Reno, NV		6 43 P
9 44 A	3539 2199	Truckee, CA ●		5 51 P
12 04 P	3643 2265	Colfax, CA ●		3 37 P
1 55 P	3730 2318	Sacramento, CA		2 27 P
2 13 P	3751 2331	Davis, CA ⊕		1 58 P
2 41 P	3795 2357	Suisun-Fairfield, CA ●		1 31 P
3 03 P	3822 2375	Martinez, CA		1 09 P
3 32 P	3853 2394	Richmond, CA ⊕ ⊕		12 38 P
4 30 P	3869 2404	Ar Oakland, CA Dp		12 25 P
5 00 P	3878 2410	Ar San Francisco, CA ⇌ (PT) Dp		11 55 A
		(Transbay Terminal)		

The San Francisco Zephyr
Chicago-Oakland/San Francisco

Services

All Reserved Train

Complete Dining and Beverage Service
Lounge Service
Sleeping Car Service—Complimentary coffee and tea served on request 6:30-9:30 AM.
Dome Coach Service
Coach Service
Baggage Service—Checked baggage handled at Chicago, Burlington, Omaha, Lincoln, Hastings, McCook, Denver, Greeley, Cheyenne, Laramie, Rock Springs, Ogden, Reno, Sacramento, Davis, Martinez, Oakland and San Francisco, also at Rawlins and Green River subject to delay. Large trunks and oversize baggage to and from San Francisco subject to delay.
For explanation of reference marks, see page 41.

Page 43

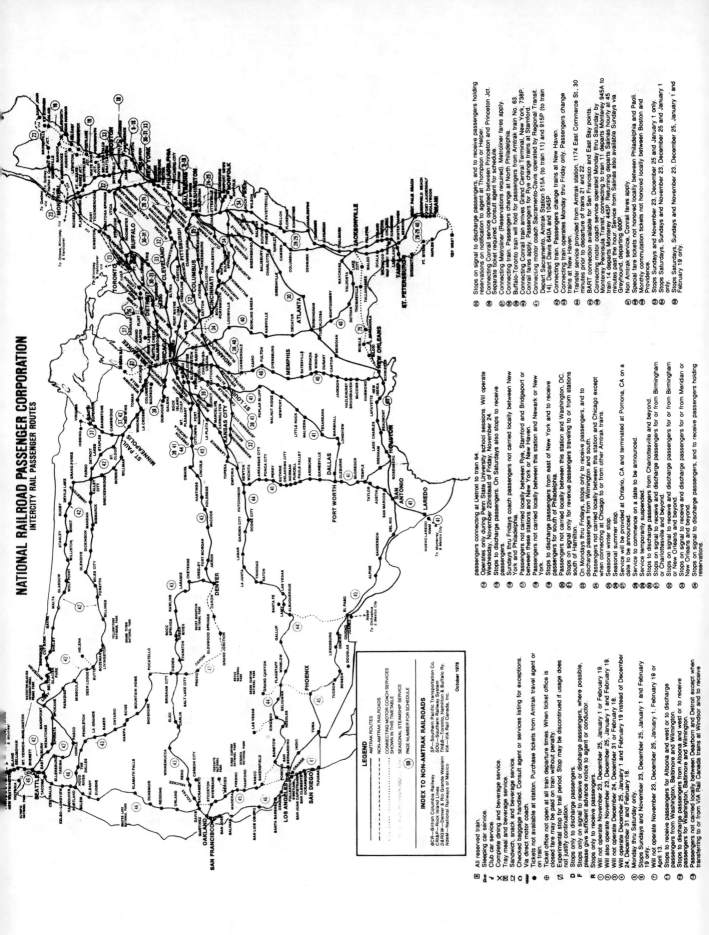

NATIONAL RAILROAD PASSENGER CORPORATION
INTERCITY RAIL PASSENGER ROUTES

LEGEND

AMTRAK ROUTES
NON-AMTRAK RAILROADS
CONNECTING MOTOR COACH SERVICES
SHOWN IN THIS TIMETABLE
SEASONAL STEAMSHIP SERVICE
⑨⑨ PAGE NUMBER FOR SCHEDULE

October 1978

INDEX TO NON-AMTRAK RAILROADS

BCR—British Columbia Railway
CRI&P—Rock Island Lines
D&RGW—Denver & Rio Grande Western
TH&B—Toronto, Hamilton & Buffalo Ry.
NdeM—National Railways of Mexico

SP—Southern Pacific Transportation Co.
SOU—Southern Railway System
TH&B—Toronto, Hamilton & Buffalo Ry.
VIA—VIA Rail Canada, Inc.

☒ All reserved train.
⌧ Sleeping car service.
✗ Club car service.
Ⓧ Complete dining and beverage service.
◨ Tray meal and beverage service.
▯ Sandwich, snack and beverage service.
Ⓒ Checked baggage handled. Consult agent or services listing for exceptions.
● Via direct motor coach.
◐ Tickets not available at station. Purchase tickets from Amtrak travel agent or on train.
◑ Ticket office not open at all train departure times. When ticket office is closed fare may be paid on train without penalty.
◿ Experimental stop for trial period. Stop may be discontinued if usage does not justify continuation.
Ⓓ Stops only to discharge passengers.
D Stops only on signal to receive or discharge passengers, where possible, please give sufficient advance notice to agent or conductor.
F Stops only to receive passengers.
Ⓡ Stops only to receive passengers.
Ⓢ Will not operate November 23, December 25, January 1 or February 19.
⑩⑩ Will also operate November 23, December 25, January 1 and February 19.
⑪⑪⑪ Will operate December 24, December 31 or February 18.
⑫⑫ Will operate December 25, January 1 and February 19 instead of December 24, December 31 and February 18.
⑬ Monday thru Saturday only.
⑭⑭ Stops Sundays and November 23, December 25, January 1 and February 19 only.
⑯ Will not operate November 23, December 25, January 1, February 19 or April 13.
⑰ Stops to receive passengers for Altoona and west or to discharge passengers from Washington, Baltimore and Wilmington.
⑱ Stops to discharge passengers from Altoona and west or to receive passengers for Washington, Baltimore and Wilmington.
⑲ Passengers not carried locally between Dearborn and Detroit except when transferring to or from VIA Rail Canada trains at Windsor and to receive

passengers connecting at Detroit to train 64.
④ Operates only during Penn State University school sessions. Will operate Wednesday, November 22 instead of Friday, November 24.
⑥ Stops to discharge passengers. On Saturdays also stops to receive passengers.
⑦ Sundays thru Fridays coach passengers not carried locally between New York and Philadelphia.
⑰ Passengers not carried locally between Rye, Stamford and Bridgeport or between these stations and New York or New Haven.
⑱ Passengers not carried locally between this station and Newark or New York.
⑲ Stops to discharge passengers from east of New York and to receive passengers for south of Philadelphia.
㉒ Passengers not carried locally between this station and Washington, DC.
㉓ Stops on signal only for revenue passengers traveling to or from stations south of Hamilton.
㉔ On Mondays thru Fridays, stops only to receive passengers, and to discharge passengers from Wilmington and south.
㉕ Passengers not carried locally between this station, and Chicago except when connecting at Chicago to or from other Amtrak trains.
㉖ Seasonal winter stop.
㉗ Seasonal summer stop.
㉘ Service will be provided at Ontario, CA, and terminated at Pomona, CA, on a date to be announced.
㉙ Service to commence on a date to be announced.
㉚ Service temporarily suspended.
㉛ Stops to discharge passengers from Charlottesville and beyond.
㉜ Stops on signal to receive and discharge passengers for or from Birmingham or Charlottesville and beyond.
㉝ Stops on signal to receive and discharge passengers for or from Birmingham or New Orleans and beyond.
㉞ Stops on signal to receive and discharge passengers for or from Meridian or New Orleans and beyond.
㉟ Stops on signal to discharge passengers, and to receive passengers holding reservations.

⑱ Stops on signal to discharge passengers, and to receive passengers holding reservations on notification to agent at Thompson or Helper.
⑱ Connecting Conrail service operated between Princeton and Princeton Jct. Separate ticket required. Consult agent for schedule.
⑱ Connecting Metroliner. (Reservations required). Metroliner fares apply.
⑱ Connecting train. Passengers change at North Philadelphia.
⑲ Buffalo-Toronto train will hold for through passengers from Amtrak train No. 63.
⑳ Connecting Conrail train arrives Grand Central Terminal, New York, 738P. Conrail fares apply. Passengers for Rye change trains at Stamford.
㊶ Connecting motor coach Sacramento-Davis operated by Regional Transit. Depart Sacramento, Amtrak Station 515A (to train 11) and 915P (to train 14). Depart Davis 640A and 1045P.
㊷ Connecting train. Passengers change trains at New Haven.
㊸ Connecting train operates Monday thru Friday only. Passengers change trains at New Haven.
㊹ Transfer service provided from Amtrak station, 1174 East Commerce St., 30 minutes prior to departure of trains 21 and 22.
㊺ BART connection available for San Francisco and East Bay points.
㊻ Connecting motor coach service operated Monday thru Saturday by Monterey Peninsula Transit. Departs Monterey for Salinas hourly at 945A to train 14 departs Monterey 445P. Returning departs Salinas hourly at 45 minutes past the hour. Service from Salinas also available Sundays via Greyhound, departing 600P.
㊼ Non Amtrak service, Conrail fares apply.
㊽ Special fare applies. Not honored locally between Philadelphia and Paoli.
㊾ Monthly commutation tickets not honored locally between Boston and Providence.
㊿ Stops Sundays and November 23, December 25 and January 1 only.
51 Stops Saturdays, Sundays and November 23, December 25 and January 1 only.
52 Stops Saturdays, Sundays and November 23, December 25, January 1 and February 19 only.

ALL-AMERICA TRAIN FARES
Edition 6

#9TH REV. PAGE (2)-35
CANCELS
7TH REV. PAGE (2)-35
Effective: MARCH 5, 1979

TABLE 4 - NEW YORK/BOSTON-BUFFALO-DETROIT/CLEVELAND-CHICAGO - Continued

- 8TH REV. PAGE (2)-35
expired September 5, 1978

BETWEEN	CITY CODE	RAIL FARES		ACCOMMODATIONS CHARGES		
		REGULAR	OFF-PEAK ROUND-TRIP COACH EXCURSION	ROOMETTE	BEDROOM	SLUMBERCOACH
	KIND OF→ FARE	OW	RE30	OW	OW	OW
HUDSON, NY	**HUD**	$ ♦	$ ♦	$ •	$ •	$ ♦
and						
ALBANY-RENSSELAER, NY	ALB					
Colonie	CSD	3.00	4.50	s3.00	.....	
■ Schenectady	SDY					
Amsterdam	AMS	6.10	9.25	s3.25	.....	
Utica	UCA	11.25	17.00	s4.75	.....	c10.00
Rome	ROM	12.25	18.50	s5.50	.....	d18.00
SYRACUSE	SYR	14.75	22.50	s7.00	.....	
ROCHESTER	ROC	23.00	34.50	s10.00	.....	
BUFFALO, NY (Central Term.)	BUF	28.50	43.00	s12.00	.....	
■ Exchange St	BFX					
■ Niagara Falls, NY	NFL	30.50	46.00	s12.00	.....	....
◪ Welland	WLD					
St. Thomas	STT	38.50	58.00	32.50	62.00	....
WINDSOR, ON	WDS	47.00	71.00	40.00	76.00	....
DETROIT, MI	DET					
Erie, PA.	ERI	31.50	.....	21.50	39.00	
CLEVELAND, OH	CLE	38.50	.....	27.00	50.00	
Elyria	ELY	40.00	.....	29.00	55.00	c10.00
TOLEDO, OH.	TOL	46.00	.....	33.00	62.00	d18.00
Elkhart, IN	EKH	56.00	.....	41.00	78.00	
South Bend, IN.	SOB	57.00	.....	42.50	80.00	
CHICAGO, IL	CHI	62.00	.....	47.00	90.00	
BOSTON, MA **(South Station and Back Bay)**	**BOS** **BBY**					
and						
†BOSTON, MA	BBY	2.00	.....	s3.10	.....	......
Back Bay						
Framingham	FRA	2.20	.....	s3.10	.....	......
WORCESTER	WOR	3.45	.....	s3.60	.....	......
SPRINGFIELD	SPG	7.10	.....	s4.85	.....	......
Pittsfield, MA.	PIT	11.50	.....	s6.25	.....	......
ALBANY-RENSSELAER, NY	ALB					
Colonie	CSD	14.75	.....	s7.75	.....	......
■ Schenectady	SDY					
Amsterdam	AMS	18.50	.....	s10.00	.....	......
Utica	UCA	23.50	.....	s11.25	.....	......
Rome	ROM	24.00	.....	s12.25	.....	......
SYRACUSE	SYR	26.00	.....	s12.75	.....	......
ROCHESTER	ROC	31.50	.....	20.50	38.50	......
BUFFALO, NY (Central Term.)	BUF	37.50	.....	23.00	42.00	......
■ Exchange St	BFX					
Erie, PA.	ERI	43.00	.....	28.50	53.00	......
CLEVELAND, OH	CLE	50.00	.....	34.00	64.00	......
Elyria	ELY	52.00	.....	36.50	68.00	......
TOLEDO, OH.	TOL	58.00	.....	40.50	77.00	......
Elkhart, IN	EKH	67.00	.....	49.00	92.00	......
South Bend, IN.	SOB	67.00	.....	49.50	93.00	......
CHICAGO, IL	CHI	73.00	.....	56.00	103.00	......

Amtrak

ALL-AMERICA TRAIN FARES
Edition 6

#10TH REV. PAGE (2)-142
CANCELS
8TH REV. PAGE (2)-142

Effective: MARCH 5, 1979

CHAPTER 2 - FARES FOR EACH AMTRAK ROUTE - Continued

TABLE 17 - CHICAGO-DENVER-OGDEN- SAN FRANCISCO - Continued

- 9TH REV. PAGE (2)-142
expired September 5, 1978

BETWEEN	CITY CODE	RAIL FARES REGU-LAR	ACCOMMODATIONS CHARGES ROOM-ETTE	BED-ROOM	SLUM-BER-COACH
	KIND OF→ FARE	OW	OW	OW	OW

ATTENTION

For complete fares locally between Chicago and Galesburg and intermediate stations please refer to Table 14.

BETWEEN	CITY CODE	REGULAR	ROOMETTE	BEDROOM	SLUMBERCOACH
CHICAGO, IL	CHI	$ ♦	$ ♦	$ ♦	$ ♦
and					
Galesburg, IL.	GBB	14.75	s5.10	......	
Monmouth, IL.	MTH	15.75	s6.10	......	
Burlington, IA.	BRL	19.00	s6.85	......	
Mt. Pleasant.	MTP	21.00	s7.35	......	
Ottumwa.	OTM	24.50	s8.75	......	{c 9.00 d16.50
Osceola.	OSC	30.00	s9.75	......	
Creston, IA.	CRN	33.00	s11.50	......	
OMAHA, NE.	OMA	41.50	{21.00 s14.00}	39.50	
LINCOLN.	LNK	43.00	21.00	39.50	
Hastings	HAS	50.00	26.00	48.00	{c10.25 d17.50
Holdrege	HLD	53.00	29.00	55.00	{c11.00 d19.50
McCook, NE	MCK	60.00	31.00	59.00	{c12.00 d21.00
Akron, CO.	AKN	70.00	38.50	69.00	{c13.00 d24.00
Fort Morgan.	FMG	74.00	38.50	69.00	{c13.50 d24.50
DENVER	DEN	77.00	42.00	78.00	{c14.00 d25.00
Greeley, CO.	GRE	83.00	43.00	80.00	......
CHEYENNE, WY	CHY	86.00	43.00	80.00	......
Laramie.	LAR	86.00	43.00	80.00	......
Rawlins.	RWL	95.00	46.50	84.00	......
Rock Springs	RSG	100.00	51.00	94.00	......
Green River.	GNR				
Evanston, WY	EVT	110.00	51.00	95.00	......
OGDEN, UT.	OGD	114.00	56.00	101.00	......
Elko, NV	ELK	129.00	67.00	121.00	......
Carlin	CRL				
Winnemucca	WNN	133.00	70.00	127.00	......
Sparks	SPX	133.00	80.00	143.00	......
RENO, NV	RNO				
Truckee, CA.	TRU	133.00	80.00	144.00	......
Colfax	COX	133.00	81.00	147.00	......
SACRAMENTO	SAC	133.00	82.00	148.00	......
Davis.	DAV				
Suisun-Fairfield	SUI	133.00	84.00	152.00	......
Martinez	MTZ				
Richmond	RIC	133.00	84.00	153.00	......
OAKLAND	OAK				
SAN FRANCISCO, CA.	SFO	135.00	......	......	
AURORA, IL	ARA				
and					
Galesburg, IL.	GBB	11.50	s4.10	......	
Monmouth, IL.	MTH	12.25	s4.85	......	
Burlington, IA	BRL	14.75	s6.85	......	
Mt. Pleasant	MTP	18.00	s6.85	......	{c 9.00 d16.50
Ottumwa.	OTM	21.00	s7.75	......	
Osceola.	OSC	26.50	s9.75	......	

BETWEEN	CITY CODE	REGULAR	ROOMETTE	BEDROOM	SLUMBERCOACH
AURORA, IL (Continued)	ARA	$ ♦	$ ♦	$ ♦	$ ♦
and					
Creston, IA.	CRN	30.00	s10.00	......	{c 9.00 d16.50
OMAHA, NE.	OMA	40.50	{20.50 s14.00}	38.50	
LINCOLN, NE.	LNK	40.50	21.00	39.50	
Hastings	HAS	47.50	25.50	47.00	{c10.25 d17.50
Holdrege	HLD	51.00	27.50	51.00	{c10.50 d18.50
McCook, NE	MCK	58.00	29.00	55.00	{c11.50 d20.50
Akron, CO.	AKN	68.00	37.00	67.00	{c13.00 d24.00
Fort Morgan.	FMG	70.00	37.00	67.00	{c13.00 d24.00
DENVER	DEN	76.00	41.00	75.00	{c14.00 d25.00
Greeley, CO.	GRE	82.00	41.00	75.00	......
CHEYENNE, WY	CHY	85.00	41.00	75.00	......
Laramie.	LAR	85.00	41.00	75.00	......
Rawlins.	RWL	91.00	46.50	84.00	......
Rock Springs	RSG	98.00	51.00	94.00	......
Green River.	GNR				
Evanston, WY	EVT	106.00	52.00	95.00	......
OGDEN, UT.	OGD	110.00	53.00	97.00	......
Elko, NV	ELK	127.00	65.00	117.00	......
Carlin	CRL				
Winnemucca	WNN	133.00	67.00	120.00	......
Sparks	SPX	133.00	79.00	140.00	......
RENO, NV	RNO				
Truckee, CA.	TRU	133.00	79.00	141.00	......
Colfax	COX	133.00	80.00	144.00	......
SACRAMENTO	SAC	133.00	81.00	146.00	......
Davis.	DAV				
Suisun-Fairfield	SUI	133.00	82.00	148.00	......
Martinez	MTZ				
Richmond	RIC	133.00	82.00	148.00	......
OAKLAND	OAK				
SAN FRANCISCO, CA.	SFO	135.00	......	......	......
GALESBURG, IL MONMOUTH, IL	GBB MTH				
and					
†Monmouth, IL.	MTH	2.10	s1.80	......	
Burlington, IA	BRL	4.45	s2.70	......	
Mt. Pleasant	MTP	6.60	s3.60	......	
Ottumwa.	OTM	11.00	s3.85	......	
Osceola.	OSC	17.00	s6.10	......	{c 9.00 d16.50
Creston, IA.	CRN	19.50	s7.10	......	
OMAHA, NE.	OMA	29.50	s9.75	......	
LINCOLN, NE.	LNK	31.00	18.00	32.50	
Hastings	HAS	38.00	21.00	39.50	
Holdrege	HLD	42.50	23.00	40.50	
McCook, NE	MCK	48.00	26.00	47.50	{c10.25 d17.50

(Continued on next page)

† - These fares apply for travel between Galesburg and Monmouth.
c - Single Slumbercoach room.
d - Double Slumbercoach room.
s - Seat in club or sleeping car.
When only a seat fare is shown above in the ROOMETTE column, the charge for a roomette will be ♦$18.00, and the charge for a bedroom will be ♦$31.50. To find seat charges not shown above, apply the Roomette fare to the scale in Chapter 5, Table E.
To find charges for seats in slumbercoaches, see Section B-1(F) of Chapter 1.

To read the timetable, first find your origin city and then read in the direction of the arrow to read the destination city. In this case we will read down. The train number is indicated at the top of left-hand column in bold print. The train departs Boston at 4:15 PM and arrives in Chicago the following afternoon at 3:05 PM. You will mark down this information on your itinerary, reservations sheet.

Refer again to the map to find the page number of the schedule for the second leg, Chicago to Denver. As you indicated on the map, you must turn to page 43 for the Chicago to Denver schedule.

In the table you see that the train your clients will be taking is train #5 which departs Chicago at 6:15 PM and arrives in Denver at 11:35 AM the following day. The schedules for the return trip are on the same pages. In this case you will find your origin cities and read up.

On their return trip the Cahill's will depart Denver at 6:20 PM and arrive Chicago the following afternoon at 1:25 PM, on train #6. They will depart Chicago on train #448 at 3:30 PM and arrive in Boston at 3:45 PM the following afternoon.

Since their trip involves overnight travel, the Cahill's have decided to travel first-class and have a bedroom.

You are now ready to call in the reservation. Give the reservationist the appropriate reservation data such as clients' name, train numbers, dates of travel, and any other booking information. The AMTRAK reservationist will give you a reservation number. Be sure to take the number down, as this number must be shown on the ticket and it is also used to retrieve the record.

After the reservation is made the reservationist will give you a ticket option date, or if you are ready to write the ticket, she will take the ticket number then, and give you the bedroom car assignment and also a "protect code" which must be entered on the ticket. The protect code entry provides evidence that related accommodations have been properly ticketed. On all AMTRAK trains that require reservations, it is mandatory to call in ticket numbers by the option date, otherwise the reservations will be automatically cancelled.

Below is the completed reservation sheet for the rail travel:

		Home Phone	Order Rec'd	Pick Up Date		
Name: Mr. & Mrs. Bernard Cahill		345-6789	9-1		Fare	
					Tax	
Res. #93769		Office Phone	Call Client	Advised Client OK unless we call −	Total	
					Passport	
					Small Pox	

DATE	DAY	ITINERARY	FL.NO.	CLASS	STATUS	LEAVE	ARRIVE		
								Option Date	
9/10	M T W TH F SA SU	BOSTON	AM 449	F A T Y K R	OK Req. List	4:15 PM	3:05 PM	Ticket No.	By
9/11	M T W TH F SA SU	CHICAGO	AM 5	F A T Y K R	OK Req. List	6:15 PM	11:35 PM	Protect Code
9/24	M T W TH F SA SU	DENVER	AM 6	F A T Y K R	OK Req. List 9-1	6:20 PM	1:25 PM	24LG
9/25	M T W TH F SA SU	CHICAGO	AM 448	F A T Y K R	OK Req. List Miss Jones	3:30 PM	3:45 PM	BOS CH1 Car 4491 BRG DEN Car 0520 BRE
	M T W TH F SA SU	BOSTON		F A T Y K R	OK Req. List	PM	PM	CH1 Car 0610 BRA BOS Car 4482 BRB

You would now go to your AMTRAK tariff to compute the fare. First, refer to the map in the front of the tariff. On the route line from Boston to Chicago there is a table number. For this portion of the fare, we will refer to Table 4.

On Table 4, you see that the one-way fare from Boston to Chicago is $68. On Table 17, you see that the one-way fare from Chicago to Denver is $72. The one-way fare is $140. We will double this for a round-trip fare of $280. for the head of the family. Since the Cahill's are not travelling on a Friday or Sunday, they are eligible for family plan travel. This entitles the wife to a 50% discount on the rail fare. The fare for Mrs. Cahill will be $140. round-trip.

Now we must add the bedroom charges to come up with the total fare. On Table 4 the bedroom charge for the Boston to Chicago leg is $103 one-way. Note that accommodation charges are not per person, but rather one amount for the accommodation. Table 17 shows that the bedroom charge from Chicago to Denver is $73. Below is our fare computation:

        $280. - Rail Fare Head of Family
         140. - Rail Fare Spouse
         103. - Bedroom Boston-Chicago
          73. - Bedroom Chicago-Denver
          73. - Bedroom Denver-Chicago
         103. - Bedroom Chicago-Boston
        $772. - Total Fare

We are now ready to write the ticket. See the completed ticket below.

U.S.A. RAIL PASS

The U.S.A. RAIL PASS is one of the most fantastic travel bargains in the United States. Available for 14, 21, or 30 days, the U.S.A. RAIL PASS is your key to American adventures. The U.S.A. RAIL PASS is good for absolutely unlimited coach travel over almost 27,000 miles of AMTRAK and Southern Railway routes throughout the United States, and on AMTRAK routes in Eastern and Western Canada, too.

Within the period of validity of the U.S.A. RAIL PASS, your clients can take as many trains as they can. They can backtrack, sidetrack, make as many stopovers as they wish. All they need do is present their PASS at an AMTRAK or Southern Railway ticket counter or ticket window to obtain a coach ticket, and then show it once again when they present their ticket aboard their train.

Your client can also use the U.S.A. RAIL PASS to upgrade to the sleeping compartments on the long distance trains, and the club cars on the new Turboliners and Amfleet trains. Or, they can upgrade to AMTRAK's special, all-reserved train, the Metroliner, which serves the route from New York City to Washington, D.C.

America is a lot more than just cities and towns ... it's all those colorful miles in between. Its majestic mountains, green and lush, arid deserts with tumbleweed, towering skylines, and the mighty ocean shores. To really see America, your clients have to see it by train.

AMTRAK is America's National Railroad Passenger System. It's over 500 cities and towns linked by over 27,000 miles of track. AMTRAK's trains follow the routes carved out by the railroad pioneers who built America's cities and towns. AMTRAK's trains are the comfortable, up-to-date way to travel. Whether it's the modern Turboliners, sleek Amfleet cars, or long distance trains, AMTRAK can take your client clear across America, from downtown-to-downtown in style.

With the U.S.A. Rail Pass your client can see as much of America as he or she wants to see. They will have a window view of the scenery as it rolls past, and a chance to look at it as they sit back and relax. And, in the near future, your clients will be able to experience the beauty of America from the new Superliners, bi-level trains which will offer the latest in train innovations on selected routes in the Midwest and Western United States. Not only do your clients get to see a lot of America with the U.S.A. Rail Pass, they can also take advantage of the Rail, Road and City Adventures, or one of the many fine tours available throughout the United States.

How to Use Your U.S.A. Rail Pass

1. Your U.S.A. RAIL PASS entitles you to regular coach travel on as many AMTRAK and Southern Railway trains and routes as your client wishes (except Metroliners), until the end date shown. However, every time your client obtains a coach ticket at an AMTRAK or Southern Railway ticket counter or downtown ticket office, he must present his signed PASS.

2. A U.S.A. RAIL PASS also entitles your client to upgrade to AMTRAK's Metroliner, club, or sleeping car services, but you must do so on a space available basis no more than one hour prior to train departure or on-board trains. Appropriate full accommodations charges must be paid to upgrade to club or sleeping car service. To upgrade to Metroliner, you simply pay the difference between regular rail fares and Metroliner fares.

3. To be sure of getting the accommodations your client desires on the train he wants to take, allow ample time to make coach reservations before departure, either in person or by calling one of the toll-free "800" numbers listed in every AMTRAK timetable. Reservations are mandatory on most long distance trains. Although reservations may not be made prior to purchase of the U.S.A. RAIL PASS, they should be made as soon as possible after purchase of the PASS. This is especially critical during peak travel periods, which include the months of June, July, August, and holiday periods such as Christmas.

4. After boarding the train, your client should have his PASS and ticket handy. He must present both and sign the ticket in the presence of a conductor or trainman, who may ask for identification to verify the signature.

5. The period of validity of the PASS is based on a start date of no more than 15 days after and including the date of purchase shown on the front of the PASS, to midnight of the 14th, 21st or 30th day of usage, depending upon the type of PASS purchased. At that time, the PASS and all tickets issued against it are considered expired. Departure from any point, including intermediate transfer points, must be made before midnight of the end date (which also appears on the front of the PASS). The PASS is not valid for a change in trains after midnight of the end date.

6. The cost of the PASS is not refundable after your client has reached the start date entered on the front of the PASS. No refunds are granted if a PASS is lost or stolen. Refunds will be made only upon surrender of a totally unused PASS prior to the start date, together with all tickets which have been issued but not used. If no start date has been entered on the PASS, application for refund must be made within six months of the date of purchase.

7. Exchange of shorter validity period PASSES for PASSES with a longer validity period will not be permitted once the start date of the original pass has begun.

8. Any alteration of the U.S.A. RAIL PASS invalidates it.

9. A U.S.A. RAIL PASS is available to citizens of all countries.

If you, as the travel agent, familiarize yourself with these simple conditions and follow them, your clients and thousands of others will be able to make the most of the U.S.A. RAIL PASS.

TICKETING A U.S.A. RAIL PASS

AMTRAK's U.S.A. Rail Pass is designed to provide unlimited coach travel within the designated period of 14, 21, or 30 days.

Current charges are as follows:

VALID	REGULAR Adult or Head of Family	Spouse or Child 12-21	FAMILY PLAN Child 2-11
14 days	$169.	$ 85.	$50.
21 days	$219.	$110.	$50.
30 days	$259.	$130.	$50.

Procedure for issuing the U.S.A. Rail Pass:

1. Circle the period of validity.

2. Enter the tariff charges and form of payment.

3. If a Family Plan Pass, print the endorsement "Family" and indicate the Family members travelling as follows:

        "F" - Head of Family
        "S" - Spouse and children 12-21
        "C" - Children 2-11

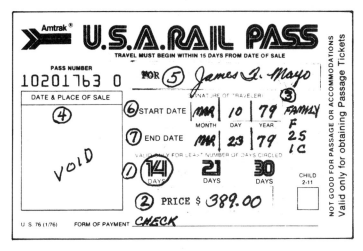

4.   Date stamp with ticket validator showing date and place of issue. The following entries may be completed by the issuing agent at the time of sale or by any AMTRAK agent at the time of first ticket issuance. (Must be within 15 days of the date of sale.)

5.   Signature of the traveller, or head of family, if Family Plan.

6.   Enter "Start Date" or date of first travel. This must be within 15 days of issued date.

7.   Enter the "End Date" or last date travel is allowed on the pass.

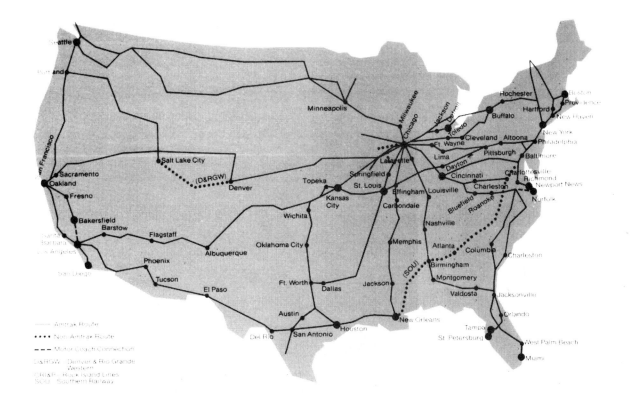

ISSUING INTERLINE RAIL TICKETS

Although the National Railroad Passenger Corporation has assumed the operation of most passenger trains in the United States a number of rail carriers continue to operate passenger trains over their own lines.

In order to provide continuity of service and as an added convenience to its customers, AMTRAK has entered into interline agreements with some of the carriers. There are a number of non-AMTRAK railroads operating passenger train service. Schedules for some of these are shown in the AMTRAK time tables under "Connecting Intercity Rail Service." A separate coupon must be included for each segment of travel over a non-AMTRAK carrier, routed 'via' the carrier's appropriate abbreviation.

Via "CR – "TH&B" – CP
Buffalo, NY – Toronto, Ontario

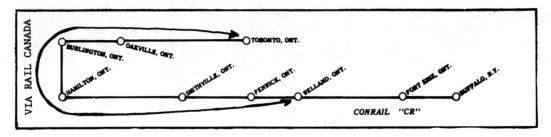

Two non-AMTRAK carriers participate in operation of through train service between Buffalo, NY, and Toronto, Ontario.

AMTRAK tickets may be issued to all stations on this line and must contain coupons routed as follows:

Between	Route
Buffalo, NY – Welland, Ont.	"CR"
Welland, Ont. – Toronto, Ont.	"VIA"

Coupons to points on this line may be incorporated as a part of through tickets issued from other AMTRAK stations beyond the Buffalo transfer point. (See example below.)

Travel to points beyond Toronto must not be included in through tickets, issue separate tickets.

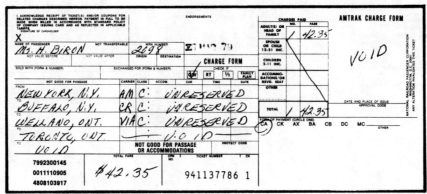

The nationwide rail passenger operations of the Canadian Railways are now officially combined under the corporate umbrella of VIA Rail Canada Incorporated. AMTRAK tickets may be issued for all trains operated by VIA Rail Canada Incorporated. AMTRAK's current agreement with the Canadian National Railway will continue in effect pending completion of VIA Rail Canada's negotiations and approval of a new joint interline agreement.

The general procedure for issuing tickets for Canadian travel remains unchanged; however, the VIA tariff contains changes in fares and related subjects.

The following arrangements will apply when issuing AMTRAK tickets for travel on trains operated by VIA Rail Canada.

Separate tickets must be issued for all travel on VIA Rail Canada. AMTRAK and VIA Rail Canada travel must not be combined on the same ticket.

The coupon requirements of AMTRAK and VIA Rail Canada are basically the same - a separate coupon for each train or bus the passenger uses; however, the ticketing scheme of VIA Rail Canada is governed by the fare collected. When regular fare is collected, issue a separate ticket for each direction of travel. When round-trip excursion fare is collected, issue a separate ticket for each round trip.

In preparing tickets in accordance with these instructions, it is permissible to include a number of adults and/or children on the same ticket.

VIA RAIL CANADA TICKET

Illustrated below is an example round-trip between Montreal and Toronto, issued on separate tickets for each direction of travel.

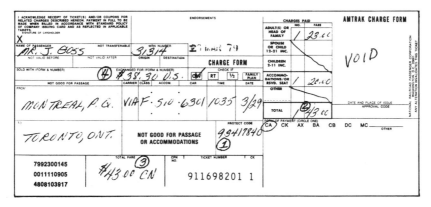

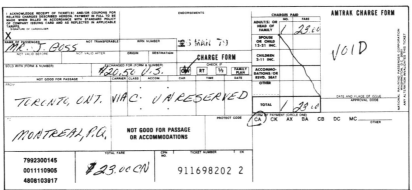

Important differences particular to VIA Rail Canada are as follows:

1. The Canadian eight digit code number must be entered for each reservation. The code will be furnished by AMTRAK Central Reservation upon advise that tickets have been issued.

2 & 3. The fares entered in these blocks must be as quoted in the Tariff in Canadian Currency.

4. Use the currency conversion scale in Table 205 of the Tariff and the current exchange rate to determine the amount to be collected in U.S. funds. AMTRAK reservations will advise the current exchange rate and percentage scale to use in currency conversion calculations.

The VIA Pass is the Canadian equivalent to our U.S.A. RAIL PASS, it provides unlimited passage on VIA trains (former CN-ONR trains) within designated territories.

"On" and "Off" season rates for each type of pass and periods of validity are shown in the chart below.

TYPE	TERRITORY IN WHICH VALID		SEASON – NUMBER OF DAYS – RATES							
			ON SEASON JUN 15 - SEP 15				OFF SEASON SEP 16 - JUN 14*			
		#DAYS	8	15	22	30	8	15	22	30
SYSTEM	ENTIRE SYSTEM	$			300	350			240	280
EAST	EAST OF WINNIPEG	$		180	225			160	200	
WEST	WEST OF WINNIPEG	$		180	225			160	200	
CORRIDOR	IN CORRIDOR ONLY	$	100	130			95	120		
MOUNTAIN	WEST OF CALGARY/EDMONTON	$	100	130			95	120		
CHILDREN 6 - 11 ONE-HALF THE ADULT CHARGES			* EXCEPT DECEMBER 18 - JANUARY 4 INC. and APRIL 12 & 16, 1979							

AMTRAK Agents may issue AMTRAK Tour Order (Form 95) as shown below to cover the sale of one or more VIA PASSES.

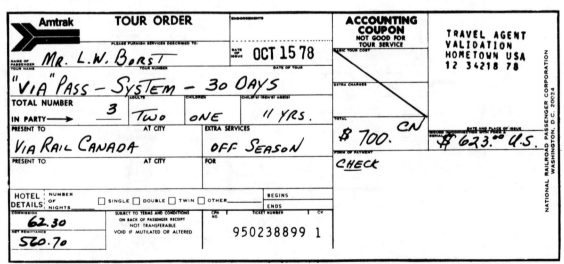

Tour Orders must be exchanged at a VIA Rail Canada Ticket Office for an actual VIA PASS before travel in Canada begins.

AMTRAK TOUR ORDERS

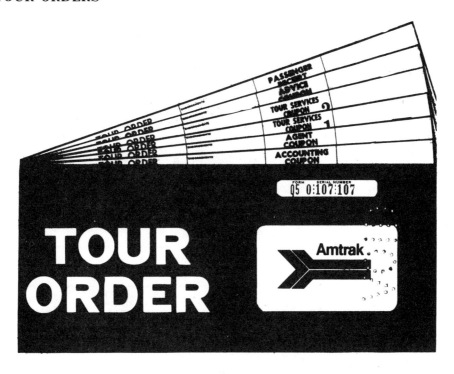

The Tour Order is an AMTRAK ticket form consisting of six coupons: Accounting, Travel Agent's, two Tour Services coupons (1 & 2), an Advice coupon and a Passenger's Receipt.

The Tour Order is specifically designed for use in connection with AMTRAK sponsored tours which may be booked and sold in advance. In general, Tour Orders are issued to cover complete tour packages without rail transportation; however, certain tours, such as Four Winds or American Rail Tours, include AMTRAK transportation. This information is contained in the tour details.

Travel Agents must exercise care in preparing Tour Orders in accordance with these guidelines including any specific instructions furnished by the booking agency.

After the Tour Order is completed, the handling and distribution of the tour service coupons becomes extremely important. Agents will be governed by the tour operators booking instruction to send coupons directly to his office or have the customer present them upon arrival at the point the tour commences.

The following page shows an Example of a Tour Order and a Tour Order with Transfer Included.

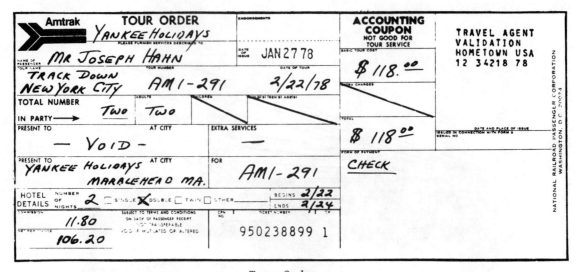

Tour Order

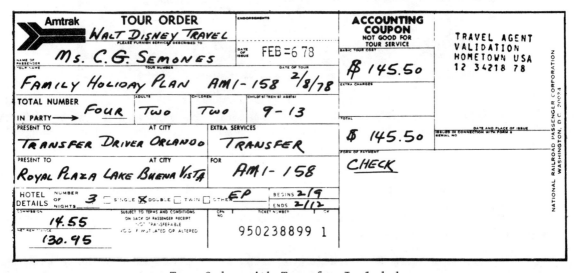

Tour Order with Transfer Included

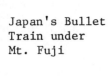

Japan's Bullet
Train under
Mt. Fuji

Bourbon Street Parade

3 Days from $66

per person, double occupancy
(rail fare not included)

Thrill to the lively sounds of Dixieland in the city where it originated. Here the soul-moving sounds of New Orleans-style jazz played by its masters. The city's "alive" with music. In famous night clubs, in lounges, in Preservation Hall and in the streets. You'll enjoy it all in New Orleans.

3 Day Tour
Price includes:
• Three days and two nights' accommodations at a selected hotel
• Top of the Mart—enjoy your choice of a standard cocktail while overlooking the city. Tax and tip included.
• Pete Fountain's—see a great show while enjoying two cocktails of your choice. Show admission, tax and tip included.
• River Queen Show atop the Marriott Hotel—be entertained while enjoying two cocktails of your choice. Show admission, tax and tip included.
• French Quarter Carriage Tour—the past comes alive as your carriage journeys through the famous Vieux Carre with its scrolled wrought iron balconies and quaint cobblestone streets steeped in history
• All local taxes.
• Charges for planning and operation. (Baggage handling not included.)

AM1-348 / AM1-351
Bourbon Street Parade / New Orleans Potpourri
(rates per person)

Hotel	Single	Twin-Double	Triple
Fountain Bay Club	$ 88.00	$ 66.00	$58.00
Chateau Motor Hotel	84.00	68.00	58.00
Grand Hotel New Orleans	96.00	70.00	62.00
Le Richelieu	100.00	74.00	64.00
Howard Johnsons-Dtwn	102.00	74.00	64.00
Warwick Hotel	108.00	74.00	64.00
Le Downtowner Vieux Carre	96.00	76.00	68.00
Le Pavillon	112.00	80.00	70.00
Chateau Le Moyne	116.00	82.00	72.00
Monteleone Hotel	116.00	82.00	72.00
Marie Antoinette	124.00	88.00	74.00
Maison Dupuy	126.00	90.00	76.00
Marriott Hotel	118.00	90.00	72.00
Fairmont Hotel	118.00	90.00	80.00
New Orleans Hilton	128.00	96.00	86.00
Royal Sonesta	152.00	104.00	88.00

*All prices per person effective Jan 1st-Dec 31st, 1978 except for Sugar Bowl, Super Bowl & Mardi Gras periods.

Philadelphia Independence

3 Days from $49

per person, double occupancy
(rail fare not included)

Almost everywhere in Philadelphia, the Cradle of Liberty, there is a sense of history. Run your fingers over the crack in the Liberty Bell. Stroll along one of the oldest streets in America, Elfreth's Alley. Feel the past come vibrantly alive in the mellowed majesty of Independence Hall. Feel the golden patina of age carry over to the vital, exciting present. Fine theatre, excellent shopping, concerts and major league sports are all here for you to enjoy in this old and new city called Philadelphia.

3 Day Tour
Price includes:
• 2 nights' first class accommodations in a selected hotel
• Historic Philadelphia escorted motorcoach tour—see Antique Row, Franklin's Grave and Society Hill. Relive the past at Independence Hall, the Liberty Bell, Christ Church and the Betsy Ross House

or

Modern Philadelphia Escorted Motorcoach Tour—see the Franklin Institute, Penn Center, J.F.K. Plaza, and the Boat House Row area. Browse through the Philadelphia Museum of Art and the new U.S. Coin Mint
• All program taxes
• Yankee "Philadelphia Visitors Welcome Information Packet"

AM1-122
Philadelphia Independence
(rates per person)

Hotels	Single	Double/Twin	Triple
Ben Franklin	$ 79.00	$ 53.00	$46.00
Extra Night	30.00	19.00	15.00
Hilton Hotel of Philadelphia	82.00	60.00	53.00
Extra Night	33.00	22.00	20.00
Penn Center Inn	77.00	49.00	34.00
Extra Night	29.00	18.00	15.00
Philadelphia Sheraton	86.00	54.00	47.00
Extra Night	35.00	20.00	16.00
The Latham	112.00	70.00	NA
Extra Night	48.00	28.00	NA
The Marriott	81.00	53.00	46.00
Extra Night	32.00	19.00	16.00

(Extra night rates include tax)

New England On Wheels

Rail/Motorhome
7 Days from $230

per person, double occupancy
(rail fare not included)

Travel from the rolling hills of Massachusetts to the rocky cliffs of Maine in a luxurious "home-on-wheels". In between, discover promising artists on Cape Cod. Catch the awe-inspiring beauty of the White Mountains of New Hampshire and the Green Mountains of Vermont. Play on the fantastic ocean beaches of Rhode Island and enjoy the unspoiled beauty of the Connecticut River Valley. New England—its sights and its pleasures—is yours with all the comforts of home.

7 Day Tour
Price includes:
• Round trip transportation from Boston Amtrak terminal to Motorhome Rental Center
• 7 days' rental of Yankee TEC Lark (or similar Motorhome)—including dinette, refrigerator, stove, bath facilities, all kitchen utensils and linen, storage space and wardrobe closet. The Lark is completely self-contained, and sleeps six in comfort. Equipped with air-conditioning, automatic heater, AM-FM stereo radio, tape deck, roof rack and carpeting.
• 800 free miles (gasoline not included)

AM1-113
New England On Wheels
(rates per person)

	Single	Double	Triple
1 Week	$435.00	$230.00	$172.00
2 Weeks	785.00	420.00	385.00
3 Weeks	1,115.00	598.00	420.00
Extra Days:	70.00	40.00	30.00

AM1-113
New England On Wheels
(rates per person)

	Quad	Five	Six
1 Week	$138.00	$117.00	$107.00
2 Weeks	234.00	197.00	174.00
3 Weeks	277.00	280.00	240.00
Extra Days:	25.00	22.00	20.00

Cancellation fee, within 15 days of departure, $100.00 per booking.

A $100 security deposit is payable on arrival, by passenger direct to rental firm. This deposit is completely refundable when Motorhome is returned by renter.

Payable by cash or Travellers Checks.

Tour Operator:
Yankee Holidays
Marblehead, MA 01945

For tour conditions and booking information, see Page 37.

RAIL TOUR OPERATORS

Abbott Tours
The Abbott Building
2609 Canal Street
New Orleans, LA 70117
(880)535-9092

Airail Rent-A-Car
(Book through AMTRAK Reservations)

American Travel Brokers
650 - 17th Street
Security Bldg., Suite 712
Denver, CO 80202
(303)433-6313

AmTour Corporation
421 Powell Street
San Francisco, CA 94120
(800)227-4248 (in states)
(800)622-0809 (CA)

Cosmopolitan Travel Service
122 Regency Square
Jacksonville, FL 32211
(904)724-7503

Educational Tour Consultants
108 N. Loudon Street Mall
Winchester, VA 22601
(800)336-2515

Fidelity Tours
P.O. Box 2277
Miami Beach, FL 33140
(800)327-8206

Fiesta Train Tours
Box 1195
Torrance, CA 90505
(213)373-4502

Finlay Fun-Time Tours
11306 Burbank Blvd.
No. Hollywood, CA 91601
(213)877-7759

Florida World Tours
999 Woodcock Road
Suite 302
Orlando, FL 32803
(800)327-2941

Floyd Chapman Leasing Corp.
4902 South Orange Avenue
Orlando, FL 32808
(305)857-3100

Four Winds Travel
175 Fifth Avenue
New York, NY 10010
(212)777-0260

Global Sports Tours
9348 Santa Monica Blvd.
Suite 301
Beverly Hills, CA 90210
(800)421-0584

Global Sports Tours/Utah
234 Atlas Building
Salt Lake City, UT 84111
(800)453-9441

Grand National Tours, Inc.
435 Galleria Bldg.
600 S.W. 10th Ave.
Portland, OR 97205
(503)227-1426

Gray Line of Albuquerque
P.O. Box 693
Albuquerque, NM 87103
(505)243-3501

Gray Line of San Diego
1670 Kettner Blvd.
San Diego, CA 92101
(714)231-9922

Grayline of Seattle
415 Seneca Street
Seattle, WA 98101
(206)682-1234

Great Western Tours
Sheraton Palace Hotel
639 Market Street
San Francisco, CA 94105
(415)398-2994

Hilton Inn Gateway
7470 Spacecoast Parkway
Kissimmee, FL 32741
(800)382-7665

Inter-American RR Tours
1820 Caminito Monrovia
La Jolla, CA 92037

Ivanhoe Holidays
3612 W. 211th Street
Olympia Fields, IL 60461
(312)995-6868

Kel-Mar World Travel Service
404-22nd Street
Oakland, CA 94612
(415)835-3800

Kneisel Travel
345 N.E. 8th Avenue
Portland, OR 97232
(503)238-9730

Let's Travel Tours
P.O. Box 2786
Riverside, CA 92506
(714)787-8350

Lincolnland Sightseeing
1026 S. Fifth Street
Springfield, IL 62703
(217)522-5547

Midwest Travel Service
2936 Bella Vista Drive
Midwest City, OK 73110
(405)732-0566

Monarch Cruise Lines, Inc.
1428 Brickell Avenue
Miami, FL 33131
(305)374-6611

Mystic Marine Aquarium
Mystic, CT
(203)536-9631

Mystic Seaport
Mystic, CT
(203)536-2631

New York Group Tours
8 W. 40th Street
New York, NY 10018
(800)223-0450

Norwegian American Line
29 Broadway
New York, NY 10006
(800)221-2400

On-the-Scene Tours
Suite 1315
205 W. Wacker Drive
Chicago, IL 60606
(312)236-9722

Prestige Resort Hotels
Box 767
Lake Worth, FL 33460
(305)588-8543

Ramada Inn, Downtown
1005 Guy Street
Montreal, Que. H3H2K4
(514)866-4611

Rodeway Inn of Kissimmee
2050 East Spacecoast Parkway
Kissimmee, FL 32741
(305)846-4545

76 Adventures, Inc.
871 Seventh Avenue
New York, NY 10019
(800)223-7501

Sheraton Mt. Royal
1455 Peel Street
Montreal, Que. H3A 1T5
(514)842-7777

Talmage Tours, Inc.
1223 Walnut Street
Philadelphia, PA 19107
(215)WA3-7100

UTL Holiday Tours
P.O. Box 219
Toronto, Ontario M5C2J3
(416)967-3355

VIA Rail Canada
Central Station
Montreal, Que. H3C3N4
(514)877-5650

VIA Rail Canada
Union Station
Toronto, Ontario M5J1E7
(416)367-4300

VIA Rail Canada
CN Station
Vancouver, B.C. V6A2X7
(604)682-5552

Walt Disney Travel Co.
Preview Center
Preview Center Boulevard
P.O. Box 22094
Lake Buena Vista, FL 32830
(305)828-3232

Washington Group Tours
Suite 112
1832 M Street, N.W.
Washington, DC 20036
(202)466-2251

Yankee Holidays
Fife & Drum Bldg.
Town House Square
Marblehead, MA 01945
(800)225-2550

German Rail

THE OFFICIAL RAILWAY GUIDE

The Official Railway Guide is normally issued monthly, except February and August, and usually contains rail timetables and other essential information for client booking. The Official Railway Guide is principally divided into separate American, Canadian and Mexican sections. The International section of condensed foreign schedules appears near the back of the Guide, preceding the passenger station index. Each section consists of a national map with passenger train routes, an index of carriers and train names, schedules of intercity service and tables of suburban service for major metropolitan areas. Timetable pages include schedules, sample fares, equipment descriptions and reference mark explanations.

Trains operating across international borders, while appearing on more than one national map, are listed in one section only and carry the appropriate table number on all maps. Table of contents, late schedule and tariff changes, other news and feature articles are located before the United States section. Located at the back of the Guide, following the Mexican section, are schedules for connecting bus and ferry service, general reference material and an index of North American passenger stations.

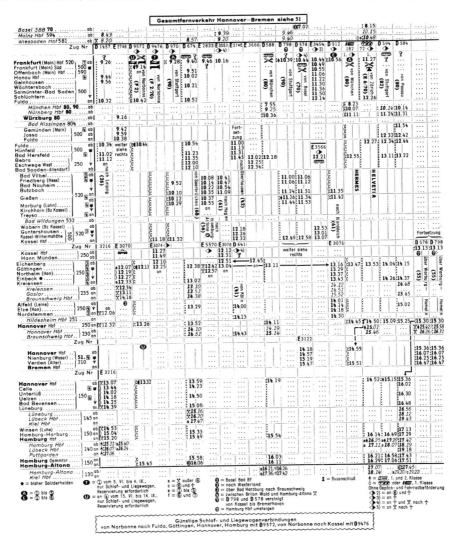

Typical European rail schedule.

THOMAS COOK INTERNATIONAL TIMETABLE

The Thomas Cook International Timetable generally contains:

800 tables of rail timings in the 24-hour clock over every European main line railway, and condensed rail schedules for the rest of the world.

Cross-Channel hovercraft services with connections to and from London and Paris.

Shipping services linking Britain, Ireland, Continental Europe and Scandinavia, and throughout the Mediterranean.

List of principal resorts not served by rail, with nearest railhead and means of access.

Quick-reference index maps of the routes covered, with their respective table numbers.

Passport and visa regulations for all countries in Europe.

Detailed, individual tables for Europe's most important trains, including the high-speed Trans-Europe-Express network and through routes from Britain to the Continent.

Plans of railway terminal for London, Paris, Rome and 55 other European cities.

Foreign geographical names with corresponding English language forms.

Monthly temperature figures and annual rainfall for many cities and resorts.

Steamer services on the Rhine, the Danube, the Gota Canal and the Swiss and Italian lakes.

Motorail (auto) trains in Britain and on the European Continent, with loading times and accommodations.

Rail links between European cities and their international airports.

ABC RAIL GUIDE

Another useful rail travel guide (in Great Britain) is the ABC Rail Guide. For well over a century, the ABC Rail Guide has been Britain's most popular rail guide. Published every month, it provides information for rail bookings throughout Great Britain, plus continental shipping services. Contents include:

Rail routes and fares from London to all stations in Great Britain.

Complete train service section for South-East England.

Separate inter-city section in quick-reference format, with over 400 point-to-point journeys between provincial centers.

Connecting lines for places not served by rail.

Cross-Channel shipping services.

Full coverage of fares (ordinary, day, weekend, and 17-day) and their validity.

BRITRAIL TRAVEL

The High Speed Trains on British Rail are now in service between London and Edinburgh. Also frequent services between London, Bath and Cardiff, New Inter-City 125 routes in 1979 from London to Exeter, Plymouth and Penzance. Unlimited rail travel in England, Scotland and Wales is available with a Britrail Pass. No matter how long your client stays in Britain, there's a BritRail Pass to suit your client's travel requirements. Travel in Britain by modern passenger train is a new experience for many North Americans that will change their ideas about the comfort, speed and service of rail travel. The famous Inter-City network (including our High Speed Trains, Inter-City 125) links major cities throughout the country with fast, frequent and comfortable services which take your client from city center to city center. Use the Pass any time WITHIN A YEAR OF THE ISSUE DATE. Choose from more than 16,000 trains daily, 1,800 of them Inter-City Expresses. No predating - just have the Pass validated at any British Rail Station before your client starts the first journey, then enjoy unlimited rail travel on CONSECUTIVE days for the following periods: 7, 14, 21 days or 1 month.

Britrail Passes are not sold in Great Britain. They must be purchased in North America.

London—Preston, Carlisle, Glasgow, Perth, Inverness   **2**

MONDAYS TO SATURDAYS

Station										SX	SO	SX	SX	SX	SX	SO	SUNDAYS								
London Euston	0745	0845	0940	1045	1145	1345	1545	1645	1745	2050	2145	2150	2235	2300	2330	2330	0915	1150	1350	1545	1725	2050	2250	2300	2330
Preston	1019	1119	1249	1315	1421	1621	1820	1915	2015	–	–	–	–	–	–	–	1306	1539	1717	1822	2005	–	–	–	–
Carlisle	1132	1232	1401	–	1534	1734	1933	2034	2128	–	–	–	–	–	0411	0547	1549	1704	1836	1937	2124	–	–	–	0411
Glasgow Central	1257	1355	–	1545	1655	1900	–	2156	2253	–	–	–	–	0514	0605	0839	1733	1831	2003	2058	2246	–	–	0514	0605
Perth	1529	–	1657	1813	1926	2112	–	0012	–	0432	0724	0529	0733	–	0829	1138	1926	1831	–	–	0048	0432	0841	0829	0829
Inverness	–	–	1945	2125	–	–	–	–	–	0805	1032	0910	–	–	1355	–	–	–	–	–	–	0805	1355	1355	1355

MONDAYS TO SATURDAYS

Station									SX	SX	SO	SX	SO	SX	SX
Inverness	–	–	–	–	–	–	1030	–	1215	1850	–	1850	2015	2015	–	–	–
Perth	–	–	–	0820	1020	1220	1328	1420	1519	2205	2212	2212	2339	2339	–	–	–
Glasgow Central	0710	0800	0910	1010	1210	1410	–	1610	1730	–	–	–	–	–	2250	2250	2310
Carlisle	0835	0943	1039	–	1331	1531	1620	1735	1851	–	–	–	–	–	0051	0051	–
Preston	0946	1105	1146	1230	1439	1639	1732	1843	1959	–	–	–	–	–	–	–	–
London Euston	1229	1407	1432	1510	1720	1917	2052	2125	2237	0622	0713	0806	0720	0843	0524	0651	0534

SUNDAYS

Inverness	–	–	–	–	–	1845	2015	–	–
Perth	–	–	–	1243	–	2215	2338	–	–
Glasgow Central	0900	1105	1330	1600	1715	–	–	2250	2310
Carlisle	1057	1301	1512	1725	1836	–	–	0051	–
Preston	1346	1549	1647	1832	1950	–	–	–	–
London Euston	1743	1839	1937	2123	2235	0713	0720	0524	0534

EXPLANATION OF SIGNS

- SX Saturdays excepted.
- SO Saturdays only.
- Sleeper service.
- R Limited accommodation, all seats reservable.
- 1st class Pullman service only (supplementary charge including reserved seat).
- (P) 1st class Pullman service (supplementary charge including reserved seat). 2nd class non-Pullman.
- Through coaches.
- • No refreshments.
- φ No refreshments on Saturdays.

If your client is 65 or older, there is a Britrail Senior Citizen Pass, i.e., FIRST CLASS train travel for the Economy rate. Senior Citizen Pass is issued for 7, 14, 21, and 30 days.

A great travel bargain for young people aged 14 through 22 is the Youth Pass. Whether your clients stay one week, three weeks or for one month, they don't have to travel every day to make the Youth Pass pay. No predating - the Youth Pass is validated at the station from which your clients start the first journey. No identification needed; the Passport will verify age. Youth Passes must be purchased in North America before leaving for 7, 14, 21, or 30 days.

The Tower of London - 900 years and standing sturdy.   British Tourist Photo

For clients travelling between Britain and Ireland, choose the inexpensive scenic way by train and Sealink Ship. For extra travel savings, clients can buy the SEAPASS (Ireland) which is an addition to the BritRail Pass that allows your customer to make one or two "one-way" journeys between London and the Irish Ports served by British Rail's Ship routes. Valid only for economy (2nd Class) travel on ships.

Clients travelling between Britain and Europe, choose the train and Sealink Ship or Seaspeed Hovercraft and can use the SEAPASS (CONTINENTAL). Valid only for economy (2nd class), and one class travel on ships and Hovercraft.

The connecting rail journeys between London and the British ports of embarkation/disembarkation are included in the cost of the SeaPass. Rail/Sea journeys can be taken outside the validity of your BritRail Pass, either before or after, as long as you use the whole ticket WITHIN SIX MONTHS OF ISSUE DATE. Children 3 through 13 half fare. The SeaPass facility applies to Youth Pass and Senior Citizen Pass prices. Savings up to 52% when compared with 2nd Class fares from London to these Continental Ports.

British Rail operates a large fleet of "drive on and off" car ferries between ports in Britain and Europe/Ireland. Reservations are normally confirmed immediately but prior notice of at least 21 days is required. Brief details of the services are provided below:

    Dover/Folkstone - Ostend, 10 sailings daily.
    Dover/Folkstone - Boulogne/Calais/Dunkirk, 15 sailings daily
    Newhaven - Dieppe, 3 sailings daily
    Weymouth - Cherbourg, 2 sailings daily
    Harwich - Hook of Holland, 2 sailings daily
    Fishguard - Rosslare, 2 sailings daily
    Holyhead - Dun Laoghaire, 2 sailings daily

EURAILPASS

Eurailpass is a single, convenient card (rail ticket) that entitles the client to unlimited 1st-class rail travel throughout 15 countries of Continental Europe. The Eurailpass must be paid for in advance. The Eurailpass gives customers unlimited mileage to travel the length and breadth of Europe, whether, in one, two or more

countries, stop where customers want. Customers can also base themselves in a city of their choice and make an unlimited number of different excursions by train each day.

European rail travel is a unique pleasure for the traveller: the trains run on time and they are modern, comfortable, fast and frequent, such as the Trans Europe Express (TEE) which are first-class track trains that permit the client to travel from one country to another in luxury and at speeds often as high as 125 mph. The table below gives an indication of some distances and travel times using a Eurailpass:

FROM	TO	DISTANCE (MILES)	TRAVEL TIME
Amsterdam	Brussels	148	2:30 hrs.
	Paris	346	5:00 hrs.
Barcelona	Avignon	294	5:23 hrs.
	Geneva	544	9:09 hrs.
Copenhagen	Hamburg	225	5:05 hrs.
	Cologne	513	9:14 hrs.
	Stuttgart	753	13:09 hrs.
Luxembourg	Zurich	281	4:29 hrs.
Milan	Florence	198	2:48 hrs.
	Rome	395	6:00 hrs.
Paris	Lyon	320	3:45 hrs.
	Marseille	539	6:35 hrs.
	Nice	680	9:05 hrs.
Vienna	Nuremberg	322	5:10 hrs.
	Cologne	618	9:57 hrs.
Zurich	Munich	221	4:16 hrs.

Austria, Belgium, Denmark, Finland, France, Germany, Greece, Italy, Luxembourg, Netherlands, Norway, Portugal, Spain, Sweden and Switzerland have more than 100,000 miles of railroad track to take your client to every corner of Europe. From the Arctic Circle to the azure Mediterranean, from the Moorish gardens of the Alhambra to the ancient splendor of the Acropolis - the trains of Europe are among the most modern in the world. They take your client from city center to city center, often in less time than air travel and at less cost than renting an automobile. Plus, when the customer travels with a Eurailpass or a Eurail Youthpass, they are not limited to train travel. For a change, take an excursion by boat on the Rhine, the Danube or on Lake Geneva - the ticket is valid on many European ferries, river and lake steamers - or try a tour by motor coach; some trips are free, others are available at substantially-reduced fares.

EURAILPASS AND EURAIL YOUTHPASS CONDITIONS

1.   Eurailpass or Eurail Youthpass may be purchased and used only if you live outside of Europe or North Africa.

2.   Eurail Youthpass is available to anyone under 26 years of age.

3.   Eurailpass and Eurail Youthpass are not sold in Europe. They have to be obtained from an issuing office or a Travel Agent before leaving.

4.   Eurailpass and Eurail Youthpass are personal and non-transferable. They are forfeited if presented by anyone other for whom they were issued, or if they bear any evidence of alteration or mutilation. Presentation of a passport to European train personnel is compulsory.

5.   Eurailpass or Eurail Youthpass have to be presented at the station where you will board the train for the first time, to have the dates of validity inscribed upon them, and to avoid a penalty charge.

6.   Eurailpass or Eurail Youthpass have to be used within six months from the date of their issuance.

7.   Eurailpass or Eurail Youthpass are vaild until midnight of the last day of validity; therefore, make sure to take a train scheduled to arrive at destination before midnight.

8.   Eurailpass is valid in 1st class; Eurail Youthpass is valid in 2nd class. Both entitle you to transportation on the national railroads and many private rail lines, steamers and ferry crossings of the following countries: Austria, Belgium, Denmark, Finland, France, Germany (Federal Republic), Greece, Holland, Italy, Luxembourg, Norway, Portugal, Spain, Sweden and Switzerland. They do not include reservation fees, meals, refreshments, sleeping accommodations, port taxes nor, in the case of the Eurail Youthpass, fees and supplements required to travel on certain trains.

9. Eurailpass and Eurail Youthpass do not assure a seat on a train. Some trains require reserved seats, obtainable for a nominal fee. Advance reservations, which must be requested early, are recommended on all major long-distance trains during holidays and the summer season; they are compulsory to travel in sleepers or couchettes. In Spain, passengers are not allowed to board express trains unless they have reserved a seat or obtained a boarding pass.

10. Eurailpass or Eurail Youthpass are not refundable if lost or stolen, or when submitted after the first day of validity, or after one year from the date of issuance. In other cases, application for refund must be submitted to the office where they were purchased. Any refund, if granted, is subject to a deduction of 10% from the price of the ticket.

11. Eurailpass or Eurail Youthpass use and carriers' responsibility are governed by the International Convention for the Transportation of Passengers and Baggage by Rail (C.I.V.).

Each year Eurailpass publishes new fares for the unlimited 1st class travel in 15 European countries for 15, 21, or 30 days; unlimited 2nd class Youthpasses are for 60 days. Other European rail passes include:

Austria Ticket: Unlimited rail travel in Austria, including steamers on Lake Constance and Lake Wolfgang for 9 and 16 days by 1st and 2nd class travel.

Benelux Tourrail: Unlimited 2nd class travel during 10 consecutive days in Holland, Belgium, and Luxembourg; only available during the period April to October.

Finnrailpass: Unlimited travel on all trains of the Finnish State Railways for 1 to 4 weeks by 1st and 2nd class travel.

France Vacances: Unlimited 1st and 2nd class travel on the French rail system for 9, 16 and 30 days by 1st and 2nd class travel.

Germanrail Tourist Card: Unlimited travel in Germany, with bonus coupon for reduced round-trip ticket to Berlin for 9 and 16 days by 1st and 2nd class travel.

Interrail Card: Sold to persons under 23 years of age. Unlimited 2nd class rail travel for 1 month. Sold in the major train stations of all 15 Eurailpass countries, plus Great Britain, Hungary, Ireland, Yugoslavia, and Morocco. While travelling in country issuing the pass, holders must purchase 2nd class tickets at 50% discount.

Italian Tourist Card: Unlimited rail travel in Italy for 8, 15, 21, 30 days by 1st and 2nd class travel.

Portuguese Rail Tourist Ticket: Personal tickets available year round at all major railroad stations in Portugal for 2nd class travel only (7, 14, and 21 days).

Rover Ticket (Holland): Unlimited rail travel throughout Netherlands rail network (purchase in Holland) for 1 day or 8 days by 1st and 2nd class travel.

Scandinavian Rail Pass: Unlimited rail travel in Denmark, Finland, Norway, and Sweden for 21 days by 1st or 2nd class travel. Not valid on Stockholm's local rail system.

Swiss Holiday Card: Unlimited rail travel in Switzerland for 4, 8, 15, 30 days by 1st and 2nd class travel.

The above listing is partial and not inclusive of all offerings of special discount tickets and passes.

As a travel agent you will want to learn all you can about the various national railways. A good book to begin with is Fodor's Railways of the World (David McKay, New York, 1977); individual timetables in the countries as well as the Thomas Cook International Timetables can provide you more understanding of rail travel around the world.

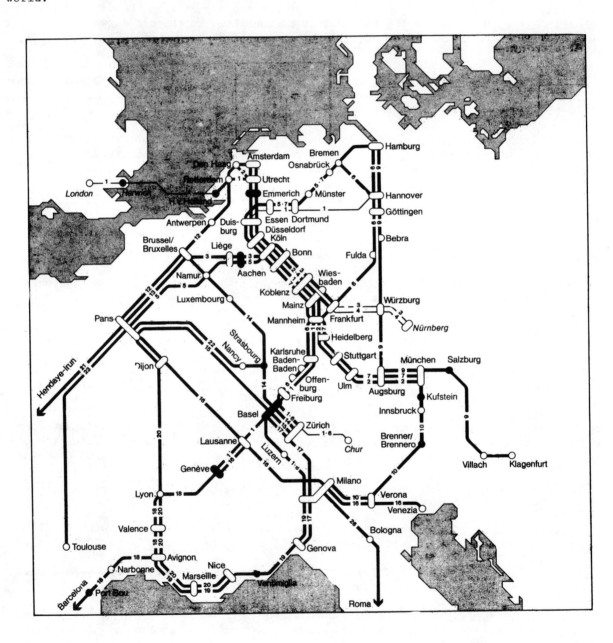

Chapter 11

BUS TRAVEL

BUS TRANSPORTATION

In the travel industry a bus is a reserved vehicle that provides scheduled service for an individually-ticketed passenger. When used to perform any tour service, the same vehicle is a motorcoach. In the United States and Canada, there are more than 400 private owned intercity bus companies; two of the largest carriers are Greyhound and Trailways.

The bus industry is an integral part of the tourism industry in this country. In 1977 alone, privately owned intercity buses carried 332 million passengers. In charters and tours alone, buses carried approximately 150 million people. This figure excludes local service operations, school bus operations, and government and military group movement. These passengers carried on bus tours and charters constitute 20 percent of the intercity passengers carried by all public transportation services last year. Travel by bus as part of a charter group is a most enjoyable experience and a very effective way for people to travel.

Intercity buses today provide the most pervasive form of service of any transportation mode in America, serving 15,000 communities in scheduled service, 14,000 of which have no alternative form of intercity public transportation.

Bus transportation is the only real alternative to the use of the private automobile serving traditional highway and secondary road systems of the nation. Tour buses can go where the hotels and motels have been built, where the attractions are located, to the heart of the urban centers or the most distant national park, and on a network of roadway systems ranging from the interstate highways to the smallest country road. The attractiveness of bus travel can be seen in the fare structure:

TYPICAL INTERCITY BUS FARES

New York, N.Y. to	Feb. 16, 1972 1-Way	Excursion	Feb. 10, 1978 1-Way	Excursion
Boston, Mass.	$10.45	$19.90	$20.40	$19.00
Philadelphia, Pa.	4.85	9.25	9.40	17.90
Washington, D.C.	11.20	21.30	20.95	39.85
Pittsburgh, Pa.	19.10	36.30	33.85	64.35
Miami, Fla.	52.45	86.55	88.30	99.00
Buffalo, N.Y.	19.40	36.90	36.10	58.85
Chicago, Ill.	36.40	69.20	64.30	80.00

| | Feb. 16, 1972 | | Feb. 10, 1978 | |
	1-Way	Excursion	1-Way	Excursion
Chicago, Ill. to				
St. Louis, Mo.	$11.05	$21.00	$19.55	$37.15
Kansas City, Mo.	18.75	35.65	33.20	63.10
Milwaukee, Wis.	3.70	7.05	6.55	11.50
Minneapolis, Minn.	13.25	25.20	23.45	44.60
Detroit, Mich.	12.70	24.15	22.45	42.70
Cincinnati, Ohio	13.80	26.25	24.40	46.40
New Orleans, La.	31.90	60.65	56.40	88.00
Los Angeles, Calif. to				
San Diego, Calif.	4.63	7.85	7.48	14.21
San Francisco, Calif.	13.56	24.41	21.72	41.27
Phoenix, Ariz.	15.95	30.35	28.25	53.70
Seattle, Wash.	38.50	73.15	68.20	110.00

In recent years the bus industry has experienced with reduced excursion fares; reduced rates during the winter period in the very long hard markets where buses do not carry a substantial volume of business, e.g., Greyhound offers seven days to anywhere and everywhere in Florida for a $75.00 fare.

Other special fares (Winter 1979) include:

Greyhound offers 10 days of unlimited travel in California for $89.50.

Greyhound and Vermont Transit take the large view of what constitutes New England, so the new seven day $49.95 New England bus pass is valid for travel between New York City and Montreal via Albany and intermediate points, as well as all of Maine, Rhode Island, Massachusetts, New Hampshire, Vermont and Connecticut.

Trailways has a go anywhere package for $69.00 and marked it down to $65.00 for trips between any two points begun on a weekday.

The unlimited travel Ameripass and Eagle Pass available at $99.50 for seven days of busing on either Trailways or Greyhound, $149.50 for 15 days and $199.50 for 30 days. Moreover, any pass can be extended for any period at a cost of $8.00 per day.

Greyhound and Trailways have discounts for passengers 65 and older. One-way tickets and the outbound portion of roundtrip tickets must be used Monday through Thursday on Greyhound, Monday through Wednesday on Trailways, but the return points of a round trip may be used any day.

Travel agents dealing in bus travel ticketing should have the current edition of RUSSELL'S BUS GUIDE. This "OAG" of the bus travel is published monthly and provides the latest timetables (schedules), current fares, and other route information required by the bus traveller.

In Melbourne, trams have been retained and provide an inexpensive and efficient means of transport. Pictured here is Collins Street, noted for its smart shops, arcades, department stores and boutiques.

Australian Tourist Photo

TICKETING

Travel agencies hold ticket stock for major bus companies such as Greyhound or Trailways. This enables the agency to sell bus travel as a means of transportation as well as a component of a tour. Below is an itinerary.

Name: MRS. ELLEN HAUGE	Home Phone	Order Rec'd	Pick Up Date	Fare	
				Tax	
29 ROCKLAND AVENUE	Office Phone	Call Client	Advised Client OK unless we call –	Total	
GOFFSTOWN, NH 03045				Passport	

DATE	DAY	ITINERARY	BUS NO.	CLASS	TABLE NO.	LEAVE	ARRIVE	Small Pox		
								Option Date		
5/8	M T (W) TH F SA SU	MANCHESTER	VERMONT TRANSIT	F A T Y K R	OK Req. List		4:50 (AM) PM	6:30 (AM) PM	Ticket No.	By
5/8	M T (W) TH F SA SU	BOSTON NEW YORK	3163	F A T Y K R	OK Req. List	116 117	8:00 (AM) PM	12:40 AM (PM)		
5/8	M T (W) TH F SA SU	CHICAGO	1307	F A T Y K R	OK Req. List	285	1:45 (PM) AM	6:30 (AM) PM	*1 night	
5/9	M (TH) F W SA SU	OMAHA	1307	F A T Y K R	OK Req. List	558	7:30 (AM) PM	7:15 AM (PM)	Stopover	
5/11	M T W TH F SA (SU)	SALT LAKE CITY	1307	F A T Y K R	OK Req. List	558	7:15 AM (PM)	6:35 AM (PM)	* o night	
5/12	(M) T W TH F SA SU	LAS VEGAS	6025	F A T Y K R	OK Req. List	557	7:05 AM (PM)	3:15 (AM) PM		
5/13	M (T) W F SA SU	SAN BERNADINO	6025	F A T Y K R	OK Req. List	556	3:45 (AM) PM	9:05 (AM) PM	*1 night	
	M T W TH F SA SU	LAS VEGAS	6034	F A T Y K R	OK Req. List	556	10:45 (AM) PM	3:55 AM (PM)	Stopover	
	M T W TH F SA SU	SALT LAKE CITY	6022	F A T Y K R	OK Req. List	557	8:00 AM (PM)	8:15 AM (PM)		
	M T W TH F SA SU	CHICAGO	1308	F A T Y K R	OK Req. List	558	9:05 AM (PM)	7:05 AM (PM)	*1 night	
	M T W TH F SA SU	NEW YORK	1300	F A T Y K R	OK Req. List	285	8:00 AM (PM)	6:25 (AM) PM	*1 night	
	M T W TH F SA SU	BOSTON	150	F A T Y K R	OK Req. List	117 116	9:30 (AM) PM	3:25 AM (PM)		
	M T W TH F SA SU	MANCHESTER	VERMONT TRANSIT	F A T Y K R	OK Req. List		5:45 (AM) PM	7:05 AM (PM)		
	M T W TH F SA SU			F A T Y K R	OK Req. List		AM PM	AM PM	$65.00 one-way	
	M T W TH F SA SU			F A T Y K R	OK Req. List		AM PM	AM PM	65.00 $130.00 RT	
	M T W TH F SA SU			F A T Y K R	OK Req. List		AM PM	AM PM	EFT 575H	
	M T W TH F SA SU			F A T Y K R	OK Req. List		AM PM	AM PM		

Bus tickets are relatively simple to issue; however, it takes a considerable amount of an agent's valuable time to read bus timetables (current schedules) and select a routing for a customer on a cross-country journey by bus. This time requirement can be costly to an agency because the bus fares are inexpensive, so the 10% commission made on the sale is not enough to pay for the agent's time. The sales investment strategy is that the little lady who goes cross-country by bus will some day go around the world on a QE2 cruise! Mrs. Ellen Hauge came into the travel agency and wanted to go to San Bernadino, California from Manchester, New Hampshire. She wanted to stop on her way out to visit relatives in Omaha, and she wanted to spend a few days in Las Vegas on her return. Greyhound had a special fare; one-way to anywhere for $65.00. Since the customer was retired, and had plenty of time and a limited budget, Mrs. Hauge chose to travel by bus.

Travel agents in serving the needs of their clients will frequently spend inordinate amounts of time searching bus schedules and destination information for an extensive trip with very little commission, i.e., bus domestic independent travel (DIT/$130 fare has a $13.00 commission) and may require several hours of coordination with the client - see actual ticket example below:

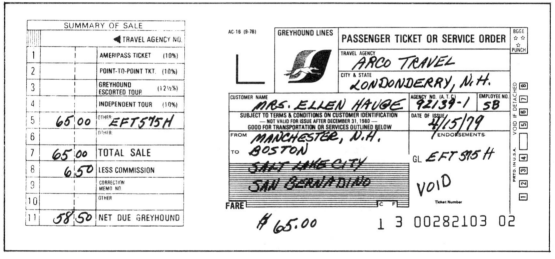

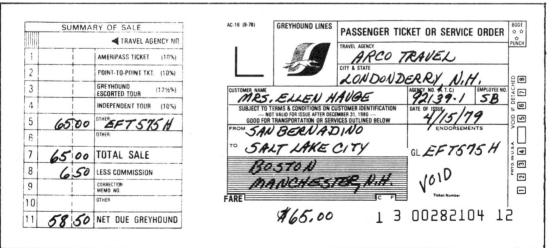

Some times a client may want to take an escorted tour for an extended period, e.g., Trailways 16 Days/15 Nights from Kansas City to Los Angeles and return.

Trailways 1977 Escorted Tour Guide

SOUTHWEST ADVENTURE

TOUR NO. CTE-1-013-4

DEPARTURE DATES

MARCH 19
APRIL 23
OCTOBER 22
NOVEMBER 19

ITINERARY

1st Day — KANSAS CITY — AMARILLO — We make stops in Wichita and Oklahoma City and continue to Amarillo, TX. Overnight: Holiday Inn.

2nd Day — AMARILLO — CARLSBAD — To Carlsbad, NM, via Palo Duro Canyon. Overnight: Holiday Inn.

3rd Day — CARLSBAD — EL PASO — Tour of Carlsbad Caverns before traveling to El Paso, TX. Take Gray Line tour of Juarez. Overnight: Holiday Inn-Downtown.

4th Day — EL PASO — TUCSON — To Tucson, AZ, with visit to Mission San Xavier Del Bac. Overnight: Sheraton Pueblo.

5th Day — TUCSON — SAN DIEGO — Travel through Yuma to San Diego, CA. Overnight: Royal Inn at the Wharf.

6th Day — SAN DIEGO — LOS ANGELES — Sightseeing tour of San Diego before departing to Los Angeles, CA. Overnight: Regency Hyatt.

7th Day — IN LOS ANGELES — Enjoy the eight-hour Gray Line tour of Los Angeles. Tour ends by visiting Universal Studios. Overnight: Regency Hyatt.

8th Day — MORE OF LOS ANGELES — Today is open for shopping and sightseeing in Los Angeles. Overnight: Regency Hyatt.

9th Day — DISNEYLAND — Enjoy several hours in Disneyland; then Knott's Berry Farm, an authentic recreation of the Old West. Overnight: Regency Hyatt.

10th Day — LOS ANGELES — LAS VEGAS — To Las Vegas, NV. Enjoy a dinner show. Overnight: Flamingo Hilton.

11th Day — LAS VEGAS — GRAND CANYON — While en route to Grand Canyon, AZ, stop and visit Hoover Dam. Overnight: Yavapai Lodge.

12th Day — AT GRAND CANYON — Morning tour of the West Rim of the Canyon. In the afternoon, tour goes to the East Rim. Overnight: Yavapai Lodge.

13th Day — GRAND CANYON — WINSLOW — Make a brief stop at the Trading Post in Cameron and see the Walnut Canyon National Monument before heading to Winslow, AZ. Overnight: Townhouse Motel.

14th Day — WINSLOW — ALBUQUERQUE — While en route to Albuquerque, NM, visits are made to the Petrified Forest and Rainbow Falls; then see the Painted Desert. Dinner and overnight: Sheraton Old Town.

15th Day — ALBUQUERQUE — LIBERAL — Sightseeing time allowed in Albuquerque before traveling to Liberal, KS. Farewell Dinner and overnight: Holiday Inn.

16th Day — HOMEWARD BOUND — Pleasant memories are in mind as we continue to end of tour.

**TOURS TO:
WESTERN U.S.A.**

**16 DAYS/15 NIGHTS FROM:
KANSAS CITY/WICHITA/OKLAHOMA CITY**

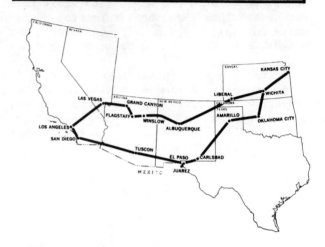

TOUR HIGHLIGHTS

CARLSBAD CAVERNS

SAN DIEGO TOUR

UNIVERSAL STUDIOS

DISNEYLAND

LAS VEGAS

GRAND CANYON

WALNUT CANYON NATIONAL MONUMENT

PETRIFIED FOREST

ALBUQUERQUE

PRICE PER PERSON

From:	Twin	Single
Kansas City/ Wichita	$595.00	$720.00
Oklahoma City	583.00	708.00

PRICE INCLUDES

(1) Transportation on Silver Eagle ® motorcoach.
(2) Rooms with private baths for 15 nights.
(3) Escort service for the entire trip.
(4) Baggage handling (including tips).
(5) Sightseeing and admissions as listed in the itinerary.
(6) 3 meals included while on tour.
(7) Twenty-four (24) hour accident insurance policy while on tour: $10,000 accidental death or dismemberment, $1,000 maximum medical benefits, $33.33 daily hospital indemnity for accident or sickness.

Tour Operator: CONTINENTAL TRAILWAYS TOURS, INC.

BUS TOURS

Motorcoach travel is a significant part of the total world of vacation planning. Bus tours offer exciting sightseeing opportunities and are sometimes the only transportation available. There are three principal types of tours to be sold by the travel agent: (1) package tour which can be any advertised tour to single or multiple destination(s) including prepaid bus transportation, accommodations and other tour elements (meals, transfers, sightseeing, etc.); (2) charter bus tours are transportation buses hired for exclusive tour use to one or more destinations; (3) sightseeing bus tours are organized as prepackaged bus programs that enable a client to tour a particular area.

HAWAII, HILO *1978 SALES TARIFF*

TOUR NO. H-526: CIRCLE ISLAND TOUR

City of Refuge, Punaluu Black Sand Beach, Volcano National Park, Lava Tube, Orchids of Hawaii, Luncheon at Naniloa Hotel in Hilo (not included), Akaka Falls (weather permitting), Macadamia Nut Factory, Parker Ranch, Mauna Kea Beach Hotel, Kona.

DEPARTURE — Daily			AM
From Kailua-Kona Hotels			7:45
From Keauhou Hotels			8:00
(Approx. 9 hours)			
	Fare	Commission	Remit
Motorcoach (Mini)	$26.00	$2.50	$23.50

TOUR NO. H-521: KONA HISTORICAL TOUR

In the morning or afternoon you will see: Historic Kona Coast — quaint interesting Island churches — Honaunau, ancient City of Refuge — Village of Napoopoo — Kealakekua Bay and Captain Cook's monument — coffee plantations — coffee mill (during season) — tropical foliage and flowers. Return to your hotel. (Please specify AM or PM)

DEPARTURE — Daily		AM	PM
From Kona		9:00	1:30
(Approx. 3½ hours)			
	Fare	Commission	Remit
Motor Coach	$ 9.36	$ .90	$ 8.46
Limousine (min. 4)	11.44	1.10	10.34

ISLANDER U-DRIVE

MAUI, HILO, KONA, KAUAI, HONOLULU

Full collision protection . . . only $3.00 per day. Rates do not include gasoline. Car must be returned with a full tank of gas. All Chevrolets are equipped with power steering and automatic transmission. All new models. Major credit cards accepted. Free delivery to nearby hotels. All rates subject to 4% State Tax. Island of Hawaii: $8.00 charge on all rentals not returned to point of origin. Island of Maui: $5.00 charge on all rentals not returned to point of origin, except Hana where drop-off charge is $40.00.

— SPECIAL FLAT RATE —

For only $14.95 a day . . . drive a Standard Datsun and forget about the mileage.   ALSO MOLOKAI!!

Style	Daily	Mileage	Code
DATSUN (Standard)	$ 6.00	11¢	A
DATSUN (Automatic)	8.00	12¢	A-1
CHEVY II	12.00	12¢	B
TORINO A/C	15.00	15¢	C
STATION WAGON A/C	17.00	17¢	D
LINCOLN CONTINENTAL	22.00	22¢	E
FURNISH OWN GAS — 12 PAX VANS ARE ALSO AVAILABLE			

EXCLUSIVE SERVICES

CHARTERED LIMOUSINES and MOTOR COACHES

For your F.I.T. clients wishing exclusive equipment, hourly rates are available on 5- and 11-passenger air-conditioned limousines. For your prestigious groups, we can offer 53- and 57-passenger air-conditioned motor coaches, all equipment provided with fully experienced driver/guides. Rates applicable to the above are as follows:

5-passenger Limousine	11-passenger Limousine	53/57-passenger Motor Coach
Per hour (min. 2 hours) $20.00	Per hour (min. 2 hours) $30.00	Per hour (min. 2 hours) $54.00

Note: Rates subject to 4% Hawaii State Tax.
For F.I.T. bookings, kindly write to each individual Gray Line Manager; Group requests should be directed to Jeanne M. White, Director of Sales, InterIsland Resorts, Transportation Division, P.O. Box 8539, Honolulu, Hawaii, 96815.

GENERAL INFORMATION

AREA SERVED: Hilo, Kona, Waimea, Island of Hawaii.
EQUIPMENT: Chauffeured limousines for 5 and 11 passengers, and Air Conditioned Motor Coaches carrying from 45 to 57 passengers.
CLIMATE: Varies with altitude from warm tropical on the Kona Coast, cooler on the slopes of Mauna Kea and in Hilo.
FEES, MEALS, ETC.: Not included in fares unless otherwise indicated.
TAXES: The 4% Hawaii State Tax has been included in the rates given above for all tours and transfers. For other service please add this item to the total.
REMITTANCE: Payment, less commission, must accompany all coupons or tour orders.
PICK UP TIMES: The pick-up times for transfer from hotels to Big Island Airports are as follows: Kailua-Kona Hotels: 1 hour prior to plane departure. Keauhou Hotels: 1¼ hours prior to plane departure. Hilo Hotels: One hour prior to plane departure for domestic flights and 1½ hours prior to plane departure for mainland flights.
GROUPS: For information relative to group programs, please write direct

to Jeanne M. White, Director of Sales, InterIsland Resorts, Transportation Division, P.O. Box 8539, Honolulu, Hawaii, 96815.
DRIVER-GUIDES: Tours are conducted by entertaining Hawaiian chauffeured guides who know Hawaii's people, its legends, its flowers, trees and its industries.
CHILDREN: Half fare rates shall apply to children under twelve years of age.
FOREIGN NARRATION: Foreign speaking narrators and guides are available. Please write direct to General Manager for cost and details.
CONFIRMATION: Should you have any questions upon arrival on the Island, please call direct to our Gray Line office in Hilo: 935-2835 or Kona: 329-1010.
SIZE: Gray Line Hilo, Gray Line Kauai and Gray Line Maui form the Transportation Division of InterIsland Resorts (Hawaii Transportation), and is the largest sightseeing system in the State of Hawaii.
KONA TOURS: For tours commencing or terminating at the Ke-ahole-Kona Airport, a transfer charge must be added to the prices of the tour.

GRAY LINE OF HILO   *InterIsland Resorts Ltd., dba Gray Line Hilo — Gray Line Kauai — Gray Line Maui — Hawaii Transportation Charles E. McCrary, Vice President*

FOR INFORMATION AND RESERVATIONS, CONTACT: *William M. Vannatta, General Manager*

PACKAGE TOURS

Travel agents should know about prearranged and advertised package tours for groups or individuals. A typical package tour would include: transportation via modern air-conditioned motor coach, lodging in leading hotels and motels, baggage handling for 1 large piece per person, competent tour escort for passengers' added pleasure and convenience, sightseeing and admissions to attractions in itinerary, and meals only when specifically indicated in itinerary and shown by underline. Package tours do not usually include meals except those specifically mentioned in the itinerary, all items of a personal nature and gratuities to maids and waiters except for meals included in tour. Also not included are gratuities to special guides, driver and tour escort. Though customary, these are not necessary tour expenses and should be extended on a voluntary individual basis. Reservations should be made well in advance of tour departure. A deposit secures the tour at the time of the reservation. Single rooms are

usually limited. Triple rooms have twin beds and a roll-away bed or two double beds. Three individual beds cannot generally be guaranteed. Passengers must select their own roommates. Final payment must be made at least 21 days prior to departure date, except some tours request final payments 30 days prior to departure date. Cancellation must usually be made at least 14 days prior to departure date to insure return of all monies paid. On shorter notice, any expenses incurred due to cancellation may be deducted from refund. Baggage allowance per passenger is one large suitcase. A small overnight bag handled directly by the passenger and placed in the overhead rack is also permissible. While every effort is made to handle baggage carefully, the tour operator cannot assume liability for damage or loss of baggage. In order that all passengers may enjoy the facilities of the motor coach equally, seating may be rotated twice daily at the direction of the tour escort. All rates and schedules are subject to change without notice. Tour operation subject to a minimum of 25 passengers is responsible only while passenger is travelling on its operation within the United States or Canada. The tour operator acts only as agent for the owners or contractors providing other means of transportation or other services, and all tickets and/or exchange orders shall be deemed to be consent to the further condition that neither operator nor its agents shall be or become liable or responsible in any way in connection with such other means of transportation or other services for any loss, injury, or damage to, or in respect of, any person or property howsoever caused or arising.

Florida Circle

FEATURING FT. LAUDERDALE, JUNGLE QUEEN DINNER CRUISE, THE GOLD COAST WALT DISNEY WORLD

FEBRUARY 19 - 16 DAYS
3 Meals Included

1st Day, Feb. 19 Welcome aboard our luxury coach. Because we're starting out in snow country, our destination today is no further than New York City and the Barbizon Plaza Hotel. There's time for a pleasant evening on the town.

2nd and 3rd Days, Feb. 20 and 21 Watch the countryside unfold as you travel to the Sun. On Feb. 20 overnight will be at the Executive Motor Inn in Richmond, Va. and on Feb. 21, at the modern Howard Johnson Motor Lodge in Walterboro, S.C.

4th Day, Feb. 22 Today's pleasant ride is through Georgia's pecan country and then—the Sunshine State! Our destination is Orlando. Accommodations for two nights are at the Quality Inn International, minutes from Walt Disney World.

5th Day, Feb. 23 You will have the entire day for the wonders of Walt Disney World, for its multitude of fascinating shows and attractions for all ages. There's so much to see that you'll have to make choices. We'll transport you to the Magic Kingdom and return.

6th Day, Feb. 24 Lovely Cypress Gardens is a "must" and first on our route today. We'll take in the famed water show and the many beautiful acres. This afternoon we are headed west to St. Petersburg. The Edgewater Beach Inn will host us for two nights.

7th Day, Feb. 25 Today, a trip to Busch Gardens in Tampa. Ride the monorail for a close-up view of hundreds of African creatures. There are cockatoo and macaw shows at the Bird Theater, acres of landscaped gardens, lagoons, flowers and exotic birds. This evening **dinner** at the popular Kapok Tree in Clearwater is included.

8th Day, Feb. 26 Leaving St. Petersburg, we travel down the West coast of Florida via the Sunshine Skyway over lower Tampa Bay, Sarasota, Fort Myers and Naples. At Fort Myers we'll tour the winter home of Thomas Edison. His gardens contain rare trees and ferns from all parts of the world. We now cross the Everglades via Alligator Alley to Ft. Lauderdale where we'll stay for three nights at the Lauderdale Surf Hotel.

9th Day, Feb. 27 Ft. Lauderdale with its many waterways has been called the Venice of America. We'll get acquainted with this resort community aboard a sightseeing tram. The afternoon is free for the pool or beach, or whatever is your pleasure. Tonight we'll board the Jungle Queen for a **dinner** cruise up the New River. The dinner is included.

10th Day, Feb. 28 This morning our coach takes us south along the Gold Coast for a look at Miami Beach's Collins Ave., Lincoln Mall and Biscayne Bay. There is more free time upon return to Ft. Lauderdale.

11th Day, Mar. 1 Follow the ocean north to wealthy Palm Beach with its stately palm-lined avenues. Our destination is Daytona Beach, known for its beautiful 23-mile beach. Our hotel is the Quality Inn on the beach.

12th Day, Mar. 2 The morning is free to enjoy the beach or a bit of shopping. This afternoon we continue north to Marineland. You'll enjoy the porpoise show and the many marine life exhibits. It's just a short distance to St. Augustine, the nation's oldest city, and the Holiday Inn of St. Augustine by-the-Sea.

13th Day, Mar. 3 The forenoon is devoted to seeing old St. Augustine and sites such as Mission Nombre de Dios and Castillo de San Marcos. A tram ride through the old streets is included. There will be time for personal sightseeing at your own pace. This afternoon we travel north and say goodbye to sunny Florida. But there's a treat in store tonight—**dinner**, included, at the Pirates' House in Old Savannah, Georgia. Overnight at the Quality Inn Oasis.

14th and 15th Days, Mar. 4 and 5 Northward we travel through the Carolinas for an overnight stop at the Holiday Inn of Emporia, Va. on Mar. 4 and at the Towne House in Woodbridge, N.J. on Mar. 5.

16th Day, Mar. 6 Homeward bound with pleasant memories. We will arrive in Bennington at approximately 2:00 PM, Brattleboro at approximately 3:00 PM, Claremont 4:00 PM, White River Jct. 4:35 PM, Barre 6:00 PM, Montpelier 6:20 PM and Burlington 7:10 PM.

Package tours can be located in CONSOLIDATED AIR TOUR MANUAL, WORLDWIDE TOUR GUIDE, GRAY LINE SALES AND TOUR GUIDE, and AMERICAN SIGHTSEEING INTERNATIONAL. Foreign tour packages are very popular with some travellers; for example, "the smart way to see Europe is travel by comfortable EUROPABUS motor coaches." Travelling by EUROPABUS only or by combining Bus and Rail travel to suit time, taste and convenience, clients can see all of Europe comfortably, effortlessly and at moderate cost and enjoy abundant stopover privileges along the way.

Created by the railways of Europe to supplement their extensive railroad systems, EUROPABUS is a vast network of international bus lines covering more than 70,000 miles of scenic routings throughout the length and breadth of Europe - from London to Sicily, from Amsterdam to Barcelona, and from Paris to Istanbul. Seeing Europe by bus, clients travel in modern, aircooled motorcoaches, with an English-speaking hostess-guide on most lines, and a specially trained, experienced driver whose intimate knowledge of highways and byways permits customers to relax completely and thoroughly enjoy a "picture window" view of Europe. What's more, travel by bus means that clients travel in restful, carefree comfort all the way because the motorcoaches provide deeply upholstered, individual seats and often, as an added convenience, feature a radio, a lavatory - even a bar.

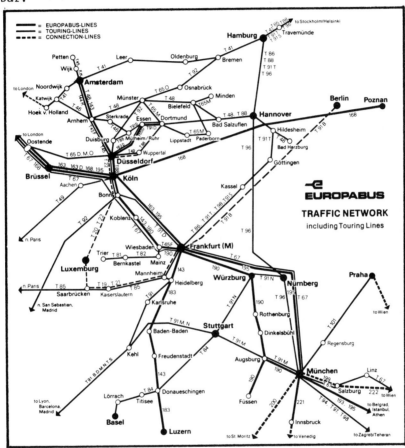

Some typical escorted EUROPABUS tours:

GRAND ALPINE TOUR
7 days - from Zurich or Geneva

SWISS HIGHLIGHTS
3 days - from Geneva

SWISS ALPS AND LAKES
4 days - from Zurich

PACKAGES IN GERMANY
Various tours

BEST OF GERMANY, AUSTRIA AND SWITZERLAND
14 days - from Frankfurt

MEDIEVAL AND MODERN GERMAN HIGHLIGHTS
14 days - from Frankfurt

JOURNEY TO EUROPE'S HEARTLAND
21 days - from Frankfurt

GERMAN SCENERY AT A GLANCE
7 days - from Frankfurt

NORTH CAPE TOUR
Stockholm, Sundsvall, Lulea, North Cape,
Rovaniemi, Helsinki, Stockholm
13 days (3500 km)

SCOTTISH HIGHLAND TOURS
5, 6 days - from Edinburgh
7, 8 days - from London

RED - WHITE - RED
Tour of Austria
7 days - from Salzburg, Vienna or
Innsbruck

WALTZ - CSARDAS
Tour of Vienna and Budapest,
excursions in Hungary
7 days - from Vienna

NORMANDY, BRITTANY AND CASTLE COUNTRY
4 days - from Paris

CASTLES OF THE LOIRE
2 days - from Paris

BEST OF BRITTANY
7 days - from Paris

THE GOLDEN RIBBON OF SICILY
7 days - from Palermo

CENTRAL AND NORTHERN ITALY
Various package tours

ANDALUSIAN TOUR
5 days - from Madrid

TOUR OF ALGARVE
6 days - from Lisbon

TOUR OF NORTHERN PORTUGAL
7 days - from Lisbon

CHARTER BUS TOURS

Travel agents frequently will organize a charter bus trip for college students, teachers, social clubs or community group. Travel agents will frequently charter a bus for an existing group if the trip is not advertised to the public or sold on a per seat basis.

It is the travel agent's responsibility to organize the group, establish the dates, travel itinerary, size of bus or buses and other land arrangements. In the United States, the agent would make the arrangements with an appropriate intrastate or interstate bus line carrier in order to determine availability and cost of the charter.

SIGHTSEEING TOURS

Gray Line, the largest sightseeing company, offers more than 1300 prepackaged bus tours. Gray Line also can process prepaid individual services for travel agents when three or more Gray Line cities are involved, providing net remittance, along with copies of prepaid orders or vouchers issued, accompany the request.

PASSENGER'S COUPON PRINTED IN U.S.A.

The GRAY LINE

GRAY LINE SIGHT-SEEING TOUR ORDER

No. -K 625414

SOLD TO Mr. + Mrs. Adolf Steinhäuser

FOR SERVICE AT Kona, Hawaii

GRAY LINE TELEPHONE NO. 329-1010

NAME OF TOUR Circle Island Tour #H-526

DATE OF SERVICE 2-16-79

PERSONS Two

VALUE OF THIS ORDER $ 52.00

Please telephone Gray Line number given on this order immediately upon arrival.

CONTACT PASSENGERS AT Kona Surf Hotel TIME 7:45 AM

ISSUED BY B. Welch - All Aboard Travel

GIVE NAME OF AGENT IN FULL TOGETHER WITH NAME OF COMPANY

STREET ADDRESS 1625 Adams Road CITY Nome STATE Alaska

Sight-seeing Tour Orders are made when the travel agent consults the pages in the GRAY LINE SALES & TOUR GUIDE for applicable tours, scheduled departures, rates and commissions. The tour coupons are instantly duplicated, since they have been printed with special carbonized paper. It is necessary to issue a separate TOUR ORDER for each tour, with the triplicate copies disposed as follows:

PASSENGER'S COUPON (white) - To be given to passenger for presentation upon arrival at Gray Line destination.

ADVICE COPY (yellow) - To be forwarded with your net remittance to the involved Gray Line company.

AGENT'S COPY (green) - To remain in book as your file or reference copy.

Gray Line Prepaid Sight-Seeing Tour Orders cannot be used unless they are prepaid! Your net remittance must accompany the yellow advice copy forwarded to the Gray Line company providing services for your clients.

The Gray Line Prepaid Sight-Seeing Tour Orders represent value once they are issued, similar to airline or steamship company ticket stock, where prepayment is an absolute must. The agency's failure to prepay could result in: difficult situations with your clients, who will be refused service which are unpaid, and/or immediate recall of your remaining stock of the PPO's.

Travel agents should read closely the Gray Line directory and/or American Sightseeing International (tour operators) for the most appropriate tour for your client. The listings provide a basic description of the tours available in a particular city, i.e., Tehran, including a list of major attractions, length of tour and time of departure. The name of tour operator is provided (including address and phone number). The tour costs are given in U.S. dollars at the time of publication and other necessary information for booking the tour. Sightseeing tours are inexpensive when compared to air fare and become an attractive way to sightsee in unfamiliar places.

IRAN   IRAN

Direct prepaid vouchers and checks to:
AMERICAN SIGHTSEEING IRAN.
P.O. Box 12/1676
Mir Emad, Corner Takhte Tavoos No. 2
Tehran, Iran
Operated by: Persian Gulf Travel Agency Ltd.

Managers: George Garek; J. Kyling
Telephone: 858271, 2, 3, 4 or 5
Cable: TRAVELGULF
Members of: ASTA, IATA, PATA, SIATTA

CODES: FR = Standard Class (luxury service).

TRANSFERS —

Including welcome or departure service, transportation, and porterage of two pieces of hand baggage per person. (FR & TU)

Each direction, between:

	RATES PER PERSON			
	PRIVATE CAR FR			PRIVATE MINI-COACH
	1 pax	2-3 pax	4-6 pax	7-12 pax
(a) Tehran airport and city hotels	$11.25 + 25%	$ 6.45 + 25%	$ 5.25 + 25%	$ 4.90 + 25%
(b) Tehran airport & Hilton, International, Miami, & Vanak hotels..	13.30 + 25%	7.65 + 25%	5.65 + 25%	4.90 + 25%
(c) Isfahan, Shiraz, Abadan, Ahwaz, & Tabriz airports & city hotels	8.05 + 25%	4.45 + 25%	4.90 + 25%	4.05 + 25%
(d) Khorramshahr Harbour & Abadan hotels	14.50 + 25%	9.65 + 25%	8.45 + 25%	7.65 + 25%
(e) Julfa (U.S.S.R. frontier) to Tabriz rail station or hotels	40.25 + 25%	28.20 + 25%	22.55 + 25%	22.55 + 25%

Note: From 8:00 P.M. to 8:00 A.M., add 25% to above rates; on holidays add 35% to above rates.

SIGHTSEEING TOURS —

Private car accommodates 1-4 pax. Passengers picked up & returned to hotels; departure times to suit convenience of clients.

Rates include multilingual guide service & entrance fees.
NOTE: Most places of interest are closed on Fridays.

	PRIVATE CAR RATES PER PERSON FR		
TEHRAN	1 pax	2-3 pax	4-6 pax
TOUR AS/104 — TEHRAN 3 hrs., Daily. Visit the Golestan Palace, Royal Museum, Ethnological Museum, and the covered bazaar of Tehran	$29.40 + 25%	$16.10 + 25%	$14.70 + 25%
TOUR AS/103F/T — PERSIAN CARPET (Mornings only), 3 hrs., Daily. Visit the Parliament or Senate Buildings, Royal Palaces Fine Arts Museum, work shop of handicrafts, and the Sepahsalar Mosque and rug washing	28.00 + 25%	14.70 + 25%	13.30 + 25%
TOUR AS/105 — CROWN JEWELS TOUR, 3 hrs., Daily, except Fridays. View the Crown Jewels Treasury at Bank Melli and the Archeological Museum	29.40 + 25%	16.10 + 25%	14.70 + 25%
TOUR AS/112 — TEHRAN BY NIGHT, 3½ hrs., Daily. Dinner included. Caviar and vodka are additional. To the famous Shekoofeh Now cabaret. European and Oriental floor shows	49.70 + 25%	28.00 + 25%	27.30 + 25%
ISFAHAN			
TOUR AS/127 — ISFAHAN TOUR, 6 hrs., Daily. Visit the Khadju Bridge, the Palace of 40 Pillars, several important mosques and bazaars. Continue to the Ali Qapu Palace, Julfa City, Armenian Cathedral, the shaking minarets, and the Zoroastrian Fire Temple	44.80 + 25%	25.20 + 25%	21.00 + 25%
SHIRAZ			
TOUR AS/135 — POETIC PERSIA, 6 hrs., Daily. Visit the Tomb of Saadi and Hafez, the Pars Museum, Vakil Mosque, the bazaars, Khan School, Khalili Garden, Juma Mosque, and the Nemazi Hospital	44.80 + 25%	25.20 + 25%	21.00 + 25%
TOUR AS/136 — PERSEPOLIS TOUR, 6 hrs., Daily. Motor to Persepolis to visit the monumental palace built by Darius the Great 2500 years ago, & Royal Tents	63.70 + 25%	36.40 + 25%	28.00 + 25%

Bus travel can be very rewarding for your clients; guided sightseeing tours provide both transportation to the destination and explanation, usually in English, of what is seen. Sightseeing tours (supplemental travel) are easy to sell and should be sold before the client begins the trip.

An intercity bus stop at the Royal Castle.   Poland Tourist Board Photo.

Chapter 12

RELATED TRAVEL SERVICES: CAR RENTALS, INSURANCE, CURRENCY AND TRAVEL DOCUMENTS

Travel agents should try to increase their commission sales base by marketing related travel services, such as car rentals, insurances, currency, and other related products such as travel books and maps. Travel agents must seek ways to increase their total sales, particularly on those services like insurance which offer a 35% or higher commission for writing a policy. The focus of this chapter is to briefly cover some of the areas where the travel agent may be involved.

CAR RENTALS

Selling domestic and international car rentals has become a major function for the travel agent, the airline reservation agent, the AMTRAK sales agent and others, i.e., hotel representatives. Agents using toll free telephone numbers are able to book these major U.S. auto rental systems:

AIRWAYS RENT A CAR SYSTEM
9420 Telstar Ave.
El Monte, CA 91731
(800) 648-5656

ALAMO RENT A CAR, INC.
P.O. Box 22776
Fort Lauderdale, FL 33335
(800) 327-9633

AMERICAN INTERNATIONAL
Rent-A-Car
9864 Monroe Drive
Dallas, TX 75220
(800) 527-6346

AUTO EUROPE
770 Lexington Ave.
New York, NY 10021
(800) 223-5125

AVIS RENT A CAR SYSTEM
North American Headquarters
900 Old Country Road
Garden City, NY 11530
(800) 331-1212

BUDGET RENT A CAR
35 East Wacker Drive
Chicago, IL 60601
(800) 228-9650

DOLLAR RENT A CAR SYS., INC.
6141 West Century Blvd.
Los Angeles, CA 90045
(800) 421-6868

ECONO-CAR
4930 W. 77th St.
Suite 260
Edina, MN 55435
(800) 228-1000

HERTZ SYSTEM INC.
660 Madison Avenue
New York, NY 10021
(800) 654-3131

NATIONAL CAR RENTAL SYSTEM
5501 Green Valley Drive
P.O. Box 35187
Minneapolis, MN 55437
(800) 328-4567

PAYLESS CAR RENTAL SYSTEM, INC.
W. 1505 4th St.
Spokane, WA 99204
(800)541-1566

THRIFTY RENT-A-CAR SYS., INC.
P.O. Box 51069
Tulsa, OK 74151
(800)331-4200

When a travel agent typically reserves a car for the client, the resulting commission is 10% to 15% of the car rental costs and the automated commission payment program assures prompt and accurate commission reporting and payment. There are several primary guides available to the travel agent:

NAOAG TRAVEL PLANNER AND HOTEL/MOTEL GUIDE contains rental car location list which permits the travel agent to suggest rental car options, e.g., airport or downtown location. The "destination index" by city indicates the names of the rental car companies located at the airport; the accompanying airport map indicates the actual location of the rentals.

OFFICIAL AIRLINE GUIDE NORTH AMERICAN EDITION –GROUND TRANSPORTATION SERVICES is published every two months and features rental car services of Avis, Budget, Dollar, Econo-car, Hertz, and National Car Rental. This OAG supplement provides car rental information at airport, cities, and other locations; the rate by the mile, by day, by hour, and unlimited mileage; and other special information. Travel agents will need to know: client's arrival time, flight numbers, reservation codes, and return date and location.

THE CONSOLIDATED AIR TOUR MANUAL (CATM) includes rental car arrangements in the particular vacation area, i.e., "...includes American International Rent-A-Car Ford Fairmont or similar sedan for three 24-hour periods."

THE TRAVEL AGENT: TRAVEL INDUSTRY PERSONNEL DIRECTORY offers a good list of "car purchase, rental, coaches and sightseeing" companies, including toll free numbers.

RENTAL CAR RESERVATIONS

The major domestic car rental agencies (Avis, Hertz, National, Budget, Dollar, and Econo-car) publish their own directories and manuals for reservations as well as rental car information. A travel agent should advise the client about rental car rates, insurance coverage, collision damage waiver, personal accident insurance, minimum age, valid driver's license and one way service options. Cost of a rental car is computed on the basis of a time charge, plus, in certain cases, a mileage charge as determined by the car's factory-installed odometer. Charges vary with the type of car used and length of time the car is rented; i.e., hourly, daily, weekly, monthly rates. Travel agents, in making rental car reservations, should state: (1) the name of client or clients; (2) where and when the rental car is to be available, i.e., date, time and place; (3) type of service (self-drive or chauffeur driven); (4) car information, (type and/or make):

E-Car	Pinto or similar	LX	Luxury Car
C-Car	Fairmont or similar	SW	9 passenger wagons
I-Car	Granada, LTD II or similar	MB	Mini Bus - 9 - 12 passengers
S-Car	LTD, Thunderbird or similar	VN	Vans - 9 - 12 passengers;

(5) dates and length of rental program; (6) when and where the client will return the car; and (7) total number in the party, include the age of the driver(s). Some rental companies the driver can be 18, others at least 21 and still others must be 25 years of age.

INTERNATIONAL RENTAL CARS

European (international) car rentals can be profitable. In addition to Avis, Budget, Pan Am's World Rent-a-Car, Hertz and National Car Rental in Europe, there is Auto Europe and the Kemwel Group. The primary agent's work is booking auto rentals; agents can arrange an auto lease for more than 30 days, e.g., a brand new car in Brussels or a used one in Frankfurt; and agents can order (purchase) a car for the client from the factory. Each auto rental firm provides full information on their policies, e.g., "...detailed information and prices on all European makes and models with U.S. or European specifications. Over 700 different models produced by 35 automobile manufacturers, including recreational vehicles, are available. The Purchase Package Plan includes factory delivery, registration and plates, overnight accommodation, shipment, marine insurance, U.S. Customs Duty, clearance and port handling." Agents can also assist their clients in shipping their own car overseas, e.g., to ship a Mercury cougar from the port of New York to Auckland would take at least 15 days or more depending on the ship and cost approximately $1500.00, insurance additional.

Rental cars in Europe can have high tax (20% or higher), surcharge for current inflation, value-added tax, and Collision Damage Waiver (CDW) fee ($4.00 or higher per day) - all of these add-ons above the basic rental charge, and client will probably purchase the gasoline at $3.00 or more per U.S. gallon. Agents should explain very carefully to clients the <u>real</u> cost of international car rental.

France

Group	TIME + MILEAGE Per Day 7 or 1 to 6	More	Per Km.	UNLIMITED MILEAGE 1 Wk.	2 Wks.	3 Wks.	Addl. Days Up to 21	Over 21
A Ford Fiesta, Renault 5 Deluxe	$ 9.35	8.50	8¢	155	309	462	22	21
B Peugeot 104, Renault 5 Sunroof*	9.65	9.00	9.5¢	162	323	483	23	22
C Renault 14, Simca 1307 Deluxe	12.45	11.50	11.5¢	199	393	585	28	27
D Peugeot 504, Peugeot 305, Ford Taunus 1600 Deluxe	14.00	12.85	12¢	245	486	725	35	34
E Renault 20 Special Deluxe	15.00	11.85	13¢	315	624	929	45	44
F VW Bus (9 pax), Peugeot 504 Stw. (7 pax)	18.00	16.30	15¢	336	669	998	48	47
G Peugeot 604 (A), Renault 30 (A)	28.70	26.50	18.5¢	370	740	1089	53	52
H Mercedes 280 (A) A/C**	51.00	49.00	32¢	—	—	—	—	—

*Available in Nice only. **Available in Nice and Paris only.

AVAILABLE at: ABBEVILLE, AIX-EN-PROVENCE, AIX-LES-BAINS, ALBI, AMIENS, ANGERS, ANGOULEME, ANNECY, ANNONAY, ANTIBES, ARLES, ARRAS, AULNEY-SOUS-BOIS, AURILLAC, AUXERRE, AVIGNON, AVRANCHES, BAR-LE-DUC, BAYONNE, BEAUCAIRE, BEAUNE, BEAUVAIS, BELFORT, BESANCON, BETHUNE, BEZIERS, BIARRITZ, BOLLENE, BORDEAUX, BOURG-EN-BRESSE, BOURGES, BOURGOIN-JALLIEU, BREST, BRIANCON, BRIVE, CAEN, CAGNES S. MER, CAHORS, CALAIS, CAMBRAI, CANNES, CARCASSONE, CARPENTRAS, CAVAILLON, CHALONS-SUR-MARNE, CHALON-SUR-SOANE, CHAMBERY, CHARLEVILLE-MEZIERES, CHARTRES, CHATEAUROUX, CHAUMONT, CHAVILLE, CHELLES, CHERBOURG, CLERMONT-FERRAND, CLUSES, COLMAR, COMPIEGNE, DAX, DEUIL-LA-BARRE, DIEPPE, DIJON, DOUAI, DRAGUIGNAN, DUNKERQUE, ENGHIEN, EPERNAY, FLERS, FORBACH, GAP, GENEVA (French side), GOLFJUAN, GRANVILLE, GRENOBLE, HAGUENAU, HENDAYE, HENIN-BEAUMONT, HYERES, JOIGNY, JUAN LES PINS, LA-CLAYETTE, LAGNY POMPONNE, LA-GRANDE-MOTTE, LANNION, LA ROCHELLE, LA ROCHE-SUR-YON, LE CREUSOT, LE HAVRE, LE LAVANDOU, LE MANS, LENS, LE PUY, LES SABLES D'OLONNE, LILLE, LIMOGES, LORIENT, LYON, MACON, MANTES LA JOLIE, MARSEILLE, MARTIGUES, MEAUX, MELUN, MENTON, METZ, MONTCEAU-LES-MINES, MONTELIMAR, MONTFERMEIL, MONTLUCON, MONTPELLIER, MOULINS, MULHOUSE, NANCY, NANTES, NARBONNE, NEVERS, NICE, NIMES, NIORT, NOGENT S. MARNE, NOISY-LE-GRAND, ORANGE, ORLEANS, PARIS (Boulogne, Courbevoie, Gare de Lyon, Montparnasse, Porte de la Chapelle, Port Maillot and at Avenue de Saxe and Paris airports (Orly, Le Bourget and Charles de Gaulle)), PAU, PERIGUEUX, PERPIGNAN, PIERRELATTE, POITIERS, PONTOISE, QUIMPER, REIMS, RENNES, ROANNE, ROUEN, ST. AVOLD, ST. BRIEUC, ST. DIZIER, ST. ETIENNE, ST. GAUDENS, ST. JEAN-DE-LUZ, ST MALO, STE. MAXIME, ST. NAZAIRE, ST. OMER, ST. RAPHAEL, ST. TROPEZ, SALLANCHES, SALON DE PROVENCE, SARREBOURG, SARREGUEMINES, SAVERNE, SEDAN, SENS, SETE, STRASBOURG, TARBES, THIERS, TOULON, TOULOUSE, TOURS, TRAPPES, TROYES, VALENCE, VALENCIENNES, VANNES, VICHY, VILLEFRANCHE-SAONE, VITRY-LE-FRANCOIS, and in CORSICA at AJACCIO, BASTIA, CALVIA and PORTO-VECCHIO. DELIVERY and RETURN: FREE between the above cities in France for all groups except F and H. For Group F, if not returned to the same delivery point - for rentals of up to 6 days, $70; up to 13 days, $35; 14 days or more FREE. For Group H, if not returned to NICE or PARIS - 19¢ per km. INSURANCE: Comprehensive with $160 deductible collision. CDW (payable in France only) - $2.35 per day, $16 per wk. AGE LIMITS: Min. - Groups A through F - 23, Groups G and H - 25. Max. - None. TAX: 17.6%. U.S. DOLLAR RATES: Calculated at Francs 4.93 - $1.00.

France & Benelux One-Way

For one-way service between BELGIUM, FRANCE, HOLLAND and LUXEMBOURG see page 7.

France

ae-conomy plan

IN and BETWEEN CALAIS, NICE and PARIS
UNLIMITED MILEAGE

Group	1 Wk.	2 Wks.	3 Wks.	Addl. Days Up to 21	Over 21
A Renault 4	$115	226	318	16.00	15.00
B Austin Mini	126	245	358	17.00	16.00
C Ford Fiesta, Honda Civic, Fiat 127	138	270	378	19.00	18.00
D Peugeot 104 Deluxe	145	281	399	20.00	19.00
E Ford Escort, Fiat 128 Special	159	312	440	22.00	21.00
F Peugeot 304, Renault 12	179	347	514	24.00	23.00
G Ford Escort (A), Simca 1307 (A)	185	367	539	26.00	25.00
H Renault 12 (A)	188	371	548	26.50	25.50
J Ford Taunus 1600 Deluxe	193	382	555	27.50	26.50
K Ford Granada Deluxe, Ford Taunus 1600 Deluxe (A)	199	396	568	28.50	27.00
L Renault 16 (A), Simca 1308 Deluxe	205	408	579	29.00	27.50
M Peugeot 504, Renault 20 Special Deluxe	217	429	597	31.00	29.00
N Ford Granada Deluxe (A)	225	448	631	32.00	30.00
O Peugeot 504 Stw.	285	564	753	40.00	35.00
P VW Bus (9 pax), Ford Bus (9 pax)	301	599	849	43.00	38.00

AVAILABLE at: CALAIS and PARIS. DELIVERY and RETURN: FREE between the above cities and FREE in NICE if the rental starts in CALAIS or PARIS. Under this plan the car must be collected from, and returned to, the downtown office during normal business hours. Airport and hotel deliveries not available. INSURANCE: Comprehensive with $200 deductible collision. CDW - $3 per day, $19 per wk. AGE LIMITS: Min. - 18. Max. - None. TAX: 17.6%. U.S. DOLLAR RATES: Calculated at Francs 4.93 = $1.00.

Riviera

and BETWEEN NICE - PARIS or CALAIS

Group	TIME + MILEAGE Per Day 7 or 1 to 6	More	Per Km.	UNLIMITED MILEAGE 1 Wk.	2 Wks.	3 Wks.	Addl. Days Up to 21	Over 21
A Austin Mini	$ 9.30	8.80	6.5¢	126	245	358	17.00	16.00
B Renault 4	9.80	9.30	7¢	134	265	361	18.50	17.50
C Peugeot 104 Deluxe	11.85	11.35	9¢	155	305	429	21.50	20.50
D Simca 1100, Renault 12	12.85	12.35	11.5¢	179	354	509	25.00	24.00
E Renault 14, Simca 1307 Deluxe	13.85	13.35	13.5¢	192	374	525	26.00	25.00
F Peugeot 504	16.00	15.50	14.5¢	212	420	586	30.00	28.00
G Peugeot 504 Stw., Renault 12 (A)	21.60	20.60	17.5¢	293	586	831	42.00	40.00
H VW Bus (9 pax)	22.00	21.00	18¢	301	599	849	43.00	41.00
J Mercedes 230 (A)	35.00	34.00	19¢	525	1016	1509	72.00	70.00
K Mercedes 230 (A) A/C	39.00	38.00	20¢	—	—	—	—	—

CONVERTIBLES

Group								
L Peugeot Deluxe Conv. (2 pax)	21.00	20.00	11¢	—	—	—	—	—
M Chevrolet Conv. (A), Buick Conv (A)	44.00	42.00	17¢	—	—	—	—	—

AVAILABLE at: CANNES, MONTE CARLO and NICE. DELIVERY and RETURN: FREE between the above cities, and for Groups A through G only, return is FREE between NICE and PARIS or CALAIS. INSURANCE: Comprehensive with $200 deductible collision, except Group L $500 deductible collision. CDW - $3 per day, $19 per wk., except Group L $6.75 per day. AGE LIMITS: Min. - 18 for Group A, otherwise 23. Max. - None. LUGGAGE RACK: 75¢ per day, $5 per wk. TAX: 17.6%. U.S. DOLLAR RATES: Calculated at Francs 4.93 = $1.00.

Opel Kadett

Opel Ascona

Peugeot 504

Opel Rekord

Renault 5

Renault 12

Volvo 244

Simca 1307/1308

VW Passat/Dasher

VW Rabbit

Some countries require an International Driving Permit; an inexpensive ($3.00) and easy document to obtain for anyone with a valid domestic driver's license. U.S. driver's licenses are accepted in all European countries, except Austria, Finland, Greece, Portugal and Spain, where an International Driving Permit is needed.

INSURANCE

APPLICATION TO THE OMAHA INDEMNITY COMPANY — ONE COPY WILL BE YOUR POLICY SCHEDULE
PLEASE COMPLETE WITH CARE — ONLY COVERAGES FOR WHICH PREMIUMS ARE SHOWN WILL BE IN EFFECT

Do Not Write On This Line ▶ Signature of Licensed Resident Agent _____

Policy Date **12 APRIL** Policy Number **H 63298**

TRIP: From **BOSTON** To **TAHITI** Return Trip Destination **LOS ANGELES** Carrier Tour **PAN AM**

Family Members Covered	Beneficiary	Relationship	Policy Form T16TP1 Travel Accident	Principal Sum	Premium
Insured **P.B. DUVAL**	**STEPHEN F.**	**SON**		$ **50,000.**	$ **31.20**
Dependent **JAMES O.**			Capital Sums are DOUBLE the Principal Sums.	$	$
Dependent **THOMAS P.**				$	$
Dependent _____				$	$

Snow Skiing Coverage (optional) $ _____

Policy to be Effective Date **30 APRIL** Hour **9:00** a.m. XXX Term of Coverage **27** Days

	Policy Form PTB248 Baggage	Amount of Coverage	Premium
PLEASE PRINT! BEAR DOWN	Subject to limitation and exclusion on certain items.	$ **1,000.**	$ **26.50**
	Policy Form T16TC1 Trip Cancellation	Benefit Amount $ **1,000.** No. of Insureds x premium per person	Premium $ **97.50**

Name of Insured **PAULINE B. DUVAL**
Address **231 S. PLYMOUTH AVENUE**
City **S. HADWICK,** State **NH** ZIP **03102**

Snow Skiing Coverage (optional)

Make Check Payable to Addressee ▶ Total Premium $ **155.20**

Signature of Insured _**Pauline B. Duval**_

5351 App

Place **S. HADWICK, NH 03102** Date **26 APRIL 1979**

Travel agents in some states can sell "personal effects and baggage insurance," "trip cancellation insurance," "air passenger insurance" without a state license. The requirements vary from state to state. Some clients will have peace of mind and therefore make their trip more enjoyable with a vacation travel insurance. As a travel agent you can offer protection against air disaster and financial distress that would upset the most carefully organized vacation fly/sea cruise.

TRAVEL ACCIDENT INSURANCE

Sometimes "travel accident insurance" is called air passenger insurance and can be written at airport vending machines. Travel accident insurance pays the amount on the policy for (1) loss of life, limb, or sight; (2) accident medical expenses; and (3) in-hospital sickness benefits; insurance covers injuries received while a passenger is on a scheduled "airline flight" or while a passenger is on any land or water carrier, i.e., train, ship, taxi, bus or other appropriate vehicle.

Benefits for Accidental Loss of Life, Limb or Sight
$10,000.00 to $100,000.00 (Capital Sum)
. . . pays the amount you select for injuries received while a passenger on a scheduled airline flight—or while a passenger on any land or water common carrier (train, ship, taxi, bus, etc.).

$5,000.00 to $50,000.00 (Principal Sum)
. . . pays the Principal Sum (50% of the Capital Sum) for injuries resulting from all other accidents, no matter when or where they occur, except as listed in the Exceptions and Limitations. Includes coverage for injuries received as a passenger on nonscheduled flights of any properly licensed United States aircraft (or its foreign equivalent) or aircraft (other than a single-engine jet) of the United States Department of Defense, United States Coast Guard, Army National Guard or Air National Guard used principally for transportation of passengers, including cargo.

Benefits under this policy are payable only for injuries received while the policy is in force and for loss occurring within 100 days of the accident.

Benefit amounts above are payable for loss of life, both hands or feet, sight or any two members. One-half the maximum benefit is payable for loss of one hand or one foot—and one-fourth the benefit amount for loss of one eye. Loss means severance of the limb and total and irrecoverable loss of sight. The maximum amount of insurance which you may have under all policies of this same type may not exceed $100,000.00.

Accident Medical Expense Benefits
$1,000.00 to $5,000.00 (maximum amount)
. . . pays up to 10% of the Principal Sum you select or $1,000.00, whichever is greater, for medical or surgical treatment by a physician, services of a registered graduate nurse or hospital care required because of accidental injuries received while the policy is in force (in Nevada, includes home health care and services as required by that state). Pays up to the maximum amount you select for as long as 52 weeks from the date of the accident.

In-hospital Sickness Benefits
$50.00 a day
Your coverage includes an In-hospital Sickness Benefit of $50.00 a day. This benefit is payable for as long as 60 days for hospital confinement beginning while the policy is in force as a result of sickness first manifesting itself while the policy is in force.

Dependents' Coverage
Dependents eligible for this coverage include the Insured's spouse and any unmarried dependent children under age 21 and living at home.

Exceptions and Limitations
This policy does not cover loss due to: suicide or attempted suicide; commission of or attempt to commit a felony or to which a contributing cause was engagement in an illegal occupation; an act of declared or undeclared war, invasion or civil war; participation in any armed service maneuvers or training exercises; snow skiing, unless additional premium is added; mountaineering, riding or driving in any kind of race, participation in any organized sporting competition as a team member, and, except in Washington, motor competition and participation in any body contact sport. In Washington, interscholastic sports are excluded.

BAGGAGE AND PERSONAL POSSESSIONS INSURANCE

Personal effects and baggage insurance covers baggage and personal possessions (not specifically or otherwise insured) for your entire trip, 24 hours a day, everywhere in the world, on land, sea or in the air. This includes clothing, luggage and recreation equipment. Not covered are animals, artificial teeth and limbs, contact lenses, credit cards, documents, furniture, rugs or carpets of any type or for any use, money, property pertaining to business or profession or occupation, securities, tickets, automobiles, auto equipment, boats, motors, motorcycles, campers, motor homes and any other conveyances or their appurtenances, except bicycles while checked as baggage with a common carrier.

The baggage and personal possessions policy insures against all risks of loss or damage except when caused by: normal wear and tear; hostile or warlike action; deterioration; vermin; insects; inherent vice; illegal act; insurrection; rebellion; revolution; radioactive or nuclear contamination; confiscation by order of authorities.

The policy requires immediate reporting of loss or damage in writing to the proper authorities (airlines, police, hotel management, etc.) and reporting as soon as possible to the Company. Failure to comply will invalidate any claim. All losses, damage and values shall be substantiated by the Insured.

A specified limit usually applies to loss of or damage to any one classification as follows: objects of art, antiques, books, cameras and equipment, china, collections or portions thereof, glass objects, furs, jewelry (including watches), paintings, or religious articles.

TRIP CANCELLATION INSURANCE

Trip cancellation insurance provides up to the maximum amount you select for non-refundable portions of travel expense (air fare, land and water common carriers such as trains, boats, etc., hotel and other land accommodations) specified and prearranged by your travel agency or other authority (airline, steamship company, rail, etc.).

For Travel Expense Loss Due to Illness or Injury

When you or a Covered Dependent require medical treatment and have to cancel or change your travel plans, this policy covers the nonrefundable expense incurred.

Prior to Departure for Entire Trip or Return Trip—If you must cancel your trip, you are covered for nonrefundable deposits paid for the trip.

During the Trip—If the trip is interrupted, benefits are provided for transportation to catch up to the trip, or transportation to the return trip destination. Transportation costs may not exceed economy class air fare, up to the amount of coverage selected.

The benefits described above apply equally if a member of your family is stricken, forcing you to cancel or interrupt your trip. Family members include spouse, children, brothers or sisters, parents, parents-in-law, grandparents or grandchildren, provided they reside in the United States or Canada.

Dependents' Coverage

Dependents eligible for this coverage include the Insured's spouse and any unmarried dependent children under age 21 and living at home.

Preexisting Conditions

Benefits are not payable for loss resulting from injuries or sickness for which the Insured or Covered Dependent received medical treatment, advice, or a prescribed medicine during the one-year period immediately prior to the date the policy application is received.

Exceptions and Limitations

Benefits are not payable for loss resulting from: an act of declared or undeclared war, invasion or civil war; accident or damage to the aircraft in which the Insured or Covered Dependent is traveling; the Insured or Covered Dependent's: suicide or attempted suicide; commission of or attempt to commit a felony or to which a contributing cause was engagement in an illegal occupation; snow skiing, unless additional premium is added; normal childbirth or normal pregnancy; participation in organized team sports, mountaineering, riding or driving in any kind of race, and except in Washington, motor competition. In Washington, interscholastic sports are excluded.

TRAVELLERS CHECKS

A travel agent may want to assist a client by providing travelers checks. American Express Travelers Cheques, Thomas Cook & Son, Bank of America, First City Bank of New York, Barclay and other banks sell travelers checks in denominations of $10, $20, $50, $100, and $500; typical charges to the purchaser are 1 percent over the face value of the checks. The commission is two-thirds of the 1 percent fee.

FOREIGN CURRENCY

Travel agents can assist travellers with foreign currency before they begin the trip. Many travel agents encourage their clients to obtain some foreign currency before leaving for Europe or other foreign destination(s). The Deak-Perera International Exchange Group has developed foreign currency systems to suit the specific needs of travel agents. Deak-Perera can pay the invoices from hotels and tour operators abroad in their local currency. This system eliminates completely the possibility of backbillings and other similar unpleasant surprises, due to the daily rate fluctuations. By the request of several travel agencies, Deak-Perera can supply agents with drafts in most currencies, which can be sent directly to the clients, together with vouchers and other pertinent instructions. "Pre-Packs" (prepackaged foreign money) is very popular with travellers, although most major airports offer exchange.

Commission checks expressed in foreign currencies have always been a problem to travel agents. Due to low exchange rates and heavy collection charges imposed by commercial banks, most or sometimes all of the commission is lost. Deak-Perera buys foreign commission checks, applies the daily exchange rate, and charges NO collection fee. The U.S. Dollar equivalent is paid to the agent immediately, which should improve profits, and facilitate bookkeeping.

Foreign currency checks also make excellent gifts, if any clients should like to send money abroad.

OTHER RELATED TRAVEL SALES

A good travel agent will want to assist clients in any reasonable way. As an agent you can sell "I Love New York" theatre packages so your customers can sit in orchestra reserved seats for a current Broadway show, e.g., "The Best Little Whorehouse in Texas."

Some travel agencies sell travel luggage and special travel bags. One problem with products, unlike travel services, customers think the merchandise is free, i.e., you give away travel luggage since they just purchased a cruise.

Other travel agencies carry outstanding travel books and maps for customers, and thereby, increase commission sales. Travel agents should make available only the better trade editions, for example; THE NICHOLSON'S GUIDES AND MAPS:

LONDON GUIDES

Nicholson's London Guide
Pocket sized packed full of information, plus many coloured maps.

Nicholson's Student's London
Pocket sized, directed specifically to the student's own needs. Maps and index.

Nicholson's Visitor's London
Specifically for the tourist. Full colour picture maps and index.

Nicholson's London Restaurants
London's best restaurants including cheap meals and pub lunches. Coloured centre maps.

Nicholson's London Nightlife
Not only the hot spots, but a practical guide to London after dark. Coloured centre maps.

Nicholson's American's Guide to London
Written by Americans for Americans in the famous Nicholson format. Coloured centre maps.

Nicholson's Guide to Children's London for Parents
All a parent needs to know to keep the kids happy and informed. Coloured centre maps.

LONDON MAPS

Nicholson's Central London Map and Index
30 square miles of central London in two colours and showing one-way streets.

Nicholson's London Street Finder
The famous and long established best seller. Two colours throughout, with large scale centre section showing one-way streets.

Nicholson's Large Street Finder
Large scale and two colour maps throughout for extra legibility.

Nicholson's Hard Back Street Finder
The handy, legible Street Finder for office or car. Two colour maps throughout.

Nicholson's Sightseer's London
An easy guide to localities wherever you are in London.

Nicholson's London Map
Large scale central London with index.

Nicholoson's 2 London Maps
Central London map with index plus London route planning map.

Nicholson's Visitor's London Map
Handy full colour fold out map with main sights in 3D.

GREAT BRITAIN GUIDES & MAPS

Nicholson's Great Britain
An easy reference guide to all the family's interests and activities. Fully illustrated and with coloured relief maps.

Nicholson's Waterway's Guides
Five regional guides to the canals of England and Wales with detailed maps.

Nicholson's Thames
Complete from source to sea with detailed maps, drawings and photographs.

Nicholson's Real Ale Guide to the Waterways
Over 1000 pubs on or near the waterways. Maps.

Nicholson's Great Britain Touring Map
Full colour map of Great Britain showing motorways and main roads.

A travel agency selling domestic and international travel books and maps will be able to order these material for the 40% trade discount. Michelin, Fodor's and Nicholson's, to name only three, are essential for any FIT client. Your client is always in need of good advice, your advice. Free travel brochures with colorful photos may sell the trip, but a good travel guide may literally save the day and bring your customer home again for another holiday.

DOCUMENTARY REQUIREMENTS

It is an exciting time for customers when they make their first international flight. An essential element of an international trip is guaranteeing that your clients will experience little or no inconvenience when crossing international boundaries. To assure this ease of travel it is necessary that your client be in possession of credentials that will permit them to leave one country and enter another and, what is just as important, to return to their country of residence. Regulations vary widely and depend upon the country, status of the traveller, purpose of the visit, length of stay and the discretionary authority of the custom officials. Be sure to inform your clients that these regulations are subject to change at any time.

The major documentary requirements are: passport, tourist card, visa, special papers, and health records (certificates). International travel requires that an individual be able to prove citizenship, prove identity, and have certain vaccination certificates. Any one of the following are Proof of Citizenship: Passport (valid or expired), Birth Certificate, Baptismal Certificate, Certificate of Naturalization or Citizenship, or any other official document issued by the government showing the person is a citizen or was born in that country. Proof of Identity is established with any document which contains signature and either a photograph or a physical description of the applicant. A driver's license, passport and identification card are some examples of Proof of Identity. Vaccination Certificate is a booklet in which records of vaccination(s) are shown. The booklet issued by the World Health Organization is accepted as the approved format by all members of the United Nations and is distributed by most carriers.

U.S. PASSPORTS

A passport is a formal document issued by a government to its citizens, subjects or nationals. It officially establishes the bearer's identity and nationality, and authorizes the bearer to travel outside of his own country.

A passport is required of U.S. citizens returning from outside of the Western Hemisphere or Guam. In addition, a passport is required for entry into some Western Hemisphere countries. See specific entry requirements of all countries to be visited and countries through which your client travels.

A U.S. passport may include: the spouse of the bearer; unmarried minor children less than age 13 (including stepchildren and adopted children) of the bearer; unmarried minor brothers and sisters of the bearer. A person included in a passport of another may not use the passport for travel unless he is accompanied by the bearer (signator). Application for passport must be made in person by anyone 13 years of age and older.

What is Needed to Obtain a U.S. Passport:

1. Proof of citizenship - An expired passport or birth certificate, (evidence of birth in the U.S. recorded soon after birth). If this is not obtainable applicant should submit statement issued by appropriate authorities that no birth records exist and secondary evidence of birth in the U.S. such as baptismal certificate, certificate of circumcision or other documentary evidence created shortly but not more than 5 years after birth. Those born outside the U.S. require either a certificate of naturalization or certificate of citizenship (when citizenship is obtained through parent) or naturalization certificate of the parent.

2. Photographs - Two duplicates, 2 inches by 2 inches, taken within six months. Black and white or color photos are acceptable. In a joint passport, the bearer must have his or her own photo alone, and all inclusions must share space in a group photo.

3. Proof of identity - Any document, such as a passport or driver's license, which contains signature and either physical description or photograph of applicant. If document is not available, an identifying witness who has known the applicant for at least two years is acceptable.

4. Fee - $13.00 ($10.00 plus $3.00 execution fee) if obtained by personal appearance at passport agency, or Clerk of Court; $10.00 for mail applications. Check or money order should be payable to "Passport Office."

5. Application for passport must be made in person unless applicant meets requirements established for securing passport by mail (see item 6 below).

6. Application by mail is allowed under following conditions: (a) mail application may be used only in the United States; (b) applicant must have been issued in his own name a U.S. passport within 8 years of the current application. Previous passport must have been issued when applicant was 13 years or over; (c) previous passport must accompany the mail application; (d) two photos, taken within 6 months, must accompany the application. Mail application may not be made for passport to include more than one person.

TOURIST CARD

A Tourist Card is a document issued to prospective tourists as a prerequisite for entry and departure. A tourist card is usually the only travel document required by the issuing country, i.e., no passport is required, but a passport without the card is insufficient.

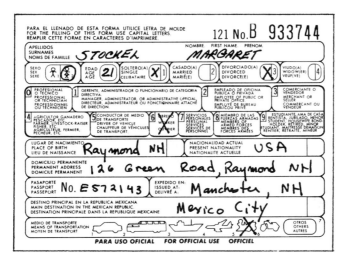

VISA

A visa is an endorsement placed in a passport or a document issued in lieu of passport by a consular or other government to indicate that the passport has been examined by such an official. A visa may be obtained from a consul representative or through a visa service agency in the country of residence prior to departure.

The visa application is an important part of preparing for a trip; for example, an incorrect application is rejected by the Soviet Embassy and can cause delay, confusion and sometimes considerable extra expense. The Soviet visa shows the name and passport number, both of which must agree with the passport presented upon arrival in the USSR. The visa will indicate dates of travel and cities of entry and exit. Should any of this information change after applying for the visa, the visa may not be valid...

SPECIAL PAPERS

Additonal requirements may take the form of a police certificate of good conduct, letter of recommendation or a ticket to leave the particular country.

HEALTH CERTIFICATES

The quarantinable disease for which vaccination certificates are required under the regulations of the World Health Organization. The travel agent should check the latest list of areas which are infected with cholera, smallpox, and/or yellow fever. These areas are subject to change at any time. Any passenger travelling or leaving these areas must be vaccinated against the particular disease. Unless otherwise indicated vaccinations are not required for transit passengers not leaving the airport. Validity of vaccination certificates and incubation periods are:

1. Upon initial vaccination

    a) Smallpox - not less than 8 days nor more than 3 years old.
Incubation period - 14 days.
    b) Cholera - not less than 6 days nor more than 6 months.
Incubation period - 5 days.
    c) Yellow Fever - not less than 10 days nor more than 10 years old.
Incubation period - 6 days.

2. Upon revaccination

    a) For smallpox, the certificate becomes valid on date of revaccination. Cholera revaccination to be valid immediately must be done within 6 months of previous vaccination. Yellow Fever vaccination to be valid immediately must be done within 10 day period.

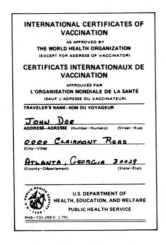

International Certificates of Vaccination must be complete in every detail.

Travellers are advised to contact their local health department, physician, or private or public agency that advises international travellers at least 2 weeks prior to departure to obtain current information on countries to be visited. Travel agents are advised to read HEALTH INFORMATION FOR INTERNATIONAL TRAVEL, DHEW - Center for Disease Control (CDC).

AREAS OF RISK FOR MALARIA TRANSMISSION – DECEMBER 1975

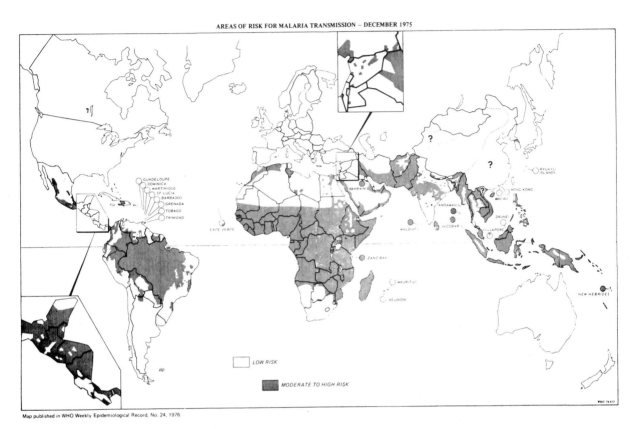

Map published in WHO Weekly Epidemiological Record, No. 24, 1976.

Because the situation with regard to the quarantinable diseases (cholera, plague, smallpox, and yellow fever) may change frequently, the Bureau of Epidemiology, CDC, distributes weekly "Blue Sheet" (Countries with Areas Infected with Quarantinable Diseases) that shows which countries are currently reporting these diseases. Some countries require vaccination against cholera, smallpox, and yellow fever only if a traveller arrives from a country infected with these diseases; therefore, it is essential that infected areas be considered in determining whether vaccinations are required.

Official changes in vaccination requirements reported by the World Health Organization (WHO) are published in the "Blue Sheet" and also in the Morbidity and Mortality Weekly Report (CDC) under "International Notes - Quarantine Measures."

As a travel agent you will be able to advise your client, for example, that a vaccination against plague is not required by any country as a condition for entry and is not recommended for travellers to most countries, even those reporting plague. Plague vaccination, however, is advisable for all persons travelling to the interior regions of Viet-Nam, Cambodia, and Laos, and for all persons whose occupation brings them into frequent and regular contact with wild rodents in plage enzootic areas of South America, Africa, or Asia.

U.S. CUSTOMS AND IMMIGRATION

Upon returning to the U.S., all passengers must show their passports when clearing immigration. After immigration, everyone must clear customs, where their bags may or may not be opened. Articles acquired abroad and brought into the United States are subject to applicable duty and internal revenue tax, but as a returning resident you are allowed certain exemptions from paying duty on items obtained while abroad. The combined value of all goods purchased while overseas, that may be imported duty-free CANNOT exceed U.S. $300.00/per person.

Your clients should read: KNOW BEFORE YOU GO: CUSTOMS HINTS FOR RETURNING U.S. RESIDENTS (U.S. Customs Service). Travel agents may want to explain the declaration, any penalties (warnings), exemption(s), articles free of duty or dutiable, prohibited and restricted articles, and other points on foreign shopping.

After a nice meal on a homeward flight, clients can complete their U.S. Customs Declaration Form.

Icelandic Loftleidir Photo

Chapter 13

THE FUTURE OF TRAVEL AGENCIES

Tomorrow's travel agent will be part of an ever changing travel agency. We now know where travel and tourism is and has been, but the future is a larger question. There is every reason to think that the days ahead will be as exciting as things are presently. We are impressed by the mass travel growth, Concorde's supersonic flight, resurgence of cruise ship travel and the other modern travel phenomenon. Retail agencies will have to adjust their planning, become more selective in their business mix in the face of open pricing, route additions and the possibility of net fares and open commissions.

TRAVEL AGENT TODAY

Sharon, a travel agent with ten years experience, meets personally with clients and discusses in a pleasant manner their travel plans. Sharon completes the reservation booking sheet; makes other trip notes; and gives the clients additional brochures to read in their leisure. After the client's exit, Sharon dials, and re-dials, a toll free number to reach the airline in order to book the air tour or the reservation. Her agency (almost $1,000,000 sales) has been thinking about ordering automatic telephone cards. Sharon knows that a computer terminal would do away with the endless hours of dialing and waiting to reserve a flight; but which one and what about the additional cost? She knows that at the present time 13% of all agencies (2,000) have a computerized reservation and ticketing system. Sharon writes a letter to her mother.

May 5

Dear Mom,

I think I'm ready to come home for a rest. You just wouldn't believe what we've been going through at the office!

Two weeks ago, one of the major airlines went on strike. We've been dialing our fingers to the bone trying to reach the other airlines that serve the same routes to reschedule people. It's unbelievable! Yesterday I spent two hours dialing and getting a busy signal before I finally got through to a recording. Then I was on hold so long that when a person finally answered, I forgot why I'd called.

It seems that we can't keep up with who is flying where anymore with all the new routes that have come about since deregulation. The new air fares come out in the newspaper before we receive any notification of them, and the airlines come up with a new set of fares almost every month.

The international fares are even worse. All the fares were quoted to us as subject to approval for April 1. By April 3, the fares still weren't approved, but we did know that if we ticketed people on these phantom fares before April 15, they would probably avoid the fuel surcharge

which would go into effect May 1 — subject to government approval of course. So we've been ticketing all of our customers who are going to Europe this summer and working 12 hours a day to save them money. However, before they leave, there are bound to be schedule changes and we'll just have to recall their tickets and do them all over again.

I used to love selling cruises, but this year even that is becoming a problem. The cruises are so heavily booked that it's becoming very difficult to get the type of space or the sailing date that my clients want. And, while a fly/cruise usually makes a very nice package, I've had some big problems arise when there are flight delays and the clients miss their ship.

This is such a crazy business. All my friends think I'm lucky to have such a great job. If they only knew, I haven't had time to take a lunch in months, and when I'm not working a twelve-hour day at the office, I'm rushing off to a seminar after work to keep up with all the new fares and tours being offered. These seminars are really important, but travel agents aren't paid for this extra time.

The thing my friends envy most is the fam trips I take. They really are a great

opportunity. How else could I have seen all five islands in Hawaii in just seven days and come home without a suntan? Then I come back to the office and my clients ask me how my "vacation" was.

Oh, by the way, there's talk around the office that we might be able to get a computer in a year or so, and our automatic telephone dialers will be installed by next month. I can't wait. Maybe when I don't have to spend all day dialing and ticketing things won't be quite as hectic.

Now that I've been a travel agent for ten years, I don't think I could go back to a normal office job. It would be too boring now. Being a travel agent drives me crazy, Mom, but it's too late now — I'm addicted to it.

See you soon.

Love,
Sharon

COMPUTERS IN TRAVEL

In twenty-five years the speed and capability of passenger aircraft have grown at an accelerated pace, i.e., from the propeller craft of yesterday to the SSTs of today. As we enter the 1980's we are faced with the challenge of the 749s with 500 passengers. Increasing passenger traffic of deregulation has placed a tremendous responsibility on the reservation system of the airline, as well as the travel agent, particularly in terms of good customer service. Because of the phenomenal growth in the airline industry, and the related problems of servicing larger numbers of passengers on additional routes of service, passenger handling systems have been hard pressed to meet the demands. This is the main reason why all the major airlines of the world are completely computerized and even commited to industry-wide reservation systems.

The introduction of electronic data processing to the travel world has produced substantial cost savings in areas where large volumes of repetitive paperwork were required; i.e., reservations, schedules, payrolls, inventory, shipping documents, invoice preparation, accounts receivables and other high volume operations. Today's computers were widely announced in 1964 and 1965, and began to come into installation in late 1965. Integrated circuitry made miniaturization possible. Real-time access and "time-sharing" capabilities were features of many central processors, providing the capability of access from remote terminals.

A computer, for example, is helping Trans World Airlines conserve more than 70 million gallons of precious fuel a year. At current prices this means a yearly saving of $24 million. The key to achieving this are an online flight planning system and a preferential fueling program. With online flight planning, information on aircraft performance and routes is stored in the computer: the system analyzes payload; fuel requirements; allowable takeoff weight; flight time; weather; and, up to five different altitudes. The system then displays fuel consumption, flight time and operating cost for every possible route/altitude combination. The system also determines power settings for climb, cruise and descent. A dispatcher reviews the alternatives and recommends the optimum least-cost route and altitude to the flight captain. The flight plan can be revised at the last minute should the weather or other conditions change.

SITA (Societe Internationale de Telecommunications Aeronautiques) is another type of a computer system which is a network of 175 international airlines. Basically, the SITA network handles two kinds of traffic. The bulk of it consists of teletypewriter messages; "Class B" traffic of lost baggage, passenger reservations, and flight servicing information. It also includes messages transmitted between and/or among the reservation computers of different member airlines. "Class A" messages are relatively short, inquiry-response type communications, between a reservation agent operating a CRT terminal and the airline's central reservation computer. The SITA network includes nine computerized switching centers located in Amsterdam, Brussels, Frankfort, Hong Kong, London, Madrid, New York, Paris and Rome. Each European airline operates their own seat reservation system. SITA provides a modern system for communications between airline reservation data bases. Assume that a client, Mr. William C. Traveller, wants to make an airplane trip that requires travel on three different airlines; Northwest, Air France, and Lufthansa, and that he places his reservations with Northwest through a travel agent using a MAARS-PLUS terminal system.

The Northwest reservation system interface will check the NW passenger data base for the appropriate flight to determine if space is available for the Northwest portion of the trip. Assuming that it is, the agent will enter inquiries in the Northwest system to determine if the space is available on Air France and Lufthansa. These data bases are not held by the Northwest system, so these transactions are forwarded to

SITA for processing since Air France and Lufthansa are European airlines: SITA determines the proper destinations for the inquiries and routes the transactions to the proper locations, e.g., Paris and Frankfort. The returning information also comes through SITA for routing back to Minneapolis.

An increasing number of travel agency managers are seeking automation as an answer to today's problems. Travel agents can use the PARS, and IBM developed system for Trans World Airlines, the APOLLO-ONE (United Airlines), SABRE (American and other carriers), Alleghany Reservations, and MAARS-PLUS (Eastern and Northwest). If an agent today selects an airline version, it will usually be from the airline which is the main carrier in his area. For example, the PARS (Programmed Airline Reservations System) offers availability for both the domestic and international as well as the hotel reservations (e.g., TWA and HILTON). The present computer system proliferations have caused the airlines to "sell" their own reservation systems in order to sell their own available seats first. In time it may be possible to have one multiple access reservation system that will allow agents to obtain unbiased airline reservation schedules and true last seat availability on any domestic airline. In the future it should be possible to make direct (real time access) connections with the computers of hotels, cruise lines, car rental agencies and related services.

COMPUTER SYSTEMS

The term "computer" can be applied logically to any calculating device. In common usage, however, the term refers specifically to the electronic computer. Early writers in the computer field frequently referred to the "automatic computer" in order to differentiate it from other calculating devices, i.e., the ending term AC as ENIAC. General definition of computers is a data processor which can perform substantial computation, including numerous arithmetic or logic operations, without intervention by a human operator during a single, continuous performance of a routine or program.

The computer has several differentiating characteristics. The computer relies largely on electronic components (transistors, resistors, diodes, and similar devices) rather than on mechanical operations. The use of modern electronics makes possible much faster operation than is possible with mechanical devices. The computer also has internal storage or memory modules for storing both the program and the date being processed by the program. Prior to its execution, the program of instructions which specifies the sequence of operations is put into the internal memory. This program makes the computer "automatic," since the entire set of steps to be taken is determined in advance and human intervention is seldom required during execution.

Another distinguishing feature of the computer is its ability to check the types of data being processed and to select from alternative sets of processing instructions. The computer is an electronic device capable of solving problems. A program of instructions directs the computer in accepting data, in performing prescribed operations, and in supplying the results of these operations as output.

Several elements make up a computer system: hardware, software, and user-written programs. Computer hardware consists of devices which can perform one or more of these functions: data preparation; input to the computer; computation, control and primary storage; secondary storage; and output from the computer.

In the simplest sense a computer is a collection of five component units: input, memory, arithmetic, control, and output. Input (I) is a means by which humans communicate with computers. Specific devices for input are: card reader, magnetic tape, switches, teletypewriters, cathode ray tubes, mechanical plotting boards, optical scanners, and paper tape.

REAL-TIME PROCESSING

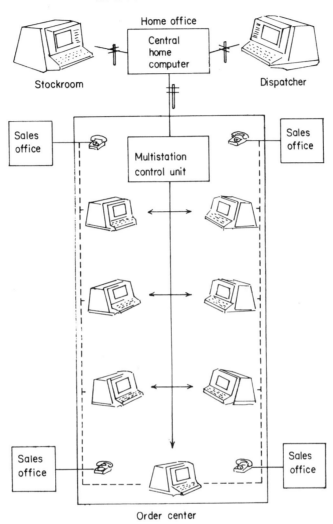

A Cathode Ray Tube (CRT Terminal) and other teleprinter devices are important communication links for conversational information between users and computers. The value of a terminal involves the over all operating efficiency, compatibility, and flexibility within the systems operations.

Teleprinters were initially used as interactive terminals because they were available before the introduction of the CRT, and because their costs were substantially below those of the early display terminals. Dramatic technological changes, large-scale integrated circuitry, have resulted in reducing equipment costs.

The CRT terminal is a high-speed I/O device which can transmit and receive several thousand characters per second, but is run at a <u>speed</u> that is compatible with the communications system in which it is used. In travel reservations CRT screen receives any output from the typewriter or function keyboard, and any input from the computer. A reservation system allows the agent to request scheduled displays of departing flights operating between most airports in the country, i.e., "electronic" OAG. The primary purpose of computerized reservations is to enable the agent to sell seats more efficiently.

Memory units are capable of storing information. An analogy could be a large collection of post office boxes each labeled with a number in which a group of iron rings mechanically chained and accessed in parallel are placed. Primary storage refers to data and instructions which have been entered into the main storage section of the central processor.

CENTRAL PROCESSING UNIT

Central Processor

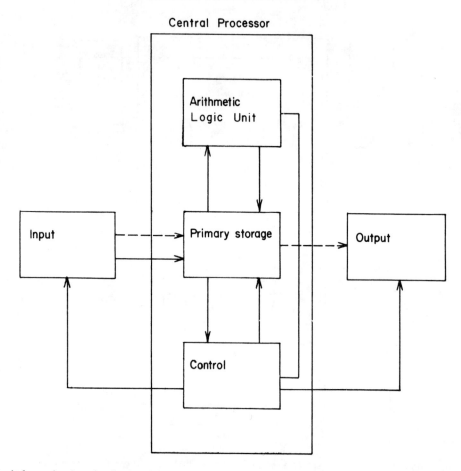

The Arithmetic-Logical device is an electronic adder that can add more than 1,000,000 numbers per second. The major difference between the arithmetic device and the standard adding machine is only the speed of operation.

The Arithmetic-Logic processor manipulates the data in accordance with the algorithm of instructions. The arithmetic-logic unit performs addition, subtraction, multiplication, division, and certain other logical operations.

Controls are required inside the CPU system to designate the input location, e.g., "what data to enter into primary storage, what file devices to access, what arithmetic-logic unit operations to perform".

The control device is the part of a computer that regulates what is happening according to a predetermined plan, a computer program. The output device is generally the same as the input device, i.e., the teletype type output.

The output (0) is the final result of the CPU operation. Output units provide an ability to exit from the computer storage information in the form of punched cards, magnetic tape, paper tape or written documents or to convert internal computer representation into a form suitable for either human interpretation, such as printed pages, or further processing or temporary storage, such as magnetic tape, paper tape or punched cards.

ELECTRONIC RESERVATIONS

The following illustrates the creation of PNR's (Passenger Name Record) and shows the necessary entries to establish an electronic reservation in PARS. An agent at Welcome Aboard Travel in Chicago receives a telephone call from a customer--"I need a one-way reservation to New York around 8:00 AM tomorrow morning, First Class."

The agent keys in the request for a display of available flights to the computer.

1. A12SEPORDNYC800A
2. Depress the ENTER key

A - Availability Entry Code
12SEP - Date of travel
ORDNYC - City or Airport Codes
800A - Approximate time of requested departure

The computer responds immediately, displaying the seat availability of the morning flights on this date, (maximum of four flights shown).

12SEP   F 70.00   Y 56.00   EX 89.00

1TW114F4Y3	ORDEWR	830A	242P	727	LL	03
2AA332F1Y4	ORDEWR	835A	117P	720	BS	02
3AA 2F5Y7	ORDJFK	845A	1246P	720	BB	00

"Yes, I can confirm a First Class seat for you on a non-stop flight, departing at 8:45 AM." The agent then specifies the flight to the computer and the inventory is adjusted.

The computer displays, for example, on line 2:

AA	Airline Code
332	Flight Number
F2Y4	Number of seats available per class of service; 2 first class and 4 coach
ORDEWR	Airport Codes, i.e., Newark Airport
835A	Time of Departure
117P	Time of Arrival
720	Type of Aircraft
BS	Meals
02	Number of Stops

Inventory Adjustment: N1F3

N	Need
1	Number of Seats
F	Class
3	Location of Desired Segment in Availability Display

The computer responds by displaying the confirmation instantly:

                1   2F 12SEP   ORDJFK   SS1   845A   1246P

"Under what name may I hold this reservation?"

"Bill Jones."

The agent keys in the name and enters it. It is preceded by an "Entry Code" that instructs the computer as to what type of information is being entered.

        -JONES/B   (- entry code for Name)

"And your home phone number, Mr. Jones?"

"Raymond 4-3201."

She keys in the number and enters it by "entry code, city, home phone":

                9CHIRA4-3201

"I'll pick up my tickets at the travel agency."

"That will be fine, Mr. Jones. We will have them ready for you."

"Mr. Jones, you hold a First Class reservation on AA flight 2 departing O'Hare at 8:45 AM tomorrow morning, and arriving in JFK airport at 12:46 PM. Is there anything else we may help you with at this time, such as rental of car, hotel, return reservation?"

"No, thank you."

"Thank you for calling Welcome Aboard Travel."

The computer edits all information sent to it. If any items of the program of information are not entered by the agent, such as Mr. Jones' phone number, the computer would have immediately reminded the agent of the error or oversight (NEED FONE).

A PNR (Passenger Name Record) has been created for Mr. Jones. No reservation card has been completed. This PNR is filed in the computer. Any agent can request later retrieval and display of Mr. Jones' or any other passenger's PNR. Changes can be made to a PNR and then it can be filed away again, i.e., rental cars, hotels, additional flights, traveling with infant, special meal, or, requires special attention.

A computer reservation system can be the travel agency's partner in providing passenger service. Any agent in the office has instant access to any Passenger Name Record in the computer even though the computer may be 3,000 miles away. In seconds the computer can display any PNR requested on the agent's screen. Necessary changes in the PNR; cancellations, rebookings, passenger name changes, etc., can be made by any agent who later speaks with the passenger.

Through the computer's automatic teletype processing, messages are sent to other airlines or received from other airlines. Through computer terminals, a travel agency is able to select not only the best available flight on all airlines, but the most advantageous fares currently applicable on a carrier basis and to furnish full and accurate pricing information. Computers permit immediate selection, booking and con-

firmation of an air fare/flights, and confirms hotel reservations and car rentals all in one swift step. To clients, this means instant confirmation of requests without wasted time on call backs.

Sales personnel no longer are required to work at conventional desks. Instead, they are now seated at reservation sets that use video screens and typewriter-like keyboards and are linked directly to the airline's main computer center. Clients can receive immediate confirmation for flights operated by over hundreds of domestic and foreign airlines, as well as hotels and car rental companies throughout the world.

Computer reservation systems provide instant confirmation of hotel reservations, including the domestic and international properties of Holiday Inns, Hilton, Hyatt, Howard Johnson, Ramada, Western International, Sheraton, Quality Inns and Americana. Leading car rental companies, available worldwide are Hertz, Avis, National, Budget, Econo Car and Dollar.

A computer reservation system enables travel agents to direct their attention and effort on knowing clients as individuals and providing that "personal touch." Automatic reservations help agents to immediately determine a customer's needs, wants, and preferences, and enables booking and ticketing to be accomplished quickly and accurately. Computers will enable travel agents to provide customers with the full courteous attention they expect and deserve.

YEAR 2001

Travel agents' roles are changing with automation. In the 1930's when the airlines first engaged in the practice of appointing travel agents to assist them in generating pleasure and business travel, they did not have the modern sales "tools" available: Toll Free Telephone Service for making it easy and convenient for potential customers to call for information and reservations; Computerized Reservations Systems to facilitate the answering of inquiries and booking of airline reservations, tours, car rentals, hotels, etc.; and, Automated Ticketing Machines for dispensing airline tickets covering each segment of the passenger's itinerary at the applicable fare. Where these technologies lead the travel agent in the next thirty years is a question for speculation.

In 2001, airplanes will travel faster; maybe it will be possible to travel anywhere on earth in less than four hours. A significant travel projection is that more and more people will be able to travel great distances in a comparatively brief span of time. Travel at the beginning of the next century will be relatively inexpensive; i.e., budget fares. The lower fares will give rise to mass travel requirements. As income levels are redistributed in the Middle East and in the developing nations of Africa, China, and India, the once scarce resources will be available for air travel and other leisure requirements. Exploration of other lands has always been the dream of every man. The wide body SSTs of the future will make untold opportunities for mankind; there will be new hotels, new air routes, and new tours for all of the workers of the world, wherever they reside.

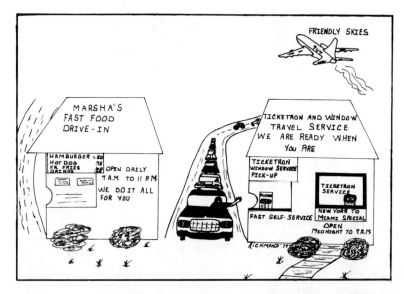

The booking and reservation requirements will remain; the 1990's computer systems will solve, finally, today's problems. Passengers will need only to give the computer travel program and answer the questions (probably voice activated since the responses are limited). An intelligent computer display or screen will provide literature (TV type brochures) of destinations; flight schedules and detailed interviews will be suggested in accordance with international air agreements (similar to IATA regulations). The client will simply indicate where and when he (she) wants to travel and as other questions are raised, the client and computer will arrive at a flight and establish the details of the trip. The computer will "sell" the ticket and suggest that the client place his credit card in the validator so the ticket can be printed (ticket printer delivers the actual ticket ready to use). The travel agent's job, as we know it, will dramatically change. If we want to understand the role of the travel agent

thirty years from now, we must know the 2001 travel agency. For some time the carriers have wanted to reduce the cost of selling tickets. Airlines have always wanted to sell all of their own seats, with no commissions, if they could; in 1978 ATC appointed travel agencies sold over $11 billion in airline passenger transportation and earned nearly $900 million in commissions. In the future the airlines may question their dependence on travel agents for the sale and ticketing of air transportation, for example, by offering toll free telephone service and ticketrons in local banks. The airlines would be in a position to motivate potential customers to call them directly for reservations and thus avoid the booking services of a travel agent. The key to the future is with the computerized reservation systems. Is it the airline sales agent or the travel agent who will have at their fingertips the schedules and fares of all carriers to nationwide/worldwide destinations in order to book reservations instaneously upon customer demand? By the end of the century the computerized reservation will probably be in the hands of the customer.

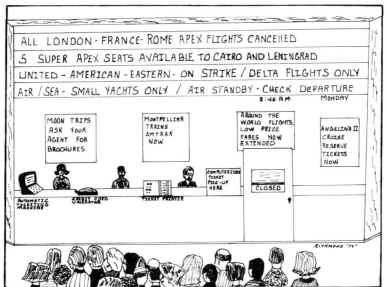

The approaching of net fares and increasing mini-computer technology should enable the travel agency to continue as the focus of airline ticket sales. New software programs and "front end" communications will enable a client (or travel agent) to ticket automatically any domestic or international travel. There will be on-line access to all airline computer systems, including hotels, wholesalers, land operators, rental cars and the like. It is anticipated that almost all "ordinary" travel will be organized and ticketed by an automatic computer terminal located in a travel agency. A credit card validator and ticket printer will be part of the airline system. Travel clerks will be required to assist with anything special, i.e., not in the data base.

It is anticipated that the customer will personally interact directly with the computer, a job presently undertaken by the airline reservations; personal computing will promote personal reservations. Clients in their homes will see and learn on television about foreign lands. In England, Teletext and Viewdata currently promote travel and tours on the television. The viewer merely uses a switching unit to call up the desired travel information on the screen from either the Teletext or Viewdata stations; the viewer is encouraged to make a booking with the wholesaler or carrier.

In the future travel agency terminals, similar to a pay telephone of today, will probably provide the agent with a lower commission on air/tour ticket sales. The airlines may be able to lease the terminals to agencies thus standardizing the hardware design and programming systems. Travel agencies will like this kind of installation as a way to eliminate today's problems of booking and ticketing (reticketing).

It is anticipated that not everyone in the future will know <u>all</u> about cruises or air travel tours to distant lands. The travel agents will continue to meet with clients and advise them, but the customers will make their own choices and write their own tickets using the automatic computer terminal facility.

Some clients will require more travel advice and will be given to domestic and international independent travel. It is anticipated that clients will have to pay a service charge (e.g., 15%) for this counseling. Travel agents in the future will have more "confidential" information to sell in regard to travel, e.g., unadvertised (not in the computer data base) inns in China or South America. By 2001 travel agents will be very specialized in foreign travel and will be viewed as consultants by their clients. It is one thing to open up the air routes and borders around the globe; it is quite another to expect all people to say "welcome" to strangers. Travellers may require introductions, prior booking and screening before becoming a "guest" in special resorts. Travel in the next century will be more exciting with ease of global air travel and modern information systems.

Gold Pavilion, Kyoto   Japan National Tourist Photo.

APPENDICES

Appendix A

WORLDWIDE EDITION OFFICIAL AIRLINE
GUIDE REVIEW

Directions: Upon completion of this review, you will be able to use the OFFICIAL
AIRLINE GUIDE Worldwide Edition (WEOAG) to prepare flight itineraries for passenger
travel; answer questions concerning flight frequencies, fares, number of stops, class
of service, and equipment types; advise passengers of correct airport of departure
and/or arrival if a city is a multiple-airport city; use the charts provided in the
WEOAG to determine minimum time required between flights in a connecting city, determine minimum connecting times between airports in multiple-airport cities, and
convert pounds into kilograms for purposes of quoting excess baggages charges. Answer
the questions in the space(s) provided; use the sample WEOAG materials and exhibits,
when necessary, at the end of the exercise.*

1. Which of the following flight schedules would not appear in the WEOAG?

   A. Detroit, Michigan to Stockholm, Sweden
   B. Montreal, Canada to Miami, Florida
   C. Honolulu, Hawaii to Osaka, Japan
   D. San Juan, Puerto Rico to London, England

2. It's easy to locate flight schedules in the WEOAG. Simply look for the name of
   your destination city across the top of the columns. You will find it printed
   in large bold face type like this:

   <u>To ROME, ITALY</u>

   At time, a "To" city listing will begin in the middle of a column instead of the
   top, but it will always be in proper alphabetical order. Schedules to Venice,
   Italy are found on Page 988. Where would you expect to find schedules to Sao
   Paulo, Brazil?

   A. Page 1017   B. Page 861

3. Having found your "To" or destination city look down the listing beneath it until
   you find your "From" or departure city in alphabetical order. If, for example,
   you were planning a trip from New York to Copenhagen, Denmark, you would first
   look for the heading "To _____." Having located it, you
   would then look down the listing beneath it until you found your "From" city, in
   this case _____.

*The WEOAG and NAOAG are reproduced here with the permission of the Reuben H. Donnelley
Corporation, publishers of the WORLDWIDE EDITION OFFICIAL AIRLINE GUIDE.

4. Due to the large number of flight schedules and the amount of information that must be displayed, codes were developed to conserve space. These codes may be found in the Worldwide Edition under Abbreviations and Reference Marks. The page on which these codes are listed appears in the Index of the WEOAG. Locate Exhibits 1 and 2 and use them to complete the following sentences: the Carrier (Airline) code "AF" stands for _____; the Jet Aircraft Code "D10" represents a _____ aircraft; and the Frequency code "4" means _____.

5. Now locate the "City/Airport Codes" which are listed alphabetically by code preceding the Quick Reference schedules section of the WEOAG (Use Exhibit 8). The three-letter code "ASP" stands for _____. "BEG" represents _____.

6. Your WEOAG at the end of the questions also contains a "Flight Itineraries" section. Each carrier's flights making at least one stop between their origin and destination are listed here in numerical order with their origin, cities en-route, and destination. Where does Swissair (SR) flight 336 originate? (Just jot down the three-letter code.) _____. What is its final destination? _____. Where else does it stop? _____.

7. Many flights operate on only specific days of the week, thereby requiring extreme caution when quoting direct flights or constructing itineraries. The days of the week are given a number code and are referred to as "Frequency Codes". Their decodes can be found in the "Abbreviations and Reference Marks" section.

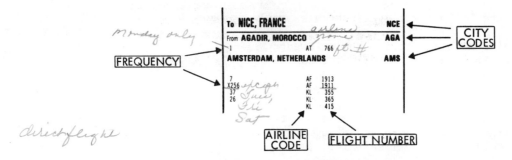

A flight will operate everyday of the week unless otherwise designated by frequency codes on the extreme left-hand side of the schedule. In the above example from Amsterdam, KL flight 355 operates only on Wednesday (3) and Sunday (7), while AF 1911 operates on Monday (1), Wednesday (3), Thursday (4), and Sunday (7) (the X256 indicates except Tuesday, Friday, and Saturday). What day(s) of the week does AF 1913 operate? _____. What day(s) of the week does KL 415 operate? _____.

8. Two other important items in any schedule are the departure and arrival times. Examine the following:

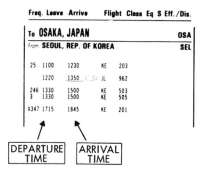

Departure and arrival times are always printed in the local time (24-hour clock) of the departure and arrival city. In the sample schedule above from Seoul to Osaka, the first flight departs Seoul at 1100 and arrives in Osaka at 1230. What day(s) of the week does KE flight 203 operate? _____.
If a passenger wishes to arrive in Osaka around 7:00 p.m. on Friday, what flight would you recommend? _____. At what time does it depart from Seoul? _____. If a passenger wishes to depart Seoul around 1:00 p.m. on a Sunday, what flight would you recommend? _____.
At what time does this flight depart? _____. When does it arrive in Osaka? _____.

9. Since most passengers are unfamiliar with the 24-hour clock, it is important that you know how to convert the 24-hour clock to the 12-hour clock (using a.m. and p.m.)

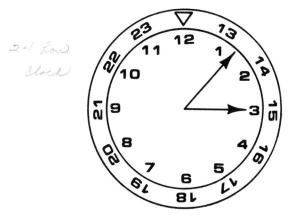

In the above example, the 12-hour clock reads 3:06 a.m. which is the equivalent of 0306 on the 24-hour clock. If this were 3:06 p.m., the time would be 1506 on the 24-hour clock. Using the "clock" above, convert the following times (use a.m. and p.m. where they apply):

24-hour clock	12-hour clock		12-hour clock	24-hour clock
0535	=		9:45 p.m.	=
1550	=		3:30 a.m.	=
2210	=		11:15 p.m.	=
0930	=		12:45 a.m.	=

10. Due to lengthy flights, time of departure, or crossing of the International Date Line, arrival at the destination is not necessarily on the same day as departure. Caution must be exercised, especially when making connections, to ensure the correct day of arrival is determined.

To AMSTERDAM, NETHERLANDS				AMS
From NEW YORK, N.Y., USA.				NYC
26	1000	0045+1	PA	100
	1815	0715+1	KL	642
14	1940	0810+1	OK	601
4	2015	0925+1	AY	102
36	2015	0925+1	AY	104
2	2030	1000+1	RO	302
	2100	1050+1	PA	102

DAY-CHANGE INDICATOR

All flights in the above schedule arrive the day after departure (shown by the "+1" following the arrival time; i.e., "+1" indicates day of arrival is one day after day of departure). If the departure at 10:00 a.m. in the above schedule was on Tuesday, the arrival would be on Wednesday at 12:45 a.m. In the above schedule from New York to Amsterdam, a passenger departing at 7:40 p.m. on Thursday would arrive in Amsterdam at _____ (time) on _____ (day). If a passenger wishes to arrive in Amsterdam on Thursday around 9:00 a.m., what flight would you recommend? _____. What time does it depart from New York? _____.

11. Examine the sample schedule below (From Auckland to Pago Pago):

Freq. Leave Arrive   Flight Class Eq S Eff./Dis.

To PAGO PAGO, SAMOA				PPG
From AUCKLAND, NEW ZEALAND				AKL
4	0800	1445-1	PA	820
6	0830	1210-1	PA	826
26	1400	1845-1	TE	526

Due to crossing the International Date Line, some eastbound flights arrive at their destination on the day before departure (shown by a "-1" after the arrival time). If a passenger departed AKL on a Saturday at 8:30 a.m., what day and time would he arrive in PPG? _____.

12. Many cities have more than one airport serving the area. Whenever this is true, the three-letter code of the departure and/or arrival airport is shown immediately following the applicable departure or arrival time. To determine the name of the airport served, refer to the City/Airport decoding pages preceding the flight schedules section. Here is part of the London to Moscow schedule:

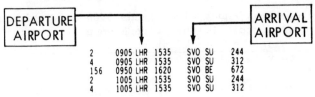

DEPARTURE AIRPORT					ARRIVAL AIRPORT	
2	0905	LHR	1535	SVO	SU	244
4	0905	LHR	1535	SVO	SU	312
156	0950	LHR	1620	SVO	BE	672
2	1005	LHR	1535	SVO	SU	244
4	1005	LHR	1535	SVO	SU	312

In this example, all the flights depart from _____ (airport code) airport and arrive at _____ (airport code) airport in Moscow.

13. Several more items are presented in this sample Bombay to New York schedule.

```
To NEW YORK, N.Y., USA.              NYC
From BOMBAY, INDIA                   BOM
     2  0100  1535     JFK AI  103  FY  747 3
     3  0100  1535     JFK AI  105  FY  747 4
     4  0100  1535     JFK AI  107  FY  747 4
     7  0100  1535     JFK AI  115  FY  747 4
     7  2115  1535+1   JFK AI  101  FY  747 5
     4  2115  1535+1   JFK AI  109  FY  747 5
     5  2115  1535+1   JFK AI  111  FY  747 5
```

NUMBER OF STOPS

CLASS(ES) OF SERVICE   TYPE OF AIRCRAFT

The three items introduced are 1) the class/classes of service offered to a passenger on each particular flight, 2) the type of aircraft, and 3) the number of stops the aircraft makes between the two points. You will recall these items are decoded on the "Abbreviations and Reference Marks" pages in front of the WEOAG. The class(es) of service is denoted by capital letters. Night service is indicated by a small "n" after the general classification. Example:

Fn = Jet Night Coach in First Class Compartment
Yn = Jet Night Coach/Economy

In the above schedule, AI 103 offers both _____ and _____ service. The airplane is a _____ and makes _____ stops between BOM and NYC.

14. Using the Paris (PAR) to New York (NYC) schedules below, let's review.

```
Freq. Leave Arrive      Flight Class Eq S Eff./Dis.

To NEW YORK, N.Y., USA.              NYC
From PARIS, FRANCE                   PAR
        1100 CDG 1225    JFK AF  015  FY  707 0
     4  1140 ORY 1535    JFK AI  107  FY  747 1
     7  1140 ORY 1535    JFK AI  115  FY  747 1
     3  1145 ORY 1535    JFK AI  105  FY  747 1
     2  1155 ORY 1535    JFK AI  103  FY  747 1
        1200 CDG 1255    JFK TW  803  FY  747 0
        1330 CDG 1515    JFK AF  077  FY  747 0
        1500 CDG 1715    JFK TW  801  FY  B3J 0
    14  1800 CDG 1945    JFK AF  017  FY  747 0
     2  1800 ORY 1900    JFK PK  703  FY  D10 0
     6  1800 ORY 1900    JFK PK  711  FY  D10 0
```

A. AF 015 leaves PAR at _____, arriving in NYC at _____. The _____ (type) aircraft offers _____ (Class/es of service) service.

B. A passenger wishes to arrive in New York around 3:30 p.m. on Wednesday, what flight would you recommend? _____. How many stops does this flight make? _____.

C. If a passenger wishes to depart from Paris (Orly Field) on Tuesday around 11:00 a.m., what flight would you recommend? _____. Does this flight make any intermediate stops? _____. What type of aircraft is used? _____.

15. Here is part of the Auckland to Papeete schedule. Please use it to answer the following questions:

To **PAPEETE, TAHITI, FR. POLYNESIA**						**PPT**
From **AUCKLAND, NEW ZEALAND**						**AKL**
1	0915 AKL 1555-1	PA	826	FY	747	0
24	1225 AKL 1925-1	PA	816	FY	707	0
35	2010 AKL 0315	TE	556	FY	D10	0
5	2300 AKL 0600	UT	584A	Y	DC8	0
6	2300 AKL 0600	UT	586A	Y	DC8	0

A. If a passenger wishes to arrive in Papeete on Monday around 4:30 p.m. what flight would you recommend? _____. What time would he actually arrive? _____. What class(es) of service does the flight offer? _____. What type of aircraft is used? _____. How many intermediate stops does the flight make? _____.

B. In the schedule, locate the UT 584A flight. This flight departs on _____ (day) at _____ (time). It arrives in Papeete on _____ (day) at _____ (time). The flight offers _____ class(es) of service on a _____ aircraft.

16. The Worldwide Edition contains an "International Standard Time Chart" which may be used to determine elapsed flying time for any given flight. It may also be used to determine the local time in any country throughout the world. For example, at 2:00 P.M. in New York, a secretary must contact her boss who is in London, England on business. She can use the chart to determine whether to contact her boss at the business telephone or at his hotel. Reproduced here is the portion of the chart the secretary must use to determine the time in London.

COUNTRY	STANDARD TIME		Countries observing Daylight Saving Time during local Summer (S) or Winter (W) season and dates of observance if available.
	Hours fast or slow of GMT	Time at 1200 hrs. GMT	
UGANDA	+ 3	15 00	
UNITED KINGDOM	GMT	12 00	(S) (+1 hr.) Mar. 16–Oct. 25
UPPER VOLTA	GMT	12 00	
URUGUAY	− 2½	09 30	
U.S.A.—Eastern Time	− 5	07 00	(S) (+1 hr.)
Central Time	− 6	06 00	(S) (+1 hr.)
Mountain Time	− 7	05 00	(S) (+1 hr.) Feb. 23, 1975
Pacific Time	− 8	04 00	(S) (+1 hr.) through
ALASKA—Ketchikan to Skagway	− 8	04 00	(S) (+1 hr.) October 25,
Skagway to 141° long. W. (Yakutat)	− 9	03 00	(S) (+1 hr.) 1975
141° long. W. to 162° long. W.	−10	02 00	(S) (+1 hr.)
162° long. W. to Western tip	−11	01 00	(S) (+1 hr.)
HAWAIIAN ISLANDS	−10	02 00	
U.S.S.R.—Moscow, Ukraine, West	+ 3	15 00	
Approximately every 15° from 30° 30' E. to 172° 30' W. add 1 hr.	+ 4	16 00	
	+12	24 00	

Compare the times shown for the United Kingdom and the Eastern Time zone of the U.S.A. Assume New York City is on Eastern Standard Time. At 7:00 A.M. in New York, it is 12:00 noon in London. The United Kingdom time is 5 hours ahead of the Eastern U.S.A. time. Therefore, at 2:00 P.M. in New York, it is 7:00 P.M. in London. The secretary should attempt to contact her boss at his hotel. At 9:00 A.M. EST in New York, it is _____ (time) in London. At 9:00 A.M. in London, it is _____ (time) EST in New York.

17.

To **AMSTERDAM, NETHERLANDS**								**AMS**
From	**FRANKFURT, GERMANY**							**FRA**
5	0645	0750	SQ	745A	FY	707	0	E-APR 2
								D-MAY 1
3	0710	0815	SQ	725A	FY	707	0	E-APR 2
								D-MAY 1
5	0710	0815	SQ	745A	FY	707	0	D-APR 1
5	0750	0855	SQ	743A	FY	747	0	E-MAY 2
7	0755	0905	KL	834	FY	D10	0	
6	0800	0910	KL	844	FY	747	0	
3	0805	0910	SQ	725A	FY	707	0	D-APR 1
	0920	1025	LH	080	FY	737	0	
2	0950	1100	GA	892	FY	D10	0	
5	0950	1100	GA	894	FY	D10	0	
X7	1100	1205	KL	242	Y	D9S	0	
137	1350	1455	LH	450	FY	707	0	D-MAY 7
X5	1350	1455	LH	450	FY	707	0	E-MAY 8
	1500	1605	KL	244	Y	DC9	0	
3	1620	1730	KL	778	FY	D10	0	
	1650	1755	LH	084	FY	727	0	D-MAR31
X67	1650	1755	LH	084	FY	727	0	E-APR 1
67	1650	1755	LH	084	FY	737	0	E-APR 1
	2130	2235	LH	086	FY	737	0	D-MAR31
	2130	2235	LH	086	FY	727	0	E-APR 1

Examining the first flight in the Frankfurt to Amsterdam schedule, you will note that the flight begins operation on April 2 and ends operation on May 1. Looking further down the schedules, you will note another SQ 745A that ended operation on April 1 (this flight operated at different times than the flight on April 2). If a passenger wishes to arrive in Amsterdam as early as possible Thursday, May 6, what flight would you recommend? _____. What time would he arrive in Amsterdam?_____. If a passenger had reservations on Wednesday, March 30, on SQ 725A and had to change departure days to Saturday, April 2, what flight would you recommend (the passenger wants to arrive around the same time)? _____.

18. Using the following schedule, let's summarize what you have learned.

To **PALMA, MALLORCA IS., SPAIN**								**PMI**
From	**LONDON, ENGLAND**							**LON**
X256	0830 LHR	1035	BE	162	Y	L10	0	E-APR 1
245	0915 LHR	1225	BE	162	Y	TRD	0	D-MAR20
245	1015 LHR	1225	BE	162	Y	TRD	0	E-MAR21
								D-MAR31
67	1120 LHR	1430	BE	164	Y	L10	0	D-MAR20
X246	1215 LHR	1520	IB	501	FY	727	0	D-MAR20
246	1215 LHR	1520	IB	503	FY	727	0	D-MAR20
67	1220 LHR	1430	BE	164	Y	L10	0	E-MAR21
								D-MAR31
	1350 LHR	1555	IB	293	FY	727	0	E-APR 1
6	1640 LHR	1845	BE	164	Y	L10	0	E-APR 1
6	2100 LHR	0020+1	IB	897	FnYn	DC9	1	E-APR 1
								D-JUN30
246	2100 LHR	0020+1	IB	897	FnYn	DC9	1	E-JUL 1
57	2145 LHR	0100+1	IB	295	FnYn	DC9	1	E-APR 1
								D-JUN30
X246	2145 LHR	0100+1	IB	295	FnYn	727	1	E-JUL 1

A. A passenger wishes to arrive in Palma (PMI) around 3:00 p.m. on Thursday, March 18. What flight would you recommend? _____. What is his actual arrival time? _____. If he were delayed until Sunday, March 21, what flight would you recommend if he still wished to arrive around 3:00 p.m.? _____. What would be his actual arrival time? _____.

B. A passenger wishes to arrive in Palma (PMI) as late as possible on Saturday, April 3. What flight would you recommend? _____. What class(es) of service are offered? _____. What type of aircraft is used? _____. At what time would the passenger arrive in Palma? _____.

C. A family of four wishes to depart for Palma on Sunday, around noon on March 7. What flight would you recommend to them? _____. When does this flight depart? _____. When will it arrive? _____.

19. Reaching his final destination often requires the passenger to make a connection from one aircraft to another at an enroute city. This might be because; a) direct flights are completely reserved; b) timing of direct flights is inconvenient; or, c) there is no direct service between the two points. Here is a sample connecting schedule:

To PANAMA CITY, PANAMA REP.					PTY
From CHICAGO, ILL., USA.					CHI
CONNECTIONS					
146 0900 ORD 2000	AA	57	FY	D10 0	
1310 MEX 1545	OP	601	S	727 0	

If you have had extensive experience using the North American Edition and can interpret the above schedule, answer the questions in this step. A passenger holding reservations on the above itinerary would depart from CHI at _____ and arrive in PTY at _____. He would depart from CHI on _____ _____ Airlines flight number _____, connect at _____ _____ (name of city) to _____ Airlines flight number _____. If the passenger traveled Economy Class on his first flight, what class of service would he travel on his second flight? _____ _____.

20. Here is another connecting schedule:

	Freq. Leave Arrive	Flight	Class	Eq	S Eff./Dis.
To NUREMBERG, GERMANY					NUE
From CHICAGO, ILL., USA.					CHI
CONNECTIONS					
1715 ORD 1025+1	LH	431	FY	D10 0	
0835 FRA 0940	LH	880	FY	727 0	
467 1815 ORD 1405+1	PA	58	FY	707 0	D-MAR30
0940 FRA 1320	LH	881	FY	727 0	

A passenger wishes to leave Chicago on Thursday, April 8 on a trip to Nuremberg, Germany. Using the above schedule, he would depart from ORD at _____ on _____ Airlines flight number _____ and arrive in _____ (connecting city) at _____ (time). He would then depart the connecting city at _____ on _____ Airlines flight number _____ and arrive in Nuremberg at _____ on _____ (day).

21. Let's review using the following schedule:

	Freq. Leave Arrive	Flight	Class	Eq	S Eff./Dis.
To AMSTERDAM, NETHERLANDS					AMS
From BUENOS AIRES, ARGENTINA					BUE
3 1125 EZE 1015+1	KL	794	FY	D8S 3	
7 1125 EZE 1135+1	KL	792	Y	OC8 4	
CONNECTIONS					
7 1135 EZE 1240+1	SK	956	FY	D8S 4	
1000 ZRH 1115	OA	151	FY	727 0	
2 1535 EZE 1545+1	AZ	577	FY	D10 2	
1145 FCO 1320	KL	348	Y	D9S 0	
6 1730 EZE 1525+1	AR	152	FY	707 0	D-MAR30
0930 MAD 1310	IB	480	FY	727 0	
2 1905 EZE 2025+1	SK	958	FY	D8S 3	D-MAR30
1640 ZRH 1900	SR	796	FY	D99 0	
7 1940 EZE 1840+1	AZ	573	FY	D10 1	D-MAR30
1400 FCO 1520	AZ	382	FY	DC9 1	
3 2200 EZE 1815+1	AR	146	FY	707 0	
1400 MAD 1555	KL	362	Y	D9S 0	
2 2200 EZE 1815+1	AR	154	FY	707 0	
1400 MAD 1555	KL	362	Y	D9S 0	

A passenger wishes to leave Buenos Aires on April 2 (Tuesday). His final destination is Amsterdam. What flight(s) would you suggest if the passenger requested an arrival time of 5:30 p.m.? _____. How many intermediate stops does this flight make (if a connection, include the connecting point)? _____. On what day does he arrive? _____. The passenger would leave Buenos Aires at _____ and arrive in Amsterdam at _____. If you suggest a connection, what city would the passenger connect at? _____.

22.   Examine the following schedule and answer the following questions:

To	AMSTERDAM, NETHERLANDS						AMS	
From	DAYTONA BEACH, FLA., USA						DAB	
			CONNECTIONS					
	1516	1005+1	NA	439	FY	727	1	E-MAR20
	1701 MIA	1820	NA	2	FY	D10	0	
	0735 LHR	0905	KL	120	Y	D9S	0	
56	1516	1115+1	NA	439	FY	727	1	D-MAR19
	1701 MIA	1820	NA	2	FY	D10	0	
	0735 LHR	0920	BE	206	Y	TRD	0	
X56	1516	1115+1	NA	439	FY	727	1	D-MAR19
	1701 MIA	1820	NA	2	FY	D10	0	
	0735 LHR	0920	BE	206	FY	TRD	0	
DELHI, INDIA							DEL	
2	2320	0820+1	KL	862	FY	747	2	
6	2320	0850+1	KL	864	FY	747	2	
			CONNECTIONS					
X156	0240	1025	LH	661	FY	D10	0	
	0700 FRA	0920	LH	080	FY	737	0	
4	1340	2235	SK	988	FY	D8S	0	
	1810 FRA	2130	LH	086	FY	737	0	

A passenger leaving Daytona Beach on Monday (March 15) would like to depart in
the early afternoon. What flight would you recommend? _____
(airline/flt. number) to _____ (airline/flt. number) to _____
___ ____ (airline/flt. number). What cities would the passenger make connections?
_____ (city code) and _____ (city code). What time
would the passenger arrive at the first connecting point? _____.
What time would he depart his second connecting point? _____.
When would he finally arrive at his final destination? _____.

23.   Fares for international travel are published in the currency of the originating
      city/country. For this reason, a fare from London, England to Paris, France
      will be published in English Pounds. A three-letter code follows the fare in-
      dicating the currency used. Fares to London from Rome are published in (LIT)
      _____. Fares from Mexico City to Zurich, Switzerland are
      published in (MEP) _____.

24.   One-way and round-trip fares are published in the currency of the origin (From)
      city for all destinations with direct service. In some cases, fares are pub-
      lished where only connecting service is shown. These fares are for your informa-
      tion and are dependent on the routing selected. All users should only use fares
      for direct service. Examine this exhibit which displays schedule and fare in-
      formation from Cairo to Amsterdam.

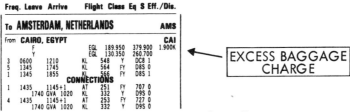

Freq.	Leave	Arrive	Flight	Class	Eq	$ Eff./Dis.

To	AMSTERDAM, NETHERLANDS						AMS
From	CAIRO, EGYPT						CAI
	F		EGL	189.950	379.900		1.900K
	Y		EGL	130.350	260.700		
3	0600	1210	KL	548	Y	DC8	1
5	1345	1745	KL	564	FY	D8S	0
1	1345	1855	KL	666	FY	D8S	1
			CONNECTIONS				
1	1435	1145+1	AT	251	FY	707	0
	1740 GVA	1020	KL	332	Y	D9S	0
4	1435	1145+1	AT	253	FY	727	0
	1740 GVA	1020	KL	332	Y	D9S	0

EXCESS BAGGAGE CHARGE

The symbols F & Y located just under the "From" city name correspond to the
classes of service available on the flights listed in the schedule. One-way and
round-trip fares in Egyptian pounds are shown to the right of the symbols F and
Y as indicated by the currency code EGL. In addition, excess baggage charges
are shown immediately below the three-letter code of the "From" city, and are
published in the currency of the "From" city. In most cases, the basis for excess baggage charges is kilograms (the code "K" follows the excess baggage
charge), but pounds are also used (an "L" is used to indicate pounds). In the
above schedule, the First Class Jet fare from CAI to AMS is _____
Egyptian pounds. The round-trip Jet Economy fare is _____ Egyptian
pounds. The excess baggage charge between CAI and AMS is _____ Egyptian
pounds per kilogram.

25. The WEOAG contains a complete Airline Index containing home office addresses of all airlines whose schedules appear in the Worldwide Edition.

INDEX OF AIRLINES
APPEARING IN THIS PUBLICATION

✦Indicates carrier's participation to the agreement relating to liability limitations of the Warsaw Convention and The Hague Protocol, which carriers have signed and filed with the Civil Aeronautics Board counterparts of the inter-carrier Agreement (CAB 18900—sometimes called the Montreal Agreement) providing for increase of liability limits to $75,000 and waiver of defense under Article 20(1) of the Warsaw Convention or The Hague Protocol, with respect to passengers.
● Operator Members and Associate Members of the Air Transport Association of Canada (A.T.A.C.)
▲ Members and Associate Members of the International Air Transport Association (I.A.T.A.)   ★ Members and Associate Members of the Air Transport Association of America (A.T.A.)

AIRLINE AND HOME OFFICE	ATA/IATA FORM NO. CABLE ADDRESS	AIRLINE AND HOME OFFICE	ATA/IATA FORM NO. CABLE ADDRESS
ACES (VX) Aerolineas Centrales De Colombia Carrera 49, No. 56-27, Medellin, Colombia Tel. 456-043, 452-618		AIR JAMAICA (1968) LTD. (JM)✦ 72-76 Harbour Street Kingston, Jamaica, W.I. Tel. 932-3460	201
AERANGOL (NG) Rua Cabral, Moncada 9, Luanda, Angola Tel. 25259		AIR LIBERIA, INC. (NL)▲ P.O. Box 2076, Monrovia, Liberia Tel. 22144	277 LNAHARBEL, Liberia
AERIAL TOURS PTY. LTD. (TI) P.O. Box 1179 Boroko, Moresby Papua, New Guinea Tel. 53499		AIR LIMOUSIN (QU) Aeroport de Limoges, Bellegarde, 87 Limoges, France Tel. 00-10-37	
AER LINGUS TEORANTA (Irish International) (EI)▲✦ (Aerlinte Eireann) (IN) Dublin Airport, (P.O.B. 180); O'Connell St., Dublin, Ireland Tel. 370011	053 AERLINGUS, Dublin	AIR LITTORAL (FU) Aerodrome de 83, Le Castellet, France Tel. (94) 98.74.11	
AERLINTE EIREANN (IRISH INTERNATIONAL) (IN)▲✦ (Aer Lingus) (EI) Dublin Airport, (P.O.B. 180), Dublin, Ireland Tel. 370011	052 AERLINTE, Dublin	AIR LOWVELD (PTY) LTD. (LE) 14th Floor Union Square 80 Plein St., Cor. Klein St., P.O. Box 3567 Johannesburg, Rep. of S. Africa Tel. 22-9641	LOWVEL DAIR, Johannesburg
AERO CHACO (Lineas Aereas Chaquenas) (CQ)▲ Santa Maria de Oro 145 Resistencia, Chaco, Argentina Tel. 5274	AEROCHACO, Resistencia	AIR MADAGASCAR (See Societe Nationale Malgache de Transports Aeriens) AIR MALAWI (QM)▲ Robins Road, (P.O.B. 84), Blantyre, Malawi Tel. Blantyre 2001	167 AIRMALAWI, Blantyre
AEROCONDOR—Aerovias Condor De Colombia Ltd. (OD) Carrera 45B, (P.O. Box 2299), Barranquilla, Colombia Tel. 27700	355 AEROCONDOR, Barranquilla	AIR MALI (MY)▲ P.O. Box 27, Bamako, Republic of Mali Tel. 27-41/2, 35-36, 33-36	091 AIRMALI, Bamako
AEROFLOT—SOVIET AIRLINES (SU) Leningradsky Prospekt, 37, Moscow, U.S.S.R Tel. 83-58-35	555 AEROFLOT, Moscow	AIR MALTA COMPANY, LTD—AIR MALTA (KM)▲ Development House, St. Anne Street Floriana, Malta Tel. 21421	AIR MALTA, Malta
AEROLINEAS ARGENTINAS (AR)▲✦ Paseo Colon 185, Buenos Aires, Argentina Tel. 30-2071	044 AEROLINEAS, Buenos Aires	AIR MAURITANIE (See Societe Nationale Air Mauritanie) AIR MAURITIUS (MK) 1 Sir William Street Port Lewis, Mauritius Tel. 2-1281	239 AIRMAURITIUS, Port Lewis
AEROLINEAS TAO (RM) Avenida 19, No. 4-20 Int., 9 Bogota, Colombia Tel. 340-592, 415-402		AIR MELANESIAE (HB) B. P. 72, Port Vila, New Hebrides Tel. 753	
AEROLINEE ITAVIA, S.P.A. (IH) Via Sicilia 43, Roma, Italy Tel. 4692	298 ITAVIA, Rome	AIR MICRONESIA (see Continental Airlines) AIR MONGOL (OM) Airport, Ulan-Bator, Mongolian People's Republic	289

If, for example, you wished the address of the home office for Air Malawi, locate Air Malawi alphabetically. The address is printed immediately below the name of the airline.

A. Air Malawi's home office is located in _____.
   (name of city & country)
B. The home office for Aerolineas Argentinas is located in _____
   _____.(name of city)

26.

To NICE, FRANCE						NCE
From FRANKFURT, GERMANY						FRA
F		DMK	445	890		4.45K
Y		DMK	313	626		
X125	1035	1200	LH	182	FY	727 0 D-MAR31
X7	1615	1740	LH	150	FY	727 0 E-APR 1
7	1615	1740	LH	150	FY	737 0 E-APR 1

Using the above example, the one-way Jet First Class fare from FRA to NCE is _____ German marks. The round-trip Jet Economy fare in German marks (DMK) is _____.

27. If a passenger traveling from Los Angeles to Geneva, Switzerland (in Exhibit 10) in First Class had 70 pounds of luggage (use normal free baggage allowance in Exhibit 3), how many pounds is he over the free baggage allowance? _____. How much will he be charged? _____. (Exhibit 5 of this review shows a chart to be used to convert pounds into kilograms when computing excess baggage charges.)

28. Fares printed in the WEOAG sometimes have special references attached to them.

To **NEW YORK, N.Y., USA.**				**NYC**
From **COLOMBO, REP. OF SRI LANKA**				**CMB**
1F	CER	10780	21560	107.80K
3F	CER	10075	20150	100.75K
1Y	CER	7061	14122	
3Y	CER	6141	12282	
1 VIA PACIFIC				
3 VIA ATLANTIC				

The CMB to NYC listing shows fares which apply via the Atlantic and separate
fares which apply to travel via the Pacific. (Fare #1 via Pacific; #3 via
Atlantic.) The fare via the Atlantic is lower because the distance is shorter
than the distance via the Pacific. The one-way Jet First Class fare from CMB
to NYC via the Atlantic is _____ Sri Lanka rupees (CER). The
round-trip Jet Economy fare via the Pacific is _____ rupees.

29. Using the "Explanation of Peak 'YH' and Winter 'YL' Economy Fares", solve the
     following problem. (Fares are the same in both directions.)

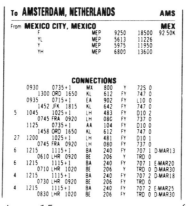

To **AMSTERDAM, NETHERLANDS**			**AMS**
From **MEXICO CITY, MEXICO**			**MEX**
F	MEP	9250	18500	92.50K
YL	MEP	5613	11226	
Y	MEP	5975	11950	
YH	MEP	6800	13600	

CONNECTIONS

	0930	0735+1	MX	800	Y	72S	0
	1300 ORD 1650	KL	612	FY	747	0	
	0935	0715+1	EA	902	FY	L10	0
	1452 JFK 1815	KL	642	FY	747	0	
5	1045	1025+1	LH	483	FY	D10	2
	0745 FRA 0920	LH	08C	FY	737	0	
	1125	0735+1	AA	104	FY	D10	0
	1458 ORD 1650	KL	612	FY	747	0	
27	1200	1025+1	LH	481	FY	D10	1
	0745 FRA 0920	LH	080	FY	737	0	
6	1215	1115+1	BA	240	FY	707	1 D-MAR13
	0610 LHR 0920	BE	206	Y	TRD	0	
6	1215	1115+1	BA	240	FY	707	1 E-MAR20
	0710 LHR 1020	BE	206	Y	TRD	0 D-MAR30	
4	1215	1115+1	BA	240	FY	707	2 D-MAR18
	0730 LHR 0920	BE	206	FY	TRD	0	
4	1215	1115+1	BA	240	FY	707	2 E-MAR25
	0830 LHR 1020	BE	206	FY	TRD	0 D-MAR30	

(Eastbound) MEX to AMS - Aug. 15 = _____ (MEP) Mexican pesos
(Westbound) AMS to MEX - Dec. 18 = _____ (MEP) Mexican pesos
The total round-trip fare is $_____ (MEP) Mexican pesos

30. The 14-21 day reference indicates a minimum stay of 14 days and a maximum of 21
     days is required. If the passengers meet all the conditions listed under one of
     these notes, then the fare corresponding to that note is charged.

To **PALMA, MALLORCA IS., SPAIN**			**PMI**
From **TORONTO, ONT., CANADA**			**YYZ**
F	CAD	653	1306	6.53K
YL	CAD	341	682	
Y	CAD	355	710	
YH	CAD	450	900	
EX 4 14-21 DAY YE	CAD	604		
EX 5 14-21 DAY YE	CAD	691		
EX 8 22-45 DAY YE	CAD	366		
EX 12 22-45 DAY YE	CAD	393		
EX 13 22-45 DAY YE	CAD	486		

CONNECTIONS

16	1745	1200+1	CP	222	FY	DC8	2
	0930 MAD 1055	AO	186	Y	CVL	0	
6	2000	1430+1	BA	600	FY	747	0 E-MAR 6
	0745 LHR 1120	BE	164	Y	L10	0 D-MAR13	
5	2000	1430+1	BA	600	FY	747	1 D-MAR12
	0925 LHR 1120	BE	164	Y	L10	0	
5	2000	1430+1	BA	600	FY	747	1 E-MAR14
	0925 LHR 1120	BE	164	Y	L10	0 D-MAR19	
56	2000	1430+1	BA	600	FY	747	1 E-MAR20
	1025 LHR 1220	BE	164	Y	L10	0 D-MAR30	
47	2000	1520+1	BA	600	FY	747	1 D-MAR12
	0925 LHR 1215	IB	501	FY	727	0	
247	2000	1520+1	BA	600	FY	747	1 E-MAR14
	0925 LHR 1215	IB	501	FY	727	0 D-MAR19	

If a passenger travelling 18 days meets all the conditions described in Note 5,
he would be charged a total of _____ (CAD) round-trip from YYZ to PMI.
If he met the Note 12 conditions, he would be charged _____ (CAD).

31.

```
To AMSTERDAM, NETHERLANDS              AMS
From ATLANTA, GA., USA                 ATL
        F    700.00 1400.00            7.00K
        YL   376.00  752.00
        Y    396.00  792.00
        YH   482.00  964.00
    EX/4  14-21 DAY YE  694.00
    EX/5  14-21 DAY YE  782.00
    EX/8  22-45 DAY YE  514.00
    EX/12 22-45 DAY YE  552.00
    EX/13 22-45 DAY YE  647.00
    EX/28-AP 22-45 DAY YE  460.00
    EX/29-AP 22-45 DAY YE  478.00
    EX/30-AP 22-45 DAY YE  574.00
    EX/35 YL · YOUTH  525.00
    EX/36 Y  · YOUTH  552.00·
    EX/37 YH · YOUTH  599.00
              CONNECTIONS
26  0611   0045+1   DL  188 FnYnB 72S 0 D-APR24
   LGA 0759 JFK 1000 PA  100  FY   747 1
 4  1220   0710+1   EA  330  FYB  727 1 D-APR24
   1513 YYZ 1810     KL  692  FY   D10 0
 2  1220   0910+1   EA  330  FYB  727 1 D-APR25
   1513 YYZ 1825     KL  678  FY   D8S 1
   1224   0715+1     DL  238  FYB  72S 0 D-APR24
   1305 ORD 1630     KL  612  FY   747 0
   1510   0715+1     EA  108  FYB  727 0 E-APR25
   1709 JFK 1915     KL  642  FY   747 0
```

Using Exhibit 3 and the schedule above, compute the fare for the following round-trip itinerary:
(Eastbound) ATL to AMS First Class July 30 = $ _____
(Westbound) AMS to ATL Economy   Sept. 28 = $ _____
The total round-trip fare is $ _____.

32. Point-to-point maximum and nonstop mileages*--separated by a / character--are published in the WEOAG following each "From" city name.

```
To PANAMA CITY, PANAMA REP.            PTY
From GUAYAQUIL, ECUADOR 933/778        GYE
        F    189.00 378.00            1.89K
        Y    127.00 254.00
    OP  S    109.00 218.00
    EU  Y    121.00 242.00
    YE 30 DAY 226.00 EFF ALL YEAR
    OP SE 30 DAY 193.00 EFF ALL YEAR
 6  0150  0330   BN  974  FY  DC8 0 E-FEB 2
 2  0205  0345   BN  974  FY  D8S 0
 6  0745  1220   EU   42  FY  720 2
 5  0815  1150   BN  906  FY  D8S 1
 4  0915  1350   EU   46  FY  720 2
 3  1005  1145   BN  906  FY  D8S 0
36  1010  1200   OP  112  S   727 0
 7  1435  1615   BN  970  FY  D8S 0
```

These mileages are used for constructing unpublished fares. If no maximum or nonstop mileage is available, a zero (0) is shown on the appropriate side of the slash. Maximum mileages are shown on the left and nonstop mileages on the right. In the above schedule, the maximum mileage from Guayaquil to Panama City is _____ miles. The nonstop mileage is _____ miles.

*Maximum mileage is defined as the allowable mileage which can be traveled for a given fare. Nonstop mileage is defined as the nonstop or direct distance between a pair of cities.

33. Exhibit 7 shows the minimum time required when making connections at most international cities. Alphabetically, locate the listing for Melbourne, Australia. The minimum connecting time between domestic services is 30 minutes, and _____ minutes between wholly international services.

34. A passenger flying from London to Adana, Turkey will make a connection in Munich, Germany. He will depart on LH 445 and connect to LH 279. What would be the minimum connecting time for this itinerary? _____.

35.

To **OSAKA, JAPAN**					**OSA**

From **OKINAWA, RYUKYU IS., JAPAN 903/753**					**OKA**
Y		JYE	22183	44366	
1000	1155	JL	910	Y	D8S 0
1145	1340	NH	100	Y	72S 0
1200	1355	JL	912	Y	D8S 0
1220	1415	NH	102	Y	72S 0
6 1320	1510	NW	22	Y	B3J 0

In the above example, a passenger wishes to arrive in Osaka at 1:30 p.m. He has reservations on NH 100, but needs a flight from Los Angeles (LAX) to Okinawa. Allowing for the minimum connecting time, what would be the latest possible arrival time for his flight from LAX? _____.

36. In the listing for London, England in Exhibit 7, we see there are two airports-- Heathrow and Gatwick--with separate connecting times for each airport. In addition, minimum connecting times are shown for passengers arriving at one airport and departing from the other. The schedule for a passenger arriving at Heathrow and departing from Gatwick must allow at least _____ minutes (direct) connecting time for international and/or domestic travel. If he chooses to make the connection via the Town Terminal, a minimum of _____ minutes must be allowed.

37. Examine the following schedule.

To **OKINAWA, RYUKYU IS., JAPAN**						**OKA**

From **HONOLULU, OAHU; HAWAII, USA 5776/0**						**HNL**
1F	730.00	1460.00				
1Y	450.00	900.00				
EX/10 14-21 DAY 1YE	846.00					
EX/16-IT 14-35 DAY 1YE	846.00					
1 VIA PACIFIC						
6 1400	2255+1	NW	9	*	747	
	NW	9	747-HND-B3J			
	NW	9	FY-HND-Y			
X135 2335	0625+2	PA	843	FY	747	
	PA	843	747-GUM-707			
135 2335	0625+2	PA	843	FY	747	
357 2335	0635+2	PA	843	FY	747	
146 2335	0635+2	PA	843	FY	747	
	PA	843	747-GUM-707			

You will note that the class of service for NW 9 has an asterisk "*". This code indicates that the flight will change its class(es) of service at some point during the flight. If there is a change of equipment enroute, an additional line (beginning with the flight number) will be located just below the flight line with all necessary information. Can a passenger on NW 9 fly first class from Honolulu to Okinawa? _____. A passenger departing on Wednesday, May 3, traveling from Honolulu to Okinawa on PA 843 would depart on a _____ jet and arrive in Okinawa on a _____ jet.

38. Transportation taxes vary considerably in the different countries of the world. Some countries levy taxes on arriving passengers and/or departing passengers. Others may tax issuance of tickets only. Exhibit 5 shows part of the WEOAG Local Tax chart. Alphabetically, locate the Greece listing. Only departing passengers are taxed; the amount is 40 Greek drachmas (DRA). A ticketed U. S. citizen vacationing in Gambia departs Bathurst Airport on his return home. He would be subject to a _____ tax of _____ Gambia Dalasi (GAD).

USE EXHIBIT 10 TO ANSWER THE FOLLOWING:

39. All flights from London, England to Geneva leave from _____ (airport code).

40. The round-trip Shoulder Economy fare from Los Angeles to Geneva is _____ U. S. dollars. A passenger flying First Class between London and Geneva one-way is charged _____ U. K. pounds. Fares in the WEOAG are published in the currency of the _____ (from/to) city.

41. A passenger wants to fly from Los Angeles to Geneva on Sunday afternoon March 21. To leave after 11:00 a.m., he must depart at _____ on _____ _____ Airlines flight number _____. He arrives at the connecting city, _____ (city code) at _____. He then departs the connecting city at _____ on _____ Airlines flight number _____ which makes _____ stop(s) and arrives in Geneva at _____ on _____ (day of week).

42. Assume a passenger meets all conditions specified in Excursion Note 13. What fare is he charged between Los Angeles and Geneva? _____. Are there any direct flights between LAX and GVA? _____.

43. What changes occur between July 7 and July 8 on British Airways flight 120 between Cairo, Egypt and London, England? _____ _____.

44. On February 21, a Kansas City plumber entered a travel agency to make reservations for a trip to Geneva, Switzerland. He planned to depart on March 17 (Wednesday) and return April 21 (Wednesday). Does this Europe-bound plumber qualify for an excursion fare (no stopovers are planned)? _____. If yes, which one and how much is the round-trip fare? _____ _____.

45. What is the minimum connecting time for a passenger arriving from London, England at Mirabel Airport in Montreal and departing Dorval Airport (Montreal) enroute to Detroit, Michigan? _____.

46. An economy passenger traveling from London, England to Naples, Italy on Alitalia Airlines has 54 pounds of luggage. Does this exceed his free baggage allowance? _____. If yes, by how many pounds? _____. What additional cost would he have to pay? _____.

47. A passenger wants to fly First Class from Calcutta, India to Geneva, Switzerland on Tuesday, April 20. Using the exhibits provided in this review, construct the most favorable schedule for him using London as a connecting point.

Depart Calcutta   (a) Carrier/flight number _____
                             (b) Time _____
                             (c) Equipment Type _____
Arrive London: (d) Time _____
Depart London: (e) Carrier/flight number _____
                             (f) Time _____
                             (g) Equipment Type _____
Arrive Geneva: (h) Time _____
Minimum Connecting Time in London   _____

48. SN flight 211 originates in _____ (city name) stops in _____ (city name) and terminates in _____.

49. A passenger traveling from Manila, Philippines to Geneva, Switzerland on a Thursday would connect at _____ (city name) and _____ (city name) and arrive in Geneva on _____ (day) at _____ _____ (time).

50. Airlines and Airports have established minimum times in which a passenger should arrive at the airport before the actual departure of his flight. This time usually takes into account: parking, check-in, and walking time (to the gates). It may also take into account those airports that use transportation vehicles between the terminal and airplane. Using the examples below, answer the following:

Check-In Time Requirements—The minimum time prior to the scheduled departure time of a flight in which passengers should report to the airport airline desk for required Check-In procedures. Duty-Free Shops—Available to departing international passengers and at some airports to connecting international passengers.	AIRPORT DUTY-FREE SHOP
AALBORG, DENMARK—SK: Dom. 10; Int. 25 mins.....................	YES
AARHUS, DENMARK—SK: Dom. 10; Int. 30 mins.....................	YES
ABADAN, IRAN—IR: Dom. 60; Int. 90 mins..........................	—
ABERDEEN, SCOTLAND—BA: 15 mins...........................	—
ABU DHABI, U.A. EMIRATES—BA: 60; GF: 45 mins..................	—
ACAPULCO, MEXICO—WA: 60; CP: 90 mins..........................	—
ACCRA, GHANA—LH: 30 mins......................................	—
ADDIS ABABA, ETHIOPIA—BA: 60; ET: Dom. 60; Int. 90; LH: Dom. 20; Int. 30 mins.......................................	YES
AGADIR, MOROCCO—BA: 30 mins.................................	—
ALGHERO, ITALY—AZ: 25 mins....................................	—
ALICANTE, SPAIN—BA, IB: 30 mins...............................	—
ALMERIA, SPAIN—BA, IB, LH: 30 mins............................	—
AMSTERDAM, NETHERLANDS—BA: 30; LY: 120; IB: 30; KL: Dom. 15; European 30; Intercontinental 60; TLV: 120; CP: 60; Int. 30; European: 35; AY; Europe 30; Intercontinental 60 mins.............	YES
ANACO, VENEZUELA—VE: 30 mins...............................	—
ANCHORAGE, ALASKA, U.S.—BA: 60; NW: Dom. 20, (747, DC10: 30); Int. 40; LH: 45 mins..	YES
ANKARA, TURKEY—LH: 20 mins..................................	—
ANTIGUA, WEST INDIES—BA, BW: 60 mins.........................	YES
ANTOFAGASTA, CHILE—LA: 90 mins..............................	—
APIA, W. SAMOA—FJ: 60 mins...................................	YES
AREQUIPA, PERU—CF: 60 mins...................................	—
ARICA, CHILE—LB: 90 mins......................................	—
ARRECIFE, CANARY IS.—IB: 30 mins..............................	—
ARUBA, NETH. ANTILLES—LM: 60 mins............................	YES
ASMARA, ETHIOPIA—BA: 60; ET: Dom. 60; Int. 90 mins.............	YES
ASUNCION, PARAGUAY—BN: 60; IB: 30; LB: 90; LH: 45 mins.........	—
ATHENS, GREECE—BA: 45; LY: 150; IB, LH: 30; TG, TW, AY, GF: 60; CP: 90 mins..................................	YES
ATLANTA, GEORGIA, U.S.—NW: Dom. 20, (747, DC10: 30); Int. 40 mins....	YES
AUCKLAND, NEW ZEALAND—TE, FJ, BA: 60 mins....................	YES
AYACUCHO, PERU—CF: 60 mins..................................	—
BAGHDAD, IRAQ—BA: 75; LH: 30; GF: 45 mins.....................	YES
BAHRAIN IS., ARABIAN GULF—BA: 60; GF: 45 mins.................	YES

A passenger flying on Iberia Airlines plans to depart Athens at 3:00 p.m. What time should the passenger arrive at the airport? _____.
Is there a duty-free shop at the airport? _____.

ABBREVIATIONS AND REFERENCE MARKS

CODE	AIRLINE
AA	AMERICAN AIRLINES
AC	AIR CANADA
AE	AIR CEYLON
AF	AIR FRANCE
AH	AIR ALGERIE
AI	AIR INDIA
AL	ALLEGHENY AIRLINES
AM	AEROMEXICO
AN	ANSETT AIRLINES OF AUSTRALIA
AO	AVIACO
AQ	AIR ANGLIA LTD.
AR	AEROLINEAS ARGENTINAS
AS	ALASKA AIRLINES
AT	ROYAL AIR MAROC
AU	AUSTRAL LINEAS AEREAS S.A.
AV	AVIANCA
AW	AIR NIGER
AY	FINNAIR
AZ	ALITALIA
BA	BRITISH AIRWAYS (OVERSEAS DIV.)
BD	BRITISH MIDLAND AIRWAYS
BE	BRITISH AIRWAYS (EUROPEAN DIV.)
BG	BANGLADESH BIMAN
BI	ROYAL BRUNEI AIRLINES
BJ	BAKHTAR AFGHAN AIRLINES
BM	AERO TRASPORTI ITALIANI
BN	BRANIFF INTERNATIONAL AIRWAYS
BO	BOURAQ INDONESIA AIRLINES
BP	AIR BOTSWANA PTY. LTD.
BQ	BUSINESS JETS PTY. LTD.
BR	BRITISH CALEDONIAN AIRWAYS
BS	BURNETT AIRWAYS
BU	BRAATHENS S.A.F.E. AIRTRANSPORT
BW	B.W.I.A. INTERNATIONAL
CA	CAAC
CE	CENTRAL AUSTRALIAN AIRWAYS PTY. LTD.
CF	FAUCETT
CI	CHINA AIRLINES
CK	CONNAIR PTY. LTD.
CM	COPA
CO	CONTINENTAL AIRLINES (AIR MICRONESIA)
CP	CP AIR
CS	BRITISH AIRWAYS (CAMBRIAN)
CU	CUBANA AIRLINES
CX	CATHAY PACIFIC AIRWAYS
CY	CYPRUS AIRWAYS
DA	DAN-AIR
DJ	AIR DJIBOUTI
DL	DELTA AIR LINES, INC.
DO	DOMINICANA DE AVIACION
DR	ADVANCE AIRLINES
DS	AIR SENEGAL
DT	TAAG-ANGOLA AIRLINES
DX	DANAIR
DY	ALYEMDA, DEMOCRATIC YEMEN AIRLINES
EA	EASTERN AIR LINES
EC	EAST AFRICAN AIRWAYS
EF	FAR EASTERN AIR TRANSPORT CORP.
EG	JAPAN ASIA AIRWAYS CO. LTD.
EI	AER LINGUS (IRISH)-AERLINTE EIREANN (IN)
EK	MASLING COMMUTER SERVICES PTY. LTD.
EO	EUROPAIR
EP	TROPIC AIR SERVICES PTY. LTD.
EQ	TAME C.A.
ET	ETHIOPIAN AIRLINES
EU	COMPANIA ECUATORIANA DE AVIACION
EW	EAST-WEST AIRLINES
EY	EUROPE AERO SERVICE
FG	ARIANA AFGHAN AIRLINES
FI	FLUGFELAG—ICELANDAIR
FJ	AIR PACIFIC
FL	FRONTIER AIRLINES
FU	AIR LITTORAL
GA	GARUDA INDONESIAN AIRWAYS
GB	AIR INTER GABON
GC	LINACONGO
GD	AIR NORTH LTD.
GF	GULF AIR
GH	GHANA AIRWAYS
GJ	ANSETT AIRLINES OF SOUTH AUSTRALIA
GL	GREENLANDAIR
GN	AIR GABON
GP	HADAG AIR SEEBAEDERFLUG G.M.B.H. & CO.
GR	AURIGNY AIR SERVICES, LTD.
GT	GIBRALTAR AIRWAYS
GU	AVIATECA
GV	TALAIR PTY. LTD.
GX	GREAT LAKES AIRLINE, LTD.
GY	GUYANA AIRWAYS
HA	HAWAIIAN AIRLINES
HB	AIR MELANESIE
HH	SOMALI AIRLINES
HM	AIR MAHE LTD.
HN	NLM-DUTCH AIRLINES
HT	AIR TCHAD
IA	IRAQI AIRWAYS
IB	IBERIA
IC	INDIAN AIRLINES
IE	SOLOMON ISLANDS AIRWAYS LTD.
IF	INTERFLUG
IG	ALISARDA
IH	ITAVIA
IJ	TOURAINE AIR TRANSPORT
IN	AERLINTE EIREANN—AER LINGUS (EI)
IQ	INTERNATIONAL CARIBBEAN AIRWAYS
IR	IRAN NATIONAL AIRLINES
IT	AIR INTER
IV	LINEAS AEREAS GUINEA ECUATORIAL
IW	INTERNATIONAL AIR BAHAMA
IY	YEMEN AIRWAYS CORP.
IZ	ARKIA-ISRAEL INLAND AIRLINES LTD.
JD	TOA DOMESTIC AIRLINES, CO., LTD.
JL	JAPAN AIR LINES COMPANY, LTD.
JM	AIR JAMAICA (1968) LTD.
JP	INEX ADRIA AIRWAYS
JU	YUGOSLAV AIRLINES—JAT
JX	BOUGAIR
KB	C.A.A. DPRK
KD	KENDELL AIRLINES
KE	KOREAN AIR LINES
KH	COOK ISLAND AIRWAYS
KL	KLM—ROYAL DUTCH AIRLINES
KM	AIR MALTA COMPANY, LTD.—AIR MALTA
KR	KAR-AIR
KU	KUWAIT AIRWAYS
LA	LAN CHILE
LB	LLOYD AEREO BOLIVIANO
LC	LOGANAIR, LTD.
LE	AIR LOWVELD (PTY.) LTD.
LF	LINJEFLYG
LG	LUXAIR—LUXEMBOURG AIRLINES
LH	LUFTHANSA GERMAN AIRLINES
LJ	SIERRA LEONE AIRWAYS
LL	ICELANDIC AIRLINES
LM	DUTCH ANTILLEAN AIRLINES
LN	LIBYAN ARAB AIRLINES
LO	LOT POLISH AIRLINES
LP	AIR ALPES
LR	LACSA
LU	SAETA
LV	LAV—LINEA AEROPOSTAL VENEZOLANA
LX	AIR LANGUEDOC
LY	EL AL ISRAEL AIRLINES
LZ	BULGARIAN AIRLINES—BALKAN
MA	MALEV—HUNGARIAN AIRLINES
MD	AIR MADAGASCAR
ME	MIDDLE EAST AIRLINES
MH	MALAYSIAN AIRLINE SYSTEM
MK	AIR MAURITIUS
MM	SOCIEDAD AERONAUTICA MEDELLIN
MN	COMMERCIAL AIRWAYS LTD. (COMAIR)
MR	AIR MAURITANIE
MS	EGYPTAIR
MT	MACKNIGHT AIRLINES
MU	MISRAIR
MV	MACROBERTSON-MILLER AIRLINE SERVICES
MW	MAYA AIRWAYS
MX	MEXICANA DE AVIACION
MY	AIR MALI
MZ	MERPATI NUSANTARA AIRLINES
NA	NATIONAL AIRLINES
NC	NORTH CENTRAL AIRLINES
ND	NORDAIR
NE	AIR NEW ENGLAND
NH	ALL NIPPON
NI	LANICA
NJ	NAMAKWALAND LUGDIENS
NL	AIR LIBERIA, INC.
NM	MT. COOK AIRLINES
NS	BRITISH AIRWAYS (NORTHEAST)
NU	SOUTHWEST AIRLINES CO., INC.
NW	NORTHWEST ORIENT AIRLINES INC.
NY	NEW YORK AIRWAYS
NZ	NEW ZEALAND NATIONAL AIRWAYS
OA	OLYMPIC AIRWAYS
OB	OPAL AIR PTY. LTD.
OD	AEROCONDOR
OH	SFO HELICOPTER AIRLINES, INC.
OJ	MARGATE AIR SERVICES
OK	CZECHOSLOVAK AIRLINES
OL	DLT LUFTVERKEHRSGESELLSCHAFT MBH OSTFRIESISCHE LUFTTRANSPORT GMBH
OM	AIR MONGOL
ON	AIR NAURU
OP	AIR PANAMA INTERNACIONAL
OR	AIR COMORES
OS	AUSTRIAN AIRLINES
OU	AERIAL TOURS PTY. LTD.
OZ	OZARK AIR LINES
PA	PAN AMERICAN WORLD AIRWAYS
PC	FUJI AIR
PH	POLYNESIAN AIRLINES
PI	PIEDMONT AVIATION
PK	PAKISTAN INTERNATIONAL
PL	AEROPERU
PO	AEROPELICAN INTERCITY COMMUTER AIR SERVICES PTY. LTD.
PR	PHILIPPINE AIRLINES
PU	PLUNA
PV	EASTERN PROVINCIAL AIRWAYS, LTD.
PW	PACIFIC WESTERN AIRLINES
PX	AIR NIUGINI
PY	SURINAM AIRWAYS
PZ	LAP—LINEAS AEREAS PARAGUAYAS
QB	QUEBECAIR INC.
QC	AIR ZAIRE
QD	TRANSBRASIL S/A LINHAS AEREAS
QF	QANTAS
QM	AIR MALAWI
QN	BUSH PILOTS AIRWAYS
QP	CASPAIR LTD.
QQ	AEROVIAS QUISQUEYANA
QZ	ZAMBIA AIRWAYS
RA	ROYAL NEPAL AIRLINES
RB	SYRIAN ARAB AIRLINES
RF	AIR SAMOA LTD.
RG	VARIG, S.A.
RH	AIR RHODESIA
RJ	ALIA-ROYAL JORDANIAN AIRLINES
RK	AIR AFRIQUE
RN	ROYAL AIR INTER
RO	TAROM—ROMANIAN AIR TRANSPORT
RS	AEROPESCA
RW	HUGHES AIRWEST
SA	SOUTH AFRICAN AIRWAYS
SC	CRUZEIRO
SD	SUDAN AIRWAYS
SH	SAHSA
SK	SAS—SCANDINAVIAN AIRLINES
SN	SABENA—BELGIAN AIRLINES
SO	SOUTHERN AIRWAYS
SP	SATA
SQ	SINGAPORE AIRLINES
SR	SWISSAIR
SU	AEROFLOT SOVIET AIRLINES
SV	SAUDI ARABIAN AIRLINES
SW	SUIDWES LUGDIENS
SY	AIR ALSACE
TA	TACA INTERNATIONAL
TE	AIR NEW ZEALAND LTD.
TG	THAI AIRWAYS INTERNATIONAL
TH	THAI AIRWAYS COMPANY
TI	TEXAS INTERNATIONAL AIRLINES, INC.
TK	TURK HAVA YOLLARI
TM	DETA
TN	TRANS-AUSTRALIA AIRLINES
TP	TAP
TU	TUNIS AIR
TW	TRANS WORLD AIRLINES
TX	TRANSPORTES AEREOS NACIONALES
TY	AIR CALEDONIE
TZ	TRANSAIR LIMITED
UA	UNITED AIRLINES
UB	BURMA AIRWAYS CORPORATION
UC	LADECO—LINEA DEL COBRE
UE	UNITED AIR SERVICES (PTY.) LTD.
UF	TONGA TOURIST DEVELOPMENT CO., LTD.
UG	NORFOLK ISLAND AIRLINES
UK	BRITISH ISLAND AIRWAYS. LTD.
UL	LANSA AIRLINES OF HONDURAS
UN	NEW ENGLAND AVIATION PTY. LTD.
UP	BAHAMASAIR (OIA)
UT	UTA—UNION DE TRANSPORTS AERIENS
UY	CAMEROON AIRLINES
UZ	AIR ROUERGUE
VC	TAC (TRANSPORTES AEREOS DEL CESAR)
VA	VIASA
VE	AVENSA
VF	BRITISH AIR FERRIES LTD.
VG	AIR SIAM
VH	AIR VOLTA
VK	PANGA AIRWAYS LIMITED
VP	VASP
VT	AIR POLYNESIE
VU	AIR IVOIRE
VX	ACES
WA	WESTERN AIRLINES
WB	SAN (SERVICIOS AEREOS NACIONALES S.A.)
WC	WIEN AIR ALASKA, INC.
WF	WIDEROES FLYVESELSKAP
⊕WG	ALAG—ALPINE LUFT TRANSPORT A. G.
⊕WK	WESTKUESTENFLUG
WT	NIGERIA AIRWAYS LTD.
WU	AVNA AIR LINES
WW	TRANS—WEST
WX	ANSETT AIRLINES OF NEW SOUTH WALES
WZ	SWAZI AIR LTD.
YK	CYPRUS TURKISH AIRWAYS
YO	BRITISH AIRWAYS (HELICOPTERS SERVICE)
YP	PAGAS AIRLINES
YT	CIVIL FLYING SERVICES
ZI	LUCAS AIR TRANSPORT
ZT	SATENA

COMMUTER AIR CARRIERS

CODE	AIRLINE
HK	SOUTH PACIFIC ISLAND AIRWAYS ♦
VQ	AIR PACIFIC INT'L INC.

REMARKS

* INDICATES CHANGE IN CLASS OF SERVICE ENROUTE, FOLLOWS FLIGHT LISTING

CONEX INDICATES BEST CONNECTION ♦ OVER 9 STOPS

CHG PLANE CHANGE OF AIRCRAFT REQUIRED AT DESIGNATED AIRPORT

EX EXCEPT ON

GOVT GOVERNMENT

NIGHT STOP (AIRPORT CODE) OVERNIGHT STOP PAID FOR BY CARRIER

OP OPERATES ON

REQ APPEARS IN PLACE OF DEPARTURE AND ARRIVAL TIMES AND INDICATES A FLAG STOP

+1 NEXT DAY
+2 SECOND DAY
+3 THIRD DAY
-1 PREVIOUS DAY

& (IN FLIGHT NUMBER COLUMN ONLY) INDICATES AIR SHUTTLE

☐ (FOLLOWING FLIGHT NUMBER) INDICATES A REPLACEMENT FLIGHT OPERATED BY A COMMUTER AIR CARRIER ON BEHALF OF A CERTIFICATED AIR CARRIER PURSUANT TO A C. A. B. APPROVED AGREEMENT.

FREQUENCY CODE

1—MONDAY
2—TUESDAY
3—WEDNESDAY
4—THURSDAY
5—FRIDAY
6—SATURDAY
7—SUNDAY
X—EXCEPT

EFFECTIVE RANGE CODE

E—EFFECTIVE ON
D—DISCONTINUED AFTER

*—Service Temporarily Suspended
⊕—Carrier performs seasonal service only
♦—Member of Commuter Airline Association, A Division of National Air Transportation Associations

ABBREVIATIONS AND REFERENCE MARKS

FARES AND CLASS
OF SERVICE

(TAXES NOT INCLUDED IN FARE)

A   PROPELLER FIRST CLASS
B   CONTROLLED INVENTORY—COACH. IDENTIFIES FLIGHTS WITH CAPACITY CONTROLLED EXCURSION AND INCLUSIVE TOUR FARES.
C   PROPELLER THRIFT AND PROPELLER STANDARD CLASS WITHIN BRAZIL
F   JET FIRST CLASS (MAY ALSO APPLY ON PROPELLER FLIGHTS OUTSIDE THE U.S.A. WHERE THERE IS NO FARE DIFFERENCE BETWEEN JET AND PROPELLER SERVICE)
Fn JET NIGHT COACH IN FIRST CLASS COMPARTMENT
J   LIMITED SERVICE CLASS-AVAILABLE MONDAY THROUGH THURSDAY ONLY, RESERVATIONS ACCEPTED UPON PURCHASE OF TICKET 7 DAYS IN ADVANCE.
K   JET THRIFT OR ECONOMY ON U.S. DOMESTIC
L   CONTROLLED INVENTORY—ECONOMY. IDENTIFIES FLIGHTS WITH CAPACITY CONTROLLED EXCURSION FARES.
R   SUPERSONIC
S   STANDARD ONE CLASS OR STANDARD CLASS JET
Sn NIGHT STANDARD ONE CLASS
T   PROPELLER TOURIST / COACH / ECONOMY
Tn PROPELLER NIGHT TOURIST/COACH
U   NO RESERVATION SERVICE
Y   JET TOURIST/COACH AND ECONOMY ON INTERNATIONAL SERVICES (MAY ALSO APPLY ON PROPELLER FLIGHTS OUTSIDE THE U.S.A. WHERE THERE IS NO FARE DIFFERENCE BETWEEN JET AND PROPELLER SERVICE)
Yn JET NIGHT COACH / TOURIST (MAY ALSO APPLY ON PROPELLER FLIGHTS OUTSIDE THE U.S.A. WHERE THERE IS NO FARE DIFFERENCE BETWEEN JET AND PROPELLER SERVICE AND TO OFF-PEAK (OP) SERVICE WITHIN THE UNITED KINGDOM)

QUALIFYING CODES USED IN FARE SECTION

E   SUFFIX TO INDICATE EXCURSION FARES
H   SUFFIX TO INDICATE PEAK SEASON TRANSATLANTIC FARES—FOR APPLICATION SEE PAGE 10
L   SUFFIX TO INDICATE LOW SEASON TRANSATLANTIC Y FARES—FOR APPLICATION SEE PAGE 10
EX/ EXCURSION FARE—FOR APPLICATION SEE PAGE 10
    A NUMBER PRECEDING FARE INDICATES ADDITIONAL INFORMATION FOLLOWS FARE LISTING

EQUIPMENT
CODE   JET AIRCRAFT

A3B   A300B—EUROPEAN AIRBUS
B11   BAC 111 (GENERAL DESIGNATOR)
B3J   BOEING 707-320 FAN JET
CRV   CORVETTE
CVL   CARAVELLE (ALL SERIES)
CVS   CARAVELLE 10, 11, & 12 SERIES
DME   DASSAULT MERCURE
DC8   DOUGLAS DC8 (ALL SERIES)
DC9   DOUGLAS DC9 (ALL SERIES)
D10   DOUGLAS DC10 (ALL SERIES)
D8S   DOUGLAS DC8 SUPER 60 SERIES
D9S   DOUGLAS DC9—SUPER
D95   DOUGLAS DC9 SUPER 50 SERIES
F28   FOKKER FELLOWSHIP JET
L10   LOCKHEED 1011 TRISTAR
M20   MYSTERE 20
SSC   SUPERSONIC CONCORDE
STV   VICKERS STANDARD VC10
SUV   VICKERS SUPER VC10
S11   BAC 111—500
TRD   HAWKER SIDDELEY TRIDENT (ALL SERIES)
T04   TUPOLEV 104 (ALL SERIES)
T1E   HAWKER SIDDELEY TRIDENT 1E
T24   TUPOLEV TU-124
T34   TUPOLEV TU-134
T54   TUPOLEV TU-154
V10   VICKERS VC10
Y40   YAK 40
Y62   ILYUSHIN IL-62
707   BOEING 707 (ALL SERIES)
72S   BOEING 727—200
720   BOEING 720 (ALL SERIES)
727   BOEING 727 (ALL SERIES)
73S   BOEING 737—200
737   BOEING 737 (ALL SERIES)
74L   BOEING 747 SP
747   BOEING 747 (ALL SERIES)
880   CONVAIR 880 (ALL SERIES)

EQUIPMENT
CODE   PROPELLER AIRCRAFT

ACD   AERO COMMANDER (GENERAL DESIGNATOR)
AVR   AVRO ANSON
A24   ANTONOV 24

BBR   BEECH BARON
BCH   BEECHCRAFT (GENERAL DESIGNATOR)
BNI   BRITTEN NORMAN ISLANDER
BNT   BRITTEN NORMAN TRI ISLANDER
B80   BEECH QUEEN 80
B99   BEECH 99

CAR   CARVAIR
CES   CESSNA (GENERAL DESIGNATOR)/ CESSNA 206
CV3   CONVAIR 340
CV4   CONVAIR 440 METROPOLITAN
CV5   CONVAIR 580 TURBO-PROP
CV6   CONVAIR 600/CONVAIR 640
C46   CURTISS COMMANDO C-46

DC3   DOUGLAS DC3/DAKOTA C47
DC4   DOUGLAS DC4/SKYMASTER C54
DC6   DOUGLAS DC6
DDV   De HAVILLAND DOVE
DHC   De HAVILLAND DHC-4 CARIBOU
DTO   De HAVILLAND TWIN OTTER
D6B   DOUGLAS DC-6B

EMB   EMB—110 BANDEIRANTE

FH7   FOKKER FRIENDSHIP TURBO-PROP FH227
F27   FOKKER FRIENDSHIP TURBO-PROP F-27

GWI   GRUMMAN G-44 WIDGEON

HLD   HANDLEY PAGE HERALD
HRN   De HAVILLAND HERON

LEC   LOCKHEED ELECTRA TURBO-PROP
L41   OMNIPOL L-410

N26   NORD 262/SUPER BROUSSARD

PAZ   PIPER AZTEC
PNV   PIPER NAVAJO
PPS   PIPER SENECA
PP6   PILATUS PORTER PC-6

ST2   SAUNDERS ST-27
S58   SIKORSKY S-58 HELICOPTER
S61   SIKORSKY S-61 HELICOPTER

T14   TUPOLEV 114

VAN   BAC VANGUARD PASSENGER AIRCRAFT
VIS   VICKERS VISCOUNT (ALL SERIES)
V70   VICKERS VISCOUNT 700 SERIES
V80   VICKERS VISCOUNT 800 SERIES

Y11   NAMCO YS-11
Y14   ILYUSHIN IL-14
Y18   ILYUSHIN IL-18

402   CESSNA 402 TWIN TURBO SYSTEM
748   HAWKER SIDDELEY 748

FREE BAGGAGE ALLOWANCES

The normal free baggage allowance for international travel is based on the fare paid regardless of the class of service used. The free baggage allowance applies to all passengers paying at least half fare. Infants carried at 10% of the fare are not entitled to any free baggage allowance. Exceptions to the normal free baggage allowance are shown below the normal free baggage allowance in two categories. The first category applies to travel (all classes unless specifically indicated) wholly within the area(s) and/or country(s) shown. The second category applies to travel on specific carriers or on specific segments of a carrier's route.

All U.S. (and several Canadian) carriers require that checked baggage have the passenger's name on the outside.

NORMAL FREE BAGGAGE ALLOWANCES

FIRST CLASS	30 kg.	66 lb.
TOURIST/ECONOMY	20 kg.	44 lb.

1—EXCEPTIONS TO NORMAL BY COUNTRY

COUNTRY	CARRIER	KG	LB
ARGENTINA	ALL	15	33
AUSTRALIA	AN, GJ, TN, WJ, WX–DOMESTIC SERVICE ONE PIECE LENGTH + WIDTH + HEIGHT NOT TO EXCEED 56 INCHES		
	CK, COMMUTER, EK, EO, EW, MV, NM	16	35
BOLIVIA	LB	15	33
BRAZIL	ALL	20	44
CHILE	ALL	15	33
COLOMBIA	AV	25	55
	MM ON T SERVICE	30	66
ECUADOR	ALL EXCEPT EU	20	44
	EU TO/FROM MIA ON Y SERVICE	30	66
GERMAN DEMO. REP.	IF	20	44
GERMANY	DOMESTIC SERVICES ALLOWED LENGTH + WIDTH + HEIGHT NOT TO EXCEED 170 cm.		

COUNTRY	CARRIER	KG	LB
GREECE	OA	15	33
GUYANA	BG	18	40
HONDURAS	ALL	20	44
HUNGARY	MA	10	22
INDIA	IC	20	44
ISRAEL	IZ	10	22
ITALY	DOMESTIC SERVICES – 2 PIECES ALLOWED LENGTH + WIDTH + HEIGHT NOT TO EXCEED 160 cm. IF 1 PIECE IS HAND BAGGAGE, DIMENSIONS SHALL NOT EXCEED: LENGTH 40 cm, HEIGHT 25 cm, WIDTH 30 cm.		
JAPAN	ALL	15	33
KOREA (Rep. of)	ALL	15	33
MEXICO (Not to/from U.S.)	ALL	25	55
NEW ZEALAND	GD, NM	16	35
PHILIPPINES	DELUXE + FIRST	18	40
	ECONOMY	9	20

COUNTRY	CARRIER	KG	LB
ROMANIA	RO	10	22
SOMALI REP.	HH	15	33
SOUTH AFRICA, REP. OF	LE	16	35
	MN	17	37
TAIWAN (FORMOSA)	CI DOMESTIC SERVICE	15	33
THAILAND	ALL	15	33
U.S.S.R.	ON TURBO-PROP + JET	30	66
	ON PISTON EQUIPMENT	20	44
UNITED KINGDOM AND CHANNEL ISLANDS	FIRST	20	44
	TOURIST	15	33
URUGUAY	PU	10	22
VENEZUELA	LV–DOMESTIC SERVICE– 5 PIECES WITH A TOTAL WEIGHT OF 30 KG.		
YEMEN (PEOP.DEM.REP.)	DY DOMESTIC ROUTES	15	33
YUGOSLAVIA	JU ON F SERVICE	20	44
	JU ON Y SERVICE	15	33

2—EXCEPTIONS TO NORMAL BY CARRIER

CARRIER		KG	LB
AF	BETWEEN MIA/NYC AND PTP AND ALL POINTS IN COLOMBIA ON Y SERVICE	30	66
AN	JOURNEYS BETWEEN AUSTRALIA AND PAPUA NEW GUINEA		
	FIRST CLASS	9.5	20
	ECONOMY CLASS	7.5	16
AR	BETWEEN BOG AND LAX OR BETWEEN LAX/MIA TO LIM ON Y SERVICE	30	66
AT	BETWEEN DAKAR AND FRANCE/ NO. AFRICA	30	66
AV	BETWEEN ALL POINTS IN CONTINENTAL U.S. AND ALL POINTS IN COLOMBIA ON Y SERVICE	30	66
AY	DOMESTIC SERVICES 3 PIECES FREE OF CHARGE.		
BE	DOMESTIC SERVICES ONE PIECE LENGTH + WIDTH + HEIGHT NOT TO EXCEED 67 INCHES (170cm) AND ONE PIECE DIMENSIONS NOT TO EXCEED 18'' X 14'' X 6''		
BN	BETWEEN ALL POINTS IN CONTINENTAL U.S. AND ALL POINTS IN COLOMBIA ON Y SERVICE	30	66
BR	BETWEEN LON AND BFS/EDI/GLA CONDITIONS SAME AS FOR BE		
CI	BETWEEN HKG AND TPE	30	66
CX	BETWEEN HKG AND TPE	30	66
DJ	DOMESTIC SERVICE	15	33
DL	BETWEEN ALL POINTS IN CONTINENTAL U.S. AND ALL POINTS IN COLOMBIA ON Y SERVICE	30	66

CARRIER		KG	LB
EU	BETWEEN MIA AND PTY, GYE, LIM AND BOG	30	66
GU	BETWEEN MIA/MSY AND GUA/SAP	30	66
HB	SOUTHERN ISLANDS SERVICE	10	22
	NORTHERN ISLANDS SERVICE	15	33
IC	BETWEEN CCU AND RGN	30	66
IE	ALL SERVICES	16	35
IV	DOMESTIC SERVICES	15	33
	BETWEEN KUNMING AND RANGOON	30	66
KL	BETWEEN NYC AND COLOMBIA ON Y SERVICE	30	66
LB	INTERNATIONAL Y SERVICE	30	66
LH	BETWEEN NYC AND COLOMBIA ON Y SERVICE	30	66
MD	BETWEEN MALAGASY REP–REUNION ISLAND	30	66
NA	BETWEEN ALL POINTS IN CONTINENTAL U.S. AND ALL POINTS IN COLOMBIA ON Y SERVICE	30	66
NI	BETWEEN MIA AND MGA/SAL	30	66
NM	BETWEEN INVERCARGILL AND STEWART ISLAND	9	20
NZ	DOMESTIC SERVICES ONE PIECE LENGTH + HEIGHT + WIDTH NOT TO EXCEED 59 INCHES (150cm.)		
OD	ALL SERVICES		
OP	BETWEEN MIA AND PTY, GYE, LIM AND BOG	30	66
PA	BETWEEN PAGO PAGO/GUAM AND POINTS IN THE U.S.–1 PIECE = 62''(LENGTH + HEIGHT + WIDTH), 1 PIECE = 55'' (LENGTH +		

CARRIER		KG	LB
PA–CONT.	HEIGHT + WIDTH) AND 1 OR MORE ADDITIONAL PIECES TOTALING TOGETHER 45'' (LENGTH + HEIGHT + WIDTH) TO BE RETAINED BY THE PASSENGER AND STOWED UNDER THE PASSENGER'S SEAT		
PK	NIGHT COACH SERVICES	14	30
PL	BETWEEN MIA AND GYE/LIM AND BETWEEN LAX/MIA/NYC AND BUE/RIO/ SAO/SCL ON Y SERVICE	30	66
PU	BETWEEN BUE AND PDP	15	33
PZ	BETWEEN ASU AND BUE/MVD ON LEC SERVICE	30	66
QF	BETWEEN AUSTRALIA/NORFOLK ISLAND	20	44
QP	ALL SERVICES	10	22
RF	ALL SERVICES	9.5	20
SA	TRAVEL WITHIN SOUTH OR SOUTHWEST AFRICA BY NORMAL OR SKY COACH DOMESTIC SERVICE	20	44
SH	ALL ECONOMY CLASS SERVICES	30	66
SP	ALL SERVICES	15	33
TG	BETWEEN HKG AND TPE	30	66
TW	BETWEEN GUAM AND POINTS IN THE U.S.– 1 PIECE = 62'' (LENGTH + HEIGHT + WIDTH), 1 PIECE = 55'' (LENGTH + HEIGHT + WIDTH), AND 1 PIECE = 45'' (LENGTH + HEIGHT + WIDTH)		
TX	ALL SERVICES	30	66

EXPLANATION OF EXCURSION FARE NOTES

EX/1—Fares are valid between U.S./Canada/Mexico and Amman, Baghdad, Beirut, Cairo, Damascus, Kuwait, Nicosia and Teheran. Fares are applicable November 1 thru March 31 Eastbound and Westbound.

Stopovers in Europe not permitted. Stopovers are permitted at the Middle East points mentioned above, except when travel is between North American points and Teheran/Kuwait (when travel is to/from Teheran a stopover is permitted in Israel but not at the Middle East points listed above). One stopover will be permitted at the North American gateway, subject to an additional charge of USD 30.

The return transatlantic travel must not commence before the 14th day after the date of commencement of outbound transatlantic travel—and travel from the last point of stopover must commence by midnight of the 21st day after the date of commencement of travel from the point of origin.

EX/2—Apply the same rules shown for EX/1 except that the period of application is: EASTBOUND: June, July, August and WESTBOUND: July, August, September.

EX/3—Fares apply only on transatlantic travel originating and sold in Canada, Mexico or the U.S. Return travel from the area of Afghanistan, Ceylon, India, Nepal and Pakistan cannot commence prior to the seventh (7th) day after arrival in such area. Also, return travel over the Atlantic Ocean cannot commence prior to the seventeenth (17th) day after the date of commencement of outbound transatlantic travel. Travel from the last continuous sector without a stopover must be commenced by midnight of the thirty-fifth (35th) day after the date of commencement of travel from the point of origin. These fares are not combinable with other excursion fares. Valid all year.

EX/4—Fares are valid for transatlantic departures EASTBOUND: 0700 Sunday thru 0700 Friday, September thru May, WESTBOUND: 0700 Monday thru 0700 Saturday, October thru June. Weekend travel is permitted at a surcharge of USD 15.00 for transatlantic crossing in each direction—i.e.: USD 30.00 for both directions. Return transatlantic travel is permitted at any time, subject to the weekend surcharge provisions, but not earlier than the 14th (from REK the 12th) day after the date of the outbound transatlantic flight and not later than the 21st day after date of travel commencement from point of origin. Normal infants', children's, agents' and tour conductors' discounts apply. Stopovers in other than the Middle East (except Israel) or Africa are limited to two in each direction in addition to the point of turnaround. For the Middle East (except Israel) a total of four stopovers will be allowed in addition to the point of turnaround, provided that not more than two stopovers are made in Europe in each direction (inbound and outbound). Africa is allowed a total of five stopovers in addition to the point of turnaround, provided that not more than two stopovers are made in Europe in each direction (inbound and outbound).

EX/5—Apply the same rules and regulations shown for EX 4 above except that the period of application is: EASTBOUND: June, July and August, and WESTBOUND: July, August and September.

EX/6—Apply the same rules shown for EX 1 except that the period of application is: EASTBOUND April, May, September, October and WESTBOUND: April, May, June, October.

EX/7—Fares are valid between U.S. Canada Mexico and Amman, Baghdad, Beirut, Cairo, Damascus, Kuwait, Nicosia and Teheran.

Fares are applicable EASTBOUND: April, May, September, October and WESTBOUND: April, May, June, October.

In Europe one stopover is permitted in each direction. In the WESTBOUND direction the passenger may either disembark and re-embark at the same point or depart from another point. However, the fare for such a side trip must be in addition to and combined with the excursion fare. Stopovers are permitted at the Middle East points mentioned above, except when travel is from North American points to Teheran and or Kuwait and return, only one stopover is permitted. When travel is to Teheran, the one en route stopover permitted in the Middle East may be made in Israel. One stopover will be permitted at the North American gateway, subject to an additional charge of USD 30.

EX/8—Fares are valid for transatlantic departures EASTBOUND: 0700 Sunday thru 0700 Friday, November thru March, WESTBOUND: 0700 Monday thru 0700 Saturday, November thru March. Weekend travel is permitted at a surcharge of USD 15.00 for transatlantic crossing in each direction—i.e.: USD 30.00 for both directions. Return transatlantic travel is permitted at any time, subject to the weekend surcharge provisions, but not earlier than the 22nd day after the date of the outbound transatlantic flight and not later than the 45th day after date of travel commencement from point of origin. Normal infants', children's, agents' and tour conductors' discounts apply. Only a stopover at the point of turnaround is allowed (for travel to/from points in the Middle East one stopover, in addition to point of turnaround, is permitted on either the outbound or inbound journey in Europe—for travel to from Israel the one additional stopover is only permitted on the return journey). No stopovers are allowed within the U.S. or Canada when travel originates or terminates in any of the following cities: ACA/ABQ/AMA/BAL/BUF/YYC/CHI/CLE/DTT/YXD/HNL/MCI/LAS/LAX/DTT/YXD/MID/MEX/MIA/MKE/MSP/OKC/OMA/YOW/PHL/PHX/PDX/STL/SLC/SAN/SFO/SEA/GEG/TPA/YYZ/TUS/TUL/YVR/WAS/YWG/—one stopover will be allowed either inbound or outbound and only at a North American gateway for an additional charge of USD 30.00.

EX/9—Available all year. Travel on the last continuous sector shall be commenced by midnight of the 28th day after the date travel commenced from point of origin. Return travel on the transpacific portion shall not be commenced prior to the 14th day after the date of arrival. Normal children's, infants' and tour conductors' discounts apply.

EX/10—Fares are valid all year via the Pacific ocean except as provided directly in connection with the fares.
Return travel on the transpacific portion shall not be commenced prior to the 14th day after the date of arrival and not later than 21 days after the date of commencement of travel.

EX/11—Apply the rules and regulations shown for EX/4 above except that all travel must be completed by the forty-fifth (45th) day after the date travel commenced from point of origin, also for travel between western hemisphere and ABJ/ACC/CKY/COO/DKR/FNA/JOS/KAN/LOS/MLW return travel must not be commenced prior to the 13th day after the date of departure of the outward journey across the Atlantic ocean.

EX/12—Apply the same rules and regulations shown for EX/8 above except that the period of application is: EASTBOUND—April, May, September and October; WESTBOUND—April, May, June and October.

EX/13—Apply the same rules and regulations shown for EX/8 above except that the period of application is: EASTBOUND: June, July and August, and WESTBOUND: July, August and September.

EX/14—Apply the same rules shown for EX 7 except that the period of application is November 1 thru March 31 for EASTBOUND or WESTBOUND travel.

EX/15—Apply the same rules shown for EX 7 except:
a.—Fares apply EASTBOUND: June, July, August;
WESTBOUND: July, August, September
b.—In Europe, no stopover is permitted EASTBOUND.

EX/16—IT—Fares are valid all year. Travel on the continuous sector shall be commenced by midnight of the 35th day after the date travel commenced from point of origin. Return travel on the transpacific portion shall not be commenced prior to 14th day after day of arrival. The total inclusive tour selling price may not be less than the applicable inclusive tour fare plus:
1) USD 200.00 (USD 100.00 from points in the North Central Pacific to points in Alaska or Hawaii) for travel to from points in the North Central Pacific area and points in the US/Canada.
2) USD 140.00 for the minimum stay in area of turnaround (U.S./Canada or North/Central/South Pacific) plus USD 10.00 for each day of the tour in excess of the minimum stay (USD 200.00 if ½ of the South Pacific EX/16—IT is combined with ½ of a Pacific round trip, circle trip or North Central Pacific EX/16—IT Fare) for travel to/from points in the South Pacific area and points in the USA/Canada.

EX/17—Fares are valid all year. Travel from the last point of stopover must commence by midnight of the 23rd day after the date travel commenced from the point of origin.

EX/18—Apply the same rules and regulations shown for EX/4 above except that all travel must be completed by the forty-fifth (45th) day after the date travel commenced from point of origin and the period of application is: EASTBOUND—June, July and August; WESTBOUND—July, August and September.

EX/19—AP—Advance purchase excursion fares are applicable all year. Return travel on the transpacific portion shall not commence prior to the 21st day and not later than 45th day after the date of arrival. A stopover will be permitted at the point of turnaround only. Reservations, payment and issuance of ticket(s) shall be completed not later than the 60th day prior to the date of commencement of travel. When payment is made under UATP or similar credit plan or under any installment plan, the down payment shall not be less than 25% of the applicable fare. After the 60th day prior to the date of commencement of outbound travel, reservations may not be changed and in the event of cancellation 25% of the applicable fare is not refundable. Exception: prior to departure, full refund will be made in case of death or illness of the passenger or a member of his immediate family.

EX/22—(WEEKEND FARES) Fares apply on Fr, Sa, Su. One-half of a "week-end" excursion fare may be combined with one-half of a "mid-week" excursion fare. Valid all year.

EX/23—(MID-WEEK FARES) Fares apply on Mo, Tu, We, Th. One-half of a "mid-week" excursion fare may be combined with one-half of a "week-end" excursion fare. Valid all year.

EX/24—(WEEKEND FARES) Fares apply on Sa, Su, Mo. One-half of a "week-end" excursion fare may be combined with one-half of a "mid-week" excursion fare. Valid all year.

EX/25—(MID-WEEK FARES) Fares apply on Tu, We, Th, Fr. One-half of a "mid-week" excursion fare may be combined with one-half of a "week-end" excursion fare. Valid all year.

EX/28—AP (APEX WINTER)—Advance purchase excursion fares are applicable November 1 thru March 31 EASTBOUND and WESTBOUND.
Return travel on the Transatlantic portion shall not commence prior to the 22nd day and not later than the 45th day after the date of arrival.
Stopovers are not permitted. Reservations, payment and issuance of ticket(s) shall be completed not later than two calendar months (including date of departure) prior to the date of commencement of outbound travel. In the event of cancellation 25% of the fare is not refundable.

EX/29—AP (APEX SHOULDER)—Apply the same rules shown for EX/28 except that the period of application is EASTBOUND: April, May, September, October and WESTBOUND: April, May, June, October.

EX/30—AP (APEX PEAK)—Apply the same rules shown for EX-28 except that the period of application is EASTBOUND: June, July, August and WESTBOUND: July, August, September.

EX/31—Discounts applicable to children's and infants' fares will not apply.

EX/32—To be sold only in the countries of origin and destination.

EX/33—Routings via points in Florida are not permitted. The mileage system may not be used to circumvent this provision.

EX/34—Fares apply during the period September 15 thru March 31 (incl.). Only one stopover outbound and one stopover inbound is permitted (these may not be taken within South America or Panama). Return travel from South America shall not be commenced prior to the 29th day after date of departure from point of origin.

EX/50—Fares are valid all year for transatlantic departures between 0701 Sunday and 0659 Friday (weekend travel permitted at a surcharge of USD 15.00 for transatlantic crossing in each direction—i.e.: USD 30.00 for both directions).
Fares apply on Icelandic airlines:
Eastbound—YLE: Originating in U.S. September 1 thru May 31
Eastbound—YHE: Originating in U.S. June 1 thru August 31
Westbound—YLE: Originating in Europe October 1 thru June 30
Westbound—YHE: Originating in Europe July 1 thru September 30
The return portion of the transatlantic trip must not begin before the 14th day nor commence after midnight of the 21st day after the commencement of the outbound travel.

EX/51—IT—Inclusive tour basing fares on Icelandic airlines apply:
Eastbound—YLE: Originating in U.S. September 1 thru May 31
Eastbound—YHE: Originating in U.S. June 1 thru August 31
Westbound—YLE: Originating in Europe October 1 thru June 30
Westbound—YHE: Originating in Europe July 1 thru September 30
Return travel across the Atlantic ocean must be commenced not later than Midnight of the 21st day after commencement of the outbound travel. Exception: for travel originating in Reykjavik the return travel shall not be commenced prior to the 6th day after commencement of outbound travel across the Atlantic.
These fares apply only when the passenger purchases a fully prepaid complete travel package. The total price of the complete package for each passenger must be not less than the applicable air fare plus USD 120.00.

EX/54—Fares are valid all year. No stopovers are permitted. Return travel from India shall not commence prior to the 14th (21st day during the months June, July and August) day after arrival in India; return travel from U.S./Canada shall not commence prior to the 14th day after arrival in the U.S./Canada.
Return travel across the Atlantic Ocean on the last continuous portion without stopover, shall be commenced by Midnight of the 120th day after the date of commencement of travel from point of origin.
These fares may be combined only with domestic fares within the U.S./Canada/India. These fares may not be used in construction of other types of round, circle or open jaw trips or around-the-world fares.

EX/67—Fares are valid all year. No stopovers are permitted. Return travel from Pakistan or from U.S. Canada cannot commence prior to the 15th day after the day of arrival.
Return travel across the Atlantic Ocean on the last continuous portion without stopover shall be commenced by midnight of the 120th day after the date of commencement of travel from point of origin.

EX/68—Not combinable with fare to from Brazil.

EX/84—Fares apply on Icelandic airlines:
Eastbound—YLE: Originating in U.S. September 1 thru May 31
Eastbound—YHE: Originating in U.S. June 1 thru August 31
Westbound—YLE: Originating in Europe October 1 thru June 30
Westbound—YHE: Originating in Europe July 1 thru September 30

LOCAL TAXES

Many countries impose Transportation Taxes of some type which are collected in addition to the regular air fares. Refer to the list of countries below to determine what taxes, if any, will be collected either at the time tickets are purchased for transportation, or upon entering or leaving countries included in your itinerary. In general, tax exemptions apply to persons holding diplomatic passports or travelling under government orders, transit passengers, and those travelling on free passage.

CHILE—Exit tax assessed in Chilean Escudos to Chilean nationals and foreign residents, as follows:
  a) **Exempt are:** children under 2 years of age and passengers destined to neighboring countries Argentina, Bolivia, Peru.
  b) Other Latin American countries including Curacao, Jamaica, Puerto Rico and Bahama Islands—average per passenger USD 50.00.
  c) USA, Europe and other countries—average USD 220.00—per passenger.

COLOMBIA—Stamp Tax and Tourist Tax (issuing office collection). Total of 10% on all tickets issued in Colombia for transportation from a Colombian port to a foreign point or from a foreign point to a Colombian port and then to another foreign point. Such taxes are applicable on the value of the transportation from the Colombian port to the foreign point.
  (1) One way tickets—on the full value thereof from the Colombian port of exit to the foreign point.
  (2) Round trip ticket and circle trip tickets—on one half of the value of the transportation from the Colombian port of exit to the Colombian port of entry. On circle trips, if there is only one foreign port of call, the taxes apply only on the portion from the Colombian port of exit to the foreign point of call.

Airport Tax (departure collection) on all passengers embarking in Colombia for destinations within Colombia COP 25.00, destinations abroad COP 200.00 (USD 10.00). **Exempt are:** infants under 2 years of age and transit passengers whose stay does not exceed 24 hours.

GABON—Airport Tax (departure collection):
  Domestic flights . . . . AFR 400
  Exempt are: infants under 2 years of age.

GAMBIA—Airport Tax (departure collection) of GAD 5.00 is levied on all passengers embarking at Bathurst Airport.

GERMANY, Federal Rep.—Passenger charge of DMK 5.00 collected at the airport of departure for a destination abroad.

GHANA—Airport Tax (departure collection) is collected from all passengers embarking at airports in Ghana: domestic flights GHN 0.50, international flights GHN 3.00.
  Exceptions: Children under 2 years and passengers transferring to another service within 24 hours.
  Ticket Tax of 10% is assessed on all tickets issued and paid for in Ghana covering transportation from Ghana to a destination abroad.
  Exceptions: Infants under 2 years.

GIBRALTAR—Passenger Tax (departure collection) GBL 0.50 levied on all passengers departing from Gibraltar.
  Exempt are: transit passengers continuing their journey within 6 hours.

GREECE—Head Tax (departure collection) DRA 40 is levied on every passenger over 12 years of age boarding in Greece and departing for a foreign destination.

EXCESS BAGGAGE CHARGES

The charge for excess baggage in international travel (except between U.S.A. and Canada), is 1% of the normal adult direct first class one way through-fare per kilo regardless of the class of service used. Special rates are available for golf and ski equipment.

In computing excess baggage charges it is necessary to determine the rate per kilo rounded off to the next higher unit of currency shown under the Official IATA Exchange Rate column of the Money and Exchange Rates table shown herein. The rounded off rate must then be multiplied by the excess weight to determine the total charge.

In applying excess baggage rates, fractions of less than one-half kilogram will be charged for as the next higher half kilogram and fractions in excess of one-half kilogram will be charged for as the next higher full kilogram. Use the following table when converting pounds to kilograms.

The following table should be used for converting from pounds to kilograms for the purposes of computing excess baggage charges:

Lbs.	Kilos	Lbs.	Kilos	Lbs.	Kilos	Lbs.	Kilos	Lbs.	Kilos	Lbs.	Kilos	Lbs.	Kilos	Lbs.	Kilos	Lbs.	Kilos	Lbs.	Kilos
1	.5	11	5.	21	10.	31	14.5	41	19.	51	23.5	61	28.	71	32.5	81	37.	91	41.5
2	1.	12	5.5	22	10.	32	15.	42	19.5	52	24.	62	28.5	72	33.	82	37.5	92	42.
3	1.5	13	6.	23	10.5	33	15.	43	20.	53	24.5	63	29.	73	33.5	83	38.	93	42.5
4	2.	14	6.5	24	11.	34	15.5	44	20.	54	24.5	64	29.5	74	34.	84	38.5	94	43.
5	2.5	15	7.	25	11.5	35	16.	45	20.5	55	25.	65	29.5	75	34.5	85	39.	95	43.5
6	3.	16	7.5	26	12.	36	16.5	46	21.	56	25.5	66	30.	76	34.5	86	39.5	96	44.
7	3.5	17	8.	27	12.5	37	17.	47	21.5	57	26.	67	30.5	77	35.	87	39.5	97	44.
8	4.	18	8.5	28	13.	38	17.5	48	22.	58	26.5	68	31.	78	35.5	88	40.	98	44.5
9	4.5	19	9.	29	13.5	39	18.	49	22.5	59	27.	69	31.5	79	36.	89	40.5	99	45.
10	5	20	9.5	30	14.	40	18.5	50	23.	60	27.5	70	32.	80	36.5	90	41.	100	45.5

MINIMUM CONNECTING TIMES

Compiled by the International Air Transport Association and The Reuben H. Donnelley Corporation

These Minimum Connecting Times are supplied for information purposes only and neither the International Air Transport Association nor the Publishers of the Official Airline Guide undertake any responsibility for the accuracy of the material. All Scheduled Airlines will accept connecting reservations based upon these established connection times; however there may be other acceptable connecting times under the following conditions:

(1) Nothing shall preclude Airlines from making bilateral agreements with shorter connection times in cases where their special arrangements make this possible.

(2) Any Airline may give notice of a special requirement when longer times are necessary.

(3) Any City/Airport not listed on these pages, allow: 20 minutes for domestic connections and: 60 minutes for international connections.

SUMMARY OF REVISIONS IN THIS ISSUE:

- ■ Aberdeen, Scotland
- ● Barbados, Barbados
- ● Cali, Colombia
- ▲ Chittagong, Bangladesh
- ▲ Dacca, Bangladesh
- ■ Fukuoka, Japan
- ▲ Georgetown, Rep. of Guyana
- ■▲ Guam Is., Mariana Island
- ■ Irtutsk, U.S.S.R.
- ■ Kagoshima, Japan
- ▲ Luanda, Angola
- ● Medellin, Colombia
- ▲ Melbourne, Vic., Australia
- ▲ Monrovia, Liberia (Robertsfield)
- ▲ Munich, Germany
- ▲ Nadi, Fiji Island
- ▲ New York, New York (J. F. Kennedy) (Helicopter)
- ▲ Panama City, Panama Rep.
- ▲ Port au Prince, Haiti
- ● Rome, Italy (Leonardo da Vinci)
- ■ Seattle, Washington
- ■ Tokyo, Japan (Haneda)
- ■ West Palm Beach, Florida

NOTES: DOMESTIC means travel between two points in the same country, territory or possessions unless otherwise specified.
EUROPE means the area comprised of the following countries: Albania, Algeria, Andorra, Austria, Azores, Belgium, Bulgaria, Canary Islands, Czechoslovakia, Denmark, Finland, France, Germany, Gibraltar, Greece, Hungary, Iceland, Ireland, Italy, Liechtenstein, Luxembourg, Madeira, Malta, Monaco, Morocco, Netherlands, Norway, Poland, Portugal, Romania, San Marino, Spain, Sweden, Switzerland, Tunisia, Turkey (in Europe and Asia), United Kingdom, USSR (west of the Ural Mountains), Yugoslavia.

▲Change ■Addition ●Deletion

City/Airport	Connecting Time Intervals: Between Domestic Services	Between Domestic and International Services: From Domestic to Internat'l	Between Domestic and International Services: From Internat'l to Domestic	Between Internat'l Services
	Minutes	Minutes	Minutes	Minutes
Livingstone, Rep. of Zambia (Z)	30	60	60	—
Ljubljana, Yugoslavia	30	30	30	30
Lome, Togo	45	45	45	45
London, England:				
Heathrow				
Terminal 1 (QQ) BD,BE,CS,CY,EI,KM,NS.	45	45	45(JJ)	45
Terminal 2 AF,AH,AT,AY,AZ,FI,IB,JU,KL,LG,LH,LL, LN,LO,LZ,MA,OA,OK,OS,RO,SK,SN,SR, SU,TK,TP,TU.	—	—	—	60
Terminal 3 AC,AE,AI,AR,BA,BG,BW,EC,ET,FG,GF,GH, IA,IR,JL,JM,KU,LY,ME,MH,MK,MS,NA,PA, PK,QF,QC,QZ,RB,RG,RJ,SA,SD,SQ,SV,TG, TW,VA,WT.	—	—	—	60(J)
Between Terminals (HH)	75	75	75	75
Gatwick (QQ)	25	30	50	40
Heathrow to Gatwick and v.v. (direct)	150	150	150	150
Heathrow to Gatwick and v.v. (via London) Town Terminal—Road and Rail	195	195	195	195
Heathrow to Luton and v.v.	130	150	150	150
Los Angeles, Calif., U.S.A.: (M)				
International Airport	50*	60(L)	90(U)	90
Lourenco Marques, Mozambique	45	120(OO)	90	90
▲Luanda, Angola	30	60	60	60
Lubumbashi, Zaire	30	60	60	60
Lulea, Sweden	30	—	—	—
Lusaka, Rep. of Zambia	30	60	60	45
Luxembourg, Luxembourg	—	—	—	(PP)
Luxor, Egypt	15	—	—	—
Lyon, France	20	35	35	35
Mackay, Qld., Australia	30	—	—	—
Madras, India	30	60	60	30
Madrid, Spain	45	75(D)	75(D)	45
Mahon, Minorca, Spain	30	—	—	—
Majunga, Malagasy Rep.	35	35	35	35
Malaga, Spain	45	75	75	45
Malmo, Sweden (Bulltofta)	30	30	30	30
Malta, Mediterranean Sea	—	—	—	30
Managua, Nicaragua	—	30	60	30
Manaus, Brazil	30	60	60	60
Manchester, England (QQ)	30	50(W)	45(W)	40
Manila, Philippines	45	75	75	60
Maracaibo, Venezuela	30	60	90	60
Mariehamn, Finland	—	15	15	—
Marseille, France	30	40	40	30
Maturin, Venezuela	20	60	60	—
Mauritius, Indian Ocean	—	—	—	45
Mazatlan, Mexico	60	60	90	—
Mbandaka, Zaire	30	—	—	—
Mbuji-Mayi, Zaire	30	—	—	—
Medan, Sumatra, Indonesia	60	60	60	60
●Medellin, Colombia (EE)	20	50	60	—
▲Melbourne, Vic., Australia	30	45	60	45
Mendoza, Argentina	60	60	60	60
Merida, Mexico	45	60	60	60
Mexico City, Mexico	45	60	75	90
Miami, Florida, U.S.A.	40*	60(P)	90(C)	90(CC)
Milan, Italy:				
Malpensa	40	40	40	40
Forlanini (Linate)	40(II)	50	50	40
Malpensa to Forlanini and v.v.	130	130	130	130
Minneapolis/St. Paul, Minn., U.S.A.	40*	40(G)	60(G)	—
Moncton, N.B., Canada	30	—	—	—
Monrovia, Liberia:				
▲Robertsfield	30	60	75	60
Sprigg Payne	—	60	60	45
Robertsfield to Sprigg Payne and v.v.	150	150	150	150
Montego Bay, Jamaica	—	45	45	60(T)
Monterrey, Mexico	60	60	90	—
Montevideo, Uruguay	30	60	60	60
Montreal, Que., Canada:				
Dorval (F)	30(Y)	—	—	—
Mirabel	—	60(LL)	90(MM)	60
Mirabel to Dorval	—	—	165(KK)	—
Dorval to Mirabel	—	165	—	165
Moscow, USSR:				
Domodedovo	60	—	—	—
Sheremetyevo	—	—	—	60
Vnukovo	60	—	—	—
Sheremetyevo to Domodedovo and v.v.	—	240	240	—
Sheremetyevo to Vnukovo and v.v.	—	180	180	—
Mulhouse, France (See Basel)				
▲Munich, Germany	35	35	35	35
Nagoya, Japan	25	60	60	—
Nairobi, Kenya	30	60	60	60
▲Nadi, Fiji Is.	—	45	60	45
Naples, Italy (Capodichino)	40	40	40	40
▲Nassau, Bahamas (H)	60	60(AA)	75(K)	90
Natal, Brazil	30	30	30	30
N'Djamena, Chad	45	45	45	45
Ndola, Rep. of Zambia	30	60	60	45
Newcastle, England (QQ)	30	45	45	30
New Delhi, India (see Delhi)				
New Orleans, La., U.S.A.	30*	60(Q)	60(Q)	60
New York, N. Y., U.S.A.: (B)				
▲John F. Kennedy Int'l	60*	75(E)	105(A)	120(X)
John F. Kennedy to La Guardia	120*	—	150	—
La Guardia to John F. Kennedy	120*	120	—	—
John F. Kennedy Int'l to Newark	180	—	210	—
Newark to John F. Kennedy Int'l	180	180	—	—
Newark Airport	40*	—	—	—
La Guardia	45*	—	—	—
La Guardia to Newark and v.v.	180	—	—	—
Niamey, Niger	45	45	45	45
Nice, France	25	40	40	30
Nicosia, Cyprus (See Larnaca)	—	—	—	—
Niigata, Japan	—	60	60	—
Norwich, England (QQ)	—	25	25	—
Noumea, New Caledonia				
Noumea	30	30	30	60
Noumea to Magenta and v.v.	—	—	150	—
Nuremberg, Germany	30	30	30	30
Oaxaca, Mexico	60	—	—	—
Okinawa, Ryukuy Is., Japan	45	60	60	60
Oran, Algeria	30	45	45	40
Osaka, Japan	30	60	60	30
Oslo, Norway	30	30	45	30
Ottawa, Ontario, Canada	30(FF)	30(FF)	90(FF)	—
Ouagadougou, Upper Volta	45	45	45	45
Pago Pago, Samoa	—	—	—	45
Palembang, Sumatra, Indonesia	60	60	60	60
Palermo, Italy	30	40	60	40
Palma, Mallorca Is., Spain	30	45	45	45
▲Panama City, Panama Rep.	—	45	45	45(S)
Papetee, Tahiti, Fr. Polynesia	45	60	60	45
Paramaribo, Surinam (Zandery)	—	—	—	45
Paris, France:				
Orly	50(DD)	60	60	50(R)
Le Bourget	30	30	30	30
C. DeGaulle	50	50	50	50
Orly to C. DeGaulle and v.v.	135	135	135	135
Orly to Le Bourget (direct) and v.v.	180	180	180	180
Le Bourget to C. DeGaulle and v.v.	65	65	65	65
Penang, Malaysia	30	45	60	—
Perth, W. Australia	30	45	60	40
Peshawar, Pakistan	15	45	45	—
Philadelphia, Pennsylvania, U.S.A. (N)	30*	90(N)	90	90
Phoenix, Ariz., U.S.A.	30*	60(I)	60(I)	—
Pittsburgh, Pennsylvania, U.S.A. (BB)	40*	—	45	—

HELICOPTER CONNECTING TIME INTERVALS IN NEW YORK CITY

Airport	From Domestic to Helicopter	From Helicopter to Domestic	From Internat'l to Helicopter	From Helicopter to Internatl.
	Minutes	Minutes	Minutes	Minutes
■La Guardia	30*	25*	—	—
■Newark	40*	40*	—	—
■John F. Kennedy International Airport	35*	25*	105(V)	35

*—For additional exceptions to U.S. City Domestic Time Intervals refer to North American Edition of the Official Airline Guide.

▲(A) TW to TW: 75 mins.; EA to EA (except from ACA/ANU/KIN/MBJ/MEX): 30 mins.; AA to AA: 90 mins.; except flights which clear customs at Chicago, Dallas, San Antonio, Honolulu and San Juan: 30 mins.; NW to All: 60 mins.; DL to DL: 30 mins.; EA to AL: 60 mins.; BN flights transiting MIA only to UA: 45 mins.; PA to PA: 60 mins.; TW to VM: 75 mins.; PA to AL: 65 mins.

(B) Flights to/from Canada, Bermuda, Puerto Rico, U.S. Virgin Is. and Nassau (except flights stopping in Freeport) are considered Domestic. JAL flights via Honolulu to San Francisco and New York are considered Domestic. NW flights via Anchorage and/or Seattle are considered Domestic.

(C) EA flights from NAS: 40 mins.; All other flights from Nassau: 60 mins.; NA to NA: 60 mins.; BN to BN: 75 mins.; EA to EA (from FPO/MBJ): 75 mins.; EA to EA(except from FPO/MBJ): 30 mins.; BA/MX to EA: 75 mins.; MI to DL: 60 mins.; PA to PA: 80 mins.; SO to SO: 70 mins.; UP (from NAS) to DL/NA/NW/UA: 40 mins.; UP (from NAS) to BN/SO/TW: 45 mins.

(D) Between IB flights: 60 mins.

(E) EA to EA: 30 mins.; AL/PA to PA: 45 mins.; TW to TW: 50 mins.; AA to OA: 45 mins.; AA to AA: 30 mins.; DL to DL: 30 mins.; UA to BN: 45 mins.; BN/UA to AY: 45 mins.; BN to DO: 45 mins.; VM to TW: 50 mins.

(F) Canada-U.S.A. and v.v.: 60 mins.; All to ND transborder flights: 30 mins.

(G) NW Int'l. flights stopping at ANC, HNL or SEA are considered domestic. Domestic to International: NW to NW: 25 mins.

(H) If flight is pre-cleared to U.S.A.: 60 mins.

(I) Flights to/from Hawaii are domestic; RW to RW (to MEXICO): 25 mins.; RW to RW (from MEXICO): 50 mins.; Domestic FL to International RW: 40 mins.

(J) TW to TW and PA to PA: 45 mins.; BA to/from BA Concorde Services: 55 mins.

(K) DL to DL: 30 mins.

(L) AA/UA to TW: 50 mins.; TW to TW: 45 mins.; from WA flights to WA flights to ACA and MEX: 20 mins.; CO/RW/TI/UA/WA to MX: 50 mins.; AA to NW: 50 mins.

(M) Domestic Connecting Time Intervals will apply to all International flights which transit to a point in the U.S. prior to arrival in Los Angeles and San Francisco. Exception: BA, QF, SK, TE and WA. Connections to/from Hawaii are Domestic.

(N) TW Domestic to TW International: 60 mins.; Flights to/from Canada (except JM), Hawaii, Puerto Rico, U.S. Virgin Islands, Bermuda, Nassau are Domestic.

(O) Flights to/from Hawaii, Canada, Puerto Rico, U.S. Virgin Islands are Domestic.

■(P) EA to EA: 30 mins.; BN to BN: 45 mins.; NA to NA: 30 mins.; EA to BA/MX: 45 mins.; DL to MI: 45 mins.; SO to SO: 30 mins.; AC/CO/NW/UA/TW to SO: 45 mins.; DL/NA/NW to UP: 40 mins.; BN/SO/TW to UP: 45 mins.; UA to UP (to NAS): 40 mins.; NA to SL: 30 mins.

(Q) TA Int'l to DL Domestic: 50 mins.; DL Domestic to DL Int'l (to CCS, MAR, MBJ): 40 mins.; DL Int'l to DL Domestic (from CCS, MAR, MBJ): 50 mins.; EA Domestic to EA Int'l (to MEX) and EA Int'l to EA Domestic (from MEX): 55 mins.

(R) TW to TW: 40 mins.

▲(S) BN to BN: 35 mins.

(T) EA to EA: 30 mins.

(U) NW to All: 50 mins.; WA flights from ACA and MEX to WA flights: 60 mins.; MX to CO/RW/TI/UA/WA: 75 mins.

(V) AA to Helicopter: 25 mins.; PA to Helicopter: 60 mins.

(W) Domestic to/from Transatlantic: 50 mins.

▲(X) BA to BA: 60 mins. PA to PA: 65 mins.

(Y) All to/from ND (except YHM/YOW/YMT/YQG/YVO): 40 mins.; AC to AC: 45 mins.

(Z) Passenger transfer Livingstone A/P—Victoria Falls A/P at Zambia/Rhodesia border points: allow minimum 3 hours (Service Temporarily Suspended).

▲(AA) DL to DL: 30 mins.

(BB) Domestic connecting times will apply to all TW International flights which transit to a point in the U.S. prior to arrival/departure. Flights to/from YUL and YYZ are considered domestic.

(CC) Between BA and EA: 75 mins.; UP (from NAS) to SO: 45 mins.

(DD) Including Geneva Cointrin French Sector.

■(EE) AV to AV Domestic: 30 mins.

(FF) Domestic to Transborder: 30 mins.; Transborder to Domestic: 30 mins.; Transborder to International: 45 mins.; International to Transborder: 90 mins.

■(HH) Between Terminal 1 and 3 BE/CS/NS to/from BA Concorde Services: 55 mins.

(II) IH to IH: 20 mins.

(JJ) Connecting flights to Belfast: 60 mins.

(KK) All to transborder: 195 mins.

(LL) QB to AC: 50 mins.

(MM) AC to QB: 80 mins.

(OO) Flights to BLZ, NBO, LUN, DAR, LAD, JNB, MTS, TNR: 75 mins.

(PP) Europe to/from Europe: 35 mins.; Europe to/from Intercontinental: 45 mins.

(QQ) Flights to the Rep. of Ireland, JER and GCI are considered domestic. Flights from those points are International.

CITY/AIRPORT CODES Listed Alphabetically by Code

A

AQJ	AQABA, JORDAN
AQP	AREQUIPA, PERU
ARC	ARCTIC VILLAGE, ALASKA, USA
ARI	ARICA, CHILE
ARM	ARMIDALE, N.S.W., AUSTRALIA
ARN	STOCKHOLM, SWEDEN-ARLANDA ARPT
ARS	ARAGARCAS, BRAZIL
ART	WATERTOWN, N.Y., USA
ARU	ARACATUBA, BRAZIL
ARW	ARAC, ROMANIA
ARX	ASBURY PARK, N.J., USA
ASA	ASSAB, ETHIOPIA
ASB	ASHKHAEAD, USSR
ASC	ASCENSION, BOLIVIA
ASD	ANDROS TOWN, BAHAMAS
ASE	ASPEN, COLO., USA
ASJ	AMAMI O SHIMA, JAPAN
ASK	YAMOUSSOUKRO, IVORY COAST
ASM	ASMARA, ETHIOPIA
ASO	ASOSA, ETHIOPIA
ASP	ALICE SPRINGS, N.T., AUSTRALIA
ASR	KAYSERI, TURKEY
ASU	ASUNCION, PARAGUAY
ASW	ASWAN, EGYPT
ASX	ASHLAND, WIS., USA
ATA	ANTA, PERU
ATB	ATEARA, SUDAN
ATC	ARTHUR'S TOWN, BAHAMAS
ATE	ANTIQUE, PHILIPPINES
ATH	ATHENS, GREECE
ATI	ARTIGAS, URUGUAY
ATL	ATLANTA, GA., USA
ATM	ALTAMIRA, BRAZIL
ATN	NAMATANAI, NEW IRELAND, N. GUI.
ATQ	AMRITSAR, INDIA
ATR	ATAR, MAURITANIA
ATS	ARTESIA, N. M., USA
ATU	ATTU IS., ALASKA, USA
ATV	ATI, CHAD
ATW	APPLETON, WIS., USA
ATY	WATERTOWN, S.D., USA
AUA	ARUBA, NETH. ANTILLES
AUC	ARAUCA, COLOMBIA
AUD	AUGUSTUS DOWNS, QLD., AUSTRALIA
AUG	AUGUSTA, ME., USA
AUH	ABU DHABI, U. A. EMIRATES
AUK	ALAKANUK, ALASKA, USA
AUO	AUBURN, ALA., USA
AUP	AGUAN, PAPUA NEW GUINEA
AUQ	ATUONA, MARQUESAS IS., PAC. OC.
AUR	AURILLAC, FRANCE
AUS	AUSTIN, TEXAS, USA
AUU	AURUKUN MISSION, QLD., AUST.
AUW	WAUSAU, WIS., USA
AUY	ANEITYUM, NEW HEBRIDES
AVL	ASHEVILLE, N.C., USA
AVP	WILKES-BARRE/SCRANTON, PA., USA
AVU	AVUAVU, SOLOMON IS.
AVX	CATALINA IS. CALIF-AVALON BAY, USA
AWA	AWASA, ETHIOPIA
AWR	AWAR, PAPUA NEW GUINEA
AWZ	AHWAZ, IRAN
AXC	ARAMAC, QLD., AUSTRALIA
AXD	ALEXANDROUPOLIS, GREECE
AXK	ATAQ, PEOP. DEM. REP. OF YEMEN
AXM	ARMENIA, COLOMBIA
AXS	ALTUS, OKLA., USA
AXT	AKITA, JAPAN
AXU	AXUM, ETHIOPIA
AYP	AYACUCHO, PERU
AYQ	AYERS ROCK, N.T., AUSTRALIA
AYT	ANTALYA, TURKEY
AZB	AMAZON BAY, PAPUA NEW GUINEA
AZD	YAZD, IRAN
AZG	APATZINGAN, MEXICO
AZO	KALAMAZOO, MICH., USA

B

BAA	BIALLA, NEW BRITAIN, N.GUINEA
BAC	BARRANCA DE UPIA, COLOMBIA
BAG	BAGUIO, PHILIPPINES
BAH	BAHRAIN IS., ARABIAN GULF
BAJ	BALI, UNEA ISLAND, NEW GUINEA
BAK	BAKU, USSR
BAL	BALTIMORE, MD., USA
BAO	BAN MAK KHAENG, THAILAND
BAP	BAIBARA, PAPUA NEW GUINEA
BAQ	BARRANQUILLA, COLOMBIA
BAS	BALALAE, SOLOMON IS.
BAU	BAURU, BRAZIL
BAY	BAIA MARE, ROMANIA
BBA	BALMACEDA, CHILE
BBG	BUTARITARI, GILBERT IS.
BBI	BHUBANESWAR, INDIA
BBN	BARIO, SARAWAK, MALAYSIA
BBO	BERBERA, SOMALIA
BBQ	BARBUDA, WEST INDIES
BBR	BASSE-TERRE, GUADELOUPE
BBU	BUCHAREST, ROM-BANESA ARPT.
BBV	BEREBY, IVORY COAST
BBZ	ZAMBEZI, REP. OF ZAMBIA
BCA	BARACOA, CUBA
BCD	BACOLOD, PHILIPPINES
BCG	BEMICHI, REP. OF GUYANA
BCI	BARCALDINE, QLD., AUSTRALIA
BCK	BOLWORRA, QLD., AUSTRALIA
BCM	BACAU, ROMANIA
BCN	BARCELONA, SPAIN
BCO	BACO, ETHIOPIA
BCY	BULCHI, ETHIOPIA
BDA	BERMUDA, ATLANTIC OCEAN
BDB	BUNDABERG, QLD., AUSTRALIA
BDC	BARRA DO CORDA, BRAZIL
BDG	BLANDING, UTAH, USA
BDI	BIRD IS., SEYCHELLES IS. INDIAN OCE.
BDJ	BANJARMASIN, BORNEO, INDONESIA
BDL	HARTFORD, CONN., USA
BDN	BADANA, SAUDI ARABIA
BDO	BANDUNG, JAVA, INDONESIA
BDP	BHADRAPUR, NEPAL
BDQ	BARODA, INDIA
BDR	BRIDGEPORT, CONN., USA
BDS	BRINDISI, ITALY
BDT	BADO LITE, ZAIRE
BDU	BARDUFOSS, NORWAY
BDW	BEDFORD DOWNS, W. AUSTRALIA
BEA	BEREINA, PAPUA NEW GUINEA
BEB	BENBECULA, HEBRIDES IS., SCOT.
BED	BEDFORD, MASS., USA
BEE	BEAGLE, QLD., AUSTRALIA
BEF	BLUEFIELDS, NICARAGUA
BEG	BELGRADE, YUGOSLAVIA
BEH	BENTON HARBOR, MICH., USA
BEI	BEICA, ETHIOPIA
BEL	BELEM, BRAZIL
BEN	BENGHAZI, LIBYA
BER	BERLIN, GERMANY
BES	BREST, FRANCE
BET	BETHEL, ALASKA, USA
BEV	BEERSHEBA, ISRAEL
BEW	BEIRA, MOZAMBIQUE
BEY	BEIRUT, LEBANON
BFD	BRADFORD, PA., USA
BFF	SCOTTSBLUFF, NEBR., USA
BFL	BAKERSFIELD, CALIF., USA
BFN	BLOEMFONTEIN, SOUTH AFRICA
BFO	BUFFALO RANGE, RHODESIA
BFS	BELFAST, N. IRELAND
BGA	BUCARAMANGA, COLOMBIA
BGB	BOOUE, GABON
BGF	BANGUI, CENTRAL AFRICAN REP.
BGH	BOGHE, MAURITANIA
BGI	BARBADOS, BARBADOS
BGL	BAGLUNG, NEPAL
BGM	BINGHAMTON, N.Y., USA
BGN	BAGABAG, PHILIPPINES
BGO	BERGEN, NORWAY
BGR	BANGOR, ME., USA
BGW	BAGHDAD, IRAQ
BGX	BAGE, BRAZIL
BGY	BERGAMO, ITALY
BHB	BAR HARBOR, ME., USA
BHE	BLENHEIM, NEW ZEALAND
BHH	BISHA, SAUDI ARABIA
BHI	BAHIA BLANCA, ARGENTINA
BHJ	BHUJ, INDIA
BHK	BUKHARA, USSR
BHL	BAHIA DE LOS ANGELES, MEX.
BHM	BIRMINGHAM, ALA., USA
BHN	BEIHAN, PEOP. DEM. REP. OF YEMEN
BHO	BHOPAL, INDIA
BHQ	BROKEN HILL, N.S.W., AUSTRALIA
BHR	BHARATPUR, NEPAL
BHS	BATHURST, N.S.W., AUSTRALIA
BHU	BHAVNAGAR, INDIA
BHX	BIRMINGHAM, ENGLAND
BHZ	BELO HORIZONTE, BRAZIL
BIA	BASTIA, CORSICA
BID	BLOCK ISLAND, R.I., USA
BIG	BIG DELTA, ALASKA, USA
BIH	BISHOP, CALIF., USA
BIK	BIAK, W. IRIAN, INDONESIA
BIL	BILLINGS, MONT., USA
BIM	BIMINI, BAHAMAS
BIN	BAMIAN, AFGHANISTAN
BIO	BILBAO, SPAIN
BIP	BULIMBA, QLD., AUSTRALIA
BIQ	BIARRITZ, FRANCE
BIR	BIRATNAGAR, NEPAL
BIS	BISMARCK, N.D., USA
BJI	BEMIDJI, MINN., USA
BJM	BUJUMBURA, BURUNDI
BJR	BAHAR DAR, ETHIOPIA
BKC	BUCKLAND, ALASKA, USA
BKE	BAKER, ORE., USA
BKI	KOTA KINABALU, SABAH, MALAYSIA
BKK	BANGKOK, THAILAND
BKL	CLEVELAND, OHIO-LAKEFRONT ARPT, USA
BKM	BAKALALAN, SARAWAK, MALAYSIA
BKO	BAMAKO, MALI
BKQ	BLACKALL, QLD., AUSTRALIA
BKU	BETIOKY, MALAGASY REP.
BKW	BECKLEY, W. VA., USA
BKX	BROOKINGS, S.D., USA
BKY	BUKAVU, ZAIRE
BKZ	BUKOBA, TANZANIA
BLA	BARCELONA, VENEZUELA
BLC	BALI, CAMEROON
BLE	BORLANGE, SWEDEN
BLF	BLUEFIELD, W. VA., USA
BLG	BELAGA, SARAWAK, MALAYSIA
BLH	BLYTHE, CALIF., USA
BLI	BELLINGHAM, WASH., USA
BLK	BLACKPOOL, ENGLAND
BLL	BILLUND, DENMARK
BLQ	BOLOGNA, ITALY
BLR	BANGALORE, INDIA
BLT	BLACKWATER, QLD., AUSTRALIA
BLZ	BLANTYRE, MALAWI
BMA	STOCKHOLM, SWEDEN-BROMMA ARPT
BMB	BUMBA, ZAIRE
BMC	BRIGHAM CITY, UTAH, USA
BMD	BELO, MALAGASY REP.
BME	BROOME, W. AUSTRALIA
BMG	BLOOMINGTON, IND., USA
BMI	BLOOMINGTON, ILL., USA
BMM	BITAM, GABON
BMO	BHAMO, BURMA
BMP	BRAMPTON ISLAND, Q. AUSTRALIA
BMY	BELEP, NEW CALEDONIA
BNA	NASHVILLE, TENN., USA
BNB	BOENDE, ZAIRE
BND	BANDAR ABBAS, IRAN
BNE	BRISBANE, QLD., AUSTRALIA
BNI	BENIN CITY, NIGERIA
BNN	BRONNOYSUND, NORWAY
BNS	BARINAS, VENEZUELA
BNT	BUNDI, PAPUA NEW GUINEA
BNY	BELLONA IS., SOLOMON IS.
BOB	BORA-BORA, SOC. IS. FR. POLYNESIA
BOC	BOCAS DEL TORO, PANAMA REP.
BOD	BORDEAUX, FRANCE
BOG	BOGOTA, COLOMBIA
BOH	BOURNEMOUTH, ENGLAND
BOI	BOISE, IDAHO, USA
BOJ	BURGAS, BULGARIA
BOM	BOMBAY, INDIA
BON	BONAIRE, NETH. ANTILLES
BOO	BODO, NORWAY
BOR	BELFORT, FRANCE
BOS	BOSTON, MASS., USA
BOY	BOBO DIOULASSO, UPPER VOLTA
BPH	BISLIG, PHILIPPINES
BPN	BALIKPAPAN, BORNEO, INDONESIA
BPP	* BABELTHAUP IS., PALAU ISLANDS
BPT	BEAUMONT/PT. ARTHUR, TEX., USA
BPY	BESALAMPY, MALAGASY REP.
BQN	AGUADILLA, PUERTO RICO
BRC	SAN CARLOS DE BARILOCHE, ARG.
BRD	BRAINERD, MINN., USA
BRE	BREMEN, GERMANY
BRI	BARI, ITALY
BRK	BOURKE, N.S.W., AUSTRALIA
BRL	BURLINGTON, IOWA, USA
BRM	BARQUISIMETO, VENEZUELA
BRN	BERNE, SWITZERLAND
BRO	BROWNSVILLE, TEXAS, USA
BRQ	BRNO, CZECHOSLOVAKIA
BRR	BARRA, HEBRIDES IS., SCOTLAND
BRS	BRISTOL, ENGLAND
BRU	BRUSSELS, BELGIUM
BRW	BARROW, ALASKA, USA
BSA	BOSASO, SOMALIA
BSB	BRASILIA, BRAZIL
BSC	BAHIA SOLANO, COLOMBIA
BSG	BATA, EQUATORIAL GUINEA
BSK	BISKRA, ALGERIA
BSL	BASEL, SWITZERLAND
BSO	BASCO, PHILIPPINES
BSR	BASRA, IRAQ
BSS	BALSAS, BRAZIL
BSU	BASANKUSU, ZAIRE
BSX	BASSEIN, BURMA
BTE	BONTHE, SIERRE LEONE
BTH	BANJUL, GAMBIA
BTI	BARTER IS., ALASKA, USA
BTJ	BANDA ACEH, SUMATRA, INDONESIA
BTL	BATTLE CREEK, MICH., USA
BTM	BUTTE, MONT., USA
BTR	BATON ROUGE, LA., USA
BTS	BRATISLAVA, CZECHOSLOVAKIA
BTT	BETTLES, ALASKA, USA
BTU	BINTULU, SARAWAK, MALAYSIA
BTV	BURLINGTON, VT., USA
BTZ	BURSA, TURKEY
BUA	BUKA IS. BOUGAINVILLE IS. SOLOMON IS
BUC	BURKETOWN, QLD., AUSTRALIA
BUD	BUDAPEST, HUNGARY
BUE	BUENOS AIRES, ARGENTINA

E

ESF	ALEXANDRIA, LA., USA
ESN	EASTON, MD., USA
ESR	EL SALVADOR, CHILE
ETE	METEMMA, ETHIOPIA
ETH	ELAT, ISRAEL
EUA	EUA, TONGA ISLAND, S. PACIFIC
EUG	EUGENE, ORE., USA
EUN	EL AAIUN, SP. SAHARA
EUX	ST. EUSTATIUS, LEEWARD IS.
EVE	NARV/HARSTAD, NORWAY
EVM	EVELETH, MINN., USA
EVN	EREVAN, USSR
EVV	EVANSVILLE, IND., USA
EWB	NEW BEDFORD, MASS., USA
EWN	NEW BERN, N.C., USA
EWO	EWO, CONGO
EWR	NEW YORK, NY-NEWARK ARPT, USA
EXT	EXETER, ENGLAND
EYP	EL YOPAL, COLOMBIA
EYW	KEY WEST, FLA., USA
EZE	BUENOS AIRES, ARG-EZEIZA ARPT.

F

FAE	FAEROE ISLANDS, DENMARK
FAG	FAGURHOLSMYRI, ICELAND
FAI	FAIRBANKS, ALASKA, USA
FAJ	FAJARDO, PUERTO RICO
FAN	FARSUND, NORWAY
FAO	FARO, PORTUGAL
FAR	FARGO, N.D., USA
FAT	FRESNO, CALIF., USA
FAY	FAYETTEVILLE, N.C., USA
FBD	FAIZABAD, AFGHANISTAN
FBM	LUBUMBASHI, ZAIRE
FCA	KALISPELL, MONT., USA
FCO	ROME, ITALY-LEONARDO DA VINCI ARPT
FDE	FORDE, NORWAY
FDF	FORT DE FRANCE, MARTINIQUE
FDU	BANDUNDU, ZAIRE
FEG	FERGANA, USSR
FEN	FERNANDO DE NORONHA, BRAZIL
FEZ	FEZ, MOROCCO
FFT	FRANKFORT, KY., USA
FGA	* FARA IS., SOLOMON IS.
FGD	F'DERIK, MAURITANIA
FGI	APIA, W. SAMOA-FAGALII ARPT.
FIH	KINSHASA, ZAIRE
FIN	FINSCHHAFEN, PAPUA NEW GUINEA
FIZ	FITZROY CROSSING, W. AUSTRALIA
FKI	KISANGANI, ZAIRE
FKJ	FUKUI, JAPAN
FKL	FRANKLIN, PA., USA
FLA	FLORENCIA, COLOMBIA
FLG	FLAGSTAFF, ARIZ., USA
FLL	FT. LAUDERDALE, FLA., USA
FLN	FLORIANOPOLIS, BRAZIL
FLO	FLORENCE, S.C., USA
FLS	FLINDERS IS., TASMANIA
FLW	SANTA CRUZ, FLORES IS., AZORES
FLY	FINLEY, N.S.W., AUSTRALIA
FMA	FORMOSA, ARGENTINA
FMI	KALEMIE, ZAIRE
FMN	FARMINGTON, N.M., USA
FMS	FORT MADISON, IOWA, USA
FMY	FORT MYERS, FLA., USA
FNA	FREETOWN, SIERRA LEONE
FNC	FUNCHAL, MADEIRA IS.
FNE	FANE, PAPUA NEW GUINEA
FNI	NIMES, FRANCE
FNJ	PYONGYANG, N. KOREA
FNT	FLINT, MICH., USA
FOA	* FORTUNA LEDGE, ALASKA, USA
FOB	FORT BRAGG, CALIF., USA
FOD	FT. DODGE, IOWA, USA
FOE	* TOPEKA, KANSAS-FORBES AFB
FOR	FORTALEZA, CEARA, BRAZIL
FOU	FOUGAMOU, GABON
FOY	FOYA, LIBERIA
FPO	FREEPORT, BAHAMAS
FRA	FRANKFURT, GERMANY
FRC	FRANCA, BRAZIL
FRG	FARMINGDALE, N.Y., USA
FRL	FORLI, ITALY
FRM	FAIRMONT, MINN., USA
FRO	FLORO, NORWAY
FRS	FLORES, GUATEMALA
FRU	FRUNZE, USSR
FRW	FRANCISTOWN, BOTSWANA
FSD	SIOUX FALLS, S.D., USA
FSM	FT. SMITH, ARK., USA
FTC	FORT COLLINS, COLO., USA
FTU	FT. DAUPHIN, MALAGASY REP.
FTV	FT VICTORIA, RHODESIA
FTX	FORT ROUSSET, CONGO
FUB	FULLEBORN, NEW BRITAIN, NEW GUINEA
FUE	FUERTEVENTURA, CANARY IS.
FUJ	FUKUE, JAPAN
FUK	FUKUOKA, JAPAN
FUL	FULLERTON, CALIF., USA
FUN	FUNAFUTI, ELLICE IS., S. PACIFIC
FWA	FT. WAYNE, IND., USA
FWL	FAREWELL, ALASKA, USA
FYT	FAYA, CHAD
FYU	FT. YUKON, ALASKA, USA
FYV	FAYETTEVILLE, ARK., USA

G

GAD	GADSDEN, ALA., USA
GAJ	YAMAGATA, HONSHU, JAPAN
GAL	GALENA, ALASKA, USA
GAM	GAMBELL, ALASKA, USA
GAO	GUANTANAMO, CUBA
GAQ	GAO, MALI
GAR	GARAINA, PAPUA NEW GUINEA
GAS	GARISSA, KENYA
GAT	GAP, FRANCE
GAU	GAUHATI, INDIA
GAW	GANGAW, BURMA
GAX	GAMBA, GABON
GBD	GREAT BEND, KAN., USA
GBE	GABORONE, BOTSWANA
GBG	GALESBURG, ILL., USA
GBJ	MARIE GALANTE, FR. ANTILLES
GBV	GIBB RIVER, W. AUSTRALIA
GBZ	GREAT BARRIER IS., NEW ZEALAND
GCC	GILLETTE, WYO., USA
GCI	GUERNSEY, CHANNEL IS., U.K.
GCK	GARDEN CITY, KAN., USA
GCM	GRAND CAYMAN, WEST INDIES
GCN	GRAND CANYON, ARIZ., USA
GDE	GODE, ETHIOPIA
GDL	GUADALAJARA, MEXICO
GDN	GDANSK, POLAND
GDO	GUASDUALITO, VENEZUELA
GDQ	GONDAR, ETHIOPIA
GDT	GRAND TURK, B.W.I.
GDV	GLENDIVE, MONT., USA
GEA	NOUMEA, NEW CAL-MAGENTA ARPT.
GED	GEORGETOWN, DEL., USA
GEG	SPOKANE, WASH., USA
GEL	SANTO ANGELO, BRAZIL
GEO	GEORGETOWN, REP. OF GUYANA
GER	NUEVA GERONA, CUBA
GES	GENERAL SANTOS, PHILIPPINES
GET	GERALDTON, W. AUSTRALIA
GEV	GALLIVARE, SWEDEN
GFF	GRIFFITH, N.S.W., AUSTRALIA
GFK	GRAND FORKS, N.D., USA
GFL	GLENS FALLS, N.Y., USA
GFN	GRAFTON, N.S.W., AUSTRALIA
GFO	BARTICA, REP. OF GUYANA
GFY	GROOTFONTEIN, S. W. AFRICA
GGD	GREGORY DOWNS, QLD., AUSTRALIA
GGG	LONGVIEW, TEXAS, USA
GGR	GAROE, SOMALIA
GGT	GEORGE TOWN, BAHAMAS
GGW	GLASGOW, MONT., USA
GHA	GHARDAIA, ALGERIA
GHB	GOVERNORS HARBOUR, BAHAMAS
GHC	GREAT HARBOUR CAY, BAHAMAS
GHT	GHAT, LIBYA
GHU	GUALEGUAYCHU, ARGENTINA
GIB	GIBRALTAR, GIBRALTAR
GIG	RIO DE JANEIRO, BRA-GALEAO ARPT.
GIS	GISBORNE, NEW ZEALAND
GIZ	GIZAN, SAUDI ARABIA
GJA	GUANAJA IS., HONDURAS
GJM	GUAJARA-MIRIM, BRAZIL
GJT	GRAND JUNCTION, COLO., USA
GKA	GOROKA, PAPUA NEW GUINEA
GKH	GORKHA, NEPAL
GKL	GREAT KEPPEL ISLAND, AUSTRALIA
GKN	GULKANA, ALASKA, USA
GLA	GLASGOW, SCOTLAND
GLD	GOODLAND, KAN., USA
GLF	GOLFITO, COSTA RICA
GLH	GREENVILLE, MISS., USA
GLI	GLEN INNES, N.S.W., AUSTRALIA
GLK	GALCAIO, SOMALIA
GLR	GLENROY, W. AUSTRALIA
GLS	GALVESTON, TEXAS, USA
GLT	GLADSTONE, QLD., AUSTRALIA
GLV	GOLOVIN, ALASKA, USA
GLY	MT. GOLDSWORTHY, W. AUSTRALIA
GMA	GEMENA, ZAIRE
GMB	GAMBELA, ETHIOPIA
GMI	GASMATA, NEW BRITAIN, N. GUI.
GMM	GAMBOMA, CONGO
GNB	GRENOBLE, FRANCE
GND	GRENADA, WINDWARD IS.
GNU	GOODNEWS BAY, ALASKA, USA
GNV	GAINESVILLE, FLA., USA
GNY	GRANBY, COLO., USA
GOA	GENOA, ITALY
GOB	GOBA, ETHIOPIA
GOH	GODTHAB, GREENLAND
GOM	GOMA, ZAIRE
GON	NEW LONDON, CONN., USA
GOO	GOONDIWINDI, QLD., AUSTRALIA
GOR	GORE, ETHIOPIA
GOT	GOTHENBURG, SWEDEN
GOU	GAROUA, CAMEROON
GOV	GOVE, N.T., AUSTRALIA
GOZ	GORNA ORJACHOVICA, BULGARIA
GPI	GUAPI, COLOMBIA
GPT	GULFPORT/BILOXI, MISS., USA
GPZ	GRAND RAPIDS, MINN., USA
GQQ	GALION, OHIO, USA
GRB	GREEN BAY, WIS., USA
GRC	GRAND CESS, LIBERIA
GRD	GREENWOOD, S.C., USA
GRH	GARUAHI, PAPUA NEW GUINEA
GRI	GRAND ISLAND, NEBR., USA
GRJ	GEORGE, SOUTH AFRICA
GRL	GRENAATBOSKOLK, SOUTH AFRICA
GRO	GERONA, SPAIN
GRQ	GRONINGEN, NETHERLANDS
GRR	GRAND RAPIDS, MICH., USA
GRS	GROSSETO, ITALY
GRU	GRAJAU, BRAZIL
GRX	GRANADA, SPAIN
GRZ	GRAZ, AUSTRIA
GSO	GREENSBORO/HIGH POINT, N.C., USA
GSP	GREENVILLE/SPARTANBURG, S.C., USA
GSR	GARDO, SOMALIA
GST	GUSTAVUS, ALASKA, USA
GSU	GEDAREF, SUDAN
GTE	GROOTE IS., N.T., AUSTRALIA
GTF	GREAT FALLS, MONT., USA
GTO	GORONTALO, CELEBES, INDONESIA
GTR	COLUMBUS, MISS., USA
GTT	GEORGETOWN, QLD., AUSTRALIA
GTW	GOTTWALDOV, CZECHOSLOVAKIA
GUA	GUATEMALA CITY, GUATEMALA
GUB	GUERRERO NEGRO, MEXICO
GUC	GUNNISON, COLO., USA
GUD	GOUNDAM, MALI
GUG	GUARI, PAPUA NEW GUINEA
GUI	GUIRIA, VENEZUELA
GUM	GUAM ISLAND, MARIANA IS.
GUP	GALLUP, N.M., USA
GUQ	GUANARE, VENEZUELA
GUR	GURNEY, PAPUA NEW GUINEA
GVA	GENEVA, SWITZERLAND
GVR	GOVERNADOR VALADARES, BRAZIL
GVX	GAVLE, SWEDEN
GWD	GWADAR, PAKISTAN
GWL	GWALIOR, INDIA
GWO	GREENWOOD, MISS., USA
GWT	WESTERLAND, GERMANY
GXF	GHURAF, PEOP. DEM. REP. OF YEMEN
GXQ	COYHAIQUE, CHILE
GXX	YAGOUA, CAMEROON
GYA	GUAYARAMERIN, BOLIVIA
GYE	GUAYAQUIL, ECUADOR
GYM	GUAYMAS, MEXICO
GYN	GOIANIA, BRAZIL
GZO	GIZO, SOLOMON IS.

H

HAC	HACHIJO JIMA ISLAND, JAPAN
HAD	HALMSTAD, SWEDEN
HAJ	HANOVER, GERMANY
HAM	HAMBURG, GERMANY
HAN	HANOI, N. VIETNAM
HAP	HAPPY BAY, QLD., AUSTRALIA
HAQ	* HASKOVO, BULGARIA
HAR	HARRISBURG, PA., USA
HAS	HAIL, SAUDI ARABIA
HAT	HEATHLANDS, QLD., AUSTRALIA
HAU	HAUGESUND, NORWAY
HAV	HAVANA, CUBA
HAZ	HATZFELDTHAFEN, PAPUA NEW GUINEA
HBA	HOBART, TASMANIA
HCA	BIG SPRING, TEXAS, USA
HCQ	HALLS CREEK, W. AUSTRALIA
HCR	HOLY CROSS, ALASKA, USA
HDD	HYDERABAD, PAKISTAN
HDF	HERINGSDORF, GERMAN DEM. REP.
HDM	HAMADAN, IRAN
HDN	STEAMBOAT SPRINGS, COLO., USA
HDY	HAADYAI, THAILAND
HEA	HERAT, AFGHANISTAN
HEH	HEHO, BURMA
HEI	HEIDE/BUESUM, GERMANY
HEL	HELSINKI, FINLAND
HER	HERAKLION, GREECE
HEZ	NATCHEZ, MISS., USA
HFA	HAIFA, ISRAEL
HFD	HARTFORD, CONN-BRAINARD FIELD, USA
HFN	HOFN, ICELAND
HFT	HAMMERFEST, NORWAY
HGA	HARGEISA, SOMALIA
HGD	HUGHENDEN, QLD., AUSTRALIA
HGH	HANGCHOW, CHINA
HGL	HELGOLAND, GERMANY
HGN	MAE HONG SON, THAILAND
HGO	KORHOGO, IVORY COAST
HGR	HAGERSTOWN, MD., USA
HGS	FREETOWN, SIERRA LEONE-HASTINGS ARP.
HGU	MT. HAGEN, PAPUA NEW GUINEA

*—UNOFFICIAL CODE

CITY/AIRPORT CODES Listed Alphabetically by Code

LON	LONDON, ENGLAND
LOS	LAGOS, NIGERIA
LOZ	LONDON, KY., USA
LPA	LAS PALMAS, CANARY IS.
LPB	LA PAZ, BOLIVIA
LPL	LIVERPOOL, ENGLAND
LPM	LAMAP, NEW HEBRIDES
LPP	LAPPEENRANTA, FINLAND
LPT	LAMPANG, THAILAND
LQM	PUERTO LEGUIZAMO, COLOMBIA
LRA	LARISSA, GREECE
LRD	LAREDO, TEXAS, USA
LRE	LONGREACH, QLD. AUSTRALIA
LRH	LA ROCHELLE, FRANCE
LRT	LORIENT, FRANCE
LRU	LAS CRUCES, N.M., USA
LSA	LOSUIA, PAPUA NEW GUINEA
LSE	LA CROSSE, WIS., USA
LSH	LASHIO, BURMA
LSI	LERWICK, SHETLAND IS., SCOTLAND
LSM	LONG SEMADO, SABAH, MALAYSIA
LSP	LAS PIEDRAS, VENEZUELA
LSS	LES SAINTES, GUADELOUPE
LST	LAUNCESTON, TASMANIA
LSU	LONG SUKANG, SARAWAK, MALAYSIA
LTD	GHADAMES, LIBYA
LTL	LASTOURVILLE, GABON
LTM	LETHEM, REP. OF GUYANA
LTN	LUTCN, ENGLAND
LTO	LORETO, MEXICO
LTQ	LE TOUQUET, FRANCE
LUB	LUBANG, PHILIPPINES
LUD	LUDERITZ, SOUTH AFRICA
LUE	LUCENEC, CZECHOSLOVAKIA
LUI	LA UNION, HONDURAS
LUM	MAPUTO, MOZAMBIQUE
LUN	LUSAKA, REP. OF ZAMBIA
LUP	KALAUPAPA, MOLOKAI; HAWAII, USA
LUQ	SAN LUIS, ARGENTINA
LUR	CAPE LISBURNE, ALASKA, USA
LUT	LAURA STATION, QLD., AUSTRALIA
LUU	LAURA, QLD., AUSTRALIA
LUX	LUXEMBOURG, LUXEMBOURG
LVB	LIVRAMENTO, BRAZIL
LVI	LIVINGSTONE, REP. OF ZAMBIA
LVO	LAVERTON, W. AUSTRALIA
LVR	LIVERMORE, CALIF., USA
LWB	GREENBRIER, W. VA., USA
LWC	LAWRENCE, KAN., USA
LWH	LAWN HILL, QLD., AUSTRALIA
LWM	LAWRENCE, MASS., USA
LWO	LWOW, USSR
LWS	LEWISTON, IDAHO, USA
LWT	LEWISTOWN, MONT., USA
LWY	LAWAS, SARAWAK, MALAYSIA
LXR	LUXOR, EGYPT
LXS	LEMNOS, GREECE
LXU	LUKULU, REP. OF ZAMBIA
LXV	LEADVILLE, COLO., USA
LYH	LYNCHBURG, VA., USA
LYP	LYALLPUR, PAKISTAN
LYR	SVALBARD, NORWAY
LYS	LYON, FRANCE
LYU	ELY, MINN., USA
LYX	LYDD, KENT, ENGLAND
LZC	LAZARO CARDENAS, MEXICO
LZR	LIZARD ISLAND, AUSTRALIA

M

MAA	MADRAS, INDIA
MAB	MARABA, BRAZIL
MAD	MADRID, SPAIN
MAF	MIDLAND/ODESSA, TEXAS, USA
MAG	MADANG, PAPUA NEW GUINEA
MAH	MAHON, MINORCA, SPAIN
MAJ	MAJURO, MARSHALL IS.
MAK	MALAKAL, SUDAN
MAM	MATAMOROS, MEXICO
MAN	MANCHESTER, ENGLAND
MAO	MANAUS, BRAZIL
MAP	MAMAI, PAPUA NEW GUINEA
MAR	MARACAIBO, VENEZUELA
MAS	MANUS IS., PAPUA NEW GUINEA
MAT	MATADI, ZAIRE
MAU	MAUPITI, SOCIETY ISLAND
MAW	MALDEN, MO., USA
MAX	MATAM, SENEGAL
MAY	MANGROVE CAY, BAHAMAS
MAZ	MAYAGUEZ, PUERTO RICO
MBA	MOMBASA, KENYA
MBB	MARBLE BAR, W. AUSTRALIA
MBH	MARYBOROUGH, QLD., AUSTRALIA
MBI	MBEYA, TANZANIA
MBJ	MONTEGO BAY, JAMAICA
MBL	MANISTEE, MICH., USA
MBO	MAMBURAO, PHILIPPINES
MBP	MOYOBAMBA, PERU
MBS	SAGINAW, MICH., USA
MBT	MASBATE, PHILIPPINES
MBU	MBAMBANAKIRA, SOLOMON IS.
MBY	MOBERLY, MO., USA
MCE	MERCED, CALIF., USA
MCG	MC GRATH, ALASKA, USA
MCI	KANSAS CITY, MO., USA
MCJ	MAICAO, COLOMBIA
MCK	MC COOK, NEBR., USA
MCN	MACON, GA., USA
MCO	ORLANDO, FLA., USA
MCP	MACAPA, AMAPA, BRAZIL
MCR	MELCHOR DE MENCOS, GUATEMALA
MCT	MUSCAT, OMAN
MCV	MAC ARTHUR RIVER, N.T., AUST.
MCW	MASON CITY, IOWA, USA
MCY	MAROOCHYDORE, QLD., AUSTRALIA
MCZ	MACEIO, ALAGOAS, BRAZIL
MDC	MENADO, INDONESIA
MDE	MEDELLIN, COLOMBIA
MDH	CARBONDALE, ILL., USA
MDK	MBANDAKA, ZAIRE
MDL	MANDALAY, BURMA
MDQ	MAR DEL PLATA, ARGENTINA
MDR	MEDFRA, ALASKA, USA
MDS	MIDDLE CAICOS, WEST INDIES
MDT	HARRISBURG, PA-INTERNATIONAL ARPT.
MDU	MENDI, PAPUA NEW GUINEA
MDW	CHICAGO, ILL-MIDWAY ARPT, USA.
MDX	MERCEDES, CORRIENTES, ARG.
MDZ	MENDOZA, ARGENTINA
MEB	MELBOURNE, VIC., AUST-ESSENDON ARPT.
MED	MEDINA, SAUDI ARABIA
MEE	MARE, LOYALTY IS., PACIFIC OCEAN
MEG	MALANGE, ANGOLA
MEH	MEHAMN, NORWAY
MEI	MERIDIAN, MISS., USA
MEL	MELBOURNE, VIC., AUSTRALIA
MEM	MEMPHIS, TENN., USA
MEO	MANTEO, N.C., USA
MES	MEDAN, SUMATRA, INDONESIA
MET	MORETON, QLD., AUSTRALIA
MEX	MEXICO CITY, MEXICO
MEY	MEGHAULI, NEPAL
MFA	MAFIA IS., TANZANIA
MFD	MANSFIELD, OHIO, USA
MFE	MC ALLEN, TEXAS, USA
MFF	MOANDA, GABON
MFI	MARSHFIELD, WIS., USA
MFQ	MARADI, NIGER
MFR	MEDFORD, ORE., USA
MFS	MIRAFLORES, COLOMBIA
MFU	MFUWE, REP. OF ZAMBIA

S

SLD	SLIAC, CZECHOSLOVAKIA
SLE	SALEM, ORE., USA
SLH	SOLA, NEW HEBRIDES, S. PACIFIC
SLI	SOLWEZI, REP. OF ZAMBIA
SLK	SARANAC LAKE, N.Y., USA
SLL	SALALAH, OMAN
SLN	SALINA, KAN., USA
SLP	SAN LUIS POTOSI, MEXICO
SLQ	SLEETMUTE, ALASKA, USA
SLS	SILISTRA, BULGARIA
SLU	ST. LUCIA, W. INDIES
SLX	SALT CAY, WEST INDIES
SLZ	SAO LUIZ, MARANHAO, BRAZIL
SMA	SANTA MARIA, AZORES
SMF	SACRAMENTO, CALIF., USA
SMI	SAMOS ISLAND, GREECE
SMK	ST. MICHAEL, ALASKA, USA
SML	STELLA MARIS, L.I., BAHAMAS
SMM	SEMPORNA, SABAH, MALAYSIA
SMP	STOCKHOLM, NEW BRITAIN, NEW GUINEA
SMR	SANTA MARTA, COLOMBIA
SMS	ST. MARIE, MALAGASY REP.
SMX	SANTA MARIA, CALIF., USA
SMY	SIMENTI, SENEGAL
SMZ	STOELMANSEILAND, SURINAM
SNA	SANTA ANA, CALIF., USA
SNG	SAN IGNACIO DE VELASCO, BOLIVIA
SNI	SINOE/GREENVILLE, LIBERIA
SNM	SAN IGNACIO DE MOXOS, BOLIVIA
SNN	SHANNON, IRELAND
SNP	ST. PAUL IS., ALASKA, USA
SNQ	SAN QUINTIN, MEXICO
SNU	SANTA CLARA, CUBA
SNV	SANTA ELENA, VENEZUELA
SNW	SANDOWAY, BURMA
SNY	SIDNEY, NEBR., USA
SOC	SOLO, JAVA, INDONESIA
SOF	SOFIA, BULGARIA
SOG	SOGNDAL, NORWAY
SOI	SOUTH MOLLE IS., Q. AUSTRALIA
SOJ	SORKJOSEN, NORWAY
SOM	SAN TOME, VENEZUELA
SON	ESPIRITU SANTO, NEW HEBRIDES
SOP	PINEHURST, N.C., USA
SOQ	SORONG, WEST IRIAN, INDONESIA
SOU	SOUTHAMPTON, ENGLAND
SOY	STRONSAY, SCOT.
SPC	SANTA CRUZ LA PALMA, CANARY IS.
SPE	SEPULOT, SABAH, MALAYSIA
SPI	SPRINGFIELD, ILL., USA
SPK	SAPPORO, JAPAN
SPN	SAIPAN, MARIANA IS.
SPS	WICHITA FALLS, TEXAS, USA
SPU	SPLIT, YUGOSLAVIA
SPW	SPENCER, IOWA, USA
SPY	SAN PEDRO, IVORY COAST
SQI	STERLING/ROCK FALLS, ILL., USA
SQK *	SAND CREEK, REP. OF GUYANA
SRB	SANTA ROSA, BOLIVIA
SRD	SAN RAMON, BOLIVIA
SRE	SUCRE, BOLIVIA
SRF	SAN RAFAEL, CALIF., USA
SRG	SEMARANG, JAVA, INDONESIA
SRH	SARH, CHAD
SRJ	SAN BORJA, BOLIVIA
SRL	SANTA ROSALIA, MEXICO
SRQ	SARASOTA/BRADENTON, FLA., USA
SRV	STONY RIVER, ALASKA, USA
SRZ	SANTA CRUZ, BOLIVIA
SSA	SALVADOR, BRAZIL
SSG	MALABO, EQUAT'L GUINEA
SSI	ST. SIMONS ISLAND, GA., USA
SSJ	SANDNESSJOEN, NORWAY
SSM	SAULT STE. MARIE, MICH., USA
SSO	SAO SIMAO, BRAZIL
SSX	SAMSUN, TURKEY
STA	STAUNING, DENMARK
STB	SANTA BARBARA, ZULIA, VENEZUELA
STE	STEVENS POINT, WIS., USA
STI *	SANTIAGO, DOMINICAN REP.
STL	ST. LOUIS, MO., USA
STM	SANTAREM, BRAZIL
STN	STANSTED, ENGLAND
STO	STOCKHOLM, SWEDEN
STP	MINNEAPOLIS/ST PAUL, MINN-DOWNTOWN
STR	STUTTGART, GERMANY
STS	SANTA ROSA, CALIF., USA
STT	ST. THOMAS, VIRGIN IS.
STW	STAVROPOL, USSR
STX	ST. CROIX, VIRGIN IS.
STY	SALTO, URUGUAY
STZ	SANTA TEREZINHA, BRAZIL
SUB	SURABAYA, JAVA, INDONESIA
SUE	STURGEON BAY, WIS., USA
SUG	SURIGAO, PHILIPPINES
SUI	SUKHUMI, USSR
SUJ	SATU MARE, ROMANIA
SUL	SUI, PAKISTAN
SUN	SUN VALLEY, IDAHO, USA
SUV	SUVA, FIJI IS.
SUX	SIOUX CITY, IOWA, USA
SVA	SAVOONGA, ALASKA, USA
SVB	SAMBAVA, MALAGASY REP.
SVC	SILVER CITY, N.M., USA
SVD	ST. VINCENT, WINDWARD IS.
SVG	STAVANGER, NORWAY
SVI	SAN VINCENTE DEL CAGUAN, COLOMBIA
SVJ	SVOLVAER, NORWAY
SVL	SAVONLINNA, FINLAND
SVO	MOSCOW, USSR-SHEREMETYEVO ARPT
SVQ	SEVILLE, SPAIN
SVS	STEVENS VILLAGE, ALASKA, USA
SVU	SAVUSAVU, FIJI IS.
SVV	SAN SALVADOR DE PAUL, VENEZUELA
SVW	SPARREVOHN, ALASKA, USA
SVZ	SAN ANTONIO, VENEZUELA
SWA	SWATOW, CHINA
SWD	SEWARD, ALASKA, USA
SWH	SWAN HILL, VIC., AUSTRALIA
SWS	SWANSEA, WALES
SXB	STRASBOURG, FRANCE
SXF	BERLIN, GER. DEM. REP.
SXG	SENANGA, REP. OF ZAMBIA
SXM	ST. MARTIN, NETH. ANTILLES
SXP	SHELDON POINT, ALASKA, USA
SXR	SRINAGAR, INDIA
SXU	SODDU, ETHIOPIA
SYA	SHEMYA IS., ALASKA, USA
SYD	SYDNEY, N.S.W., AUSTRALIA
SYR	SYRACUSE, N.Y., USA
SYY	STORNOWAY, SCOTLAND
SYZ	SHIRAZ, IRAN
SZC	SANTA CRUZ, COSTA RICA
SZG	SALZBURG, AUSTRIA
SZK	SKUKUZA, SOUTH AFRICA
SZR	STARA-ZAGORA, BULGARIA
SZS	STEWART ISLAND, NEW ZEALAND
SZZ	SZCZECIN, POLAND

T

TAB	TOBAGO, TRINIDAD AND TOBAGO
TAC	TACLOBAN, PHILIPPINES
TAE	TAEGU, REP. OF KOREA
TAG	TAGBILARAN, PHILIPPINES
TAH	TANNA ISLAND, NEW HEBRIDES
TAI	TAIZ, YEMEN
TAK	TAKAMATSU, JAPAN
TAL	TANANA, ALASKA, USA
TAM	TAMPICO, MEXICO
TAP	TAPACHULA, MEXICO
TAQ	TARCOOLA, S. AUSTRALIA
TAS	TASHKENT, USSR
TAT	TATRY/POPRAD, CZECHOSLOVAKIA
TBF	TABITEUEA, TARAWA, GILBERT IS.
TBG	TABUBIL, PAPUA NEW GUINEA
TBL	TABLELAND, W. AUSTRALIA
TBN	FT. LEONARD WOOD, MO., USA
TBO	TABORA, TANZANIA
TBP	TUMBES, PERU
TBS	TBILISI, USSR
TBU	TONGATAPU, S. PACIFIC
TBZ	TABRIZ, IRAN
TCA	TENNANT CREEK, N.T., AUSTRALIA
TCB	TREASURE CAY, BAHAMAS
TCE	TULCEA, ROMANIA
TCF	TOCOA, HONDURAS
TCH	TCHIBANGA, GABON
TCI	TENERIFE, CANARY IS.
TCL	TUSCALOOSA, ALA., USA
TCN	TEHUACAN, MEXICO
TCO	TUMACO, COLOMBIA
TCQ	TACNA, PERU
TCT	TAKOTNA, ALASKA, USA
TDA	TRINIDAD, COLOMBIA
TDD	TRINIDAD, BOLIVIA
TDG	TANDAG, PHILIPPINES
TEB	TETERBORO, N.J., USA
TED	THISTED, DENMARK
TEO	TERAPO, PAPUA NEW GUINEA
TER	TERCEIRA, AZORES
TET	TETE, MOZAMBIQUE
TEU	TE ANAU, NEW ZEALAND
TEY	THINGEYRI, ICELAND
TEZ	TEZPUR, INDIA
TFF	TEFE, BRAZIL
TFI	TUFI, PAPUA NEW GUINEA
TGD	TITOGRAD, YUGOSLAVIA
TGG	KUALA TRENGGANU, MALAYSIA
TGH	TONGOA, NEW HEBRIDES
TGI	TINGO MARIA, PERU
TGJ	TIGA, LOYALTY IS.
TGM	TIRGU MURES, ROMANIA
TGR	TOUGGOURT, ALGERIA
TGT	TANGA, TANZANIA
TGU	TEGUCIGALPA, HONDURAS
TGV	TARGOVISHTE, BULGARIA
TGZ	TUXTLA GUTIERREZ, MEXICO
THC	TCHIEN, LIBERIA
THE	TERESINA, PIAUI, BRAZIL
THI	TICHITT, MAURITANIA
THL	TACHILEK, BURMA
THR	TEHRAN, IRAN
THT	TAMCHACKETT, MAURITANIA
THZ	TAHOUA, NIGER
TIA	TIRANA, ALBANIA
TIE	TIPPI, ETHIOPIA
TIF	TAIF, SAUDI ARABIA
TIJ	TIJUANA, MEXICO
TIP	TRIPOLI, LIBYA
TIQ	TINIAN, MARIANA ISLAND
TIR	TIRUPATI, INDIA
TIS	THURSDAY IS., QLD., AUSTRALIA
TIU	TIMARU, NEW ZEALAND
TIV	TIVAT, YUGOSLAVIA
TIY	TIDJIKJA, MAURITANIA
TIZ	TARI, PAPUA NEW GUINEA
TJA	TARIJA, BOLIVIA
TJI	TRUJILLO, HONDURAS
TJQ	TANJUNG APANDAN, INDONESIA
TKC	TIKO, CAMEROON
TKG	TELUKBETUNG, SUMATRA, INDONESIA
TKJ	TOK, ALASKA, USA
TKK	TRUK, CAROLINE IS., PAC. OCEAN
TKM	TIKAL, GUATEMALA
TKN	TOKUNO SHIMA, JAPAN
TKP	TAKAPOTO, TUAMOTU IS. S. PAC. OC.
TKQ	KIGOMA, TANZANIA
TKR	THAKURGAON, BANGLADESH
TKS	TOKUSHIMA, JAPAN
TKU	TURKU, FINLAND
TLA *	TELLER, ALASKA, USA
TLE	TULEAR, MALAGASY REP.
TLH	TALLAHASSEE, FLA., USA
TLL	TALLINN, USSR
TLN	TOULON/HYERES, FRANCE
TLO	TOL, NEW BRITAIN, NEW GUINEA
TLS	TOULOUSE, FRANCE
TLT	TULUKSAK, ALASKA, USA
TLV	TEL AVIV-YAFO, ISRAEL
TLW	TALASEA, NEW BRITAIN, N. GUI.
TME	TAME, COLOMBIA
TMG	TOMANGGONG, MALAYSIA
TMI	TUMLINGTAR, NEPAL
TML	TAMALE, GHANA
TMM	TAMATAVE, MALAGASY REP.
TMO	TUMEREMO, VENEZUELA
TMP	TAMPERE, FINLAND
TMR	TAMANRASSET, ALGERIA
TMS	SAO TOME IS., GULF OF GUINEA
TMT *	TEMORA, N.S.W., AUSTRALIA
TMW	TAMWORTH, N.S.W., AUSTRALIA
TMX	TIMIMOUN, ALGERIA
TNA	TSINAN, CHINA
TNC	TIN CITY, ALASKA, USA
TNE	TANEGASHIMA, JAPAN
TNG	TANGIER, MOROCCO
TNJ	TANJUNG PINANG, BINTAN, INDONESIA
TNK	TUNUNAK, ALASKA, USA
TNN	TAINAN, TAIWAN
TNR	TANANARIVE, MALAGASY REP.
TOB	TOBRUK, LIBYA
TOG	TOGIAK, ALASKA, USA
TOL	TOLEDO, OHIO, USA
TOM	TOMBOUCTOU, MALI
TOP	TOPEKA, KAN., USA
TOS	TROMSO, NORWAY
TOU	TOUHO, NEW CALEDONIA
TOY	TOYAMA, JAPAN
TPA	TAMPA, FLA., USA.
TPE	TAIPEI, TAIWAN
TPI	TAPINI, PAPUA NEW GUINEA
TPJ *	KINGSTON, JAMAICA-TINSON PEN
TPL	TEMPLE, TEXAS, USA
TPP	TARAPOTO, PERU
TPR	TOM PRICE, W. AUSTRALIA
TPS	TRAPANI, ITALY
TQS	TRES ESQUINAS, COLOMBIA
TRA	TARAMAJIMA, JAPAN
TRB	TURBO, COLOMBIA
TRC	TORREON, MEXICO
TRD	TRONDHEIM, NORWAY
TRE	TIREE ISLAND, SCOTLAND
TRG	TAURANGA, NEW ZEALAND
TRI	TRI-CITY AIRPORT, TENN., USA
TRK	TARAKAN, BORNEO, INDONESIA
TRN	TURIN, ITALY
TRO	TAREE, N.S.W., AUSTRALIA
TRR	TRINCOMALEE, REP. OF SRI LANKA
TRS	TRIESTE, ITALY
TRT	TREMONTON, UTAH, USA
TRU	TRUJILLO, PERU
TRV	TRIVANDRUM, INDIA
TRW	TARAWA, GILBERT IS., S. PACIFIC
TRY	TREVISO, ITALY
TRZ	TRICHINOPOLY, INDIA
TSH	TSHIKAPA, ZAIRE
TSJ	TSUSHIMA, JAPAN
TSK	TASKUL, NEW IRELAND, NEW GUINEA
TSM	TAOS, N.M., USA
TSR	TIMISOARA, ROMANIA
TST	TRANG, THAILAND
TSV	TOWNSVILLE, QLD., AUSTRALIA

Y

YMM	FT. MCMURRAY, ALTA., CANADA
YMO	MOOSONEE, ONTARIO, CANADA
YMS	YURIMAGUAS, PERU
YMX	MONTREAL, QUE.-MIRABEL INT'L. ARPT.
YNA	NATASHQUAN, QUE., CANADA
YNC	PAINT HILLS, QUE., CANADA
YND	YANDINA, SOLOMON IS.
YNE	NORWAY HOUSE, MAN., CANADA
YNG	YOUNGSTOWN, OHIO, USA
YNM	MATAGAMI, QUEBEC, CANADA
YOJ	HIGH LEVEL, ALBERTA, CANADA
YOL	YOLA, NIGERIA
YOP	RAINBOW LAKE, ALTA., CANADA
YOW	OTTAWA, ONTARIO, CANADA
YPA	PRINCE ALBERT, SASK., CANADA
YPE	PEACE RIVER, ALTA., CANADA
YPH	PORT HARRISON, QUE., CANADA
YPL	PICKLE LAKE, ONT., CANADA
YPQ	PETERBOROUGH, ONT., CANADA
YPR	PRINCE RUPERT, B.C., CANADA
YPW	POWELL RIVER, B.C., CANADA
YPX	POVUNGNITUK, QUEBEC, CANADA
YPY	FT. CHIPEWYAN, ALTA., CANADA
YQB	QUEBEC, QUE., CANADA
YQD	THE PAS, MAN., CANADA
YQF	RED DEER, ALTA., CANADA
YQG	WINDSOR, ONT., CANADA
YQH	WATSON LAKE, Y.T., CANADA
YQI	YARMOUTH, N.S., CANADA
YQK	KENORA, ONT., CANADA
YQL	LETHBRIDGE, ALTA., CANADA
YQM	MONCTON, N.B., CANADA
YQQ	COMOX, B.C., CANADA
YQR	REGINA, SASK., CANADA
YQT	THUNDER BAY, ONT., CANADA
YQU	GRANDE PRAIRIE, ALBERTA, CANADA
YQX	GANDER, NFLD., CANADA
YQY	SYDNEY, N.S., CANADA
YQZ	QUESNEL, B.C., CANADA
YRB	RESOLUTE, N.W.T., CANADA
YRL	RED LAKE, ONT., CANADA
YRT	RANKIN INLET, N.W.T., CANADA
YSB	SUDBURY, ONT., CANADA
YSF	STONEY RAPIDS, SASK., CANADA
YSJ	SAINT JOHN, N.B., CANADA
YSM	FT. SMITH, N.W.T., CANADA
YTA	PEMBROKE, ONT., CANADA
YTH	THOMPSON, MAN., CANADA
YTN	RIVIERE AU TONNERRE, QUE., CAN.
YTS	TIMMINS, ONT., CANADA
YUB	TUKTOYAKTUK, N.W.T., CANADA
YUL	MONTREAL, QUE., CANADA
YUM	YUMA, ARIZ., USA
YUX	HALL BEACH, N.W.T., CANADA
YUY	ROUYN - NORANDA, QUE., CANADA
YVA	MORONI, COMORO IS.
YVC	LAC LA RONGE, SASK., CANADA
YVO	VAL D'OR, QUE., CANADA
YVP	FT. CHIMO, QUE., CANADA
YVQ	NORMAN WELLS, N.W.T., CANADA
YVR	VANCOUVER, B.C., CANADA
YVT	BUFFALO NARROWS, SASK., CANADA
YWG	WINNIPEG, MAN., CANADA
YWH *	WHALEHEAD, QUE., CANADA
YWJ	FORT FRANKLIN, N.W.T., CANADA
YWK	WABUSH, NFLD., CANADA
YWL	WILLIAMS LAKE, B.C., CANADA
YWN	WINISK, ONTARIO, CANADA
YWY	WRIGLEY, N.W.T., CANADA
YXC	CRANBROOK, B.C., CANADA
YXD	EDMONTON, ALTA., CANADA
YXE	SASKATOON, SASK., CANADA
YXH	MEDICINE HAT, ALTA., CANADA
YXJ	FT. ST. JOHN, B.C., CANADA
YXK	RIMOUSKI, QUE., CANADA
YXL	SIOUX LOOKOUT, ONT., CANADA
YXR	EARLTON, ONT., CANADA
YXS	PRINCE GEORGE, B.C., CANADA
YXT	TERRACE, B.C., CANADA
YXU	LONDON, ONT., CANADA
YXY	WHITEHORSE, Y.T., CANADA
YXZ	WAWA, ONTARIO, CANADA
YYB	NORTH BAY, ONT., CANADA
YYC	CALGARY, ALTA., CANADA
YYD	SMITHERS, B.C., CANADA
YYE	FT. NELSON, B.C., CANADA
YYF	PENTICTON, B.C., CANADA
YYG	CHARLOTTETOWN, P.E.I., CANADA
YYJ	VICTORIA, B.C., CANADA
YYL	LYNN LAKE, MAN., CANADA
YYQ	CHURCHILL, MAN., CANADA
YYR	GOOSE BAY, NFLD., CANADA
YYT	ST. JOHNS, NFLD., CANADA
YYU	KAPUSKASING, ONT., CANADA
YYY	MONT JOLI, QUE., CANADA
YYZ	TORONTO, ONT., CANADA
YZF	YELLOWKNIFE, N.W.T., CANADA
YZH	SLAVE LAKE, ALTA., CANADA
YZP	SANDSPIT, B.C., CANADA
YZR	SARNIA, ONT., CANADA
YZS	CORAL HARBOUR, N.W.T., CANADA
YZT	PORT HARDY, B.C., CANADA
YZV	SEVEN ISLANDS, QUE., CANADA

Z

ZAA	ALICE ARM, B.C., CANADA
ZAD	ZADAR, YUGOSLAVIA
ZAG	ZAGREB, YUGOSLAVIA
ZAH	ZAHEDAN, IRAN
ZAM	ZAMBOANGA, PHILIPPINES
ZAZ	ZARAGOZA, SPAIN
ZBO	BOWEN, QLD., AUSTRALIA
ZEL	BELLA BELLA, B.C., CANADA
ZEM	EAST MAIN, QUEBEC, CANADA
ZFB	OLD FORT BAY, QUE., CANADA
ZFM	FT. MCPHERSON, N.W.T., CANADA
ZFN	FT. NORMAN, N.W.T., CANADA
ZGF	GRAND FORKS, B.C., CANADA
ZGI	GODS RIVER, MAN., CANADA
ZGM	NGOMA, REP. OF ZAMBIA
ZGS	GETHSEMANI, QUE., CANADA
ZIG	ZIGUINCHOR, SENEGAL
ZIH	ZIHUATANEJO, MEXICO
ZKB	KASABA BAY, REP. OF ZAMBIA
ZKG	KEGASKA, QUE., CANADA
ZLO	MANZANILLO, MEXICO
ZLT	LA TABATIERE, QUE., CANADA
ZMT	MASSET, B.C., CANADA
ZND	ZINDER, NIGER
ZNE	NEWMAN, W. AUSTRALIA
ZNU	NAMU, B.C., CANADA
ZNZ	ZANZIBAR, TANZANIA
ZOF	OCEAN FALLS, B.C., CANADA
ZQN	QUEENSTOWN, NEW ZEALAND
ZQS	QUEEN CHARLOTTE, B.C., CANADA
ZRH	ZURICH, SWITZERLAND
ZRR	ARCTIC RED RIVER, N.W.T., CANADA
ZSA	SAN SALVADOR, BAHAMAS
ZSP	ST. PAUL, QUE., CANADA
ZSS	SASSANDRA, IVORY COAST
ZST	STEWART, B.C., CANADA
ZTH	ZAKINTHOS, GREECE
ZTS	TAHSIS, B.C., CANADA
ZUM	CHURCHILL FALLS, NFLD., CANADA
ZVA	MIANDRIVAZO, MALAGASY REP.
ZWA	ANDAPA, MALAGASY REP.
ZWL	WOLLASTON LAKE, SASK., CANADA
ZYL	SYLHET, BANGLADESH
ZZU	MZUZU, MALAWI

*—UNOFFICIAL CODE

FLIGHT ITINERARIES

(Flights with Intermediate Stops Only) Numbers following itinerary indicate day/s of the week flight departs origin airport.

FLIGHT

RK—AIR AFRIQUE

102 DKR ABJ COO
103 COO ABJ DKR
121 LBV DLA COO ABJ ROB DKR
122 DKR ROB ABJ COO DLA LBV
157 NDJ BGF FIH
158 FIH BGF NDJ
300 DKR BKO BOY OUA NIM
301 NIM OUA BOY DKR
302 DKR BOY OUA NIM
303 NIM OUA BOY BKO DKR
465 LBV POG PNR
474 PNR POG LBV
500 ABJ LFW LOS DLA
502 DKR BKO ABJ
503 COO LFW ABJ BKO DKR
504 DKR OUA ABJ LFW COO
505 ABJ FNA CKY DKR
506 DKR CKY FNA ABJ
510 ABJ ACC COO
511 DLA LOS LFW ACC ABJ
512 ABJ LFW COO
513 COO LFW ABJ
515 COO LFW ACC ABJ
516 ABJ ACC LFW COO
517 COO LFW ACC ABJ
519 BZV LBV LFW ABJ
520 ABJ LFW LOS LBV BZV
522 ABJ COO LBV BZV
523 BZV LBV LOS COO ABJ
641 LFW POG LBV

RN—ROYAL AIR INTER

212 AGA RAK CAS
213 CAS RAK AGA
215 CAS RAK AGA
216 AGA RAK CAS
217 CAS RAK AGA
218 AGA RAK CAS
219 CAS RAK AGA
220 AGA RAK CAS
221 CAS RAK AGA
236 OZZ RAK CAS
237 CAS RAK OZZ
242 CAS RBA TTU.AHU
245 GIB TTU RBA CAS
248 CAS RBA FEZ OUD ORN
249 ORN OUD FEZ RBA CAS
260 CAS FEZ TNG GIB
267 GIB TNG FEZ CAS
272 AGA RAK CAS
290 OZZ AGA RAK CAS
291 CAS RAK AGA OZZ
292 OZZ AGA RAK CAS
293 CAS RAK AGA OZZ
295 CAS RAK AGA TTA
296 TTA AGA RAK CAS
297 CAS AGA TTA
298 TTA AGA CAS
840 CMN FEZ OUD ORN
841 ORN OUD FEZ CMN
880 AGA RAK CMN
883 CMN RAK AGA
885 CMN RAK AGA
886 AGA RAK CMN
888 AGA RAK CMN
889 CMN RAK AGA

RO—TAROM—ROMANIAN AIR TRANSPORT

1 BBU BCM IAS
2 IAS BCM BBU
3 BBU BCM IAS
4 IAS BCM BBU
201 BUH SXF CPH
202 CPH SXF BUH
203 BUH SOF ATH
204 ATH SOF BUH
205 BUH BRU LHR
206 LHR BRU BUH
209 BUH VIE AMS
210 AMS VIE BUH
223 BUH ZRH ALG
224 ALG ZRH BUH
225 BUH BUD WAW
226 WAW BUD BUH
237 BUH ZRH MAD
238 MAD ZRH BUH
241 BUH ATH CAI
242 CAI ATH BUH
253 BUH DAM KWI
254 KWI DAM BUH
301 BUH AMS JFK
302 JFK AMS BUH
311 BUH ATH KHI PEK
312 PEK KHI ATH BUH

RS—AEROPESCA

212 PSO PPN BOG
213 BOG PPN PSO
214 BOG EJA CUC BAQ CUC MDE
215 MDE CUC BAQ CUC EJA BOG
216 MDE CUC BAQ
217 BAQ CUC MDE

SA—SOUTH AFRICAN AIRWAYS

102 JNB GBE FRW
103 FRW GBE JNB
104 JNB GBE FRW
105 FRW GBE JNB
121 JNB MTS DUR
122 DUR MTS JNB
192 JNB DUR RUN MRU
193 MRU RUN DUR JNB
205 JNB GIG JFK
206 JFK GIG JNB
207 JNB SID JFK
208 JFK SID JNB
209 JNB SID JFK
210 JFK SID JNB
220 JNB SID LIS FCO ATH 3
DIS AFT APR10
220 JNB LIS FCO ATH 3
MAY 1 - MAY29
221 ATH FCO LIS JNB

CONT. NEXT COLUMN

FLIGHT

SA—SOUTH AFRICAN AIRWAYS

222 JNB SID LIS FCO ATH 6
DIS AFT APR 9
222 JNB LIS FCO ATH 6
MAY 1 - MAY28
223 ATH FCO LIS JNB
224 JNB SAY SID LHR
225 LHR LPA SAY JNB
226 JNB SID LHR
227 LHR LPA JNB
228 JNB SAY SID LHR
229 LHR LPA SAY JNB
230 JNB SID ORY LHR
231 LHR ORY LPA JNB 5
DIS AFT APR 9
231 LHR ORY JNB 5
AUG 1 - SEP25
232 JNB SID LHR 5
DIS AFT JUL31
232 JNB UTN LHR 5
EFF AUG 1
233 LHR MAD LPA JNB 6
DIS AFT APR 9
233 LHR MAD JNB 6
EFF AUG 1
234 JNB SID ORY LHR
236 JNB SID LHR
237 LHR ORY LPA JNB 7
DIS AFT APR 9
237 LHR ORY JNB 7
AUG 1 - SEP25
238 JNB WDH SID ZRH FRA 2
DIS AFT JUL31
238 JNB WDH ZRH FRA 2
EFF AUG 1
239 FRA ZRH LIS WDH JNB 3
DIS AFT JUL31
239 FRA ZRH WDH JNB 3
EFF AUG 1
241 SYD PER MRU JNB
242 JNB MRU PER SYD
246 JNB SEZ HKG
247 HKG SEZ JNB
250 JNB WDH SID ZRH FRA 5
DIS AFT JUL31
250 JNB WDH ZRH FRA 5
EFF AUG 1
251 FRA ZRH LIS WDH JNB 6
DIS AFT JUL31
251 FRA ZRH WDH JNB 6
EFF AUG 1
254 JNB SID FRA AMS
255 AMS FRA LIS JNB 7
DIS AFT JUL31
255 AMS FRA JNB 7
EFF AUG 1
256 JNB SID FRA AMS
257 AMS FRA LIS JNB 5
DIS AFT JUL31
257 AMS FRA JNB 5
EFF AUG 1
258 JNB SID MAD LHR
264 JNB LBV MAD BRU LUX
265 LUX BRU MAD LBV JNB
301 JNB BFN CPT
302 CPT BFN JNB
303 JNB KIM CPT
304 CPT KIM JNB
308 CPT BFN JNB
309 JNB KIM CPT
312 CPT KIM JNB
314 CPT BFN JNB
315 JNB BFN CPT
317 JNB KIM CPT
318 CPT BFN JNB
325 JNB BFN CPT
326 CPT BFN JNB
327 JNB KIM CPT
332 CPT KIM JNB
337 JNB BFN CPT
338 CPT KIM JNB
339 JNB KIM CPT
341 JNB BFN CPT
346 CPT BFN JNB
400 PLZ ELS JNB
402 PLZ ELS BFN JNB
403 JNB ELS PLZ
404 PLZ ELS KIM JNB
405 JNB ELS PLZ
408 PLZ ELS JNB
409 JNB KIM ELS PLZ
410 PLZ ELS BFN JNB
411 JNB BFN ELS PLZ
412 PLZ ELS KIM JNB
414 PLZ ELS JNB
415 JNB KIM ELS PLZ
417 JNB BFN ELS PLZ
418 PLZ ELS JNB
419 JNB ELS PLZ
421 JNB ELS PLZ
423 JNB ELS PLZ
424 PLZ ELS JNB
425 JNB ELS PLZ
426 PLZ ELS BFN JNB
428 PLZ ELS JNB
429 JNB ELS PLZ
436 PLZ ELS BFN JNB
442 PLZ ELS JNB
600 CPT PLZ ELS DUR
601 DUR ELS PLZ CPT
602 CPT ELS DUR
604 CPT PLZ DUR
605 DUR ELS PLZ CPT
606 CPT PLZ ELS DUR
607 DUR PLZ CPT
608 CPT ELS DUR
609 DUR PLZ CPT
610 CPT PLZ DUR
611 DUR ELS CPT
612 CPT PLZ DUR
613 DUR ELS CPT
615 DUR PLZ CPT
616 CPT ELS DUR
618 CPT ELS DUR
650 CPT OUH.GRJ PBZ PLZ
651 PLZ PBZ GRJ OUH CPT
701 JNB UTN WDH
702 WDH UTN JNB
709 JNB UTN WDH

CONT. NEXT COLUMN

FLIGHT

SA—SOUTH AFRICAN AIRWAYS

710 WDH UTN JNB
713 JNB UTN WDH
714 WDH UTN JNB
716 WDH UTN JNB
741 JNB KIM UTN KMP WDH
742 WDH KMP UTN BFN JNB
743 JNB BFN UTN KMP WDH
744 WDH KMP UTN KIM JNB
746 WDH KMP UTN BFN JNB
760 WDH UTN CPT
761 CPT KMP WDH
762 WDH UTN CPT
763 CPT UTN WDH
765 CPT UTN WDH
766 WDH KMP CPT

SC—CRUZEIRO

200 CGH GIG BSB MAO
201 MAO BSB GIG CGH
210 GIG CGH CGB MAO
211 MAO CGB CGH GIG
214 GIG CGH CGR CGB PVH MAO
215 MAO PVH CGB CGR CGH GIG
220 BEL STM MAO
222 BEL STM MAO
223 MAO STM BEL
230 GIG CGH CGR CGB
231 CGB CGR CGH GIG
240 MAO TFF CZS
241 CZS TFF MAO
300 GIG SSA REC FOR SLZ BEL MAO
301 MAO BEL SLZ FOR REC SSA GIG
432 GIG BHZ BSB
433 BSB BHZ GIG
434 GIG BHZ BSB
435 BSB BHZ GIG
436 GIG BHZ BSB
437 BSB BHZ GIG
614 GIG CGH POA EZE
615 EZE POA CGH GIG
616 GIG CGH EZE
617 EZE CGH GIG
618 GIG CGH POA MVD
619 MVD POA CGH GIG
620 CGH IGU EZE
621 EZE IGU CGH GIG
622 GIG IGU EZE
623 EZE IGU GIG
640 GIG CGH SRZ LPB
641 LPB SRZ CGH GIG
670 MAO LET IQT
671 IQT LET MAO
672 MAO LET IQT
673 IQT LET MAO
680 BEL CAY PBM
681 PBM CAY BEL

SD—SUDAN AIRWAYS

102 KRT CAI BEY
103 BEY CAI KRT
110 KRT CAI TIP
111 TIP CAI KRT
112 KRT CAI FCO LHR
113 LHR FCO CAI KRT
116 KRT ATH FCO LHR
117 LHR FCO ATH KRT
118 KRT FCO FRA LHR
119 LHR FRA FCO KRT
120 KRT FCO LHR
121 LHR FCO KRT
124 KRT ATB MWE DOG
125 DOG MWE ATB KRT
126 KRT ATB DDD
127 DDD ATB KRT
128 KRT CAI FRA LHR
129 LHR FRA CAI KRT
130 KRT ATB MWE DDD
131 DDD MWE ATB KRT
214 KRT PZU JED
215 JED PZU KRT
216 KRT ATB PZU
217 PZU ATB KRT
224 KRT JED AUH
225 AUH JED KRT
226 KRT JED BAH
227 BAH JED KRT
302 KRT MAK JUB
303 JUB MAK KRT
308 KRT JUB EBB
309 EBB JUB KRT
312 KRT WUU JUB
313 JUB WUU KRT
322 KRT MAK WUU
323 WUU MAK KRT
408 KRT EBD ELF
409 ELF EBD KRT
412 KRT ELF UYL EGN
413 EGN UYL ELF KRT
414 KRT UYL EGN
415 EGN UYL ELF KRT

SH—SAHSA

50 SAP LCE RTB
51 RTB LCE SAP
52 SAP LCE UII RTB GJA
53 GJA RTB UII LCE SAP
108 LCE OAN TCF
414 SJO MGA TGU SAP BZE MSY
415 MSY BZE SAP TGU MGA SJO
416 PTY SJO MGA TGU SAP BZE MSY
417 MSY BZE SAP TGU MGA SJO PTY
52A SAP LCE UII RTB GJA
602 TGU AHS BHG PEU
603 PEU BHG AHS TGU
900 PTY ADZ TGU
901 TGU ADZ PTY
903 TGU ADZ PTY

SK—SAS—SCANDINAVIAN AIRLINES

101 KRN LLA ARN
104 ARN LLA KRN
107 KRN LLA ARN
112 ARN LLA KRN

CONT. NEXT COLUMN

FLIGHT

SK—SAS—SCANDINAVIAN AIRLINES

341 TOS EVE BOO OSL
342 OSL TRD BOO EVE TOS
343 TOS ANX BOO OSL
344 OSL TRD BOO EVE BDU
345 BDU EVE BOO TRD OSL
347 EVE TRD OSL
348 OSL TRD BOO ANX TOS X67
348 OSL TRD BOO TOS 67
350 OSL TOS ALF
351 ALF TOS BDU BOO TRD OSL
352 OSL TOS ALF KKN
353 KKN LKL ALF TOS EVE OSL
354 OSL EVE TOS ALF LKL KKN
355 KKN LKL ALF TOS EVE BOO OSL
357 ALF TOS OSL
358 OSL BOO BDU TOS ALF
392 EVE ANX BDU TOS
393 TOS BDU ANX EVE
443 NRK JKG CPH
444 CPH JKG NRK
445 NRK JKG CPH
448 CPH JKG NRK
462 CPH GOT OSL
463 OSL GOT CPH
464 CPH GOT OSL
465 OSL GOT CPH
468 CPH GOT OSL
469 OSL GOT CPH
470 CPH AAL KRS
472 CPH SVG BGO
473 BGO KRS CPH
474 CPH SVG BGO
475 BGO SVG CPH
476 CPH KRS BGO
477 BGO SVG CPH
479 KRS AAL CPH
513 OSL SVG LHR
514 LHR SVG OSL
515 BGO SVG LHR
516 LHR SVG BGO
517 BGO SVG LHR
518 LHR SVG BGO
520 LHR BGO OSL
531 CPH SVG GLA
532 GLA SVG CPH
537 CPH MAN DUB
538 DUB MAN CPH
541 OSL CPH BRU
542 BRU CPH OSL
545 OSL SVG AMS
546 AMS SVG OSL
551 GOT CPH AMS
553 ARN CPH AMS
554 AMS CPH ARN
557 ARN CPH BRU
558 BRU CPH ARN
568 CDG CPH OSL
569 OSL CPH CDG
581 ARN CPH MAD
582 MAD CPH ARN
585 CPH NCE LIS
586 LIS NCE CPH
591 CPH BGO KEF
592 KEF BGO CPH
601 OSL CPH ZRH
602 ZRH CPH OSL
603 ARN CPH ZRH
607 ARN CPH BSL GVA
608 GVA BSL CPH ARN
611 OSL CPH DUS
632 FRA CPH OSL
635 OSL CPH FRA MUC
636 MUC FRA CPH ARN
642 HAM CPH ARN
643 OSL GOT CPH HAM
644 HAM CPH GOT
647 OSL CPH HAM
648 HAM CPH OSL
681 OSL CPH FCO
682 FCO CPH ARN
685 ARN CPH LIN
686 LIN CPH ARN
711 CPH KEF UAK
712 UAK KEF CPH
734 CPH ARN HEL
735 HEL ARN OSL
738 OSL ARN HEL
739 HEL ARN CPH
762 CPH ARN LED
763 LED ARN CPH
768 CPH ARN SVO
769 SVO ARN CPH
783 CPH PRG BUD
784 BUD PRG CPH
785 CPH PRG BUD
786 BUD PRG CPH
791 CPH ZAG BEG
792 BEG ZAG CPH
821 CPH BEG IST
822 IST BEG CPH
823 CPH BUH IST
824 IST BUH CPH
831 OSL CPH ATH BEY
832 BEY ATH CPH
861 OSL CPH ATH BEY BGW
862 BGW DAM BEY ATH CPH
871 OSL CPH ATH BEY CAI
872 CAI BEY ATH CPH
873 CPH ATH CAI
874 CAI ATH CPH
911 ARN CPH JFK
912 JFK CPH ARN
914 JFK BGO CPH
915 CPH BGO JFK
918 JFK SVG CPH
933 CPH SEA LAX
934 LAX SEA CPH
941 CPH YMX ORD
942 ORD YMX CPH
951 CPH ZRH BGI POS
952 POS BGI ZRH CPH
955 CPH ZRH LIS GIG VCP MVD EZE SCL
956 SCL EZE MVD VCP GIG LIS ZRH CPH
957 CPH ZRH ROB GIG MVD EZE SCL
958 SCL EZE MVD GIG ROB ZRH CPH
961 CPH VIE ATH NBO JNB
962 JNB NBO ATH VIE CPH
963 CPH ZRH NBO DAR

CONT. NEXT COLUMN

FLIGHT

SK—SAS—SCANDINAVIAN AIRLINES

964 DAR NBO ZRH CPH
965 CPH DUS MAD ROB ABJ
966 ABJ ROB MAD DUS CPH
967 CPH DUS LOS
968 LOS DUS CPH
971 CPH BKK SIN
972 SIN BKK THR CPH 3
972 BKK THR CPH 5
973 CPH TAS BKK KUL HLP
974 HLP BKK TAS CPH
980 HND ANC CPH
981 CPH SVO HND
982 HND SVO CPH
983 CPH ZRH FCO ATH BGW KHI BKK MNL HND
984 HND MNL BKK KHI BGW ATH FCO ZRH CPH
985 CPH FRA ZRH FCO THR KHI CCU BKK MNL HND
986 HND MNL BKK CCU KHI THR FCO ZRH FRA CPH
987 CPH FRA DEL BKK SIN
988 SIN BKK DEL FRA CPH
989 CPH ANC HND

SN—SABENA—BELGIAN AIRLINES

211 BRU ATH BEY
225 BRU ATH BEY DAM
226 DAM BEY ATH BRU
227 BRU ATH THR DHA
228 DHA THR ATH BRU
243 BRU ATH CAI
244 CAI ATH BRU
247 BRU IST CAI
248 CAI IST BRU
251 BRU DXB BOM BKK HND
252 HND BKK BOM DXB BRU
261 BRU ANC HND
262 HND ANC BRU
271 BRU AUH BOM BKK SIN
272 SIN BKK BOM AUH BRU
273 BRU ATH BOM BKK MNL
274 MNL BKK BOM ATH BRU
285 BRU AUH BOM KUL HLP
286 HLP KUL BOM DXB BRU
287 BRU DXB BOM KUL SIN HLP
288 HLP SIN KUL BOM AUH BRU
327 BRU LBV FIH JNB
328 JNB FIH LBV BRU 4
DIS AFT JUN11
328 JNB FIH BRU 4
JUN17 - SEP17
329 BRU FIH JNB
330 JNB FIH BRU
342 FIH LBV BRU
363 BRU ATH FIH
364 FIH ATH BRU
375 BRU LOS FIH
376 FIH LOS BRU
387 BRU TNG CMN
388 CMN TNG BRU
421 BRU CKY ABJ ROB
422 ROB ABJ BRU
423 BRU CKY ROB
437 BRU KAN DLA
438 DLA KAN BRU
491 BRU NBO KGL
492 KGL NBO EBB ATH BRU
493 BRU BJM KGL
494 KGL BJM NBO ATH BRU
495 BRU ATH EBB BJM
496 BJM KGL EBB BRU
497 BRU EBB NBO DAR
498 DAR BJM KGL ATH BRU
503 BRU YMX MEX
504 MEX YMX BRU
505 BRU YMX MEX GUA
506 GUA MEX YMX BRU
507 BRU YMX HAV MEX
508 MEX HAV YMX BRU
531 BRU YMX JFK
532 JFK YMX BRU
571 BRU DKR MVD EZE SCL
572 SCL EZE MVD DKR BRU
761 BRU CPH ARN
762 ARN CPH BRU
787 BRU BSL ZRH
875 BRU WAW SVO
876 SVO WAW BRU

SP—SATA

200 SMA PDL TER HOR
201 HOR TER PDL SMA
202 SMA PDL TER HOR
203 HOR TER PDL SMA
204 SMA PDL TER HOR
205 HOR TER PDL SMA
500 PDL TER HOR
501 HOR TER PDL
503 HOR TER PDL
505 HOR TER PDL
600 SMA PDL TER
602 SMA PDL TER

SQ—SINGAPORE AIRLINES

581 SIN CMB MAA
582 MAA CMB SIN
631 OSA HKG BKK SIN
632 SIN BKK HKG OSA
637 HND TPE HKG SIN
638 SIN HKG TPE HND
641 SEL TPE HKG BKK SIN
642 SIN BKK HKG TPE SEL

CONT. NEXT COLUMN

FLIGHT

SQ—SINGAPORE AIRLINES

643 HKG BKK SIN
644 SIN BKK HKG
645 HKG KUL SIN
646 SIN KUL HKG
701 NAN AKL NOU SIN
702 SIN NOU AKL NAN
713 MEL SYD SIN
722 SIN HLP SYD
723 SYD HLP SIN
732 SIN SYD MEL
733 MEL SYD SIN
742 SIN SYD MEL
743 SYD HLP SIN
752 SIN SYD MEL
762 SIN SYD MEL
763 MEL SYD SIN
772 SIN HLP SYD
773 MEL SYD SIN
712A LHR AMS ATH BAH BOM SIN 1
DIS AFT APR10
712A LHR AMS FCO BAH BKK SIN 1
MAY 1 - MAY29
713A SIN BKK BAH ATH AMS LHR 1
DIS AFT APR10
713A SIN BOM BAH ATH ORY LHR 1
MAY 1 - SEP25
722A LHR AMS FRA BAH BKK SIN
723A SIN CMB BAH ZRH LHR 2
DIS AFT APR30
723A SIN BKK BAH FCO FRA LHR 2
MAY 1 - MAY29
725A SIN BKK BAH FRA AMS LHR 2
DIS AFT APR30
725A SIN CMB BAH ZRH AMS 2
EFF MAY 1
732A LHR ZRH BAH CMB SIN 3
DIS AFT APR30
732A LHR FRA FCO BAH BKK SIN 3
MAY 1 - MAY29
733A SIN BKK BAH FCO FRA LHR 3
DIS AFT APR30
733A SIN BKK BAH FRA AMS LHR 3
EFF MAY 1
734A LHR FRA FCO BAH BKK SIN 3
DIS AFT APR30
734A AMS ZRH BAH CMB SIN 3
EFF MAY 1
742A LHR AMS FCO BAH BKK SIN 4
DIS AFT APR30
742A LHR AMS FRA BAH BKK SIN 4
EFF MAY 1
743A SIN BAH ATH LHR 4
DIS AFT APR10
743A SIN BKK BAH FRA AMS LHR 4
EFF MAY 1
745A SIN BOM BAH FRA AMS LHR
752A LHR ATH BAH SIN 5
DIS AFT APR10
752A LHR ORY ATH BAH BOM SIN 5
MAY 1 - SEP25
753A SIN BKK BAH FCO AMS LHR
754A LHR AMS FRA BAH BOM SIN
762A LHR FRA FCO BAH BKK SIN
763A SIN CMB BAH ZRH LHR 6
DIS AFT APR30
763A SIN BOM BAH ATH ORY LHR 6
MAY 1 - SEP24
765A SIN CMB BAH ZRH AMS
772A LHR ZRH BAH CMB SIN 7
DIS AFT APR30
772A LHR ORY ATH BAH BOM SIN 7
MAY 1 - SEP25
773A SIN BOM BAH FCO FRA LHR 7
DIS AFT APR30
773A SIN BKK BAH FCO FRA LHR 7
MAY 1 - MAY29
774A AMS ZRH BAH CMB SIN

SR—SWISSAIR

100 GVA ZRH JFK
110 ZRH GVA JFK
111 JFK GVA ZRH
164 ZRH BOS ORD
165 ORD BOS ZRH
170 ZRH YMX YYZ
171 YYZ YMX ZRH
200 ZRH GVA DKR GIG VCP SCL
201 SCL VCP GIG DKR GVA ZRH
202 ZRH GVA DKR GIG VCP EZE
203 EZE VCP GIG DKR GVA ZRH
204 ZRH GVA DKR GIG VCP EZE
205 EZE VCP GIG DKR GVA ZRH
232 ZRH GVA ALG
233 ALG GVA ZRH
236 ZRH GVA ORN
237 ORN GVA ZRH
238 ZRH GVA CMN
239 CMN GVA ZRH
242 ZRH GVA TUN
243 TUN GVA ZRH
251 ACC LOS GVA ZRH
252 ZRH GVA LOS ACC
254 ZRH GVA ABJ ROB
255 ROB ABJ GVA ZRH
258 ZRH GVA ABJ ROB
259 ROB ABJ GVA ZRH

CONT. NEXT PAGE

1-Monday 2-Tuesday 3-Wednesday 4-Thursday 5-Friday 6-Saturday 7-Sunday X-Except

FLIGHT ITINERARIES

(Flights with Intermediate Stops Only) Numbers following itinerary indicate day/s of the week flight departs origin airport.

FLIGHT

SR—SWISSAIR

262 ZRH GVA DLA LBV
263 LBV DLA GVA ZRH
266 ZRH LOS ACC
267 ACC LOS ZRH
272 ZRH GVA ATH KRT
273 KRT ATH GVA ZRH
282 ZRH GVA FIH JNB
283 JNB FIH ZRH
284 ZRH GVA FIH JNB
285 JNB FIH ZRH
286 ZRH GVA NBO DAR
JNB
287 JNB DAR NBO ZRH
300 GVA ZRH VIE ATH
KHI BOM BKK HKG
301 HKG BKK BOM VIE
ZRH
302 GVA ZRH ATH BOM
BKK HKG
303 HKG BKK BOM GVA
ZRH
304 ZRH GVA ATH KHI
BKK HKG HND
305 HND HKG BKK KHI
ATH GVA ZRH
306 GVA ZRH ATH BKK
HKG HND
307 HND HKG BKK KHI
ATH ZRH
308 ZRH GVA BOM BKK
MNL
309 MNL BKK BOM ATH
GVA ZRH
311 HND HKG BOM ZRH
312 GVA ZRH BOM HKG
HND
314 ZRH GVA BOM CMB
SIN
315 SIN CMB BOM ZRH
GVA
316 ZRH GVA ATH BOM
PEK SHA
317 SHA PEK BOM ATH
GVA ZRH
318 ZRH GVA BOM CMB
SIN
319 SIN CMB BOM GVA
ZRH
326 ZRH GVA IST
328 ZRH GVA IST
336 ZRH GVA TLV
342 ZRH GVA ATH CAI
343 CAI ATH GVA ZRH
344 ZRH GVA CAI
345 CAI GVA ZRH
346 ZRH GVA CAI
347 CAI GVA ZRH
356 ZRH GVA ATH
359 ATH GVA ZRH
372 ZRH GVA BEY THR
373 THR BEY GVA ZRH
374 GVA BEY THR
375 THR BEY GVA ZRH
376 ZRH IST THR
377 THR IST GVA ZRH
384 ZRH GVA ATH DAM
BGW
385 BGW DAM ATH GVA
ZRH
388 ZRH ATH BGW
389 BGW ATH GVA
392 ZRH ATH KWI DXB
393 DXB KWI ATH ZRH
394 ZRH ATH DHA AUH
395 AUH DHA ATH ZRH
396 ZRH ATH DHA
397 DHA ATH ZRH
398 ZRH ATH AUH DXB
399 DXB AUH ATH ZRH
410 ZRH ARN HEL
411 HEL ARN ZRH
418 ZRH CPH ARN
419 ARN CPH ZRH
422 GVA CPH OSL
423 OSL CPH GVA
432 BSL ZRH VIE
433 VIE ZRH BSL
436 BSL ZRH VIE
437 VIE ZRH BSL
452 ZRH ZAG BEG
453 BEG ZAG ZRH
490 ZRH WAW SVO
491 SVO WAW ZRH
548 GVA BSL FRA
566 GVA BSL MUC
600 BSL ZRH FCO
605 FCO ZRH BSL
609 FCO GVA ZRH
612 BSL GVA FCO
642 BSL GVA LIN
656 ZRH GVA MAD
657 MAD GVA ZRH
670 BSL ZRH PMI
671 PMI ZRH BSL
682 ZRH GVA AGP
683 AGP GVA ZRH
693 LIS GVA ZRH
742 ZRH BSL ORY
749 ORY BSL ZRH
772 ZRH BSL BRU

SU—AEROFLOT-SOVIET AIRLINES

33 SVO OMS IKT KHV
34 KHV IKT OMS SVO
121 DME OMS IKT
122 IKT OMS DME
123 DME OMS IKT
124 IKT OMS DME
153 SVO KBP BUH
154 BUH KBP SVO
211 SVO ARN OSL
212 OSL ARN SVO
217 SVO ARN CPH
218 CPH ARN SVO
269 SVO KBP ZRH
270 ZRH KBP SVO
287 SVO MXP MRS
288 MRS MXP SVO
290 MXP KBP SVO
295 SVO SOF ATH
296 ATH SOF SVO
301 SVO CDG YMX
302 YMX CDG SVO
303 SVO KBP CDG YMX
304 YMX CDG KBP SVO
311 SVO LHR JFK
312 JFK LHR SVO
313 SVO CDG JFK
314 JFK CDG SVO
317 SVO CDG IAD
318 IAD CDG SVO
331 SVO FRA LIS HAV
332 HAV LIS FRA SVO
333 SVO CMN HAV
334 HAV CMN SVO
CONT. NEXT COLUMN

FLIGHT

SU—AEROFLOT-SOVIET AIRLINES

335 SVO FRA LIS HAV
LIM
336 LIM HAV LIS FRA
SVO
337 SVO LIS HAV
338 HAV LIS SVO
409 SVO BUD ALG
410 ALG BUD SVO
411 SVO BUD DKR CKY
412 CKY DKR BUD SVO
413 SVO BUD RBA NDB
BXO
414 BXO NDB RBA BUD
SVO
415 SVO BUD TUN BKO
BXO
416 BXO BKO TUN BUD
SVO
417 SVO ODS TIP NDJ
SSG
418 SSG NDJ TIP ODS
SVO
421 SVO VIE TIP LOS
422 LOS TIP VIE SVO
431 SVO BEY CAI KRT
BGF BZV
432 BZV BGF KRT CAI
BEY SVO
433 SVO BEY KRT BGF
BZV
434 BZV BGF KRT BEY
SVO
445 SVO ODS CAI KRT
EBB NBO DAR
446 DAR NBO EBB KRT
CAI SVO
447 SVO CAI ADE MGQ
DAR
448 DAR MGQ ADE CAI
SVO
451 SVO ODS CAI SAH
ADE
452 ADE CAI SVO
453 SVO ODS CAI ADE
MGQ
454 MGQ SAH ADE CAI
SVO
502 IST ESB SVO
503 SVO ESB IST
505 SVO BEY AMM
506 AMM BEY SVO
507 SVO LCA DAM
508 DAM LCA SVO
509 SVO EVN BEY
510 BEY EVN SVO
517 SVO ODS DAM
518 DAM ODS SVO
519 SVO ODS LCA
520 LCA ODS SVO
531 SVO TAS KBL
532 KBL TAS SVO
536 DEL TAS SVO
541 SVO THR BOM RGN
VTE HAN
542 HAN VTE RGN BOM
THR SVO
543 SVO THR KHI CMB
544 CMB KHI THR SVO
545 SVO KWI CMB
546 CMB KWI SVO
547 SVO DEL KUL
548 KUL DEL SVO
549 SVO BGW BOM DAC
550 DAC BOM BGW SVO
551 CPH SVO THR BKK
552 BKK THR SVO CPH
553 CPH SVO THR BKK
554 BKK THR SVO CPH
555 SVO KHI KUL
556 KUL KHI SVO
557 SVO DEL SIN
558 SIN DEL SVO
559 SVO KHI SIN JKT
560 JKT SIN KHI SVO
561 SVO OMS IKT
562 IKT OMS SVO
563 SVO OMS IKT ULN
564 ULN IKT OMS SVO
567 SVO OMS IKT FNJ
568 FNJ IKT OMS SVO
575 CDG SVO HND
576 HND SVO CDG
577 FRA SVO HND
578 HND SVO FRA
579 CPH SVO HND
580 HND SVO CPH
581 LHR SVO HND
582 HND SVO LHR
583 FCO SVO HND
584 HND SVO FCO
585 AMS SVO HND
586 HND SVO AMS
603 LED VNO WAW
604 WAW VNO LED
617 LED WAW BUD
618 BUD WAW LED
633 LED ARN AMS
634 AMS ARN LED
635 LED ARN OSL
636 OSL ARN LED
637 LED CPH LHR
638 LHR CPH LED
643 SVO LED LBG
644 LBG LED SVO
687 DME SKD BHK
688 BHK SKD DME
3719 IKT OVB ALA TAS
3720 TAS ALA OVB IKT
4201 ALA BAK MRV AER
4202 AER MRV BAK ALA
4687 FRU BAK MRV
4688 MRV BAK FRU
4853 DYU ASB BAK
4854 BAK ASB DYU
4883 DYU AER SIP KBP
4884 KBP SIP AER DYU
4999 TAS UGC MRV
5000 MRV UGC TAS
5035 TAS MRV ODS
5036 ODS MRV TAS
5151 ASB ALA OVB
5152 OVB ALA ASB
5225 ASB TBS AER ODS
5226 ODS AER TBS ASB
6233 VOG HRK MSQ
6234 MSQ HRK VOG
6297 KRR DOK IEV
6298 IEV DOK KRR
6307 KRR ROV HRK
6308 HRK ROV KRR
6361 MRV ROV LWO
6362 LWO ROV MRV
6551 BAK TAS OVB
6552 OVB TAS BAK
6673 BAK KRR ODS
6674 ODS KRR BAK
6677 BAK SIP LWO
CONT. NEXT COLUMN

FLIGHT

SU—AEROFLOT-SOVIET AIRLINES

6678 LWO SIP BAK
6684 KBP ROV BAK
6685 BAK ROV KBP
6961 SUI TBS BAK
6962 BAK TBS SUI
6999 SUI DOK HRK
7000 HRK DOK SUI
7051 BUS ROV HRK
7052 HRK ROV SUI BUS
7067 BUS SIP ODS
7068 ODS SIP SUI BUS
7105 EVN TAS ALA
7106 ALA TAS EVN
7189 EVN KBP LWO
7190 LWO KBP EVN
7287 KBP TBS SUI
7297 KBP DOK AER
7298 AER DOK KBP
7759 MSQ ROV TBS
7760 TBS ROV MSQ
7791 MSQ SIP AER
7792 AER SIP MSQ
7997 VNO KBP ROV
7998 ROV KBP VNO
8017 VNO ODS SIP
8018 SIP ODS VNO
8161 RIX HRK VOG TAS
8162 TAS VOG HRK RIX
8171 RIX DOK TBS
8172 TBS DOK RIX
8175 RIX HRK KRR EVN
8176 EVN KRR HRK RIX
8185 RIX OZH MRV
8186 MRV OZH RIX
8187 RIX ODS AER
8188 AER ODS RIX
8195 RIX KBP ROV
8196 ROV KBP RIX
8199 RIX SIP SUI
8200 SUI SIP RIX
8257 RIX VNO MSQ
8258 MSQ VNO RIX
8367 TLL KBP AER
8368 AER KBP TLL
8371 TLL KBP SIP
8372 SIP KBP TLL
8373 TLL ODS SIP
8374 SIP ODS TLL

SV—SAUDI ARABIAN AIRLINES

100 JED RUH DHA 7
100 JED RUH KHI 45
105 DHA RUH JED 7
105 KHI RUH JED 5
174 LHR CDG JED RUH
180 LHR FCO JED RUH
183 KHI DXB RUH
187 RUH JED CDG LHR
195 JED FCO LHR
212 JED MED HAS AJF
BDN TUI AMM
213 AMM TUI URY BDN
AJF HAS JED
219 TUU MED JED
220 JED MED HAS ELQ
AQI
222 JED MED TUU
223 AQI ELQ RUH
224 TUU BDN RAH AQI
RUH
226 TUU URY TUI BDN
HAS RUH
228 JED MED EJH TUU
229 RUH ELQ RAH BDN
URY TUU
230 BDN AJF HAS AQI
RUH
232 JED EJH TUU AJF
BDN
233 AQI ELQ HAS MED
JED
234 JED MED HAS BDN
236 JED MED TUU HAS
ELQ AQI RUH
237 RUH AQI HAS RAH
BDN AJF MED JED
238 RUH ELQ AQI
239 RUH AQI BDN TUI
URY TUU
240 BDN HAS ELQ RUH
241 TUU MED JED
243 RUH HAS BDN TUI
URY TUU
244 JED EJH TUU URY
TUI BDN HAS RUH
245 RUH AQI ELQ HAS
BDN
246 BDN RAH AQI RUH
247 RUH ELQ HAS BDN
AJF TUU MED JED
248 BDN RAH HAS ELQ
RUH
249 RUH AQI RAH BDN
251 TUU MED JED
263 RUH HAS AJF BDN
265 BDN RAH HAS JED
700 JED RUH DHA
701 DHA RUH JED
702 JED RUH DHA BGW
703 BGW DHA RUH JED
705 DHA RUH JED
707 DHA RUH JED
708 KRT JED RUH DHA
710 DHA DXB KHI
711 KHI MCT DHA RUH
JED
716 JED RUH DHA KWI
DAM
718 CAI MED DHA
719 DHA MED CAI
722 JED RUH DHA KWI
724 JED RUH DHA BEY
728 JED MED AMM
732 RUH DHA BEY
733 KWI DHA RUH
734 RUH DHA BEY
735 BEY DHA RUH
736 JED RUH BEY
737 BEY RUH JED
738 DHA RUH BEY
739 AUH DOH DHA RUH
740 RUH DHA DOH AUH
741 JED BEY TIP TUN
ALG CAS
742 CAS ALG TUN TIP
BEY JED
743 RUH BEY TIP TUN
744 TUN TIP BEY RUH
750 DHA DXB BOM
751 BOM DXB DHA
752 KRT JED RUH DHA
753 KHI DXB DHA
754 JED DXB KHI
757 DHA RUH JED
CONT. NEXT COLUMN

FLIGHT

SV—SAUDI ARABIAN AIRLINES

758 JED DHA DXB KHI
BOM
759 BOM KHI DXB DHA
RUH JED
760 JED RUH DHA
761 KHI DXB JED
762 CAI DHA RUH
764 DHA DXB KHI
769 DHA RUH JED
771 DHA CAI CDG
772 LHR FCO RUH DHA
773 DHA RUH JED LHR
774 LHR FCO JED RUH
DHA
776 RUH DHA MCT KHI
777 IST DAM AMM JED
778 JED AMM DAM IST
780 JED RUH DHA
791 DHA RUH JED FCO
LHR
792 CDG CAI JED RUH
DHA
793 RUH DHA FCO LHR
794 LHR JED RUH
795 DHA RUH JED GVA
LHR
796 LHR GVA JED RUH
DHA
797 KHI DXB DHA
800 JED RUH DHA
801 DHA RUH JED
806 JED RUH DHA SYZ
807 SYZ DHA RUH TIF
JED 7
807 SYZ DHA RUH JED
4
810 PZU JED RUH DHA
811 RUH TIF JED PZU
812 JED TIF RUH DHA
813 DHA RUH JED
821 RUH ELQ MED JED
822 AHB JED MED RUH
823 DHA RUH ELQ MED
JED
824 JED MED ELQ RUH
825 DHA RUH HAS AJF
TUU EJH JED
827 DHA RUH AJF TUU
EJH MED JED
829 RUH HAS AJF TUU
MED JED
830 SAH JED RUH DHA
KWI
835 KWI RUH MED JED
836 JED MED TUU BEY
837 BEY TUU MED JED
840 GIZ AHB RUH
841 RUH JED PZU
842 PZU JED RUH DHA
846 JED MED TUU HAS
RUH
852 JED GIZ SAH
853 DHA RUH EAM SAH
862 AHB BHH RUH
863 GIZ AHB JED
864 JED AHB GIZ
870 JED AHB GIZ
876 JED TIF BHH AHB
GIZ EAM SHW RUH
877 GIZ AHB BHH TIF
JED
880 JED TIF BHH AHB
GIZ EAM SHW RUH
881 RUH BHH AHB JED
KRT
882 JED BHH AHB EAM
SHW RUH
883 RUH BHH AHB
885 DHA RUH AHB GIZ
887 RUH SHW EAM GIZ
AHB JED
889 DHA RUH SHW EAM
AHB BHH JED
890 JED BHH AHB RUH
908 JED TIF RUH
910 JED RUH DHA
912 GIZ AHB JED MED
ELQ RUH
915 AMM MED JED
920 RUH DHA DOH AUH
921 AUH DOH DHA RUH
JED
922 DHA RUH AMM
923 SAH EAM RUH DHA
AMM
924 JED EJH TUU AJF
HAS RUH
926 GIZ AHB JED TUU
AMM
927 AMM TUU MED JED
929 AMM RUH DHA
931 DAM MED JED GIZ
932 GIZ JED RUH DAM
936 JED MED TUU DAM
937 DAM DHA RUH TIF
JED
938 GIZ AHB BHH JED
MED DAM
939 DAM KWI DHA RUH
JED
943 SAH GIZ JED
944 JED MED TUU AJF
RUH
952 AHB RUH DHA
953 RUH ELQ MED JED
958 AHB JED MED EJH
TUU
959 TUU MED JED GIZ
971 DHA RUH JED 1
971 DHA RUH TIF JED
5
975 RUH AHB JED
978 JED TIF RUH DHA
980 JED RUH DHA
985 DHA RUH AHB GIZ
990 JED RUH DHA
993 JED MED TUU CAI
994 CAI TUU MED JED

SW—SUIDWES LUGDIENS

901 ERS WVB LUD ALJ
CPT
902 CPT ALJ WVB
903 WVB ALJ CPT
904 CPT ALJ LUD WVB
ERS
905 ERS WVB ALJ CPT
906 CPT ALJ WVB ERS
907 ERS WVB LUD ALJ
CPT
908 CPT ALJ LUD WVB
ERS
909 ERS ADI WVB
910 WVB ADI ERS
911 ERS WDH ADI WVB
CONT. NEXT COLUMN

FLIGHT

SW—SUIDWES LUGDIENS

912 WVB ADI ERS

SY—AIR ALSACE

250 CMR EPL LBG
251 LBG EPL CMR
258 CMR EPL LBG
259 LBG EPL CMR
606 CMR ENC LGW
887 LGW ENC CMR
2074 CMR EPL LBG
2078 CMR EPL LBG
2173 LBG EPL CMR
2177 LBG EPL CMR

TA—TACA INTERNATIONAL

110 SJO MGA SAL BZE
MSY
111 MSY BZE SAL MGA
SJO 267
111 MSY BZE SAL 345
210 SAL GUA MEX
211 MEX GUA SAL
309 GUA SAL MGA SJO
310 PTY SJO MGA SAL
BZE MIA 23
310 PTY SJO MGA SAL
MIA 6
311 MIA BZE SAL MGA
SJO PTY
350 SAL BZE KIN
351 KIN BZE SAL

TE—AIR NEW ZEALAND, LTD.

221 AKL SYD HKG
222 HKG SYD AKL
502 CHC WLG NAN
503 NAN WLG CHC
506 WLG AKL PPG
507 PPG AKL WLG
508 WLG AKL PPG
509 PPG AKL WLG
555 LAX PPT AKL 35
DIS AFT APR24
555 LAX HNL AKL X345
EFF APR25
555 LAX HNL NAN AKL
4
DIS AFT APR24
556 AKL NAN HNL LAX
4
DIS AFT APR24
556 AKL HNL LAX 126
DIS AFT APR24
556 AKL PPT LAX 35
DIS AFT APR24
556 CHC AKL HNL LAX
7
DIS AFT APR24
561 LAX HNL NAN AKL
CHC
562 AKL NAN HNL LAX
574 CHC WLG NAN RAR
575 RAR NAN WLG CHC

TG—THAI AIRWAYS INTERNATIONAL

301 BKK RGN CCU
302 CCU RGN BKK
303 BKK DAC DEL
304 DEL DAC BKK
311 BKK CCU KTM
312 KTM CCU BKK
411 BKK BWH SIN
412 SIN BWH BKK
413 BKK SIN HLP
414 HLP SIN BKK
415 BKK KUL SIN
416 SIN KUL BKK
423 BKK SIN HLP DPS
424 DPS HLP SIN BKK
600 BKK HKG TPE HND
601 HND TPE HKG BKK
610 BKK HKG TPE OSA
611 OSA TPE HKG BKK
620 BKK MNL OSA
621 OSA MNL BKK
900 BKK KHI FCO LHR
1
900 BKK KHI AMS LHR
4
900 BKK FCO LHR 5
901 LHR AMS KHI BKK
2
901 LHR FCO KHI BKK
5
901 LHR FCO BKK 6
902 BKK FRA CPH
903 CPH FRA BKK 7
903 CPH FRA DEL BKK
3
904 BKK DEL ATH CDG
1
DIS AFT APR10
904 BKK FRA CDG 4
905 CDG ATH BKK 2
DIS AFT APR10
905 CDG FRA BKK 5
981 BKK SIN SYD
982 SYD SIN BKK
992 BKK FRA CPH

TH—THAI AIRWAYS COMPANY

121 BKK PHS PRH LPT
CNX
122 BKK PHS PRH NNT
CNX
123 BKK PHS PRH LPT
CNX
124 BKK PHS NNT CNX
125 BKK PHS PRH NNT
CNX
126 BKK PHS NNT CNX
127 BKK PHS PRH LPT
CNX
131 CNX LPT PRH PHS
BKK
132 CNX NNT PRH PHS
BKK
133 CNX LPT PRH PHS
BKK
134 CNX NNT PHS BKK
135 CNX NNT PRH PHS
BKK
136 CNX NNT PHS BKK
137 CNX LPT PRH PHS
BKK
221 BKK KKC BAO LOE
KOP
CONT. NEXT COLUMN

FLIGHT

TH—THAI AIRWAYS COMPANY

222 BKK KKC BAO UBP
KOP
223 BKK KKC BAO KOP
224 BKK KKC BAO KOP
225 BKK KKC BAO UBP
KOP
226 BKK KKC BAO KOP
227 BKK KKC BAO KOP
231 KOP BAO KKC BKK
232 KOP BAO KKC BKK
233 KOP BAO KKC BKK
234 KOP LOE BAO KKC
BKK
235 KOP BAO KKC BKK
236 KOP BAO KKC BKK
237 KOP UBP BAO KKC
BKK
321 BKK HKT TST HDY
322 BKK HKT HDY
323 BKK HKT TST HDY
324 BKK HKT HDY PAN
325 BKK HKT TST HDY
326 BKK HKT HDY PAN
327 BKK HKT TST HDY
331 HDY TST HKT BKK
333 HDY TST HKT BKK
334 PAN HDY BKK
335 HDY TST HKT BKK
336 PAN HDY BKK
337 HDY TST HKT BKK
342 BKK HDY PEN
344 BKK HDY PEN
346 BKK HDY PEN
352 PEN HDY HKT BKK
354 PEN HDY HKT BKK
356 PEN HDY HKT BKK
361 BKK HDY PAN
363 BKK HDY PAN
364 BKK TST HDY
371 PAN HDY BKK
373 PAN HDY BKK
374 HDY TST HKT BKK
385 BKK HDY PAN
387 BKK HDY PAN
395 PAN HDY BKK
397 PAN HDY BKK
141A BKK CNX CEI 137
141A BKK LPT CNX CEI
X137
151A CEI CNX BKK 137
151A CEI CNX LPT BKK
X137

TK—TURK HAVA YOLLARI

262 ESB DIY VAN
263 VAN DIY ESB
822 ESB ADA BEY
823 BEY ADA ESB
859 IST FCO LIN
860 LIN FCO IST
865 IGL FCO LIN
866 LIN FCO IGL
873 AYT FCO LIN
874 LIN FCO AYT
889 ESB IST MUC
893 ESB IST MUC CPH
894 CPH MUC IST
903 IST FRA BRU
904 BRU FRA IST
905 IST FRA AMS
906 AMS FRA IST
910 ZRH GVA IST
911 IST ZRH LYS
912 ZRH GVA IST 13
DIS AFT MAY 1
912 LYS ZRH IST 57
EFF MAY 2
915 IGL ZRH BRU 7
EFF MAY 2
915 IZM ZRH FRA 6
DIS AFT MAY 1
916 BRU ZRH IGL 7
EFF MAY 2
916 FRA ZRH IZM 6
DIS AFT MAY 1
929 IST ORY LHR
930 LHR ORY IST
971 IST SXF CPH
972 CPH SXF IST

TM—DETA

400 LUM BEW APL
401 APL UEL BEW LUM
402 BEW UEL APL MNC
POL
403 APL VXC VHO TET
BEW
404 LUM BEW TET
405 TET UEL BEW LUM
408 LUM BEW UEL APL
409 APL BEW LUM
412 LUM BEW APL
413 APL BEW LUM
414 BEW TET VHO VXC
APL MNC POL
415 POL MNC APL ANO
UEL BEW
420 LUM BEW UEL APL
4
420 LUM BEW APL 5
424 LUM INH VNX BEW
425 APL UEL BEW LUM
3
425 APL BEW LUM 5
430 TET VXC APL POL
431 POL APL VXC TET
432 LUM BEW TET
433 TET UEL BEW LUM
434 BEW TET VHO VXC
APL
435 POL MNC APL VXC
VHO TET BEW
436 LUM BEW TET
437 TET UEL BEW LUM
438 LUM BEW APL
439 APL UEL BEW LUM
446 BEW TET VXC APL
447 POL APL VXC TET
BEW
450 LUM BEW UEL APL
451 APL UEL BEW LUM
453 APL VXC VHO TET
BEW
461 LMB ANO APL
463 ANO LMB APL
464 BEW UEL ANO APL
POL
470 LUM BEW APL
471 APL BEW LUM
473 BEW VNX INH LUM
503 TET BEW LUM
520 LUM BEW LAD
521 LAD LUN LUM
CONT. NEXT COLUMN

1-Monday 2-Tuesday 3-Wednesday 4-Thursday 5-Friday 6-Saturday 7-Sunday X-Except

Freq. Leave Arrive Flight Class Eq S Eff./Dis.

To GENEVA, SWITZERLAND GVA

From EDMONTON, ALTA., CANADA-CONT. YXD
2 1905 YEG 1430+1 AC 852 FY DC8 0
1115 LHR 1305 BE 576 FY TRD 0
5 1950 YEG 1720+1 AC 852 FY DC8 1
1315 LHR 1555 SR 813 FY D9S 0

EL PASO, TEXAS, USA 6775/0 ELP
CONNECTIONS
0735 0920+1 AA 116 FYB 727 2 E-APR25
LGA 1622 JFK 2100 SR 111 FY 747 0
0840 0920+1 AA 164 FYB 707 1 D-APR24
1556 JFK 2000 SR 111 FY 747 0

FT. LAUDERDALE, FLA., USA 5882/0 FLL
CONNECTIONS
1340 0920+1 DL 1072 FYJ L10 0 D-APR24
1600 JFK 2000 SR 111 FY 747 0
1430 0920+1 EA 750 FYBJ 727 0 D-APR24
1703 JFK 2000 SR 111 FY 747 0
1712 0920+1 DL 374 FYJ 72S 0 E-APR25
1930 JFK 2100 SR 111 FY 747 0

FRANKFURT, GERMANY 344/287 FRA
F DMK 286 572 2.90
Y DMK 213 426
0925 1030 LH 240 FY 737 0
1625 1730 SR 543 FY D9S 0
X6 2055 2200 LH 242 FY 737 0

GRAZ, AUSTRIA 734/0 GRZ
F AUS 3120 6240 32
Y AUS 2290 4580
CONNECTIONS
0700 1205 OS 221 Y D9S 0
0730 VIE 1040 OS 211 FY D9S 0

GUADALAJARA, MEXICO 7291/0 GDL
CONNECTIONS
257 1100 1105+1 AF 070 FY 707 1 E-MAY 3
0755 CDG 1110 AF 662 FY 72S 0
AF 070 707-JFK-747
X346 1100 1105+1 AF 070 FY 707 1 E-APR25
0755 CDG 1110 AF 662 FY 72S 0 D-MAY 2
AF 070 707-JFK-747
X346 1225 1105+1 AF 070 FY 707 1 D-APR24
0855 CDG 1110 AF 662 FY 72S 0
AF 070 707-JFK-747

GUAYAQUIL, ECUADOR 7471/0 GYE
CONNECTIONS
5 1310 1730+1 LH 493 FY D10 2
1125 FRA 1625 SR 543 FY D9S 0
3 1710 1735+1 KL 774 FY D10 3
1555 ZRH 1655 SR 656 FY D9S 0

HARTFORD, CONN., USA 4534/0 BDL
F 652.00 1304.00 6.52
YL 350.00 700.00
Y 363.00 726.00
YH 455.00 910.00
EX/4 14-21 DAY YE 633.00
EX/5 14-21 DAY YE 719.00
EX/8 22-45 DAY YE 436.00
EX/12 22-45 DAY YE 466.00
EX/13 22-45 DAY YE 569.00
EX/28-AP 22-45 DAY YE 377.00
EX/29-AP 22-45 DAY YE 396.00
EX/30-AP 22-45 DAY YE 501.00
EX/35 YL - YOUTH 417.00
EX/36 Y - YOUTH 434.00
EX/37 YH - YOUTH 479.00
CONNECTIONS
1550 BDL 1105+1 DL 123 FYB 72S 0 D-APR24
LGA 1627 JFK 1900 AF 070 FY 747 0
0855 CDG 1110 AF 662 FY 72S 0
1550 BDL 1105+1 DL 123 FYB 72S 0 E-APR25
LGA 1627 JFK 1900 AF 070 FY 747 0
0755 CDG 1110 AF 662 FY 72S 0
X6 1745 BDL 0920+1 TW 11 FYB 707 0 D-APR24
1833 JFK 2000 SR 111 FY 747 0
6 1745 BDL 0920+1 TW 43 FYB 707 0 D-APR24
1833 JFK 2000 SR 111 FY 747 0
X136 1745 BDL 1055+1 TW 11 FYB 707 0 D-APR24
1833 JFK 2000 TW 832 FYB B3J 1
X136 1745 BDL 1005+1 TW 11 FYB 707 0 E-APR25
1833 JFK 2000 TW 832 FYB B3J 1
1835 BDL 0920+1 AL 279 SB D9S 0 E-APR25
1914 JFK 2100 SR 111 FY 747 0
14 1911 BDL 1305+1 DL 959 FYB D8S 0 E-APR25
1952 JFK 2200 AF 022 FY 747 0 D-MAY15
1055 CDG 1300 AF 664 FY CVL 0
X256 1911 BDL 1305+1 DL 959 FYB D8S 0 E-MAY16
1952 JFK 2200 AF 022 FY 747 0
1055 CDG 1300 AF 664 FY CVL 0

HILO, HAWAII; HAWAII, USA ITO
CONNECTIONS
6 0935 1145+2 TS 393 F 737 1
1049 HNL 1245 VG 909 FY D10 2
0015 BKK 0205 SR 305 FY D10 2
6 0935 1145+2 TS 393 F 737 1 D-APR16
1049 HNL 1245 VG 909 FY D10 1
2040 HKG 2220 SR 305 FY D10 3
6 0935 1145+2 TS 393 F 737 1
1049 HNL 1245 VG 909 FY D10 0
1600 HND 1755 SR 305 FY D10 4
6 0935 1145+2 TS 393 F 737 1 E-APR17
1049 HNL 1245 VG 909 FY D10 1
2040 HKG 2320 SR 305 FY D10 3

HONG KONG, HONG KONG 8227/0 HKG
F HKD 8267 16534 82.67
Y HKD 4826 9652
6 1725 HKG 0510+1 SR 303 FY D10 2 D-APR17
6 1825 HKG 0510+1 SR 303 FY D10 2 E-APR18
7 2220 HKG 1145+1 SR 305 FY D10 3 D-APR17
7 2320 HKG 1145+1 SR 305 FY D10 3 E-APR18
CONNECTIONS
35 0650 HKG 2145 TG 603 FY DC8 0 D-APR17
0930 BKK 1015 SK 972 FY D10 1
1735 CPH 1855 SK 607 FY DC9 1
17 0650 HKG 2145 TG 603 FY DC8 0 D-APR17
0930 BKK 1015 SK 974 FY D8S 1
1720 CPH 1855 SK 607 FY DC9 1
4 0650 HKG 2200 TG 603 FY DC8 0 D-APR17
0930 BKK 1015 SK 988 FY D8S 1
1730 FRA 2055 LH 242 FY 737 0
35 0750 HKG 2145 TG 603 FY DC8 0 E-APR18
0930 BKK 1015 SK 972 FY D10 1
1735 CPH 1855 SK 607 FY DC9 1
17 0750 HKG 2145 TG 603 FY DC8 0 E-APR18
0930 BKK 1015 SK 974 FY D8S 1
1720 CPH 1855 SK 607 FY DC9 1
4 0750 HKG 2200 TG 603 FY DC8 0 E-APR18
0930 BKK 1015 SK 988 FY D8S 1
1730 FRA 2055 LH 242 FY 737 0
6 1450 HKG 1030+1 TG 611 FY D8S 0 D-APR17
1730 BKK 1815 SK 986 FY D8S 5
0710 FRA 0925 LH 240 FY 737 0

CONT. NEXT COLUMN

To GENEVA, SWITZERLAND GVA

From HONG KONG, HONG KONG-CONT. HKG
3 1450 HKG 1200+1 TG 611 FY D8S 0 D-APR17
1730 BKK 1815 SK 984 FY D8S 5
0830 CPH 1005 SR 423 FY D9S 0
6 1550 HKG 1030+1 TG 611 FY D8S 0 E-APR18
1730 BKK 1815 SK 986 FY D8S 5
0710 FRA 0925 LH 240 FY 737 0
3 1550 HKG 1200+1 TG 611 FY D8S 0 E-APR18
1730 BKK 1815 SK 984 FY D8S 5
0830 CPH 1005 SR 423 FY D9S 0
4 1750 HKG 1010+1 AZ 777 FY D10 3 D-APR17
0625 FCO 0850 SR 611 FY D9S 0
15 1750 HKG 1010+1 AZ 789 FY D10 3 D-APR17
0605 FCO 0850 SR 611 FY D9S 0
46 1845 HKG 1010+1 KE 601 FY A3B 0 D-MAY28
2135 BKK 2315 QF 5 FY 747 2
0750 FCO 0850 SR 611 FY D9S 0
6 1850 HKG 1010+1 AF 193 FY 747 0 D-APR17
2135 BKK 2315 QF 5 FY 747 2
0750 FCO 0850 SR 611 FY D9S 0
4 1850 HKG 1010+1 AZ 777 FY D10 3 E-APR18
0625 FCO 0850 SR 611 FY D9S 0 D-MAY28
15 1850 HKG 1010+1 AZ 789 FY D10 3 E-APR18
0605 FCO 0850 SR 611 FY D9S 0 D-MAY28
15 1850 HKG 1010+1 AZ 789 FY D10 3 E-MAY29
0705 FCO 0950 SR 611 FY D9S 0
1 1925 HKG 1010+1 AF 193 FY 747 0 D-APR17
2210 BKK 2315 QF 5 FY 747 2
0750 FCO 0850 SR 611 FY D9S 0
6 1950 HKG 1010+1 AF 193 FY 747 0 E-APR18
2135 BKK 2315 QF 5 FY 747 2 D-MAY28
0750 FCO 0850 SR 611 FY D9S 0
1 2025 HKG 1010+1 AF 193 FY 747 0 E-APR18
2210 BKK 2315 QF 5 FY 747 2 D-MAY28
0750 FCO 0850 SR 611 FY D9S 0

HONOLULU, OAHU; HAWAII, USA 9463/0 HNL
F 965.00 1930.00 9.65
YL 582.00 1164.00
Y 595.00 1190.00
YH 687.00 1374.00
EX/4 14-21 DAY YE 985.00
EX/5 14-21 DAY YE 1071.00
EX/8 22-45 DAY YE 737.00
EX/12 22-45 DAY YE 767.00
EX/13 22-45 DAY YE 870.00
EX/28-AP 22-45 DAY YE 696.00
EX/29-AP 22-45 DAY YE 715.00
EX/30-AP 22-45 DAY YE 835.00
EX/35 YL - YOUTH 733.00
EX/36 Y - YOUTH 750.00
EX/37 YH - YOUTH 810.00
CONNECTIONS
X2 1415 2145+1 NW 86 FYK 747 0 D-APR24
2125 SEA 2225 SK 934 FY D10 0
1650 CPH 1855 SK 607 FY DC9 1
X13 1415 2145+1 NW 86 FYK 747 0 E-MAY17
2125 SEA 2325 SK 934 FY D10 0
1650 CPH 1855 SK 607 FY DC9 1
X2 1415 2145+1 NW 86 FYK 747 0 E-APR25
2125 SEA 2325 SK 934 FY D10 0 D-MAY16
1650 CPH 1855 SK 607 FY DC9 1
2300 0920+2 UA 22 • 747 1 E-APR25
1640 JFK 2100 SR 111 FY 747 0 D-MAY 2
UA 22 747-SFO-D10
UA 22 FYK-SFO-FYB
2300 0920+2 UA 22 • 747 1 E-MAY 3
1650 JFK 2100 SR 111 FY 747 0
UA 22 747-SFO-D10
UA 22 FYK-SFO-FYB
2350 0920+2 UA 22 • 747 1 D-APR23
1640 JFK 2000 SR 111 FY 747 0
UA 22 747-SFO-D10
UA 22 FYK-SFO-FYB

HOUSTON, TEXAS, USA 6326/0 IAH
F 754.00 1508.00 7.54
YL 434.00 868.00
Y 447.00 894.00
YH 539.00 1078.00
EX/4 14-21 DAY YE 806.00
EX/5 14-21 DAY YE 892.00
EX/8 22-45 DAY YE 598.00
EX/12 22-45 DAY YE 628.00
EX/13 22-45 DAY YE 731.00
EX/28-AP 22-45 DAY YE 539.00
EX/29-AP 22-45 DAY YE 558.00
EX/30-AP 22-45 DAY YE 663.00
EX/35 YL - YOUTH 559.00
EX/36 Y - YOUTH 588.00
EX/37 YH - YOUTH 658.00
CONNECTIONS
1225 IAH 0920+1 DL 224 FYB 72S 0 D-APR24
1625 JFK 2000 SR 111 FY 747 0
1225 IAH 0920+1 DL 224 FYB 72S 0 E-APR25
1625 JFK 2100 SR 111 FY 747 0
X136 1225 IAH 1055+1 DL 224 FYB 72S 0 D-APR24
1625 JFK 2000 TW 832 FYB B3J 1
X136 1225 IAH 1005+1 DL 224 FYB 72S 0 E-APR25
1625 JFK 2000 TW 832 FYB B3J 1
X12 1235 IAH 0945+1 KL 682 FY 747 1 D-APR24
0645 AMS 0825 KL 331 Y DC9 0
1250 IAH 0920+1 EA 64 FnYnB L10 0 E-MAY 1
1700 JFK 2100 SR 111 FY 747 0
X136 1250 IAH 1005+1 EA 64 FnYnB L10 0 E-MAY 1
1700 JFK 2000 TW 832 FYB B3J 1
X12 1335 IAH 0945+1 KL 682 FY 747 1 E-APR25
0645 AMS 0825 KL 331 Y DC9 0
X257 2200 IAH 1705+1 AF 066 FY 747 0 D-APR24
1510 CDG 1700 AF 666 FY CVL 0
X257 2300 IAH 1705+1 AF 066 FY 747 0 E-APR25
1510 CDG 1700 AF 666 FY CVL 0

INDIANAPOLIS, IND., USA 5342/0 IND
F 719.00 1438.00 7.19
YL 398.00 796.00
Y 411.00 822.00
YH 503.00 1006.00
EX/4 14-21 DAY YE 726.00
EX/5 14-21 DAY YE 812.00
EX/8 22-45 DAY YE 506.00
EX/12 22-45 DAY YE 536.00
EX/13 22-45 DAY YE 639.00
EX/28-AP 22-45 DAY YE 450.00
EX/29-AP 22-45 DAY YE 469.00
EX/30-AP 22-45 DAY YE 574.00
EX/35 YL - YOUTH 467.00
EX/36 Y - YOUTH 484.00
EX/37 YH - YOUTH 529.00
CONNECTIONS
1334 0920+1 AL 174 SB D9S 0 D-APR24
1515 JFK 2000 SR 111 FY 747 0
X136 1334 1005+1 AL 174 SB D9S 0 E-APR25
1515 JFK 2000 TW 832 FYB B3J 1

CONT. NEXT COLUMN

To GENEVA, SWITZERLAND GVA

From INDIANAPOLIS, IND., USA-CONT. IND
X136 1620 1055+1 TW 416 FYB 727 0 D-APR24
LGA 1800 JFK 2000 TW 832 FYB B3J 1
X136 1620 1005+1 TW 416 FYB 727 0 E-APR25
LGA 1800 JFK 2000 TW 832 FYB B3J 1

ISTANBUL, TURKEY 1426/1189 IST
F TUL 4078 8156 40.80
Y TUL 2984 5968
2 1020 1115 IR 735 FY 727 0 D-APR13
6 1105 1325 TK 917 Y DC9 0 E-MAY 1
5 1110 1210 SR 377 FY D10 0
7 1600 1705 SR 327 FY D9S 0

JAKARTA, JAVA, INDONESIA 8930/0 JKT
F 1533.70 3067.40 15.34
Y 941.70 1883.40
CONNECTIONS
4 1630 HLP 1010+1 GA 894 FY D10 1 D-MAY28
2110 BKK 2315 QF 5 FY 747 2
0750 FCO 0850 SR 611 FY D9S 0
16 1715 HLP 1010+1 TG 424 FY D8S 1 D-MAY28
2130 BKK 2315 QF 5 FY 747 2
0750 FCO 0850 SR 611 FY D9S 0

JEDDAH, SAUDI ARABIA 3039/2523 JED
F ARI 2234 4468 22.35
Y ARI 1590 3180
5 1215 1610 SV 795 FY 707 0
1 1235 1740 AT 251 FY 707 1
4 1235 1740 AT 253 FY 727 1
CONNECTIONS
4 0830 1455 ME 365 FY 707 0
0950 BEY 1145 ME 215 FY 707 0
7 0830 1455 ME 365 FY 707 0
0950 BEY 1145 ME 227 FY 707 0
6 0830 1455 ME 369 FY 707 0
0950 BEY 1145 ME 215 FY 707 0
5 0830 1455 ME 369 FY 707 0
0950 BEY 1145 ME 227 FY 707 0
1 0830 1455 ME 375 FY 707 0
0950 BEY 1145 ME 215 FY 707 0
3 0830 1455 ME 375 FY 707 0
0950 BEY 1145 ME 227 FY 707 0

JOHANNESBURG, SOUTH AFRICA 6326/0 JNB
F SAR 851.60 1703.20 8.52
Y SAR 515.40 1030.80
CONNECTIONS
7 1950 JNB 1010+1 AZ 815 FY D10 1 D-MAY28
0630 FCO 0850 SR 611 FY D9S 0
7 1950 JNB 1010+1 AZ 815 FY D10 1 E-MAY29
0730 FCO 0950 SR 611 FY D9S 0
2 1950 JNB 1010+1 AZ 827 FY D10 1 D-MAY28
0600 FCO 0850 SR 611 FY D9S 0
5 2000 JNB 1050+1 OA 102 FY 707 1 D-APR 9
0620 ATH 0910 OA 131 FY 720 0
5 2000 JNB 1050+1 OA 102 FY 707 1 E-APR11
0720 ATH 1010 OA 131 FY 720 0
5 2350 JNB 1310+1 AZ 823 FY D10 1 D-MAY28
0955 FCO 1150 AZ 410 FY DC9 0

KABUL, AFGHANISTAN 4780/0 KBL
CONNECTIONS
3 0800 1830 FG 705 Y 727 2 D-MAY29
1345 FCO 1710 AZ 408 FY DC9 0

KAHULUI, MAUI; HAWAII, USA OGG
CONNECTIONS
6 1050 1145+2 TS 391 F 737 0
1117 HNL 1245 VG 909 FY D10 2
0015 BKK 0205 SR 305 FY D10 2
6 1050 1145+2 TS 391 F 737 0 D-APR16
1117 HNL 1245 VG 909 FY D10 1
2040 HKG 2220 SR 305 FY D10 3
6 1050 1145+2 TS 391 F 737 0
1117 HNL 1245 VG 909 FY D10 0
1600 HND 1755 SR 305 FY D10 4
6 1050 1145+2 TS 391 F 737 0 E-APR17
1117 HNL 1245 VG 909 FY D10 1
2040 HKG 2320 SR 305 FY D10 3

KANSAS CITY, MO., USA 5754/0 MCI
F 760.00 1520.00 7.60
YL 426.00 852.00
Y 439.00 878.00
YH 531.00 1062.00
EX/4 14-21 DAY YE 782.00
EX/5 14-21 DAY YE 868.00
EX/8 22-45 DAY YE 567.00
EX/12 22-45 DAY YE 597.00
EX/13 22-45 DAY YE 700.00
EX/28-AP 22-45 DAY YE 495.00
EX/29-AP 22-45 DAY YE 514.00
EX/30-AP 22-45 DAY YE 619.00
EX/35 YL - YOUTH 507.00
EX/36 Y - YOUTH 524.00
EX/37 YH - YOUTH 569.00
1325 MCI 0850+1 TW 830 FYB B3J 2 E-JUN10
CONNECTIONS
1325 MCI 0920+1 TW 800 FYB 707 1 D-APR24
1819 JFK 2000 SR 111 FY 747 0
1325 MCI 0920+1 TW 800 FYB B3J 1 E-APR25
1821 JFK 2100 SR 111 FY 747 0
X136 1330 MCI 1055+1 TW 152 FYB 72S 1 D-APR24
LGA 1759 JFK 2000 TW 832 FYB B3J 1
X136 1330 MCI 1005+1 TW 152 FYB 72S 1 E-APR25
LGA 1759 JFK 2000 TW 832 FYB B3J 1
X26 1400 MCI 1105+1 TW 414 FYB 72S 0 D-APR24
1515 ORD 1630 AF 030 FY 747 1
1020 CDG 1110 AF 662 FY 72S 0
X26 1450 MCI 1105+1 BN 138 FYB 72S 0 E-APR25
1600 ORD 1730 AF 030 FY 747 1
1020 CDG 1110 AF 662 FY 72S 0

KARACHI, PAKISTAN 4760/3633 KHI
F PAR 9056 18112 90.60
Y PAR 5858 11716
1 0600 1145 SR 305 FY D10 1 E-APR 2
CONNECTIONS
6 0250 1010 PR 824 FY D10 0 E-APR 2
0600 FCO 0850 SR 611 FY D9S 0 D-MAY29
2 0300 1010 PR 822 FY D10 0 E-APR 2
0610 FCO 0850 SR 611 FY D9S 0 D-MAY29
6 0600 1445 RJ 193 FY B3J 1
0845 AMM 1100 RJ 151 FY B3J 0

KHARTOUM, SUDAN 3132/0 KRT
F SUL 212.900 425.800 2.130
Y SUL 159.100 318.200
7 1020 1615 SR 273 FY DC8 1
CONNECTIONS
1 0515 1455 ME 375 FY 707 1
0950 BEY 1145 ME 215 FY 707 0
3 0515 1455 ME 375 FY 707 1
0950 BEY 1145 ME 227 FY 707 0
5 0645 1455 ME 373 FY 707 0
1005 BEY 1145 ME 227 FY 707 0

To GENEVA, SWITZERLAND GVA

From KINGSTON, JAMAICA 6172/0 KIN
CONNECTIONS
5 1345 KIN 1110+1 BA 210 FY 707 2 E-APR 2
0735 LHR 0945 BE 574 FY TRD 0 D-APR23
1 1435 KIN 1235+1 BA 230 FY 707 2 E-APR 5
0840 LHR 1110 SR 811 FY D9S 0 D-APR19
5 1445 KIN 1110+1 BA 210 FY 707 2 E-APR30
0735 LHR 0945 BE 574 FY TRD 0
1 1535 KIN 1235+1 BA 230 FY 707 2 E-APR26
0840 LHR 1110 SR 811 FY D9S 0
6 1900 KIN 1435+1 BA 210 FY 747 1 E-APR 3
1115 LHR 1305 BE 576 Y S11 0 D-APR24
6 1900 KIN 1435+1 BA 210 FY 747 1 E-MAY 1
1015 LHR 1305 BE 576 Y S11 0
3 2045 KIN 1720+1 BA 210 FY 747 1 E-APR 7
1315 LHR 1555 SR 813 FY D9S 0 D-APR21
3 2045 KIN 1720+1 BA 210 FY 747 1 E-APR28
1215 LHR 1555 SR 813 FY D9S 0

KINSHASA, ZAIRE 4256/3545 FIH
F ZAI 428 856 4.280
Y ZAI 303 606
1 0900 1615 QC 080 FY D10 0

KONA, HAWAII; HAWAII, USA KOA
CONNECTIONS
6 1015 1145+2 TS 393 F 737 0
1049 HNL 1245 VG 909 FY D10 2
0015 BKK 0205 SR 305 FY D10 2
6 1015 1145+2 TS 393 F 737 0 D-APR16
1049 HNL 1245 VG 909 FY D10 1
2040 HKG 2220 SR 305 FY D10 3
6 1015 1145+2 TS 393 F 737 0
1049 HNL 1245 VG 909 FY D10 0
1600 HND 1755 SR 305 FY D10 4

KUWAIT, KUWAIT 3132/0 KWI
F KUD 182.400 364.800 1.825
Y KUD 127.600 255.200
2 1130 1700 KU 195 FY 707 1
CONNECTIONS
6 0730 1445 RJ 805 FY B3J 0
0840 AMM 1100 RJ 151 FY B3J 0
146 0800 1455 ME 403 FY 707 0
0920 BEY 1145 ME 215 FY 707 0
35 0800 1455 ME 403 FY 707 0
0920 BEY 1145 ME 227 FY 707 0
5 1520 1445+1 RJ 805 FY 72S 0
1630 AMM 1100 RJ 151 FY B3J 0

LAGOS, NIGERIA 3294/2745 LOS
F NGN 474.90 949.80 4.75
Y NGN 293.90 587.80
3 1045 1625 SR 251 FY D10 0

LAS VEGAS, NEV., USA. 7039/0 LAS
F 856.00 1712.00 8.56
YL 493.00 986.00
Y 506.00 1012.00
YH 598.00 1196.00
EX/4 14-21 DAY YE 867.00
EX/5 14-21 DAY YE 953.00
EX/8 22-45 DAY YE 631.00
EX/12 22-45 DAY YE 671.00
EX/13 22-45 DAY YE 819.00
EX/28-AP 22-45 DAY YE 547.00
EX/29-AP 22-45 DAY YE 571.00
EX/30-AP 22-45 DAY YE 706.00
EX/35 YL - YOUTH 613.00
EX/36 Y - YOUTH 630.00
EX/37 YH - YOUTH 675.00
CONNECTIONS
X136 0735 1055+1 TW 192 FYB B3J 1 D-APR24
1620 JFK 2000 TW 832 FYB B3J 1
X136 0735 1005+1 TW 192 FYB B3J 1 E-APR25
1635 JFK 2000 TW 832 FYB B3J 1
0810 0920+1 UA 120 FYB DC8 1 D-APR24
1723 JFK 2000 SR 111 FY 747 0
X6 1100 0920+1 UA 74 FYB DC8 0 D-APR 5
1835 JFK 2000 SR 111 FY 747 0
1100 0920+1 UA 74 FYB DC8 0 E-APR 6
1835 JFK 2000 SR 111 FY 747 0 D-APR24
1100 0920+1 UA 74 FYB DC8 0 E-APR25
1835 JFK 2100 SR 111 FY 747 0

LIBREVILLE, GABON 3804/3170 LBV
F AFR 204650 409300 2050
Y AFR 140800 281600
5 0910 1655 SR 263 FY DC8 1
7 1030 1700 RK 82 FY D8S 0

LIHUE, KAUAI; HAWAII, USA LIH
CONNECTIONS
6 1055 1145+2 TS 324 F 737 0
1122 HNL 1245 VG 909 FY D10 2
0015 BKK 0205 SR 305 FY D10 2
6 1055 1145+2 TS 324 F 737 0 D-APR16
1122 HNL 1245 VG 909 FY D10 1
2040 HKG 2220 SR 305 FY D10 3
6 1055 1145+2 TS 324 F 737 0
1122 HNL 1245 VG 909 FY D10 0
1600 HND 1755 SR 305 FY D10 4
6 1055 1145+2 TS 324 F 737 0 E-APR17
1122 HNL 1245 VG 909 FY D10 1
2040 HKG 2320 SR 305 FY D10 3

LIMA, PERU 8019/0 LIM
CONNECTIONS
5 1350 1430+1 BA 260 FY 707 2
1100 LHR 1305 BE 576 Y TRD 0
3 1350 1435+1 BA 260 FY 707 2 E-APR 7
1045 LHR 1305 BE 576 Y S11 0
3 1440 1735+1 KL 774 FY D10 4
1555 ZRH 1655 SR 656 FY D9S 0
6 1455 1935+1 KL 776 FY D10 4
1650 ZRH 1855 SR 942 FY D9S 0
KL 776 CUR-KL 786

LISBON, PORTUGAL 1116/930 LIS
F ESP 5225 10450 52.30
Y ESP 3950 7900
1510 1725 SR 693 FY D9S 0

LONDON, ENGLAND 548/457 LON
F UKL 77.00 154.00 .77
Y UKL 51.50 103.00
0945 LHR 1110 BE 574 FY TRD 0
3 1105 LHR 1230 SV 796 FY 707 0
1110 LHR 1235 SR 811 FY D9S 0
1 1120 LHR 1245 KU 196 FY 707 0
357 1145 LHR 1300 IR 750 FY 727 0
6. 1145 LHR 1310 AI 122 FY 707 0
135 1305 LHR 1430 BE 576 FY TRD 0
6 1305 LHR 1430 BE 576 Y TRD 0
247 1305 LHR 1435 BE 576 Y S11 0
1555 LHR 1720 SR 813 FY D9S 0
X6 1730 LHR 1855 BE 578 FY TRD 0
3 1900 LHR 2025 AI 126 FY 707 0
1955 LHR 2120 SR 819 FY D9S 0

Freq. Leave Arrive Flight Class Eq S Eff./Dis.

To GENEVA, SWITZERLAND GVA

From LONDON, ONT., CANADA 4904/0 YXU
CONNECTIONS
4 1600 0945+1 GX 816 Y CV4 0 D-APR24
1635 YYZ 1810 KL 692 FY D10 0
0710 AMS 0825 KL 331 Y DC9 0
7 1600 0945+1 GX 816 Y CV4 0 D-APR24
1635 YYZ 1835 KL 692 FY 747 0
0735 AMS 0825 KL 331 Y DC9 0
4 1715 0945+1 AC 326 FY D9S 0 E-APR25
1745 YYZ 1910 KL 692 FY D10 0
0710 AMS 0825 KL 331 Y DC9 0
7 1715 0945+1 AC 326 FY D9S 0 E-APR25
1745 YYZ 1935 KL 692 FY 747 0
0735 AMS 0825 KL 331 Y DC9 0

LOS ANGELES, CALIF., USA 7092/0 LAX
8.76K
F 876.00 1752.00
YL 499.00 998.00
Y 512.00 1024.00
YH 604.00 1208.00
EX/4 14-21 DAY YE 805.00
EX/5 14-21 DAY YE 891.00
EX/8 22-45 DAY YE 569.00
EX/12 22-45 DAY YE 609.00
EX/13 22-45 DAY YE 757.00
EX/28-AP 22-45 DAY YE 485.00
EX/29-AP 22-45 DAY YE 509.00
EX/30-AP 22-45 DAY YE 644.00
EX/35 YL - YOUTH 637.00
EX/36 Y - YOUTH 654.00
EX/37 YH - YOUTH 714.00
0800 LAX 0850+1 TW 830 FYB B3J 3 E-JUN10
CONNECTIONS
0845 LAX 0920+1 AA 2 FYB D10 0 D-APR24
1639 JFK 2000 SR 111 FY 747 0
0845 LAX 0920+1 UA 6 FYB D10 0 D-APR24
1645 JFK 2000 SR 111 FY 747 0
0845 LAX 0920+1 UA 6 FYB D10 0 E-APR25
1645 JFK 2100 SR 111 FY 747 0
X136 0845 LAX 1055+1 UA 6 FYB D10 0 D-APR24
1645 JFK 2000 TW 832 FYB B3J 1
X136 0845 LAX 1005+1 UA 6 FYB D10 0 E-APR25
1645 JFK 2000 TW 832 FYB B3J 1
0930 LAX 0920+1 AA 74 FYB 707 2 E-APR25
1944 JFK 2100 SR 111 FY 747 0
X234 1015 LAX 1105+1 AF 004 FY 747 1 E-MAY20
0745 CDG 1110 AF 662 FY 72S 0
1230 LAX 1110+1 TW 760 FYB 747 0 D-APR24
0740 LHR 0945 BE 574 FY TRD 0
1230 LAX 1110+1 TW 760 FYB 747 0 E-APR25
0640 LHR 0945 BE 574 FY TRD 0
1730 LAX 1720+1 BA 598 FY D10 0 D-APR24
1240 LHR 1555 SR 813 FY D9S 0
1830 LAX 1720+1 BA 598 FY D10 0 E-APR25
1240 LHR 1555 SR 813 FY D9S 0
X2 1900 LAX 2145+1 SK 934 FY D10 1 D-APR24
1650 CPH 1855 SK 607 FY DC9 1
X13 2000 LAX 2145+1 SK 934 FY D10 1 E-MAY17
1650 CPH 1855 SK 607 FY DC9 1
X2 2000 LAX 2145+1 SK 934 FY D10 1 E-APR25
1650 CPH 1855 SK 607 FY DC9 1 D-MAY16
46 2030 LAX 1855+1 AF 002 FY 707 0 D-APR24
1725 CDG 1900 AF 668 FY 72S 0
7 2030 LAX 1855+1 AF 002 FY 707 0 D-APR24
1725 CDG 1900 AF 668 FY 707 0
X123 2030 LAX 2040+1 AF 002 FY 707 0 D-APR24
CDG 1725 ORY 2045 SR 729 FY D9S 0
46 2130 LAX 1855+1 AF 002 FY 707 0 E-APR25
1725 CDG 1900 AF 668 FY 72S 0 D-MAY15
7 2130 LAX 1855+1 AF 002 FY 707 0 E-APR25
1725 CDG 1900 AF 668 FY 707 0 D-MAY15
X123 2130 LAX 2040+1 AF 002 FY 707 0 E-APR25
CDG 1725 ORY 2045 SR 729 FY D9S 0 D-MAY15

LOUISVILLE, KY., USA 5395/0 SDF
CONNECTIONS
1237 0920+1 AL 174 SB D9S 1 D-APR24
1515 JFK 2000 SR 111 FY 747 0
X136 1237 1005+1 AL 174 SB D9S 1 E-APR25
1515 JFK 2000 TW 832 FYB B3J 1
X136 1605 1055+1 TW 396 FYB 72S 0 D-APR24
LGA 1742 JFK 2000 TW 832 FYB B3J 1
X136 1605 1005+1 TW 396 FYB 72S 0 E-APR25
LGA 1742 JFK 2000 TW 832 FYB B3J 1

LUBUMBASHI, ZAIRE 5414/0 FBM
F ZAI 539 1078 5.390
Y ZAI 332 664
1 0630 1615 QC 080 • 737 1
QC 080 737-FIH-D10
QC 080 Y-FIH-FY

MADRID, SPAIN 753/628 MAD
F PTS 9450 18900 95
Y PTS 7200 14400
0800 0940 SR 657 FY D9S 0 D-APR10
0900 0940 SR 657 FY D9S 0 E-APR11
2 1055 1240 OK 773 Y T34 0 D-APR10
5 1055 1410 OK 773 Y T34 1 D-APR10
2 1155 1240 OK 773 Y T34 0 E-APR11
5 1155 1410 OK 773 Y T34 1 E-APR11
135 1355 1540 LO 392 Y T34 0 D-APR10
36 1420 1640 RG 752 FY 707 1 E-APR 2
135 1455 1540 LO 392 Y T34 0 E-APR11
1555 1740 IB 284 FY 727 0 D-APR10
1655 1740 IB 284 FY 727 0 E-APR11

MALAGA, SPAIN 1028/857 AGP
F PTS 11550 23100 116
Y PTS 9050 18100
46 0900 1110 IB 572 FY DC9 0 D-APR10
357 0915 1240 IB 512 FY DC9 1 D-APR10
46 1000 1110 IB 572 FY DC9 0 E-APR11
D-JUN30
246 1000 1110 IB 572 FY DC9 0 E-JUL 1
D-AUG31
46 1000 1110 IB 572 FY DC9 0 E-SEP 1
357 1015 1240 IB 512 FY DC9 1 E-APR11
D-JUN30
X246 1015 1240 IB 512 FY DC9 1 E-JUL 1
D-AUG31
357 1015 1240 IB 512 FY DC9 1 E-SEP 1
X234 1515 1725 SR 683 FY D9S 0 D-APR10
X234 1615 1725 SR 683 FY D9S 0 E-APR11

MANCHESTER, ENGLAND 741/618 MAN
F UKL 96.00 192.00 .96
Y UKL 64.00 128.00
126 1045 1225 BE 952 Y S11 0

MANILA, PHILIPPINES 9069/0 MNL
F 1553.20 3106.40 15.53
Y 927.40 1854.80
5 1615 0520+1 SR 309 • DC8 3
SR 309 FY-ATH-FYn
CONT. NEXT COLUMN

To GENEVA, SWITZERLAND GVA

From MANILA, PHILIPPINES-CONT. MNL
CONNECTIONS
4 1710 1010+1 SN 274 FY D10 0 D-MAY28
1945 BKK 2315 QF 5 FY 747 2
0750 FCO 0850 SR 611 FY D9S 0
1 1950 1010+1 PR 822 FY D10 2 D-MAY28
0610 FCO 0850 SR 611 FY D9S 0
1 1950 1010+1 PR 822 FY D10 2 E-MAY30
0710 FCO 0950 SR 611 FY D9S 0
5 1950 1010+1 PR 824 FY D10 2 D-MAY28
0600 FCO 0850 SR 611 FY D9S 0

MARSEILLE, FRANCE 238/199 MRS
F FFR 521 1042 5.21
Y FFR 366 732
5 1420 1410 OK 773 Y T34 0 D-SEP25
1625 1715 SR 763 FY D9S 0 E-SEP26
1725 1715 SR 763 FY D9S 0 D-SEP25

MELBOURNE, VIC., AUSTRALIA 12766/0 MEL
CONNECTIONS
36 1230 MEL 1010+1 AZ 761 FY D10 3 D-MAY28
0515 FCO 0850 SR 611 FY D9S 0
36 1230 MEL 1010+1 AZ 761 FY D10 3 E-MAY29
0615 FCO 0950 SR 611 FY D9S 0
2 1300 MEL 1010+1 AZ 1789 FY D10 4 D-MAY28
0720 FCO 0850 SR 611 FY D9S 0
146 1545 MEL 1010+1 QF 5 FY 747 3 D-MAY28
0750 FCO 0850 SR 611 FY D9S 0

MEMPHIS, TENN., USA 5778/0 MEM
CONNECTIONS
1340 0920+1 BN 118 FYB 72S 1 D-APR24
1725 JFK 2000 SR 111 FY 747 0
1340 0920+1 BN 118 FYB 72S 1 E-APR25
1725 JFK 2100 SR 111 FY 747 0

MERIDA, MEXICO 6747/0 MID
CONNECTIONS
5 1300 1030+1 LH 483 FY D10 1
0745 FRA 0925 LH 240 FY 737 0

MEXICO CITY, MEXICO 7134/0 MEX
CONNECTIONS
5 1030 1030+1 LH 483 FY D10 2
0745 FRA 0925 LH 240 FY 737 0
27 1145 1030+1 LH 481 FY D10 1
0745 FRA 0925 LH 240 FY 737 0
6 1215 1110+1 BA 240 FY 707 1
0710 LHR 0945 BE 574 FY TRD 0
4 1215 1110+1 BA 240 FY 707 1
0735 LHR 0945 BE 574 FY TRD 0
2 1215 1235+1 BA 240 FY 707 2
0835 LHR 1110 SR 811 FY D9S 0
X257 1850 1705+1 AF 066 FY 747 1
1510 CDG 1700 AF 666 FY CVL 0

MIAMI, FLA., USA. 5858/0 MIA
6.81
F 681.00 1362.00
YL 384.00 768.00
Y 397.00 794.00
YH 489.00 978.00
EX/4 14-21 DAY YE 663.00
EX/5 14-21 DAY YE 749.00
EX/8 22-45 DAY YE 444.00
EX/12 22-45 DAY YE 474.00
EX/13 22-45 DAY YE 577.00
EX/28-AP 22-45 DAY YE 425.00
EX/29-AP 22-45 DAY YE 444.00
EX/30-AP 22-45 DAY YE 549.00
EX/35 YL - YOUTH 572.00
EX/36 Y - YOUTH 589.00
EX/37 YH - YOUTH 634.00
CONNECTIONS
1350 0920+1 DL 478 FYJ 72S 0 D-APR24
1612 JFK 2000 SR 111 FY 747 0
1350 1105+1 DL 478 FYJ 72S 0 D-APR24
1612 JFK 1900 AF 070 FY 747 0
0855 CDG 1110 AF 662 FY 72S 0
1350 1105+1 DL 478 FYJ 72S 0 E-APR25
1612 JFK 1900 AF 070 FY 747 0
0755 CDG 1110 AF 662 FY 72S 0
1400 1105+1 EA 20 FYBJ L10 0 D-APR24
LGA 1637 JFK 1900 AF 070 FY 747 0
0855 CDG 1110 AF 662 FY 72S 0
1400 1105+1 EA 20 FYBJ L10 0 E-APR25
LGA 1637 JFK 1900 AF 070 FY 747 0 D-APR30
0755 CDG 1110 AF 662 FY 72S 0
1400 1105+1 EA 20 FYBJ 727 0 E-MAY 1
LGA 1637 JFK 1900 AF 070 FY 747 0
0755 CDG 1110 AF 662 FY 72S 0
1500 0920+1 EA 22 FYBJ D9S 0 D-APR24
1748 JFK 2000 SR 111 FY 747 0
X136 1500 1055+1 EA 22 FYBJ D9S 0 D-APR24
1748 JFK 2000 TW 832 FYB B3J 1
X136 1500 1005+1 EA 22 FYBJ D9S 0 E-APR25
1748 JFK 2000 TW 832 FYB B3J 1
1700 0920+1 DL 472 FYJ 72S 0 E-APR25
1922 JFK 2100 SR 111 FY 747 0
1700 0920+1 EA 26 FYBJ L10 0 E-APR25
1922 JFK 2100 SR 111 FY 747 0
14 1730 1305+1 NA 98 FYJ D10 0 E-APR25
2003 JFK 2200 AF 022 FY 747 0 D-MAY15
1055 CDG 1300 AF 664 FY CVL 0
X256 1730 1305+1 NA 98 FYJ D10 0 E-MAY16
2003 JFK 2200 AF 022 FY 747 0
1055 CDG 1300 AF 664 FY CVL 0
47 1730 1740+1 IB 978 FY D10 1 D-APR 9
1020 MAD 1555 IB 284 FY 727 0
47 1730 1740+1 IB 978 FY D10 1 E-APR11
1120 MAD 1655 IB 284 FY 727 0 D-APR24
X37 1820 1110+1 NA 2 FY D10 0 E-APR25
0735 LHR 0945 BE 574 FY TRD 0 D-MAY15
X7 1820 1110+1 NA 2 FY D10 0 E-MAY16
0735 LHR 0945 BE 574 FY TRD 0
2 1820 1230+1 NA 2 FY D10 0 D-APR24
0835 LHR 1105 SV 796 FY 707 0
X37 1820 1235+1 NA 2 FY D10 0 D-APR24
0835 LHR 1110 SR 811 FY D9S 0
47 1830 1740+1 IB 978 FY D10 1 E-APR25
1120 MAD 1655 IB 284 FY 727 0
X23 1930 1235+1 BA 660 FY 747 0 D-APR24
0945 LHR 1110 SR 811 FY D9S 0
X23 1930 1235+1 BA 660 FY 747 0 E-APR25
0845 LHR 1110 SR 811 FY D9S 0 D-MAY15
X2 1930 1235+1 BA 660 FY 747 0 E-MAY16
0845 LHR 1110 SR 811 FY D9S 0

MILAN, ITALY 176/147 MIL
F LIT 56100 112200 600
Y LIT 40400 80800
0820 LIN 0905 AZ 412 FY DC9 0 D-MAY29
0820 LIN 0905 AZ 412 FY DC9 0 E-SEP26
0920 LIN 0905 AZ 412 FY DC9 0 E-MAY30
D-SEP25
1115 MXP 1100 TW 831 FYB B3J 0 E-JUN10
1630 LIN 1715 SR 643 FY D9S 0 D-MAY29
1630 LIN 1715 SR 643 FY D9S 0 E-SEP26
1730 LIN 1715 SR 643 FY D9S 0 E-MAY30
D-SEP25

To GENEVA, SWITZERLAND GVA

From MILWAUKEE, WIS., USA 5350/0 MKE
7.25
F 725.00 1450.00
YL 403.00 806.00
Y 416.00 832.00
YH 508.00 1016.00
EX/4 14-21 DAY YE 736.00
EX/5 14-21 DAY YE 822.00
EX/8 22-45 DAY YE 515.00
EX/12 22-45 DAY YE 545.00
EX/13 22-45 DAY YE 648.00
EX/28-AP 22-45 DAY YE 443.00
EX/29-AP 22-45 DAY YE 462.00
EX/30-AP 22-45 DAY YE 567.00
EX/35 YL - YOUTH 459.00
EX/36 Y - YOUTH 476.00
EX/37 YH - YOUTH 521.00
CONNECTIONS
1345 0920+1 NW 220 FYB 747 0 D-APR24
1640 JFK 2000 SR 111 FY 747 0
1345 0920+1 NW 220 FYB 747 0 E-APR25
1640 JFK 2100 SR 111 FY 747 0
X26 1420 1105+1 NC 294 SB CV5 0 D-APR24
1450 ORD 1630 AF 030 FY 747 1
1020 CDG 1110 AF 662 FY 72S 0
X26 1535 1105+1 NC 815 SB CV5 0 E-APR25
1605 ORD 1730 AF 030 FY 747 1
1020 CDG 1110 AF 662 FY 72S 0

MINNEAPOLIS/ST PAUL, MINN., USA 5671/0 MSP
7.51
F 751.00 1502.00
YL 420.00 840.00
Y 433.00 866.00
YH 525.00 1050.00
EX/4 14-21 DAY YE 743.00
EX/5 14-21 DAY YE 829.00
EX/8 22-45 DAY YE 493.00
EX/12 22-45 DAY YE 523.00
EX/13 22-45 DAY YE 626.00
EX/28-AP 22-45 DAY YE 479.00
EX/29-AP 22-45 DAY YE 498.00
EX/30-AP 22-45 DAY YE 603.00
EX/35 YL - YOUTH 482.00
EX/36 Y - YOUTH 499.00
EX/37 YH - YOUTH 544.00
CONNECTIONS
1200 MSP 0920+1 NW 220 FYB 747 1 D-APR24
1640 JFK 2000 SR 111 FY 747 0
1200 MSP 0920+1 NW 220 FYB 747 1 E-APR25
1640 JFK 2100 SR 111 FY 747 0
X136 1200 MSP 1055+1 NW 220 FYB 747 1 D-APR24
1640 JFK 2000 TW 832 FYB B3J 1
X136 1200 MSP 1005+1 NW 220 FYB 747 1 E-APR25
1640 JFK 2000 TW 832 FYB B3J 1
X26 1355 MSP 1105+1 NW 716 FYB 72S 0 D-APR24
1500 ORD 1630 AF 030 FY 747 1
1020 CDG 1110 AF 662 FY 72S 0
X26 1455 MSP 1105+1 UA 680 FYB 72S 0 E-APR25
1605 ORD 1730 AF 030 FY 747 1
1020 CDG 1110 AF 662 FY 72S 0
257 1655 MSP 1220+1 NW 288 FYB 727 0 D-APR24
2019 BOS 2145 SR 165 FY D10 0
1050 ZRH 1140 SR 232 FY D9S 0
1 1655 MSP 1305+1 NW 288 FYB 727 0 D-APR24
2019 BOS 2145 SR 165 FY D10 0
1050 ZRH 1220 SR 252 FY D10 0
3 1655 MSP 1305+1 NW 288 FYB 727 0 D-APR24
2019 BOS 2145 SR 165 FY D10 0
1050 ZRH 1220 SR 262 FY DC8 0
X3 1655 MSP 1315+1 NW 288 FYB 727 0 D-APR24
2019 BOS 2145 SR 165 FY D10 0
1050 ZRH 1235 SR 928 FY D9S 0
257 1655 MSP 1220+1 NW 288 FYB 727 0 E-APR25
2019 BOS 2245 SR 165 FY D10 0
1050 ZRH 1140 SR 232 FY D9S 0
1 1655 MSP 1305+1 NW 288 FYB 727 0 E-APR25
2019 BOS 2245 SR 165 FY D10 0
1050 ZRH 1220 SR 252 FY D10 0
3 1655 MSP 1305+1 NW 288 FYB 727 0 E-APR25
2019 BOS 2245 SR 165 FY D10 0
1050 ZRH 1220 SR 262 FY DC8 0
X3 1655 MSP 1315+1 NW 288 FYB 727 0 E-APR25
2019 BOS 2245 SR 165 FY D10 0
1050 ZRH 1235 SR 928 FY D9S 0

MONROVIA, LIBERIA 3636/0 MLW
F LID 791 1582 7.91
Y LID 491 982
7 0745 ROB 1635 SR 255 FY DC8 1
4 0745 ROB 1635 SR 259 FY DC8 1

MONTERREY, MEXICO 6853/0 MTY
CONNECTIONS
X257 1600 1705+1 MX 721 Y 72S 0
1705 MEX 1850 AF 066 FY 747 1
1510 CDG 1700 AF 666 FY CVL 0

MONTREAL, QUE., CANADA 4419/0 YUL
F CAD 596 1192 5.96
YL CAD 324 648
Y CAD 337 674
YH CAD 429 858
EX/4 14-21 DAY YE CAD 571
EX/5 14-21 DAY YE CAD 657
EX/8 22-45 DAY YE CAD 358
EX/12 22-45 DAY YE CAD 377
EX/13 22-45 DAY YE CAD 473
EX/28-AP 22-45 DAY YE CAD 321
EX/29-AP 22-45 DAY YE CAD 340
EX/30-AP 22-45 DAY YE CAD 436
EX/35 YL - YOUTH CAD 328
EX/36 Y - YOUTH CAD 345
EX/37 YH - YOUTH CAD 390
CONNECTIONS
X136 1640 YUL 1055+1 EA 159 FYB 727 0 D-APR24
1800 JFK 2000 TW 832 FYB B3J 1
X136 1640 YUL 1005+1 EA 159 FYB 727 0 E-APR25
1800 JFK 2000 TW 832 FYB B3J 1
X12 1810 YMX 0945+1 KL 682 FY 747 0 D-APR24
0645 AMS 0825 KL 331 Y DC9 0
6 1810 YMX 1215+1 KL 682 FY 747 0 D-APR24
0645 AMS 0945 RJ 152 FY B3J 1
1 1850 YMX 0945+1 CP 208 FY 747 0 D-APR24
0730 AMS 0825 KL 331 Y DC9 0
X12 1910 YMX 0945+1 KL 682 FY 747 0 E-APR25
0645 AMS 0825 KL 331 Y DC9 0
6 1910 YMX 1215+1 KL 682 FY 747 0 E-APR25
0645 AMS 0945 RJ 152 FY B3J 1
1 1915 YMX 0945+1 CP 282 FY 747 0 E-APR26
0700 AMS 0825 KL 331 Y DC9 0
124 1920 YMX 1030+1 LH 445 FY 707 0 D-APR24
0830 FRA 0925 LH 240 FY 737 0
4 1935 YMX 1200+1 SK 940 FY D8S 0 D-APR24
0835 CPH 1005 SR 423 FY D9S 0
X256 1945 YMX 1030+1 LH 441 FY 707 0 E-MAY16
0755 FRA 0925 LH 240 FY 737 0
CONT. NEXT COLUMN

To GENEVA, SWITZERLAND GVA

From MONTREAL, QUE., CANADA-CONT. YUL
4 2020 YMX 1030+1 LH 445 FY 707 0 E-MAY 1
0830 FRA 0925 LH 240 FY 737 0 D-MAY15
12 2020 YMX 1030+1 LH 445 FY D10 0 E-MAY 1
0830 FRA 0925 LH 240 FY 737 0 D-MAY15
124 2020 YMX 1030+1 LH 445 FY 707 0 E-APR25
0830 FRA 0925 LH 240 FY 737 0 D-APR30
4 2035 YMX 1200+1 SK 940 FY D8S 0 E-APR25
0835 CPH 1005 SR 423 FY D9S 0 D-MAY16
14 2035 YMX 1200+1 SK 940 FY D8S 0 E-MAY17
0835 CPH 1005 SR 423 FY D9S 0
X26 2045 YMX 1105+1 AF 030 FY 747 0 D-APR24
1020 CDG 1110 AF 662 FY 72S 0
6 2045 YMX 1105+1 AF 032 FY 747 0 D-APR24
1020 CDG 1110 AF 662 FY 72S 0
2 2045 YMX 1215+1 CP 282 FY 747 0 E-APR27
0830 AMS 0945 RJ 152 FY B3J 1
2 2050 YMX 1150+1 SR 171 FY D10 0 D-APR24
0955 ZRH 1110 SR 236 FY D9S 0
SR 236 PENDING GOVT APPROVAL
67 2050 YMX 1150+1 SR 171 FY D10 0 D-APR24
0955 ZRH 1110 SR 682 FY D9S 0
16 2050 YMX 1215+1 SR 171 FY D10 0 D-APR24
0955 ZRH 1135 SR 242 FY D9S 0
3 2125 YMX 1510+1 SN 504 FY 707 0
0910 BRU 1400 SN 793 FY 737 0
7 2125 YMX 1510+1 SN 508 FY 707 0
0910 BRU 1400 SN 793 FY 737 0
X26 2145 YMX 1105+1 AF 030 FY 747 0 E-APR25
1020 CDG 1110 AF 662 FY 72S 0
6 2145 YMX 1105+1 AF 032 FY 747 0 E-APR25
1020 CDG 1110 AF 662 FY 72S 0 D-MAY 7
2 2150 YMX 1150+1 SR 171 FY D10 0 E-APR25
0955 ZRH 1110 SR 236 FY D9S 0
SR 236 PENDING GOVT APPROVAL
67 2150 YMX 1150+1 SR 171 FY D10 0 E-APR25
0955 ZRH 1110 SR 682 FY D9S 0
16 2150 YMX 1215+1 SR 171 FY D10 0 E-APR25
0955 ZRH 1135 SR 242 FY D9S 0
2210 YMX 1235+1 BA 600 FY 747 0 E-APR25
0925 LHR 1110 SR 811 FY D9S 0 D-MAY22
56 2210 YMX 1235+1 BA 610 FY 707 0 E-MAY28
0930 LHR 1110 SR 811 FY D9S 0
23 2210 YMX 1235+1 BA 610 FY V10 0 E-MAY25
0930 LHR 1110 SR 811 FY D9S 0
147 2210 YMX 1235+1 BA 610 FY 747 0 E-MAY23
0925 LHR 1110 SR 811 FY D9S 0
5 2210 YMX 1430+1 BA 600 FY 747 0 D-APR24
1025 LHR 1305 BE 576 Y TRD 0
247 2210 YMX 1430+1 BA 600 FY 747 0 D-APR24
1025 LHR 1305 BE 576 FY TRD 0
136 2210 YMX 1435+1 BA 600 FY 747 0 D-APR24
1025 LHR 1305 BE 576 Y S11 0

MOSCOW, USSR 1800/1499 MOW
F ROU 304.20 608.40 3.05
Y ROU 207.50 415.00
6 0925 SVO 1105 SU 271 FY T54 0

MUSCAT, OMAN 4041/0 MCT
CONNECTIONS
6 0600 1445 RJ 601 FY 72S 1
0820 AMM 1100 RJ 151 FY B3J 0
46 0640 1455 ME 439 FY 747 1
0935 BEY 1145 ME 215 FY 707 0

NAIROBI, KENYA 4548/3783 NBO
F KES 7610 15220 76.10
Y KES 4618 9236
CONNECTIONS
6 0055 NBO 1010 AZ 849 FY D8S 0 E-APR 2
0550 FCO 0850 SR 611 FY D9S 0 D-MAY29
6 0130 NBO 1050 OA 102 FY 707 0 D-APR10
0620 ATH 0910 OA 131 FY 720 0
6 0130 NBO 1050 OA 102 FY 707 0 E-APR12
0720 ATH 1010 OA 131 FY 720 0
1 0135 NBO 1010 AZ 815 FY D10 0 D-MAY29
0630 FCO 0850 SR 611 FY D9S 0
1 0135 NBO 1010 AZ 815 FY D10 0 E-MAY30
0730 FCO 0950 SR 611 FY D9S 0
4 0955 NBO 1830 AZ 829 FY D8S 1 D-MAY29
1615 FCO 1710 AZ 408 FY DC9 0
7 1140 NBO 2135 AZ 1813 FY D8S 0 D-MAY29
1635 FCO 2015 SR 609 FY D9S 0
7 1140 NBO 2135 AZ 1813 FY D8S 0 E-MAY30
1735 FCO 2115 SR 609 FY D9S 0

NASHVILLE, TENN., USA 5540/0 BNA
CONNECTIONS
0834 0920+1 AA 606 FYB 727 0 D-APR24
1120 LGA 1617 NY 944 A S61 0
1624 JFK 2000 SR 111 FY 747 0
0834 0920+1 AA 606 FYB 727 0 E-APR25
1120 LGA 1603 NY 940 A S61 0
1610 JFK 2100 SR 111 FY 747 0
0950 0920+1 AA 540 FYB 727 2 D-APR24
1435 LGA 1913 NY 970 A S61 0
1920 JFK 2000 SR 111 FY 747 0
0950 0920+1 AA 540 FYB 727 2 E-APR25
1435 LGA 1913 NY 970 A S61 0
1920 JFK 2100 SR 111 FY 747 0
1045 0920+1 AA 414 FYB 727 1 D-APR24
1430 LGA 1913 NY 970 A S61 0
1920 JFK 2000 SR 111 FY 747 0
1045 0920+1 AA 414 FYB 727 1 E-APR25
1430 LGA 1913 NY 970 A S61 0
1920 JFK 2100 SR 111 FY 747 0
1445 0920+1 BN 118 FYB 72S 0 D-APR24
1725 JFK 2000 SR 111 FY 747 0
1445 0920+1 BN 118 FYB 72S 0 E-APR25
1725 JFK 2100 SR 111 FY 747 0

NASSAU, BAHAMAS 5781/0 NAS
CONNECTIONS
5 1600 NAS 1110+1 BA 210 FY 707 1 E-APR 2
0735 LHR 0945 BE 574 FY TRD 0 D-APR23
6 1700 NAS 1110+1 BA 240 FY 707 0 D-APR24
0710 LHR 0945 BE 574 FY TRD 0
5 1700 NAS 1110+1 BA 210 FY 707 1 E-APR30
0735 LHR 0945 BE 574 FY TRD 0
2 1700 NAS 1235+1 BA 240 FY 707 1 D-APR20
0835 LHR 1110 SR 811 FY D9S 0
6 1800 NAS 1110+1 BA 240 FY 707 0 E-MAY 1
0710 LHR 0945 BE 574 FY TRD 0
2 1800 NAS 1235+1 BA 240 FY 707 1 E-APR27
0835 LHR 1110 SR 811 FY D9S 0
3 2320 NAS 1720+1 BA 210 FY 747 0 E-APR 7
1315 LHR 1555 SR 813 FY D9S 0 D-APR21
3 2320 NAS 1720+1 BA 210 FY 747 0 E-APR28
1215 LHR 1555 SR 813 FY D9S 0

Freq.	Leave	Arrive	Flight	Class	Eq S	Eff./Dis.

To LJUBLJANA, YUGOSLAVIA — LJU

Freq.	Leave	Arrive	Flight	Class	Eq S	Eff./Dis.
From LONDON, ENGLAND-CONT.						**LON**
27	1305 LHR	1605	JU 213	Y	DC9 0	E-OCT24
5	1305 LHR	1605	JU 213	Y	727 0	E-OCT24
27	1405 LHR	1605	JU 213	Y	DC9 0	D-OCT23
5	1405 LHR	1605	JU 213	Y	727 0	D-OCT23
MALTA, MEDITERRANEAN SEA 1035/716						**MLA**
5	1445	1650	JU 455	Y	DC9 0	E-SEP20
5	1545	1650	JU 455	Y	DC9 0	D-SEP19
NEW YORK, N.Y., USA. 5058/0						**NYC**
		CONNECTIONS				
X356	1945 JFK	1350+1	LH 401	FY	747 0	
	0810 FRA	1240	JU 353	Y	DC9 0	
1	2215 JFK	1350+1	KL 644	FY	747 0	
	1015 AMS	1215	JU 225	Y	DC9 0	
3	2300 JFK	1355+1	LH 491	FY	D10 0	
	1125 FRA	1240	JU 355	Y	DC9 0	
5	2300 JFK	1355+1	LH 493	FY	D10 0	
	1125 FRA	1240	JU 355	Y	DC9 0	
6	2300 JFK	1355+1	LH 495	FY	D10 0	
	1125 FRA	1240	JU 355	Y	DC9 0	
PARIS, FRANCE 710/591						**PAR**
	F		FFR 905		1810	9.05K
	Y		FFR 660		1320	
57	1955 ORY	2145	AF 245	Y	DC9 0	
PRAGUE, CZECHOSLOVAKIA 322/269						**PRG**
	F		CKR 571		1142	5.75K
	Y		CKR 438		876	
3	1745	1845	JU 333	Y	DC9 0	
6	1745	1845	JU 335	Y	DC9 0	
SKOPJE, YUGOSLAVIA						**SKP**
	Y		YUD 490		980	4.90K
2	0800	1020	JU 905	Y	DC9 1	
SPLIT, YUGOSLAVIA 0/206						**SPU**
	Y		YUD 274		548	2.75K
1	0840	0930	JU 384	FY	727 0	
1	0840	0930	JU 900	FY	727 0	
2	0930	1020	JU 905	Y	DC9 0	
4	1500	1555	JU 900	Y	CVL 0	E-JUN 1 D-SEP30
57	1605	1655	JU 900	Y	DC9 0	
TORONTO, ONT., CANADA 5179/0						**YYZ**
		CONNECTIONS				
4	2000	1605+1	BA 600	FY	747 1	D-MAY22
	0925 LHR	1405	JU 213	Y	727 0	
16	2000	1605+1	BA 600	FY	747 1	D-MAY22
	0925 LHR	1405	JU 213	Y	DC9 0	
ZURICH, SWITZERLAND 351/293						**ZRH**
	F		SFR 383		766	3.90K
	Y		SFR 275		550	
X46	1130	1235	JU 323	Y	DC9 0	

To LOANI, PAPUA NEW GUINEA — LNP

ARPT LOANI 10.0MI/16.1KM 30MIN

Freq.	Leave	Arrive	Flight	Class	Eq S	Eff./Dis.
From AMAZON BAY, PAPUA NEW GUINEA						**AZB**
	F		NGK 17.00		34.00	.17K
4	0930	1105	GV 812	F	CES 3	
BAIBARA, PAPUA NEW GUINEA						**BAP**
4	1020	1105	GV 812	F	CES 1	
MAMAI, PAPUA NEW GUINEA						**MAP**
4	0955	1105	GV 812	F	CES 2	
PORT MORESBY, PAPUA NEW GUINEA						**POM**
	F		NGK 41.00		82.00	.38K
4	0800	1105	GV 812	F	CES 4	
SAGARAI, PAPUA NEW GUINEA						**SGJ**
	F		NGK 9.50		19.00	.09K
4	1050	1105	GV 812	F	CES 0	

To LOCK, S. AUSTRALIA — LOC

ARPT LOCK 6.0MI/9.7KM 8MIN

Freq.	Leave	Arrive	Flight	Class	Eq S	Eff./Dis.
From ADELAIDE, S. AUSTRALIA						**ADL**
	F		AUD 26.75		53.50	
1	0750	0920	CE 460	F	DDV 1	
5	1300	1420	CE 464	F	BBR 1	
CLEVE, S. AUSTRALIA 0/44						**CVC**
	F		AUD 10.00		20.00	
1	0910	0920	CE 460	F	DDV 0	
5	1410	1420	CE 464	F	BBR 0	
MINNIPA, S. AUSTRALIA						**MIN**
	F		AUD 11.00		22.00	
1	1105	1140	CE 461	F	DDV 1	
5	1605	1640	CE 465	F	BBR 1	
STREAKY BAY, S. AUSTRALIA						**KBY**
	F		AUD 15.00		30.00	
1	1045	1140	CE 461	F	DDV 2	
5	1545	1640	CE 465	F	BBR 2	
WUDINNA, S. AUSTRALIA 0/41						**WUD**
	F		AUD 10.00		20.00	
1	1125	1140	CE 461	F	DDV 0	
5	1625	1640	CE 465	F	BBR 0	

To LODJA, ZAIRE — LJA

ARPT LODJA 7.5MI/12.0KM 45MIN

Freq.	Leave	Arrive	Flight	Class	Eq S	Eff./Dis.
From KANANGA, ZAIRE 0/188						**KGA**
	Y		ZAI 32.65		65.30	.46K
2	1015	1120	QC 631	Y	F27 0	
KINDU, ZAIRE 0/162						**KND**
	Y		ZAI 28.55		57.10	.40K
7	1615	1715	QC 415	Y	F27 0	
KINSHASA, ZAIRE 0/568						**FIH**
	Y		ZAI 67.20		134.40	.95K
5	0500	0840	QC 140	Y	F27 0	
7	0530	0910	QC 160	Y	F27 0	
KISANGANI, ZAIRE						**FKI**
	Y		ZAI 52.65		105.30	.74K
2	1350	1520	QC 360	Y	F27 0	

To LOEI, THAILAND — LOE

ARPT LOEI 3.0MI/4.8KM 10MIN

Freq.	Leave	Arrive	Flight	Class	Eq S	Eff./Dis.
From BANGKOK, THAILAND						**BKK**
	Y		BHT 495		990	5.00K
1	0820	1105	TH 221	Y	748 2	
BAN MAK KHAENG, THAILAND 0/71						**BAO**
	Y		BHT 115		230	1.20K
1	1040	1105	TH 221	Y	748 0	
KHON KAEN, THAILAND						**KKC**
	Y		BHT 205		390	2.10K
1	0945	1105	TH 221	Y	748 1	
NAKHON PHANOM, THAILAND 0/199						**KOP**
4	1140	1240	TH 234	Y	748 0	

To LOERIESFONTEIN, SOUTH AFRICA — LOM

Freq.	Leave	Arrive	Flight	Class	Eq S	Eff./Dis.
From CALVINIA, SOUTH AFRICA 0/487						**CLV**
5	0805	0820	NJ 531	S	PNV 0	
2	0905	0920	NJ 231	S	PNV 0	
CAPETOWN, SOUTH AFRICA 0/583						**CPT**
5	0700 CPT	0820	NJ 531	S	PNV 1	
2	0800 CPT	0920	NJ 231	S	PNV 1	
GRENAATBOSKOLK, SOUTH AFRICA						**GRL**
4	1600	1640	NJ 434	S	PNV 0	
5	1600	1640	NJ 532	S	PNV 0	
KENHARDT, SOUTH AFRICA 0/417						**KEH**
4	1525	1640	NJ 434	S	PNV 1	
5	1525	1640	NJ 532	S	PNV 1	
UPINGTON, SOUTH AFRICA						**UTN**
4	1500	1640	NJ 434	S	PNV 2	
5	1500	1640	NJ 532	S	PNV 2	

To LOIKAW, BURMA — LIW

Freq.	Leave	Arrive	Flight	Class	Eq S	Eff./Dis.
From HEHO, BURMA 0/81						**HEH**
	Y		BUR 40.00		80.00	40L
4	1430	1500	UB 604	Y	F27 0	
135	1440	1510	UB 602	Y	F27 0	
LASHIO, BURMA						**LSH**
	Y		BUR 95.00		190.00	95L
135	1225	1510	UB 602	Y	F27 2	
MANDALAY, BURMA						**MDL**
	Y		BUR 95.00		190.00	95L
135	1345	1510	UB 602	Y	F27 1	
RANGOON, BURMA 0/207						**RGN**
	Y		BUR 85.00		170.00	85L
135	0800	0900	UB 601	Y	F27 0	
4	1200	1300	UB 603	Y	F27 0	

To LOJA, ECUADOR — LOH

Freq.	Leave	Arrive	Flight	Class	Eq S	Eff./Dis.
From CUENCA, ECUADOR 0/83						**CUE**
	T		SUC 150		300	
X7	1130	1210	WB 833	T	DC3 0	
QUITO, ECUADOR						**UIO**
	T		SUC 450		900	
146	1015	1210	WB 833	T	V70 1	
		WB 833 V70-CUE-DC3				

To LOME, TOGO — LFW

ARPT LOME 2.5MI/4.0KM 30MIN

Freq.	Leave	Arrive	Flight	Class	Eq S	Eff./Dis.
From ABIDJAN, IVORY COAST 434/362						**ABJ**
	F		AFR 20900		41800	210K
	Y		AFR 16700		33400	
5	0630	0735	RK 106	FY	DC8 0	E-MAY 7
6	0630	0830	RK 516	FY	CVL 1	E-MAY 8
6	0700	0900	RK 516	Y	CVL 1	D-MAY 7
7	1130	1240	RK 524	FY	CVL 0	E-MAY 6
3	1215	1325	RK 520	Y	CVL 0	D-MAY 4
7	1220	1325	RK 50	FY	DC8 0	D-MAY 7
1	1335	1445	QC 051	Y	73S 0	
1	1500	1610	RK 500	Y	CVL 0	D-MAY 3
4	1545	1650	RK 104	FY	DC8 0	E-MAY 6
2	1845	1955	RK 500	FY	CVL 0	E-JUL 6 D-SEP21
5	1945	2050	RK 131	FY	DC8 0	
2	1945	2055	RK 500	FY	CVL 0	E-SEP28
2	2015	2125	RK 500	FY	CVL 0	E-MAY 4 D-JUN29
2	2015	2125	RK 512	Y	CVL 0	D-APR30
2	2015	2125	RK 512	FY	CVL 0	E-MAY 1
4	2100	2210	RK 504	Y	CVL 0	D-MAY 5
ACCRA, GHANA 126/105						**ACC**
	F		GHC 43		86	43K
	Y		GHC 35		70	
1	0730	0800	GH 550	FY	F28 0	
6	0800	0830	RK 516	FY	CVL 0	E-MAY 8
6	0830	0900	RK 516	Y	CVL 0	D-MAY 7
BORDEAUX, FRANCE						**BOD**
6	0050	0605	UT 837	FY	DC8 1	D-MAY 1
6	1150	1640	UT 837	FY	D10 1	E-MAY 8 D-SEP25
6	1150	1740	UT 837	FY	D10 1	E-SEP26
BRAZZAVILLE, CONGO 1447/0						**BZV**
	F		AFR 65300		130600	655K
	Y		AFR 52200		104400	
4	0600	0855	RK 519	Y	CVL 1	D-MAY 5
4	0700	1145	RK 105	FY	DC8 2	E-MAY 6
1	0830	1130	RK 84	FY	D10 1	D-MAY 9
5	1600	2020	RK 521	FY	CVL 2	E-MAY 7
1	2000	2300	RK 84	FY	D10 1	E-MAY10 D-SEP20
1	2100	2359	RK 84	FY	D10 1	E-SEP27
CHICAGO, ILL., USA.						**CHI**
		CONNECTIONS				
5	1520 ORD	1640+1	TW 800	•	707 1	E-MAY 7
	0825 CDG	0940	UT 837	FY	D10 2	D-JUN 9
		TW 800 707-JFK-747				
		TW 800 FYB-JFK-FY				
COTONOU, PEOPLES REPUBLIC OF BENIN 94/79						**COO**
	F		AFR 6500		13000	65K
	Y		AFR 5200		10400	
3	0600	0530	RK 503	Y	CVL 0	D-APR30
3	0600	0530	RK 503	FY	CVL 0	E-MAY 1
6	1645	1615	RK 531	FY	CVL 0	E-MAY 8 D-SEP25
6	1745	1715	RK 531	FY	CVL 0	E-OCT 2
6	1930	1900	RK 517	Y	CVL 0	D-MAY 8
5	2050	2020	RK 521	FY	CVL 0	E-MAY 7
DAKAR, SENEGAL 1792/0						**DKR**
	F		AFR 71700		143400	720K
	Y		AFR 57400		114800	
7	0715	1325	RK 50	FY	DC8 2	D-MAY 7
1	1000	1445	QC 051	Y	73S 1	
2	1430	1955	RK 500	FY	CVL 1	E-JUL 6 D-SEP21
2	1530	2055	RK 500	FY	CVL 1	E-SEP28
4	1530	2210	RK 504	Y	CVL 2	D-MAY 5
2	1600	2125	RK 500	FY	CVL 1	E-MAY 4 D-JUN29
DOUALA, CAMEROON 722/602						**DLA**
	F		AFR 39600		79200	400K
	Y		AFR 31700		63400	
5	1125	1155	RK 49	FY	DC8 0	D-MAY 6
5	1830	2020	RK 521	FY	CVL 1	E-MAY 7
KINSHASA, ZAIRE 1466/0						**FIH**
	F		ZAI 144		288	1.440K
	Y		ZAI 116		232	
7	0700	1015	QC 050	Y	73S 1	
LAGOS, NIGERIA 176/147						**LOS**
	F		NGN 25.00		50.00	.25K
	Y		NGN 20.00		40.00	
1	1045	1100	GH 551	FY	F28 1	
4	1200	1145	RK 105	FY	DC8 0	E-MAY 6

To LOME, TOGO — LFW

Freq.	Leave	Arrive	Flight	Class	Eq S	Eff./Dis.
From LIBREVILLE, GABON 825/688						**LBV**
	F		AFR 49400		98800	495K
	Y		AFR 39500		79000	
4	0810	0855	RK 519	Y	CVL 0	D-MAY 5
7	0915	1015	QC 050	Y	73S 0	
4	0925	1145	RK 105	FY	DC8 1	E-MAY 6
5	0945	1155	RK 49	FY	DC8 1	D-MAY 6
1	1050	1130	RK 84	FY	D10 0	D-MAY 9
1	2220	2300	RK 84	FY	D10 0	E-MAY10 D-SEP20
1	2320	2359	RK 84	FY	D10 0	E-SEP27
LOS ANGELES, CALIF., USA						**LAX**
		CONNECTIONS				
5	1015 LAX	1640+1	AF 004	FY	747 1	E-MAY20
	0745 CDG	0940	UT 837	FY	D10 2	
MONROVIA, LIBERIA 984/0						**MLW**
	F		LID 173		346	1.73K
	Y		LID 138		276	
7	0950 ROB	1325	RK 50	FY	DC8 1	D-MAY 7
MONTREAL, QUE., CANADA						**YUL**
		CONNECTIONS				
6	1340 YUL	1325+1	AC 746	FY	D9S 0	D-MAY 6
	1455 JFK	1800	RK 50	FY	DC8 3	
6	1446 YUL	1325+1	EA 397	FY	727 0	E-MAY 1
	LGA 1550 JFK	1800	RK 50	FY	DC8 3	D-MAY 6
NEW YORK, N.Y., USA. 6367/0						**NYC**
	F 948.00 1896.00					9.48K
	YO 605.00 1210.00					
	YH 664.00 1328.00					
	EX/11 14-45 DAY YE 833.00					
	EX/18 14-45 DAY YE 957.00					
6	1800 JFK	1325+1	RK 50	FY	DC8 3	D-MAY 6
		CONNECTIONS				
5	1930 JFK	1640+1	TW 800	FY	747 0	E-MAY 7
	0825 CDG	0940	UT 837	FY	D10 2	
NIAMEY, NIGER 757/0						**NIM**
	F		AFR 30900		61800	310K
	Y		AFR 24700		49400	
6	0540	0605	UT 837	FY	DC8 0	D-MAY 1
6	1620	1640	UT 837	FY	D10 0	E-MAY 8 D-SEP25
6	1720	1740	UT 837	FY	D10 0	E-SEP26
OTTAWA, ONTARIO, CANADA						**YOW**
		CONNECTIONS				
6	1145	1325+1	ND 650	Y	FH7 0	D-MAY 6
	1220 YUL	1340	AC 746	FY	D9S 0	
	1455 JFK	1800	RK 50	FY	DC8 3	
6	1300	1325+1	AC 530	Y	DC9 0	E-MAY 1
	1330 YUL	1446	EA 397	FY	727 0	D-MAY 6
	LGA 1550 JFK	1800	RK 50	FY	DC8 3	
OUAGADOUGOU, UPPER VOLTA 0/467						**OUA**
	F		AFR 35500		71000	355K
	Y		AFR 28400		56800	
4	1845	2210	RK 504	Y	CVL 1	D-MAY 5
PARIS, FRANCE 3541/2951						**PAR**
	F		FFR 3925		7850	39.25K
	Y		FFR 2510		5020	
1	0830 CDG	1230	RK 83	FY	D10 0	E-MAY10 D-SEP20
1	0830 CDG	1330	RK 83	FY	D10 0	E-SEP27
6	0940 CDG	1640	UT 837	FY	D10 2	E-MAY 8 D-SEP25
6	0940 CDG	1740	UT 837	FY	D10 2	E-SEP26
7	2030 CDG	0030+1	RK 83	FY	D10 0	D-MAY 9
5	2240 CDG	0605+1	UT 837	FY	DC8 2	D-APR30
TORONTO, ONT., CANADA						**YYZ**
		CONNECTIONS				
6	1510	1325+1	AC 778	FY	D9S 0	D-MAY 6
	1635 JFK	1800	RK 50	FY	DC8 3	
VANCOUVER, B.C., CANADA						**YVR**
		CONNECTIONS				
6	0630	1325+1	PW 350	Y	73S 0	D-MAY 2
	0700 SEA	0845	UA 40	FYB	D10 0	
	1635 JFK	1800	RK 50	FY	DC8 3	
WASHINGTON, D.C., USA						**WAS**
		CONNECTIONS				
5	1825 IAD	1640+1	TW 890	FY	B3J 0	E-MAY 7
	0805 CDG	0940	UT 837	FY	D10 2	

To Londolovit, New Ireland, New Guinea — LNV

ARPT LONDOLOVIT

Freq.	Leave	Arrive	Flight	Class	Eq S	Eff./Dis.
From Kamiraba, New Ireland, New Guinea						**KJU**
	S		NGK 12.00		24.00	.13K
3	0645	0710	VK 526	S	PAZ 0	
KAVIENG, NEW IRELAND, N. GUI.						**KVG**
	S		NGK 28.00		56.00	.28K
3	0600	0710	VK 526	S	PAZ 1	
NAMATANAI, NEW IRELAND, N. GUI. 0/45						**ATN**
	S		NGK 13.00		26.00	.15K
3	1320	1340	VK 527	S	PAZ 0	
RABAUL, NEW BRITAIN, N. GUINEA						**RAB**
	S		NGK 18.00		36.00	.21K
3	1300	1340	VK 527	S	PAZ 1	

To LONDON, ENGLAND — LON

ARPT HEATHROW-LHR-15.0MI/24.1KM 35MIN
TERMINAL 1-BD, BE, CS, CY, EI, KM & NS
TERMINAL 2-AF, AH, AT, AY, AZ, FI, IB, JU, KL, LG, LH, LL, LN, LO, LZ, MA, OA, OK, OS, RO, SK, SN, SR, SU, TK, TP & TU
TERMINAL 3-AC, AE, AI, AR, BA, BG, BW, EC, ET, FG, GF, GH, IA, IR, JL, JM, KU, LY, ME, MH, MK, MS, NA, PA, PK, QC, QF, QZ, RB, RG, RJ, SA, SD, SQ, SV, TG, TW, VA & WT
ARPT GATWICK-LGW-28.0MI/43.2KM 40MIN

Freq.	Leave	Arrive	Flight	Class	Eq S	Eff./Dis.
From ABADAN, IRAN 3848/0						**ABD**
	F		UKL 242.50		485.00	2.43K
	Y		UKL 168.00		336.00	
246	1430	2000 LHR	IR 755	FY	727 1	D-MAY31
X357	1430	2000 LHR	IR 755	FY	727 1	E-JUN 1 D-OCT23
X357	1430	1900 LHR	IR 755	FY	727 1	E-OCT24
ABERDEEN, SCOTLAND 0/415						**ABZ**
	Y		UKL 29.00		58.00	
X7	0735	0855 LHR	BE 8553	Y	B11 0	
X7	0930	1045 LHR	BE 8557	Y	TRD 0	
7	1015	1130 LHR	BE 8559	Y	TRD 0	
X67	1315	1430 LHR	BE 8563	Y	TRD 0	
7	1520	1635 LHR	BE 8567	Y	TRD 0	
6	1520	1640 LHR	BE 8567	Y	B11 0	
X67	1715	1830 LHR	BE 8569	Y	TRD 0	
X7	1940	2055 LHR	BE 8571	Y	TRD 0	

To LONDON, ENGLAND — LON

Freq.	Leave	Arrive	Flight	Class	Eq S	Eff./Dis.
From ABIDJAN, IVORY COAST 3894/0						**ABJ**
	F		AFR 202100		404200	2025K
	Y		AFR 125400		250800	
		CONNECTIONS				
6	0050	1055 LHR	AZ 831	FY	D10 0	E-JUN17
	0820 FCO	0935	AZ 282	FY	DC9 0	
5	2210	1055+1 LHR	AZ 841	FY	D10 1	D-MAY28
	0635 FCO	0835	AZ 282	FY	DC9 0	
5	2210	1055+1 LHR	AZ 841	FY	D10 1	E-MAY30
	0735 FCO	0935	AZ 282	FY	DC9 0	
ABU DHABI, U. A. EMIRATES 4290/3413						**AUH**
	F		ADH 3063		6126	30.65K
	Y		ADH 2154		4308	
27	0105	0645 LHR	GF 121	FY	V10 1	
5	0215	0650 LHR	BA 749	FY	V10 0	D-OCT22
5	0215	0550 LHR	BA 749	FY	V10 0	E-OCT29
7	0335	0810 LHR	BA 861	FY	V10 0	D-OCT17
7	0335	0710 LHR	BA 861	FY	V10 0	E-OCT24
4	0800	1455 LHR	BA 443	FY	V10 2	D-OCT21
4	0800	1355 LHR	BA 443	FY	V10 2	E-OCT28
5	0840	1530 LHR	BA 357	FY	V10 1	D-OCT22
5	0840	1430 LHR	BA 357	FY	V10 1	E-OCT29
3	0850	1315 LHR	BA 485	FY	L10 0	E-MAY12 D-MAY26
136	0850	1450 LHR	BA 485	FY	L10 1	E-JUN 2 D-OCT23
136	0850	1350 LHR	BA 485	FY	L10 1	E-OCT25
4	0850	1455 LHR	GF 003	FY	L10 1	
2	0850	1455 LHR	GF 003	FY	V10 1	
6	1025	1455 LHR	GF 007	FY	V10 0	
3	1320	1745 LHR	BA 485	FY	L10 0	D-MAY 5
		CONNECTIONS				
6	0730	1530 LHR	RJ 181	FY	B3J 0	
	0830 AMM	1200	RJ 111	FY	B3J 0	
3	0745	1530 LHR	RJ 191	FY	B3J 0	D-MAY26
	0845 AMM	1200	RJ 111	FY	B3J 0	
246	0805	1630 LHR	ME 419	FY	707 0	
	0925 BEY	1230	ME 201	FY	747 0	
X246	0805	1630 LHR	ME 419	FY	747 0	
	0925 BEY	1230	ME 201	FY	747 0	
6	0815	1540 LHR	RB 514	FY	707 0	
	0920 DAM	1100	RB 405	FY	707 1	
ACAPULCO, MEXICO 6859/0						**ACA**
		CONNECTIONS				
567	0700	0640+1 LHR	EA 902	FY	L10 1	D-APR30
	1452 JFK	1900	PA 2	FY	747 0	
6	0910	0710+1 LHR	AM 302	Y	D9S 0	E-MAY 1
	0955 MEX	1215	BA 240	FY	707 1	D-JUN 9
46	0910	0710+1 LHR	AM 302	Y	D9S 0	E-JUN10
	0955 MEX	1215	BA 240	FY	707 1	
4	0910	0735+1 LHR	AM 302	Y	D9S 0	E-APR29
	0955 MEX	1215	BA 240	FY	707 1	D-JUN 3
2	0910	0835+1 LHR	AM 302	Y	D9S 0	E-APR27
	0955 MEX	1215	BA 240	FY	707 2	
ACCRA, GHANA 3790/3159						**ACC**
	F		GHC 1031		2062	10.31K
	Y		GHC 640		1280	
246	1055	1825 LGW	BR 362	FY	B3J 0	
1	2030	0610+1 LHR	GH 702	FY	STV 1	
4	2030	0710+1 LHR	GH 706	FY	STV 2	
		CONNECTIONS				
6	0015	1055 LHR	AZ 841	FY	D10 0	D-MAY29
	0635 FCO	0835	AZ 282	FY	DC9 0	

CONT. NEXT PAGE

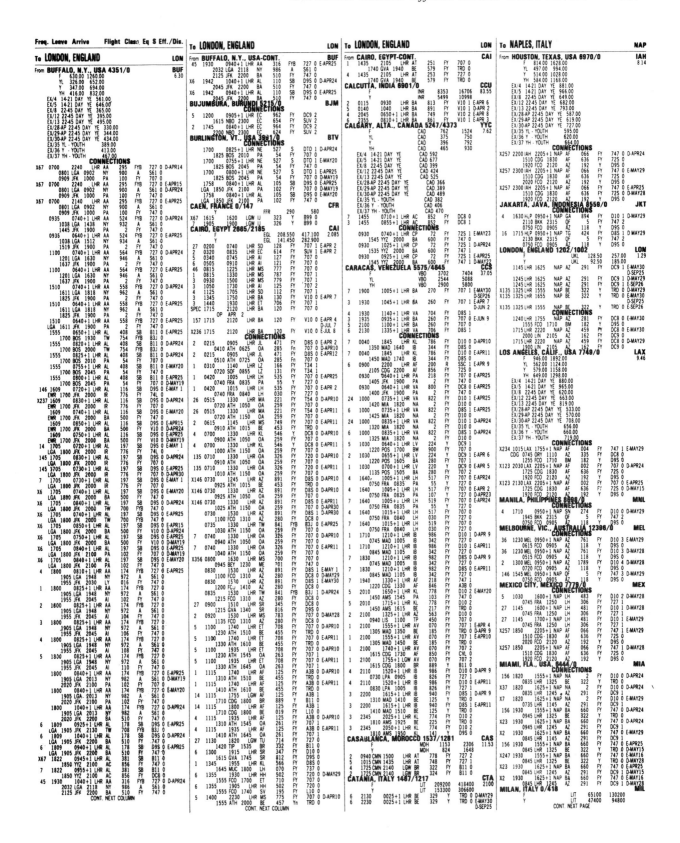

Freq. Leave Arrive   Flight Class Eq $ Eff./Dis.

To LONDON, ENGLAND — LON
From **BUFFALO, N.Y., USA 4351/0** — BUF

To LONDON, ENGLAND — LON
From **BUFFALO, N.Y., USA-CONT.** — BUF
CAEN, FRANCE 0/147 — CFR
CAIRO, EGYPT 2065/2185 — CAI

To LONDON, ENGLAND — LON
From **CAIRO, EGYPT-CONT.** — CAI
CALCUTTA, INDIA 6901/0 — CCU
CALGARY, ALTA., CANADA 5247/4373 — YYC
CARACAS, VENEZUELA 5575/4645 — CCS
CASABLANCA, MOROCCO 1537/1281 — CAS
CATANIA, ITALY 1467/1217 — CTA

To NAPLES, ITALY — NAP
From **HOUSTON, TEXAS, USA 8970/0** — IAH
JAKARTA, JAVA, INDONESIA 8559/0 — JKT
LONDON, ENGLAND 1202/1002 — LON
LOS ANGELES, CALIF., USA 7749/0 — LAX
MANILA, PHILIPPINES 8698/0 — MNL
MELBOURNE, VIC., AUSTRALIA 12396/0 — MEL
MEXICO CITY, MEXICO 7779/0 — MEX
MIAMI, FLA., USA 5644/0 — MIA
MILAN, ITALY 0/418 — MIL

CONT. NEXT COLUMN

CONT. NEXT PAGE

WEAOG ANSWERS

1. (B) Montreal, Canada to Miami,
    Florida. (While travel from Montreal
    to Miami is across an international
    border (Canada to the United States)
    both cities are located in North
    America. For flight schedules wholly
    within North America, consult the
    North American Edition of the OFFI-
    CIAL AIRLINE GUIDE.)

2. (B) Page 861

3. to COPENHAGEN, DENMARK

    from NEW YORK, N.Y., USA

4. Air France; Douglas DC-10; Thursday

5. Alice Springs, Australia; Belgrade,
    Yugoslavia

6. ZRH (Zurich, Switzerland); TLV (Tel
    Aviv, Israel); GVA (Geneva, Switzer-
    land)

7. Only on Sunday; All week (Monday
    through Sunday)

8. Tuesday and Friday; KE 201; 1715
    (5:15 p.m.); JL 962; 1220 (12:20
    p.m.); 1350 (1:50 p.m.)

9. 5:35 a.m.   2145
    3:50 p.m.   0330
    10:10 p.m.   2315
    9:30 a.m.   0045

10. 8:10 a.m.; Friday; AY 104; 8:15 p.m.

11. Friday at 12:10 p.m.

12. LHR (Heathrow); SVO (Sheremetyevo)

13. Jet First Class; Jet Economy; Boeing
    747 Jet; 3 Stops

14. (A) 11:00 a.m.; 12:25 p.m.; Boeing
    707; Jet First Class & Jet Economy
    (B) AF 077 (Departs nearly 2 hours
    after AI 105)
    (C) AI 103; One; Boeing 747

15. (A) PA 816; 7:25 p.m.; Jet First
    Class/Jet Economy; Boeing 707;
    None; (Did you remember the "-1"
    means the flight arrives the day
    before it departs?)
    (B) Friday; 11:00 p.m.; Friday;
    6:00 a.m.; Jet Economy; Douglas DC8

16. 2:00 P.M.; 4:00 A.M.

17. LH 080; 10:25 a.m.; KL 844

18. (A) IB 503; 3:20 p.m.; BE 164;
    2:30 p.m.
    (B) BE 164; Jet Economy; Lock-
    heed L1011; 6:45 p.m.
    (C) IB 501; 12:15 p.m.; 3:20 p.m.

19. 9:00 a.m.; 8:00 p.m.; American; 57;
    Mexico City; Air Panama Int'l; 601;
    Standard One Class Service

20. 5:15 p.m.; Lufthansa 431; Frankfurt;
    8:35 a.m.; 9:40 a.m.; Lufthansa 880;
    10:25 a.m.; Friday

21. AR 154/KL 362; One; Wednesday;
    10:00 p.m.; 6:15 p.m.; Madrid

22. NA 439; NA 2; BE 206; MIA (Miami);
    LHR (London); 5:01 p.m.; 9:20 a.m.;
    11:15 a.m.

23. Italian lira; Mexican pesos

24. 189.950; 260.700; 1.900

25. (A) Blantyre, Malawi
    (B) Buenos Aires

26. 445; 626

27. 4 pounds; $17.52 (2 X 8.76) Excess
    baggage charges from the United
    States are based on kilograms.

28. 10075; 14122

29. (Eastbound) 6800 (YH); (Westbound)
    5613 (YL); (Total) 12413

30. 691; 393

31. (Eastbound) $700.00; (Westbound) $482.00; (Total) $1182.00

32. 933; 778

33. 45

34. 35 minutes

35. 10:45 a.m. (NH 100 departure time minus 60 minutes)

36. 150; 195

37. No (only coach class is offered between HND and OKA); Boeing 747; Boeing 747

38. Airport (departure collection); 5.00 GAD

39. LHR

40. 1024.00; 77.00; from

41. 12:30 p.m.; TW 760; LHR; 7:40 a.m.; 9:45 a.m.; BE 574; no (zero); 11:10 a.m.; Monday

42. $757.00; Yes

43. An additional day of operation is begun on July 8. Flight 120 will now operate on Monday, Thursday, Friday and Sunday

44. Yes; EX/8 22-45 DAY $567.00 (Note: EX/28-AP 22-45 DAY $495.00 cannot be used because ticket must be purchased 60 days in advance.)

45. 195 minutes

46. Yes; 10 pounds; 6.45 UKL (English pounds)

47. British Airways 813; 1:15 a.m.; Vickers VC10; 9:30 a.m.; Swissair 811; 11:10 a.m.; Douglas DC9-Super; 12:35 p.m.; 75 minutes (Between Terminals)

48. Brussels, Belgium; Athens, Greece; Beirut, Lebanon

49. Bangkok, Thailand; Rome, Italy; Friday; 10:10 a.m.

50. 2:30 p.m.; Yes

Appendix B

NORTH AMERICAN EDITION OFFICIAL
AIRLINE GUIDE REVIEW

Directions: Upon completion of this review, you will be able to improve your use of the North American Edition (NAOAG) to prepare passenger flight itineraries; correctly answer passenger's questions concerning flight frequencies, fares, number and location of stops, class of service, meals, equipment types and general transportation; advise passengers of correct airport of departure and of arrival if a city is a multiple-airport city; determine minimum time required between flights in a connecting city; and, determine minimum connecting times between airports in multiple-airport cities. Answer the questions in the space(s) provided; use the sample NAOAG materials when necessary, for the exercise.

1. Schedules appearing in the North American Edition of the OFFICIAL AIRLINE GUIDE represent flights betweeen cities in Canada, the U.S.A. (including Alaska and Hawaii), Mexico, and all adjacent Atlantic and Caribbean Islands including Bermuda, Aruba, Curacao, and Trinidad. For example, the North American Edition lists flight schedules to Chicago from such cities as Acapulco, Mexico; Denver, Colorado; Fairbanks, Alaska; Honolulu, Hawaii; Ottawa, Ontario; and Kingston, Jamaica. It does not list flight schedules to Chicago from such cities as Buenos Aires, Argentina; London, England; or Manila, Republic of the Phillippines because these cities are not located in North America. Which of the following flight schedules would not appear in the NAOAG?

    A. Cleveland, Ohio to Dallas, Texas
    B. Toronto, Ontario to Montreal, Quebec
    C. Honolulu, Hawaii to Sydney, Australia
    D. San Juan, Puerto Rico to Washington, D. C.

2. It's easy to locate flight schedules in the NAOAG. Simply look for the name of your destination city across the top of the columns. You will find it printed in large bold face type like this:

    <u>To SALT LAKE CITY, UTAH</u>

    At times, a "To" city listing will begin in the middle of a column instead of the top, but it will always be in correct alphabetical order. If schedules to Phoenix are found on Page 615, where would you expect to find schedules to San Francisco?

    A. Page 509   B. Page 712

3. If you were planning a trip from New York to Detroit, Mich., you would first look for the heading "To _____." Having located it, you would then look down the listing beneath it until you found your "From" city, in this case _____.

A. to DETROIT, MICH.   B. From NEW YORK, N.Y.

4. To be able to present all the necessary information for a flight schedule, it is
    necessary to condense this information into codes. Example: United Airlines is
    coded "UA". These codes can be found under "Abbreviations and Reference Marks"
    in the front pages of the NAOAG. Locate them now in your sample NAOAG and use
    them to answer the following questions: the Carrier (Airline) Code "NC" stands
    for _____ Airlines; the Jet Aircraft Code "D10" represents a _____
    _____ aircraft; and, the Frequency Code "4" means _____ .

5. All origin or destination cities are spelled out for easy reference, but each is
    given a three-letter code to standardize this information. These three-letter
    codes can be found in the "City/Airport Codes" in the front pages of the NAOAG.
    Now locate this section in your Sample (back pages) NAOAG and answer the follow-
    ing questions: "CHA" stands for what city? _____ ?
    "KOA" stands for what city? _____ ?

6. Your Sample NAOAG also contains a "Flight Itineraries" section. Each carrier's
    flights are listed here in numeric order with their origin, destination and en-
    route cities, if any. Please turn to these pages in your sample NAOAG and lo-
    cate Eastern Air Lines Flight 569 listed under the Carrier Code EA. Note the
    flight itinerary is expressed in three-letter codes. Eastern's Flight 569 flies
    from BOS (Boston, Mass) to IAH (Houston, Texas) with a stop enroute in MSY (New
    Orleans, La.). Where does Frontier Airlines (FL) Flight 61 originate? (Just jot
    down the three-letter code.) _____ . What is its final stop? _____ .
    Where else does it stop? _____ .

7. Many flights operate on only specific days of the week, thereby requiring extreme
    caution when constructing itineraries. The days of the week are given a number
    code and are referred to as "Frequency Codes". Their decodes can be found in the
    "Abbreviations and Reference Marks" section. (Refer to the Sample NAOAG.)

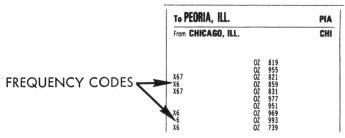

A flight will operate every day of the week unless otherwise designated by frequency codes on the extreme left hand side of the schedule. In the above example,
OZ flight 859 operates every day <u>except</u> Saturday (shown by X6 in the frequency
column). When frequency codes appear without an X preceding the day code, the
flight will operate on that day (or those days) only. Referring to the above
table, OZ 993 operates on day 6 (Saturday) only. OZ 969 operates _____
_____ . Does OZ 831 operate on Sunday? _____ .
OZ 819 operates _____ .

8. Departure and arrival times are located between the frequency and carrier codes.
    (Note: Immediately to the left of the 3-letter city code is the time zone of
    the "To" city and the "From" city.) Examine the following:

TIME ZONE

CITY CODE

DEPARTURE TIMES

ARRIVAL TIMES

	To PITTSBURGH, PA.			EDT PIT
	From WASHINGTON, D.C.			EDT WAS
X7	7:03a	8:00a	AL	629
X7	7:15a	8:06a	NW	323
	8:15a	9:08a	UA	649
X7	9:30a	11:30a	AL	633
X67	10:00a	10:52a	NW	311
X7	10:33a	11:30a	AL	620
X6	12:35p	1:27p	NW	341
X6	1:33p	2:30p	AL	619
	2:25p	4:00p	AL	626
	3:03p	4:00p	AL	626
	3:55p	4:48p	NW	355
X6	6:33p	7:30p	AL	625
	6:55p	7:48p	UA	699
X6	6:59p	9:02p	AL	739
	8:07p	8:55p	AL	823
	9:15p	10:08p	NW	389
	10:00p	10:50p	AL	557

Departure and arrival times are always printed in the local time of the departure and arrival cities. In the sample schedule above, the first morning flight leaves Washington at 7:03 a.m. and arrives in Pittsburgh at 8:00 a.m. local time. AL 633 leaves Washington at _____ and arrives in Pittsburgh at _____ _____. What day(s) of the week does it operate? _____ _____. If the passenger wants to arrive at the Pittsburgh airport near 10:00 a.m. on Sunday, what flight would you suggest to him? _____. Does AL 619 operate on Sunday? _____.

9.   Many cities have more than one airport serving the area. Whenever this is true, a one-letter symbol representing the departure and/or arrival airport is shown immediately following the applicable departure or arrival time. This symbol is decoded in the heading of the "To" and the "From" listings.

	To CHICAGO, ILL.					CDT CHI
	C-CGX (MEIGS FIELD) O-ORD (O'HARE)					
	M-MDW (MIDWAY)					
	From WASHINGTON, D.C.					EDT WAS
	D-IAD, N-DCA, I-BAL					

DEPARTURE AIRPORT CODE

ARRIVAL AIRPORT CODE

	7:25a	D	9:20a	O	UA	659
	7:30a	N	8:19a	O	AA	563
X7	7:40a	N	9:25a	O	NW	39
X7	8:00a	N	8:49a	O	TW	237
	8:10a	I	9:00a	O	UA	253
	8:10a	N	9:02a	O	UA	271
X7	8:30a	I	9:14a	O	TW	117
	8:30a	N	9:24a	O	AA	285
X7	8:50a	N	11:29a	O	AA	429
	10:00a	N	11:46a	O	UA	285
	10:10a	N	11:02a	O	UA	327
	10:20a	N	11:09a	O	TW	183
	10:20a	D	11:15a	O	NW	3
	10:30a	N	11:17a	O	AA	223
	11:15a	N	12:03p	O	UA	277
	11:20a	I	12:10p	O	UA	171
	11:30a	N	12:21p	O	AA	423
	12:10p	N	12:59p	O	TW	377
	12:15p	I	12:59p	O	TW	445
	12:15p	N	1:57p	O	UA	493
X6	12:30p	N	1:16p	O	AA	525
X6	12:35p	N	2:57p	M	NW	341

A.   In the example above, all AA flights depart from _____ Airport. What airport does NW 341 arrive at? _____.

B.   If a passenger wanted to make a reservation for a flight leaving Washington's National Airport on a Sunday around 8:00 a.m., what flight should he take? _____. He would arrive at _____ Airport at _____.

10. Several more items are introduced in this sample SFO to MSY schedule.

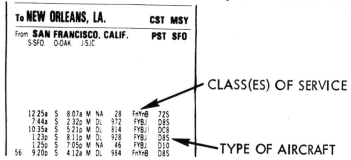

The two items introduced are 1) the class(es) of service offered to a passenger on each particular flight and 2) the type of aircraft. You will recall both of these items are decoded in the "Abbreviations and Reference Marks" section in the front of the NAOAG. Using this section, we determine flight number 972 is operated by _____(name of airline). To determine class(es) of service--every "capital" letter represents a class of service on a given flight. To indicate "night" service, an "n" is used; i.e., Fn - Night Coach Class in First Class Compartment and Yn - Night Coach Class Service. What classes of service are offered on National Airlines flight 28? _____ _____. What type of equipment is used? _____.

11. USING THE NYC TO PHL SCHEDULES BELOW, LET'S REVIEW:

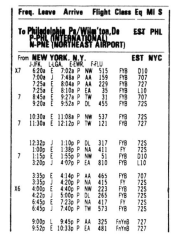

A. DL Flight 455 leaves EWR at _____, arriving in PHL at _____.
   The _____(type) aircraft offers _____(class/es) of service).
B. The earliest time on a Saturday one can depart JFK for PHL is at _____.
C. A passenger wishes to leave from EWR on Saturday afternoon around 2:00 p.m. What flight could you offer to him? _____. At what time will he leave Newark? _____. At what time will he arrive in PHL? _____.

12.　Here is part of the RST to CHI schedule.

Freq.	Leave	Arrive		Flight	Class	Eq	MI	S
To CHICAGO, ILL.							CST	CHI
C-CGX (MEIGS FIELD)　O-ORD (O'HARE)								
M-MDW (MIDWAY)								
From ROCHESTER, MINN.							CST	RST
	8:10a	9:04a	O NW	206	FYB	727		
	9:16a	10:20a	O NC	700	SB	CV5		
	10:30a	11:19a	O NW	740	FYB	72S		
	11:38a	12:30p	O NC	295	SB	D9S		
	2:00p	2:50p	O NW	352	FYB	727		
X6	3:35p	4:27p	O NC	704	SB	D9S		
	5:45p	6:43p	O NW	416	FYB	727		

A.　A passenger wants to depart RST at approximately 9:00 a.m. on a Saturday. What flight closely meets his needs? _____.　The aircraft is a _____ (type) leaving Rochester, Minn. at _____, arriving in CHI at _____.　The class(es) of service offered is/are _____.

B.　Does the flight departure at 5:45 p.m. operate on Sunday? _____. What is the latest flight on Saturday with Jet Custom or Standard Class Service? _____.　What type of plane is it? _____ _____(code).

13.

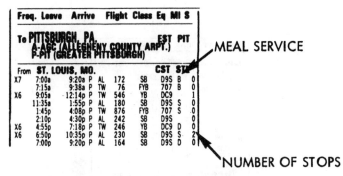

Freq.	Leave	Arrive		Flight	Class	Eq	MI	S
To PITTSBURGH, PA.							EST	PIT
A-AGC (ALLEGHENY COUNTY ARPT.)								
P-PIT (GREATER PITTSBURGH)								
From ST. LOUIS, MO.							CST	STL
X7	7:00a	9:20a	P AL	172	SB	D9S	B	0
	7:15a	9:38a	P TW	76	FYB	707	B	0
X6	9:05a	12:14p	P TW	546	YB	DC9		1
	11:35a	1:55p	P AL	180	SB	D9S	S	0
	1:45p	4:08p	P TW	876	FYB	707	S	0
	2:10p	4:30p	P AL	242	SB	D9S		0
X6	4:55p	7:18p	P TW	246	YB	DC9	D	0
X6	6:50p	10:35p	P AL	230	SB	D9S	S	2
	7:00p	9:20p	P AL	164	SB	D9S	D	0

MEAL SERVICE

NUMBER OF STOPS

In the schedule above, the symbol "B" has been added to the listing for AL 172 just to the right of the equipment code.　A look at the Abbreviations and Reference Marks--"Food Service" section of your Sample NAOAG shows the "B" representing _____.　The last column on the right indicates the number of stops the flight makes.　How many stops does TW 546 make? _____. What type of meal is served on TW 246? _____.　How many stops does AL 230 make between PIT and STL? _____.

14. Examine the following schedule.

Freq.	Leave	Arrive		Flight	Class	Eq	MlS	
To CHICAGO, ILL C-CGX (MEIGS FIELD) O-ORD (O'HARE) M-MDW (MIDWAY)							CST CHI	
From NASHVILLE, TENN.							CST BNA	
	7:50a	9:04a	O	DL	760	FYB	D9S	B	0
	9:46a	10:58a	O	EA	258	FYB	727	S	0
	12:05p	1:19p	O	DL	568	FYB	D9S	L	0
	3:40p	4:54p	O	DL	668	FYB	D9S		0
	4:39p	6:00p	O	EA	894	FYB	DC9	S/	0
X6	6:55p	8:09p	O	DL	566	FYB	D9S	D/S	0

On some flights, only passengers in First Class receive complimentary meal service. On others, passengers in the Coach cabin do not receive the same type of meal service as passengers traveling in First Class. In the above schedule, when traveling First Class on DL 566, passengers receive a full dinner while Coach passengers are served a snack ("B" class passengers receive the same meals as Coach passengers). On EA 894, First Class passengers receive a snack; Coach passengers are not served a meal (no code follows the slash (/)--See Abbreviations and Reference Marks). When only one letter appears with no slash (/), passengers in all compartments (except K/J/L classes) receive the same type of meal service. Do passengers in Coach receive a meal when traveling on EA 258?

_____.

15. Because the aircraft makes stops enroute, some passengers may receive a meal on part of the trip and another meal on another part of the trip.

Freq.	Leave	Arrive		Flight	Class	Eq	MlS	
To HOUSTON, TEXAS I-IAH (INTERCONTINENTAL ARPT) H-HOU (HOBBY ARPT)							CST IAH	
From SEATTLE/TACOMA, WASH. S-SEA, B-BFI							PST SEA	
	12:25a	S	9:03a	I	CO	430	FnYnB	72S	B	3
	12:35a	S	7:50a	I	BN	96	FnYnB	727	S	1
	7:45a	S	3:02p	I	CO	984	FYKBL	D10	BL	1
	12:00n	S	7:22p	I	CO	988	FYKBL	D10	LD	1
	1:50p	S	10:32p	I	CO	452	FYKBL	72S	SD	3
	3:00p	S	10:12p	I	CO	724	FYKBL	72S	SD	1

In this schedule, passengers on CO 984 receive both a breakfast and lunch. This is shown by the symbols B and L, not separated by a "/" symbol. What meal service is available on CO 452? _____. Do passengers in both First Class and Coach receive the same type of meal? _____. Do Coach passengers on BN 96 receive any meal service? _____.

16. Using the following schedule,

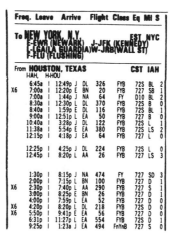

Freq.	Leave	Arrive		Flight	Class	Eq	MlS	
To NEW YORK, N.Y. E-EWR (NEWARK) J-JFK (KENNEDY) L-LGA (LA GUARDIA) W-JRB (WALL ST) F-FLU (FLUSHING)							EST NYC	
From HOUSTON, TEXAS I-IAH, H-HOU							CST IAH	
	6:45a	I	12:49p	J	DL	326	FYB	72S	BL	2
X6	7:00a	I	12:20p	E	BN	20	FYB	727	SB	1
	7:00a	I	1:44p	J	NA	64	FY	D10	BL	2
	8:30a	I	12:30p	L	DL	370	FYB	72S	B	0
	8:40a	I	1:59p	E	DL	116	FYB	72S	BL	1
	9:00a	I	12:51p	L	EA	50	FYB	727	B	0
	10:40a	I	3:28p	J	DL	122	FYB	72S	L	1
	11:38a	I	5:54p	E	EA	380	FYB	72S	LS	2
	12:15p	I	4:18p	J	EA	64	FYB	727	L	0
	12:25p	I	4:25p	J	DL	224	FYB	72S	L	0
	12:45p	I	8:20p	L	AA	26	FYB	727	LS	3
	1:30p	I	8:15p	J	NA	474	FY	727	SD	3
	2:00p	I	7:15p	L	BN	100	FYB	727	D	1
X6	2:30p	I	7:40p	L	AA	290	FYB	727	S	1
	3:00p	I	8:25p	E	BN	26	FYB	727	D	1
	4:00p	I	7:59p	L	EA	52	FYB	727	D	0
X6	4:20p	I	8:20p	L	DL	218	FYB	72S	D	0
X6	5:50p	I	9:41p	E	EA	56	FYB	727	D	0
	6:31p	I	11:27p	L	EA	554	FYB	72S	D	1
	9:25p	I	1:23a	J	EA	494	FnYnB	727	S	0

A. Does the 2:30 p.m. departure from IAH operate on Friday? _____.
    What type of aircraft is it? _____. How many stops does
    it make? _____. What airline operates the flight? _____
    _____. Do they offer Coach service on this flight? _____.
B. At what airport does NA 474 arrive? _____.
C. A passenger has an engagement in New York at 1:00 p.m. What flight would
    you offer him? _____.
    What is the departure time? _____.
D. What type of meal is served on NA 474? _____.

17. The Standard off-line connecting time at O'Hare Airport is 50 minutes. Shorter
connecting times are printed for those airlines who share the same area in the
airport. At O'Hare, AA, DL and NC share the same wing of the terminal. Only
40 minutes are required for transfer between these airlines. What is the minimum
connecting time at ORD for transfer from Air Canada (AC) to TWA? _____.
If a passenger arrived at O'Hare on Continental Airlines at 4:00 p.m., at what
time could he leave if his transfer was to Eastern Air Lines? _____.
If a passenger arrived at O'Hare on Delta Air Lines at 4:00 p.m., at what time
could he leave on another Delta Air Lines flight? _____.

18. Here is a connecting schedule:

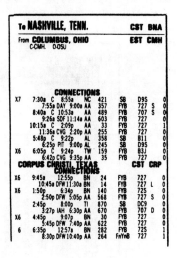

In this schedule, the passenger leaves Chicago's O'Hare Airport at _____,
arriving at Pocatello at _____. The flight number from ORD to the connecting city _____, (name of city) is _____
(carrier code and number). The _____ (type) aircraft arrives in the
connecting city at _____. There the passenger changes to _____
_____ (carrier name) Airlines flight number _____ leaving at
_____. This flight makes _____ stop/s. What class/es of ser-
vice is/are available on AA 563? _____.
Is there meal service on AA 563? _____.

19. In the NAOAG, direct schedules are shown prior to the connecting schedules. If
no direct schedules exist, only connections will be shown.

If a passenger wishes to leave Columbus as late as possible on Saturday, what departure time would you suggest to him? _____. At what time would he arrive in Nashville? _____.

20.

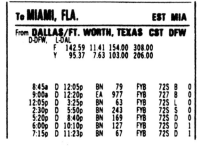

Schedules for Commuter and Intra-State carriers can be found directly after "CONNECTIONS" and use the same format as a direct flight of a Certificated Air Carrier (if no connections are published, then Commuter and Intra-State carriers are located directly after "Certificated Direct Flights"). In the above example, Midstate Airlines (IU) operates between Chicago and Stevens Point with one stop. What type of aircraft does Midstate Airlines use? _____.

21. One-way and round-trip fares for direct flights are published immediately preceeding the direct flight schedules. These fares will only apply to direct flights. Connection fares will be discussed later.

Freq.	Leave		Arrive		Flight	Class	Eq	MI	S
To **MIAMI, FLA.**							**EST**	**MIA**	
From **DALLAS/FT. WORTH, TEXAS**					**CST**	**DFW**			
D-DFW,	L-DAL								
		F	142.59	11.41	154.00	308.00			
		Y	95.37	7.63	103.00	206.00			
	8:45a	D	12:05p		BN	79	FYB	72S B	0
	9:00a	D	12:20p		EA	977	FYB	727 B	0
	12:05p	D	3:25p		BN	63	FYB	72S L	0
	2:30p	D	5:50p		BN	243	FYB	72S S	0
	5:20p	D	8:40p		BN	169	FYB	72S D	0
	6:00p	D	10:10p		BN	127	FYB	72S D	1
	7:15p	D	11:23p		BN	67	FYB	72S D	1

The first fare line contains the Jet First Class fares (designated by the letter F.) The one-way fare, shown as the first item immediately following the letter designating the type of service, is published without tax, followed by the amount of tax and then the <u>total one-way fare</u>. The last amount in the column is the round-trip fare, published <u>only</u> with tax included. In the above example, the First Class one-way jet fare from DFW to MIA is $142.59 U. S. dollars. The tax on this amount is shown as $11.41 and the total one-way First Class fare is published as $154.00. The round-trip Jet First Class fare is $308.00 including tax. One-way Jet Coach is $95.37. The tax one-way is _____ and the total one-way Jet Coach fare is _____. The round-trip Jet Coach fare including tax is _____.

22. Many times numerous fares will appear in the heading. The fare to be selected from the group is the one corresponding to the class of service the passenger is using.

In the above schedule, if a passenger were flying on NC 450 "S" class one-way, his fare would be $39.81 (plus tax). However, if his reservation was on IU 10, which offers "A" (Propeller First Class) only, he must pay the "A" fare of $33.33 (plus tax). The "A" fare would be charged only if he were traveling on an "IU" (a Commuter Air Carrier) flight.

A. If a passenger had an "S" class reservation on NC 576, what fare would he pay for round-trip travel including tax? _____. If another passenger traveled round-trip on "IU", what fare would apply? _____.

B. If a passenger was flying to his destination on NC "S" and returning on IU, his total round-trip fare before tax would be $ _____. (Just add NC's one-way S fare to IU's A fare).

23. Coach and Economy Fares to or from Hawaii and Puerto Rico are based on the day of the week travel commences.

    YH—Peak—Applies 12:01 a.m. Friday thru midnight Sunday unless otherwise noted with fare.
    YL—Off Peak—Applies 12:01 a.m. Monday thru midnight Thursday unless otherwise noted with fare.

The fares are published without U. S. Transportation Taxes. Taxes on Hawaiian travel (other than $3.00 International Travel Tax) must be computed by using charts in the front of the NAOAG.

To HONOLULU, OAHU; HAWAII				HST	HNL	
From SEATTLE/TACOMA. WASH.				PST	SEA	
S-SEA, B-BFI						
TAX NOT INCL-SEE PGS 10-11						
	F	201.41		402.82		
	YL	123.41		246.82		
	YH	139.41		278.82		
	KL	116.41		232.82		
	KH	131.41		262.82		
	YM	104.41				
8:45a S	12:30p	NW	87	FYK	747 L	0
9:00a S	12:45p	CO	981	FYK	D10 SL	0
9:15a S	12:55p	PA	895	FYK	747 L	0
X6 1:05p S	6:10p	NW	95	FYK	D10 D	1
6 1:05p S	7:35p	NW	95	FYK	D10 D	2

A passenger flying Jet Coach between Seattle and Honolulu on Thursday pays $123.41 one-way before tax. If travel was on Saturday, the round-trip Jet Coach fare before tax would be _____.

24. Many discounted fares are also published in the fares section of each listing.

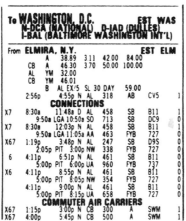

The reduced fare for Military Reservation passengers is coded YM. Reduced fares are listed one-way, <u>including tax</u>. In the Dubuque to Chicago schedule above, the Military Reservation fare on OZ is $25.00, including tax. "XV" offers a "Youth Fare" (YZ); how much is it? _____ .

25. Also published in the fares section of each listing are Excursion fares (if any) which are coded EX/(number), this number corresponds to a note number in the "Excursion Fare Note Explanation" pages in your NAOAG. All Excursion fares are published for round-trip travel and are always shown including tax. In the above schedule, from DBQ to CHI, an EX/33 Excursion fare is _____ . For what carrier does EX/33 apply? _____ .

26. Review the following schedule:

A. If a passenger wishes to arrive in Washington (National Airport) around noon, what flight/flights would you recommend? _____ .
On what type of equipment would the passenger fly? _____ .
How many stops would he make? _____ .

B. A passenger wishes to depart Elmira at 3:00 p.m. What flight/flights would you recommend? _____ . What would be his "normal" one-way fare including tax? _____ . At what airport would he arrive? _____ .

C. What would be the Military Reservation fare for an army captain flying to DCA on CB (Commuter Airlines)? _____ . On what days could the captain travel? _____ .

27. Determining fares for connecting service in the new NAOAG is a simple procedure. First, select the connection flight and class of service as before. For example, if the passenger wishes to leave Houston some time before 9:00 a.m., using the schedule shown below you would suggest the flight departing at _____ a.m. This flight arrives in the connecting city at _____ a.m. and arrives in Akron at _____ p.m. The classes of service offered on both flights are _____ _____ .

To AKRON/CANTON, OHIO					EST CAK		
From HOUSTON, TEXAS					CST IAH		
HAH, H-HOU							
CONNECTIONS							
6 45a I 12:26p	DL	326	FYB	72S	B	0	
9:18a ATL 10:55a	UA	600	FYB	737	S	0	
11:38a I 6:27p	EA	380	FYB	72S	L	0	
2:20p ATL 5:00p	UA	570	FYB	727	D	0	
11:45a I 6:43p	DL	156	FYB	72S	L	0	
1:50p ORD 3:45p	AL	222	SB	D9S		1	
3:00p I 7:54p	AA	146	FYB	707	D	0	
6:22p PIT 7:26p	AL	187	SB	D9S		0	

28. When the connecting flights and classes of service have been selected, note the Fare Code Identifier located in the parentheses immediately to the left of the connecting city arrival time (on the second line of the connection). For the flight departing from Houston at 6:45 a.m. and arriving in the connecting city at 9:18 a.m., the Fare Code Identifier is BD@.

@ = other

To AKRON/CANTON, OHIO	EST CAK
From HOUSTON, TEXAS	CST IAH
HAH, H-HOU	
CONNECTIONS	

CONNECTION FARE LOCATION

FARE CODE IDENTIFIER

6:45a I 12:26p	DL	326	FYB	72S	B	0
(BD@) 9:18a ATL 10:55a	UA	600	FYB	737	S	0
11:38a I 6:27p	EA	380	FYB	72S	L	0
(BD@) 2:20p ATL 5:00p	UA	570	FYB	727	D	0
11:45a I 6:43p	DL	156	FYB	72S	L	0
(AC@) 1:50p ORD 3:45p	AL	222	SB	D9S		1
3:00p I 7:54p	AA	146	FYB	707	D	0
(BD@) 6:22p PIT 7:26p	AL	187	SB	D9S		0

What is the Fare Code Identifier for the flight leaving Houston at 11:45 a.m. and arriving in the connecting city at 1:50 p.m.? _____ .

29. Examine the connecting schedules below. On CO flight 274 to DL flight 704, the Fare Code Identifier for F (first class) service on both flights is _____? The Fare Code Identifier for Y (coach) service is _____. The Fare Code Identifier for K (economy) - Y (coach) service is _____. Is there a fare for "B" and "L" service? _____. On CO flight 36 to DL flight 384, the Fare Code Identifier "A" represents _____ class of service, "G" represents _____ service and "H" represents _____ service. What Fare Code Identifier represents S service on TI flight 904 to F service on DL flight 16? _____ .

To ATLANTA, GA.						EST ATL		
8.0 MI S 60 MIN L $3.00 RA								
From ALBUQUERQUE, N.M.						MST ABQ		
CONNECTIONS								

CONNECTION FARE LOCATION

1 1:33a 9:23a	FL	776	SnB	73S		0	
(DJ@) 3:56a DFW 6:40a	DL	884	FYB	DC8	B	0	
X7 8:00a 2:04p	TI	829	SKB	DC9	B	0	
(EJ@) 10:24a DFW 11:20a	DL	704	FYB	D9S	L	0	
8:20a 2:04p	CO	274	FYKBL	72S	B	0	
(BJK@) 10:45a DFW 11:20a	DL	704	FYB	D9S	L	0	
11:00a 5:55p	TI	993	SKB	DC9		0	
(FJ@) 1:24p DFW 3:15p	EA	120	FYB	727	S	0	
1:15p 7:13p	CO	270	FYKBL	72S	L	0	
(BJK@) 3:40p DFW 4:30p	DL	1110	FYB	L10	D	0	
1:58p 9:38p	TI	904	SB	DC9	S	2	
(EJ@) 5:30p DFW 6:55p	CO	16	FYB	747	D	0	
2:55p 9:33p	CO	90	FYKBL	72S		1	
(BJK@) 6:20p IAH 6:50p	EA	794	FYB	D9S	D	0	
4:25p 11:41p	TI	952	SKB	DC9	D	0	
(JL@) 6:49p DFW 9:00p	EA	666	FnYnB	727		0	
X6 5:40p 11:43p	CO	278	FYKBL	72S	D	0	
(CJL@) 8:05p DFW 9:00p	DL	1116	FnYnB	L10		0	
7:52p 5:11a	CO	36	FYKBL	72S		1	
(AGH@) 11:48p MCI 1:45a	DL	384	FnYnB	72S		1	
345 10:57p 5:18a	FL	76	SnB	73S		0	
(JM@) 1:20a DFW 2:35a	DL	986	FnYnB	D8S		0	

30. To determine the fare for a connecting schedule, refer to the Fare Codes listed in alphabetical order directly above the connecting schedules. Next to each Fare Code is the one-way fare excluding tax, immediately followed by the tax amount and the total one-way fare. What is the one-way fare excluding tax for code B? _____. What is the amount of tax for code B? _____. The total one-way for code B? _____. What is the total one-way fare for code D? _____. What is the tax amount for code F? _____. What is the one-way fare excluding tax for code H? _____.

CONNECTIONS

A	116.37	9.31	125.68
B	105.56	8.44	114.00
C	98.15	7.85	106.00
D	96.30	7.70	104.00
E	92.59	7.41	100.00
F	90.74	7.26	98.00
G	89.52	7.16	96.68
H	86.74	6.94	93.68
J	75.93	6.07	82.00
K	73.15	5.85	79.00
L	70.37	5.63	76.00
M	69.44	5.56	75.00

31. A passenger traveling jet coach to Austin at 7:15 p.m. on a Saturday will pay $ _____ plus tax. The fare level used to construct this fare is _____. A passenger traveling jet coach to Austin at 7:15 p.m. on Wednesday evening will pay $ _____ plus tax. The fare level used to construct this fare is _____. What service class level is used to construct the fare for the line identified by Fare Code "F"? _____.

To AUSTIN, TEXAS CST AUS

From **HONOLULU, OAHU; HAWAII** HST HNL
CONNECTIONS
TAX NOT INCL-SEE PGS 10-11

A	345.93		345.93	F				
B	310.41		310.41	F				
C	303.26		303.26					
D	238.97		238.97	H				
D	222.97		222.97	L				
E	215.41		215.41	YH				
E	199.41		199.41	YL				
F	204.41		204.41	KH				
F	188.41		188.41	KL				
1	12:01a	2:25p	PA	828	FY	707	S	0
(AD⊛)	11:20a DFW	1:45p	BN	105	FYB	727		0
	1:40p	8:13a	CO	602	FYK	D10	L	0
(CE⊛F)	8:44p LAX 12:10a	CO	56	FnYnB	72S	B/S	4
X56	4:45p	8:13a	CO	606	FYK	D10	D	0
(CE⊛F)	11:49p LAX 12:10a	CO	56	FnYnB	72S	B/S	4
	7:15p	9:10a	BN	502	FY	747	D	0
(BE⊛)	6:00a DFW	8:30a	BN	167	FYB	72S	S	0
5	9:00p	12:40p	PA	826	FY	707	SB	0
(AD⊛)	8:20a DFW 12:00n	BN	7	FYB	72S		0

32. Examine the following schedule:

To ATLANTA, GA. EDT ATL

SACRAMENTO, CALIF. PDT SMF
CONNECTIONS

A	200.00	16.00	216.00	F					
B	150.93	12.07	163.00	Y					
C	137.96	11.04	149.00	Y					

DISCONTINUED AFTER OCT 7

C	141.67	11.33	153.00	Y	

EFFECTIVE OCT 8-OCT14

C	152.78	12.22	165.00	Y	

EFFECTIVE OCT15

	7:00a	4:02p	WA	476	FK	72S		0
(AB⊛)	8:00a LAX 9:10a	EA	82	FYB	727	B	0
	7:00a	5:00p	RW	903	SB	D9S		0
(AB⊛)	7:30a SFO 8:30a	DL	1124	FYB	L10	BS	1

Fare Code "C" represents what total fare on October 12? $ _____.
Fare Code "C" represents what total fare on October 18? $ _____.

33. Examine the following schedule:

```
To AUSTIN, TEXAS              CST  AUS
From SAN FRANCISCO, CALIF.    PST  SFO
   S-SFO,  O-OAK,  J-SJC
              CONNECTIONS
A  227.77   18.22  245.99    F    CC
B  175.93   14.07  190.00    F    JT
C  164.81   13.18  177.99         CC
D  160.19   12.82  173.01         CC
E  138.89   11.11  150.00    Y    CC-T
F  137.96   11.04  149.00    K    CC
G  125.00   10.00  135.00    Y    JT
H  117.59    9.41  127.00    Y    JT
       12:05a  S  9:10a  AA   84  FnYnB  707   S   0
(DH@)   5:04a DFW 8:30a BN  167  FYB    72S   S   1
       12:25a  S  7:51a  NA   28  FnYnB  72S   S   0
(CGG@•) 6:34a IAH 7:12a CO   51  FYKBL  72S   S   1
X7     12:25a  S  8:48a  NA   28  FnYnB  72S   S   1
(GG@)   6:34a IAH 8:12a TI  986  SKB    DC9       0
        3:10a  S  1:33p  WA  651  FnYnB  720       0
(BHH@•) 4:14a LAX 7:00a CO  226  FYKBL  72S   BS  3
        7:10a  S  2:25p  AA  296  FYB    727   B   0
(BH@)  12:16p DFW 1:45p BN  105  FYB    727       0
X6      8:30a  S  3:20p  DL 1124  FYB    L10   B   0
(BH@)   1:27p DFW 2:40p BN  163  FYB    727       0
        8:30a  S  4:03p  DL 1124  FYB    L10   B   0
(BH@)   1:27p DFW 3:20p TI  925  SKB    DC9       0
        9:00a  S  4:07p  AA  146  FYKBL  707   B   0
(AEF@•) 2:29p IAH 3:28p CO   69  FYKBL  72S       0

       12:35p  S  7:15p  AA  140  FYB    D10   L   0
(BH@)   5:38p DFW 6:35p BN   37  FYB    72S       0
        1:23p  S  8:13p  DL  928  FYB    D8S   L   0
(BH@)   6:20p DFW 7:30p TI  952  SKB    DC9       0
        4:45p  S  1:20p  AA  264  FYB    727   D   0
(BH@)   9:49p DFW 10:40p BN  187  FYB    72S       0
```

A. A passenger asks for a flight departing around 10:00 a.m. You suggest the connecting schedule that departs from San Francisco at _____, arrives in the connecting city at _____ and arrives in Austin at _____. The Fare Code Identifier is _____.

B. The 1st Fare Code represents _____. Its one-way fare is _____.

C. The 2nd Fare Code represents _____. Its one-way fare is _____.

D. The 3rd Fare Code represents _____. Its one-way fare is _____.

E. The 4th Fare Code represents _____. Its one-way fare is _____.

F. The 5th Fare Code represents _____. Its one-way fare is _____.

34. The fare for UA flight 869 to UA flight 436, was constructed on a THRU basis; that is, UA has published a through fare between Denver and Sacramento, via the connecting city. The fare construction code used to indicate a through fare published by a single carrier is _____. The code which indicates a through fare published by two carriers is _____. If the online through fare and the interline joint fare are identical, then the basis for construction is displayed as _____.

```
To SACRAMENTO, CALIF.        PST  SMF
From DENVER, COLO.           MST  DEN
   D-DEN,  B-WBI-
         F  122.22   9.78  132.00  264.00
         Y   81.48   6.52   88.00  176.00
      UA  YM  66.00
       B  UA EX/5  YL 30 DAY        123.00
   2:00p  D  3:15p  UA  719  FYB  DC8  S   0
   7:45p  D  9:00p  UA  441  FYB  727  S   0
              CONNECTIONS
A  126.85   10.15  137.00    F    JT/THRU
B  125.00   10.00  135.00    F    JT
C   84.26    6.74   91.00    Y    JT/THRU
D   83.33    6.67   90.00    Y    JT
X6 12:20p  D  3:32p  WA  579  YB   720   L   0
(D@)   1:45p SFO 3:00p RW  722  SB   DC9       0
6  12:20p  D  5:15p  WA  579  YB   720   L   0
(D@)   1:45p SFO 4:45p RW  922  SB   DC9       0
6   2:35p  D  5:15p  TW  389  FYB  B3J   S   0
(AC@)  4:04p SFO 4:45p RW  922  SB   DC9       0
6   3:45p  D  6:39p  UA  869  FYB  737   S   0
(AC@)  5:15p SFO 6:05p UA  436  FYB  D8S       0
6   4:40p  D  8:30p  UA  963  FYB  72S   D   0
(BD@)  6:03p SFO 8:00p RW  236  SB   D9S       0
   4:45p  D  9:35p  WA  675  FYB  72S   S   2
(BD@)  8:04p SFO 9:05p RW  904  SB   D9S       0
   6:40p  D 10:29p  WA  493  YB   73S   S   1
(BD@)  9:00p SFO 9:55p UA   57  FYB  D8S       0
```

35. The fare construction code indicating two local fares have been combined is
_____. The code indicating a connection allowance amount has been
deducted from a combination of two local fares is _____.

```
To RALEIGH/DURHAM, N.C.          EST RDU
From MIAMI, FLA.                        EST MIA
              F   101.85  8.15 110.00 220.00
              Y    69.44  5.56  75.00 150.00
         EA  YM    56.00
                   EA EX/39'Y MIDWEEK   120.00
         6:05a  10:41a  EA   630   FYB   72S  *  2
                        EA 630 * MEALS SB/S
         8:35a   1:23p  EA   538   FYB   72S  S  2
        11:50a   1:35p  EA   898   FYB   D9S  L  0
        12:30p   4:21p  EA   594   FYB   72S  L  1
                    CONNECTIONS
   A  130.55  10.44 140.99  F   CC
   B  101.85   8.15 110.00  F   THRU
   C   99.07   7.93 107.00  F   JT
   D   75.00   6.00  81.00  Y   CC-T
   E   69.44   5.56  75.00  Y   THRU
   F   67.59   5.41  73.00  Y   JT
         3:25a   7:54a  DL  1090  FnYn  L10  S  0
  (CF@)  5:04a ATL 7:00a EA   592  FYB   727  S  0
         7:00a  10:41a  EA   678  FYB   727  B  0
  (BE@)  8:47a ATL 9:40a EA   630  FYB   72S     0
         9:40a   1:23p  DL   960  FY    D8S  S/ 0
  (CF@) 11:19a ATL 12:20p EA  538  FYB   72S  S  0
         9:40a   1:23p  EA   252  FYB   D9S  S/ 0
  (BE@) 11:30a ATL 12:20p EA  538  FYB   72S  S  0
         1:15p   4:40p  EA   730  FYB   D9S  L  0
  (AD@)  3:07p GSO 4:16p DL  530  FYB   D9S     0
         3:35p   7:47p  EA   616  FYB   72S  S/ 0
  (BE@)  5:25p ATL 6:45p EA  576  FYB   72S  S  0
         3:49p   7:09p  EA   726  FYB   727  S  0
  (CF@)  5:25p CLT 6:32p PI  960  SB    Y11     0
         7:59p  11:16p  EA   602  FYB   727  S/ 0
  (BE@)  9:42a ATL 10:20p EA 488  FnYnB 727     0
```

36. When a point beyond either the city of origin or final destination or both is
used in fare construction, the point beyond is enclosed in _____.

```
To LAS VEGAS, NEV.              PST LAS
From HOUSTON, TEXAS             CST IAH
                    CONNECTIONS
   A  187.96  15.04 203.00  F   ((MSY)(LAX))
   B  187.96  15.04 203.00  F   ((OAK))
   C  173.15  13.85 187.00  F   ((RNO))
   D  163.89  13.11 177.00  F   (AMA)
   E  150.00  12.00 162.00  F   JT
   F  125.00  10.00 135.00  Y   ((MSY)(LAX))
   G  125.00  10.00 135.00  Y   ((OAK))
   H  122.22   9.78 132.00  Y   CC
   J  115.74   9.26 125.00  Y   ((RNO))
   K  115.74   9.26 125.00  Y   ((MSY))
   L  100.00   8.00 108.00  Y   JT
         7:45a  10:15a  CO   983  FYKBL D10  B  0
  (ELL@) 8:55a DEN 9:35a FL    7  SB    73S  S  0
  X23    7:45a  10:36a  CO   983  FYKBL D10  B  0
  (AFF@) 8:55a DEN 10:00a UA  753  FYB   727  S  0
         7:45a  11:33a  CO   983  FYKBL D10  B  0
  (AFF@) 8:55a DEN 10:50a UA  249  FYB   D10  S  0
         9:50a   1:00p  CO   959  FYKBL D10  L  0
  (CJJ@*)11:07a LAX 12:10p RW  204  SB    D9S     0
        10:00a  12:43p  BN    95  FYB   727     0
  (EL@) 10:50a DFW 12:05p DL   15  FYB   747  L  0
        11:45a   2:50p  CO   975  FYKBL D10  L  0
  (BGG@*) 1:07p LAX 2:00p WA  226  YB    73S     0
```

37. In the connection UA 852 to UA 269 shown below, both the first class and coach
fares were constructed by using a published local between _____ and
_____, a published local fare between _____ and _____
_____ via the connecting point _____. Was a "terminal
charge" deducted? _____?

```
To ATLANTA, GA.                EST ATL
From MILWAUKEE, WIS.            CST MKE
              F    99.07  7.93 107.00 214.00
              Y    67.59  5.41  73.00 146.00
             YM    55.00
         EA  YM    54.00
              B   EX/5  YL 30 DAY  102.00
         7:15a  10:08a  EA   789  FYB   D9S  B  0
        10:45a   2:26p  NW   704  FYB   727  L  1
         4:37p   7:26p  EA   787  FYB   D9S  D  0
                    CONNECTIONS
   A  116.67   9.33 126.00  F   (SBN)-T
   B   95.37   7.63 103.00  F   JT
   C   75.00   6.00  81.00  Y   (SBN)-T
   D   64.81   5.19  70.00  Y   JT
         7:11a  11:32a  UA   852  FYB   727  B  0
  (AC@)  9:15a CLE 9:50a UA  269  FYB   72S  S  0
         7:15a  11:30a  NC   902  SB    D9S     0
  (BD@)  7:45a ORD 8:55a DL  345  FYB   72S  S  0
         8:15a  12:56p  OZ   901  SB    D9S  S  0
  (BD@)  9:15a STL 10:35a EA 273  FYB   D9S  L  0
         8:30a  12:58p  NC   971  SB    CV5     0
  (BD@)  9:00a ORD 10:10a EA 243  FYB   D9S  L  0
```

38. When only a through Y fare is published for a connection although F service is available for one segment, the basis for fare construction would be indicated by _____. The fare amount is found by adding the difference between F and Y service to the through _____ fare.

Freq.	Leave	Arrive	Flight	Class	Eq	MI	S
To CALGARY, ALTA.					**MST**	**YYC**	
From MIAMI, FLA.						**EST**	**MIA**
		CONNECTIONS					
A	281.00	22.48	303.48	F	THRU		
B	274.00	21.92	295.92	F	JT		
C	260.00	20.80	280.80		DIFF.		
D	194.00	15.52	209.52	Y	JT/THRU		
67	4:15a	10:25a	AC 919	Y	747	S	0
(CD)	7:10a	YYZ 8:30a	AC 117	FY	L10	L	0
67	4:15a	11:35a	AC 919	Y	747	S	0
(CD)	7:10a	YYZ 9:45a	CP 63	FY	727	L	0
	1:05p	9:15p	BN 72	FYB	72S	L	1
(BD●)	4:05p	DEN 7:00p	WA 603	FY	72S	D	0
	2:00p	7:55p	AC 915	FY	747	L	0
(AD)	4:55p	YYZ 6:00p	AC 141	FY	L10	D	0
	2:00p	10:40p	AC 915	FY	747	L	0
(AD)	4:55p	YYZ 8:05p	CP 75	FY	72S	D	1

39. To review the coding system used for fare construction, match the construction codes below with their corresponding definitions.

THRU	A.	A published joint through fare
JT	B.	A combination of two local fares less the connection allowance amount.
JT/THRU	C.	A point beyond
CC	D.	A full combination of local fares
CC-T	E.	A carrier's published through fare
( )	F.	A combination of two local fares and one joint fare
( ) ( )	G.	A local fare to a hidden point plus a joint fare to a point beyond used in constructing the interline connection.
(( ))	H.	Identical joint and through fares
(( )) (( ))	I.	A combination of one local fare and one joint fare.
( ) (( ))	J.	Points beyond both the city of origin and final destination used in fare construction
DIFF	K.	A differential construction used when a class of service is not available on a through basis.

40. Complete the following exercise to see if you understand the procedure for determining connecting schedule fares. Use the schedule below:

Freq.	Leave	Arrive	Flight	Class	Eq	MI	S
To BURLINGTON, VT.						**EST**	**BTV**
From SAN FRANCISCO, CALIF.						**PST**	**SFO**
S-SFO,	O-OAK,	J-SJC					
		CONNECTIONS					
A	287.04	22.96	310.00	F	JT		
B	281.48	22.52	304.00	F	((MHT))		
C	243.52	19.48	263.00		CC		
D	235.18	18.81	253.99		CC		
E	188.89	15.11	204.00	Y	JT		
F	185.19	14.81	200.00	Y	((MHT))		
G	182.41	14.59	197.00		(PHL)		
H	182.41	14.59	197.00		CC		
J	180.56	14.44	195.00		(CHI)		
K	177.77	14.22	191.99		CC		
	9:00a	S 8:10p	AA 92	FYB	707	B	0
(BF●)	4:11p	DTW 6:05p	DL 548	FYB	D9S	D	1

A. Flight _____ to flight _____ leaves _____ at _____ and arrives in the connecting city at _____.
B. It leaves the connecting city at _____ and arrives in _____ _____ at _____.
C. The Fare Code Identifier for this connection is _____.
D. The first letter represents _____ service; the second letter represents _____ service; the third letter represents _____ service; for jet coach class service, therefore, you would refer to fare code _____.
E. The one-way fare excluding tax is _____, the transportation tax is _____, and the total one-way fare is _____.

F. The fare level used to construct this fare is _____.

G. The code indicating the basis for fare construction is _____,
which means _____.
(explanation)

41.

```
To SEATTLE, WASH.              PDT SEA
B-BFI (BOEING FIELD)
S-SEA (SEATTLE/TACOMA)
SEA
14.0 MI S  25 MIN L  $2.00 RA
BFI
 5.0 MI S  25 MIN L  $1.50 RA
```

Looking at the "To SEA" listing above, how many miles is the airport (SEA) from
the city and in what direction? _____. What ground transportation
is available, in addition to rental cars and Air Taxi? _____.
How much does it cost? _____.

42.

CITY	OFF LINE	ON LINE
CHICAGO, ILL.		
ORD DOMESTIC		
STANDARD	:50	
(FLIGHTS TO/FROM ALASKA, CANADA, HAWAII, BERMUDA, NASSAU, PUERTO RICO & U.S. VIRGIN IS. ARE DOMESTIC EXCEPTION: AF AND BA FLIGHTS VIA CANADA AND JM FLIGHTS FROM NAS ARE CONSIDERED INTERNATIONAL)		
BETWEEN AA/DL/NC	:40	
BETWEEN AA/AL	:40	
AC TO TW	:40	
BETWEEN AL/NC	:40	
EA/NW TO/FROM CO	:30	
BETWEEN OZ/UA	:40	
AA, DL, EA		:30
UA		:40
NC, OZ		:20
NW, TW		:25
ORD INTERNATIONAL		
DOMESTIC TO INT'L	1:15	
ALL TO BN	:50	
ALL TO JM	:45	
ALL TO NW	1:00	
NW/UA TO DL	:50	
UA TO BA	1:00	
ALL TO TW	:50	:45
TW-DOMESTIC CONNECTING TIMES WILL APPLY TO ALL TW INT'L FLIGHTS WHICH TRANSIT TO A POINT IN THE U.S. PRIOR TO ARRIVAL/DEPARTURE		
ALL TO AA	:50	:30
EA, NW		:30
INT'L TO DOMESTIC	1:30	
FROM BN (WITH STOP AT DFW, IAH, SAT)	:50	
FROM AA (WITH STOP AT DFW, HNL, SAT)	:50	:30
NW TO ALL	:50	
FROM ALL TO TW	1:00	1:00
MX TO UA	1:15	
AA (FROM ACA OR MEX NONSTOP)		1:00
EA		:30
NW		:25
INT'L TO INT'L	1:30	
MDW STANDARD	:25	
NC		:10
TW, UA		:20
INTER-AIRPORT SURFACE CONNECTIONS:		
MDW TO/FROM ORD	2:40	

If a passenger was arriving at O'Hare on North Central from Milwaukee and was
transferring to Pan American to London, the "DOMESTIC TO INT'L." off-line time
of 75 minutes (1:15) must be used. What is the minimum time if the passenger
was transferring to American Airlines for Mexico? _____.

43. The phrase "MINIMUM CONNECTING TIME" means the minimum time required when making transfers from one aircraft to another. These charts are published for each city and can be located in the front pages of the NAOAG. It must be remembered these are the <u>minimum times</u> required for connections and they may <u>not</u> be reduced.

OFF LINE	ON LINE	CITY	OFF LINE	ON LINE	CITY	OFF LINE	ON LINE	CITY	OFF LINE
:10		**BIG SPRING, TEXAS** STANDARD	:20		**CHICAGO, ILL.** ORD DOMESTIC			**DALLAS/FT. WORTH, TEXAS-CONT.** BETWEEN BN AND FY	:30
:20		TT		:15	STANDARD	:50		BETWEEN FL AND OZ/TT/XO	:30
	:15	**BILLINGS, MONT.** STANDARD	:30		(FLIGHTS TO/FROM ALASKA, CANADA, HAWAII, BERMUDA,			BETWEEN OZ AND TT/XO	:30
1:00		NW		:25	NASSAU, PUERTO RICO &			BETWEEN TT AND XO	:15
1:00		FL, WA		:20	U.S. VIRGIN IS. ARE			BETWEEN CO AND DL/ZK	:30
1:30		**BINGHAMTON, N.Y.** STANDARD	:25		DOMESTIC EXCEPTION: AF AND BA			AA, BN, DL	
1:30		**BIRMINGHAM, ALA.** STANDARD	:30		FLIGHTS VIA CANADA AND JM FLIGHTS FROM NAS			CO FL	
:30		EA, SO, UA		:20	ARE CONSIDERED			TT	
	:25	**BISMARCK, N.D.**			INTERNATIONAL)			FLIGHTS TO/FROM HAWAII	
	:20	NC	:20		BETWEEN AA/DL/NC	:40		ARE DOMESTIC	
		BLOOMINGTON, IND.		:10	BETWEEN AA/AL	:40		DFW INTERNATIONAL	
:30		STANDARD	:25		AC TO TW	:40		DOMESTIC TO INT'L	
	:10	**BOISE, IDAHO**			BETWEEN AL/NC	:40		BETWEEN AA/EA	
	:20	STANDARD	:30		EA/NW TO/FROM CO	:30		AA, BN	
	:15	BETWEEN RW AND TJ	:25		BETWEEN OZ/UA	:40		INT'L TO DOMESTIC	1:
:20		RW		:15	AA, DL, EA		:30	AA TO EA	1:0
	:15	UA		:20	UA		:40	AA	
:20		**BOSTON, MASS.** DOMESTIC			NC, OZ		:20	FROM AA (WITH STOP AT SAT)	:50
	:25	STANDARD	:40		NW, TW		:25	FROM BN (WITH STOP IAH OR SAT)	:50
:10		DL TO/FROM DD/PM/PT/ QO/DE/NE/ZM	:30		ORD INTERNATIONAL DOMESTIC TO INT'L	1:15		ALL OTHER BN	
:20		AA, AL, EA		:30	ALL TO BN	:50		INT'L TO INT'L	1:10
	:15	DL		:25	ALL TO JM	:45		BN	
		TW, UA		:20	ALL TO NW	1:00		DAL STANDARD	:20
		FLIGHTS TO/FROM BERMUDA, HAWAII, MONTREAL,			NW/UA TO DL	:50		**DAYTON, OHIO**	
:20		TORONTO, NASSAU, AND			UA TO BA	1:00		STANDARD	:30
:15		PUERTO RICO ARE DOMESTIC			ALL TO TW	:50	:45	AL	
	:10	INTERNATIONAL			TW-DOMESTIC CONNECTING			NC	
	:15	DOMESTIC TO INT'L	1:00		TIMES WILL APPLY TO ALL			TW	
		ALL TO AA	:40		TW INT'L FLIGHTS WHICH			**DENVER, COLO.**	
1:00		DL		:25	TRANSIT TO A POINT IN			DOMESTIC	
1:00		PA		:40	THE U.S. PRIOR TO			STANDARD	
1:00		TW		:30	ARRIVAL/DEPARTURE			BETWEEN BN AND UA	
	:45	INT'L TO DOMESTIC	1:00		ALL TO BN	:50	:30	BETWEEN NC AND TT	
		DL		:25	EA, NW		:30	WA (FROM CANADA)	
:45		PA		1:05	INT'L TO DOMESTIC	1:30		CO, NC	
:45	:30	**BRADFORD, PA.** STANDARD	:25		FROM BN (WITH STOP AT DFW, IAH, SAT)	:50		TT	
:45	:30	**BRAINERD, MINN.** STANDARD	:10		FROM AA (WITH STOP AT DFW, HNL, SAT)	:50	:30	FL	
	:30	**BRIDGEPORT, CONN.** STANDARD	:20		NW TO ALL	:50		TW, UA	
:20		AL		:25	FROM ALL TO TW	1:00	1:00	WA (EXCEPT FROM CANADA) FLIGHTS TO/FROM HAWAII	
:45		**BROOKINGS, S.D.** STANDARD	:10		MX TO UA	1:15		ARE DOMESTIC	
:45		**BROWNSVILLE, TEXAS** STANDARD	:20		AA (FROM ACA OR MEX NONSTOP)		1:00	INTERNATIONAL DOMESTIC TO INT'L	
:40		IF CONNECTION INVOLVES			EA		:30	BETWEEN UA AND MX	1:00
:30		TRANSFER BETWEEN			NW		:25	TW-DOMESTIC CONNECTING	
	:30	BROWNSVILLE AND MAT-			INT'L TO INT'L	1:30		TIMES WILL APPLY TO ALL	
	:25	AMOROS AIRPORTS	1:15		MDW STANDARD	:25		TW INT'L FLIGHTS WHICH	
	:15				NC		:10	TRANSIT TO A POINT IN THE U.S. PRIOR TO	
					TW, UA		:20	ARRIVAL/DEPARTURE	
					INTER-AIRPORT SURFACE CONNECTIONS:			INT'L TO DOMESTIC	
					MDW TO/FROM ORD	2:40		BETWEEN MX AND UA	1:00
					CINCINNATI, OHIO			**DES MOINES, IOWA**	
					STANDARD	:40		STANDARD	:20
					BETWEEN AL/NC/PI	:30		OZ	:10

"Off-line" connecting time must be used when a change of airlines is made. "On-line" connecting time is observed when the arriving and departing airlines are the same (connection is made on the same airline).

In the above listings separate times are published for Midway (MDW) and for O'Hare (ORD) airports in Chicago. The minimum time is also published for surface transportation between the two airports if a passenger is arriving at one airport and departing from the other. Refer again to the minimum connecting lines for Chicago. If a passenger was scheduled to arrive at Midway Airport at 1:30 p.m. on United Air Lines, the minimum time required for a scheduled connection to an American Airlines flight is 25 minutes (Standard off-line time). Therefore, he may make a reservation on any American Airlines flight leaving at 1:55 p.m. or later. If the passenger arriving at MDW on United Air Lines at 1:30 p.m. were departing on another United Air Lines flight from MDW, he must be scheduled to leave at 1:50 p.m. or later because _____

_____.

44. In cases where no logical connecting point is suggested, it is best to consult a map. Find a large city near the destination with the least deviation from a direct line between the origin and destination. Turn to the pages in the NAOAG containing schedules <u>to</u> the final destination and determine if service is available from the selected connecting point to the final destination. If no schedules exist, select another city and check the NAOAG flight listings to the destination.
NOTE: If several cities may be used as the connecting city, select the city with the most nonstop service in order to reduce flying time for the passenger. Assume a passenger wanted to fly from Buffalo, N.Y. to Grand Rapids, Mich. Using a map provided by NAOAG, what city should be used as the connecting point?
_____ .

45. Minimum connecting times between airports in multiple-airport cities are also printed in the listings. This minimum connecting time includes travel times between airports, time for the passenger to claim baggage at the arrival airport, and check-in time at the departure airport. If a passenger arrived at O'Hare at 2:00 P.M., the earliest time he could be scheduled to depart on a flight from Midway Airport is _____ .

46. Examine the following schedule:

```
To SEATTLE/TACOMA, WASH.    PST SEA
From HONOLULU, OAHU; HAWAII       MST HNL
              TAX NOT INCL-SEE PGS 10-11
          F  201.41              402.82
          YL 123.41              246.82
          YH 139.41              278.82
          KL 116.41              232.82
          KH 131.41              262.82
          YM 104.41
      11:00a   7:15p S PA  830    FYK   747 L   0
                    PA 830 EFFECTIVE APR25
       2:10p   9:28p S CO  982    FYK   D10 L   0
       2:15p   9:25p S NW   86    FYK   747 D   0
       2:30p   9:45p S PA  896    FYK   747 L   0
                    PA 896 DISCONTINUED AFTER APR24
                         •
      X14 9:20p   6:49a S NW   94    FYK   D10 S   1
                    NW 94 EFFECTIVE APR24
      X14 10:20p  6:49a S NW   94    FYK   D10 S   1
                    NW 94 DISCONTINUED AFTER APR23
```

Occasionally, additional information pertinent to a flight must be shown on a second line. This line of information will always refer <u>only</u> to the flight listed directly <u>above</u> it.

The additional information shown in conjunction with PA 830 indicates the flight is "EFFECTIVE APR 25". This, of course, means PA 830 will not operate prior to April 25. What is the additional information concerning PA 896? _____
_____. What additional information is shown for NW 94? _____
_____
_____.

47. The NAOAG occasionally suggests such a logical connecting point or points with the words "CONEX VIA..." under the departure city. You can use the city or cities listed to determine a suitable schedule. Examine this Columbus to Wichita schedule.

To WICHITA, KAN. 6.0 MI SW 20 MIN L $2.65 RA				CDT ICT				
From COLUMBUS, OHIO CONEX VIA CHI, MCI/STL				EDT CMH				
	Y	67.59	5.41	73.00	146.00			
TW	YM	55.00						
4:10p		8:01p		TW	547	Y	DC9 S	3

This schedule lists one direct flight from Columbus to Wichita. The listing also suggests connections should be made at _____, _____ _____ or _____.

48. Assume a passenger flying from Buffalo to Grand Rapids wanted to arrive in Grand Rapids as early on a Wednesday morning as possible. The arrival time at the destination is critical to the passenger. Examine the schedule below from Detroit to Grand Rapids. NC 971 is the earliest arrival, leaving at 7:10 a.m. and arriving at 7:44 a.m. Now examine the schedules from Buffalo to Detroit. AA 23 is the earliest departure but it arrives in Detroit at 8:55 a.m., too late to connect to NC 971. Therefore, he must use a later DTW to GRR flight. Since the offline minimum connecting time at DTW is 45 minutes, his North Central flight to GRR must leave no earlier than 9:40 a.m. to be a valid connection. The passenger's itinerary should be AL 421 BUF-DTW and _____ (flight number) DTW-GRR.

To DETROIT, MICH.			EST DTT				
From BUFFALO, N.Y.			EST BUF				
F	50.00	4.00	54.00	108.00			
S	35.19	2.81	38.00	76.00			
Y	35.19	2.81	38.00	76.00			
YM	29.00						
	AL EX/11 S WEEKEND		57.00				
B	AL EX/5 SL 30 DAY		53.00				
B	AA EX/5 YL 30 DAY		53.00				
	AA EX/11 Y WEEKEND		57.00				
8:00a	8:55a M	AA	23	FYB	707 S	0	
9:40a	10:35a M	AL	421	SB	B11	0	
3:35p	4:27p M	AL	423	SB	D9S	0	
7:55p	8:47p M	AL	137	SB	D9S	0	

To GRAND RAPIDS, MICH.				EST GRR			
From DETROIT, MICH.-CONT. D-DET, M-DTW, R-YIP							
	A	23.15	1.85	25.00	50.00		
	S	28.70	2.30	31.00	62.00		
NC	YM	23.00					
	B ·	NC EX/5 SL 30 DAY		43.00			
7:10a	M	7:44a	NC	971	SB	CV5 S	0
8:10a	M	9:10a	NC	343	SB	CV5	1
12:35p	M	1:35p	NC	908	SB	CV5	1
1:40p	M	2:14p	NC	345	SB	CV5	0
X6 2:10p	M	2:45p	NC	989	SB	CV5	0
X6 4:15p	M	4:49p	NC	979	SB	CV5	0
X6 5:25p	M	5:59p	NC	983	SB	CV5	0
6:45p	M	7:45p	NC	347	SB	D9S	1
X6 9:00p	M	9:34p	NC	987	SB	CV5	0
COMMUTER AIR CARRIERS							
X67 9:25a	M	10:10a	JB	202	A	899	0
X67 10:45a	M	11:45a	JB	102	A	899	1
X67 3:50p	M	4:35p	JB	206	A	899	0
X6 6:00p	M	7:00p	JB	208	A	899	1

49. A passenger wishes to fly from Peoria, Illinois to Harrisburg, Pennsylvania. He wishes to depart on a Friday, as late in the day as possible. Using the schedules that follow and Chicago as a connecting point, determine the most convenient schedule for this passenger.

To HARRISBURG, PA.			EDT HAR			
From CHICAGO, ILL. M-MDW, O-ORD, C-CGX			CDT CHI			
F	69.44	5.56	75.00	150.00		
S	53.70	4.30	58.00	116.00		
Y	53.70	4.30	58.00	116.00		
YM	43.00					
AL EX/11 S WEEKEND			87.00			
7:00a	O 10:31a H	AL	876	SB	D9S B	1
9:10a	O 12:27p H	AL	878	SB	D9S	1
11:45a	O 3:41p H	AL	908	FYB	D9S	1
1:10p	O 3:41p H	TW	30	SB	72S L	0
1:45p	O 5:11p H	AL	976	SB	D9S S	1
3:45p	O 7:11p H	AL	890	FYB	D9S	1
6:45p	O 10:21p H	AL	884	SB	D9S D	1
8:45p	O 12:16a H	AL	944	SB	D9S	1

To CHICAGO, ILL.				CDT CHI			
From PEORIA, ILL.				CDT PIA			
	S	23.15	1.85	25.00	50.00		
OZ	YM	19.00					
	7:02a	7:40a O	OZ	920	SB	D9S	0
X7	7:32a	8:20a O	OZ	860	SB	FH7	0
X67	10:12a	11:00a O	OZ	816	SB	FH7	0
	11:37a	12:15p O	OZ	956	SB	D9S	0
X6	1:45p	2:23p O	OZ	928	SB	D9S	0
67	2:57p	3:45p O	OZ	890	SB	FH7	0
X67	3:42p	4:30p O	OZ	826	SB	FH7	0
	4:37p	5:15p O	OZ	976	SB	D9S	0
X6	7:11p	7:59p O	OZ	809	SB	FH7	0
X6	7:49p	9:14p O	OZ	858	SB	FH7	1

A. The last flight from Peoria to Chicago is OZ 858, which arrives in Chicago at 9:14 p.m. Since the minimum off-line connecting time at O'Hare Airport is 50 minutes (determined from the Minimum Connecting Time Section in the front pages of the NAOAG), we must check the Chicago-Harrisburg listings for a flight departing O'Hare at 10:04 p.m. or later.

B. Examine the Chicago-Harrisburg listings. The latest flight on a Friday is AL 944, which departs at 8:45 p.m. We must find an earlier PIA-CHI flight.

C. Now that you know the latest flight to Harrisburg leaves O'Hare at 8:45 p.m., simply look for a PIA-CHI flight which arrives at O'Hare earlier than 7:55 p.m. (minimum connecting time subtracted from the departure time).

D. OZ 809 does not satisfy the minimum connecting time requirements. Even though the difference is only 4 minutes, the minimum time may not be reduced.

E. OZ 976 is the next earlier PIA-CHI flight. It is the latest flight from PIA-CHI the passenger may take in order to make the connection to Harrisburg.

F. The passenger's itinerary, then, is OZ 976 PIA-CHI and AL 944 ORD-HAR. Or, is it? With this itinerary, the passenger has a 3 1/2 hour wait at ORD. Perhaps there is another ORD-HAR flight a little earlier so we could reduce the waiting time. Please recheck the ORD-HAR schedule.

G. The next earlier ORD-HAR flight is AL 884 departing at 6:45 p.m. This flight satisfies the minimum connecting time requirement, and the passenger would only have to wait 1 1/2 hours at O'Hare. The passenger's itinerary should be OZ 976 and _____ ORD-HAR.

Assuming the passenger wanted to arrive in HAR as early on a Saturday as possible, answer the following:

H. The flight from the origin to the connecting city should be _____ Airlines flight number _____.

I. The flight from the connecting city to Harrisburg should be _____ Airlines flight number _____.

50. The NAOAG contains a complete Airline Index containing home office addresses of all airlines whose schedules appear in the North American Edition.

INDEX OF CERTIFICATED AIR CARRIERS
APPEARING IN THIS PUBLICATION

✦Indicates carrier's participation to the agreement relating to liability limitations of the Warsaw Convention and The Hague Protocol, which carriers have signed and filed with the Civil Aeronautics Board counterparts of the inter-carrier Agreement (CAB 18900—sometimes called the Montreal Agreement) providing for increase of liability limits to $75,000 and waiver of defense under Article 20(1) of the Warsaw Convention or The Hague Protocol, with respect to passengers.

▲ Members and Associate Members of the International Air Transport Association (I.A.T.A.)
★ Members and Associate Members of the Air Transport Association of America (A.T.A.)
● Operator Members and Associate Members of the Air Transport Association of Canada (A.T.A.C.)

ATA/IATA Form Numbers Follow Two Letter Codes.

AIRLINE AND HOME OFFICE	AIRLINE AND HOME OFFICE	AIRLINE AND HOME OFFICE	AIRLINE AND HOME OFFICE
AEROLINEAS DEL PACIFICO S.A. (PN) Esqverro 40-B La Paz, Baja California, Mexico Tel. 2-01-72	✦▲BRANIFF INTERNATIONAL AIRWAYS (BN) 002 Braniff Airways Building, Exchange Park Dallas, Texas 75235 Tel. 214—358-6011	**JAMAICA AIR TAXI, LTD. (JQ)** P.O. Box 218 Montego Bay, Jamaica Tel. 3205, 3416	✦▲PHILLIPPINE AIRLINES (PR) 079 6780 Ayala Avenue Pal Bldg. Makati, Rizal, Philippines Tel. 88-10-61
✦▲●**AEROMEXICO (AM)** 139 Blvd. Aeropuerto Central 161 Mexico 9, D. F. Tel. 903—571-3000	✦▲BRITISH AIRWAYS BRITISH OVERSEAS AIRWAYS CORP. London Airport (BA) 061 Hounslow, Middlesex, England Tel. 759-5511	✦▲JAPAN AIR LINES, LTD. (JL) 131 Tokyo Bldg. 2-3-2 Marunouchi Tokyo, Japan Tel. (03) 213-6211	✦★PIEDMONT AVIATION, INC. (PI) 030 Smith Reynolds Airport Winston-Salem, N.C. 27102 Tel. 919—767-5100
AERONAVES ALIMENTADORAS Av. Revolucion No. 1608 Despacho 203 Mexico 20, D.F. Tel. 903—71-20-11	BRITISH OVERSEAS AIRWAYS CORP. (SEE BRITISH AIRWAYS)	✦▲KLM—ROYAL DUTCH AIR LINES (KL) 074 Schipol Int'l. Airport P.O. Box 7700 Netherlands Tel. Amsterdam 020-499123	✦▲QANTAS AIRWAYS, LTD. (QF) 081 Qantas House, 70 Hunter St. P.O. Box 489 Sydney, N.S.W., Australia Tel. 20369
AERONAVES del CENTRO, S.A. (JZ) **AERONAVES DEL MAYAB (JR)** **AERONAVES del OESTE, S.A. (JO)** **AERONAVES del SUR, S.A. (JS)** **AERONAVES DEL SURESTE (JH)** c/o AERONAVES ALIMENTADORAS	✦▲BRITISH WEST INDIAN AIRWAYS, LTD. (BW) 106 Kent House, Long Circular Rd. Maraval, Port of Spain, Trinidad Tel. 21241	KODIAK WESTERN ALASKA AIRLINES P.O. Box 2457 (KO) 366 Kodiak, Alaska 99615 Tel. 907—486-3271	✦▲●QUEBECAIR INC. (QB) 330 P.O. Box 490 Montreal Int'l Airport Dorval, Quebec, Hhy 1B5, Canada Tel. 418—631-9802
AEROSERVICIOS DE CALIFORNIA (YM) APDO, Postal 299 Ensenada. B. Cfa., Mexico Tel. 9-1844, 9-1825	✦CAYMAN AIRWAYS, LTD. (KX) 378 P.O. Box 11 Grand Cayman, B.W.I. Tel. 9-2311	✦LACSA—LINEAS AEREAS COSTARRICENSES, S.A. (LR) 133 P. O. Box 1531 San Jose, Costa Rica Tel. 217315	REEVE ALEUTIAN AIRWAYS, INC. (RV) P.O. Box 559 338 Anchorage, Alaska 99510 Tel. 272-9426
✦AEROVIAS QUISQUEYANA (QQ) 442 El Conde 80 Santo Domingo, Dominican Republic Tel. 689-7291/3	▲CHICAGO HELICOPTER AIRWAYS, INC. 5313 W. 63rd St. (CH) 328 Midway Airport Chicago, Ill. 60638 Tel. 312—735-0200	✦ALAN CHILE—LINEA AEREA NACIONAL DE CHILE (LA) Casilla (P.O. Box) 147-D Santiago, Chile Tel. 572233	SFO HELICOPTER AIRLINES, INC. (OH) P.O. Box 2525 352 Metropolitan Oakland Int'l Airport Oakland, Calif. 94614 Tel. 415—635-2222
AIR BVI, LTD. (BL) 644 Box 85 Roadtown, Tortola, British Virgin Islands	✦CHINA AIRLINES LTD. (CI) 297 26, Sec. III Nanking East Rd. Taipei, Taiwan, Rep. of China Tel. 571111	✦LEEWARD ISLAND AIR TRANSPORT SERVICES, LTD. (LI) 140 Coolidge Airport Antigua, West Indies Tel. 30140/30141	✦▲SABENA BELGIAN WORLD AIRLINES (SN) 082 (Societe Anonyme Belge D'Exploitation De La Navigation Aerienne) 35 Rue Cardinal Mercier Brussels, Belgium Tel. 119060
✦★▲●AIR CANADA (AC) 014 Place Ville Marie Montreal 113, Quebec, Canada	✦★▲CONTINENTAL AIR LINES, INC. International Airport 005 Los Angeles, Calif. 90009 Tel. 213—646-2810	LIAT (See LEEWARD ISLANDS AIR TRANSPORT SERVICES LTD.)	

If, for example, you wished the address of the home office for Piedmont Aviation, locate Piedmont alphabetically. The address is printed immediately below the name of the airline.

A. Piedmont's home office is located in _____.
B. Continental's home office is located in _____.

Sample NAOAG

ABBREVIATIONS AND REFERENCE MARKS

These sample pages are intended for illustrative purposes only. Refer to the latest edition of the NAOAG for current schedules and fares information.

REMARKS

*	INDICATES CHANGE IN CLASS OF SERVICE ENROUTE, FOLLOWS FLIGHT LISTING
CHG PLANE	CHANGE OF AIRCRAFT REQUIRED AT DESIGNATED AIRPORT
CONEX	INDICATES BEST CONNECTION
VIA	CITIES FOR TRAVEL FROM CITIES NOT SHOWN
#	OVER 9 STOPS
DIS	DISCONTINUED AFTER
EFF	EFFECTIVE ON
EX	EXCEPT ON
GOVT	GOVERNMENT
OP	OPERATES ON
SPB	SEAPLANE BASE
&	(IN FLIGHT NUMBER COLUMN ONLY) INDICATES "AIR SHUTTLE"
☐	(FOLLOWING FLIGHT NUMBER) INDICATES A REPLACEMENT FLIGHT OPERATED BY A COMMUTER AIR CARRIER ON BEHALF OF A CERTIFICATED AIR CARRIER PURSUANT TO A C.A.B. APPROVED AGREEMENT

GROUND TRANSPORTATION

L	LIMOUSINE	R	RENTAL CAR
T	TAXI	A	AIR TAXI

FREQUENCY CODE

1—MONDAY		5—FRIDAY	
2—TUESDAY		6—SATURDAY	
3—WEDNESDAY		7—SUNDAY	
4—THURSDAY		X—EXCEPT	

"SPEC" IN A FREQUENCY COLUMN INDICATES THE FLIGHT WILL OPERATE ON THE DATES SPECIFIED ON THE FOLLOWING LINE.

FOOD SERVICE

B	BREAKFAST
D	DINNER
L	LUNCH
S	SNACK
*	(IN MEAL COLUMN) INDICATES REMARK CONCERNING FOOD SERVICE FOLLOWS FLIGHT LISTING.

Note 1. A / SYMBOL SHOWN WITH THE FOOD SERVICE DESIGNATOR INDICATES MEAL SERVICE DIFFERS DEPENDING ON CLASS OF SERVICE. NORMALLY A FOOD SERVICE INDICATOR TO THE LEFT OF THE / SYMBOL INDICATES SERVICE APPLICABLE TO THE FIRST CLASS COMPARTMENT OF THE AIRCRAFT. A FOOD SERVICE INDICATOR TO THE RIGHT OF THE SLASH SYMBOL INDICATES SERVICE APPLICABLE TO THE COACH AND/OR ECONOMY COMPARTMENT OF THE AIRCRAFT. IF NO / SYMBOL IS SHOWN THE FOOD SERVICE INDICATOR APPLIES TO ALL CLASSES OF SERVICE SHOWN WHICH ARE ELIGIBLE FOR FOOD SERVICE.

Note 2. MEAL SERVICE FOR K CLASS VARIES ACCORDING TO INDIVIDUAL AIRLINE POLICY. NORMALLY NO MEALS ARE SERVED FOR K CLASS PASSENGERS ON AA/CO/DL/TI/TW/UA.

CLASS OF SERVICE

A	PROPELLER FIRST CLASS
An	PROP NIGHT FIRST CLASS
B	CONTROLLED INVENTORY—COACH. IDENTIFIES FLIGHTS WITH CAPACITY CONTROLLED EXCURSION FARES.
C	PROPELLER THRIFT
F	JET FIRST CLASS (MAY ALSO APPLY ON PROPELLER FLIGHTS AT SAME FARE)
Fn	JET NIGHT COACH IN FIRST CLASS COMPARTMENT
Fo	FIRST CLASS OFF PEAK
J	LIMITED SERVICE CLASS—AVAILABLE MONDAY THROUGH THURSDAY ONLY, RESERVATIONS ACCEPTED UPON PURCHASE OF TICKET 7 DAYS IN ADVANCE
K	JET THRIFT (ECONOMY—WITHIN U.S.)
Kn	JET NIGHT ECONOMY

L	CONTROLLED INVENTORY—ECONOMY. IDENTIFIES FLIGHTS WITH CAPACITY CONTROLLED EXCURSION FARES.
S	JET CUSTOM CLASS/ONE CLASS STANDARD SERVICE (MAY ALSO APPLY ON PROPELLER FLIGHTS AT SAME FARE)
Sn	NIGHT STANDARD ONE CLASS
T	PROPELLER COACH
Tn	PROPELLER NIGHT COACH
U	NO RESERVATION SERVICE
Y	JET COACH (MAY ALSO APPLY TO PROPELLER FLIGHTS AT SAME FARE)
Yn	JET NIGHT COACH IN OTHER THAN FIRST CLASS COMPARTMENT

FARES

ADG	GOVERNMENT FIRST CLASS TRAVEL FARES (GTR REQUIRED)
AU	ADULT STANDBY—SEE PAGE 17
CAD	CANADIAN DOLLARS
EX/99	EXCURSION FARE—NUMBER REFERS TO NOTE ON PAGES 18 & 19
KDG	GOVERNMENT COMMUTER CLASS TRAVEL FARES (GTR REQUIRED)
KH	PEAK—APPLIES 12:01A.M. FRIDAY THRU MIDNIGHT SUN. UNLESS OTHERWISE NOTED WITH FARE
KL	OFF-PEAK—APPLIES 12:01A.M. MON THRU MIDNIGHT THURS UNLESS OTHERWISE NOTED WITH FARE
KM	MILITARY RESERVATION FARE—SEE PAGE 16
KU	ADULT STANDBY—SEE PAGE 16
M	MILITARY STANDBY FARES—SEE PAGE 16
MEP	MEXICAN PESOS
SDG	GOVERNMENT STANDARD CLASS TRAVEL FARES (GTR REQUIRED)
SU	ADULT STANDBY—SEE PAGE 17
SW	OFF-PEAK—APPLIES SATURDAY OR SUNDAY
YH	PEAK—APPLIES 12:01 A.M. FRI THRU MIDNIGHT SUN. UNLESS OTHERWISE NOTED WITH FARE
YL	OFF-PEAK—APPLIES 12:01A.M. MON THRU MIDNIGHT THURS UNLESS OTHERWISE NOTED WITH FARE
YM	MILITARY RESERVATION FARE—SEE PAGE 16
YW	OFF-PEAK—APPLIES 12:01A.M. SAT. THRU 3:01P.M. SUN. OTHERWISE NOTED WITH FARE. NOT VALID JUNE 28, 29; DEC. 20, 21, 1975; JAN. 3 AND 4, 1976.
YZ	YOUTH RESERVATION FARE—SEE PAGE 17
Z	YOUTH STANDBY FARE—SEE PAGE 17
U.S.	48 CONTIGUOUS STATES (NOT INCLUDING ALASKA AND HAWAII) UNLESS OTHERWISE NOTED
1	NUMERAL PRECEDING CLASS OF SERVICE INDICATES ADDITIONAL INFORMATION FOLLOWS FARE.
INTRASTATE	THESE FARES ARE TO BE USED ONLY WHEN TRAVEL ORIGINATES AND TERMINATES WITHIN A STATE.
INTERSTATE	THESE FARES ARE TO BE USED WHEN THE ORIGIN AND DESTINATION POINTS ARE NOT IN THE SAME STATE.

BASIS FOR FARE CONSTRUCTION—DECODES

1.	JT	PUBLISHED JOINT FARE.
2.	THRU	PUBLISHED LOCAL FARE.
3.	JT/THRU	A JOINT FARE AND A LOCAL FARE AT THE SAME DOLLAR AMOUNT CONSOLIDATES INTO ONE FARE LINE TO CONSERVE SPACE. JT APPLIES TO AN INTERLINE CONNECTION AND THRU APPLIES TO AN ONLINE CONNECTION.
4.	CC	FULL COMBINATION OF LOCAL FARES.
5.	CC-T	COMBINATION OF TWO LOCAL FARES MINUS A TERMINAL CHARGE.
6.	( )	COMBINATION OF A LOCAL FARE TO THE CITY IN ( ) AND A LOCAL OR JOINT FARE FOR THE REMAINDER OF THE ITINERARY.
7.	( )—T	COMBINATION OF A LOCAL FARE TO THE CITY IN ( ) AND A LOCAL OR JOINT FARE FOR THE REMAINDER OF THE ITINERARY MINUS A TERMINAL CHARGE.
8.	( ) ( )	A LOCAL FARE TO THE FIRST CITY IN ( ), PLUS A JOINT FARE TO THE SECOND CITY IN ( ), PLUS A LOCAL FARE FOR THE REMAINDER OF THE ITINERARY.
9.	(( ))	POINT BEYOND—A PUBLISHED FARE TO/FROM THE CITY IN (( )).
10.	(( )) (( ))	DOUBLE POINT BEYOND—A PUBLISHED FARE WHICH IS USED WITH BOTH THE ORIGIN AND DESTINATION OF THE FARE BEING BEYOND THE ORIGIN AND DESTINATION OF THE CONNECTION.
11.	(( )) ( )	JOINT FARE FROM THE CITY IN (( )) TO THE CITY IN ( ), PLUS A LOCAL FARE FOR THE REMAINDER OF THE ITINERARY.
12.	( ) (( ))	REVERSE OF #11, ABOVE. A LOCAL FARE TO THE CITY IN ( ), PLUS A JOINT FARE TO THE CITY IN (( )).
13.	DIFF	DIFFERENTIAL CONSTRUCTION USED IN CALCULATING CHANGE OF CLASS.

ABBREVIATIONS AND REFERENCE MARKS

CERTIFICATED AIR CARRIERS

CODE	CARRIER
AA	AMERICAN AIRLINES
AC	AIR CANADA
AF	AIR FRANCE
AL	ALLEGHENY AIRLINES
AM	AEROMEXICO
AP	ASPEN AIRWAYS, INC.
AS	ALASKA AIRLINES
AT	ROYAL AIR MAROC
AV	AVIANCA
AZ	ALITALIA
BA	BRITISH AIRWAYS (OVERSEAS DIVISION)
BH	TURKS AND CAICOS AIRWAYS
BL	AIR BVI, LTD.
BN	BRANIFF INTERNATIONAL AIRWAYS
BT	AIR MARTINIQUE (SATAIR)
BW	B.W.I.A. INTERNATIONAL
CD	TRANS—PROVINCIAL AIRLINES LTD.
CI	CHINA AIRLINES
CO	CONTINENTAL AIRLINES
CP	CP AIR
CU	CUBANA
DG	ARROW AVIATION, LTD.
DL	DELTA AIR LINES, INC.
DO	DOMINICANA DE AVIACION
EA	EASTERN AIR LINES
EM	GOLFE AIR QUEBEC, LTD.
FL	FRONTIER AIRLINES
FO	AEROVIAS CARIBE
FW	WRIGHT AIRLINES
GU	AVIATECA
GX	GREAT LAKES AIRLINES, LTD.
HA	HAWAIIAN AIR LINES
HC	HAITI AIR INTER
HF	BRADLEY AIR SERVICES, LTD.
HS	HOOKER AIR SERVICES, LTD.
HU	TRINIDAD AND TOBAGO AIR SERVICES LTD.
IB	IBERIA
JH	AERONAVES DEL SURESTE
JL	JAPAN AIR LINES CO., LTD.
JM	AIR JAMAICA (1968) LTD.
JO	AERONAVES DEL OESTE
JQ	TRANS-JAMAICAN AIRLINES LTD.
JR	AERONAVES DEL MAYAB
JS	AERONAVES DEL SUR
JZ	AERONAVES DEL CENTRO
KI	TIME AIR, LTD.
KL	KLM
KO	KODIAK WESTERN ALASKA AIRLINES
KX	CAYMAN AIRWAYS, LTD.
LA	LAN CHILE
LH	LUFTHANSA GERMAN AIRLINES
LI	LIAT (1974) LTD.
LM	DUTCH ANTILLEAN AIRLINES
LR	LACSA
MG	WEST COAST AIR SERVICES LTD.
MX	MEXICANA DE AVIACION
NA	NATIONAL AIRLINES
NC	NORTH CENTRAL AIRLINES
ND	NORDAIR
NE	AIR NEW ENGLAND
NK	NORCANAIR
NN	NORTHWARD AIRLINES LTD.
NR	NORONTAIR
NW	NORTHWEST ORIENT AIRLINES, INC.
NY	NEW YORK AIRWAYS
OA	OLYMPIC AIRWAYS
OD	AEROCONDOR
OG	AIR GUADELOUPE
OH	SFO HELICOPTER AIRLINES, INC.
OP	AIR PANAMA INTERNACIONAL
OZ	OZARK AIR LINES
PA	PAN AMERICAN WORLD AIRWAYS
PD	PEM AIR LIMITED
PI	PIEDMONT AVIATION
PN	AEROLINEAS DEL PACIFICO, S.A.
PR	PHILIPPINE AIRLINES
PV	EASTERN PROVINCIAL AIRWAYS
PW	PACIFIC WESTERN AIRLINES
PY	SURINAM AIRWAYS LTD
QB	QUEBECAIR
QF	QANTAS AIRWAYS LTD.
QQ	AEROVIAS QUISQUEYANA
RV	REEVE ALEUTIAN AIRWAYS
RW	HUGHES AIRWEST
SH	SAHSA—SERVICIO AEREO DE HONDURAS, S.A.
SO	SOUTHERN AIRWAYS
SQ	SINGAPORE AIRLINES
TE	AIR NEW ZEALAND LIMITED
TI	TEXAS INTERNATIONAL AIRLINES, INC.
TS	ALOHA AIRLINES
TW	TRANS WORLD AIRLINES
TZ	TRANSAIR LIMITED
UA	UNITED AIRLINES
UH	AUSTIN AIRWAYS LTD.
UP	BAHAMASAIR
UW	MIDWEST AIRLINES, LTD.
VA	VIASA *[Argentine]*
VG	AIR SIAM
VY	ALAS DEL CARIBE
WA	WESTERN AIRLINES
WC	WIEN AIR ALASKA, INC.
WM	WINDWARD ISLAND AIRWAYS INTERNATIONAL N.V.
WS	NORTHERN WINGS LTD. (SUBSIDIARY OF QUEBECAIR)
WY	WAGNER AVIATION INC.
XY	MUNZ NORTHERN AIRLINES, INC.
YB	BAYVIEW AIR SERVICE LTD.
ZC	ATLANTIC CENTRAL AIRLINES LTD.

COMMUTER AIR CARRIERS

CODE	CARRIER
AD	ANTILLES AIR BOATS, INC.
AG	AIR SUNSHINE ►
AJ	ALL ISLAND AIR, INC.
AK	ALTAIR AIRLINES, INC. ►
BF	HORIZON AIRWAYS, INC.
BK	CHALK'S INTERNATIONAL AIRLINE, INC. ►
CB	COMMUTER AIRLINES, INC.
CG	SOUTH CENTRAL AIR TRANSPORT INC.
CJ	COLGAN AIRWAYS CORP. ► ◄
CT	CATALINA—VEGAS AIRLINES
CZ	CASCADE AIRWAYS ►
DD	COMMAND AIRWAYS, INC. ►
DE	DOWNEAST AIRLINES, INC. ►
DH	CARDINAL AIRLINES, INC. ► ◄
DK	CALIFORNIA AIR COMMUTER ► ◄
DN	SKYSTREAM AIRLINES, INC.
DP	COCHISE AIRLINES ►
EB	PENNSYLVANIA COMMUTER ►
EE	AIR EXEC
EJ	NEW ENGLAND AIRLINES, INC. ►
ES	CLIPPER AIR INTERNATIONAL CORP.
EV	EXECUAIR AIRLINES, INC. ►
FD	AIR GEMINI, INC.
FE	FLORIDA AIRLINES, INC. ► & AIR SOUTH, INC. ► & SHAWNEE AIRLINES, INC. ►
FH	MALL AIRWAYS ►
FN	AIR CAROLINA ► ◄
FP	AIR CATALINA ►
FS	SUN VALLEY KEY ►
FY	METROFLIGHT AIRLINES ►
FZ	AERIE AIRLINES
GM	SCHEDULED SKYWAYS SYSTEM ►
GO	GCS AIRLINES
GW	GOLDEN WEST AIRLINES, INC. ►
GZ	ROSWELL AIRLINES
HD	AIR MONT, INC.
HG	HARBOR AIRLINES ►
HI	HENSLEY FLYING SERVICE, INC.
HO	AIR ATLANTIC INC.
HP	ISLAND PACIFIC AIR
HQ	HANKINS AIRWAYS INC. ► ◄
HR	EASTERN CARIBBEAN AIRWAYS ◄
HW	LAKE HAVASU AIR SERVICE
HY	METRO AIRLINES ►
ID	APOLLO AIRWAYS, INC ► ◄
II	IMPERIAL AIRLINES ►
IK	EUREKA AERO INDUSTRIES, INC ►
IU	MIDSTATE AIRLINES ►
JB	AIR METRO AIRLINES
JC	ROCKY MOUNTAIN AIRWAYS ►
JI	GULL AIR INC ►
JV	NORTH CAY AIRWAYS
JW	ASTRO AIRWAYS CORP.
KC	AEROMECH, INC.
KF	CATSKILL AIRWAYS
KG	CATALINA AIRLINES, INC. ►
KJ	BAJA AIRLINES, INC.
KN	AIR KENTUCKY
KW	DORADO WINGS ►
LS	MARCO ISLAND AIRWAYS
MF	FEDERAL CARRIERS
MI	MACKEY INTERNATIONAL AIRLINES ►
MJ	S.M.B. STAGE LINES, INC. ►
NF	NEWPORT AERO ◄
NG	COASTAL AIRWAYS
NP	NOR-CAL AVIATION INC.
NQ	CUMBERLAND AIRLINES ►
NT	AIR NEW ULM
OF	TYEE AIRLINES, INC. ►
OO	SUN AIRE LINES ►
OQ	ROYALE AIR LINES, INC ►
OW	TRANS MOUNTAIN AIR LTD.
OX	PRIORITY AIR TRANSPORT, INC.
✈ OY	CANNON AVIATION CO., INC ► ◄
PE	POLAR AIRWAYS, INC.
PF	PALMAS AIR CORPORATION
PM	PILGRIM AIRLINES ►
PP	PHILLIPS AIRLINES
PQ	PUERTO RICO INT'L AIRLINES ►
PT	PROVINCETOWN-BOSTON AIRLINE & NAPLES AIRLINE DIVISION ►
QA	TRANS AMERICA AIRWAYS, INC. ►
QG	SKY WEST AVIATION ►
QO	BAR HARBOR AIRLINES ►
QS	VALLEY AIRPARK, INC. ◄
QT	COLUMBIA AIRLINE ►
QW	LOS ANGELES HELICOPTER AIRLINES ►
§RL	CROWN INTERNATIONAL AIRLINES
RX	CAPITOL AIR SERVICES, INC. ►
SE	SOUTHEAST SKYWAYS, INC.
SL	SOUTHEAST AIRLINES, INC. ►
ST	SAINT THOMAS TAX-AIR
SX	SEAPLANE SHUTTLE TRANSPORT, INC.
SZ	SIERRA PACIFIC AIRLINES ►
TB	TRANS REGIONAL AIRLINES
TT	BUSINESS AIRCRAFT CORPORATION
UD	BROWER AIRWAYS, INC. ►
UO	SUN BASIN AIRLINES
UQ	SUBURBAN AIRLINES ►
UR	EMPIRE AIRLINES ◄
UU	WINGS AIRLINES, INC. ►
UV	VALLEY COMMUTER ►
UX	AIR ILLINOIS
VB	STOL AIR, INC. ►
VD	NEVADA AIRLINES, INC. ◄
VI	VIEQUES AIR LINK ►
VJ	BALTIMORE AIRWAYS, INC.
VL	RESORT COMMUTER AIRLINES ► ◄
VM	MONMOUTH AIRLINES ►
VN	COMMUTAIRE INTERNATIONAL AIRWAYS, INC.
VV	SEMO AVIATION ►
WE	WESTERN AIR STAGES
WH	COASTAL AIR LTD. ►
WI	SWIFT—AIRE LINES ►
WJ	ALASKA SOUTHCOAST AIRWAYS
WL	COMUT AIRE OF MICHIGAN INC. ►
WP	AIR SPEED, INC. ◄
WR	WHEELER FLYING SERVICE, INC.►
WV	BRANDT AIR
XJ	MESABA AVIATION ►
XO	RIO AIRWAYS ►
XQ	SKYLINE AVIATION, INC. ►
XU	TRANS MO AIRLINES, INC. ►
XV	MISSISSIPPI VALLEY AIRWAYS, INC. ►
YC	ALASKA AERONAUTICAL INDUSTRIES ►
YE	PEARSON AIRCRAFT, INC. ►
YH	AMISTAD AIRLINES, INC. ►
YJ	MID-CONTINENT AIRWAYS
§YL	MONTAUK CARIBBEAN AIRWAYS INC. ► ◄
YN	ISLAND AIR
YQ	OAHU & KAUAI AIRLINES ►
YR	SCENIC AIRLINES INC ►
YS	SAN JUAN AIRLINES
YX	SUN AIRLINE, INC.
ZD	ROSS AVIATION, INC. ►
ZE	MERRIMACK AIRWAYS ►
ZF	AIR CARIBBEAN
ZH	ROYAL HAWAIIAN AIRWAYS ►
ZK	DAVIS AIRLINES, INC. ►
ZM	WINNIPESAUKEE AVIATION, INC.
ZN	TRINITY AIRWAYS ►
ZP	VIRGIN AIR, INC.
ZQ	LAWRENCE AVIATION, INC. ►
ZR	STAR AVIATION CORP.
§ZS	GRAND CANYON AIRLINES, INC. ►
ZU	ZIA AIRLINES ►
ZV	AIR MIDWEST ►
ZW	AIR WISCONSIN ►
ZY	SKYWAY AVIATION, INC. ►

SCHEDULED INTRA-STATE AIR CARRIERS

JE	YOSEMITE AIRLINES
OC	AIR CALIFORNIA
PS	PSA-PACIFIC SOUTHWEST AIRLINES
QH	AIR FLORIDA
QX	AIR ILLINOIS
WN	SOUTHWEST AIRLINES

CAR RENTAL COMPANIES

ALCR	ALAMO RENT-A-CAR
ATCR	ATLANTIC RENT A CAR
OLCR	OLINS RENT A CAR
RCCR	RAMADA RENT A CAR
TRCR	TROPICAL RENT A CAR
ZACR	AIRWAYS RENT A CAR
ZDCR	BUDGET CAR RENTAL
ZECR	HERTZ
ZICR	AVIS RENT A CAR
ZLCR	NATIONAL CAR RENTAL
ZRCR	DOLLAR-A-DAY

PROPELLER AIRCRAFT

CODE	EQUIPMENT
ACD	AERO COMMANDER
A24	ANTONOV 24
A50	AERO COMMANDER 500
BBR	BEECH BARON
BNI	BRITTEN NORMAN-ISLANDER
BNT	BRITTEN NORMAN-TRISLANDER
BTP	BEECHCRAFT TURBO PROP
B18	BEECHCRAFT D-18 (ALL SERIES)
B80	BEECH QUEEN 80
B99	BEECH 99
CES	CESSNA/CESSNA 206
CNA	CESSNA (ALL SERIES)
CON	L749 CONSTELLATION
CVR	CONVAIR (GENERAL DESIGNATOR)
CV2	CONVAIR 240
CV4	CONVAIR 440 METROPOLITAN
CV5	CONVAIR 580 TURBO-PROP
CV6	CONVAIR 600/CONVAIR 640
DBV	De HAVILLAND BEAVER
DC3	DOUGLAS DC-3—DAKOTA C-47
DC6	DOUGLAS DC-6
DDV	De HAVILLAND DOVE
DHC	De HAVILLAND DHC-4 CARIBOU
DHO	De HAVILLAND OTTER
DTO	De HAVILLAND TWIN OTTER
FH7	FOKKER FRIENDSHIP TURBO-PROP FH227
F27	FOKKER FRIENDSHIP TURBO-PROP F-27
GGM	GRUMMAN MALLARD
GGS	GRUMMAN G-21A GOOSE
HRN	De HAVILLAND HERON
LEC	LOCKHEED ELECTRA TURBO-PROP
LJT	LEAR JET
MR4	MARTIN 404
MU2	MITSUBISHI MU-2G
N26	NORD 262/SUPER BROUSSARD
PAZ	PIPER AZTEC
PCB	CESSNA 207 TURBO SYSTEM
PCH	PIPER CHEROKEE
PDS	De HAVILLAND SKYLINER
PHP	HANDLEY—PAGE 137 JETSTREAM
PNV	PIPER NAVAJO
PPS	PIPER SENECA
PRP	PROP AIRCRAFT TYPE VARIES
PR4	De HAVILLAND RILEY 400
PTC	PIPER TWIN COMANCHE
SWM	SWEARINGEN METRO
S55	SIKORSKY S-55 HELICOPTER
561	SIKORSKY S-61 HELICOPTER
TB8	TWIN BEECH 18
TS4	TURBO-STAR 400
Y11	NAMCO YS-11
Y14	ILYUSHIN IL-14
Y18	ILYUSHIN IL-18
402	CESSNA 402 TWIN TURBO SYSTEM
601	AEROSTAR 601
748	HAWKER SIDDELEY 748

JET AIRCRAFT

A3B	A300B EUROPEAN AIRBUS
B11	BAC 111 (GENERAL DESIGNATOR)
B3J	BOEING 707-320 FAN JET
DC8	DOUGLAS DC8 (ALL SERIES)
DC9	DOUGLAS DC9 (ALL SERIES)
D10	DOUGLAS DC10 (ALL SERIES)
D8S	DOUGLAS DC8 SUPER 60 SERIES
D9S	DOUGLAS DC9-SUPER
D95	DOUGLAS DC9 SUPER 50 SERIES
F28	FOKKER FELLOWSHIP JET F28
L10	LOCKHEED 1011 TRISTAR
S11	BAC 111-500
V10	VICKERS VC10
707	BOEING 707 (ALL SERIES)
725	BOEING 727-200
720	BOEING 720 (ALL SERIES)
727	BOEING 727 (ALL SERIES)
73S	BOEING 737-200
737	BOEING 737 (ALL SERIES)
747	BOEING 747 (ALL SERIES)

TIME ZONES

HOURS FROM GREENWICH MEAN TIME (GMT)

		STAND-ARD (S)	DAY-LIGHT (D)
A	ATLANTIC	—4	—3
A	ALASKA	—10	—9
B	BERING	—11	—10
C	CENTRAL	—6	—5
E	EASTERN	—5	—4
H	HAWAII	—10	
M	MOUNTAIN	—7	—6
N	NEWFOUNDLAND	—3 1/2	—2 1/2
P	PACIFIC	—8	—7
Y	YUKON	—9	—8
D	DAYLIGHT		
S	STANDARD		
T	TIME		

EST—EASTERN STANDARD TIME
(—) HOURS SLOW FROM GREENWICH MEAN TIME (GMT)

See page 3 for INDEX of Guide contents. Explanation of "HOW TO USE" OAG will be found following schedule listings.

► — COMMUTER AIRLINE ASSOCIATION OF AMERICA   ◄ — NATIONAL AIR TRANSPORTATION ASSOCIATION, INC

✈ — SERVICE TEMPORARILY SUSPENDED   § — CARRIER PERFORMS SEASONAL SERVICE ONLY

CITY/AIRPORT CODES Listed Alphabetically by Code (For Schedules Included In This Guide)

A
ABE ALLENTOWN, PA.
ABI ABILENE, TEXAS
ABL AMBLER, ALASKA
ABQ ALBUQUERQUE, N.M.
ABR ABERDEEN, S.D.
ABY ALBANY, GA.
ACA ACAPULCO, MEXICO
ACK NANTUCKET, MASS.
ACT WACO, TEXAS
ACV EUREKA/ARCATA, CALIF.
ADK ADAK IS., ALASKA
ADQ KODIAK, ALASKA-KODIAK ARPT.
AET ALLAKAKET, ALASKA
AGN ANGOON, ALASKA
AGS AUGUSTA, GA.
AGU AGUASCALIENTES, MEXICO
AHN ATHENS, GA.
AIA ALLIANCE, NEBR.
AIN WAINWRIGHT, ALASKA
AIY ATLANTIC CITY, N.J.
AIZ LAKE OF THE OZARKS, MO.
AKI AKIAK, ALASKA
AKK AKHIOK, ALASKA
AKN KING SALMON, ALASKA
AKP ANAKTUVUK PASS, ALASKA
ALB ALBANY, N.Y.
ALM ALAMOGORDO, N.M.
ALN ALTON, ILL.
ALO WATERLOO, IOWA
ALS ALAMOSA, COLO.
ALW WALLA WALLA, WASH.
ALZ ALITAK, ALASKA
AMA AMARILLO, TEXAS
AMT * ATMAUTLUAK, ALASKA
ANB ANNISTON, ALA.
ANC ANCHORAGE, ALASKA
ANI ANIAK, ALASKA
ANU ANTIGUA, WEST INDIES
ANV ANVIK, ALASKA
AOO ALTOONA, PA.
APC NAPA, CALIF.
APF NAPLES, FLA.
APN ALPENA, MICH.
ARC ARCTIC VILLAGE, ALASKA
ARE ARECIBO, PUERTO RICO
ART WATERTOWN, N.Y.
ARX ASBURY PARK, N.J.
ASD ANDROS TOWN, BAHAMAS
ASE ASPEN, COLO.
AST ASTORIA, ORE.
ASX ASHLAND, WIS.
ATC ARTHUR'S TOWN, BAHAMAS
ATL ATLANTA, GA.
ATU ATTU IS., ALASKA
ATW APPLETON, WIS.
ATY WATERTOWN, S.D.
AUA ARUBA, NETH. ANTILLES
AUG AUGUSTA, ME.
AUK ALAKANUK, ALASKA
AUS AUSTIN, TEXAS
AUW WAUSAU, WIS.
AVL ASHEVILLE, N.C.
AVP WILKES-BARRE/SCRANTON, PA.
AVX CATALINA IS. CALIF-AVALON BAY
AXS ALTUS, OKLA.
AYS WAYCROSS, GA.
AZG APATZINGAN, MEXICO
AZO KALAMAZOO, MICH.

B
BAL BALTIMORE, MD.
BBQ BARBUDA, WEST INDIES
BBR BASSE-TERRE, GUADELOUPE
BCA BARACOA, CUBA
BDA BERMUDA, ATLANTIC OCEAN
BDL HARTFORD, CONN.
BDR BRIDGEPORT, CONN.
BEC BEDFORD, MASS.
BEH BENTON HARBOR, MICH.
BET BETHEL, ALASKA
BFD BRADFORD, PA.
BFF SCOTTSBLUFF, NEBR.
BFL BAKERSFIELD, CALIF.
BFT BEAUFORT, S.C.
BGI BARBADOS, WEST INDIES
BGM BINGHAMTON, N.Y.
BGR BANGOR, ME.
BHB BAR HARBOR, ME.
BHL BAHIA DE LOS ANGELES, MEX.
BHM BIRMINGHAM, ALA.
BIC BLOCK ISLAND, R.I.
BIG BIG DELTA, ALASKA
BIH BISHOP, CALIF.
BIL BILLINGS, MONT.
BIM BIMINI, BAHAMAS
BIS BISMARCK, N.D.
BJI BEMIDJI, MINN.
BKC BUCKLAND, ALASKA
BKE BAKER, ORE.
BKL CLEVELAND,OHIO-LAKEFRONT ARPT
BKW BECKLEY, W. VA.
BKX BROOKINGS, S.D.
BLF BLUEFIELD, W. VA.
BLH BLYTHE, CALIF.
BLI BELLINGHAM, WASH.
BMC BRIGHAM CITY, UTAH
BMG BLOOMINGTON, IND.
BMI BLOOMINGTON, ILL.
BNA NASHVILLE, TENN.
BOI BOISE, IDAHO
BON BONAIRE, NETH. ANTILLES
BOS BOSTON, MASS.
BPT BEAUMONT/PT. ARTHUR, TEX.
BQN AGUADILLA, PUERTO RICO
BRD BRAINERD, MINN.
BRL BURLINGTON, IOWA
BRO BROWNSVILLE, TEXAS
BRW BARROW, ALASKA
BTI BARTER IS., ALASKA
BTL BATTLE CREEK, MICH.
BTM BUTTE, MONT.
BTR BATON ROUGE, LA.
BTT BETTLES, ALASKA
BTV BURLINGTON, VT.
BUF BUFFALO, N.Y.
BUR BURBANK, CALIF.
BWD BROWNWOOD, TEXAS
BWG BOWLING GREEN, KY.
BZN BOZEMAN, MONT.
BZS WASHINGTON,DC-BUZZARDS PT.SPB

C
CAE COLUMBIA, S.C.
CAK AKRON/CANTON, OHIO
CAP CAP HAITIEN, HAITI
CBE CUMBERLAND, MD.
CCR CONCORD, CALIF.
CCV CORDOVA, ALSK.-CITY ARPT.
CDB COLD BAY, ALASKA
CDC CEDAR CITY, UTAH
CDI ISLA DE CEDROS, MEXICO
CDR CHADRON, NEBR.
CDV CORDOVA, ALASKA
CEC CRESCENT CITY, CALIF.
CEL CAPE ELEUTHERA, BAHAMAS
CEM CENTRAL, ALASKA
CEN CIUDAD OBREGON, MEXICO
CEZ CORTEZ, COLO.
CFG CIENFUEGOS, CUBA
CFT CLIFTON, ARIZ.
CGA CRAIG, ALASKA
CGI CAPE GIRARDEAU, MO.
CGX CHICAGO, ILL-MEIGS FIELD
CHA CHATTANOOGA, TENN.
CHI CHICAGO, ILL.
CHO CHARLOTTESVILLE, VA.
CHP CIRCLE HOT SPGS., ALASKA
CHS CHARLESTON, S.C.
CIB * CATALINA IS., CALIF.
CIC CHICO, CALIF.
CID CEDAR RAPIDS/IOWA CITY, IA.
CIK CHALKYITSIK, ALASKA
CIL COUNCIL, ALASKA
CIT * NORTH CAICOS, WEST INDIES
CJS CIUDAD JUAREZ, MEXICO
CKB CLARKSBURG, W. VA.
CKD CROOKED CREEK, ALASKA
CKO * CANCUN, MEXICO
CKV CLARKSVILLE, TENN.
CLC CLEAR LAKE CITY, TEXAS
CLE CLEVELAND, OHIO
CLL COLLEGE STATION, TEXAS
CLM PORT ANGELES, WASH.
CLP CLARKS POINT, ALASKA
CLQ COLIMA, MEXICO
CLS CHEHALIS, WASH.
CLT CHARLOTTE, N.C.
CME CIUDAD DEL CARMEN, MEXICO
CMH COLUMBUS, OHIO
CMI CHAMPAIGN, ILL.
CMW CAMAGUEY, CUBA
CMX HANCOCK, MICH.
CNM CARLSBAD, N.M.
CNY MOAB, UTAH
COD CODY, WYO.
COS COLORADO SPRINGS, COLO.
COU COLUMBIA, MO.
CPE CAMPECHE, MEXICO
CPR CASPER, WYO.
CPX CULEBRA, PUERTO RICO
CRC CIRCLE, ALASKA
CRE MYRTLE BEACH, S.C.
CRI CROOKED ISLAND, BAHAMAS
CRP CORPUS CHRISTI, TEXAS
CRU CARRIACOU, WINDWARD IS.
CRW CHARLESTON, W. VA.
CSG COLUMBUS, GA.
CSH CAPE SARICHEF, ALASKA
CTM CHETUMAL, MEXICO
CUL CULIACAN, MEXICO
CUR CURACAO, NETH. ANTILLES
CUU CHIHUAHUA, MEXICO
CVG CINCINNATI, OHIO
CVM CIUDAD VICTORIA, MEXICO
CVN CLOVIS, N.M.
CWA WAUSAU,WISC-CENTRAL WIS ARPT.
CWI CLINTON, IOWA
CXC CHITINA, ALASKA
CXY CAT CAY, BAHAMAS
CYA CAYES, HAITI
CYB CAYMAN BRAC, WEST INDIES
CYF CHEFORNAK, ALASKA
CYS CHEYENNE, WYO.
CYT CAPE YAKATAGA, ALASKA
CZF CAPE ROMANZOF, ALASKA
CZM COZUMEL, MEXICO
CZN CHISANA, ALASKA

D
DAB DAYTONA BEACH, FLA.
DAL DALLAS/FT. WORTH, TEXAS- LOVE FIELD
DAN DANVILLE, VA.
DAY DAYTON, OHIO
DBN DUBLIN, GA.
DBQ DUBUQUE, IOWA
DCA WASHINGTON, DC-NATIONALARPT.
DDC DODGE CITY, KAN.
DEC DECATUR, ILL.
DEN DENVER, COLO.
DET DETROIT, MICH-CITY ARPT
DFB DRIFTWOOD BAY, ALASKA
DFW DALLAS/FT. WORTH, TEXAS
DGO DURANGO, MEXICO
DGW DOUGLAS, WYO.
DHN DOTHAN, ALA.
DLG DILLINGHAM, ALASKA
DLH DULUTH, MINN.
DMO SEDALIA, MO.
DNV DANVILLE, ILL.
DOM DOMINICA, WEST INDIES
DOV DOVER, DEL.
DRG DEERING, ALASKA
DRO DURANGO, COLO.
DRT DEL RIO, TEXAS
DSD LA DESIRADE, GUADELOUPE
DSM DES MOINES, IOWA
DTH DEATH VALLEY, CALIF.
DTT DETROIT, MICH.
DTW DETROIT,MICH-METROPOLITANAPT
DUG DOUGLAS, ARIZ.
DUJ DU BOIS, PA.
DUT DUTCH HARBOR, ALASKA
DVL DEVILS LAKE, N.D.

E
EAA EAGLE, ALASKA
EAR KEARNEY, NEBR.
EAT WENATCHEE, WASH.
EAU EAU CLAIRE, WIS.
ECG ELIZABETH CITY, N.C.
EEK EEK, ALASKA
EEN KEENE, N.H.
EGE VAIL/EAGLE, COLO.
EGP EAGLE PASS, TEXAS
EGX * EGEGIK, ALASKA
EHM CAPE NEWENHAM, ALASKA
EIS TORTOLA, VIRGIN IS.
EKA EUREKA/ARCATA, CALIF.- MURRAY FLD.
EKI ELKHART, IND.
EKN ELKINS, W. VA.
EKO ELKO, NEV.
ELD EL DORADO/CAMDEN, ARK.
ELH NORTH ELEUTHERA, BAHAMAS
ELI ELIM, ALASKA
ELM ELMIRA, N.Y.
ELP EL PASO, TEXAS
ELY ELY, NEV.
EMK EMMONAK, ALASKA
EMP EMPORIA, KAN.
ENA KENAI, ALASKA
ENL CENTRALIA, ILL.
EOK KEOKUK, IOWA
EPH EPHRATA, WASH.
ERI ERIE, PA.
ESC ESCANABA, MICH.
ESE ENSENADA, MEXICO
ESF ALEXANDRIA, LA.
ESN EASTON, MD.
EUG EUGENE, ORE.
EUX ST. EUSTATIUS, LEEWARD IS.
EVM EVELETH, MINN.
EVV EVANSVILLE, IND.
EWB NEW BEDFORD, MASS.
EWN NEW BERN, N.C.
EWR NEW YORK, NY-NEWARK ARPT
EYW KEY WEST, FLA.

F
FAI FAIRBANKS, ALASKA
FAJ FAJARDO, PUERTO RICO
FAR FARGO, N.D.
FAT FRESNO, CALIF.
FAY FAYETTEVILLE, N.C.
FCA KALISPELL, MONT.
FDF FORT DE FRANCE, MARTINIQUE
FHU FT. HUACHUCA/SR.VISTA, ARIZ.
FKL FRANKLIN, PA.
FLG FLAGSTAFF, ARIZ.
FLL FT. LAUDERDALE, FLA.
FLO FLORENCE, S.C.
FLT FLAT, ALASKA
FMN FARMINGTON, N.M.
FMS FORT MADISON, IOWA
FMY FORT MYERS, FLA.
FNT FLINT, MICH.
FOA * FORTUNA LEDGE, ALASKA
FOD FT. DODGE, IOWA
FPO FREEPORT, BAHAMAS
FRM FAIRMONT, MINN.
FSD SIOUX FALLS, S.D.
FSM FT. SMITH, ARK.
FUL FULLERTON, CALIF.
FWA FT. WAYNE, IND.
FWL FAREWELL, ALASKA
FYU FT. YUKON, ALASKA
FYV FAYETTEVILLE, ARK.

G
GAD GADSDEN, ALA.
GAL GALENA, ALASKA
GAM GAMBELL, ALASKA
GAO GUANTANAMO, CUBA
GBD GREAT BEND, KAN.
GBG GALESBURG, ILL.
GBJ MARIE GALANTE, FR. ANTILLES
GCC GILLETTE, WYO.
GCK GARDEN CITY, KAN.
GCM GRAND CAYMAN, WEST INDIES
GCN GRAND CANYON, ARIZ.
GDL GUADALAJARA, MEXICO
GDT GRAND TURK, B.W.I.
GDV GLENDIVE, MONT.
GED GEORGETOWN, DEL.
GEG SPOKANE, WASH.
GER NUEVA GERONA, CUBA
GFK GRAND FORKS, N.D.
GFL GLENS FALLS, N.Y.
GGG LONGVIEW, TEXAS
GGT GEORGE TOWN, BAHAMAS
GGW GLASGOW, MONT.
GHB GOVERNORS HARBOUR, BAHAMAS
GHC GREAT HARBOUR CAY, BAHAMAS
GJT GRAND JUNCTION, COLO.
GKN GULKANA, ALASKA
GLD GOODLAND, KAN.
GLH GREENVILLE, MISS.
GLS GALVESTON, TEXAS
GLV GOLOVIN, ALASKA
GND GRENADA, WINDWARD IS.
GNU GOODNEWS BAY, ALASKA
GNV GAINESVILLE, FLA.
GNY GRANBY, COLO.
GON NEW LONDON, CONN.
GPT GULFPORT/BILOXI, MISS.
GPZ GRAND RAPIDS, MINN.
GQQ GALION, OHIO
GRB GREEN BAY, WIS.
GRI GRAND ISLAND, NEBR.
GRR GRAND RAPIDS, MICH.
GSB GOLDSBORO, N.C.
GSO GREENSBORO/HIGH POINT, N.C.
GSP GREENVILLE/SPARTANBURG, S.C.
GST GUSTAVUS, ALASKA
GTF GREAT FALLS, MONT.
GTR COLUMBUS, MISS.
GUB GUERRERO NEGRO, MEXICO
GUC GUNNISON, COLO.
GUP GALLUP, N.M.
GWO GREENWOOD, MISS.
GYM GUAYMAS, MEXICO

H
HAR HARRISBURG, PA.
HAV HAVANA, CUBA
HAY HAYCOCK, ALASKA
HCA BIG SPRING, TEXAS
HCR HOLY CROSS, ALASKA
HDN STEAMBOAT SPRINGS, COLO.
HEZ NATCHEZ, MISS.
HGR HAGERSTOWN, MD.
HGZ HOGATZA, ALASKA
HHH HILTON HEAD ISLAND, S.C.
HIB HIBBING, MINN.
HKP KAANAPALI, MAUI; HAWAII
HKY HICKORY, N.C.
HLN HELENA, MONT.
HMO HERMOSILLO, MEXICO
HNC HATTERAS, N.C.
HNH HOONAH, ALASKA
HNL HONOLULU, OAHU; HAWAII
HNM HANA, MAUI; HAWAII
HNS HAINES, ALASKA
HOB HOBBS, N.M.
HOG HOLGUIN, CUBA
HOM HOMER, ALASKA
HON HURON, S.D.
HOT HOT SPRINGS, ARK.
HOU HOUSTON, TEXAS-HOBBY ARPT.
HPB HOOPER BAY, ALASKA
HPN WHITE PLAINS, N.Y.
HQM HOQUIAM, WASH.
HRL HARLINGEN, TEXAS
HRO HARRISON, ARK.
HSI HASTINGS, NEBR.
HSL HUSLIA, ALASKA
HSP HOT SPRINGS, VA.
HSV HUNTSVILLE/DECATUR, ALA.
HTS HUNTINGTON, W. VA.
HUF TERRE HAUTE, IND.
HUM HOUMA, LA.
HUS HUGHES, ALASKA
HUT HUTCHINSON, KAN.
HVN NEW HAVEN, CONN.
HVR HAVRE, MONT.
HYA HYANNIS, MASS.
HYG HYDABURG, ALASKA
HYR HAYWARD, WIS.
HYS HAYS, KAN.
HZL HAZLETON, PA.

I
IAD WASHINGTON, DC-DULLES ARPT.
IAH HOUSTON, TEXAS
IAN KIANA, ALASKA
ICR NICARO, CUBA
ICT WICHITA, KAN.
IDA IDAHO FALLS, IDAHO
IGA INAGUA, BAHAMAS
IGG IGIUGIG, ALASKA
IGM KINGMAN, ARIZ.
IJX JACKSONVILLE, ILL.
IKO NIKOLSKI, ALASKA
ILE KILLEEN, TEXAS
ILG WILMINGTON, DEL.
ILI ILIAMNA, ALASKA
ILM WILMINGTON, N.C.
IMT IRON MOUNTAIN, MICH.
IND INDIANAPOLIS, IND.
INL INT'L FALLS, MINN.
INT WINSTON SALEM, N.C.
INW WINSLOW, ARIZ.
IPL EL CENTRO, CALIF.
IPT WILLIAMSPORT, PA.
IRK KIRKSVILLE, MO.
ISJ ISLA MUJERES, MEXICO
ISN WILLISTON, N.D.
ISO KINSTON, N.C.
ISP ISLIP, N.Y.
ISW WISCONSIN RAPIDS, WIS.
ITH ITHACA, N.Y.
ITO HILO, HAWAII; HAWAII
IWD IRONWOOD, MICH.
IYK INYOKERN, CALIF.
IZT IXTEPEC, MEXICO

J
JAC JACKSON, WYO.
JAK JACMEL, HAITI
JAN JACKSON/VICKSBURG, MISS.
JAX JACKSONVILLE, FLA.
JBR JONESBORO, ARK.
JEE JEREMIE, HAITI
JEF JEFFERSON CITY, MO.
JEM EMERYVILLE, CALIF.
JFK NEW YORK,NY-KENNEDY INT ARPT
JHW JAMESTOWN, N.Y.
JLN JOPLIN, MO.
JMC MARIN COUNTY HELIPORT, CAL.
JMS JAMESTOWN, N.D.
JNU JUNEAU, ALASKA
JRB NEW YORK, NY-WALL STREET HELIPORT, U
JSE JUNEAU, ALSK-SEAPLANE BSE.
JST JOHNSTOWN, PA.
JUC * JUNCTION CITY, KAN.
JVL BELOIT/JANESVILLE, WIS.
JXN JACKSON, MICH.

K
KAL KALTAG, ALASKA
KBC BIRCH CREEK, ALASKA
KCN CHERNOFSKI, ALASKA
KDF * KAUPULEHU, HAWAII; HAWAII
KDK KODIAK, ALASKA
KEK EKWOK, ALASKA
KFP FALSE PASS, ALASKA
KGK KOLIGANEK, ALASKA
KGX GRAYLING, ALASKA
KIN * KINGSTON, JAMAICA
KIO KINO, MEXICO
KKA KOYUK, ALASKA
KKB KITOI, ALASKA
KKH KONGIGANAK, ALASKA
KKI AKIACHAK, ALASKA
KKK KALAKAKET CREEK, ALASKA
KKU EKUK, ALASKA
KLG KALSKAG, ALASKA
KLL LEVELOCK, ALASKA
KLN LARSON BAY, ALASKA
KLW KLAWOCK, ALASKA
KMO MANOKOTAK, ALASKA
KMY MOSER BAY, ALASKA
KNT KENNETT, MO.
KNW NEW STUYAHOK, ALASKA
KOA KONA, HAWAII; HAWAII
KOT KOTLIK, ALASKA
KOY OLGA BAY, ALASKA
KOZ OUZINKIE, ALASKA
KPC PORT CLARENCE, ALASKA
KPK PARKS, ALASKA
KPN KIPNUK, ALASKA
KPR PORT WILLIAMS, ALASKA
KPY PORT BAILEY, ALASKA
KQA AKUTAN, ALASKA
KSM ST. MARY'S, ALASKA
KTN KETCHIKAN, ALASKA
KTS BREVIG MISSION, ALASKA
KTY TERROR BAY, ALASKA
KVC KING COVE, ALASKA
KVL KIVALINA, ALASKA
KWG KWIGUK, ALASKA
KWK KWIGILLINGOK, ALASKA
KWN KWINHAGAK, ALASKA
KWP WEST POINT, ALASKA
KWT KWETHLUK, ALASKA
KYK KARLUK, ALASKA
KYU KOYUKUK, ALASKA
KZB ZACHAR BAY, ALASKA

L
LAA LAMAR, COLO.
LAF LAFAYETTE, IND.
LAK AKLAVIK, N.W.T., CANADA
LAL LAKELAND, FLA.
LAN LANSING, MICH.
LAP LA PAZ, MEXICO
LAR LARAMIE, WYO.
LAS LAS VEGAS, NEV.
LAW LAWTON, OKLA.
LAX LOS ANGELES, CALIF.
LBB LUBBOCK, TEXAS
LBF NORTH PLATTE, NEBR.
LBL LIBERAL, KAN.
LCA * LAZARO CARDENAS, MEXICO
LCH LAKE CHARLES, LA.
LCI LACONIA, N.H.
LEB LEBANON, N.H.
LEN LEON, MEXICO
LEW LEWISTON, ME.
LEX LEXINGTON, KY.
LFK LUFKIN, TEXAS
LFT LAFAYETTE, LA.
LGA NEW YORK, NY-LA GUARDIA ARPT.
LGB LONG BEACH, CALIF.
LGD LA GRANDE, OREGON
LGI DEADMAN'S CAY, L.I., BAHAMAS
LGU LOGAN, UTAH
LHU LAKE HAVASU CITY, ARIZ.
LIH LIHUE, KAUAI; HAWAII
LIT LITTLE ROCK, ARK.
LJN LAKE JACKSON, TEXAS
LMM LOS MOCHIS, MEXICO
LMT KLAMATH FALLS, ORE.
LNK LINCOLN, NEBR.
LNS LANCASTER, PA.
LNY LANAI CITY, LANAI; HAWAII
LOI LAREDO, TEXAS
LOZ LONDON, KY.
LRU LAS CRUCES, N.M.
LSE LA CROSSE, WIS.
LSS LES SAINTES, GUADELOUPE
LTO LORETO, MEXICO
LUP KALAUPAPA, MOLOKAI; HAWAII
LUR CAPE LISBURNE, ALASKA
LWB GREENBRIER, W. VA.
LWC LAWRENCE, KAN.
LWS LEWISTON, IDAHO
LWT LEWISTOWN, MONT.
LXV LEADVILLE, COLO.
LYB LITTLE CAYMAN, W. INDIES
LYH LYNCHBURG, VA.

M
MAF MIDLAND/ODESSA, TEXAS
MAM MATAMOROS, MEXICO
MAW MALDEN, MO.
MAY MANGROVE CAY, BAHAMAS
MAZ MAYAGUEZ, PUERTO RICO
MBJ * MONTEGO BAY, JAMAICA
MBL MANISTEE, MICH.
MBS SAGINAW, MICH.
MCE MERCED, CALIF.
MCG MC GRATH, ALASKA
MCI KANSAS CITY, MO.
MCK MC COOK, NEBR.
MCN MACON, GA.
MCO ORLANDO, FLA.
MCW MASON CITY, IOWA
MDH CARBONDALE, ILL.
MDO MIDDLETON IS., ALASKA
MDR MEDFRA, ALASKA
MDS MIDDLE CAICOS, WEST INDIES
MDT HARRISBURG, PA- INTERNATIONAL ARPT.
MDW CHICAGO, ILL-MIDWAY ARPT
MEI MERIDIAN, MISS.
MEM MEMPHIS, TENN.
MEO MANTEO, N.C.
MEX MEXICO CITY, MEXICO
MFD MANSFIELD, OHIO
MFE MC ALLEN, TEXAS
MFI MARSHFIELD, WIS.
MFR MEDFORD, ORE.
MGC MICHIGAN CITY, IND.
MGM MONTGOMERY, ALA.
MGR MOULTRIE/THOMASVILLE, GA.
MGW MORGANTOWN, W. VA.
MHE MITCHELL, S.D.
MHH MARSH HARBOUR, BAHAMAS
MHK MANHATTAN, KAN.
MHT MANCHESTER, N.H.
MHV MOJAVE, CALIF.
MIA MIAMI, FLA.
MID MERIDA, MEXICO
MIE MUNCIE, IND.
MKC KANSAS CITY, MO.-KANSAS CITY ARPT.
MKE MILWAUKEE, WIS.
MKG MUSKEGON, MICH.
MKK KAUNAKAKAI, MOLOKAI; HAW.

CITY/AIRPORT CODES Listed Alphabetically by Code (For Schedules Included In This Guide)

MKL	JACKSON, TENN.
MKO	MUSKOGEE, OKLA.
MKT	MANKATO, MINN.
MLB	MELBOURNE, FLA.
MLC	MC ALESTER, OKLA.
MLI	MOLINE, ILL.
MLM	MORELIA, MEXICO
MLS	MILES CITY, MONT.
MLU	MONROE, LA.
MLY	MANLEY HOT SPGS., ALASKA
MMH	MAMMOTH LAKES, CALIF.
MMU	MORRISTOWN, N.J.
MNI	MONTSERRAT, LEEWARD IS.
MNM	MENOMINEE, MICH.
MNT	MINTO, ALASKA
MOA	MOA, CUBA
MOB	MOBILE AL/PASCAGOULA, MS.
MOD	MODESTO, CALIF.
MOT	MINOT, N.D.
MOU	MOUNTAIN VILLAGE, ALASKA
MPV	MONTPELIER, VT.
MQB	MACOMB, ILL.
MQS	MUSTIQUE, WINDWARD ISLAND
MQT	MARQUETTE, MICH.
MRB	MARTINSBURG, W. VA.
MRH	MOREHEAD CITY, N.C.
MRK	MARCO ISLAND, FLA.
MRY	MONTEREY, CALIF.
MSB	MARIGOT, ST. MARTIN, NETH. ANTILLES
MSL	MUSCLE SHOALS, ALA.
MSN	MADISON, WIS.
MSO	MISSOULA, MONT.
MSP	MINNEAPOLIS/ST PAUL, MINN.
MSS	MASSENA, N.Y.
MSY	NEW ORLEANS, LA.
MTH	MARATHON, FLA.
MTJ	MONTROSE, COLO.
MTO	MATTOON, ILL.
MTT	MINATITLAN, MEXICO
MTW	MANITOWOC, WIS.
MTY	MONTERREY, MEXICO
MUE	KAMUELA, HAWAII; HAWAII
MUG	MULEGE, MEXICO
MVN	MOUNT VERNON, ILL.
MVQ	* MACKINAC ISLAND, MICH.
MVY	MARTHA'S VINEYARD, MASS.
MWA	MARION, ILL.
MXL	MEXICALI, MEXICO
MXY	MC CARTHY, ALASKA
MYG	MAYAGUANA, BAHAMAS
MYU	MEKORYUK, ALASKA
MYV	MARYSVILLE, CALIF.
MZO	MANZANILLO, CUBA
MZT	MAZATLAN, MEXICO
N	
NAS	NASSAU, BAHAMAS
NEV	NEVIS, LEEWARD IS.
NGD	ANEGADA, VIRGIN ISLANDS
NLD	NUEVO LAREDO, MEXICO
NPT	* NEWPORT, R.I.
NUL	NULATO, ALASKA
NUP	NUNAPITCHUK, ALASKA
NYC	NEW YORK, N.Y.
O	
OAJ	JACKSONVILLE, N.C.
OAK	OAKLAND, CALIF.
OAX	OAXACA, MEXICO
OBR	* BORREGO SPRINGS, CALIF.
OBU	KOBUK, ALASKA
OCF	OCALA, FLA.
OCJ	* OCHO RIOS, JAMAICA
ODM	OAKLAND, MD.
ODW	* OAK HARBOR, WASH.
OFK	NORFOLK, NEBR.
OGD	OGDEN, UTAH
OGG	KAHULUI, MAUI; HAWAII
OGS	OGDENSBURG, N.Y.
OHC	NORTH EAST CAPE, ALASKA
OJC	OLATHE, KAN.
OKC	OKLAHOMA CITY, OKLA.
OKK	KOKOMO, IND.
OLF	WOLF POINT, MONT.
OLH	OLD HARBOR, ALASKA
OLM	OLYMPIA, WASH.
OLU	COLUMBUS, NEBR.
OMA	OMAHA, NEBR.
OME	NOME, ALASKA
ONA	WINONA, MINN.
ONH	* ONEONTA, N.Y.
ONT	ONTARIO, CALIF.
OOK	TOKSOOK, ALASKA
ORD	CHICAGO, ILL-OHARE ARPT
ORF	NORFOLK, VA.
ORH	WORCESTER, MASS.
ORI	PORT LIONS, ALASKA
ORT	NORTHWAY, ALASKA
ORV	NOORVIK, ALASKA
OSH	OSHKOSH, WIS.
OTG	WORTHINGTON, MINN.
OTH	NORTH BEND, ORE.
OTM	OTTUMWA, IOWA
OTZ	KOTZEBUE, ALASKA
OWB	OWENSBORO, KY.
OXR	OXNARD, CALIF.
P	
PAH	PADUCAH, KY.
PAP	PORT AU PRINCE, HAITI
PAQ	PALMER, ALASKA
PAX	PORT DE PAIX, HAITI
PAZ	POZA RICA, MEXICO
PBF	PINE BLUFF, ARK.
PBI	WEST PALM BEACH, FLA.
PCK	PORCUPINE CREEK, ALASKA
PDT	PENDLETON, ORE.
PDX	PORTLAND, ORE.
PEC	PELICAN, ALASKA
PFN	PANAMA CITY, FLA.
PGA	PAGE, ARIZ.
PGD	PUNTA GORDA, FLA.
PGL	PASCAGOULA, MISS.
PGV	GREENVILLE, N.C.
PHF	NEWPORT NEWS, VA.
PHL	PHILADELPHIA PA/WILM'TON.DE
PHO	POINT HOPE, ALASKA
PHX	PHOENIX, ARIZ.
PIA	PEORIA, ILL.
PIB	LAUREL/HATTIESBURG, MISS.
PIC	PINE CAY, B.W.I.
PIE	ST. PETERSBURG, FLA.
PIH	POCATELLO, IDAHO
PIP	PILOT POINT, ALASKA
PIR	PIERRE, S.D.
PIT	PITTSBURGH, PA.
PKA	NAPASKIAK, ALASKA
PKB	PARKERSBURG, W. VA.
PLB	PLATTSBURGH, N.Y.
PLI	PALM ISLAND, WINDWARD IS.
PLN	PELLSTON, MICH.
PLS	* PROVIDENCIALES, WEST INDIES
PLY	PLYMOUTH, IND.
PMD	PALMDALE, CALIF.
PML	PORT MOLLER, ALASKA
PNC	PONCA CITY, OKLA.
PNE	PHILADELPHIA, PA-NE ARPT
PNO	PINOTEPA, MEXICO
PNS	PENSACOLA, FLA.
POE	FT. POLK, LA.
POF	POPLAR BLUFF, MO.
POJ	* PILOT STATION, ALASKA
POS	PORT OF SPAIN, TRINIDAD
POT	* PORT ANTONIO, JAMAICA
POU	POUGHKEEPSIE, N.Y.
PPE	* PUERTO PENASCO, MEXICO
PPF	PARSONS, KAN.
PQI	PRESQUE ISLE, ME.
PRB	PASO ROBLES, CALIF.
PRC	PRESCOTT, ARIZ.
PRX	PARIS, TEXAS
PSB	PHILIPSBURG, PA.
PSC	PASCO, WASH.
PSE	PONCE, PUERTO RICO
PSF	PITTSFIELD, MASS.
PSG	PETERSBURG, ALASKA
PSK	PULASKI, VA.
PSP	PALM SPRINGS, CALIF.
PTH	PORT HEIDEN, ALASKA
PTP	POINTE A PITRE, GUADELOUPE
PTU	PLATINUM, ALASKA
PUB	PUEBLO, COLO.
PUC	PRICE, UTAH
PUH	POCHUTLA, MEXICO
PUO	PRUDHOE BAY/SAG RIV., ALSK.
PUW	PULLMAN, WASH.
PVC	* PROVINCETOWN, MASS.
PVD	PROVIDENCE, R.I.
PVR	PUERTO VALLARTA, MEXICO
PVU	PROVO, UTAH
PWM	PORTLAND, ME.
PWT	BREMERTON, WASH.
PXM	* PUERTO ESCONDIDO, MEXICO
R	
RAD	TORTOLA, ROAD TOWN,VIRGIN IS.
RAL	RIVERSIDE, CALIF.
RAP	RAPID CITY, S.D.
RBL	RED BLUFF, CALIF.
RBY	RUBY, ALASKA
RDD	REDDING, CALIF.
RDG	READING, PA.
RDM	REDMOND, ORE.
RDU	RALEIGH/DURHAM, N.C.
RDV	RED DEVIL, ALASKA
REX	REYNOSA, MEXICO
RFD	ROCKFORD, ILL.
RHI	RHINELANDER, WIS.
RIC	RICHMOND, VA.
RIW	RIVERTON, WYO.
RKD	ROCKLAND, ME.
RKS	ROCK SPRINGS, WYO.
RLA	ROLLA, MO.
RLD	RICHLAND, WASH.
RMP	RAMPART, ALASKA
RNO	RENO, NEV.
ROA	ROANOKE, VA.
ROC	ROCHESTER, N.Y.
ROW	ROSWELL, N.M.
RSD	ROCK SOUND, BAHAMAS
RSH	RUSSIAN MISSION, ALASKA
RST	ROCHESTER, MINN.
RUT	RUTLAND, VT.
RWI	ROCKY MOUNT/WILSON, N.C.
RWL	RAWLINS, WYO.
S	
SAA	SARATOGA, WYO.
SAB	SABA, NETH. ANTILLES
SAC	SAFFORD, ARIZ.
SAF	SANTA FE, N.M.
SAN	SAN DIEGO, CALIF.
SAQ	SAN ANDROS, BAHAMAS
SAT	SAN ANTONIO, TEX.
SAV	SAVANNAH, GA.
SBA	SANTA BARBARA, CALIF.
SBH	ST. BARTHELEMY, LEEWARD IS.
SBM	SHEBOYGAN, WIS.
SBN	SOUTH BEND, IND.
SBP	SAN LUIS OBISPO, CALIF.
SBS	STEAMBOAT SPRINGS, COLO-MUN.
SBY	SALISBURY, MD.
SCE	STATE COLLEGE, PA.
SCK	STOCKTON, CALIF.
SCM	SCAMMON BAY, ALASKA
SCU	SANTIAGO, CUBA
SDF	LOUISVILLE, KY.
SDP	SAND POINT, ALASKA
SDQ	SANTO DOMINGO, DOM. REP.
SDY	SIDNEY, MONT.
SEA	SEATTLE, WASH.
SFO	SAN FRANCISCO, CALIF.
SGF	SPRINGFIELD, MO.
SGU	ST. GEORGE, UTAH
SGY	SKAGWAY, ALASKA
SHD	STAUNTON, VA.
SHG	SHUNGNAK, ALASKA
SHH	SHISHMAREF, ALASKA
SHN	SHELTON, WASH.
SHR	SHERIDAN, WYO.
SHV	SHREVEPORT, LA.
SHX	SHAGELUK, ALASKA
SIG	SANJUAN,P.R.-ISLAGRANDE ARPT
SIT	SITKA, ALASKA
SJC	SAN JOSE, CALIF.
SJF	ST. JOHN, VIRGIN IS.
SJT	SAN ANGELO, TEXAS
SJU	SAN JUAN, PUERTO RICO
SKB	ST. KITTS, LEEWARD IS.
SKJ	SITKINAK, ALASKA
SKK	SHAKTOOLIK, ALASKA
SKW	SKWENTNA, ALASKA
SLC	SALT LAKE CITY, UTAH
SLE	SALEM, ORE.
SLK	SARANAC LAKE, N.Y.
SLN	SALINA, KAN.
SLP	SAN LUIS POTOSI, MEXICO
SLQ	SLEETMUTE, ALASKA
SLU	ST. LUCIA, W. INDIES
SLX	SALT CAY, WEST INDIES
SMF	SACRAMENTO, CALIF.
SMK	ST. MICHAEL, ALASKA
SML	STELLA MARIS,L.I., BAHAMAS
SMX	SANTA MARIA, CALIF.
SNA	SANTA ANA, CALIF.
SNP	ST. PAUL IS., ALASKA
SNU	SANTA CLARA, CUBA
SNY	SIDNEY, NEBR.
SOL	SOLOMON, ALASKA
SPG	ST.PETERSBURG-WHITTED ARPT,FLA.
SPI	SPRINGFIELD, ILL.
SPS	WICHITA FALLS, TEXAS
SPW	SPENCER, IOWA
SQI	STERLING/ROCK FALLS, ILL.
SRL	SANTA ROSALIA, MEXICO
SRQ	SARASOTA, FLA.
SRV	STONY RIVER, ALASKA
SSI	ST. SIMONS ISLAND, GA.
SSM	SAULT STE MARIE, MICH.
STE	STEVENS POINT, WIS.
STI	* SANTIAGO, DOMINICAN REP.
STL	ST. LOUIS, MO.
STP	MINNEAPOLIS/ST PAUL, MINN-DOWNTOWN
STS	SANTA ROSA, CALIF.
STT	ST. THOMAS, VIRGIN IS.
STX	ST. CROIX, VIRGIN IS.
SUE	STURGEON BAY, WIS.
SUN	SUN VALLEY, IDAHO
SUX	SIOUX CITY, IOWA
SVA	SAVOONGA, ALASKA
SVC	SILVER CITY, N.M.
SVD	ST. VINCENT, WINDWARD IS.
SVS	STEVENS VILLAGE, ALASKA
SVW	SPARREVOHN, ALSK.
SWD	SEWARD, ALASKA
SWO	STILLWATER, OKLA.
SXM	ST. MARTIN, NETH. ANTILLES
SXP	SHELDON POINT, ALASKA
SYA	SHEMYA IS., ALASKA
SYR	SYRACUSE, N.Y.
T	
TAB	TOBAGO, TRINIDAD AND TOBAGO
TAL	TANANA, ALASKA
TAM	TAMPICO, MEXICO
TAP	TAPACHULA, MEXICO
TBN	FT. LEONARD WOOD, MO.
TCB	TREASURE CAY, BAHAMAS
TCL	TUSCALOOSA, ALA.
TCN	TEHUACAN, MEXICO
TCT	TAKOTNA, ALASKA
TEB	TETERBORO, N.J.
TGZ	TUXTLA GUTIERREZ, MEXICO
TIJ	TIJUANA, MEXICO
TIW	TACOMA, WASH.
TKJ	TOK, ALASKA
TLA	* TELLER, ALASKA
TLH	TALLAHASSEE, FLA.
TLT	TULUKSAK, ALASKA
TMA	TIFTON, GA.
TNC	TIN CITY, ALASKA
TNK	TUNUNAK, ALASKA
TOG	TOGIAK, ALASKA
TOL	TOLEDO, OHIO
TOP	TOPEKA, KAN.
TPA	TAMPA, FLA.
TPJ	* KINGSTON, JAMAICA-TINSONPEN
TPL	TEMPLE, TEXAS
TRC	TORREON, MEXICO
TRI	TRI-CITY AIRPORT, TENN.
TRT	* TORTOLA, WESTEND, VIRGIN IS.
TSP	TEHACHAPI, CALIF.
TTN	TRENTON, N.J.
TUL	TULSA, OKLA.
TUP	TUPELO, MISS.
TUS	TUCSON, ARIZ.
TVC	TRAVERSE CITY, MICH.
TVF	THIEF RIVER FALLS, MINN.
TVI	THOMASVILLE, GA.
TVL	LAKE TAHOE, CALIF.
TWF	TWIN FALLS, IDAHO
TWH	CATALINAIS,CALIF-TWO HARBORS
TXK	TEXARKANA, ARK.
TYR	TYLER, TEXAS
TYS	KNOXVILLE, TENN.
TZN	SOUTH ANDROS, BAHAMAS
U	
UBL	* CHUB CAY, BAHAMAS
UCA	UTICA, N.Y.
UGA	UGASHIK, ALASKA
UGS	* UGSONOKLE, ALASKA
UIN	QUINCY, ILL.
ULM	NEW ULM, MINN.
UMB	UMNAK IS., ALASKA
UNK	UNALAKLEET, ALASKA
UOX	UNIVERSITY, MISS.
UPN	URUAPAN, MEXICO
UPP	UPOLU POINT, HAWAII; HAWAII
UTO	UTOPIA CREEK, ALASKA
UVF	ST.LUCIA,W.I.-HEWANORRA ARPT.
V	
VAE	VALLES, MEXICO
VAK	CHEVAK, ALASKA
VCT	VICTORIA, TEXAS
VDZ	VALDEZ, ALASKA
VEE	VENETIE, ALASKA
VEL	VERNAL, UTAH
VER	VERACRUZ, MEXICO
VIB	V. CONSTITUCION, MEXICO
VIJ	VIRGIN GORDA, VIRGIN IS.
VIS	VISALIA, CALIF.
VLD	VALDOSTA, GA.
VPS	EGLIN A.F. BASE, FLA.
VPZ	VALPARAISO, IND.
VQS	VIEQUES, PUERTO RICO
VRB	VERO BEACH, FLA.
VSA	VILLAHERMOSA, MEXICO
W	
WAA	WALES, ALASKA
WAS	WASHINGTON, D.C.
WBB	STEBBINS, ALASKA
WBH	* COMMERCE/MONTEBELLO, CALIF.
WBQ	BEAVER, ALASKA
WBV	* EASTSOUND, WASH.
WBY	* LOSANGELES,CALIF-DOWNTOWNLA.
WCF	* LOPEZ ISLAND, WASH.
WCG	* FRIDAY HARBOR, WASH.
WCR	CHANDALAR, ALASKA
WDG	ENID, OKLA.
WIV	* RUPERT HOUSE, QUE., CANADA
WKH	* PORT HARRISON, QUE., CANADA
WKK	ALEKNAGIK, ALASKA
WKV	* PHILADELPHIA, PA-PENNS LANDING SPB.
WKW	* NEW YORK,N.Y-PIER 8 SPB EAST RIVER
WLF	* TAOS, N.M.
WLK	SELAWIK, ALASKA
WMO	WHITE MOUNTAIN, ALASKA
WMQ	* SAN FELIPE, MEXICO
WMW	* HUMACAO, PUERTO RICO
WNA	NAPAKIAK, ALASKA
WOU	* MANASSAS, VA.
WPI	* ST. MARTIN, NETH. ANTILLES-ESPERANCE
WRF	* PAINT HILLS, QUEBEC, CANADA
WRG	WRANGEL, ALSK.
WRL	WORLAND, WYO.
WRM	* SAN RAFAEL, CALIF.
WSJ	SAN JUAN, ALASKA
WSL	* CANGER BAY, ALASKA
WSM	WISEMAN, ALASKA
WSN	SOUTH NAKNEK, ALASKA
WSO	* PUNTA CHIVATO, MEXICO
WST	WESTERLY, R.I.
WSV	* SAN FRANCISQUITO, MEXICO
WSW	* SAN QUINTIN, MEXICO
WSX	* MELING RANCH, MEXICO
WTB	* SAN IGNACIO, MEXICO
WTC	* ABREOJOS, MEXICO
WTD	WEST END, BAHAMAS
WTK	NOATAK, ALASKA
WTL	TUNTUTULIAK, ALSK.
WTO	* AMOOK, ALASKA
WUK	* POCAHONTAS, IOWA
WUQ	* OCEAN SHORES, WASH.
WUV	* FAIRBANKS,ALASKA-METRO FIELD
WVH	* MANDEVILLE, JAMAICA
WVL	WATERVILLE, ME.
WWD	CAPE MAY, N.J.
WWT	NEWTOK, ALASKA
WWW	* ST. CROIX, VIRGIN IS.-SEAPLANE BASE
WWZ	* ST. THOMAS, VIRGIN IS.-SEAPLANE BASE
WXI	* PRINCE RUPERT,B.C.-SEALCOVE
WXT	* LA VEGA, DOMINICAN REP.
WXU	* PUERTO PLATA, DOMINICAN REP.
WXV	* CABO ROJO, DOMINICAN REP.
WXW	* BARAHONA, DOMINICAN REP.
WXY	* SABANA DE LA MAR, D. REP.
WXZ	* LA ROMANA, DOMINICAN REP.
WYK	* SAN PEDRO, CALIF.
WYL	* PUNTA CANA, DOMINICAN REP.
WYO	* SAN JUAN DE LA M., D. REP.
WYU	* SANTO DOMINGO, DOM. REP.-HERRERA APT
WZW	* OCEAN CITY, MD.
WZY	* NASSAU,BAHAMAS-SEAPLANE BASE
WZZ	* BIMINI, BAHAMAS-NORTH SEAPLANE BASE
X	
XSC	SOUTH CAICOS, B.W.I.
Y	
YAK	YAKUTAT, ALASKA
YAM	SAULT STE MARIE, ONT.,CANADA
YAT	ATTAWAPISKAT, ONT., CANADA
YAY	ST. ANTHONY, NFLD., CANADA
YBC	BAIE COMEAU, QUE., CANADA
YBE	URANIUM CITY, SASK., CANADA
YBG	SAGUENAY, QUE., CANADA
YBK	BAKER LAKE, N.W.T., CANADA
YBL	CAMPBELL RIVER, B.C., CANADA
YBV	BERENS RIVER, MAN., CANADA
YBX	BLANC SABLON, QUE., CANADA
YCB	CAMBRIDGE BAY,N.W.T.,CANADA
YCG	CASTLEGAR, B.C., CANADA
YCH	CHATHAM, N.B., CANADA
YCL	CHARLO, N.B., CANADA
YCR	CROSS LAKE, MAN., CANADA
YDA	DAWSON CITY, Y.T., CANADA
YDF	DEER LAKE, NFLD., CANADA
YDQ	DAWSON CREEK, B.C., CANADA
YEG	EDMONTON, ALTA-INT APT, CANADA
YEV	INUVIK, N.W.T., CANADA
YFA	FORT ALBANY, ONTARIO, CANADA
YFB	FROBISHER BAY, N.W.T., CANADA
YFC	FREDERICTON, N.B., CANADA
YFO	FLIN FLON, MAN., CANADA
YFR	FT. RESOLUTION, N.W.T., CANADA
YFS	FT. SIMPSON, N.W.T., CANADA
YGA	GAGNON, QUEBEC, CANADA
YGH	FT. GOOD HOPE, N.W.T., CANADA
YGK	KINGSTON, ONT., CANADA
YGL	LA GRANDE, QUEBEC, CANADA
YGO	GODS NARROWS, MAN., CANADA
YGP	GASPE, QUE., CANADA
YGV	HAVRE ST. PIERRE, QUE., CANADA
YGW	GREAT WHALE, QUE., CANADA
YGX	GILLAM, MAN., CANADA
YGY	DECEPTION BAY, QUE., CANADA
YHD	DRYDEN, ONT., CANADA
YHM	HAMILTON, ONT., CANADA
YHR	HARRINGTON HARBOUR, QUE., CAN.
YHY	HAY RIVER, N.W.T., CANADA
YHZ	HALIFAX, N.S., CANADA
YIF	ST. AUGUSTIN, QUE., CANADA
YIK	IVUGIVIK, QUEBEC, CANADA
YIM	* ILES DE MADELEINE,QUE.,CANADA
YJT	STEPHENVILLE, NFLD., CANADA
YKA	KAMLOOPS, B.C., CANADA
YKF	* KITCHENER, ONT., CANADA
YKL	SCHEFFERVILLE, QUE., CANADA
YKM	YAKIMA, WASH.
YKN	YANKTON, S.D.
YKU	FORT GEORGE, QUEBEC, CANADA
YKX	KIRKLAND LAKE, ONT., CANADA
YLP	MINGAN, QUE., CANADA
YLW	KELOWNA, B.C., CANADA
YMA	MAYO, Y.T., CANADA
YME	MATANE, QUE., CANADA
YMM	FT. MCMURRAY, ALTA., CANADA
YMO	MOOSONEE, ONTARIO, CANADA
YMY	MONTREAL-VICTORIASTOLPORT,CAN.
YNA	NATASHQUAN, QUE., CANADA
YNE	NORWAY HOUSE, MAN., CANADA
YNG	YOUNGSTOWN, OHIO
YNM	MATAGAMI, QUEBEC, CANADA
YOC	OLD CROW, Y.T., CANADA
YOH	OXFORD HOUSE, MAN., CANADA
YOJ	HIGH LEVEL, ALBERTA, CANADA
YOW	OTTAWA, ONTARIO, CANADA
YPA	PRINCE ALBERT, SASK., CANADA
YPE	PEACE RIVER, ALTA., CANADA
YPQ	PETERBOROUGH, ONT., CANADA
YPR	PRINCE RUPERT, B.C., CANADA
YPW	POWELL RIVER, B.C., CANADA
YPX	POVUNGNITUK, QUEBEC, CANADA
YPY	FT. CHIPEWYAN, ALTA., CANADA
YQB	QUEBEC, QUE., CANADA
YQD	THE PAS, MAN., CANADA
YQF	RED DEER, ALTA., CANADA
YQG	WINDSOR, ONT., CANADA
YQH	WATSON LAKE, Y.T., CANADA
YQI	YARMOUTH, N.S., CANADA
YQK	KENORA, ONT., CANADA
YQL	LETHBRIDGE, ALTA., CANADA
YQM	MONCTON, N.B., CANADA
YQQ	COMOX, B.C., CANADA
YQR	REGINA, SASK., CANADA
YQT	THUNDER BAY, ONT., CANADA
YQU	GRANDE PRAIRIE,ALBERTA,CANADA
YQX	GANDER, NFLD., CANADA
YQY	SYDNEY, N.S., CANADA
YQZ	QUESNEL, B.C., CANADA
YRB	RESOLUTE, N.W.T., CANADA
YRL	RED LAKE, ONT., CANADA
YRO	OTTAWA-ROCKCLIFFESTOLPORT,CAN.
YRS	RED SUCKER LAKE, MAN., CANADA
YRT	RANKIN INLET, N.W.T., CANADA
YSB	SUDBURY, ONT., CANADA
YSF	STONEY RAPIDS, SASK., CANADA
YSJ	SAINT JOHN, N.B., CANADA
YSM	FT. SMITH, N.W.T., CANADA
YST	ST. THERESE PT., MAN., CANADA
YTA	PEMBROKE, ONT., CANADA
YTH	THOMPSON, MAN., CANADA
YTN	RIVIERE AU TONNERRE, QUE.,CAN.
YTS	TIMMINS, ONT., CANADA
YUB	TUKTOYAKTUK, N.W.T., CANADA
YUL	MONTREAL, QUE., CANADA
YUM	YUMA, ARIZ.
YUY	ROUYN - NORANDA, QUE., CANADA
YVC	LAC LA RONGE, SASK., CANADA
YVO	VAL D'OR, QUE., CANADA
YVP	FT. CHIMO, QUE., CANADA
YVQ	NORMAN WELLS, N.W.T., CANADA
YVR	VANCOUVER, B.C., CANADA
YVT	BUFFALO NARROWS, SASK., CANADA
YWG	WINNIPEG, MAN., CANADA
YWH	* WHALEHEAD, QUEBEC, CANADA
YWJ	FORT FRANKLIN, N.W.T., CANADA
YWK	WABUSH, NFLD., CANADA
YWL	WILLIAMS LAKE, B.C., CANADA
YWN	WINISK, ONTARIO, CANADA
YWY	WRIGLEY, N.W.T., CANADA
YXC	CRANBROOK, B.C., CANADA
YXD	EDMONTON, ALTA., CANADA
YXE	SASKATOON, SASK., CANADA
YXH	MEDICINE HAT, ALTA., CANADA
YXJ	FT. ST. JOHN, B.C., CANADA
YXK	RIMOUSKI, QUE., CANADA
YXR	EARLTON, ONT., CANADA
YXS	PRINCE GEORGE, B.C., CANADA
YXT	TERRACE, B.C., CANADA
YXU	LONDON, ONT., CANADA
YXY	WHITEHORSE, Y.T., CANADA
YYB	NORTH BAY, ONT., CANADA
YYC	CALGARY, ALTA., CANADA
YYD	SMITHERS, B.C., CANADA
YYE	FT. NELSON, B.C., CANADA
YYF	PENTICTON, B.C., CANADA
YYG	CHARLOTTETOWN, P.E.I., CANADA
YYJ	VICTORIA, B.C., CANADA
YYL	LYNN LAKE, MAN., CANADA
YYQ	CHURCHILL, MAN., CANADA
YYR	GOOSE BAY, NFLD., CANADA
YYT	ST. JOHNS, NFLD., CANADA
YYU	* KAPUSKASING, ONT., CANADA
YYY	MONT JOLI, QUE., CANADA
YYZ	TORONTO, ONT., CANADA
YZF	YELLOWKNIFE, N.W.T., CANADA
YZG	SUGLUK, QUEBEC, CANADA
YZP	SANDSPIT, B.C., CANADA
YZR	SARNIA, ONT., CANADA
YZS	CORAL HARBOUR, N.W.T., CANADA
YZT	PORT HARDY, B.C., CANADA
YZV	SEVEN ISLANDS, QUE., CANADA
Z	
ZAA	ALICE ARM, B.C., CANADA
ZEM	EAST MAIN, QUEBEC, CANADA
ZFB	OLD FORT BAY, QUE., CANADA
ZFM	FT. MCPHERSON, N.W.T., CANADA
ZFN	FT. NORMAN, N.W.T., CANADA
ZGF	GRAND FORKS, B.C., CANADA
ZGI	GODS RIVER, MAN., CANADA
ZGN	* GARDEN HILL, CANADA
ZGR	LITTLE GRAND RAPIDS,MAN.,CANADA
ZGS	GETHSEMANI, QUEBEC, CANADA
ZIH	ZIHUATANEJO, MEXICO
ZKG	KEGASKA, QUEBEC, CANADA
ZLO	MANZANILLO, MEXICO
ZLT	LA TABATIERE, QUEBEC, CANADA
ZMT	MASSET, B.C., CANADA
ZNG	NEGGINAN, MAN., CANADA
ZRR	ARCTIC RED RIVER,N.W.T.,CANADA
ZSA	SAN SALVADOR, BAHAMAS
ZSP	ST. PAUL, QUEBEC, CANADA
ZST	STEWART, B.C., CANADA
ZUM	CHURCHILL FALLS, NFLD., CANADA
ZWL	WOLLASTON LAKE, SASK., CANADA

MINIMUM CONNECTING TIMES

The minimum connecting times shown in this section indicate the "legal" connecting times for construction of all connections, domestic and international, for travel within, and to and from the area covered in this publication. On-line connecting times will be the same as off-line connecting times except where specific times are shown. For connecting times at cities not covered in this publication refer to the International Edition. For any city not listed allow 20 minutes.

CITY	OFF LINE	ON LINE
ABERDEEN, S.D.		
STANDARD	:10	
ABILENE, TEXAS		
STANDARD	:20	
TT		:15
ACAPULCO, MEXICO		
DOMESTIC	1:00	
DOMESTIC TO INT'L	1:00	
INT'L TO DOMESTIC	1:30	
INT'L TO INT'L	1:30	
AKRON/CANTON, OHIO		
STANDARD	:30	
AL		:25
UA		:20
ALBUQUERQUE, N.M.		
STANDARD	:30	
CO		:10
FL		:20
TT, TW		:15
ALEXANDRIA, LA.		
STANDARD	:20	
TT		:15
ALLENTOWN, PA.		
STANDARD	:20	
AL		:25
ALPENA, MICH.		
STANDARD	:10	
AMARILLO, TEXAS		
STANDARD	:20	
TT		:15
ANCHORAGE, ALASKA		
DOMESTIC		
STANDARD	:20	
BETWEEN AS AND RV	:15	
AS		:10
WC (FROM FAI)		:15
INTERNATIONAL		
DOMESTIC TO INT'L	1:00	
NW		:45
INT'L TO DOMESTIC	1:00	
INT'L TO INT'L	1:00	
NW		:45
ANTIGUA, WEST INDIES		
DOMESTIC TO INT'L	:45	
LI		:30
INT'L TO DOMESTIC	:45	
LI		:30
INT'L TO INT'L	:45	
LI		:30
ARUBA, NETH. ANTILLES		
DOMESTIC	:20	
DOMESTIC TO INT'L	:45	
INT'L TO DOMESTIC	:45	
ATLANTA, GA.		
DOMESTIC		
STANDARD	:40	
DL/EA/UA TO/FROM KQ	:30	
DL, EA, UA		:30
NW		:25
PI		:15
SO, TW		:20
FLIGHTS TO/FROM HAWAII		
AND PUERTO RICO ARE		
DOMESTIC		
INTERNATIONAL		
DOMESTIC TO INT'L	:40	
EA		:30
INT'L TO DOMESTIC	1:00	
ATLANTIC CITY, N.J.		
STANDARD	:15	
AUGUSTA, GA.		
STANDARD	:30	
AUSTIN, TEXAS		
STANDARD	:20	
CO		:10
TT		:15
BAIE COMEAU, QUE.		
STANDARD	:20	
QB		:15
BALTIMORE, MD.		
FLIGHTS TO/FROM BERMUDA,		
CANADA, NASSAU AND		
PUERTO RICO ARE DOMESTIC		
DOMESTIC		
STANDARD	:30	
AL, UA		:25
NA, TW		:20
INTERNATIONAL		
DOMESTIC TO INT'L	:30	
INT'L TO DOMESTIC	1:00	
EA (EXCEPT FROM FPO,		
KIN, MBJ)		:30
INT'L TO INT'L	1:30	
EA (FROM MBJ, KIN TO		
YUL)		1:00
IF CONNECTION INVOLVES		
TRANSFER BETWEEN:		
BAL-DCA	2:20	
BAL-IAD	3:00	
VIA MOTOR COACH FROM BAL		
TO 16TH AND K STS., N.W.		
WASHINGTON TRANSFERRING		
TO LIMOUSINE FOR		
NATIONAL OR DULLES		
AIRPORTS.		
BARBADOS, WEST INDIES		
DOMESTIC	:45	
DOMESTIC TO INT'L	:45	
INT'L TO DOMESTIC	:45	
INT'L TO INT'L	:45	
BATON ROUGE, LA.		
STANDARD	:20	
TT		:15
BEAUMONT/PT. ARTHUR, TEX.		
STANDARD	:20	
TT		:15
BECKLEY, W. VA.		
STANDARD	:20	
PI		:15
BELOIT/JANESVILLE, WIS.		
STANDARD	:10	
BEMIDJI, MINN.		
STANDARD	:10	
BENTON HARBOR, MICH.		
STANDARD	:10	
BERMUDA, ATLANTIC OCEAN		
STANDARD	1:00	
BIG SPRING, TEXAS		
STANDARD	:20	
TT		:15
BILLINGS, MONT.		
STANDARD	:30	
NW		:25
FL, WA		:20
BINGHAMTON, N.Y.		
STANDARD	:25	
BIRMINGHAM, ALA.		
STANDARD	:30	
EA, UA		:20
SO		:15
BISMARCK, N.D.		
STANDARD	:20	
NC		:10
BLOOMINGTON, IND.		
STANDARD	:25	
BOISE, IDAHO		
STANDARD	:30	
BETWEEN RW AND TJ	:25	
RW		:15
UA		:20
BOSTON, MASS.		
FLIGHTS TO/FROM BERMUDA,		
HAWAII, MONTREAL,		
TORONTO, NASSAU, AND		
PUERTO RICO ARE DOMESTIC		
DOMESTIC		
STANDARD	:40	
DL TO/FROM DD/PM/PT/		
QO/DE/NE/ZM	:30	
AA, AL, EA		:30
DL		:25
TW, UA		:20
INTERNATIONAL		
DOMESTIC TO INT'L	1:00	
ALL TO AA	:40	
DL		:25
PA		:40
TW		:30
INT'L TO DOMESTIC	1:00	
DL		:25
PA		1:05
INT'L TO INT'L	1:00	
BRADFORD, PA.		
STANDARD	:25	
BRAINERD, MINN.		
STANDARD	:10	
BRIDGEPORT, CONN.		
STANDARD	:20	
AL		:25
BROOKINGS, S.D.		
STANDARD	:10	
BROWNSVILLE, TEXAS		
STANDARD	:20	
IF CONNECTION INVOLVES		
TRANSFER BETWEEN		
BROWNSVILLE AND MAT-		
AMOROS AIRPORTS	1:15	
BROWNWOOD, TEXAS		
STANDARD	:20	
TT		:15
BUFFALO, N.Y.		
FLIGHTS TO/FROM CANADA		
AND HAWAII ARE DOMESTIC		
STANDARD	:35	
BETWEEN AA AND UA	:30	
BETWEEN AL AND EA	:30	
AA, AL, UA		:25
BURBANK, CALIF.		
STANDARD	:30	
CALGARY, ALTA.		
DOMESTIC		
STANDARD	:30	
RW/WA TO AC/CP/PW	:45	
INTERNATIONAL		
INT'L TO DOMESTIC	1:00	
INT'L TO INT'L	1:00	
CAMAGUEY, CUBA		
DOMESTIC		:30
DOMESTIC TO INT'L		:45
INT'L TO DOMESTIC		1:00
INT'L TO INT'L		1:00
CAPE MAY, N.J.		
STANDARD	:20	
AL		:25
CARLSBAD, N.M.		
STANDARD	:20	
TT		:15
CASPER, WYO.		
STANDARD	:30	
BETWEEN FL AND WA	:25	
FL		:20
WA		:10
CEDAR RAPIDS/IOWA CITY, IA.		
STANDARD	:20	
OZ		:10
CHARLESTON, S.C.		
STANDARD	:30	
NA, SO		:20
CHARLESTON, W. VA.		
STANDARD	:25	
AA, UA		:20
PI		:15
CHARLOTTE, N.C.		
STANDARD	:30	
DL, UA		:20
PI		:15
CHARLOTTESVILLE, VA.		
STANDARD	:20	
PI		:15
CHATTANOOGA, TENN.		
STANDARD	:30	
SO, UA		:20
CHICAGO, ILL.		
FLIGHTS TO/FROM ALASKA,		
CANADA, HAWAII, BERMUDA,		
NASSAU, PUERTO RICO &		
U.S. VIRGIN IS. ARE		
DOMESTIC		
ORD DOMESTIC		
STANDARD	:50	
CONT. NEXT COLUMN		
CHICAGO, ILL.-CONT.		
EXCEPTION: AF AND BA		
FLIGHTS VIA CANADA AND		
JM FLIGHTS FROM NAS		
ARE CONSIDERED		
INTERNATIONAL)		
BETWEEN AA/DL/NC	:40	
BETWEEN AA/AL	:40	
AC TO TW	:40	
BETWEEN AL/NC	:40	
EA/NW TO/FROM CO	:30	
BETWEEN OZ/UA	:40	
AA, DL, EA, TW		:30
AL, UA		:40
NC, OZ		:20
NW		:25
ORD INTERNATIONAL		
DOMESTIC TO INT'L	1:15	
ALL TO BN	:50	
ALL TO JM	:45	
ALL TO NW	1:00	
NW/UA TO DL	:50	
UA TO BA	1:00	
ALL TO TW	:50	:45
TW-DOMESTIC CONNECTING		
TIMES WILL APPLY TO ALL		
TW INT'L FLIGHTS WHICH		
TRANSIT TO A POINT IN		
THE U.S. PRIOR TO		
ARRIVAL/DEPARTURE		
ALL TO AA	:50	:30
EA, NW		:30
INT'L TO DOMESTIC	1:30	
FROM BN (WITH STOP AT		
DFW, IAH, SAT)	:50	
FROM AA (WITH STOP AT		
DFW, HNL, SAT)	:50	:30
NW TO ALL	:50	
FROM ALL TO TW	1:00	1:00
MX TO UA	1:15	
AA (FROM ACA OR MEX		
NONSTOP)		1:00
EA		:30
NW		:25
INT'L TO INT'L	1:30	
MDW STANDARD	:25	
NC		:10
TW, UA		:20
INTER-AIRPORT SURFACE		
CONNECTIONS:		
MDW TO/FROM ORD	2:40	
CINCINNATI, OHIO		
STANDARD	:40	
BETWEEN AL/NC/PI	:30	
AA, AL		:25
DL		:30
NC		:10
PI		:15
TW		:20
CLARKSBURG, W. VA.		
STANDARD	:25	
CLEVELAND, OHIO		
FLIGHTS TO/FROM CANADA		
ARE DOMESTIC		
CLE DOMESTIC		
STANDARD	:30	
AA*		:30
AL		:25
NC		:10
NW, UA		:25
TW		:20
*EXCEPTIONS: AA ON		
FLIGHTS ORIGINATING BUF		
OR CVG		:20
CLE INTERNATIONAL		
DOMESTIC TO INT'L	:30	
TW-DOMESTIC CONNECTING		
TIMES WILL APPLY TO ALL		
TW INT'L FLIGHTS WHICH		
TRANSIT TO A POINT IN		
THE U.S. PRIOR TO		
ARRIVAL/DEPARTURE		
INT'L TO DOMESTIC	:30	
NW		:25
INT'L TO INT'L	:30	
BKL STANDARD	:20	
CLOVIS, N.M.		
STANDARD	:20	
TT		:15
COLD BAY, ALASKA		
STANDARD	:20	
RV		:15
COLORADO SPRINGS, COLO.		
STANDARD	:20	
CO		:10
COLUMBIA, S.C.		
STANDARD	:30	
DL, SO		:20
PI		:15
COLUMBUS, GA.		
STANDARD	:20	
SO		:15
COLUMBUS, OHIO		
STANDARD	:30	
AL		:25
NC		:10
TW		:20
CORPUS CHRISTI, TEXAS		
STANDARD	:20	
TT		:15
CURACAO, NETH. ANTILLES		
DOMESTIC	:40	
DOMESTIC TO INT'L	:40	
INT'L TO DOMESTIC	:40	
INT'L TO INT'L	:40	
ALL WIDE-BODY AIRCRAFT	1:00	
DALLAS/FT. WORTH, TEXAS		
FLIGHTS TO/FROM HAWAII		
ARE DOMESTIC		
DFW DOMESTIC		
STANDARD	:50	
BETWEEN AA AND EA	:30	
BETWEEN BN AND FY	:30	
BETWEEN CO AND DL/ZK	:30	
BETWEEN DL AND ZK	:30	
CONT. NEXT COLUMN		
DALLAS/FT. WORTH, TEXAS-CONT.		
BETWEEN FL AND OZ/TT/XO	:30	
BETWEEN OZ AND TT/XO	:30	
BETWEEN TT AND XO	:15	
AA, BN, DL		:30
CO		:10
FL		:20
TT		:15
DFW INTERNATIONAL		
DOMESTIC TO INT'L	:50	
BETWEEN AA/EA	:30	
AA, BN		:30
INT'L TO DOMESTIC	1:10	
AA TO EA	1:00	
AA		1:00
FROM AA (WITH STOP AT		
SAT)	:50	:30
FROM BN (WITH STOP IAH		
OR SAT)	:50	:30
ALL OTHER BN		:50
INT'L TO INT'L	1:10	
BN		:50
DAL STANDARD	:20	
DAYTON, OHIO		
STANDARD	:30	
AL		:25
NC		:10
TW		:20
DENVER, COLO.		
FLIGHTS TO/FROM HAWAII		
ARE DOMESTIC		
DOMESTIC		
STANDARD	:40	
BETWEEN BN AND UA	:35	
BETWEEN NC AND TT	:30	
WA (FROM CANADA)	1:00	
CO, NC		:10
TT		:15
FL		:20
TW, UA		:25
WA (EXCEPT FROM CANADA)		:20
INTERNATIONAL		
DOMESTIC TO INT'L		
BETWEEN UA AND MX	1:00	
TW-DOMESTIC CONNECTING		
TIMES WILL APPLY TO ALL		
TW INT'L FLIGHTS WHICH		
TRANSIT TO A POINT IN		
THE U.S. PRIOR TO		
ARRIVAL/DEPARTURE		
INT'L TO DOMESTIC		
BETWEEN MX AND UA	1:00	
DES MOINES, IOWA		
STANDARD	:20	
OZ		:10
DETROIT, MICH.		
FLIGHTS TO/FROM CANADA,		
HAWAII, BERMUDA, AND		
PUERTO RICO ARE DOMESTIC		
DTW DOMESTIC		
STANDARD	:45	
AA/DL TO/FROM NW	:30	
DL TO/FROM AL	:30	
NC TO/FROM BN	:30	
NW TO/FROM ZW	:30	
BETWEEN NC AND UA	:30	
AA, NW, TW, UA		:25
AL, DL		:30
NC		:15
DTW INTERNATIONAL		
DOMESTIC TO INT'L	1:00	
NW TO AA	:30	
AA		:25
INT'L TO DOMESTIC	1:30	
AA (WITH STOP AT ORD,		
DFW, SAT)	:45	:25
IF CONNECTION INVOLVES		
TRANSFER BETWEEN DTW		
AND YOG AIRPORTS	2:30	
DET STANDARD	:20	
DEVILS LAKE, N.D.		
STANDARD	:10	
DULUTH, MINN.		
STANDARD	:20	
NC		:10
EARLTON, ONT.		
STANDARD	:15	
EAU CLAIRE, WIS.		
STANDARD	:10	
EDMONTON, ALTA.		
YEG STANDARD	:30	
INT'L TO DOMESTIC	1:00	
INT'L TO INT'L	1:00	
YXD STANDARD	:30	
INTER-AIRPORT SURFACE		
CONNECTIONS YEG-YXD:		
DOMESTIC	1:20	
DOMESTIC TO INT'L	1:20	
INT'L TO DOMESTC	2:00	
INT'L TO INT'L	2:00	
EL DORADO/CAMDEN, ARK.		
STANDARD	:20	
TT		:15
ELMIRA, N.Y.		
STANDARD	:25	
EL PASO, TEXAS		
STANDARD	:20	
CO		:10
TT		:15
IF CONNECTION INVOLVES		
TRANSFER BETWEEN		
EL PASO AND CIUDAD		
JUAREZ AIRPORTS	2:00	
ERIE, PA.		
STANDARD	:25	
ESCANABA, MICH.		
STANDARD	:10	
EUREKA/ARCATA, CALIF.		
ACV STANDARD	:20	
RW		:15
EVANSVILLE, IND.		
STANDARD	:20	
AL		:25
FAIRBANKS, ALASKA		
FAI DOMESTIC		

CONT. NEXT PAGE

MINIMUM CONNECTING TIMES

The minimum connecting times shown in this section indicate the "legal" connecting times for construction of all connections, domestic and international, for travel within, and to and from the area covered in this publication. On-line connecting times will be the same as off-line connecting times except where specific times are shown. For connecting times at cities not covered in this publication refer to the International Edition. For any city not listed allow 20 minutes.

CITY	OFF LINE	ON LINE
FAIRBANKS, ALASKA-CONT.		
STANDARD	1:00	
WC		:15
FAI INTERNATIONAL		
DOMESTIC TO INT'L	1:00	
INT'L TO DOMESTIC	1:00	
INT'L TO INT'L	1:00	
FAIRMONT, MINN.		
STANDARD	:10	
FARGO, N.D.		
STANDARD	:20	
NC		:10
FAYETTEVILLE, N.C.		
STANDARD	:20	
PI		:15
FLINT, MICH.		
STANDARD	:20	
NC		:10
FLORENCE, S.C.		
STANDARD	:20	
PI		:15
FORT DE FRANCE, MARTINIQUE		
DOMESTIC	1:00	
DOMESTIC TO INT'L	1:00	
INT'L TO DOMESTIC	1:00	
BETWEEN INT'L	1:00	
FT. LAUDERDALE, FLA.		
FLIGHTS FROM NAS ARE DOMESTIC		
DOMESTIC		
STANDARD	:30	
EA, UA		:20
INTERNATIONAL		
DOMESTIC TO INT'L	:30	
INT'L TO DOMESTIC	:50	
FREDERICTON, N.B.		
STANDARD	:20	
AC		:30
TRANS-BORDER FLIGHTS		
AC (U.S. TO CANADA)		:45
FREEPORT, BAHAMAS		
DOMESTIC	:30	
DOMESTIC TO INT'L	:40	
INT'L TO DOMESTIC	1:00	
INT'L TO INT'L	1:00	
GANDER, NFLD.		
STANDARD	:20	
AC		:30
TRANS-BORDER FLIGHTS		
AC (U.S. TO CANADA)		:45
GOOSE BAY, NFLD.		
STANDARD	:30	
GRAND CANYON, ARIZ.		
STANDARD	:20	
RW		:15
GRAND CAYMAN, WEST INDIES		
STANDARD	:45	
GRAND FORKS, N.D.		
STANDARD	:20	
NC		:10
GRAND RAPIDS, MICH.		
STANDARD	:30	
AL		:25
NC		:10
UA		:20
GREAT FALLS, MONT.		
STANDARD	:20	
WA (FROM CANADA)	:30	:25
FL		:20
WA		:15
GREEN BAY, WIS.		
STANDARD	:20	
NC		:10
GREENSBORO/HIGH POINT, N.C.		
STANDARD	:25	
PI		:15
GUADALAJARA, MEXICO		
DOMESTIC	1:00	
DOMESTIC TO INT'L	1:00	
INT'L TO DOMESTIC	1:30	
MX		:50
INT'L TO INT'L	1:30	
HALIFAX, N.S.		
DOMESTIC		
STANDARD	:20	
AC, PV		:30
TRANS-BORDER FLIGHTS		
AC (U.S. TO CANADA)		:45
INTERNATIONAL		
DOMESTIC TO INT'L		
AC		:45
INT'L TO DOMESTIC		
AC		1:30
INT'L TO INT'L		
AC (WESTBOUND)		1:30
HANCOCK, MICH.		
STANDARD	:10	
HARLINGEN, TEXAS		
DOMESTIC		
STANDARD	:20	
TT		:15
INT'L TO DOMESTIC		
TT		:45
HARRISBURG, PA.		
MDT STANDARD	:20	
AL		:25
TW		:15
HAR STANDARD	:20	
HARTFORD, CONN.		
FLIGHTS TO/FROM BERMUDA ARE DOMESTIC		
BDL DOMESTIC		
STANDARD	:30	
AL, TW		:25
UA		:20
BDL INTERNATIONAL		
DOMESTIC TO INT'L		
TW-DOMESTIC CONNECTING TIMES WILL APPLY TO ALL TW INT'L FLIGHTS WHICH TRANSIT TO A POINT IN THE U.S. PRIOR TO ARRIVAL/DEPARTURE		
HAVANA, CUBA		
DOMESTIC	1:00	
CONT. NEXT COLUMN		
HAVANA, CUBA-CONT.		
DOMESTIC TO INT'L	1:30	
INT'L TO DOMESTIC	1:30	
INT'L TO INT'L	1:30	
HIBBING, MINN.		
STANDARD	:10	
HILO, HAWAII; HAWAII		
U.S. MAINLAND TO HAWAIIAN ISLANDS	:30	
HAWAIIAN ISLANDS TO U.S. MAINLAND	1:00	
HOBBS, N.M.		
STANDARD	:20	
TT		:15
HONOLULU, OAHU; HAWAII		
INTER-ISLAND		
BETWEEN HA AND TS	:30	
HA		:15
TS		:30
BETWEEN HAWAIIAN ISLANDS AND U.S. MAINLAND	1:00	
DOMESTIC TO INT'L	1:00	
TS TO ALL	1:15	
AA TO AA (WESTBOUND)		:20
CO TO VG	:50	
PA		:50
INT'L TO DOMESTIC	1:30	
AA		:40
PA		:50
INT'L TO INT'L	1:30	
HOT SPRINGS, ARK.		
STANDARD	:20	
TT		:15
HOUSTON, TEXAS		
FLIGHTS TO/FROM HAWAII ARE DOMESTIC		
IAH DOMESTIC		
STANDARD	:45	
BETWEEN AA/BN/DL	:30	
BETWEEN CO/EA/NA/TT	:30	
BETWEEN CO AND HY	:10	
DL TO/FROM ZK	:20	
HY TO/FROM AA/BN/DL	:40	
HY TO/FROM EA/NA/TT	:30	
AA, BN, EA, NA		:20
CO		:10
DL		:30
TT		:15
IAH INTERNATIONAL		
DOMESTIC TO INT'L	1:00	
AA/DL TO AF/AM/BN/KL/PA	:45	
BN TO AF/AM/KL/PA	:45	
TT		:15
BN		:30
INT'L TO DOMESTIC	1:00	
AF/AM/BN/KL/PA TO AA/DL	:45	
AF/AM/KL/PA TO BN	:45	
BN, TT		:45
INT'L TO INT'L	1:15	
HOU STANDARD	:20	
HUNTINGTON, W. VA.		
STANDARD	:20	
AL		:25
PI		:15
HURON, S.D.		
STANDARD	:10	
IDAHO FALLS, IDAHO		
STANDARD	:20	
WA		:10
INDIANAPOLIS, IND.		
STANDARD	:30	
AA, DL, TW		:20
AL		:25
INT'L FALLS, MINN.		
STANDARD	:10	
IRON MOUNTAIN, MICH.		
STANDARD	:10	
IRONWOOD, MICH.		
STANDARD	:10	
ISLIP, N.Y.		
STANDARD	:20	
AL		:25
JACKSON, MICH.		
STANDARD	:10	
JACKSON/VICKSBURG, MISS.		
STANDARD	:20	
TT		:15
JACKSONVILLE, FLA.		
STANDARD	:30	
BETWEEN UA AND FE	:20	
NA, UA		:20
JAMESTOWN, N.Y.		
STANDARD	:25	
JONESBORO, ARK.		
STANDARD	:20	
TT		:15
JOPLIN, MO.		
STANDARD	:25	
OZ		:10
JUNEAU, ALASKA		
JNU STANDARD	:20	
AS		:10
JNU TRANS-BORDER FLIGHTS		
WC (FROM YXY) TO ALL	1:00	
JSE STANDARD	:10	
KALAMAZOO, MICH.		
STANDARD	:10	
KANSAS CITY, MO.		
MCI DOMESTIC		
STANDARD	:45	
BETWEEN CO/NC/OZ/UA	:30	
BETWEEN BN/FL	:30	
CO, NC, OZ		:10
FL		:20
TW		:25
BN, DL, UA		:30
MCI INTERNATIONAL		
DOMESTIC TO INT'L		
TW-DOMESTIC CONNECTING TIMES WILL APPLY TO ALL TW INT'L FLIGHTS WHICH TRANSIT TO A POINT IN THE U.S. PRIOR TO ARRIVAL/DEPARTURE		
MKC STANDARD	:20	
KINGSTON, JAMAICA		
KIN DOMESTIC	:45	
KIN DOMESTIC TO INT'L	:45	
KIN INT'L TO DOMESTIC	:45	
KIN INT'L TO INT'L	:45	
EA		:30
TPJ STANDARD	:20	
KINSTON, N.C.		
STANDARD	:20	
PI		:15
KNOXVILLE, TENN.		
STANDARD	:30	
AA, UA		:25
SO		:20
LA CROSSE, WIS.		
STANDARD	:10	
LAFAYETTE, IND.		
STANDARD	:20	
AL		:25
LAFAYETTE, LA.		
STANDARD	:20	
TT		:15
LAKE CHARLES, LA.		
STANDARD	:20	
TT		:15
LANCASTER, PA.		
STANDARD	:20	
AL		:25
LANSING, MICH.		
STANDARD	:20	
NC		:10
LAREDO, TEXAS		
STANDARD	:20	
TT		:15
LAS VEGAS, NEV.		
DOMESTIC		
STANDARD	:35	
BETWEEN FL/RW	:25	
BETWEEN TW/RW	:30	
RW, TW, WA		:20
INTERNATIONAL		
DOMESTIC TO INT'L		
TW-DOMESTIC CONNECTING TIMES WILL APPLY TO ALL TW INT'L FLIGHTS WHICH TRANSIT TO A POINT IN THE U.S. PRIOR TO ARRIVAL/DEPARTURE		
LEWISTON, IDAHO		
STANDARD	:20	
RW		:15
LEXINGTON, KY.		
STANDARD	:20	
AL		:25
PI		:15
LITTLE ROCK, ARK.		
STANDARD	:30	
TT		:15
LONDON, ONT.		
STANDARD	:30	
LONGVIEW, TEXAS		
STANDARD	:20	
TT		:15
LOS ANGELES, CALIF.		
FLIGHTS TO/FROM ALASKA, CANADA, HAWAII, AND PUERTO RICO ARE DOMESTIC		
LAX DOMESTIC		
STANDARD	:50	
BETWEEN AA/NW	:30	
BETWEEN CO/DL/RW	:30	
BETWEEN EA AND TW/GW	:30	
AA/NW TO GW	:40	
GW TO AA/NW	:30	
NA TO TW	:40	
TW TO/FROM GW	:30	
BETWEEN TT/UA	:30	
AA, DL, UA		:30
CO, NA, WA		:20
WA (FROM YVR)	1:30	1:00
EA, RW, TW		:25
TT		:15
HAWAII FLIGHTS ONLY		
BETWEEN NA/PA	:30	
BETWEEN PA/TW	:40	
LAX INTERNATIONAL		
DOMESTIC TO INT'L	1:00	
AA/UA TO TW	:50	
CO/RW/TT/UA/WA/ TO MX	:50	
TW TO MX	:45	
TW		:45
TW-DOMESTIC CONNECTING TIMES WILL APPLY TO ALL TW INT'L FLIGHTS WHICH TRANSIT TO A POINT IN THE U.S. PRIOR TO ARRIVAL/DEPARTURE		
UA TO MX	:50	
WA (TO ACA, MEX)		:20
INT'L TO DOMESTIC	1:30	
MX TO CO/RW/TT/TW/UA/WA	1:15	
NW TO ALL	:50	
WA (FROM ACA, MEX)		1:00
INT'L TO INT'L	1:30	
BUR STANDARD	:30	
ONT STANDARD	:20	
LOUISVILLE, KY.		
STANDARD	:30	
AA, AL		:25
TW		:20
LUBBOCK, TEXAS		
STANDARD	:20	
CO		:10
TT		:15
LUFKIN, TEXAS		
STANDARD	:20	
TT		:15
LYNCHBURG, VA.		
STANDARD	:20	
PI		:15
MADISON, WIS.		
STANDARD	:20	
NC, OZ		:10
MANISTEE, MICH.		
STANDARD	:10	
MANITOWOC, WIS.		
STANDARD	:10	
MANKATO, MINN.		
STANDARD	:10	
MANSFIELD, OHIO		
STANDARD	:20	
AL		:30
MARQUETTE, MICH.		
STANDARD	:10	
MAZATLAN, MEXICO		
DOMESTIC	1:00	
DOMESTIC TO INT'L	1:00	
INT'L TO DOMESTIC	1:30	
MC ALLEN, TEXAS		
DOMESTIC		
STANDARD	:20	
TT		:15
INT'L TO DOMESTIC		
TT		:45
MEMPHIS, TENN.		
STANDARD	:30	
BETWEEN EA AND BN	:25	
AA, AL, DL		:25
BN, FL, UA		:20
SO, TT		:15
MENOMINEE, MICH.		
STANDARD	:10	
MERIDA, MEXICO		
DOMESTIC	:45	
DOMESTIC TO INT'L	1:00	
INT'L TO DOMESTIC	1:00	
INT'L TO INT'L	1:00	
MEXICO CITY, MEXICO		
DOMESTIC	:45	
DOMESTIC TO INT'L	1:00	
INT'L TO DOMESTIC	1:15	
INT'L TO INT'L	1:30	
MIAMI, FLA.		
FLIGHTS TO/FROM CANADA, PUERTO RICO, U.S. VIRGIN ISLANDS AND HAWAII ARE DOMESTIC.		
DOMESTIC		
STANDARD	:40	
BETWEEN NA AND SL	:35	
BETWEEN EA AND LS/PT	:30	
DL, EA		:30
NA, TW, UA		:20
INTERNATIONAL		
DOMESTIC TO INT'L	1:00	
DL TO MI	:45	
EA TO BA/MX	:45	
TW TO SO	:45	
BN		:45
EA, NA, SO		:30
INT'L TO DOMESTIC	1:30	
FROM NAS	1:00	
BA/MX TO EA	1:15	
MI TO DL	1:00	
BN		1:15
EA (FROM FPO)		1:15
EA (EXCEPT FROM FPO)		:30
NA		1:00
PA		1:20
SO		1:10
INT'L TO INT'L	1:30	
BA TO EA	1:15	
EA TO BA	:45	
MIDLAND/ODESSA, TEXAS		
STANDARD	:20	
CO		:10
TT		:15
MILWAUKEE, WIS.		
STANDARD	:30	
BETWEEN EA AND NC	:20	
NC, OZ		:10
NW, UA		:25
MINNEAPOLIS/ST PAUL, MINN.		
FLIGHTS TO/FROM HAWAII AND CANADA ARE DOMESTIC		
MSP DOMESTIC		
STANDARD	:40	
BN, WA		:20
NC		:15
NW (EXCEPT FROM FLIGHT 458)		:25
NW (FROM FLIGHT 458)	1:00	:40
MSP INTERNATIONAL		
NW DOMESTIC TO INT'L		:30
INT'L TO DOMESTIC	1:00	
NW INT'L TO DOMESTIC		:25
NW PASSENGERS CLEARING CUSTOMS AT ANC, HNL OR SEA		:40
MINOT, N.D.		
STANDARD	:20	
NC		:10
MITCHELL, S.D.		
STANDARD	:10	
MOLINE, ILL.		
STANDARD	:20	
OZ		:10
MONCTON, N.B.		
STANDARD	:20	
AC		:30
MONROE, LA.		
STANDARD	:20	
TT		:15
MONTEGO BAY, JAMAICA		
DOMESTIC	:45	
DOMESTIC TO INT'L	:45	
INT'L TO DOMESTIC	:45	
INT'L TO INT'L	:45	
EA		:30
MONTERREY, MEXICO		
DOMESTIC	1:00	
DOMESTIC TO INT'L	1:00	
INT'L TO DOMESTIC	1:30	

FOR ANY CITY NOT LISTED ALLOW 20 MINUTES

FLIGHT ITINERARIES

Itineraries may include city/airport codes not listed in the section preceding flight itineraries. Consult International Edition decode list.

Numbers following itinerary indicate day/s of the week flight departs origin airport.

FLIGHT

EA—EASTERN AIR LINES

458 PNS BHM ATL
459 EWR DCA ATL PNS
461 MCO MIA
462 ATL SDF IND
463 DTW TPA FLL
464 TPA DTW
465 CLE MIA
466 SRQ TPA ORD
467 DTW MIA
468 FLL ORD
469 ORD FLL
471 ATL MCO FLL
473 BAL DCA MIA
475 LGA PBI MIA
476 PNS BHM ATL TPA
477 JFK FLL
479 ATL MCN
480 SRQ TPA PHL EWR
481 EWR PHL TPA
482 MIA PIT CLE
483 CLE PIT MIA
487 ATL MIA
488 ATL PHL
489 GSO ATL
490 MCO ATL
491 BOS JFK ATL
492 ATL EWR
494 IAH JFK BOS
495 JFK IAH SAT
497 MGM ATL
498 MIA DFW
499 DFW MIA
500 MCO TPA DFW
501 DFW TPA MCO ORD
504 LEX DCA EWR
505 BOS EWR SDF EVV STL
507 EWR DCA STL
508 EVV SDF DCA
510 STL DCA CAE
511 SYR PHL
512 CLT RDU DCA
514 STL DCA EWR BOS
516 EWR BDL
518 DCA EWR
521 SAT MSY MIA
524 MIA MSY SAT
526 FLL TPA DFW
529 DFW TPA FLL MIA
530 MIA CLE
531 YUL JFK
532 MIA DFW ATL
533 BOS ATL BHM PNS
534 IAH ATL BOS
535 BOS EWR
537 BOS ATL
538 MIA MLB JAX ATL RDU DCA EWR
540 MOB BHM LGA
541 LGA BHM PNS
543 LGA ATL TLH
544 SAT ATL LGA
545 LGA CLT AGS
546 TPA ATL PVD
547 LGA ATL MOB
548 IAH MSY BOS
549 EWR RDU ATL MLB MIA
550 IAH PHL JFK
551 PHL IAH
552 IAH IAD PHL
553 PHL IAD MSY
554 IAH IAD BAL
555 BAL IAD IAH
556 IAH MSY PHL BOS
557 SYR ATL MKE
558 MSY IAD EWR
559 EWR IAD IAH
560 CLT RDU BAL
561 SYR PHL ATL JAX DAB MIA
562 RIC LGA YUL
563 LGA RIC
564 PNS ATL RDU LGA
565 LGA RDU
566 MOB ATL GSP DCA
567 RIC ATL DFW
568 RDU LGA
569 BOS MSY IAH
571 JFK RIC ATL DFW
572 ATL RIC
573 BAL RDU CLT CAE
574 AGS CLT LGA
575 BOS PHL MSY IAH
576 ATL RDU DCA
577 LGA RIC ATL DFW
578 ATL GSP GSO
579 PHL CLT GSP
580 TPA ATL GSO LGA
581 ATL MGM
582 SRQ ATL
583 DCA RDU
584 RDU LGA
585 RDU ATL MIA
586 GNV ATL RIC JFK
587 YUL LGA
588 CAE DCA
589 DCA GSO ATL DFW
590 AGS CLT PHL
591 ATL PNS
592 ATL RDU
593 BDL DCA ATL
594 CAE EWR
595 LGA GSO
596 CAE CLT PHL SYR
597 LGA RIC ATL JAX
598 DFW ATL BDL
599 BOS BDL ATL
601 BOS MCO
602 MIA TPA TLH ATL BNA
604 MCO BOS
606 MOB ATL EVV SDF EWR BOS
609 STL EVV ATL FLL MIA
610 MCO ORD
614 SRQ CVG ORD
615 ORD CVG SRQ
616 DFW ATL RIC LGA
617 GSP ATL MIA
618 PIT YYZ
619 GSO ATL IND
620 ATL BNA
622 MCN ATL
624 TPA ATL BNA
626 ATL RIC EWR BOS
627 ATL MOB
628 MIA ATL
629 BNA ATL
630 MLB ATL RDU
631 BOS EWR RIC
633 BAL ATL
634 TPA ATL BDL PVD
635 DTW MCO
637 ORD MCO
638 MCN ATL
639 DTW TPA
642 PBI DTW
643 DTW PBI
644 MOB ATL GSP
645 ATL TLH TPA MIA

CONT. NEXT COLUMN

FLIGHT

EA—EASTERN AIR LINES

647 ATL CSG
649 MSP ATL MSY
652 CSG ATL
653 EWR DCA SDF
655 EWR DCA LEX
660 ATL MEM
661 MEM ATL
662 ATL MEM
663 MEM ATL
664 DFW ATL
665 ATL MGM
669 EWR BAL MCO TPA
670 MIA ATL BNA
671 BNA ATL TLH
672 MIA MCO
673 SYR MIA NAS
674 PNS ATL STL EVV
676 ATL RDU
678 PBI ATL SYR
681 ATL MOB
685 DTW JAX SRQ
686 SRQ JAX DTW
687 BAL ATL
689 PHL PBI FLL
690 FLL MIA STL
695 BNA ATL FLL
699 STL ATL
700 FLL BUF YYZ
701 YYZ BUF FLL
702 STT SJU
703 SJU STT
712 ATL SDF
715 ATL CSG
720 MGM ATL MSP
722 STT SJU
725 EVV STL
727 PVD ATL MCO
729 CLE CAK CLT CHA ATL
730 MIA CLT GSO ROA PIT CLE
731 CLE PIT ROA GSO CLT MIA
735 MSP TPA MCO
736 MCO TPA MSP
737 SDQ SJU
738 PHL RDU GSO PIT DTW
739 DTW PIT GSO RDU PHL
740 MIA FLL EWR
741 LGA FLL
742 FLL LGA YUL
743 JFK FLL
745 EWR FLL
748 FLL LGA YUL
749 LGA FLL
750 FLL JFK
752 FLL EWR
753 JFK FLL
754 FLL LGA
756 NAS FLL JFK
757 JFK FLL MIA
759 BOS EWR FLL
760 SJU SDQ
763 SDQ SJU
768 SJU SDQ
769 SDQ SJU
772 STX SJU
773 SJU STT
774 POS UVF ANU STX SJU 47
774 POS PTP ANU STX SJU 26
774 POS FDF ANU STX SJU 135
775 SJU STX ANU UVF POS 47
775 SJU STX ANU PTP POS 26
775 SJU STX ANU FDF POS 135
776 PSE SJU
778 SJU SDQ
779 SJU PSE
780 SXM SJU
781 SJU SXM
782 SAT IAH ATL CLT
784 ATL RIC
785 SJU ANU
786 ANU SJU
787 MKE ATL MGM
788 MSY ATL MKE
789 MKE ATL MSY
790 MIA FLL ORD
791 ORD FLL
793 MSP ATL MIA NAS
794 MCO ATL
795 ORD FLL
796 FLL ORD
803 ORD DTW BDA
804 BDA DTW ORD
806 BDA EWR ATL TPA
807 JFK BDA
808 BDA BAL PHL
809 PHL BAL BDA
810 BDA JFK
811 MIA MCO ATL EWR BDA
829 MIA FPO
838 FPO MIA
840 NAS FPO BAL
841 PHL BAL NAS
842 NAS BAL PHL
843 BAL NAS FPO
844 FPO NAS PHL
845 PHL FPO NAS
847 FLL NAS
848 DAB LGA BOS
849 BOS LGA DAB
852 FLL PBI DCA STL
853 MCO MIA NAS
861 JFK MCO MIA
862 MCO LGA YUL
863 RIC RDU MIA
864 MIA FLL BOS
867 BOS PBI
868 PBI BOS
870 MCO PHL
871 LGA PHL MCO
873 PHL FLL
874 MCO DCA
875 EWR DCA MCO
876 FLL PHL
878 DAB JAX DCA BOS
879 PVD MIA
880 FLL BOS
881 BOS FLL
882 TPA BOS
883 JFK PBI MIA
884 MIA PBI LGA BDL
885 BOS TPA SRQ
886 FLL PBI PHL
887 JFK SRQ
888 MIA PVD
889 DCA PBI FLL
890 PBI EWR
891 ORD BNA BHM MIA
892 MIA LGA
893 EWR PBI
894 MIA BHM BNA ORD
896 SRQ JFK

CONT. NEXT COLUMN

FLIGHT

EA—EASTERN AIR LINES

897 BOS FLL
898 MIA RDU RIC LGA
899 PVD BDL FLL
900 ACA MEX JFK
901 JFK MEX ACA
902 ACA MEX JFK
903 JFK MEX ACA
904 MEX ATL DCA
905 DCA ATL MEX
906 MEX MSY MIA
907 MIA MSY MEX
914 SJU PHL BUF YYZ
915 MIA SJU
916 SJU EWR
917 BDL EWR SJU
918 ACA ATL LGA
919 LGA ATL ACA
920 SJU JFK
922 SJU JFK
923 JFK SJU
924 SJU JFK
927 JFK SJU
928 SJU JFK
929 JFK SJU
939 JFK SJU
940 SJU PHL
941 YYZ BUF PHL SJU
943 BOS EWR SJU
944 SJU BOS
945 EWR BOS SJU
946 SJU BAL BDL JFK
947 BDL BAL SJU
948 SJU ORD
949 ORD SJU
952 SJU MIA DTW
953 DTW MIA SJU
954 SJU ATL ORD
955 MIA SJU
956 SRQ MCO CLE
967 ORD ATL SJU
958 SJU MIA
959 CLE MCO SRQ
960 SJU EWR
961 GSO ATL SJU
962 SJU ATL GSO
963 PHL SJU
966 SJU MIA
971 SJU CUR AUA
974 POS BGI SJU
975 SJU BGI POS
978 AUA CUR SJU
980 ATL MEM OKC DEN EA 980-MEM-BN 980
981 DEN MEM ATL BN 981-MEM-EA 981
982 ATL MEM DEN EA 982-MEM-BN 982
983 DEN OKC MEM ATL BN 983-MEM-EA 983
984 SXM SJU JFK
985 JFK SJU SXM
986 SJU PIT CLE
987 CLE PIT SJU
988 MBJ ATL PIT BUF
989 BUF PIT ATL MBJ
990 MBJ JFK BOS
991 BOS JFK MBJ
993 DFW MIA STT SJU
994 SJU PAP KIN MBJ BAL EWR BOS
995 EWR BAL MBJ KIN PAP SJU
998 SJU STT STX MIA

AIR - SHUTTLE
BOS LGA
LGA DCA
LGA BOS
DCA LGA

EB—PENNSYLVANIA COMMUTER AIRLINES COMMUTER AIR CARRIER

430 SCE HAR DCA SCE EB 430-DCA-EB 431
431 SCE HAR DCA SCE EB 430-DCA-EB 431
700 SCE DCA HAR SCE EB 700-DCA-EB 701
701 SCE DCA HAR SCE EB 700-DCA-EB 701

EE—AIR EXEC—COMMUTER AIR CARRIER

101 WZW GED BAL DCA WZW EE 101-BAL-EE 102
102 WZW GED BAL DCA WZW EE 101-BAL-EE 102
105 WZW GED DCA
106 DCA GED WZW
113 DOV GED WZW DCA
114 DCA WZW GED DOV
201 WZW GED BAL
203 WZW GED BAL
204 BAL GED WZW
212 BAL GED WZW
301 WZW GED DOV PHL
302 PHL DOV GED DCA
303 WZW GED DOV PHL
304 PHL DOV GED WZW
311 DCA GED DOV PHL
312 PHL DOV GED WZW
401 WZW GED BAL ORF
402 ORF BAL
403 GED BAL ORF
404 ORF BAL GED WZW
411 BAL GED ORF X67
411 DOV GED ORF X67
412 ORF GED BAL X67
412 ORF GED DOV X67

EJ—NEW ENGLAND AIRLINES, INC.—COMMUTER AIR CARRIER

121 BID WST
122 WST BID
125 BID WST
126 WST BID
129 BID WST
130 WST BID
221 BID WST
222 WST BID
225 BID WST
226 WST BID
231 BID WST
232 WST BID
327 BID WST
328 WST BID
331 BID WST
332 WST BID

EL—EASTERN CARIBBEAN AIRWAYS—COMMUTER AIR CARRIER

101 STX NEV
102 NEV STX

FLIGHT

EM—GOLFE AIR QUEBEC, LTD.

101 YBC YXK YYY YBC
111 YBC YME YBC
121 YBC YXK YYY YBC X67
121 YBC YYY YXK 6
121 YBC YYY YXK YBC 7
131 YBC YME YBC X67
131 YXK YYY YBC 6
141 YBC YYY YXK X67
141 YBC YME YYY 6
151 YXK YYY YBC
161 YBC YME YBC
171 YBC YYY YXK YBC

EV—EXECUAIR, INC. COMMUTER AIR CARRIER

201 RLD SEA
202 SEA RLD
203 RLD SEA
204 SEA RLD
205 RLD SEA
211 RLD SEA
212 SEA RLD
213 RLD SEA
214 SEA RLD
216 SEA RLD
401 RLD PDX
402 PDX RLD
403 RLD PDX
404 PDX RLD
405 RLD PDX
406 PDX RLD
411 RLD PDX
412 PDX RLD
520 RLD PUW BOI
521 BOI PUW RLD
522 RLD PUW BOI
523 BOI PUW RLD

EZ—AIRTRANSIT CANADA

801 YRO YMY
802 YMY YRO
901 YRO YMY
902 YMY YRO
1001 YRO YMY
1002 YMY YRO
1101 YRO YMY
1102 YMY YRO
1201 YRO YMY
1202 YMY YRO
1301 YRO YMY
1302 YMY YRO
1401 YRO YMY
1402 YMY YRO
1501 YRO YMY
1502 YMY YRO
1601 YRO YMY
1602 YMY YRO
1701 YRO YMY
1702 YMY YRO
1801 YRO YMY
1802 YMY YRO
1901 YRO YMY
1902 YMY YRO
2001 YRO YMY
2002 YMY YRO
2101 YRO YMY
2102 YMY YRO
2201 YRO YMY
2202 YMY YRO

FE—FLORIDA AIRLINES COMMUTER AIR CARRIER

1 TPA SRQ FMY
2 PGD SRQ TPA
3 SRQ PGD
16 FMY TPA
17 GNV OCF
18 OCF GNV JAX
19 TPA SRQ FMY
20 FMY TPA OCF GNV JAX TLH
25 TPA SRQ
41 GNV OCF TPA
42 FMY PGD TPA OCF GNV JAX
43 TPA FMY
45 JAX TPA SRQ PGD FMY
46 FMY TPA OCF GNV
47 TPA SRQ
100 GNV TLH
109 TLH GNV OCF TPA
331 SRQ FMY MIA
332 MIA FMY TPA
333 JAX GNV OCF TPA SRQ FMY MIA
334 MIA FMY PGD SRQ TPA
335 SRQ FMY MIA
336 MIA PGD SRQ TPA JAX
819 SRQ FMY
821 SRQ FMY
823 TPA PGD FMY
824 FMY SRQ TPA
825 TPA FMY
826 FMY SRQ

FH—MALL AIRWAYS COMMUTER AIR CARRIER

50 ALB BGM ELM ITH BGM ALB FH 50-ELM-FH 55
55 ALB BGM ELM ITH BGM ALB FH 50-ELM-FH 55
60 ALB BGM ITH ELM
65 ELM ITH BGM ALB
70 ALB BGM ELM ITH BGM ALB FH 70-ELM-FH 75
75 ALB BGM ELM ITH BGM ALB FH 70-ELM-FH 75

FL—FRONTIER AIRLINES

4 LAS DEN MCI
7 MCI DEN LAS
8 LAS DEN STL
10 LAS DEN MCI STL
11 STL DEN LAS
12 PUB COS DEN STL
14 SLC DEN MCI
15 DEN LAS
17 STL DEN SLC BZN MSO FCA
19 STL DEN MOT YWG
21 MCI DEN LAS
22 FCA MSO BZN SLC DEN STL X7
22 LAS DEN STL 7
23 MCI DEN ABQ TUS PHX

CONT. NEXT COLUMN

FLIGHT

FL—FRONTIER AIRLINES

25 STL MCI DEN
27 STL DEN COS PHX
29 STL LNK DEN LAS
32 LAS DEN LNK STL
36 PHX TUS ABQ DEN
38 PHX TUS ABQ
41 LNK OMA MCI DFW
46 DFW MCI OMA LNK
54 DEN DFW
55 DFW DEN SLC
57 DFW DEN SLC
58 DEN DFW
60 SLC DEN MOT YWG X6 EFF JAN15
60 SLC DEN RAP BIS X6 DIS AFT JAN14
61 DFW DEN SLC
62 SLC DEN DFW
63 DEN GJT
65 DFW DEN SLC
66 SLC DEN DFW
70 DEN RAP
71 YWG MOT DEN
76 LAS ABQ DFW
77 DFW ABQ LAS
80 GTF BIL CPR DEN DFW
81 DFW DEN CPR BIL GTF
86 GTF BIL CPR DEN DFW
87 DFW DEN CPR BIL GTF
90 ABQ DEN LNK OMA
91 BIS RAP DEN ABQ TUS PHX
92 GJT DEN RAP MOT
93 DEN PUB
94 LAS DEN BIS YWG
95 RAP DEN
96 PHX TUS ABQ DEN
97 MOT RAP DEN MCI
98 LAS DEN RAP BIS
99 YWG BIS DEN ABQ TUS PHX
100 PHX DEN MCI 6
100 PHX DEN MCI STL X6 DIS AFT JAN14
101 GRI LNK OMA DEN PHX TUS
102 TUS PHX COS DEN
103 OMA DEN PHX TUS
104 TUS PHX DEN OMA
105 LNK OMA DEN PHX TUS
106 TUS PHX DEN OMA LNK GRI
107 DEN PHX TUS
108 TUS PHX DEN
206 DEN CYS
207 CYS DEN
208 DEN CYS LAR DEN
220 GTF LWT BIL MLS GDV SDY ISN
221 ISN SDY GDV MLS BIL LWT GTF
222 GTF HVR GGW OLF ISN MOT
223 MOT ISN OLF GGW HVR GTF
241 CDR AIA BFF SNY DEN
242 DEN SNY BFF AIA CDR
245 CDR AIA SNY DEN
248 DEN SNY BFF AIA CDR
501 DEN LBL OKC TUL MKO FSM HOT LIT MEM
503 BIL COD WRL RIW LAR CYS DEN
504 DFW OKC LBL DEN
505 WDG OKC DFW
507 OKC LAW DFW
508 PHX FLG GUP FMN CEZ DRO DEN
509 DEN ALS FMN GUP FLG PHX
510 SLC JAC BIL
511 BIL JAC SLC
512 ELP ALM ABQ FMN GJT SLC
514 DRO CEZ FMN ALS DEN
515 SLC GJT FMN ABQ ALM ELP
517 BIL BZN MSO SLC
518 ABQ FMN
521 FCA MSO BZN BIL JAC SLC 7
521 BIL JAC SLC X7
522 DEN CYS LAR RIW WRL COD
524 SLC BIL
525 DEN LBL OKC
526 MEM LIT FSM TUL OKC LBL DEN
531 JAC DEN
532 DEN JAC
541 MCI JLN FYV FSM PRX DFW
542 ICT MHK TOP MCI
543 FSM HOT MEM
544 MEM LIT HOT FSM FYV JLN MCI OMA OLU GRI HSI EAR MCK DEN
546 FSM FYV JLN MCI
548 MEM FSM FYV JLN MCI
552 DEN MCK EAR HSI GRI OLU OMA MCI STL
555 MCI TOP MHK
556 MHK TOP MCI
557 MCI TOP ICT X67
557 MCI TOP MHK 67
560 ICT TOP MCI
561 MCI OMA LNK GRI LBF BFF DEN
564 DEN BFF LBF GRI LNK OMA MCI
565 MEM LIT FSM MKO TUL OKC AMA PUB COS DEN
566 DEN BFF LBF GRI OLU OMA MCI JLN FYV FSM
567 STL MCI OMA OLU GRI LBF BFF DEN
568 DEN PUB AMA OKC TUL FSM LIT MEM
569 MCI TOP ICT
570 DFW FSM FYV HRO TBN STL
571 STL FYV FSM
572 MTJ GUC DEN
573 DEN GUC MTJ

CONT. NEXT COLUMN

FLIGHT

FL—FRONTIER AIRLINES

575 STL TBN HRO FYV FSM DFW
576 DFW FSM FYV OKC
577 STL TBN HRO FYV FSM DFW
578 JAC SLC VEL RKS HDN DEN 57
578 SLC VEL RKS HDN DEN X567
578 JAC SLC GJT HDN DEN 6
579 DEN HDN GJT SLC 6
579 DEN HDN RKS VEL SLC X6
580 LAA PUB DEN
581 FMN GUP ABQ SVC
582 SVC ABQ
587 ABQ ALM
588 ALM ABQ
589 ABQ SVC
591 DEN COS PUB LAA
593 MCI MHK SLN HYS GCK GLD DEN
594 DEN GLD GCK HYS SLN MHK MCI X6
594 DEN GLD GCK HYS SLN MHK TOP MCI 6
595 FLG PHX
596 PHX FLG
601 LAW DFW
602 SLC JAC
603 DEN CYS CPR RIW RKS VEL SLC
604 DEN CPR RIW WRL BIL
605 BFF LBF LNK MCI PPF PNC WDG SWO OKC LAW DFW X6
605 BFF LBF LNK MCI PPF PNC WDG OKC LAW DFW 6
607 COD WRL RIW CPR CYS DEN
608 FMN DRO ALS DEN
609 DEN DRO CEZ FMN PHX
610 DFW LAW OKC WDG PNC PPF MCI LNK 6
610 DFW LAW OKC SWO WDG PNC PPF MCI LNK X6
612 DFW LAW OKC WDG
614 SLC MSO BZN BIL
617 DEN ALS DRO CEZ FMN
618 SVC ABQ GUP FMN DRO DEN
619 DEN ALS DRO FMN ABQ
620 OKC TUL FYV LIT MEM
622 DEN LAR CYS DEN
624 SLC VEL RKS RIW CPR CYS DEN
628 DFW OKC LAW
629 MEM LIT HOT TUL OKC AMA
638 AMA OKC TUL FSM MEM
640 RKS HDN DEN
641 DEN HDN RKS
647 DEN CYS LAR DEN
650 DFW FSM FYV STL
651 MCI JLN FYV FSM DFW
652 SLN MHK MCI STL
655 LNK MCI TOP
657 MCI MHK SLN
658 TOP MCI
663 STL MCI LNK OMA GRI LBF BFF
670 DFW PRX FSM FYV HRO TBN STL
671 DEN GJT
672 CNY GJT DEN
673 DEN GJT MTJ GUC DEN
674 CNY GJT DEN
675 DEN GJT CNY
677 DEN GJT MTJ DEN
678 GJT DEN
679 DEN GJT CNY
688 HDN DEN
689 DEN HDN
690 COS DEN
691 DEN COS
692 COS DEN
693 DEN COS PUB
694 PUB COS DEN
695 DEN COS PUB
696 COS DEN
697 DEN COS
698 PUB DEN
699 DEN COS
706 LAS DEN
725 STL MCI DEN SLC
767 DFW GUC GJT DFW
768 SLC DFW
769 DFW SLC
771 DEN ABQ
809 DEN CEZ DRO PHX
822 DFW LAW
823 LAW DFW
826 DFW LAW
827 LAW DFW
834 SLC BIL BZN MSO FCA
836 PHX DRO
838 PHX FMN
844 OMA OLU GRI HSI EAR MCK DEN
866 MCI JLN FYV FSM
871 DEN HDN
872 HDN DEN
873 DEN HDN
875 DEN MTJ GJT
876 HDN DEN
881 DRO FMN GUP ABQ
884 GUC DEN
887 DEN GUC
2054 DEN GJT DFW

FN—FLORENCE AIRLINES COMMUTER AIR CARRIER

101 FLO CLT
104 CLT FLO
105 FLO CLT
204 CLT FLO
205 FLO CLT
206 CLT FLO
207 FLO CLT
208 CLT FLO

FO—FLIGHTWAYS CORPORATION—COMMUTER AIR CARRIER

160 ILG PHL JFK
161 JFK PHL ILG

CONT. NEXT PAGE

1-Monday 2-Tuesday 3-Wednesday 4-Thursday 5-Friday 6-Saturday 7-Sunday X-Except

NAOAG ANSWERS

1. (C) Honolulu, Hawaii to Sydney, Australia

2. (B) Page 712

3. To DETROIT, MICH.

    From NEW YORK, N.Y.

4. North Central; Douglas DC-10; Thursday

5. Chattanooga, Tenn.; Kona, Hawaii

6. DFW (Dallas/Ft. Worth); SLC (Salt Lake City); DEN (Denver)

7. Every day except Saturday; No; Every day of the week

8. 9:30 a.m.; 11:30 a.m.; Every day except Sunday; UA 649; Yes

9. (A) National Airport (see decode of DCA); Midway
    (B) UA 271; O'Hare; 9:02 a.m.

10. Delta Airlines; Night Coach Class in First Class Compartment/Night Coach Class/Controlled Inventory - Coach; Boeing 727-200

11. (A) 9:20 a.m.; 9:52 a.m.; Boeing 727-200; Jet First Class/Jet Coach Service/Controlled Inventory-Coach
    (B) 7:00 a.m.
    (C) NA 411 (EA 810 departs JFK) (NW 51 operates Sunday only); 1:00 p.m.; 1:38 p.m.

12. NC 700; CV5 (Convair 580); 9:16 a.m.; 10:20 a.m.; One Class Standard Service;Controlled Inventory-Coach

13. Breakfast; One; Dinner; Two

14. Yes (Snack)

15. Snack and Dinner; Yes; Yes (Snack)

16. (A) Yes; Boeing 727 Jet; One; American Airlines; Yes
    (B) JFK (Kennedy)

(C) DL 370; 8:30 a.m. (EA 50 arrives in New York at 12:51 p.m. which would not allow the passenger enough time to get into the city. BN 20 and DL 326 arrive around the same time as DL 370, but both leave much earlier--an inconvenience to the passenger).
(D) Snack and Dinner

17. 40 minutes; 4:30 p.m.; 4:30 p.m.

18. 9:15 a.m.; 2:15 p.m.; Salt Lake City; AA 563; Boeing 727; 11:28 a.m.; Western; 406; 1:40 p.m.; 0; Jet First Class, Jet Coach and Controlled Inventory-Coach; Yes (Breakfast)

19. 5:48 p.m.; 9:22 p.m.

20. B99 (Beech 99)

21. $7.63; $103.00; $206.00

22. (A) $86.00; $72.00
    (B) $73.14

23. $278.82

24. $25.00

25. $43.00; XV (Mississippi Valley Airways, Inc.)

26. (A) AL 458 connecting at LGA to AA 463; B11 and 727; 2(LGA+1)
    (B) AL 318; $42.00; National
    (C) $46.01; Monday thru Friday

27. 6:45 a.m.; 9:18 a.m.; 12:26 p.m.; Jet First Class/Jet Coach/Controlled Inventory - Coach

28. AC @

29. B; J; K; No; F-FN; Y-YN; K-YN; E

30. $105.56; $8.44; $114.00; $104.00; $7.26; $86.74

31. $215.41; YH; $199.41; YL; K (the H indicates high and the L indicates low)

32. $153.00; $165.00

33. (A) 9:00 a.m.; 2:29 p.m.; 4:07 p.m.:
    AEF@*
    (B) Jet First Class; $245.99
    (C) Jet Coach Class; $150.00
    (D) Jet Economy Class; $149.00
    (E) Controlled Inventory-Coach;
    No Fare
    (F) Controlled Inventory-Economy;
    No Fare

34. THRU; JT; JT/THRU (THRU, therefore,
    refers to an online connection in
    which a single carrier is used for
    both the originating and connecting
    flights and JT refers to an inter-
    line connection in which different
    carriers are used for the originat-
    ing and connecting flights. To con-
    serve space in the NAOAG, identical
    JT and THRU fares are signified by
    the single code entry JT/THRU. A
    slash (/) is used to separate the
    two construction codes.

35. CC; CC-T (The construction code
    "CC" is used to indicate a combina-
    tion of local fares, i.e., for each
    segment of the connection the local
    fares were added together to estab-
    lish the fare shown. The construc-
    tion code "CC-T" indicates that a
    connection allowance amount (terminal
    charge) has been deducted from the
    combination of local fares in accord-
    ance with the tariff rules.

36. Double Parentheses

37. Milwaukee - SBN (South Bend); SBN -
    Atlanta; CLE (Cleveland); Yes

38. DIFF; Y (NOTE: Differential con-
    structions apply only to Canadian
    and International travel).

39. (A) JT
    (B) CC-T
    (C) (( ))
    (D) CC
    (E) THRU
    (F) ( ) ( )
    (G) ( ) (( ))
    (H) JT/THRU
    (I) ( )

(J) (( )) (( ))
(K) DIFF

40. (A) AA 92; DL 548; San Francisco;
    9:00 a.m.; 4:11 p.m.
    (B) 6:05 p.m.; Burlington; 8:10
    p.m.
    (C) BF@
    (D) F - F; Y - Y; B - B; F
    (E) $185.19; $14.81; $200.00
    (F) Y
    (G) ((MHT)); Manchester is point
    beyond (using a published joint fare
    that allows Burlington)

41. 14.0 Miles South; Limousine; $2.00

42. 50 minutes (:50)

43. The on-line connecting time (20
    minutes) must be used.

44. Detroit

45. 4:40 P.M.

46. PA 896 will discontinue service
    after April 24; NW 94 will terminate
    service departing 10:20 p.m. from
    Honolulu after April 23; On April
    24 it will depart at 9:20 p.m.

47. CHI (Chicago); MCI (Kansas City);
    STL (St. Louis)

48. NC 908

49. (G) AL 884
    (H) Ozark; 860
    (I) Allegheny; 878

50. (A) Winston-Salem, N.C.
    (B) Los Angeles, California

Appendix C

NORTH AMERICAN CITY AND AIRPORT CODES
UNITED STATES, CANADA, MEXICO
AND THE CARIBBEAN

ABE	Allentown, Pennsylvania	ANV	Anvik, Alaska
ABI	Abilene, Texas	AOO	Altoona, Pennsylvania
ABL	Ambler, Arkansas	APC	Napa, California
ABQ	Albuquerque, New Mexico	APF	Naples, Florida
ABR	Aberdeen, South Dakota	APN	Alpena, Michigan
ABY	Albany, Georgia	ARC	Arctic Village, Alaska
ACA	Acapulco, Mexico	ART	Watertown, New York
ACK	Nantucket, Massachusetts	ARX	Asbury Park, New Jersey
ACT	Waco, Texas	ASD	Andros Town, Bahamas
ACV	Eureka/Arcata, California	ASE	Aspen, Colorado
ADK	Adak Island, Arkansas	AST	Astoria, Oregon
ADQ	Kodiak, Arkansas (Kodiak Airport)	ASX	Ashland, Wisconsin
ADR	Andrews, South Carolina	ATL	Atlantic, Georgia
AET	Allakaket, Arkansas	ATO	Athens, Ohio
AGN	Angoon, Arkansas	ATT	Atmautluak, Alaska
AGS	Augusta, Georgia	ATU	Attu Island, Alaska
AHN	Athens, Georgia	ATW	Appleton, Wisconsin
AIA	Alliance, Nebraska	ATY	Watertown, South Dakota
AIN	Wainwright, Arkansas	AUA	Aruba, Neth. Antilles
AIY	Atlantic City, New Jersey	AUG	Augusta, Maine
AIZ	Lake of the Ozarks, Missouri	AUK	Alakanuk, Alaska
AKI	Akiak, Arkansas	AUO	Auburn/Opelika, Alabama
AKK	Akhiok, Arkansas	AUS	Austin, Texas
AKN	King Salmon, Arkansas	AUW	Wausau, Wisconsin
AKP	Anaktuvuk Pass, Arkansas	AVL	Asheville, North Carolina
AKV	Akulivik, N.W.T., Canada	AVP	Wilkes-Barre/Scranton,
ALB	Albany, New York		Pennsylvania
ALE	Alpine, Texas	AVX	Catalina Island, California-
ALM	Alamogordo, New Mexico		Avalon Bay
ALO	Waterloo, Iowa	AXA	Anguilla, West Indies
ALS	Alamosa, Colorado	AXN	Alexandria, Minnesota
ALW	Walla Walla, Washington	AXS	Altus, Oklahoma
ALZ	Alitak, Arkansas	AZO	Kalamazoo, Michigan
AMA	Amarillo, Texas		
AMK	Durango, Colorado-Animas Air Park	BAL	Baltimore, Maryland
ANB	Anniston, Alabama	BAM	Battle Mountain, Nevada
ANC	Anchorage, Arkansas	BBQ	Barbuda, West Indies
AND	Anderson, South Carolina	BBR	Basse-Terre, Guadeloupe
ANI	Aniak, Alaska	BBX	Blue Bell, Pennsylvania
ANN	Annette Island, Alaska	BDA	Bermuda, Atlantic Ocean
ANU	Antigua, West Indies	BDG	Blanding, Utah

BDL	Hartford, Conneticut/Springfield, Massachusetts	BVX	Batesville, Arkansas
BDR	Bridgeport, Connecticut	BVY	Beverly, Massachusetts
BDY	Bandon, Oregon	BWD	Brownwood, Texas
BED	Bedford, Massachusetts	BWG	Bowling Green, Kentucky
BEH	Benton Harbor, Michigan	BXS	Borrego Springs, California
BET	Bethel, Alaska	BYI	Burley, Idaho
BFB	Blue Fox Bay, Alaska	BZN	Bozeman, Montana
BFD	Bradford, Pennsylvania		
BFF	Scottsbuluff, Nebraska	CCZ	Chub Cay, Bahamas
BFI	Seattle, Washington-Boeing Field	CDB	Cold Bay, Alaska
BFL	Bakersfield, California	CDC	Cedar City, Utah
BFT	Beaufort, South Carolina	CDR	Chadron, Nebraska
BGI	Barbados, Barbados	CDV	Cordova, Alaska
BGM	Binghamton, New York	CEC	Crescent City, California
BGR	Bangor, Maine	CEM	Central, Alaska
BHB	Bar Harbor, Maine	CEN	Ciudad Obregon, Mexico
BHC	Bullhead City, Arizona	CEZ	Cortez, Colorado
BHM	Birmingham, Alabama	CFG	Cienfuegos, Cuba
BID	Block Island, Rhode Island	CGA	Craig, Alaska
BIH	Bishop, California	CGI	Cape Girardeau, Missouri
BIL	Billings, Montana	CGX	Chicago, Illinois-Meigs Field
BIM	Bimini, Bahamas	CHA	Chattanooga, Tennessee
BIS	Bismarck, North Dakota	CHI	Chicago, Illinois
BJI	Bemidji, Minnesota	CHO	Charlottesville, Virginia
BKC	Buckland, Alaska	CHP	Circle Hot Springs, Alaska
BKE	Baker, Oregon	CHS	Charleston, South Carolina
BKL	Cleveland, Ohio-Lakefront Airport	CIC	Chico, California
		CID	Cedar Rapids/Iowa City, Iowa
BKW	Beckley, West Virginia	CIG	Craig, Colorado
BKX	Brookings, South Dakota	CIK	Chalkyitsik, Alaska
BLF	Bluefield, West Virginia	CIL	Council, Alaska
BLH	Blythe, California	CIU	Sault Ste. Marie, Michigan, USA-Chippewa
BLI	Bellingham, Washington	CJS	Ciudad Juarez, Mexico
BMG	Bloomington, Indiana	CKB	Clarksburg, West Virginia
BNA	Nashville, Tennessee	CKD	Crooked Creek, Alaska
BNO	Burns, Oregon	CKE	Clear Lake, California
BOI	Boise, Idaho	CKV	Clarksville, Tennessee
BOK	Brookings, Oregon	CLC	Clear Lake City, Texas
BON	Bonaire, Neth. Antilles	CLD	Carlsbad, California
BOS	Boston, Massachusetts	CLE	Cleveland, Ohio
BPT	Beaumont/Point Arthur, Texas	CLL	College Station, Texas
BQN	Aguadilla, Puerto Rico	CLM	Port Angeles, Washington
BRD	Brainerd, Minnesota	CLP	Clarks Point, Alaska
BRL	Burlington, Iowa	CLT	Charlotte, North Carolina
BRO	Brownsville, Texas	CMH	Columbus, Ohio
BRW	Barrow, Alaska	CMI	Champaign, Illinois
BRX	Barahona, Dominican Republic	CMW	Camaguey, Cuba
BTI	Barter Island, Alaska	CMX	Hancock, Michigan
BTL	Battle Creek, Michigan	CNM	Carlsbad, New Mexico
BTM	Butte, Montana	CNY	Moab, Utah
BTR	Baton Rouge, Louisiana	COA	Columbia, California
BTT	Bettles, Alaska	COD	Cody, Wyoming
BTV	Burlington, Vermont	CON	Concord, New Hampshire
BUF	Buffalo, New York	COS	Colorado Springs, Colorado
BUR	Burbank, California	COU	Columbia, Missouri

CPR	Casper, Wyoming	DRT	Del Rio, Texas
CPX	Culebra, Puerto Rico	DSD	La Desirade, Guadeloupe
CRC	Circle, Alaska	DSM	Des Moines, Iowa
CRI	Crooked Island, Bahamas	DTA	Delta, Utah
CRP	Corpus Christi, Texas	DTL	Detroit Lakes, Minnesota
CRW	Charleston, West Virginia	DTT	Detroit, Michigan
CRX	Corinth, Mississippi	DTW	Detroit, Mich-Metropolitan
CSE	Crested Butte, Colorado		Airport
CSG	Columbus, Georgia	DUJ	Du Bois, Pennsylvania
CSH	Cape Sarichef, Alaska	DUQ	Duncan/Quamichan Lake, B.C.,
CSN	Carson City, Nevada		Canada
CTM	Chetumal, Mexico	DUT	Dutch Harbor, Alaska
CUL	Culiacan, Mexico	DVL	Devils Lake, North Dakota
CUN	Cancun, Mexico		
CUR	Curacao, Neth. Antilles	EAA	Eagle, Alaska
CUU	Chihuahua, Mexico	EAR	Kearney, Nebraska
CVG	Cincinnati, Ohio	EAT	Wenatchee, Washington
CVN	Clovis, New Mexico	EAU	Eau Claire, Wisconsin
CVO	Corvallis, Oregon	EEK	Eek, Alaska
CWA	Wausau, Wisconsin-Central	EEN	Keene, New Hampshire
	Wisconsin Airport	EGE	Vail/Eagle, Colorado
CWI	Clinton, Iowa	EGX	Egegik, Alaska
CXH	Vancouver, BC, Canada-Coal	EHM	Cape Newenham, Alaska
	Harbour SPB	EIS	Tortola, British Virgin Island
CXL	Calexico, California	EKA	Eureka/Arcata, California-
CXY	Cat Cay, Bahamas		Murray Field
CYA	Cayes, Haiti	EKI	Elkhart, Indiana
CYB	Cayman Brac, West Indies	EKN	Elkins, West Virginia
CYF	Chefornak, Alaska	EKO	Elko, Nevada
CYS	Cheyenne, Wyoming	ELD	El Dorado/Camden, Arkansas
CZF	Cape Romanzof, Alaska	ELH	North Eleuthera, Bahamas
CZM	Cozumel, Mexico	ELI	Elim, Alaska
		ELM	Elmira, New York
DAB	Daytona Beach, Florida	ELP	El Paso, Texas
DAL	Dallas/Fort Worth, Texas-Love	ELV	Elfin Cove, Alaska
	Field	ELY	Ely, Nevada
DAN	Danville, Virginia	EMK	Emmonak, Alaska
DAY	Dayton, Ohio	EMP	Emporia, Kansas
DBQ	Dubuque, Iowa	ENA	Kenai, Alaska
DCA	Washington, DC-National Airport	EOK	Keokuk, Iowa
DDC	Dodge City, Kansas	ERI	Erie, Pennsylvania
DEC	Decatur, Illinois	ESC	Escanaba, Michigan
DEN	Denver, Colorado	ESD	Eastsound, Washington
DEO	Dearborn, Michigan	ESF	Alexandria, Louisiana
DET	Detroit, Michigan-City Airport	EUG	Eugene, Oregon
DFW	Dallas/Fort Worth, Texas	EUX	St. Eustatius, Neth. Antilles
DGO	Durango, Mexico	EVV	Evansville, Indiana
DHN	Dothan, Alabama	EWB	New Bedford, Massachusetts
DLG	Dillingham, Alaska	EWN	New Bern, North Carolina
DLH	Duluth, Minnesota	EWR	New York, NY-Newark Airport
DLS	The Dalles, Oregon	EXI	Excursion Inlet, Alaska
DMC	Sedalia, Montana	EYW	Key West, Florida
DNV	Danville, Illinois		
DOM	Dominica, West Indies	FAI	Fairbanks, Alaska
DRG	Deering, Alaska	FAJ	Fajardo, Puerto Rico
DRO	Durango, Colorado	FAR	Fargo, North Dakota

FAT	Fresno, California	GGT	George Town, Bahamas
FAY	Fayetteville, North Carolina	GGW	Glasgow, Montana
FCA	Kalispell, Montana	GHB	Governors Harbour, Bahamas
FDF	Fort De France	GHC	Great Harbour Cay, Bahamas
FFT	Frankfort, Kentucky	GHL	Garden Hill, Man., Canada
FHU	Ft. Huachuca/Sr. Vista, Arizona	GJT	Grand Junction, Colorado
FID	Fishers Island, New York	GKN	Gulkana, Alaska
FIL	Fillmore, Utah	GLD	Goodland, Kansas
FKL	Franklin, Pennsylvania	GLH	Greenville, Mississippi
FLG	Flagstaff, Arizona	GLR	Gaylord, Michigan
FLL	Fort Lauderdale, Florida	GLS	Galveston, Texas
FLC	Florence, South Carolina	GLV	Golovin, Alaska
FLT	Flat, Alaska	GMU	Greenville/Spartanburg-Grnv
FMN	Farmington, New Mexico		Dwtn
FMS	Fort Madison, Iowa	GND	Grendada, Windward Island
FMY	Fort Myers, Florida	GNU	Goodnews Bay, Alaska
FNR	Funter Bay, Alaska	GNV	Gainsville, Florida
FNT	Flint, Michigan	GNY	Granby, Colorado
FOD	Fort Dodge, Iowa	GOL	Gold Beach, Oregon
FOE	Topeka, Kansas	GON	New London, Connecticut
FOK	Westhampton, New York	GPT	Gulfport/Bioloxi, Mississippi
FPO	Freeport, Bahamas	GPZ	Grand Rapids, Minnesota
FRD	Friday Harbor, Washington	GQQ	Galion, Ohio
FRG	Farmingdale, New York	GRB	Green Bay, Wisconsin
FRM	Fairmont, Minnesota	GRD	Greenwood, South Carolina
FRY	Fryeburg, Maine	GRI	Grand Island, Nebraska
FSD	Sioux Falls, South Dakota	GRR	Grand Rapids, Michigan
FSM	Fort Smith, Arkansas	GSO	Greensboro/High Point,
FTC	Fort Collins, Colorado		North Carolina
FTL	Fortuna Ledge, Alaska	GSP	Greenville/Spartanburg,
FUL	Fullerton, California		South Carolina
FWA	Fort Wayne, Indiana	GST	Gustavus, Alaska
FWL	Farewell, Alaska	GTF	Great Falls, Montana
FYU	Fort Yukon, Alaska	GTR	Columbus, Mississippi
FYV	Fayetteville, Arkansas	GUC	Gunnison, Colorado
		GUP	Gallup, New Mexico
GAD	Gadsden, Alabama	GWO	Greenwood, Mississippi
GAL	Galena, Alaska	GYM	Guaymas, Mexico
GAM	Gambell, Alaska		
GAO	Guantanamo, Cuba	HAV	Havana, Cuba
GBD	Great Bend, Kansas	HAY	Haycock, Alaska
GBG	Galesburg, Illinois	HCR	Holy Cross, Alaska
GBJ	Marie Galante, Fr. Antilles	HDN	Steamboat Springs, Colorado
GCC	Gillette, Wyoming	HES	Hermiston, Oregon
GCK	Garden City, Kansas	HEX	Santo Domingo, Domingo Republic-
GCM	Grand Cayman, West Indies		Herrera
GCN	Grand Canyon, Arizona	HEZ	Natchez, Mississippi
GDL	Guadalajara, Mexico	HGR	Hagerstown, Maryland
GDT	Grand Turk, B. W. I.	HHH	Hilton Head Island, South
GDV	Glendrive, Montana		Carolina
GED	Georgetown, Delaware	HIB	Hibbing, Minnesota
GEG	Spokane, Washington	HKP	Kaanapali, Maui; Hawaii
GER	Nueva Gerona, Cuba	HKY	Hickory, North Carolina
GFK	Grand Forks, North Dakota	HLG	Wheeling, West Virginia
GFL	Glens Falls, New York	HLN	Helena, Montana
GGG	Longview, Texas	HMC	Hermosillo, Mexico

HNC	Hatteras, North Carolina	ISM	Orlando, Florida-Kissimmee Airport
HNH	Hoonah, Alaska		
HNL	Honolulu, Oahu; Hawaii	ISN	Williston, North Dakota
HNM	Hana, Maui; Hawaii	ISO	Kinston, South Carolina
HNS	Haines, Alaska	ISP	Islip, New York
HOB	Hobbs, New Mexico	ISS	Wiscasset, Maine
HOG	Holguin, Cuba	ISW	Wisconsin Rapids, Wisconsin
HOM	Homer, Alaska	ITH	Ithaca, New York
HON	Huron, South Dakota	IWD	Ironwood, Michigan
HOT	Hot Springs, Arkansas	IYK	Inyokern, California
HOU	Houston, Texas-Hobby Airport		
HPB	Hooper Bay, Alaska	JAC	Jackson, Wyoming
HPN	White Plains, New York	JAN	Jackson/Vicksburg, Mississippi
HPV	Hanalei, Kauai; Hawaii	JAX	Jacksonville, Florida
HRL	Harlingen, Texas	JBR	Jonesboro, Arkansas
HRO	Harrison, Arkansas	JDA	John Day, Oregon
HSI	Hastings, Nebraska	JEE	Jeremie, Haiti
HSL	Huslia, Alaska	JFK	New York, NY-Kennedy International Airport
HSP	Hot Springs, Virginia		
HSV	Huntsville/Decatur, Alabama	JHW	Jamestown, New York
HTH	Hawthorne, Nevada	JLN	Joplin, Montana
HTC	East Hampton, New York	JMS	Jamestown, North Dakota
HTS	Huntington, West Virginia	JNU	Juneau, Alaska
HUC	Humacaco, Puerto Rico	JST	Johnstown, Pennsylvania
HUF	Terre Haute, Indiana	JVL	Beloit/Janesville, Wisconsin
HUM	Houma, Louisiana	JXN	Jackson, Michigan
HUS	Hughes, Alaska		
HUT	Hutchinson, Kansas	KAE	Kake, Alaska
HVN	New Haven, Connecticut	KAL	Kaltag, Alaska
HVR	Havre, Montana	KBC	Birch Creek, Alaska
HYA	Hyannis, Massachusetts	KDK	Kodiak, Alaska
HYG	Hydaburg, Alaska	KEK	Ekwok, Alaska
HYR	Hayward, Wisconsin	KFP	False Pass, Alaska
HYS	Hays, Kansas	KGK	Koliganek, Alaska
		KGX	Grayling, Alaska
IAD	Washington, DC-Dulles Airport	KIN	Kingston, Jamaica
IAH	Houston, Texas	KKA	Koyuk, Alaska
IAN	Kiana, Alaska	KKB	Kitoi, Alaska
ICR	Nicaro, Cuba	KKH	Kongiganak, Alaska
ICT	Wichita, Kansas	KKI	Akiachak, Alaska
IDA	Idaho Falls, Idaho	KKK	Kalakaket Creek, Alaska
IGA	Inagua, Bahamas	KKU	Ekuk, Alaska
IGG	Igiugig, Alaska	KLG	Kalskag, Alaska
IGM	Kingman, Arizona	KLL	Levelock, Alaska
IJX	Jacksonville, Illinois	KLN	Larson Bay, Alaska
IKO	Nikolski, Alaska	KLW	Klawock, Alaska
ILE	Killeen, Texas	KMO	Manokotak, Alaska
ILG	Wilmington, Delaware	KMY	Moser Bay, Alaska
ILI	Iliamna, Alaska	KNB	Kanab, Utah
ILM	Wilmington, North Carolina	KNW	New Stuyahok, Alaska
IMT	Iron Mountain, Michigan	KOA	Kona, Hawaii; Hawaii
IND	Indianapolis, Indiana	KOT	Kotlik, Alaska
INT	Winston Salem, North Carolina	KOY	Olga Bay, Alaska
IPL	El Centro, California	KOZ	Ouzinkie, Alaska
IPT	Williamsport, Pennsylvania	KPK	Parks, Alaska
IRK	Kirksville, Missouri	KPN	Kipnuk, Alaska

KPY	Port Bailey, Alaska		LPO	La Porte, Indiana
KQA	Akutan, Alaska		LPS	Lopez Island, Washington
KSM	St. Mary's Alaska		LRD	Laredo, Texas
KTN	Ketchikan, Alaska		LRU	Las Cruces, New Mexico
KTP	Kingston, Jamaica-Tinson		LSE	La Crosse, Wisconsin
KTY	Terror Bay, Alaska		LSS	Les Saintes, Guadeloupe
KVC	King Cove, Alaska		LTC	Loreto, Mexico
KVL	Kivalina, Alaska		LUP	Kalaupapa, Molokai; Hawaii
KWK	Kwigillingok, Alaska		LUR	Cape Lisburne, Alaska
KWN	Kwinghagak, Alaska		LWB	Greenbrier, West Virginia
KWP	West Point, Alaska		LWC	Lawrence, Kansas
KWT	Kwethluk, Alaska		LWL	Wells, Nevada
KYK	Karluk, Alaska		LWS	Lewiston, Idaho
KYU	Koyukuk, Alaska		LWT	Lewistown, Montana
KZE	Zachar Bay, Alaska		LXN	Lexington, Nebraska
			LXV	Leadville, Colorado
LAA	Lamar, Colorado			
LAF	Lafayette, Indiana		MAF	Midland/Odessa, Texas
LAK	Aklavik, N.W.T., Canada		MAM	Matamoros, Mexico
LAM	Lake Minchumina, Alaska		MAW	Malden, Montana
LAN	Lansing, Michigan		MAY	Mangrove Cay, Bahamas
LAP	La Paz, Mexico		MAZ	Mayaguez, Puerto Rico
LAR	Laramie, Wyoming		MBJ	Montego Bay, Jamaica
LAS	Las Vegas, Nevada		MBL	Manistee, Michigan
LAW	Lawton, Oklahoma		MBS	Saginaw, Michigan
LAX	Los Angeles, California		MCE	Merced, California
LBB	Lubbock, Texas		MCG	Mc Grath, Alaska
LBE	Latrobe, Pennsylvania		MCI	Kansas City, Montana
LBF	North Platte, Nebraska		MCK	Mc Cook, Nebraska
LBL	Liberal, Kansas		MCL	Mc Kinley National Park, Alaska
LCH	Lake Charles, Louisiana		MCN	Macon, Georgia
LCI	Laconia, New Hampshire		MCO	Orlando, Florida
LEB	Lebanon, New Hampshire		MCW	Mason City, Iowa
LEN	Leon, Mexico		MDH	Carondale, Illinois
LEW	Lewiston, Maine		MDJ	Madras, Oregon
LEX	Lexington/Frankfort, Kentucky		MDR	Medfra, Alaska
LFK	Lufkin, Texas		MDS	Middle Caicos, B.W.I.
LFT	Lafayette, Louisiana		MDT	Harrisburg, Pennsylvania
LGA	New York, NY-La Guardia Airport		MDW	Chicago, Illinois-Midway Airport
LGB	Long Beach, California		MEI	Meridian, Mississippi
LGD	La Grande, Oregon		MEM	Memphis, Tennessee
LGI	Deadman's Cay, L.I., Bahamas		MEO	Manteo, North Carolina
LGU	Logan, Utah		MEX	Mexico City, Mexico
LIIU	Lake Ilavasu City, Arizona		MFD	Mansfield, Ohio
LIH	Lihue, Kauai; Hawaii		MFE	Mc Allen, Texas
LIT	Little Rock, Arkansas		MFI	Marshfield, Wisconsin
LJN	Lake Jackson, Texas		MFR	Medford, Oregon
LKE	Seattle, Washington-Lake Union		MGC	Michigan City, Indiana
LKV	Lakeview, Oregon		MGM	Montgomery, Alabama
LMT	Klamath Falls, Oregon		MGR	Moultrie/Thomasville, Georgia
LNK	Lincoln, Nebraska		MGW	Morgantown, West Virginia
LNP	Wise, Virginia		MHE	Mitchell, South Dakota
LNS	Lancaster, Pennsylvania		MHH	Marsh Harbour, Bahamas
LNY	Lanai City, Lanai; Hawaii		MHK	Manhattan, Kansas
LOL	Lovelock, Nevada		MHT	Manchester, New Hampshire
LOZ	London, Kentucky		MHV	Mojave, California

MIA	Miami, Florida	MWA	Marion, Illinois
MID	Merida, Mexico	MWH	Moses Lake, Washington
MIE	Muncie, Indiana	MXC	Monticello, Utah
MIV	Millville, New Jersey	MXL	Mexicali, Mexico
MKC	Kansas City, Missouri-Kansas City Airport	MYG	Mayaguana, Bahamas
		MYR	Myrtle Beach, South Carolina
MKE	Milwaukee, Wisconsin	MYU	Mekoryuk, Alaska
MKG	Muskegon, Michigan	MZO	Manzanillo, Cuba
MKK	Molokai/Kaunakakai, Hawaii	MZT	Mazatlan, Mexico
MKL	Jackson, Tennessee		
MKT	Mankato, Minnesota	NAS	Nassau, Bahamas
MLB	Melbourne, Florida	NCA	North Caicos, B.W.I.
MLC	Mc Alester, Oklahoma	NEG	Negril, Jamaica
MLF	Milford, Utah	NEV	Nevis, Leeward Island
MLI	Moline, Illinois	NEW	New Orleans, La-Lakefront Airport
MLS	Miles City, Montana		
MLU	Monroe, Louisiana	NGD	Anegada, British Virgin Islands
MLY	Manley Hot Springs, Alaska	NLD	Nuevo Laredo, Mexico
MMH	Mammoth Lakes, California	LMC	Norman's Cay, Bahamas
MML	Marshall, Minnesota	NOT	Novato, California
MNI	Montserrat, Montserrat	NPT	Newport, Rhode Island
MNM	Menominee, Michigan	NSB	Bimini, Bahamas-North Seaplane Base
MNT	Minto, Alaska		
MNZ	Manassas, Virginia	NUL	Nulato, Alaska
MOA	Moa, Cuba	NUP	Nunapitchuk, Alaska
MOB	Mobile Al/Pascagoula, Mississippi	NYC	New York City, New York/Newark, New Jersey
MOD	Modesto, California		
MOT	Minot, North Dakota		
MOU	Mountain Village, Alaska	OAJ	Jacksonville, North Carolina
MPV	Montpelier, Vermont	OAK	San Francisco, California-Oakland Airport
MQB	Macomb, Illinois		
MQT	Marquette, Michigan	OAX	Oaxaca, Mexico
MRK	Marco Island, Florida	OBU	Kobuk, Alaska
MRY	Monterey, California	OCE	Ocean City, Maryland
MSL	Muscle Shoals, Alabama	OCH	Nacogdoches, Texas
MSN	Madison, Wisconsin	OCJ	Ocho Rios, Jamaica
MSO	Missoula, Montana	ODM	Oakland, Maryland
MSP	Minneapolis/St. Paul, Minnesota	ODW	Oak Harbor, Washington
MSS	Massena, New York	OFK	Norfolk, Nebraska
MSV	Catskill Mts./Sullivan Co., New York	OGA	Ogallala, Nebraska
		OGG	Kahului, Maui; Hawaii
MSY	New Orleans, Louisiana	OGS	Ogdensburg, New York
MTH	Marathon, Florida	OHG	Oghsenokale, Alaska
MTJ	Montrose, Colorado	OKC	Oklahoma City, Oklahoma
MTO	Mattoon, Illinois	OKK	Kokomo, Indiana
MTP	Montauk Point, New York	OLF	Wolf Point, Montana
MTT	Minatitlan, Mexico	OLH	Old Harbor, Alaska
MTW	Manitowoc, Wisconsin	OLM	Olympia, Washington
MTX	Fairbanks, Alaska-Metro Field	OLU	Columbus, Nebraska
MTY	Monterrey, Mexico	OMA	Omaha, Nebraska
MUE	Kamuela, Hawaii; Hawaii	OME	Nome, Alaska
MUG	Mulege, Mexico	ONA	Winona, Minnesota
MVJ	Mandeville, Jamaica	ONH	Oneonta, New York
MVN	Mount Vernon, Illinois	ONO	Ontario, Oregon
MVW	Mount Vernon, Washington	ONT	Ontario, California
MVY	Martha's Vineyard, Massachusetts	OOK	Toksook, Alaska

ORD	Chicago, Illinois-Ohare Airport	POS	Port of Spain, Trin. & Tob.
ORF	Norfolk, Virginia	POT	Port Antonio, Jamaica
ORH	Worcester, Massachusetts	POU	Poughkeepsie, New York
ORI	Port Lions, Alaska	POY	Powell, Wyoming
ORT	Northway, Alaska	PPD	Humacao, Puerto Rico-Palmas Del Mar
ORV	Noorvik, Alaska		
OSB	Osage Beach, Missouri	PPF	Parsons, Kansas
OSC	Oscoda, Michigan	PQI	Presque Isle, Maine
OSH	Oshkosh, Wisconsin	PQS	Pilot Station, Alaska
OTH	North Bend, Oregon	PRB	Paso Robles, California
OTM	Ottumwa, Iowa	PRC	Prescott, Arizona
OTZ	Kotzebue, Alaska	PRX	Paris, Texas
OWB	Owensboro, Kentucky	PSB	Philipsburg, Pennsylvania
OXR	Oxnard, California	PSC	Pasco, Washington
OYS	Yosemite National Park, California	PSE	Ponce, Puerto Rico
		PSF	Pittsfield, Massachusetts
PAH	Paducah, Kentucky	PSG	Petersburg, Alaska
PAP	Port Au Prince, Haiti	PSP	Palm Springs, California
PBF	Pine Bluff, Arkansas	PTH	Port Heiden, Alaska
PBI	West Palm Beach, Florida	PTN	Morgan City/Patterson, Louisiana
PCT	Princeton, New Jersey	PTP	Pointe A Pitre, Guadeloupe
PDT	Pendleton, Oregon	PTU	Platinum, Alaska
PDX	Portland, Oregon	PUB	Pueblo, Colorado
PEC	Pelican, Alaska	PUC	Price, Utah
PFN	Panama City, Florida	PUO	Prudhoe Bay/Sag Riv., Alaska
PGA	Page, Arizona	PUW	Pullman, Washington
PGD	Punta Gorda, Florida	PVC	Provincetown, Massachusetts
PGV	Greenville, North Carolina	PVD	Providence, Rhode Island
PHF	Newport News, Virginia	PVR	Puerto Vallarta, Mexico
PHL	Philadelphia Pennsylvania/ Wilm'ton, Delaware	PWM	Portland, Maine
		PWT	Bremerton, Washington
PHO	Point Hope, Alaska	PXL	Polacca, Arizona
PHX	Phoenix, Arizona		
PIA	Peoria, Illinois	QBC	Bella Coola, B.C., Canada
PIB	Laurel/Hattiesburg, Mississippi		
PIC	Pine Cay, B.W.I.	RAD	Tortola, Br. Virgin Islands-Road Town Airport
PIE	St. Petersburg, Florida		
PIH	Pocatello, Idaho	RAL	Riverside, California
PIP	Pilot Point, Alaska	RAP	Rapid City, South Dakota
PIR	Pierre, South Dakota	RBG	Roseburg, Oregon
PIT	Pittsburgh, Pennsylvania	RBY	Ruby, Alaska
PKA	Napaskiak, Alaska	RDD	Redding, California
PKB	Parkersburg, West Virginia	RDG	Reading, Pennsylvania
PLB	Plattsburgh, New York	RDM	Redmond, Oregon
PLN	Pellston, Michigan	RDU	Raleigh/Durham, North Carolina
PLS	Providenciales, West Indies	RDV	Red Devil, Alaska
PMD	Palmdale, California	RED	Reedsville, Pennsylvania
PML	Port Moller, Alaska	REX	Reynosa, Mexico
PNC	Ponca City, Oklahoma	RFD	Rockford, Illinois
PNE	Philadelphia, Pennsylvania-North Philadelphia	RHI	Rhinelander, Wisconsin
		RIC	Richmond, Virginia
PNS	Pensacola, Florida	RIF	Richfield, Utah
POE	Fort Polk, Louisiana	RIW	Riverton, Wyoming
POF	Poplar Bluff, Missouri	RKD	Rockland, Maine
POH	Pocahontas, Iowa	RKS	Rock Springs, Wyoming
POP	Puerto Plata, Dominican Republic	RLA	Rolla, Missouri

RLD	Richland, Washington	SJC	San Jose, California
RLU	Bornite, Alaska	SJD	San Jose Del Cabo, Mexico
RMP	Rampart, Alaska	SJF	St. John, Virgin Islands
RNO	Reno, Nevada	SJM	San Juan De La M., Dominican Republic
ROA	Roanoke, Virginia		
ROC	Rochester, New York	SJT	San Angelo, Texas
ROL	Roosevelt, Utah	SJU	San Juan, Puerto Rico
ROW	Roswell, New Mexico	SKB	St. Kitts, Leeward Island
RSD	Rock Sound, Bahamas	SKJ	Sitkinak, Alaska
RSH	Russian Mission, Alaska	SKK	Shaktoolik, Alaska
RST	Rochester, Minnesota	SKW	Skwentna, Alaska
RUI	Ruidoso, New Mexico	SLC	Salt Lake City, Utah
RUT	Rutland, Vermont	SLE	Salem, Oregon
RWI	Rocky Mount, North Carolina	SLK	Saranac Lake, New York
RWL	Rawlins, Wyoming	SLN	Salina, Kansas
		SLQ	Sleetmute, Alaska
SAA	Saratoga, Wyoming	SLT	Salida, Colorado
SAB	Saba, Neth. Antilles	SLU	St. Lucia, West Indies
SAF	Santa Fe, New Mexico	SLX	Salt Cay, British West Indies
SAN	San Diego, California	SMF	Sacramento, California
SAQ	San Andros, Bahamas	SMK	St. Michael, Alaska
SAT	San Antonio, Texas	SML	Stella Maris, L.I., Bahamas
SAV	Savannah, Georgia	SMX	Santa Maria, California
SBA	Santa Barbara, California	SNA	Orange County, California
SBH	St. Barthelemy, Leeward Island	SNP	St. Paul Island, Alaska
SBM	Sheboygan, Wisconsin	SNU	Santa Clara, Cuba
SBN	South Bend, Indiana	SNY	Sidney, Nebraska
SBP	San Luis Obispo, California	SOL	Solomon, Alaska
SBS	Steamboat Springs, Colorado- Steamboat Springs	SOP	Pinehurst, North Carolina
		SPA	Greenville/Spartanburg-Dwtn Memphis Airport
SBY	Salisbury, Maryland		
SCE	State College, Pennsylvania	SPB	St. Thomas, Virgin Islands- Seaplane Base
SCK	Stockton, California		
SCM	Scammon Bay, Alaska	SPI	Springfield, Illinois
SCU	Santiago, Cuba	SPQ	San Pedro, California
SDF	Louisville, Kentucky	SPS	Wichita Falls, Texas
SDP	Sand Point, Alaska	SPW	Spencer, Iowa
SDQ	Santo Domingo, Dominican Republic	SQI	Sterling/Rock Falls, Illinois
SDY	Sidney, Montana	SRQ	Sarasota/Bradenton, Florida
SEA	Seattle/Tacoma, Washington	SRV	Stony River, Alaska
SFG	St. Maarten, Neth. Ant.- Esperance	SSB	St. Croix, Virgin Islands- Seaplane Base
SFD	San Francisco/Oakland, California	SSI	St. Simons Island, Georgia
SGF	Springfield, Missouri	SSM	Sault Ste. Marie, Michigan
SGU	St. George, Utah	STE	Stevens Point, Wisconsin
SGW	Saginaw, Alaska	STI	Santiago, Dominican Republic
SGY	Skagway, Alaska	STK	Sterling, Colorado
SHD	Staunton, Virginia	STL	St. Louis, Missouri
SHG	Shungnak, Alaska	STS	Santa Rosa, California
SHH	Shishmaref, Alaska	STT	St. Thomas, Virgin Islands
SHR	Sheridan, Wyoming	STX	St. Croix, Virgin Islands
SHV	Shreveport, Louisiana	SUE	Sturgeon Bay, Wisconsin
SHX	Shageluk, Alaska	SUM	Sumter, South Carolina
SIG	San Juan, Puerto Rico-Isla Grande Airport	SUN	Sun Valley, Idaho
		SUS	St. Louis, Missouri-Spirit of St. Louis
SIT	Sitka, Alaska		

SUX	Sioux City, Iowa
SVA	Savoonga, Alaska
SVC	Silver City, New Mexico
SVD	St. Vincent, Windward Island
SVS	Stevens Village, Alaska
SWD	Seward, Alaska
SXM	St. Maarten, Neth. Antilles
SXP	Sheldon Point, Alaska
SXQ	Soldotna, Alaska
SXY	Sidney, New York
SYA	Shemya Island, Alaska
SYB	Seal Bay, Alaska
SYR	Syracuse, New York
TAB	Tobago, Trinidad & Tobago
TAL	Tanana, Alaska
TAM	Tampico, Mexico
TAP	Tapachula, Mexico
TBI	The Bight, Bahamas
TBN	Ft. Leonard Wood, Maryland
TCB	Treasure Cay, Bahamas
TCL	Tuscaloosa, Alabama
TCT	Takotna, Alaska
TEK	Tatitlek, Alaska
TGE	Tuskegee, Alabama
TGZ	Tuxtla Gutierrez, Mexico
TIJ	Tijuana, Mexico
TKA	Talkeetna, Alaska
TKE	Tenakee, Alaska
TKJ	Tok, Alaska
TLA	Teller, Alaska
TLH	Tallahassee, Florida
TLT	Tuluksak, Alaska
TNC	Tin City, Alaska
TNK	Tununak, Alaska
TOG	Togiak, Alaska
TOL	Toledo, Ohio
TOV	Tortola, British Virgin Islands-West End Spb
TPA	Tampa, Florida
TPH	Tonopah, Nevada
TPL	Temple, Texas
TRC	Torreon, Mexico
TRI	Tri-City Airport, Tennessee
TTN	Trenton, New Jersey
TUL	Tulsa, Oklahoma
TUP	Tupelo, Mississippi
TUS	Tucson, Arizona
TVC	Traverse City, Michigan
TVF	Thief River Falls, Minnesota
TVL	Lake Tahoe, California
TWF	Twin Falls, Idaho
TWH	Catalina Island, California
TXK	Texarkana, Arkansas
TYR	Tyler, Texas
TYS	Knoxville, Tennessee

TZN	South Andros, Bahamas
UCA	Utica, New York
UGI	Uganik, Alaska
UIN	Quincy, Illinois
UKI	Ukiah, California
ULM	New Ulm, Minnesota
UNK	Unalakleet, Alaska
UOX	University, Mississippi
UPP	Upolu Point, Hawaii; Hawaii
UTO	Utopia Creek, Alaska
UVF	St. Lucia, West Indies-Hewanorra Airport
VAK	Chevak, Alaska
VCT	Victoria, Texas
VDZ	Valdez, Alaska
VEE	Venetie, Alaska
VEL	Vernal, Utah
VER	Veracruz, Mexico
VIJ	Virgin Gorda, British Virgin Islands
VIS	Visalia, California
VLD	Valdosta, Georgia
VNY	Los Angeles, Ca-Van Nuys Airport
VPS	Eglin Air Force Base, Florida
VPZ	Valparaiso, Indiana
VQS	Vieques, Puerto Rico
VSA	Villahermosa, Mexico
VSF	Springfield, Vermont
WAA	Wales, Alaska
WAS	Washington, D.C.
WBB	Stebbins, Alaska
WBI	Boulder, Colorado-Broker Inn
WBQ	Beaver, Alaska
WBU	Boulder, Colorado
WCD	Roche Harbor, Washington
WCR	Chandalar, Alaska
WDG	Enid, Oklahoma
WGS	Los Alamos, New Mexico
WHH	Boulder, Colorado-Hiltons Harvest House
WJA	Hanna, Wyoming
WKK	Aleknagik, Alaska
WLK	Selwakik, Alaska
WMC	Winnemucca, Nevada
WMO	White Mountain, Alaska
WNA	Napakiak, Alaska
WOV	Madawaska/Fort Kent, Maine
WOZ	Mountain Home, Arkansas
WPC	Pincher Creek, Alberta, Canada
WPO	Paonia, Colorado
WRG	Wrangell, Alaska
WRL	Worland, Wyoming

WSG	Washington, Pennsylvania	YGK	Kingston, Ontario, Canada
WSH	Shirley, New York	YGL	La Grande, Quebec, Canada
WSM	Wiseman, Alaska	YGO	Gods Narrows, Man., Canada
WSN	South Naknek, Alaska	YGP	Gaspe, Quebec, Canada
WST	Westerly, Rhode Island	YGR	Iles De Madeleine, Que., Canada
WTC	New York, New York World Trade Center	YGW	Great Whale, Quebec, Canada
		YGX	Gillam, Man., Canada
WTK	Noatak, Alaska	YHC	Victoria, BC Can-Vic, Inner Harb Spb
WTL	Tuntatuliak, Alaska		
WVL	Waterville, Maine	YHD	Dryden, Ontario, Canada
WWD	Cape May, New Jersey	YHM	Hamilton, Ontario, Canada
WWT	Newtok, Alaska	YHR	Harrington Harbour, Que., Canada
WYS	West Yellowstone, Montana	YHY	Hay River, N.W.T., Canada
WZY	Nassau, Bahamas-Seaplane Base	YHZ	Halifax, N.S., Canada
		YIB	Atikokan, Ontario, Canada
XAL	Alamos, Mexico	YIF	St. Augustin, Quebec, Canada
XCC	Cochrane, Ontario, Canada	YIK	Ivugivik, Quebec, Canada
XSC	South Caicos, British West Indies	YJT	Stephenville, Nfld., Canada
XSM	St. Mary's, Maryland	YKA	Kamloops, B.C., Canada
		YKL	Schefferville, Quebec, Canada
YAF	Asbestos Hill, Que., Canada	YKM	Yakima, Washington
YAG	Fort Frances, Ont., Canada	YKN	Yankton, South Dakota
YAK	Yakutat, Alaska	YKQ	Rupert House, Quebec, Canada
YAM	Sault Ste. Marie, Ont., Canada	YKU	Fort George, Quebec, Canada
YAT	Attawapiskat, Ont., Canada	YKX	Kirkland Lake, Ont., Canada
YAZ	Tofino, B.C., Canada	YLD	Chapleau, Ontario, Canada
YBC	Baie Comeau, Que., Canada	YLP	Mingan, Quebec, Canada
YBE	Uranium City, Sask., Canada	YLW	Kelowna, B.C., Canada
YBG	Saguenay, Que., Canada	YMA	Mayo, Y.T., Canada
YBJ	Baie Johan Beetz, Que., Canada	YML	Murray Bay, Quebec, Canada
YBK	Baker Lake, N.W.T., Canada	YMM	Ft. McMurray, Alta., Canada
YBL	Campbell River, B.C., Canada	YMO	Moosonee, Ontario, Canada
YBV	Berens River, Man., Canada	YMT	Chibougamau, Quebec, Canada
YBX	Blanc Sablon, Que., Canada	YMX	Montreal, Que.-Mirabel Int'l Airport
YCB	Cambridge Bay, N.W.T., Canada		
YCD	Nanaimo, B.C., Canada	YNA	Natashquan, Quebec, Canada
YCG	Castlegar, B.C., Canada	YNC	Paint Hills, Quebec, Canada
YCH	Chatham, N.B., Canada	YNE	Norway House, Man., Canada
YCL	Charlo, N.B., Canada	YNG	Youngstown, Ohio
YCR	Cross Lake, Man., Canada	YNM	Matagami, Quebec, Canada
YDA	Dawson City, Y.T., Canada	YOH	Oxford House, Man., Canada
YDF	Deer Lake, NFLD., Canada	YOJ	High Level, Alberta, Canada
YDQ	Dawson Creek, B.C., Canada	YOW	Ottawa, Ontario, Canada
YEG	Edmonton, Alta-Int'l Airport, Canada	YPA	Prince Albert, Sask., Canada
		YPE	Peace River, Alta., Canada
YEK	Eskimo Point, N.W.T., Canada	YPH	Port Harrison, Que., Canada
YEL	Elliot Lake, Ontario	YPL	Pickle Lake, Ontario, Canada
YEV	Inuvik, N.W.T., Canada	YPN	Port Menier, Quebec, Canada
YFA	Fort Albany, Ontario	YPQ	Peterborough, Ont., Canada
YFB	Frobisher Bay, N.W.T., Canada	YPR	Prince Rupert, B.C., Canada
YFC	Fredericton, N.B., Canada	YPW	Powerll River, B.C., Canada
YFO	Flin Flon, Man., Canada	YPX	Povungnituk, Quebec, Canada
YFS	Ft. Simpson, N.W.T., Canada	YPY	Ft. Chipewyan, Alta., Canada
YGA	Gagnon, Quebec, Canada	YQB	Quebec, Que., Canada
YGB	Gillies Bay, B.C., Canada	YQD	The Pas, Man., Canada
YGH	Ft. Good Hope, N.W.T., Canada	YQF	Red Deer, Alta., Canada

YQG	Windsor, Ontario, Canada
YQH	Watson Lake, Y.T., Canada
YQI	Yarmouth, N.S., Canada
YQK	Kenora, Ontario, Canada
YQL	Lethbridge, Alta., Canada
YQM	Moncton, N.B., Canada
YQQ	Comox, B.C., Canada
YQR	Regina, Sask., Canada
YQT	Thunder Bay, Ont., Canada
YQU	Grande Prairie, Alberta, Canada
YQX	Gander, Nfld., Canada
YQY	Sydney, N.S., Canada
YQZ	Quesnel, B.C., Canada
YRB	Resolute, N.W.T., Canada
YRI	Riviere Du Loup, Que., Canada
YRJ	Roberval, Que., Canada
YRL	Red Lake, Ontario, Canada
YRS	Red Sucker Lake, Man., Canada
YRT	Rankin Inlet, N.W.T., Canada
YSB	Sudbury, Ontario, Canada
YSC	Sherbrooke, Que., Canada
YSF	Stoney Rapids, Sask., Canada
YSJ	Saint John, N.B., Canada
YSK	Sanikluaq, N.W.T., Canada
YSM	Ft. Smith, N.W.T., Canada
YSR	Strathcona Sound, N.W.T., Canada
YTA	Pembroke, Ontario, Canada
YTE	Cape Dorset, N.W.T., Canada
YTH	Thompson, Man., Canada
YTS	Timmins, Ontario, Canada
YTZ	Toronto, Ont., Can-Toronto Island Airport
YUB	Tuktoyaktuk, N.W.T., Canada
YUL	Montreal, Que., Canada
YUM	Yuma, Arizona
YUX	Hall Beach, N.W.T., Canada
YUY	Rouyn - Noranda, Que., Canada
YVB	Bonaventure, Que., Canada
YVC	Lac La Ronge, Sask., Canada
YVO	Val D'or, Que., Canada
YVQ	Norman Wells, N.W.T., Canada
YVR	Vancouver, B.C., Canada
YWG	Winnipeg, Man., Canada
YWJ	Fort Franklin, N.W.T., Canada
YWK	Wabush, Nfld., Canada
YWL	Williams Lake, B.C., Canada
YWN	Winisk, Ontario, Canada
YXC	Cranbrook, B.C., Canada
YXD	Edmonton, Alta., Canada
YXE	Saskatoon, Sask., Canada
YXH	Medicine Hat, Alta., Canada
YXJ	Ft. St. John, B.C., Canada
YXR	Earlton, Ontario, Canada
YXS	Prince George, B.C., Canada
YXT	Terrace, B.C., Canada
YXU	London, Ontarior, Canada

YXY	Whitehorse, Y.T., Canada
YXZ	Wawa, Ontario, Canada
YYB	North Bay, Ontario, Canada
YYC	Calgary, Alta., Canada
YYD	Smithers, B.C., Canada
YYE	Ft. Nelson, B.C., Canada
YYF	Penticton, B.C., Canada
YYG	Charlottetown, P.E.I., Canada
YYJ	Victoria, B.C., Canada
YYL	Lynn Lake, Man., Canada
YYQ	Churchill, Man., Canada
YYR	Goose Bay, Nfld., Canada
YYT	St. Johns, Nfld., Canada
YYU	Kapuskasing, Ont., Canada
YYY	Mont Joli, Que., Canada
YYZ	Toronto, Ont., Canada
YZF	Yellowknife, N.W.T., Canada
YZG	Sugluk, Quebec, Canada
YZP	Sandspit, B.C., Canada
YZR	Sarnia, Ontario, Canada
YZS	Coral Harbour, N.W.T., Canada
YZT	Port Hardy, B.C., Canada
YZV	Seven Islands, Que., Canada
ZAA	Alice Arm, B.C., Canada
ZEL	Bella Bella, B.C., Canada
ZEM	East Main, Quebec, Canada
ZFB	Old Fort Bay, Que., Canada
ZFM	Ft. McPherson, N.W.T., Canada
ZFN	Ft. Norman, N.W.T., Canada
ZGF	Grand Forks, B.C., Canada
ZGI	Gods River, Man., Canada
ZGR	Little Grand Rapids, Man., Canada
ZGS	Gethsemani, Que., Canada
ZIH	Zihuatanejo, Mexico
ZKE	Kaschechewan, Ontario, Canada
ZKG	Kegaska, Quebec, Canada
ZLO	Manzanillo, Mexico
ZLT	La Tabatiere, Que., Canada
ZMT	Masset, B.C., Canada
ZNA	Nanaimo, B.C.-Harbour Airport
ZNU	Namu, B.C., Canada
ZOF	Ocean Falls, B.C., Canada
ZSA	San Salvador, Bahamas
ZSP	St. Paul, Que., Canada
ZST	Stewart, B.C., Canada
ZSW	Prince Rupert, B.C.-Seal Cove
ZTB	Tete A La Baleine, Que., Canada
ZTS	Tahsis, B.C., Canada
ZUM	Churchill Falls, Nfld., Canada
ZWL	Wollaston Lake, Sask., Canada

Appendix D

DEFINITIONS AND ABBREVIATIONS

Travel is a systematized process employing the many elements of transportation in logical sequence in a purposeful manner and means movements in a geographically planned pattern. A brief glossary of travel terms should enhance communication and understanding of the industry.

A means a superior class under which boats are registered at Lloyds.

ABOARD means same as on board and used instead of on or in a boat or ship.

ABOUT means when the ship turns around.

ABSORPTION means the difference between a regular and a lesser fare received caused by a joint rate.

ABOVE BOARD means deck above the water line.

ADD-ON or ARBITRARY means fares published for use in combination with other air fares for the construction of through fares.

ADJOINING ROOMS means two or more hotel rooms located next to each other; the rooms may be adjoining with connecting doors.

ADVANCE PURCHASE EXCURSION means the APEX or Super-Apex fares, are heavily discounted excursion fares which require booking and ticketing well in advance of departure. There is a penalty for cancellation after tickets have been purchased. No land arrangements are required.

ADVERTISED TOUR means a tour meeting the airline requirements for an inclusive tour number. This tour is printed in a brochure.

AFFINITY CHARTER means the rental of an airplane, train, steamship, bus or sightseeing vehicle on an exclusive basis for the carriage of a common interest group (affinity) with the renter paying a flat over-all rental for the entire vehicle.

AFFINITY GROUP means a group travelling together that has been formed for purposes other than travel.

AFT means near, toward or in the stern.

AIRLINE CODES means system of abbreviations for airlines, airports, or fares used by airlines and travel agents throughout the world.

AIRPORT TAXES means airport service and user charges are levied by local authorities in certain international cities and islands. Where levied, they are collected at the airport from each departing passenger.

AIR-SEA means a cruise or travel program in which one or more transportation legs are provided by air and one or more by sea, including hotel arrangements.

AIR-TAXI means an aircraft carrying up to 19 passengers and operating under less restrictive CAB regulations than scheduled or supplemental carriers, usually with a 250-mile radius.

AIR TRAFFIC CONFERENCE means a domestic agency which establishes standards and other airline business practices; concerned with policy and procedural matters as they pertain to approval of projected fare requests and tour basing problems, as well as the connection of the travel agent with the air industry. A.T.C. enters the rate and tariff problem areas; approves agencies to hold and sell tickets; and is concerned with <u>domestic</u> carriers.

AIR TRAFFIC CONFERENCE AREAS means IATA divisions of the world for rate and rule-making purposes. Area One: North and South America are adjacent islands; Greenland, Bermuda, West Indies and Caribbean Islands, Hawaiian Islands, Midway, and Palmyra. Area Two: Europe (including USSR west of the Ural Mountains) and adjacent islands, Iceland, Azores, Africa and adjacent islands, Ascension Island, Middle East. Area Three: Asia and adjacent islands, except parts included in Area Two, East Indies, Australia, New Zealand and adjacent islands, Pacific Ocean islands except those included in Area One.

A LA CARTE means restaurant or hotel dining room menu on which each item or course is selected and priced separately.

ALL EXPENSE TOUR means a tour that covers almost all expenses and refers to the terms and conditions of the tour contract included in prepaid tour arrangements.

AMERICAN BREAKFAST means full breakfast including juice or fruit, eggs or other entree, bread and butter, coffee or tea.

AMERICAN SOCIETY OF TRAVEL AGENTS means a professional association, of retail agents (with some wholesalers) which recommends ethical standards in the travel industry. ASTA is a national group which meets annually in a different place and which has regional and local branch associations.

AMTRAK means the National Railroad Passenger Corporation, which operates almost all U.S. passenger trains under contract with individual railroads.

ASHORE means on the ground after or before the ship sails.

AVAILABILITY means a conditional status, e.g., space available.

BACK-TO-BACK means a program of multiple air charters with arrivals and departures coordinated to eliminate deadheading or waiting, i.e., when one group is delivered, another is ready to depart from that airport.

BAGGAGE ALLOWANCE means the volume or weight of baggage that may be carried by a passenger without an additional charge.

BAGGAGE CHECK means stub or claim receipt with a baggage identification number.

BAREBOAT CHARTER means a rental yacht without crew or supplies.

BASING POINT means a point, to and from which fares are established and is used in constructing air fares between other points.

BEAM means the breadth of the ship at its widest point.

BED AND BREAKFAST means a room and English or Continental breakfast; used throughout the United Kingdom and Europe.

BERTH means a bunk in a cabin, or the ship's place at anchor or dock.

BOARD means to go on the ship.

BOARDING PASS means printed pass issued at the check-in or boarding counter when your ticket coupon is taken, giving your flight and seat number.

BONDING means the purchase, for a premium, of a guarantee of protection for a supplier or a customer; in the travel industry certain bonding programs are mandatory. ATC insists that travel agents be bonded to protect the airlines against defaults; the CAB forces the operators of inclusive tour charters to carry bonds to protect their customers against default.

BOOKING means making reservations for a flight. When your reservations are confirmed, you are "booked" on that flight.

BOOKING FORM means a document for purchasers of tours in order to give the operator full particulars about who is buying the tour, including the acknowledgment of the liability clause.

BOW means the front of the ship, or the sides of the forward part of a boat.

BOW THRUSTER means an underwater extension to the bow of a ship designed to reduce pitch.

BRITISH PASS means railroad pass for visitors to the U.K.; offers unlimited Second or First Class transportation (reservations and sleeping facilities extra) for specified numbers of days.

BUMP means to displace a passenger by virtue of holding a reservation with a higher priority (a regular fare passenger will bump a standby passenger).

CHART means a map of the sea.

CHARTER FLIGHT means a journey with stopovers that return to the point of departure without retracing its route.

CHILD means child rates, for air travel, include anyone from 2 to 11 years of age, except in Australia, which defines child as anyone from 3 years to 15 years. Child rates are variably defined.

CIRCLE FARE means special fare, lower than the sum of the point-to-point fares for individual segments, of a circle trip.

CIRCLE TRIP means a journey with stopovers that return to the point of departure without retracing its route.

CITY TERMINAL means an airline ticket office, not located at an airport, where a passenger may check-in for a flight, check his baggage, receive his seat assignment and secure ground transportation to the airport.

CIVIL AERONAUTICS BOARD means the Federal air "regulatory body", dealing with domestic route matters (including tariffs) and infractions of rules. Recently "de-regulating" air fares has been a prime function.

CLASS OF SERVICE means the name used to identify different types of service offered to airline passengers; for example, First Class and Coach.

COMMERCIAL RATE means a special rate agreed upon by a company (or other multipurchaser) and a hotel.

COMMISSION means a certain cash percentage paid to the travel agent by various suppliers of goods and services which normally comprise the elements of the travel agent's finished product (itinerary) such as airline, bus, rail, and/or sightseeing tickets, hotel, steamship reservations, auto rentals, guide, and escort services.

COMMON RATED FARE means two or more destinations, usually near each other, for which the fare from one point of origin is the same.

COMPASS means the instrument which determines direction.

CONDUCTED OR ESCORTED TOUR means a prearranged travel program escorted by a courier or a sightseeing program conducted by a guide.

CONEX-ON-LINE-OFF-LINE means (on-line) a connection changing airplanes but using the same airline on both flights. An off-line connection is changing from one airline to another.

CONFERENCE APPOINTMENTS means the granting to an agent (or wholesaler) by air, sea, rail or motor coach carriers, the privilege of acting in the capacity of ticketing agent. Major regulatory agencies such as A.T.C., I.A.T.A., or AMTRAK have appointments.

CONFIGURATION means the arrangement of seats on a vehicle or airplane.

CONJUNCTION TICKETS means when two or more tickets are issued together for one flight itinerary.

CONNECTING SERVICE means service between point of origin and destination on which the passengers change planes at an intermediate or connecting point; also, any flight carrying passengers connecting to another aircraft or airline.

CONSOLIDATED AIR TOUR MANUAL means a trade catalogue of tours.

CONTINENTAL BREAKFAST means a beverage (coffee, tea, or milk) and rolls or toast; sometimes includes fruit juice; and maybe cheese, cold meat or fish.

CONTINENTAL PLAN means a hotel rate that includes bed and continental breakfast.

COURIER means a professional travel escort assigned within one country.

CRANE means a derrick used for raising and lowering heavy weights on board a vessel.

CRUISING ALTITUDE means the altitude at which the aircraft is flown after the climb from takeoff.

CUSTOMS means an official government agency where travellers must declare all foreign-purchased items upon entry to a country.

DEBARK means the abbreviation of disembark which means to land, to go ashore from a ship.

DEMI-PENSIONE means hotel rate that includes breakfast and dinner.

DENIED BOARDING COMPENSATION means the penalty paid to a traveller by an airline that has not honored a confirmed reservation.

DIRECT FLIGHT means a flight which does not require a passenger to change planes, but may have intermediate stops enroute.

DISCOVER AMERICAN TRAVEL ORGANIZATIONS, INC. means a non-profit association of companies and government organizations formed to promote travel to and within the United States.

DOCK means waterspace alongside a pier, where a ship floats while being loaded or unloaded.

DOME CAR means railroad observation car with glass roof on upper deck for sightseeing.

DOMESTIC FLIGHTS means all flights within the U.S.

DOMESTIC INDEPENDENT TOUR means a program of travel that originate and terminates within the continental United States based on individual rates.

DOWN-LINE means all segments of the itinerary after the originating flight.

DRAFT means the depth of water a ship draws.

DUTY FREE means imported goods sold at low prices in countries and islands whose governments do not impose duty or customs charges. Also, goods you bring into the U.S. that fall within your personal merchandise allotment.

EMBARK means to go aboard a ship.

ENGLISH BREAKFAST means generally served in the U.S. and Ireland, and usually includes fruit or fruit juice; hot or cold cereal; bacon, ham, sausages or kippers; eggs; toast; butter; jam or marmalade, and tea or coffee.

ESCROW ACCOUNTS means funds placed in the custody of licensed financial institutions for safe-keeping; inclusive tour charter operators maintain escrow accounts.

EURAILPASS means a railroad pass sold for a flat rate for a specified number of days, and provides unlimited First Class travel through 13 European countries.

EXCESS BAGGAGE means baggage that is over free per-passenger allowance, in bulk or weight, and subject to a surcharge by item or weight.

EXCHANGE ORDER (EXO) means a type of voucher sold to the passenger of a tour which he can surrender for the service prescribed, e.g., sightseeing tour or hotel room. This is sometimes paid for by the passenger with a "miscellaneous charge order" which is sold to him by an airline or travel agency for an entire tour, and which is surrendable to a tour operator (for which he receives the EXO).

EXCURSION means a trip that returns to its starting point.

FAIR WIND means a wind blowing in the same direction the ship is traveling.

FAM TRIP means a reduced rate familiarization tour for travel agents and airline employees designed to stimulate travel to the area visited.

FATHOM means a measure of length containing six feet used chiefly in measuring the depth of water by soundings.

FEEDER LINES means regularly scheduled (usually regional) airlines normally providing service from sparsely populated areas to major cities connecting with trunk carriers.

FOREIGN INDEPENDENT TOUR means a program for a small number of persons (less than 15 persons) based on individual (non-group or non-charter) rates which carries the passengers to a destination outside the continental United States.

GALLEY means the kitchen on board ship.

GANGWAY means portable stairway or ramp used for entering or leaving ship.

GATE means the airport terminal area where you can check in (if you have not checked in at the front ticket counter), board and deplane.

GATEWAY means a key arrival point for a major tour origination.

GROSS REGISTER TON means a measure, not of weight, but of the cubical content of the enclosed spaces on a ship and is the measurement used in giving the size of passenger vessels, e.g., 100 cubic feet equals one gross register ton.

GROUND OPERATOR means a company providing hotel accommodations, sightseeing, transfers, point to point transportation within a given country, state or city.

GROUP means fifteen persons or more, but less than whatever number is qualified to qualify as a CHARTER.

GUARANTEED RESERVATION means a hotel reservation secured by the guest's agreement to pay for his room whether he uses it or not.

HEAD means another name for facilities, it's the toilet.

HOLD means interior of a vessel below decks where cargo is stored.

HOSPITALITY SUITE means a suite set aside at a hotel for the purpose of entertaining a tour or convention group.

HOSTEL means supervised, inexpensive accommodations, usually for young people.

HOTEL means a building which provides the general public with pre-reserved sleeping accommodations, meeting rooms and food and beverage service for a daily, weekly, or monthly rental, per room.

HULL means the body or frame of a ship.

INCENTIVE TRAVEL OPERATOR means an organization which sells travel programs and judges sales competitions (or contests) to and/or for industrial and commercial business concerns for purposes of incentives to the employees. This operator carries out these programs and maintains production and sales records for its clients as well as the counter displays, literature and general promotion of the contest.

INCLUSIVE TOUR (I.T.) means a number designation for a tour identification, by the wholesaler operator with approval of the government regulatory agency.

INCLUSIVE TOUR CHARTER (I.T.C.) means a non-affinity charter with tour program elements in a pre-planned itinerary, including hotel accommodations, sightseeing tours, meals, etc.

INTERLINE means a cooperative relationship and/or reciprocal acceptance of tickets between airlines.

INTERNATIONAL AIR TRANSPORT AUTHORITY (I.A.T.A.) means an agency which regulates fares and other airline business practices for international lines. An association (committee) which acts as a regulatory body, comprised of representative air carriers authorized by Federal governments to fly from and to the U.S.A. over strictly prescribed routes.

INTERSTATE COMMERCE COMMISSION (I.C.C.) means a federal regulatory agency with the power to approve the rights of companies to engage in the crossing of state and city lines via common carrier means, such as motor coach, truck, automobile, for the purpose of transportation of passengers and their baggage or other freight. The I.C.C. approves requested fares and schedules between points, delineates routes and rights, and appoints tour brokers, issuing broker's licenses.

INTOURIST means government travel agency of the USSR.

JET BRIDGE/JETWAY means a covered walkway that goes directly from the terminal boarding area to the airplane.

KEEL means the structure which runs from stem to stern along the bottom center of the vessel.

KNOT means a speed unit equivalent to 1.15 land miles per hour.

LASH means to bind or tie something with ropes.

LATITUDE means the distance north or south of the equator.

LEEWARD means the side facing away from the wind.

LEG/SEGMENT means a portion of a flight. For example, American Flight #80 goes from San Diego to Phoenix to New York. From San Diego to Phoenix is the first leg or segment; Phoenix to New York is the second leg or segment.

LOAD FACTOR means the ratio, expressed as a percentage of carrier capacity sold to total capcity offered for sale, i.e., a 100-seat aircraft carries 75 paying passengers, that flight is operated at a 75% load factor.

LOG means the official daily record of the ship's speed and progress.

LONGITUDE means the distance east or west expressed in degrees of the First Meridian.

MANIFEST means a list of the ship's passengers and cargo which must be supplied in every foreign port.

MINIMUM CONNECTING TIME means the time, separately established for every commercial airport, required to leave one scheduled flight and board another.

MINIMUM LAND PACKAGE means the minimum cost and ingredients of a tour that must be purchased to qualify a passenger for an airline inclusive tour, including certain number of nights lodging, and/or car rental.

MISCELLANEOUS CHARGER ORDER (M C O) is used by the airlines to indicate that the traveller has prepaid for rooms and sightseeing, taxi transfer, meals, or motor coach transportation or other services.

MOTEL means a smaller hotel (under 250 rooms) which usually locates itself "on the fringe" of a city often on a main highway.

NATIONAL TOUR BROKERS ASSOCIATION (N.T.B.A.) means a fraternal organization composed of holders of tour broker's licenses, such as motor coach tour carriers.

NET FARE means a per person or per vehicle rate quoted for a needed service to the agent or wholesaler which is non-commissionable and to which the agent or wholesaler must add a mark-up (gross profit).

NONSTOP means a flight made from one city/airport to another, with no stops en route.

OFFICIAL AIRLINE GUIDE (O.A.G.) means a periodic publication subscribed to by appointed travel agents and contains current air schedules as approved by the air carriers to the conferences.

OPEN-JAW means a round trip itinerary in which the arrival point is different from the departure point, usually has a surface segment.

OPERATOR means one who specializes in the physical carrying out of the produce as prepared by the wholesalers for both the wholesaler and the retail travel agent for profit.

OVER-BOOKING means the sale of more units for a given date and time than the seller actually has vacant and availabe for sale, e.g., rooms and seats.

OVERRIDE means any additional cash percentage which is extraordinary (over ten percent).

OVERSTAY means an additional night(s) spent at a hotel above and beyond the specifically outlined projected stay, usually paid for in cash on departure by the guest.

PACKAGE means a tour including various tour elements as well as accommodations.

PACKET means a small mail boat.

PASSPORT means an official government document that proves identity and citizenship of an individual and gives permission to travel abroad.

PEAK AND OFF-PEAK means the times of day or seasons when certain fares or hotel rates apply.

PENSION means a guest boarding house in Europe; of American hotels and motels, and meals usually taken at communal table and included in room rate.

PORT means the left side of the ship when you are facing forward.

PROMOTIONAL FARE means any tariff below regular levels established to stimulate traffic.

RAIL TRAVEL PROMOTION AGENCY is an assocication of U.S. railroads organized to promote pleasure travel by train. Disbanded since the advent of AMTRAK.

RATE means official rate number given by an airline rate desk.

RECONFIRMATION means a call to the airlines to verify your reservation for a return or continuing flight. Reconfirmation is optional on domestic flights, but is required on international flights at least 72 hours (3 days) in advance of your departure.

REGISTRY means the country in which the ship is registered, or the official nationality of the ship.

REP means a representative of an airline, steamship line, or tour operator.

RESORT HOTEL means an establishment (over 250 rooms but less than 600 rooms) which is a hotel, including golf and/or other recreational facilities, with full meal plans included in room rental cost.

RESPONSIBILITY CLAUSE means a portion of a tour brochure which states conditions under which a tour is sold.

RETAIL TRAVEL AGENT means one who engages in the service of providing the general public with preplanned travel and transportation for profit.

REVALIDATION STICKER means a sticker which is attached to a flight coupon to show a change from the original reservation.

RISE AND SHINE means up and at 'em.

ROUND TRIP means any flight or fare based on travel in both directions between two cities.

ROUTING means a geographically logical sequence of point to point destinations.

RUSSELL'S GUIDE means a periodic schedule for the Bus Industry and its agents.

SALOON means the main lounge on a passenger ship.

SINGLE PLANE SERVICE means the same as DIRECT FLIGHT.

SINGLE SUPPLEMENT means an additional charge for single accommodations on a tour. (Most brochure prices are for double occupancy.)

SPLIT RATES means two or more sets of rates quoted by a resort (hotel) which reflect high and low seasons.

STABILIZER means a device designed to eliminate or dampen a ship's tendency to roll.

STANDBY FARE means a reduced rate fare for a passenger who cannot board a plane until all reserved passengers have boarded.

STARBOARD means the right side of the ship when you are facing forward.

STERN means the back of the ship.

STOPOVER means a stop along the route of a journey (usually 24 hours or more).

STOWAWAY means an illegal passenger.

SUPPLEMENTAL CARRIERS means airlines not operating on established schedules, e.g., freight hauling, affinity charters.

SURFACE means a segment of a trip by land rather than by air.

TABLE d'HORTE means a full course meal served at a fixed price; may or may not offer alternatives.

TARIFF means a published list of fares and rules of a supplier.

THROUGH CHECKING means baggage checked through from your departure city to your final destination.

TOUR means a preplanned program of travel employing prepaid reservations of at least one night's hotel accommodations, one sightseeing tour and/or a transfer from airport to hotel, and/or a breakfast.

TOUR OPERATOR means a company that puts together tour packages and sells them either wholesale to a travel agent or directly to the public.

TRANSFERS means local ground transportation usually from the airport to the hotel.

TRUNK CARRIERS means the major Domestic scheduled air carriers.

UPGRADE means to be changed from a lower class of service or accommodation to a higher one.

VALIDATION means making a ticket legal by imprinting it with the appropriate airline plate.

VALIDATOR means a small machine (sometimes provided by the airlines, rail, steamship or bus companies) which is an identification system unique to a particular agent in order to "validate" and stamp the back of tickets and vouchers.

VISA means official document issued through the government embassy or consulate of any foreign country, giving a non-citizen authorization to travel and/or stay in that country.

VOUCHER means a document issued by your travel agent or airlines, stating that you have paid for and are entitled to certain accommodations or services. Vouchers are issued for hotels, car rentals, sightseeing trips and other pre-paid vacation features.

WAITLIST means a list of passengers who are waiting for cancellations so that they may be accommodated on a flight or tour that is sold out.

WAKE means the ship's sea tracks.

WALK means the referral of a prospective guest who has a written confirmation to another hotel or motel, by the hotel who made the original confirmation.

WEIGH means to lift the anchor from the bottom of the sea.

WHEELSMAN means the sailor who handles the wheel.

WHOLESALER means the one who provides the retail travel agent with the produce for the general public (i.e., preplanned, travel and transportation programs of air tickets, hotel accommodations, sightseeing, and other itineraries, as depicted in prepared literature and brochures).

WINDWARD means facing into the wind.

ABBREVIATIONS AND SYMBOLS

AAA means American Automobile Association which offers services pertaining to automobile travel; also AAA Worldwide Travel.

AAR means against all risks.

AAR means Association of American Railroads .

ABTA means Association of British Travel Agents.

ABTB means Trade Association of U.S. bank-operated travel agencies.

A/C means air conditioning in rental cars.

ACTO means the Association of Caribbean Tour Operators.

ACTOA means the Airline Charter Tour Operators Association, a trade association of operators of affinity and other charters.

AFTA means the Australian Federation of Travel Agents.

AGT means agent, travel agent.

AGTE means the Association of Group Travel Executives.

AH&MA means American Hotel and Motel Association, a trade association covering the lodging industry in U.S., Canada, Mexico, and Central and South America.

ALPA means Air Line Pilots Association.

ALTA means Association of Local Transportation Airlines.

AMAV means Association Mexicana de Agencias de Viajes (Mexican Travel Agents' Association).

AMHA means American Motor Hotel Association.

ARNK means arrival unknown.

ARR means arrival.

ARTA means Association of Retail Travel Agents, a trade association of American travel agents, restricted to retailers.

ASI means American Sightseeing International.

ASTA means American Socity of Travel Agents; a trade association of travel agencies and related industries.

ATA means Air Transport Association (U.S.A.).

ATAC means Air Transport Association of Canada.

ATBEC means Association of Tourist Boards of the Eastern Caribbean.

ATC means Air Traffic Conference (U.S.A.).

A3B means European Airbus A300B, jet aircraft equipment.

ATX means air taxi.

AX means American Express (credit card).

BA means Visa (credit card, formerly called Bankamericard).

BB means Barclaycard (credit card).

BHA means Bahamas Hotel Association.

BAB means British Airways Board. (Great Britain's government agency that controls British Airways.)

BTA means British Tourist Authority (Great Britain's official government agency for promotion of travel.)

BP means Bermuda Plan (A hotel plan which includes a full American breakfast.)

CA means Master Charge (credit card).

CAB means Civil Aeronautics Board.

CATM means Consolidated Air Tour Manual.

CB means Carte Blanche (credit card).

CCA means Caribbean Cruise Association.

CCR means compact car.

CERR means conference of European Railroad Representatives.

CF means car ferry.

CHA means Caribbean Hotel Association.

CHTR means charter.

CL means flight closed, waitlist open.

CLIA means Cruise Lines International Association.

CONV means convertible car.

CP means contintental breakfast.

CTA means Caribbean Tourism Association.

CTC means Certified Travel Counselor (accreditation of travel agents awarded by the ICTA).

CTC means contact.

CTO means City ticket office.

CTOA means Creative Tour Operators of America.

CTRC means Caribbean Tourism Research Centre.

CWGN means compact stationwagon.

DATO means Discover America Travel Organization.

DBLB means double room with bath.

DBLN means double room without bath or shower.

DBLS means double room with shower.

DC means Diner's Club (credit card).

DEP means departure.

DET means domestic escorted tour.

DIT means domestic independent travel, a prepaid, unescorted individual tour within a country.

DOT means U.S. Department of Transportation.

DP means Demi-pension.

DSM means District Sales Manager (of an airline, steamship co., tour operator, etc.).

E&OE means errors and omissions excepted.

EB means eastbound.

EC means Eurocard (credit card).

EP means European plan.

ETA means estimated time of arrival.

ETC means European Travel Commission.

ETD means estimated time of departure.

FAA means Federal Aviation Administration.

FCU means fare construction unit.

FET means foreign escorted tour.

FGTO means French Government Tourist Office.

FHTL means first class hotel.

FIT means foreign independent travel, an international, prepaid trip, usually unescorted, planned to individual clients' specifications.

FP means full pension; hotel rate including three meals daily, as in American plan.

FN means deluxe night coach.

GIT means group inclusive tour.

GMT means Greenwich Mean Time.

GSA means general sales agent.

HL means have waitlisted.

HN means requesting (have need).

HSMA means Hotel Sales Management Association.

HTL means hotel.

IACA means International Air Carrier Association.

IATA means International Air Transport Association.

IATC means Inter-American Travel Congress.

IATM means International Association of Tour Managers.

ICAO means International Civil Aviation Organization.

ICC means Interstate Commerce Commission.

ICCA means International Congress and Convention Association.

ICTA means Institute of Certified Travel Agents.

IHA means International Hotel Association.

IN means followed by date, indicates check-in date.

INF means infant.

IPSA means International Passenger Ship Association.

ISTA means International Sightseeing and Tours Association.

IT means inclusive tour.

ITC means inclusive tour charter.

ITX means inclusive tour excursion, British and European term for an inclusive tour fare.

IUOTO means International Union of Official Travel Organizations, the former association of travel organizations now known as World Tourism Organization.

JET means an aircraft with jet engines.

JTO means joint tour operators.

K means thrift class.

KH means peak thrift.

KK means confirming.

KL means off-peak thrift or confirming from waitlist.

KN means night thrift.

KSML means Kosher meal request.

LCAR means luxury car.

LHTL means luxury class hotel.

LWGN means luxury stationwagon.

MAA means Motel Association of America.

MAP means modified American plan.

MAXR means maximum room rate desired.

MCO means miscellaneous charges order.

MINR means minimum room rate desired.

MODR means moderate room rate desired.

MPM means maximum permitted mileage.

MV means motor vessel.

NACA means National Air Carrier Association.

NARP means National Association of Railroad Passengers.

NATO means National Association of Travel Organizations.

NB means northbound.

NPTA means National Passenger Traffic Association

NTBA means National Tour Brokers Association.

NTSB means National Transportation Safety Board.

NV means nuclear vessel.

OAG means Official Airline Guide.

OHRG means <u>Official Hotel and Resort Guide</u>.

OK means reservation confirmed (used in ticketing).

OMFG means <u>Official Meeting Facilities Guide</u>.

OTC means a one-stop inclusive tour charter.

Orbis means Polish National Travel Bureau.

OW means one-way.

PATA means Pacific Area Travel Association.

PATCO means Professional Air Traffic Controllers Organization.

PAX or PSGR means passengers.

PTA means prepaid ticket advice.

PTM means passenger traffic manager.

Q means surcharge.

R/T means round trip.

Routing means a route structure.

RPM means revenue passenger mile.

RSM means regional sales manager.

RTPA means Rail Travel Promotion Agency (AMTRAK).

SATW means Society of American Travel Writers.

SFML means sea food meal request.

SST means supersonic transport, type of aircraft operating faster than speed of sound.

Suite means a double room with bath and sitting room.

SUR means surface travel.

SWB means single with bath.

SWGN means standard stationwagon.

TC means travel card or tourist class accommodations as on a ship

TGC means travel group charter.

THTL means tourist class hotel.

TPPC means Transpacific Passenger Conference.

TRPB means triple room with bath.

TRPN means triple room without bath or shower.

TRPS means triple room with shower.

TS means turbine electric ship.

TSS means turbine steamship.

TUR means tour.

TWIN means hotel room having two single beds.

TWNB means double room with twin beds, and bath.

TWNN means double room with twin beds, but without shower or bath.

TWNS means double room with twin beds, and shower.

TWU means Transport Workers Union of America.

UATP means Universal Air Travel Plan (credit card and carrier-sponsored charge plan).

U-DRIVE means Automobile rented without a driver.

UFTAA means Universal Federation of Travel Agents Associations.

USTOA means United States Tour Operators' Association.

USTS means United States Travel Service.

VAL means value.

VES means vessel.

WATA means World Association of Travel Agencies.

WB means westbound.

WL means waitlist.

WTO means World Tourism Organization.

XO means exchange order.

XS means Access (credit card).

XX means cancel.

Y means coach.

MAJOR AIRLINES

AER LINGUS-IRISH INTERNATIONAL AIRLINES
564 5th Avenue
New York, New York 10036
Res. Phone: (212) 575-8200

Routes: In conjunction with Aerlinte Eireann a network of international routes is operated from Dublin, Shannon and Cork, to New York, Boston, Chicago, Montreal, London, Paris, Amsterdam, Frankfurt, Rome.
Aircraft: 707, 737, 747, BAC-111

AEROFLOT
545 5th Avenue
New York, New York 10017
Res. Phone: (212) 661-4050

Routes: The world's largest airline, Aeroflot provides international services to Europe, Africa, Asia, Cuba, Canada and the USA.
Aircraft: An-2, An-12, An-22, An-24; Il-18, Il-62, Il-76, Il-86; Polish-Soviet M-15; Tu-104, Tu-144, Tu-114, Tu-124, Tu-134, Tu-154, Tu-154A; Yak-40, Yak-18T

AEROLINEAS ARGENTINAS
9 Rockefeller Plaza
New York, New York 10020
Res. Phone: (212) 397-1800

Routes: Domestic system organized in regions. International services from Buenos Aires to Madrid, Rome, Zurich, Frankfurt, Paris, London, New York, Los Angeles, Miami, Mexico City, Bogota, Lima, Santiago, Rio de Janeiro, Sao Paulo.
Aircraft: 707, 737, 747, HS-748

AEROMEXICO
500 5th Avenue
New York, New York 10036
Res. Phone: (212) 221-8704

Routes: Domestic services to more than 40 cities operated on a regional basis by smaller carriers under Aeromexico's control. International services from Mexico City to Los Angeles, Tuscon, New York, Washington, Miami, Detroit, Toronto, Montreal, Madrid, Paris, and Caracas.
Aircraft: DC-8, DC-9, DC-10

AIR AFRIQUE
683 5th Avenue
New York, New York 10022
Res. Phone: (212) 758-6300

Routes: Internal services to 22 African states. International flights to Bordeaux, Lyon, Marseille, Paris, Nice, Geneva, Zurich, Rome, Las Palmas, and New York.
Aircraft: DC-3, DC-8, DC-10, Caravelle

AIR ALGERIE
One Place Maurice Audin
Algiers, Algeria

Routes: Extensive domestic system. International services to North and West Africa, France, Belgium, Spain, Italy, Germany, Switzerland, Egypt, UK, USSR, Bulgaria, Czechoslovakia, Libya.
Aircraft: 727, 737, Caravella, CV-640

AIR CALIFORNIA
3636 Birch Street
Newport Beach, California 92660
Res. Phone: (714) 752-1000

Routes: Intra-state passenger service between Orange County and Disneyland, San Francisco, San Diego, Oakland, San Jose, Palm Springs, Sacramento and Ontario.
Aircraft: 737, Lockheed Electra

AIR CANADA
600 Madison Avenue, 4th Floor
New York, New York 10022
Res. Phone: (212) 935-7172

Routes: Domestic transcontinental services. International flights to Europe, USA, Bermuda, the Caribbean and Bahamas.
Aircraft: 727, 747; DC-8, DC-9; TriStar; Viscount; L1101s

AIR CEYLON
PO Box 692, Lower Chatham Street
Colombo, Sri Lanka

Routes: Domestic services and International services from Colombo to Bombay, London, Rome, Singapore, Bangkok, Paris.
Aircraft: DC-8, DC-3; Trident; HS-748

AIR FRANCE
1350 Ave. of the Americas
New York, New York 10019
Res. Phone: (212) 759-9000

Routes: International services throughout Europe, to Africa, the Middle East, North and South America, the Caribbean, the People's Republic of China and the Far East.
Aircraft: 707, 727, 737, 747; DC-4; Caravelle; Fokker F.27; Transall C-160; Airbus A300; Concorde SST

AIR INTER
232 Rue de Rivoli
Paris 1, France

Routes: Extensive domestic system between Paris and most major cities in France.
Aircraft: Caravelle; Viscount; Fokker F.27; Dassault Mercure

AIR INDIA
666 5th Avenue
New York, New York 10019
Res. Phone: (212) 751-6200

Routes: International flights from Bombay, Calcutta and Delhi to Europe, Africa, the Far and Middle East, the USA and Australia.
Aircraft: 707, 747; Caravelle

AIR JAMAICA
19 East 49th Street
New York, New York 10017
Res. Phone: (212) 688-1212

Routes: International flights linking Kingston and Montego Bay with New York, Miami, Chicago, Philadelphia, Toronto, Nassau, Detroit and London.
Aircraft: DC-9 and DC-8

AIR MADAGASCAR
21 Avenue de l'Independence
Tananarive, Malagasy

Routes: Extensive domestic system.
Intercontinental services to Paris,
Marseille and Rome via Djibouti.
Aircraft: 707, 737; DC-4, DC-3; Nord 262;
Twin Otter; Navajo; Aztec; Cherokee Six

AIR MALAWI
PO Box 84
Chileka International Airport
Blantyre, Malawi

Routes: Domestic and regional services.
International service to London.
Aircraft: VC-10; BAC-111; HS-748;
Viscount; Islander

AIR MALTA
Luqa Airport
Malta

Routes: Service to London, Birmingham,
Manchester.
Aircraft: 720, 727

AIR NEW ZEALAND
245 Park Avenue
New York, New York 10017
Res. Phone: (212) 661-7444

Routes: International flights join
Auckland, Wellington and Christchurch to
Papeete, Honolulu, Los Angeles, Hong Kong,
Singapore, Melbourne, Sydney, Pago Pago.
Aircraft: DC-8, DC-10

AIR PACIFIC
CML Buildings
Victoria Parade
Suva, Fiji

Routes: Local and regional services with-
in the Fiji Islands, the Gilbert and
Ellice Islands, the New Hebrides, the
Solomon Islands, Samoa, Brisbane.
Aircraft: BAC-111; HS-748; Heron;
Britten-Norman Trislander

AIR RHODESIA
PO Box AP1
Salisbury Airport
Salisbury, Rhodesia

Routes: In addition to domestic system,
international services are from Salisbury,
Victoria Falls and Bulawayo to Johannesburg, Durban, Blantyre, Beira.
Aircraft: DC-3; Boeing 720; Viscount 700

AIR SIAM
1643/5 New Petchburi Road
Bangkok, Thailand

Routes: International flights from
Bangkok to Hong Kong, Tokyo and Honolulu.
Aircraft: 707, 747; Airbus 300B; DC-10

AIR VIETNAM
27B Phan-dinh-Phung
Saigon, South Vietnam

Routes: Domestic and regional services.
International flights to Laos, Cambodia,
Formosa, Japan, Phillippine Islands,
Singapore, Malaysia, Hong Kong and Thailand.
Aircraft: 707, 727; DC-6, DC-4, DC-3;
Cessna 185, Cessna 206

AIR ZAIRE
4 Avenue du Port
Kinshasa
Republic of Zaire

Routes: Extensive domestic system.
International services to Brussels, Dakar,
Entebbe, Frankfurt, Geneva, Madrid, Paris
and Rome.
Aircraft: 747, 737; DC-10, DC-8, DC-4;
Caravelle; Fokker F.27

ALIA (ROYAL JORDANIAN AIRLINES)
280 Madison Avenue
New York, New York 10016
Res. Phone: (212) 725-0044

Routes: Services, with emphasis on tourism, are from Amman to Beirut, Cairo, Istanbul, Kuwait, Teheran, Karachi, Athens, Rome, Paris, Frankfurt, Madrid, London and Copenhagen.
Aircraft: 707, 720, 727; Caravelle

ALITALIA
666 5th Avenue
New York, New York 10019
Res. Phone: (212) 582-8900

Routes: International flights to Europe, Africa, North and South America, the Middle and Far East and Australia. Also a domestic system between principal Italian cities.
Aircraft: 747; DC-8, DC-9, DC-10; Caravelle

ALLEGHENY AIRLINES
595 5th Avenue
New York, New York 10022
Res. Phone: (212) 736-3228

Routes: Domestic system in North-Eastern United States and Montreal and Toronto.
Aircraft: DC-9, BAC-111, Convair CV-580

ALL NIPPON AIRWAYS
Kasumigaseki Building
3-2-5
Kasumigaseki, Tokyo, Japan

Routes: Domestic and regional flights.
Aircraft: TriStar, 727, 737; YS-11A; Fokker F.27; Navajo; Sikorsky S-61N; Kawasaki KH-4

AMERICAN AIRLINES
633 Third Avenue
New York, New York 10017
Res. Phone: (212) 661-4242

Routes: Extensive system linking US cities plus to Toronto, Mexico City, Hawaii, Puerto Rico, the US Virgin Islands, Aruba, Curacao and Haiti.
Aircraft: 707, 727, 747; DC-10

ANSETT AIRLINES OF AUSTRALIA
One Rockefeller Plaza
New York, New York 10017
Res. Phone: (212) 489-0011

Routes: Virtually a domestic system covering all of Australia's states.
Aircraft: 727; DC-9, DC-4; Fokker F.27, F.28; Electra freighter; Carvair; Twin Otter; Sikorsky S-61N and Jet Ranger

ARIANA AFGHAN AIRLINES
Kabul, Afghanistan

Routes: To France, Germany, Great Britain, Italy, Iran, Iraq, Lebanon, Turkey, Syria, India, Pakistan, USSR.
Aircraft: 727, 720

AUSTRIAN AIRLINES
608 5th Avenue
New York, New York 10020
Res. Phone: (212) 265-6350

Routes: International flights from Vienna to major cities in West Germany, Switzerland, France, UK, Italy, Rumania, Greece, Bulgaria, Turkey, Lebanon, Israel, Poland, Hungary, Czechoslovakia, East Germany and USSR.
Aircraft: DC-9

AVIANCA AIRLINES
6 West 49th Street
New York, New York 10020
Res. Phone: (212) 586-6040

Routes: This, the largest airline in South America, has an extensive system from Bogota, plus international flights to Madrid, Paris, Frankfurt, Zurich, Miami, New York, Los Angeles, Mexico.
Aircraft: 707, 720, 727, HS-748, DC-3, DC-4

BANGLADESH BIMAN
507 5th Avenue
New York, New York 10017
Res. Phone: (212) 687-4438

Routes: Flights from Dacca to Chittagong, Calcutta, Bangkok, Kathmandu and London.
Aircraft: 707 and Fokker F.27

BRANIFF INTERNATIONAL AIRWAYS
135 East 42nd Street
New York, New York 10017
Res. Phone: (212) 972-4690

Routes: Domestic services cover central and western US. Also South American service to many major cities and flights to Mexico City and Acapulco.
Aircraft: 727, 747, 707, 720; DC-8

BRITANNIA AIRWAYS
Luton Airport
Luton, Bedfordshire
England

Routes: Passenger and cargo charters and inclusive-tour flights.
Aircraft: 737

BRITISH AIRWAYS
245 Park Avenue
New York, New York 10017
Res. Phone: (212) 687-1600

Routes: Scheduled services cover all major European cities and several cities in the Middle East. The Overseas Div. is the world's largest route system and links the UK with major cities in every continent and includes several round-the-world services.
Aircraft: 747, 707; VC-10; Concorde

BRITISH CALEDONIAN AIRWAYS
415 Madison Avenue
New York, New York 10017
Res. Phone: (212) 935-9550

Routes: Domestic flights from Gatwick to Belfast, Edinburgh, Glasgow, Manchester. Also extensive European and international services (principally to Africa).
Aircraft: 707; VC-10; BAC-111

BRITISH ISLAND AIRWAYS
Berkeley House
51-53 High Street
Redhill, Surrey, England

Routes: System of short-haul passenger and cargo services within the British Isles and to Paris, Antwerp, Hanover and Dusseldorf.
Aircraft: Herald

BRITISH MIDLAND AIRWAYS
East Midlands Airport
Castle Donington
Derby, England

Routes: Scheduled services from the East Midlands and London to Paris, Glasgow, Belfast, Dublin, Amsterdam, Brussels. Also charter and tour flights.
Aircraft: 707; Herald; Viscount

BRITISH WEST INDIAN AIRWAYS
610 5th Avenue
Rockefeller Center
New York, New York 10020
Res. Phone: (212) 581-1610

Routes: Passenger and cargo services to cities in the Caribbean and to New York, Toronto, Miami, Guyana and London.
Aircraft: 707

CAMEROON AIRLINES
Douala, Cameroon

Routes: Domestic and regional, Cameroon-France.
Aircraft: 707, 737; DC-4; Convair

CATHAY PACIFIC AIRWAYS
548 5th Avenue
New York, New York 10036
Res. Phone: (212) 541-9750

Routes: Passenger flights from Hong Kong
to Tokyo, Seoul, Osaka, Manila, Bangkok,
Saigon, Singapore, Jakarta and Perth.
Aircraft: 707; TriStar

CESKOSLOVENSKE AEROLINIE
Prague, Czechoslovakia

Routes: Extensive domestic, Eastern
and Western European system as well as
New York and Havana.
Aircraft: IL-14, 18, 62s, Tu-104, 134S

CHINA AIRLINES
620 5th Avenue
New York, New York 10020
Res. Phone: (212) 581-6500

Routes: Domestic flights within Taiwan.
International services from Taipei to
Hong Kong, Tokyo, San Francisco, Seoul,
Bangkok, Manila, Saigon, Singapore,
Honolulu, Los Angeles and Djakarta.
Aircraft: 707, 727; Caravelle III; YS-11A;
DC-4, DC-4

CIVIL AVIATION ADMINISTRATION OF CHINA
15 Chang An Street East
Peking, Peoples Republic of China

Routes: Domestic flights and Internation-
al services to Hanoi, Tirana (Albania) via
Teheran, Bucharest and Moscow.
Aircraft: 707; Trident One, Two and Three;
Viscount 800; Ilyushin Il-62, Il-18, Il-14,
Il-12; Antonov An-12, An-24, An-2, An-14;
Lisunov Li-2; Super Aero 45; Mil Mi-2

CP AIR (Canadian Pacific-Air)
489 5th Avenue
New York, New York 10017
Res. Phone: (212) 697-4504

Routes: Throughout Canada, Amsterdam,
Italy, Israel, Mexico, Spain, USA,
Australia, Fiji, Greece, Portugal, Spain.
Aircraft: DC-8, 727, 737, 747

CONTINENTAL AIR LINES
9 Rockefeller Plaza
New York, New York 10020
Res. Phone: (212) 582-6111

Routes: Service links southwest US with
Pacific northwest; flights from Houston
to Los Angeles; from Chicago to Los
Angeles; and from Los Angeles to Hawaii.
Aircraft: 747, 720, 727; DC-10, DC-9, DC-6

CRUZEIRO BRAZILIAN AIRLINES
Rio de Janeiro
Brazil

Routes: Domestic and to most South
American countries, Trinidad and Tobago.
Aircraft: 727, Caravelle, YS-11, DC-3
737

CYPRUS AIRWAYS
21 Athanassiou Dhiakou Street
Nicosia, Cyprus

Routes: Flights from Nicosia to Beirut,
Tel-Aviv, Cairo, Brussels, Istanbul,
Athens, Rome, Frankfurt, London.
Aircraft: Trident One and Two

DAN-AIR SERVICES
Bibao House
36-38 New Broad Street
London EC2, England

Routes: Extensive domestic system.
Aircraft: 707, 727; Comet; BAC 1-11;
HS-748

DELTA AIR LINES
One Penn Plaza
New York, New York 10001
Res. Phone: (212) 239-0700

Routes: National services to major
cities in the US. International services
to Canada, Bermuda, the Bahamas,
Caribbean and South America.
Aircraft: 747, 727; DC-10, DC-9, DC-8;
TriStar; Fokker F.27

DETA (Deta Mozambique Airlines)
Lourenco Marques
Mozambique

Routes: Domestic and to neighboring
southeast Africa nations.
Aircraft: 737, F-27, 707

EAST AFRICAN AIRWAYS
Sadler House
Koinange Street
Nairobi, Kenya

Routes: Extensive domestic system from
Nairobi, Mombasa, Arusha and Entebbe.
International flights to Addis Ababa,
Athens, Bombay, Copenhagen, Frankfurt,
London, Zurich, Rome.
Aircraft: 747; VC-10; DC-9, DC-3; F-27

EASTERN AIR LINES
10 Rockefeller Plaza
New York, New York 10020
Res. Phone: (212) 986-5000

Routes: Domestic service to more than
100 US cities, with an Air-Shuttle service
between Boston, Washington and New York.
International flights to Canada, Mexico,
Puerto Rico, the Bahamas, Jamaica, the
Virgin Islands and Bermuda.
Aircraft: TriStar; DC-9, DC-8; 727;
Electra

EAST-WEST AIRLINES
PO Box 249
Tamworth 2340
New South Wales, Australia

Routes: A domestic operation providing
services to 29 points in New South Wales,
Queensland, Victoria and Northern
Territory.
Aircraft: Fokker F.27

EGYPTAIR
720 5th Avenue
New York, New York 10019
Res. Phone: (212) LT 1-5600

Routes: Domestic flights and International services to cities in the Middle East,
Africa, Eastern and Western Europe and
to Bombay, Bangkok, Hong Kong, Manila
and Tokyo.
Aircraft: 707, 737; Comet 4C; An-24

EL AL ISRAEL AIRLINES
610 5th Avenue
New York, New York 10020
Res. Phone: (212) 486-2600

Routes: Regional services to Teheran,
Istanbul and Cyprus. International routes
from New York to Europe, Tel-Aviv to
Europe and African routes linking Tel-Aviv
to Nairobi, Addis Ababa and Johannesburg.
Aircraft: 707, 747, 720

EMPRESA CONSOLIDADA CUBANA DE AVIACION
Havana
Cuba

Routes: Domestic and to Spain, East
Germany, Czechoslovakia, Mexico, Peru
and Chile.
Aircraft: IL-14, 62; Bristol Britannia;
DC-8

ECUATORIANA (Compania Ecuatoriana de
Aviacion, S.A.)
Quito
Ecuador

Routes: Intercontinental serving Miami,
Mexico City, Panama City, Bogota, Quito,
and Lima. Also domestic flights.
Aircraft: 707, 720

ETHIOPIAN AIRLINES, S.C.
200 East 42nd Street
New York, New York 10017
Res. Phone: (212) 867-3830

Routes: Domestic system linking remote
areas. International services to cities
in Africa, Europe, the Middle East, India,
and Pakistan.
Aircraft: DC-6, DC-3; 707, 720

FINNAIR
10 East 40th Street
New York, New York 10016
Res. Phone: (212) 689-9300

Routes: Domestic services in Finland.
Regional services from Helsinki to
European cities including Moscow and
Leningrad. International service to
New York.
Aircraft: DC-10, DC-9, DC-8; Super
Caravelle; CV-440; Beech Debonair

THE FLYING TIGER LINE
7401 World Way West
Los Angeles International Airport
Los Angeles, California 90009

Routes: Coast-to-coast cargo flights
within the US and, internationally, to
Tokyo, Hong Kong, Seoul, Manila, Saigon.
Aircraft: DC-8; 747

GARUDA INDONESIAN AIRWAYS
Djakarta
Indonesia
Res. Phone: (212) 759-2400

Routes: Domestic and international
services from Djakarta to Hong Kong,
Sydney, South East Asia and Europe.
Aircraft: F.27, F.28; DC-8, DC-9, DC-10;
Convair CV-340

GHANA AIRWAYS
Accra
Ghana

Routes: Domestic and regional services.
International services from Accra to
Lagos, Beirut, London and Rome.
Aircraft: DC-3, DC-9; VC-10; F.28;
Viscount; HS-748

GULF AIR
245 Park Avenue
New York, New York 10017
Res. Phone: (212) 986-4500

Routes: Basic route is London-Beirut-
Bahrain-Bombay. Also local routes in
Persian Gulf.
Aircraft: VC-10; BAC 1-11; Fokker F.27

HUGHES AIRWEST
250 Park Avenue
New York, New York 10017
Res. Phone: (212) 682-2451

Routes: Passenger and cargo services to
western US cities and to Canada and
Mexico.
Aircraft: DC-9; Fokker F.27

IBERIA
565 5th Avenue
New York, New York 10036
Res. Phone: (212) 793-5000

Routes: Domestic flights between main
cities and tourist centers. International services to major western European
cities, to London, Glasgow, Dublin, and
to South and Central America, Africa and
the USA.
Aircraft: DC-10, DC-9, DC-8, DC-3; 747,
727; Caravelle; F-27, F-28; Airbus A300

ICELANDAIR
610 5th Avenue
New York, New York 10020
Res. Phone: (212) PL 7-8585

Routes: Domestic services from Reykjavik
and International services to Copenhagen,
Oslo, Frankfurt, Glasgow and London.
Aircraft: F-27; 727; DC-8

ICELANDIC AIRLINES
Reykjavik
Iceland

Routes: International services joining
New York and Reykjavik to Glasgow, London,
Luxembourg, Copenhagen, Stockholm, Oslo.
Aircraft: 727; DC-8

IRAN AIR
345 Park Avenue
New York, New York 10022
Res. Phone: (212) 949-8230

Routes: Domestic and regional services.
International services to London, Paris,
Athens, Geneva, Rome, Moscow, Istanbul,
India, Pakistan, Afghanistan.
Aircraft: 707, 727, 737, 747; DC-6

IRAQI AIRWAYS
New International Airport
Baghdad
Iraq

Routes: Flights from Baghdad to Basra,
London, Paris, Berlin, Geneva, Prague,
Vienna, Athens, Istanbul, Beirut, Cairo,
Teheran, Kuwait, New Delhi.
Aircraft: Trident One; Viscount; An-12,
An-24; 707, 737

INDIAN AIRLINES
New Delhi
India

Routes: Principally domestic. Interna-
tional services to Bangladesh, Burma,
Nepal.
Aircraft: 727; F-27; HS-748; Caravelle;
Viscount; 737

INVICTA INTERNATIONAL AIRLINES
Manston Airport
Ramsgate
Kent, England

Routes: Passenger and cargo charter
flights from Manston and Luton.
Aircraft: 720; Vanguard

JAPAN AIR LINES
655 5th Avenue
New York, New York 10036
Res. Phone: (212) 575-8200

Routes: Domestic services to major cities
in Japan and Okinawa. Extensive interna-
tional system to cities in Asia, Australia,
North and Central America, the Middle
East and Europe.
Aircraft: 727, 747; DC-10, DC-8; Beech 18

JUGOSLOVENSKI AEROTRANSPORT
630 5th Avenue
New York, New York 10020
Res. Phone: (212) 757-9676

Routes: Domestic system linking main
cities. International services from
Belgrade and Zagreb to Athens, Beirut,
Cairo, Copenhagen, Munich, Paris, London,
Rome, Budapest, Moscow, Warsaw, East
Berlin, Amsterdam, Stockholm, Istanbul.
Aircraft: 707, 727; DC-9; Caravelle;
SE-210, CV-440

KLM—ROYAL DUTCH AIRLINES
609 5th Avenue
New York, New York 10017
Res. Phone: (212) 759-3600

Routes: International services from Amsterdam and Rotterdam to Europe, North and Latin America, the Near, Middle and Far East, Africa and Australia.
Aircraft: DC-10, DC-9, DC-8; 747; F-27

KOREAN AIRLINES
350 5th Avenue
New York, New York 10001
Res. Phone: (212) 244-8330

Routes: Domestic system from Seoul to principal cities. International services to Tokyo, Osaka, Hong Kong, Bangkok, Honolulu, and Los Angeles.
Aircraft: 727, 707, 747; DC-9, DC-8; YS-11A; F-27

KUWAIT AIRWAYS
30 Rockefeller Plaza
New York, New York 10020
Res. Phone: (212) 581-9412

Routes: Services to many Middle East capital cities; to Bombay, Delhi, and to London via Frankfurt, Rome, Athens, Geneva and Paris.
Aircraft: 707

LAKER AIRWAYS
PO Box One
JFK Airport
New York 11430
Res. Phone: (212) 995-3862

Routes: Contract inclusive-tour and charter operations.
Aircraft: DC-10; 707; BAC 1-11

LAN-CHILE INTERNATIONAL AIRLINES
505 5th Avenue
New York, New York 10017
Res. Phone: (800) 327-9676

Routes: Serves most South American capitals, North American capitals, Central America, France, Germany, Spain, Portugal, Tahiti.
Aircraft: 707, 727; Caravelle

LIBYAN ARAB AIRLINES
Tripoli
Libya

Routes: Malta, Paris, Rome, London, Athens, Cairo, Beirut, Damascus and domestic services.
Aircraft: F-27; 727; Caravelle

LOT-POLISH AIRLINES
500 5th Avenue
New York, New York 10036
Res. Phone: (212) 869-1074

Routes: Domestic services from Warsaw to major cities. International services to Europe, the USA, Egypt, Iraq, Syria, Lebanon.
Aircraft: Il-62, Il-18; Tu-134; An-24B

LUFTHANSA
680 5th Avenue
New York, New York 10019
Res. Phone: (212) 357-8400

Routes: Domestic flights between major West German cities. Extensive world-wide services to Europe, North and South America, Africa, the Near, Middle and Far East, and Australia.
Aircraft: 747, 707, 727, 737; DC-10; A300

LUXAIR
PO Box 2203
Luxembourg Airport
Luxembourg

Routes: Mainly a local service and a feeder line. Services from Luxembourg to Amsterdam, Brussels, Geneva, London, Paris, Rome and several resort areas.
Aircraft: 707; Caravelle; F-27

MALAYSIAN AIRLINE SYSTEM
609 5th Avenue
New York, New York 10017
Res. Phone: (212) 371-7170

Routes: Domestic services and International services to Singapore, Bangkok, Jakarta, Hong Kong, trunk routes to London and Tokyo.
Aircraft: 707, 737; F-27; BN-2A Islander

MALEV HUNGARIAN AIRLINES
630 5th Avenue
New York, New York 10020
Res. Phone: (212) 757-6480

Routes: International services to major cities in Europe, also Scandinavia, USSR, the Middle East and North Africa.
Aircraft: Tu-154; Tu-134; Il-18

MEXICANA AIRLINES
60 East 42nd Street
New York, New York 10017
Res. Phone: (212) 973-5275

Routes: Between 21 cities in Mexico, to Los Angeles, Denver, Dallas, St. Louis, San Antonio, Chicago, Miami, Jamaica and Puerto Rico.
Aircraft: DC-6 and 727

MIDDLE EAST AIRLINES
680 5th Avenue
New York, New York 10019
Res. Phone: (212) 489-5400

Routes: System of services from Beirut to cities in the Middle East, Asia, Europe and Africa.
Aircraft: 747, 707, 720; Caravelle

MONARCH AIRLINES
Luton Airport
Luton, Beds.
England

Routes: Inclusive-tour and world-wide charter services offered.
Aircraft: 720

MOUNT COOK AIRLINES OF NEW ZEALAND
510 West 6th Street
Los Angeles, California 90014
Res. Phone: (213) 626-4574

Routes: Domestic services link Christchurch with major cities and islands. Also tourist and charter services.
Aircraft: HS-748; DC-3; BN-2A Islander; Grumman Super Goose, Widgeon; FU-24; Cessna 180, 185

NATIONAL AIRLINES
630 Third Avenue
New York, New York 10017
Res. Phone: (212) 490-8122

Routes: Services from Miami up Atlantic coast to New York and Boston, along the Gulf of Mexico, to New Orleans, Houston, San Diego, Los Angeles, and San Francisco. Also daily service to London.
Aircraft: 727, 747; DC-10, DC-8

NEW ZEALAND NATIONAL AIRWAYS
510 West 6th Street, Suite 1017
Los Angeles, California 90014
Res. Phone: (213) 689-4690

Routes: Services to 25 cities on New Zealand's North and South Islands.
Aircraft: 737; Viscount; F-27

NIGERIA AIRWAYS
30 Rockefeller Plaza
New York, New York 10020
Res. Phone: (212) 765-5005

Routes: Domestic services to principal cities in Nigeria. International services to London, Rome, Zurich, Madrid, Freetown, Beirut, New York.
Aircraft: 707, 737, 727; F-27, F-28; Aztec

NORTHWEST AIRLINES
537 5th Avenue
New York, New York 10017
Res. Phone: (212) 594-0320

Routes: Extensive services covering the United States, including Alaska, and Canada. Also to Japan, South Korea, Okinawa, Manila, Taiwan, and Hong Kong.
Aircraft: 747, 707, 727; DC-10

OLYMPIC AIRWAYS
888 7th Avenue
New York, New York 10019
Res. Phone: (212) 956-8400

Routes: Domestic services between main Greek cities and islands. International flights to Australia, Cyprus, Egypt, France, Germany, Israel, Italy, Lebanon, Turkey, UK, USA, Netherlands, Switzerland.
Aircraft: 747, 707, 720, 727; YS-11A

OVERSEAS NATIONAL AIRWAYS
645 Madison Avenue
New York, New York 10022
Res. Phone: (212) 759-1050

Routes: Charter flights undertaken on a domestic basis and to the Caribbean, Europe and India.
Aircraft: DC-10, DC-9, DC-8; Electra freighter

PAKISTAN INTERNATIONAL AIRLINES CORP.
551 5th Avenue
New York, New York 10017
Res. Phone (212) 949-0477

Routes: Domestic services to major cities. International services to Europe, USSR, the Middle and Far East, Peking and New York.
Aircraft: 707, 720, 747; DC-10; F-27

PACIFIC SOUTHWEST AIRLINES
3225 North Harbor Drive
Lindbergh Field
San Diego, California 92112
Res. Phone: (714) 297-4781

Routes: Intra-state services to San Diego, Long Beach, Los Angeles, San Jose, San Francisco, Sacramento, Hollywood.
Aircraft: 727; TriStar

PAN AMERICAN WORLD AIRWAYS
Pan Am Building
New York, New York 10017
Res. Phone: (212) 973-4000

Routes: World-wide system of routes to major cities in every continent. Also local services in Germany. No domestic services within the USA.
Aircraft: 747, 707, 727

PHILIPPINE AIRLINES
556 5th Avenue
New York, New York 10017
Res. Phone: (212) 575-7850

Routes: Domestic services link Manila and major cities within the islands. International services to the USA, Australia, Japan, Hong Kong, Taiwan, Singapore, Thailand, Pakistan, Italy, the Netherlands and West Germany.
Aircraft: DC-10, DC-8, DC-3; HS-748; BAC-111

QANTAS AIRWAYS
542 5th Avenue
New York, New York 10036
Res. Phone: (212) 764-0200

Routes: Services incorporate Melbourne, Sydney, Brisbane and Perth within the international system to London via Singapore and cities in the Far, Middle, and Near East and Europe; to Vancouver via Fiji, Honolulu and San Francisco; to New Zealand, New Guinea, Manila, Hong Kong, Tokyo, Norfolk Island.
Aircraft: 747, 707; DC-4; HS-125

SABENA BELGIAN WORLD AIRLINES
680 5th Avenue
New York, New York 10017
Res. Phone: (212) 397-2825

Routes: International services to major European cities; to Bombay, Bangkok, Singapore, Tokyo, Montreal, New York, Mexico City, Buenos Aires, to the Middle East and Africa.
Aircraft: DC-10; 747, 707, 727, 737; Caravelle; F-27; Cessna 310; SF-260

SAUDI ARABIAN AIRLINES
747 Third Avenue
New York, New York 10017
Res. Phone: 758-4727

Routes: Domestic and to London, Rome, Geneva, Frankfurt, parts of North Africa, East Africa, Eastern Mediterranean, Arab Peninsula, Bombay.
Aircraft: 707, 737; Convair 340; DC-3

SCANDINAVIAN AIRLINES
138-02 Queens Blvd.
Jamaica, New York 11435
Res. Phone (212) 657-7700

Routes: Current flights are operated within Scandinavia and Europe, USSR, Africa, the Middle and Far East, and to North, Central and South America.
Aircraft: 747; DC-10, DC-9, DC-8; Caravelle; CV-440

SINGAPORE AIRLINES
500 5th Avenue
New York, New York 10036
Res. Phone: (212) 947-2683

Routes: Services from Singapore to Kuala, Lumpur, Saigon, Manila, Madras, London via Bombay, Athens, Rome, Zurich, Amsterdam and Frankfurt; to Tokyo, Sydney and Perth.
Aircraft: 747, 707, 737

SOUTH AFRICAN AIRWAYS
605 5th Avenue
New York, New York 10017
Res. Phone: (212) 826-1245

Routes: Domestic and regional routes within Africa. International services Sydney, Rio de Janeiro and New York; Buenos Aires; and Lisbon, Madrid, Rome, Athens, Frankfurt, Vienna, Paris, Amsterdam, London and Ilha de Sol.
Aircraft: 747, 707, 727, 737; HS-748

SUDAN AIRWAYS
Khartoum
Sudan

Routes: Domestic in most of Africa; England, Greece and Italy.
Aircraft: 707; F-27; Twin Otter; DC-3

SWISSAIR
608 5th Avenue
New York, New York 10020
Res. Phone: (212) 995-3800

Routes: International services to main cities in Europe, to Africa, the Middle and Far East, and to North and South America.
Aircraft: 747; DC-10, DC-9, DC-8; CV-990 Coronado; Piagglio; SIAT 223

SYRIAN ARAB AIRLINES
Damascus
Syria

Routes: Throughout the Persian Gulf and Arabic countries.
Aircraft: Caravelle Super 10; 707

TAP (Transportes Aeros Portugueses)
1140 Avenue of the Americas
New York, New York 10036
Res. Phone: (212) 421-8500

Routes: Domestic services from Lisbon.
International services to Amsterdam,
Brussels, Buenos Aires, Boston, Frankfurt,
Geneva, London, Madrid, Montreal, New
York, Paris, Rio de Janeiro, Zurich.
Aircraft: 747, 707, 727; Caravelle

THAI AIRWAYS INTERNATIONAL
630 5th Avenue
New York, New York 10020
Res. Phone: (212) 489-1634

Routes: Services from Bangkok to Hong
Kong, Calcutta, Dacca, Delhi, Jakarta,
Manila, Saigon, Singapore, Tokyo,
Copenhagen, London and Frankfurt.
Aircraft: DC-10, DC-8

TRANS-AUSTRALIA AIRLINES
230 Park Avenue
New York, New York 10017
Res. Phone: (212) 689-4705

Routes: Extensive domestic network
throughout the states of Australia.
Aircraft: 727; DC-9, DC-3; F-27; Twin
Otter

TRANS WORLD AIRLINES
605 Third Avenue
New York, New York 10016
Res. Phone: (212) 695-6000

Routes: Operates a transcontinental and
inter-state system within the USA, and a
round-the-world service to cities in
Europe, Africa, and the Middle and Far
East.
Aircraft: 747, 707, 727, 737; TriStar;
DC-9

TURK HAVA YOLLARI
Cumhuriyet Caddesi 199-201
Harbiye-Istanbul
Turkey

Routes: Domestic and International
services to principal Turkish cities and
to Vienna, Athens, Rome, Paris, Zurich,
Geneva, Frankfurt, Amsterdam, London,
Tel-Aviv and Beirut.
Aircraft: 707, 727; DC-10, DC-9; F-28

TUNIS AIR
Tunis
Tunisia

Routes: Domestic and to Northern Africa,
most of Southern Europe, France and
Great Britain.
Aircraft: 707, 727, Caravelle, Nord 262

UNION DE TRANSPORTS AERIENS
50 Rue Arago
92-Puteaux
France

Routes: Services from Paris via Bordeaux,
Lyons, Marseille or Nice to cities in
West, Central and South Africa. Also
services to South-east Asia, Australia,
New Zealand to Los Angeles.
Aircraft: 747, 727; DC-10, DC-8

UNITED AIRLINES
1221 Avenue of the Americas
New York, New York 10020
Res. Phone: (212) 867-3000

Routes: Extensive system within the USA,
linking cities along the Atlantic coast
and providing trans-continental services
to cities on the Pacific coast with links
from Mexico to Vancouver and Hawaii.
Aircraft: 747, 727, 737, 720; DC-10, DC-8

VARIG
485 Lexington Avenue
New York, New York 10017
Res. Phone: (212) 883-6161

Routes: Extensive system of services
throughout Central and South America and
international services to the USA,
Europe, Africa and Asia.
Aircraft: 707, 727, 737; Electra;
HS-748; DC-10

VIASA (Venezolana Internacional de
Aviacion, S.A.)
Caracas
Venezuela

Routes: To Colombia, Peru, parts of
the Caribbean, parts of Central America,
Canary Islands, parts of Europe, coasts
of the US.
Aircraft: DC-8, DC-9

WARDAIR CANADA
26th Floor
C. N. Tower
Edmonton, Alberta, Canada

Routes: Domestic and international
charter services.
Aircraft: 747, 707, Twin Otter; Bristol
Freighter

WESTERN AIRLINES
609 5th Avenue
New York, New York 10017
Res. Phone: (212) 421-6177

Routes: Network serves 12 western states,
Alaska and Hawaii, Canada and Mexico.
Aircraft: 707, 720, 727, 737; DC-10

WORLD AIRWAYS
666 5th Avenue
New York, New York 10017
Res. Phone: (212) 757-4207

Routes: World-wide passenger and cargo
charter services from Oakland, California.
Aircraft: 747, 707, 727; DC-8

ZAMBIA AIRWAYS
One Rockefeller Plaza
New York, New York 10020
Res. Phone: (212) 582-6637

Routes: Passenger services from Lusaka
to Zambia's provinces. International
services to London, Rome, Nicosia,
Nairobi.
Aircraft: DC-8; BAC 1-11; HS-748; 707, 737

Appendix F

GOVERNMENT AND STATE TOURIST OFFICES

Afghan Tourist Organization
535 Fifth Avenue
New York, NY 10017
Phone: (212) 697-3660

Alabama Bureau of Publicity and
    Information
Room 403, State Highway Building
Montgomery, AL 36130
Phone: (205) 832-5510

Alaska Division of Tourism, Pouch E
Juneau, AK 99811
Phone: (907) 465-2010

American Samoa Office of Tourism
P.O. Box 1147
Pago Pago, SA 96799
Phone: 633-5187

Antigua Tourist Board
Eastern Caribbean Tourist Assn.
220 East 42nd Street
New York, NY 10017
Phone: (212) 986-9370

Argentina Consulate Tourist Dept.
1600 New Hampshire Avenue
Washington, DC 20009
Phone: (202) 332-7100

Arizona Office of Tourism
1700 W. Washington, Rm. 501
Phoenix, AZ 85007
Phone: (602) 271-3618

Arkansas Dept. of Parks & Tourism
149 State Capitol Building
Little Rock, AR 72201
Phone: (501) 371-1087

Australian Tourist Commission
1270 Avenue of the Americas
New York, NY 10020
Phone: (212) 489-7550

Austrian National Tourist Office
545 Fifth Avenue
New York, NY 10017
Phone: (212) 697-0651

Bahamas Tourist Offices
30 Rockefeller Plaza
New York, NY 10020
Phone: (212) 757-1611

Barbados Tourist Board
800 Second Avenue
New York, NY 10017
Phone: (212) 986-6516

Belgian National Tourist Office
720 Fifth Avenue
New York, NY 10019
Phone: (212) 582-1750

Benin, People's Republic of (Dahomey)
Permanent Mission to the U.N.
4 East 73rd Street
New York, NY 10021
Phone: (212) 861-2166

Bermuda Department of Tourism
P.O. Box 465, Front Street
Hamilton, Bermuda
Phone: (809) 292-0023

Bonaire Information Office
685 Fifth Avenue
New York, NY 10022
Phone: (212) 838-1797

Brazilian Government Trade Bureau
551 Fifth Avenue
New York, NY 10017
Phone: (212) 682-1055

British Tourist Authority
680 Fifth Avenue
New York, NY 10019
Phone: (212) 581-4708

Bulgarian Tourist Office
50 East 42nd Street
Suite 1508
New York, NY 10017
Phone: (212) 661-5733

Cameroon, United Republic of
Office National Camerounais du Touriste
Boite Postale 266
Yaounde, Cameroons

Canadian Government Office of Tourism
150 Kent Street
Ottawa, Canada
Phone: (613) 992-3166

Canal Zone Government
Executive Secretary
Balboa Heights
Canal Zone

Cancun Information Bureau
485 Madison Avenue
New York, NY 10022
Phone: (212) 421-9220

Cayman Islands Department of Tourism
250 Catalonia Avenue, Suite 604
Coral Gables, FL 33134
Phone: (305) 444-6551

Ceylon Tourist Board
609 Fifth Avenue
New York, NY 10017
Phone: (212) 935-0369

Chicago Convention and Tourist
    Bureau, Inc.
332 South Michigan Avenue
Chicago, IL 60604
Phone: (312) 922-3530

Chilean National Tourist Board
630 Fifth Avenue, 8th Floor
New York, NY 10020
Phone: (212) 582-3250

China, Republic of, Tourism Bureau
159 Lexington Avenue
New York, NY 10016
Phone: (212) 725-4950

Colombia Government Tourist Office
140 East 57th Street
New York, NY 10022
Phone: (212) 688-0151

Colorado Division of Commerce and
    Development
1313 Sherman Street
Denver, CO 80203
Phone: (303) 892-3045

Costa Rica Tourist Board
200 SE First Street
Miami, FL 33131
Phone: (305) 358-2150

Cyprus Tourist Office
820 Second Avenue
New York, NY 10017
Phone: (212) 986-3362

Czechoslovak Travel Bureau - CEDOK
10 East 40th Street
New York, NY 10016
Phone: (212) 689-9720

Danish National Tourist Office
75 Rockefeller Plaza
New York, NY 10019
Phone: (212) 582-2802

Delaware Division of Economic
    Development
630 State College Road
Dover DE 19901
Phone: (302) 678-4254

District of Columbia: Washington Area
    Convention and Visitors Association
1129 20th Street, NW
Washington, DC 20036
Phone: (202) 659-6460

Dominica Tourist Association
Eastern Caribbean Tourist Assoc.
220 East 42nd Street
New York, NY 10017
Phone: (212) 986-9370

Dominican Republic Tourist Office
64 West 50th Street
New York, NY 10020
Phone: (212) 581-2117

Dominican Tourist Information Center
485 Madison Avenue
New York, NY 10022
Phone: (212) 826-0750

Ecuador Tourist Agents
500 Fifth Avenue
New York, NY 10036
Phone: (212) 730-7878

Egypt Government Tourist Office
630 Fifth Avenue
New York, NY 10020
Phone: (212) 246-6960

El Salvador Tourist Commission
200 West 58th Street
New York, NY 10019
Phone: (212) 265-0727

Ethiopian Tourist Organization
P.O. Box 2183
Addis Ababa
Phone: 447470

Fiji Visitor's Bureau
c/o Holmes Associates
P.O. Box 126
Ross, CA 94957
Phone: (415) 457-7222

Finland National Tourist Office
75 Rockefeller Plaza
New York, NY 10019
Phone: (212) 582-2802

Florida Division of Tourism
107 West Gaines Street, Room 505
Tallahassee, FL 32304
Phone: (904) 488-5606

French Government Tourist Office
610 Fifth Avenue
New York, NY 10020
Phone: (212) 757-1125

French West Indies Tourist Board
610 Fifth Avenue
New York, NY 10020
Phone: (212) 757-1125

Georgia Bureau of Industry and Trade
P.O. Box 1776
Atlanta, GA 30301
Phone: (404) 656-3590

German National Tourist Office
630 Fifth Avenue
New York, NY 10020
Phone: (212) 757-8570

Ghana Tourist Office
445 Park Avenue, Suite 903
New York, NY 10022
Phone: (212) 688-8350

Greek National Tourist Organization
645 Fifth Avenue, Olympic Tower
New York, NY 10022
Phone: (212) 421-5777

Grenada Tourist Information Office
866 Second Avenue
New York, NY 10017
Phone: (212) 579-9675

Guam Visitors Bureau
P.O. Box 3520
Agana, GU 96910
Phone: 472-6014

Guatemala Tourist Commission
929 Sunrise Lane
Ft. Lauderdale, FL 33304
Phone: (305) 565-1828

Consulate of the Republic of Guyana
165 Eglington Avenue, E., Suite 501
Toronto, ON

Haiti Government Tourist Bureau
30 Rockefeller Plaza
New York, NY 10020
Phone: (212) 757-3517

Hawaii Visitors Bureau
2270 Kalakaua Avenue, Suite 801
Honolulu, HI 96815
Phone: (808) 923-1811

Honduras Tourist Bureau
530 West Sixth Street, Room 401
Los Angeles, CA 90014
Phone: (213) 485-0285

Hong Kong Tourist Association
548 Fifth Avenue
New York, NY 10036
Phone: (212) 947-5008

Hungarian Tourist Office
630 Fifth Avenue
New York, NY 10020
Phone: (212) 757-6446

Icelandic National Tourist Office
75 Rockefeller Plaza
New York, NY 10019
Phone: (212) 582-2802

Idaho Division of Tourism and
    Industrial Development
Room 108, State Capitol Building
Boise, ID 83720
Phone: (208) 384-2470

Illinois Office of Tourism
Department of Business and Eco. Dev.
222 S. College Street
Springfield, IL 62706
Phone: (217) 782-7500

India Government Tourist Office
30 Rockefeller Plaza
N. Mezzanine, Suite 15
New York, NY 10020
Phone: (212) 586-4901

Indiana Division of Tourism
336 State House
Indianapolis, IN 46204
Phone: (317) 633-5423

Indonesian Tourist Promotion Board
323 Greary Street, Ste. 305
San Francisco, CA 94102
Phone: (415) 981-3584

Iowa Development Commission
250 Jewett Building
Des Moines, IA 50309
Phone: (515) 281-3401

Iran Information and Tourism Center
10 West 49th Street
New York, NY 10020
Phone: (613) 757-1945

Iraqi Interest Section
1801 P Street, NW
Washington, DC 20036
Phone: (202) 483-7500

Irish Tourist Office
Ireland House
590 Fifth Avenue
New York, NY 10036
Phone: (212) 246-7400

Israel Government Tourist Office
488 Madison Avenue
New York, NY 10022
Phone: (212) 754-0140

Italian Government Travel Office
630 Fifth Avenue
New York, NY 10020
Phone: (212) 245-4822

Jamaica Tourist Board
200 Park Avenue
New York, NY 10017
Phone: (212) 682-8973

Japan National Tourist Organization
45 Rockefeller Plaza
New York, NY 10020
Phone: (212) 757-5640

Jordan Tourist Office
866 U.N. Plaza, Dept. C.T.
New York, NY 10017
Phone: (212) 759-1950

Kansas Department of Economic
    Development
503 Kansas Avenue, 6th Floor
Topeka, KS 66603
Phone: (913) 296-3487

Kentucky Department of Public Informa-
    tion and Travel
Capitol Annex Building
Frankfort, KY 40601
Phone: (502) 564-4930

Kenya Tourist Office
15 East 51st Street
New York, NY 10022
Phone: (212) 486-1300

Korea National Tourism Corporation
460 Park Avenue, Room 628
New York, NY 10022
Phone: (212) 688-7543

Lebanon Tourist and Information Office
405 Park Avenue
New York, NY 10022
Phone: (212) 421-2201

Embassy of Lesotho, Tourist Board
1601 Connecticut Avenue, NW
Washington, DC 20009

Louisiana Tourist Development
   Commission
P.O. Box 44291
Baton Rouge, LA 70804
Phone: (504) 389-5981

Luxembourg Tourist Information Office
One Dag Hammarskjold Plaza
New York, NY 10017
Phone: (212) 751-9650

Macau Tourist Information Bureau
3133 Lake Hollywood Drive
c/o Furman Associates
Los Angeles, CA 90068
Phone: (213) 851-3400

Maine State Development Office
State Capitol Building
Augusta, ME 04333
Phone: (207) 289-2656

Malaysian Tourist Information Center
600 Montgomery Street, 36th Floor
San Francisco, CA 94111
Phone: (415) 788-3344

Malta Government Tourist Board
9 Merchants Street
Valletta, Malta
Phone: 24444

Maryland Division of Tourist
   Development
1748 Forest Drive
Annapolis, MD 21401
Phone: (301) 269-2680

Massachusetts Department of Commerce
   and Development
Division of Tourism
Leverett Saltonstall Building
100 Cambridge Street
Boston, MA 02202
Phone: (617) 727-3204

Mexican National Tourist Council
405 Park Avenue
New York, NY 10022
Phone: (212) 755-7212

Michigan Travel Bureau, Department
   of Commerce
P.O. Box 30226
Lansing, MI 48909
Phone: (517) 373-0670

Minnesota Department of
   Economic Development
480 Cedar Street, Hanover Building
St. Paul, MN 55101
Phone: (612) 296-5027

Mississippi Agricultural and
   Industrial Board
P.O. Box 849
Jackson, MS 39205
Phone: (601) 354-6715

Missouri Division of Tourism
P.O. Box 1055
Jefferson City, MO 65101
Phone: (314) 751-3051

Monaco Government Tourist Office
115 East 64th Street
New York, NY 10021
Phone: (212) 472-0212

Mongolian People's Republic
Permanent Mission to the UN
6 East 77th Street
New York, NY 10021
Phone: (212) 861-9460

Montana Travel Promotion Unit
Department of Highways
Helena, MY 59601
Phone: (406) 449-2654

Montserrat Tourist Board
20 East 46th Street
New York, NY 10017
Phone: (212) 682-0435

Moroccan National Tourist Office
521 Fifth Avenue, Suite 2800
New York, NY 10017
Phone: (212) 421-5771

Nepal Tourist Information Centre
776 Sugata Chen Basantpur
Kathmandu, Nepal

Nebraska Department of Economic
    Development
Travel and Tourism Division
P.O. Box 94666, State Capitol
Lincoln, NE 68509
Phone: (402) 477-8984

Netherlands National Tourist Office
576 Fifth Avenue
New York, NY 10036
Phone: (212) 245-5320

Nevada Department of Economic
    Development
Capitol Complex
Carson City, NV 89710
Phone: (702) 885-4322

New Caledonia Tourism Information
700 South Flower Street, Suite 1704
Los Angeles, CA 90017
Phone: (213) 488-9878

New Hampshire Department of Resources
    and Economic Development
Box 856
Concord, NH 03301
Phone: (603) 271-2666

New Jersey Office of Tourism and
    Promotion
P.O. Box 400
Trenton, NJ 08625
Phone: (609) 292-2470

New Mexico Department of Development
113 Washington Avenue
Santa Fe, NM 87503
Phone: (505) 827-3101

New York City Convention and Visitors
    Bureau
90 East 42nd Street
New York, NY 10017
Phone: (212) 687-1300

New York State Department of Commerce
99 Washington Avenue
Albany, NY 12245
Phone: (518) 474-4116

New Zealand Government Tourist Office
630 Fifth Avenue, Suite 530
New York, NY 10020
Phone: (212) 586-0060

Consulate General of Nicaragua
1270 Avenue of The Americas
New York, NY 10020
Phone: (212) 247-1020

Nigerian Tourist Association
47 Marina, Box 2944
Lagos, Nigeria
Phone: 20335-22674

North Carolina Department of Natural
    and Economic Resources
P.O. Box 27687
Raleigh, NC 27611
Phone: (919) 733-4171

North Dakota Highway Department
Capitol Grounds
Bismarck, ND 58501
Phone: (701) 224-2525

Norwegian National Tourist Office
75 Rockefeller Plaza
New York, NY 10019
Phone: (212) 582-2802

Ohio Department of Economic and
    Community Development
30 East Broad Street
Columbus, OH 43215
Phone: (614) 466-8844

Oklahoma Tourism and Recreation
    Department, Tourism Promotion
    Division
500 Will Rogers Building
Oklahoma City, OK 73105
Phone: (405) 521-2406

Oregon Department of Transportation,
   Travel Information Section
101 Transportation Building
Salem, OR 97310
Phone: (503) 378-6309

Pakistan Mission to the United Nations
8 East 65th Street
New York, NY 10021
Phone: (212) 879-8600

Panama Government Tourist Bureau
630 Fifth Avenue
New York, NY 10020
Phone: (212) 246-5841

Pennsylvania Department of Commerce,
   Travel Development Bureau
423 So. Office Building
Harrisburg, PA 17120
Phone: (717) 787-4881

Philadelphia Convention and Visitors
   Bureau
1525 John F. Kennedy Blvd.
Philadelphia, PA 19102
Phone: (215) 864-1976

Philippine Department of Tourism
556 Fifth Avenue
New York, NY 10036
Phone: (212) 575-7915

Polish National Tourist Office
500 Fifth Avenue
New York, NY 10036
Phone: (212) 354-1487

Portuguese National Tourist Office
548 Fifth Avenue
New York, NY 10036
Phone: (212) 354-4403

Puerto Rico, Commonwealth of
Tourism Development Company
1290 Avenue of the Americas
New York, NY 10019
Phone: (212) 541-6630

Rhode Island Department of Economic
   Development
One Weybosset Hill
Providence, RI 02903
Phone: (401) 277-2601

Rumanian National Tourist Office
500 Fifth Avenue, Room 328
New York, NY 10036
Phone: (212) 354-1368

Scandinavian National Tourist Office
75 Rockefeller Plaza
New York, NY 10019
Phone: (212) 582-2802

Senegal Government Tourist Bureau
Pan Am Building, West Lobby
200 Park Avenue
New York, NY 10017
Phone: (212) 682-4695

Seychelles Tourism Division
P.O. Box 56
Victoria, Mahe, Seychelles

Singapore Tourist Promotion Board Office
251 Post Street
San Francisco, CA 94108
Phone: (415) 391-8476

Solomon Islands Tourist Authority
P.O. Box 321
Honiara, Solomon Islands

South African Tourist Corporation
Tourist Information Bureau
610 Fifth Avenue
New York, NY 10020
Phone: (212) 245-3720

South Carolina Department of Parks,
   Recreation and Tourism
Suite 113, Brown Building
1205 Pendleton Street
Columbia, SC 29201
Phone: (803) 758-2536

South Dakota Division of Tourism
Joe Foss Building, Room 217
Pierre, SD 57501
Phone: (605) 244-3301

Spanish National Tourist Office
665 Fifth Avenue
New York, NY 10022
Phone: (212) 759-8822

Ceylon (Sri Lanka) Tourist Board
609 Fifth Avenue, Suite 308
New York, NY 10017
Phone: (212) 935-0369

St. Kitts-Nevis-Anguilla Tourist Board
20 East 46th Street
New York, NY 10017
Phone: (212) 682-0435

St. Lucia Tourist Board
220 East 42nd Street, #405
New York, NY 10017
Phone: (212) 867-2950

St. Maarten, Saba and St. Eustatius
   Information Office
4 West 58th Street
New York, NY 10019
Phone: (212) 688-8350

St. Vincent and Grenadines Tourist
   Board
Eastern Caribbean Tourist Assoc.
220 East 42nd Street
New York, NY 10017
Phone: (212) 986-9370

Sudanese Tourist Corporation
P.O. Box 2424
Khartoum
D. R. of Sudan

Surinam Tourist Bureau
One Rockefeller Plaza, Room 1408
New York, NY 10020
Phone: (212) 581-3063

Swedish National Tourist Office
75 Rockefeller Plaza
New York, NY 10019
Phone: (212) 582-2802

Swiss National Tourist Office
608 Fifth Avenue
New York, NY 10020
Phone: (212) 757-5944

Tahiti Tourist Board
200 East 42nd Street
New York, NY 10017
Phone: (212) 972-9444

Tanzania Tourist Corporation
P.O. Box 2485
Dar es Salaam
Tanzania, East Africa

Tennessee Department of Tourist
   Development
505 Fesslers Lane
Nashville, TN 37210
Phone: (615) 741-1904

Texas Tourist Development Agency
Box 12008, Capitol Station
Austin, TX 78711
Phone: (512) 475-4326

Tourist Organization of Thailand
5 World Trade Center, Suite 2449
New York, NY 10048
Phone: (212) 432-0433

Tonga Visitors Bureau
c/o TC1
700 South Flower Street, Ste. 1704
Los Angeles, CA 90017
Phone: (213) 488-9150

Trinidad and Tobago Tourist Board
400 Madison Avenue
New York, NY 10017
Phone: (212) 838-7750

Tunisian National Tourist Office
630 Fifth Avenue, Ste. 863
New York, NY 10020
Phone: (212) 582-3670

Turkish Tourism and Information Office
821 U.N. Plaza
New York, NY 10017
Phone: (212) 687-2194

Turks and Caicos Tourist Office
7777 W. Talcott
Chicago, IL 60631
Phone: (312) 763-2008

Uganda Tourist Information
801 Second Avenue
New York, NY 10017
Phone: (212) 689-3780

United States Travel Service
U.S. Department of Commerce
Washington, DC 20230
Phone: (202) 377-4752

Union of the Soviet Socialist Republics
Intourist Information Office
45 East 49th Street
New York, NY 10017
Phone: (212) 371-6953

U.S. Virgin Islands Government
   Information Centers
10 Rockefeller Plaza
New York, NY 10020
Phone: (212) 582-4520

Venezuelan Government Tourist Bureau
450 Park Avenue
New York, NY 10022
Phone: (212) 355-1101

Vermont Agency of Development and
   Community Affairs
61 Elm Street
Montpelier, VT 05602
Phone: (802) 828-3236

Virginia State Travel Service
6 North Sixth Street
Richmond, VA 23219
Phone: (804) 786-2051

Washington Department of Commerce
   and Economic Development
General Administration Building
Olympia, WA 98504
Phone: (202) 753-5774

West Virginia Department of Commerce
Travel Department Division
1900 Washington Street East
Charleston, WV 25305
Phone: (304) 348-2286

Wisconsin Department of Business
   Development, Division of Tourism
123 West Washington Avenue
Madison, WI 53702
Phone: (608) 266-7621

Wyoming Travel Commission
1-25 at Etchepare Circle
Cheyenne, WY 82002
Phone: (307) 777-7777

Yugoslav National Tourist Office
630 Fifth Avenue, Suite 210
New York, NY 10020
Phone: (212) 757-2801

Zaire (Republic of) Tourism
B.P. 2466
Bukavu

Zambia National Tourist Bureau
150 East 58th Street
New York, NY 10022
Phone: (212) 758-9450

Appendix G

TRAVEL JOURNALS AND PERIODICALS

Travel Weekly
P.O. Box 278
Neptune, NJ 07753

Travel Trade
605 Fifth Avenue
New York, NY 10017

The Travel Agent
2 West 46th Street
New York, NY 10036

Selling Travel
111 Pears Avenue
Toronto, Ontario M5R 1S9
Canada

RHD Travel Media
Travel Age East and Travel Age West
888 Seventh Avenue
New York, NY 10019

Canadian Travel News
1450 Don Mills Road
Don Mills, Ontario M3B 2X7
Canada

Journal of Travel Research
Business Research Division
University of Colorado
Boulder, CO 80302

International Tourism Quarterly of
    the Economist
    Intelligence Unit
27 St. James Place
London, SW1A 1NT, England

Pacific Travel News
274 Brannan Street
San Francisco, CA 94107

Appendix H

MAJOR INTERNATIONAL HOTELS

AFGHANISTAN*

KABUL
Inter-Continental Kabul
(Inter-Continental)

ANDORRA

LES ESCALDES
Eden Roc
President
Princep
(Utell International)

ANTIGUA

Admiral's Inn
Runaway Beach Hotel
Sugar Mill
(American International)

Antigua Beach
Blue Waters Beach Hotel
Curtain Bluff Hotel
Halycon Cove
(T.C.I. Hotels)

Long Bay
White Sands Hotel
(Utell International)

Hyatt Regency
(Hyatt)

ARGENTINA

BUENOS AIRES
Buenos Aires Sheraton
(Sheraton Hotels)
City Hotel
Plaza
(Utell International)
Claridge
Lancaster
Alvear Palace
Plaza
Regidor
(Estur)

AUSTRALIA

ADELAIDE
Parkroyal
(Travelodge)

BRISBANE
Brisbane Parkroyal
Chermside Caravilla
Rockhampton Caravilla
(Travelodge)

MELBOURNE
Melbourne Hilton
(Hilton)
Sheraton Motor Inn
(Sheraton)
St. Kilda Road Travelodge
(Travelodge)

*Overseas hotels and major U.S. Hotel chains linked to a nationwide toll free number
and/or hotel representative in New York City. All Travelodge hotels and motels are
affiliated with the Trust Houses Forte Hotels; worldwide reservations can be made
through all THF facilities.

425

AUSTRALIA
(continued)

SYDNEY
Hyatt Kingsgate
(Hyatt)
Marquee Sheraton
Sheraton Motor Hotel
(Sheraton)
Sydney Hilton
*Hilton
Town House Hotel
(Tourex)

AUSTRIA

INNSBRUCK
Europa
(SRS Hotels)
Hotel Goldener Adler
(American International)
Holiday Inn
(Holiday Inns)

SALZBURG
Erzherzog Johann
Goldener Hirsch
Kaserer Hof
(American International)

VIENNA
Alpha
Atlanta
De France
Kummer
Savoy
(Utell International)
Inter-Continental Vienna
(Inter-Continental Hotels)
Wien Hilton
(Hilton)

BAHAMAS

ABACO
Guana Harbor Club
(American International)
Treasure Cay Beach Hotel and Villas
(T.C.I. Hotels)

ANDROS
San Andros Inn and Tennis Club
(Wolfe International)
Small Hope Bay Lodge
(American International)

GRAND BAHAMA
Bahamas Princess
Bahamas Princess Tower
(Princess Hotels)
Castaways Resort
Freeport Inn
(Utell International)
Holiday Inn
(Holidays Inns)
Xanadu Princess
(Hughes Resort Hotel)

NASSAU
Atlantis
Gleneagles
Ocean Spray
(Utell International)
Beach Inn
Britannia Beach Hotel
Ocean Club
(Loews Reservations)
Sheraton-British Colonial
(Sheraton)
Towne Hotel
(Wolfe International)

BAHRAIN

MANAMA
Bahrain Hilton
(Hilton)

BARBADOS

Barbados Beach Village
(Trust Houses Forte Hotels)
The Barbados Hilton
(Hilton)
Blue Water Beach
Riviera Beach
Rockley Beach
(Utell International)
Colony Club
Discovery Bay Inn
(T.C.I. Hotels)
Eastry House Hotel and Beach Club
Super Mare Hotel
(Wolfe International)

BELGIUM

BRUSSELS
Brussels Hilton
(Hilton)
Hyatt Regency Brussels
(Hyatt)

BERMUDA

Ariel Sands
Buena Vista Guest House
Montgomery Villas
(Utell International)
Banana Beach Apartments
Cabana Vacation Apartments
(Wolfe International)
The Belmont Hotel and Golf Club
Bermudiana Hotel
Harmony Hall Hotel
(Trust Houses Forte)
Princess Hotel, Golf & Tennis Club
(Princess Hotels)
Holiday Inn (St. George's)
(Holiday Inns)

BOLIVIA

LA PAZ
Copacabana
El Liberator
(Estur)
Sheraton Hotel
(Sheraton)
Crillon
(Utell International)

SANTA CRUZ
Holiday Inn
(Holiday Inns)

BOTSWANA

GABARONE
Holiday Inn
(Holiday Inns)

BRAZIL

BRASILIA
Brasilia Palace
Das Americas
Eron Brasilia
(Estur)

CAMPINAS
Holiday Inn
(Holiday Inns)

RIO DE JANEIRO
Continental Palace
Everest Rio
Flamenco Palace
(Estur)

Inter-Continental Rio
(Inter-Continental)

SAO PAULO
Brasilton Sao Paulo
(Hilton)
Ramada Inn
(Ramada Inns)
Gran Hotel Ca'D'Oro
(Estur)

BURMA

RANGOON
Strand
(Tourex)

CAMBODIA

PHNOM-PENH
Hotel Monorom
(Tourex)

CAMEROON

DOUALA
Relais Hotel
(Meridien Hotels)

YAOUNDE
Sheraton-Mont Febe Palace
(Sheraton)

CANADA

CALGARY
Calgary Holiday Inn
(Holiday Inns)
Sheraton Calgary Hotel
(Sheraton)

EDMONTON
Edmonton Plaza
(Utell International)
The Macdonald
(Hotels Unlimited)

HALIFAX
Holiday Inn
(Holiday Inns)
The Nova Scotian
(Hotels Unlimited)

CANADA
(continued)

MONTREAL
Auberge Richelieu
(Hotels Unlimited)
Montreal Airport Hilton
The Queen Elizabeth
(Hilton)
Laurentian
Sheraton Le St. Laurent
(Sheraton)

OTTAWA
Beacon Arms
(Utell International)
Holiday Inn
(Holiday Inns)

QUEBEC
Chateau Frontenac
Le Concorde
Hotel Saskatchewan
(Loew's Reservations)
Ramada Inn
(Ramada Inns)

SHERBROOKE
Le Baron
(Loew's Reservations)
Holiday Inn
(Holiday Inns)

TORONTO
Holiday Inn-Downtown
Holiday Inn-East
Holiday Inn-West
Holiday Inn-International Airport
(Holiday Inns)
King Edward-Sheraton
Sheraton-Landmark
Sheraton Plaza
Sheraton Villa Inn
(Sheraton)
Skyline Toronto
Bayshore Inn
(Utell International)

CAYMAN ISLANDS

GRAND CAYMAN
Holiday Inn
(Holiday Inns)

CEYLON

COLUMBO
Oberoi Lanka
(Loew's Reservations)
Pegasus Reef
(Trust Houses Forte)

CHAD

FORT-LAMY
Relais Hotel
(Meridien Hotels)

CHILE

SANTIAGO
Carrera Sheraton
Sheraton San Cristobal
(Sheraton)
Crillon Conquistador
Tupahue
(Estur)

COLOMBIA

BOGOTA
Bogota Hilton
(Hilton)
El Presidente
(Estur)

CALI
Inter-Continental Cali
(Inter-Continental)

MEDELLIN
Hotel Europa-Normandie
(Tourex)

REP. OF CONGO

BRAZZAVILLE
Relais Hotel
(Meridien Hotels)

COSTA RICA

SAN JOSE
Balmoral Continental
(Hoteline)
Chorotega Tower
(Utell International)
Suites Royal Dutch
Vista Palace
(Estur)

CYPRUS

FAMAGUSTA
Golden Sands
(Trust Houses Forte)

NICOSIA
Cyprus Hilton
(Hilton)

CZECHOSLOVAKIA

PIESTANY
Piestany Spa
(Tourex)

PRAGUE
Inter-Continental Prague
(Inter-Continental)

DENMARK

COPENHAGEN
Imperial
(Trust Houses Forte)
Sheraton-Copenhagen
(Sheraton)
Scandinavia
(Utell International)
Arthur Frommer
(Loew's Reservations)

DOMINICA, W.I.

PLM Anchorage
(PLM Hotels)
Riviera La Croix Estate Hotel
(RR Hotel Reps.)

DOMINICAN REPUBLIC

SANTO DOMINGO
Embajador Intercontinental
(Inter-Continental Hotels)
Loews Dominicana
(Loews Reservations)
Punta Cana Club
(Wolfe International)

ECUADOR

QUITO
Colon Internacional
(Utell International)
Humboldt Capitol
(Estur)

EGYPT

CAIRO
Cairo-Sheraton
(Sheraton Hotels)
Meridien La Caire
(Meridien Hotels)
Nile Hilton
(Hilton)
Merra House
(Loews Reservations)

EL SALVADOR

SAN SALVADOR
Camino Real
(Utell International)
Pacific Paradise
(Wolfe International)
El Salvador Sheraton
(Sheraton Hotels)
Ritz Continental
(Estur)

ENGLAND AND WALES

BIRMINGHAM
The Albany
(Strand Hotels)
City Centre Holiday Inn
(Holiday Inns)
Imperial Centre
(American International)

LONDON
Inter-Continental London
The Portman
(Inter-Continental Hotels)
Kensington Hilton
London Hilton
(Hilton Hotels)
Holiday Inn-Heathrow Airport
Holiday Inn-Marble Arch
Holiday Inn-Swiss Cottage
(Holiday Inns)
Ivanhoe
(American International)

STRATFORD-UPON-AVON
Stratford Hilton
(Hilton Hotels)
The Shakespeare
(Trust Houses Forte)
Falcon
(Utell International)

ETHIOPIA

ADDIS ABABA
Addis Ababa Hilton
(Hilton Hotels)

FIJI ISLANDS

PACIFIC HARBOUR
Beachcomber
Pacific Harbour Villas
(Trust Houses Forte)

FINLAND

HELSINKI
Inter-Continental Helsinki
(Inter-Continental Hotels)
Kalastajatorppa
Marski
(SRS Hotels)

FRANCE

CANNES
Carlton
Miramir
(Utell International)

LYON
Holiday Inn
(Holiday Inns)
Meridien Lyon
(Meridien Hotels)

MARSEILLE
Hotel Astoria
(Tourex)

PARIS
Ambassador Hotel
(SRS Hotels)
Holiday Inn Orly
Holiday Inn Roissy
Holiday Inn Porte de Versailles
(Holiday Inns)
Paris Hilton
(Hilton Hotels)
Paris Sheraton
(Sheraton Hotels)
Ramada Inn
(Ramada Inns)
Raphael
(American International)
Hotel de la Tremoille
(Trust Houses Forte)

GABON

LIBREVILLE
Inter-Continental
Okoume Palace
(Inter-Continental Hotels)

PORT-GENTIL
Relais Hotel
(Meridien Hotels)

GERMANY (WEST)

BERLIN
Berlin Ambassador
(BTH Hotels)
Europaeischer Hof
Palace
(Utell International)
Hotel Hamburg
(American International)

FRANKFURT
Frankfurt Intercontinental
(Inter-Continental Hotels)
Ramada Inn
(Ramada Inns)
Steinberger Hotel
(SRS Hotels)

MUNICH
City Hotel Metropol
(American International)
Munchen Hilton
(Hilton Hotels)
Olympiapark
(Utell International)
Vier Jahreszeiten
(Inter-Continental Hotels)

GIBRALTAR

Holiday Inn
(Holiday Inns)

GREECE

ATHENS
Athens Hilton
(Hilton Hotels)
King George
(SRS Hotels)
Marmara
(Utell International)

GREECE
(continued)

RHODES
Hotel Golden Beach
(Tourex)

THESSALONIKI
Makedonia Palace
(Utell International)
Mediterranean Palace
(HRI Hotels)

GREENLAND

ANGMAGSSALIK
Hotel Angmagssalik
(Hanns Ebensten)

GRENADA, W.I.

Holiday Inn
(Holiday Inns)
Silver Sands Hotel and Beach Club
(Wolfe International)

GUADELOUPE, F.W.I.

Novotel Fleur D'Epee
(Wolfe International)
Meridien Guadeloupe
(Meridien Hotels)

GUAM

AGANA
Guam Hilton
(Hilton Hotels)

GUATEMALA

GUATEMALA CITY
Camino Real
(Utell International)
Del Centro
(Estur)
El Dorado Americana
(Americana Hotels)

GUYANA

Guyana Pegasus Hotel
(Trust Houses Forte)

HAITI

PORT-AU-PRINCE
Castelhaiti
(Wolfe International)
El Rancho
Kyona Beach Club
(Utell International)
Haiti Holiday Hotel
(Hoteline)
Royal Haitian
(T.C.I. Hotels)

HOLLAND

AMSTERDAM
Amsterdam Hilton
Schiphol Hilton
(Hilton Hotels)
Amsterdam Marriott
(Marriott)
Apollo
(Trust Houses Forte)
Ramada Inn
(Ramada Inns)
Sheraton Schiphol Inn
(Sheraton Inns)

ROTTERDAM
Atlanta
(Utell International)
Parkhotel
(SRS Hotels)
Rotterdam Hilton
(Hilton Hotels)

HONDURAS

SAN PEDRO SULA
Gran Hotel Bolivar
(Tourex)

HONG KONG

August Moon Hotel
(American International Hotels)
Empress
(SRS Hotels)
Furama Inter-Continental
(Inter-continental Hotels)
Holiday Inn
(Holiday Inns)
Hong Kong Hilton
(Hilton Hotels)
Sheraton Hong Kong Hotel
(Sheraton Inns)

HUNGARY

BUDAPEST
Budapest Hilton
(Hilton Hotels)
Grand Hotel
(Trust Houses Forte)
Hotel Volga
Hotel Gellert
(SRS Hotels)

ICELAND

REYKJAVIK
Loftleider Hotel
(American International Hotels)

INDIA

BOMBAY
Holiday Inn
(Holiday Inns)
Ramada Inn
(Ramada Inns)
Oberoi-Sheraton
(Sheraton Hotels)

CALCUTTA
Chandigash
Oberoi Mountain View
(Loews Reservations)

NEW DELHI
Ashoka
(Utell International)
Imperial
(Inter-Continental Hotels)

INDONESIA

DJAKARTA
Hotel Asoka
(Tourex)
Horizon Hotel
(SRS Hotels)
Jakarta Hilton
(Hilton Hotels)
Sahid Jaya
(Trust Houses Forte)

IRAN

TEHRAN
Arya-Sheraton
(Sheraton Hotels)
Hyatt Crown Prince
(Hyatt)

IRELAND

BELFAST
Conway
(Trust Houses Forte)

CORK
Jurys
(Utell International)

DUBLIN
Fitzpatrick's Castle
(American International)
International Airport Hotel
(Trust Houses Forte)
Royal Hibernian
(SRS Hotels)

ISRAEL

JERUSALEM
Diplomat
(Utell International)
Jerusalem Hilton
(Hilton Hotels)
Jerusalem Inter-Continental
(Inter-Continental Hotels)

TEL AVIV
Basel Hotel
City Hotel
(Alexander Associates)
Ramada Inn
(Ramada Inns)
Tel Aviv Sheraton
(Sheraton Inns)

ITALY

FLORENCE
Anglo-American Hotel
(American International Hotels)
The Savoy
(HRI Hotels)
Villa Medici
(SRS Hotels)

GENOA
Savoia Majestic
(American International Hotels)

MILAN
Aerhotel Executivo
Aerhotel Fieramilano
Cavour
(Utell International)

ITALY
(continued)

MILAN
Michaelangelo
(SRS Hotels)

NAPLES
Ambassador
(American International Hotels)
Parker's
(Utell International)
Hotel Vesuvio
(SRS Hotels)

ROME
Ambasciatori Palace
(Trust Houses Forte)
Cavalieri Hilton
(Hilton Hotels)
Hotel Eden
(Tourex)
Holiday Inn-Parco Dei Medici
Holiday Inn-St. Peter's
(Holiday Inns)
Regency
(T.C.I. Hotels)
Villa del Parco
(Alexander Associates)

TRIESTE
Duchi d'Aosta
(Utell International)

VENICE
Hotel Ala
(Tourex)
Grand Hotel
(SRS Hotels)
Monaco and Grand Canal
(American International Hotels)

REPUBLIC OF IVORY COAST

ABIDJAN
Hotel Ivoire
(Inter-continental Hotels)
Relais Hotel
(Meridien Hotels)

JAMAICA

KINGSTON
Courtleigh Manor
(Utell International)

Sheraton Kingston
(Sheraton Hotels)

MONTEGO BAY
Bay Roc
Carlyle Beach
Hotel Coral Cliff
(Utell International)
Holiday Inn
(Holiday Inns)
Montego Bay Club
The Palms at Rose Hall
(Wolfe International)
Rose Hall Inter-Continental
(Inter-Continental Hotels)

OCHO RIOS
Hyatt Regency
(Hyatt Hotels)
Inter-Continental Ocho Rios
(Inter-Continental Hotels)

JAPAN

HIROSHIMA
Hiroshima Grand
(Utell International)

KYOTO
Holiday Inn
(Holiday Inns)
Kyoto Grand
(Sheraton Hotels)
The Miyako
(Western International Hotels)

OKINAWA
Hilton
(Hilton Hotels)

TOKYO
Grand Palace
(T.C.I. Hotels)
Keio Plaza
(Inter-Continental Hotels)
New Otani
(Utell International)

JORDAN

AMMAN
Jordan Intercontinental
(Inter-continental Hotels)

KENYA

NAIROBI
Hotel Ambassador
(Tourex)
Hotel Inter-Continental Nairobi
(Inter-Continental Hotels)
Nairobi Hilton
(Hilton Hotels)

KOREA

SEOUL
Chosun
(Americana Hotels)
Metro Hotel
(Tourex)

KUWAIT

Bristol
Messilah Beach
(Utell International)
Kuwait Hilton
(Hilton Hotels)
Kuwait Sheraton
(Sheraton Hotels)

LEBANON

BEIRUT
Beirut Carlton
(Utell International)
Beirut Hilton
(Hilton Hotels)
Holiday Inn
(Holiday Inns)
Martinez Hotel
(Tourex)
Phoenicia Intercontinental
(Inter-continental Hotels)

LESOTHO

MASERU
Lesotho Hilton
(Hilton Hotels)
Holiday Inn
(Holiday Inns)

LIBERIA

MONROVIA
Ducor Intercontinental
(Inter-continental Hotels)

LIECHTENSTEIN

TRIESENBERG
Tourotel
(Hoteline)

LUXEMBOURG

LUXEMBOURG
Hotel Aerogolf
Grand Hotel Cravat
Central Hotel Molitor
(American International Hotels)
Holiday Inn
(Holiday Inns)

MALAGASY REPUBLIC

TANNANARIVE
Madagascar Hilton
(Hilton Hotels)

MALAYSIA

KUALA LUMPUR
Federal
Merlin
(Utell International)
Holiday Inn
(Holiday Inns)
Kuala Lumpur Hilton
(Hilton Hotels)

MALTA

SLIEMA
Hotel Imperial
(Trust Houses Forte)

VALLETTA
The Malta Hilton
(Hilton Hotels)
Hotel Phoenicia
(Trust Houses Forte)

MARTINIQUE, W.I.

Hotel de L'Europe
Hotel Malmaison
(American International Hotels)
Frantel Martinique
Meridien Martinique
(Loews Reservations)
Hotel Les Alizes
(PLM Hotels)
Martinique Hilton
(Hilton Hotels)

MEXICO

ACAPULCO
Acapulco Continental
(Loews Reservations)
Acapulco Malibu
Condesa del Mar
El Presidente
Fiesta Tortuga
(Utell International)
Acapulco Princess
(Princess Hotels)
El Matador Hotel
Maraliza
(Estur)
Hyatt Regency Acapulco
(Hyatt Hotels)
Torreblanca
(Wolfe International)

GUADALAJARA
Aranzula
Roma
(Estur)
Camino Real
(Utell International)
Gran Hotel
(American International Hotels)
Hotel Roma
(Tourex)

MEXICO CITY
Alameda
Camino Real
Del Prado
(Utell International)
Casa Blanca
Continental
(Estur)
Holiday Inn (Airport)
Holiday Inn (Downtown)
(Holiday Inns)
Hotel Guadalupe
(Alexander Associates)
Metropol
(T.C.I. Hotels)

MONTERREY
Gran Hotel Ancira
(Utell International)
Holiday Inn
(Holiday Inns)
Ramada Inn
(Ramada Inns)

TIJUANA
Ramada Inn
(Ramada Inns)

MONACO

MONTE CARLO
Hotel Hermitage
(Princess Hotels)
Holiday Inn
(Holiday Inns)
Loews Monte Carlo
(Loews Reservations)
Metropole
(Utell International)

MONTSERRAT

Vue Pointe Hotel
(Utell International)

MOROCCO

CASABLANCA
Agedir
El Jadida
(First French Hotels)
Marhaba
(BTH Hotels)

TANGIER
Rif Hotel
(Tourex)
Tanjah Flandria
(Golden Tulip)

MUSCAT AND OMAN

MUSCAT

Inter-Continental Oman
(Inter-Continental Hotels)

NEPAL

KATHMANDU
Hotel de L'Annapurna
(Tourex)
Oberoi Soaltee
(Loews Reservations)

NETHERLANDS-ANTILLES

ARUBA
Aruba Caribbean Hotel/Casino
(Executive House Hotels)
Americana Aruba
(Hotels Unlimited)
Aruba Sheraton Hotel and Casino
(Sheraton Hotels)
Divi Divi
Tamarjin
(Utell International)

CURACAO
Arthur Frommer
(Loews Reservations)
Avila Beach Hotel
(Utell International)
Curacao Hilton
(Hilton Hotels)

ST. MAARTEN
Caravanserai
(Resort Representation Service)
Concord
(Loews Reservations)
Mullet Bay Beach Resort
(Marriott)

NEVIS

Croney's Old Manor Estate
(Wolfe International)
Zetland Plantation
(ITR, Inc.)

NEW CALEDONIA

Chateau Royal
(First French Hotels)
Isle De France Hotel
(Trust Houses Forte)

NEW GUINEA

PAPUA
Waijuga Resort, Wanigela
(Hanns Ebensten)

MADANG
Smuggler's Inn
(Trust Houses Forte)

RABAUL
Rabaul Travelodge
(Trust Houses Forte)

NEW HEBRIDES

Port Villa Inter-Continental
Island Inn
(Inter-Continental Hotels)

NEW ZEALAND

AUCKLAND
Auckland Travelodge
(Trust Houses Forte)
Hotel Inter-Continental Auckland
(Inter-Continental Hotels)

CHRISTCHURCH
White Heron Travelodge
(Trust Houses Forte)

WELLINGTON
Wellington Travelodge
(Trust Houses Forte)

NICARAGUA

MANAGUA
Hotel Inter-Continental Managua
(Inter-Continental Hotels)
Las Mercedes
(Estur)

NORWAY

OSLO
Grand
(SRS Hotels)
Scandinavia
(Utell International)

PAKISTAN

DACCA
Inter-Continental Dacca
(Inter-continental Hotels)

KARACHI
Hyatt Regency
(Hyatt)
Karachi Intercontinental
(Inter-continental Hotels)

PANAMA

PANAMA CITY
El Continental
(Utell International)
Holiday Inn
(Holiday Inns)

PANAMA
(continued)

PEARL ISLAND
Contadora Hotel Beach
(Estur)
Contadora Hotel
(Holiday Inns)

PARAGUAY

ASUNCION
Casino Ita Enramada
(Estur)
Gran Parana
(Tourex)
ITA Enramada
(Golden Tulip)

PERU

LIMA
Hotel Alcazar
(Tourex)
Columbus
Continental
Country Club
(Estur)
Lima Sheraton
(Sheraton Hotels)

PHILIPPINES

MANILA
Aloha Hotel
(Tourex)
Holiday Inn
(Holiday Inns)
Hyatt Regency Manila
(Hyatt Hotels)
Manila Peninsula
(SRS Hotels)
Ramada Inn
(Ramada Inns)
Silahis International
(Utell International)

POLAND

KRAKOW
Holiday Inn
(Holiday Inns)

WARSAW
Hotel Forum Warsaw
(Forum Hotels)

Inter-Continental Warsaw
(Inter-Continental Hotels)

PORTUGAL

LISBON
Altis
Diplomatico
(Golden Tulip)
Eduardo VII
Lutecia
Penta
(Utell International)
Lisbon Sheraton
(Sheraton Hotels)
Hotel de Reno
(Tourex)
Tivoli
(Trust Houses Forte)

PUERTO RICO

SAN JUAN
Americana
(Americana Hotels)
Borinquen
(Wolfe International)
Caribe Hilton
(Hilton Hotels)
Diplomat
(American International Hotels)
Excelsior
(Estur)
Holiday Inn-Condado
(Holiday Inns)
Puerto Rico Sheraton
(Sheraton Hotels)
Ramada Inn
(Ramada Inns)

RHODESIA

BULAWAYO
Holiday Inn
(Holiday Inns)

ROMANIA

BUCHAREST
Hotel Athenee Palace
Hotel Continental
Hotel Dorobant
Hotel Pare
Hotel Union
Hotel Modern
(Centroturist)

ST. KITTS, W.I.

Fairview Inn
(Wolfe International)
Ocean Terrace
(American International Hotels)

ST. LUCIA, B.W.I.

Anse Chastanet
(Tourex)
Cariblue Hotel
(Wolfe International)
Halcyon Beach Club
(T.C.I. Hotels)
Steigenberger Cariblue Hotel
(SRS Hotels)

ST. MARTIN, F.W.I.

Grand St. Martin Beach Hotel
(Alexander Associates)
La Galion Beach
St. Tropez
(ITR, Inc.)

ST. VINCENT AND THE GRENADINES

Blue Lagoon
(Alexander Associates)
Sunset Shores
(American International Hotels)

SAIPAN

Royal Taga
(Tourex)
Saipan Beach Inter-Continental Inn
(Inter-Continental Hotels)

SAUDI ARABIA

MECCA
Hotel Inter-Continental
(Inter-Continental Hotels)

RIYADH
Inter-Continental Riyadh
(Inter-Continental Hotels)

SCOTLAND

ABERDEEN
Sheraton Inn-Aberdeen
(Sheraton Inns)

DUNDEE
Queen's Hotel
(Trust Houses Forte)

EDINBURGH
Carlton
(Trust Houses Forte)
George Hotel
(Utell International)
Grosvenor Centre
(American International Hotels)

GLASGOW
Albany
(Golden Tulip)
Excelsior
(Trust Houses Forte)
Glasgow Centre
Hull Centre
(American International Hotels)

INVERNESS
Culloden House
(Trust Houses Forte)

SENEGAL

DAKAR
des Almadies
(SRS Hotels)
Teranga
(First French Hotels)

SINGAPORE

SINGAPORE
Equatorial
(Alexander Associates)
Holiday Inn
(Holiday Inns)
Hyatt Singapore
(Hyatt)
Shangri-La
(Utell International)
Singapore Hilton
(Hilton Hotels)

REPUBLIC OF SOUTH AFRICA

CAPETOWN
Heerengracht
(SRS Hotels)
Holiday Inn
(Holiday Inns)
Mount Nelson
(Loews Reservations)

REPUBLIC OF SOUTH AFRICA
(continued)

DURBAN
Cabana Beach
(SRS Hotels)
Park View Hotel
(Trust Houses Forte)

EASTERN TRANSVAAL
Mala Mala Game Reserve
(SRS Hotels)

HLUHLUWE, ZULULAND
Holiday Inn
(Holiday Inns)

JOHANNESBURG
Carlton Hotel
(Utell International)
The President
(Trust Houses Forte)
Southern Sun
(T.C.I. Hotels)

SPAIN

BARCELONA
Apolo
Arenas
Avenida Palace
Condor
La Rotunda
Presidente
(Utell International)

CORDOBA
Cordoba Melia Hotel
(Melia Hotels)

GRANADA
Melia Granada
(Melia Hotels)

MADRID

Carlton Hotel
Hotel Suecia
(Alexander Associates)
Castellana
The Claridge
Serraano
(Utell International)
Hotel Sanvy
(American International Hotels)

SUDAN

KHARTOUM
Khartoum Hilton
(Hilton Hotels)
Meridien Khartoum
(Meridien Hotels)

SURINAM

PARAMARIBO
Krasnapolsky
Surinam Torarico
(Golden Tulip)
Surinam Torarica Hotel/Casino
(Executive House Hotels)

SWAZILAND

MBABANE
Holiday Inn
(Holiday Inns)

SWEDEN

STOCKHOLM
Anglais Hotel
(SRS Hotels)
Diplomat
Palace
(Utell International)
Holiday Inn
(Holiday Inns)
Ramada Inn
(Ramada Inns)
Sheraton-Stockholm
(Sheraton Hotels)

SWITZERLAND

GENEVA
Amat-Carlton
D'Auteuil
Phenicia
(Utell International)
Hotel Intercontinental Geneve
(Inter-continental Hotels)
Ramada Inn
(Ramada Inns)
Windsor
(Tourex)

INTERLAKEN
Beau Rivage
(Utell International)

SWITZERLAND
(continued)

LAUSANNE
Alpha Palmiers
(American International Hotels)
De La Paix
(Utell International)

LUCERNE
Carlton Tivoli
Chateau Guetsch
Wilden Mann
(Utell International)

ST. MORITZ
Albania
Kulm Hotel
(American International Hotels)
Carlton
(SRS Hotels)

ZURICH
Ascot Hotel
Hotel Zurich
(American International Hotels)
Engematthof
Nova Park
(Utell International)
Hotel Zurich
(Trust Houses Forte)
Zurich Continental
(SRS Hotels)

SYRIA

DAMASCUS
Hotel Meridien Damascus
(Meridien Hotels)
Damascus Sheraton
(Sheraton Hotels)

TAHITI

MOOREA
Aimeo Hotel
(T.C.I. Hotels)
Kia Ora
(First French Hotels)

PAPEETE
Holiday Inn
(Holiday Inns)
Maera Beach
(First French Hotels)

TAIWAN

TAIPEI
Ambassador
(Utell International)
Hotel China
(Tourex)
Taipei Hilton
(Hilton Hotels)

TANZANIA

Zanzibar
Dar Es Salaam
Hotel Kilimanjaro
(Golden Tulip)
Oberoi Ya Bwanani
(Loews Reservations)

THAILAND

BANGKOK
Hotel Amarin
(Tourex)
Dusit'Thani
(Utell International)
Hyatt Rama Bangkok
(Hyatt)
Sheraton-Bangkok
(Sheraton Hotels)

TOBAGO

Arnos Vale
(Utell International)
Crown Reef Hotel
(Wolfe International)
Turtle Beach Hotel
(T.C.I. Hotels)

TONGA

International Dateline Hotel
(Wolfe International)

TRINIDAD

PORT-OF-SPAIN
Bretton Hall
(American International)
Chaconia Inn
(Alexander Associates)
Trinidad Hilton
(Hilton Hotels)

TUNISIA

HAMMAMET
Hammamet-Sheraton
(Sheraton Hotels)

TUNIS
Meridien Tunis
(Meridien Hotels)
The Tunis Hilton
(Hilton Hotels)

TURKEY

ISTANBUL
Inter-Continental Istanbul
(Inter-Continental Hotels)
Istanbul Hilton
(Hilton Hotels)
Istanbul Sheraton
(Sheraton Hotels)

UNITED ARAB EMIRATES

ABU DHABI
Abu Dhabi Hilton
(Hilton Hotels)

AL AIN
Al Ain Hilton
(Hilton Hotels)

DUBAI
Dubai Inter-Continental
(Inter-Continental Hotels)

SHARJAH
Holiday Inn
(Holiday Inns)

URUGUAY

MONTEVIDEO
Columbia Palace
(Utell International)
Lancaster
Victoria Plaza
(Estur)

VENEZUELA

CARACAS
Avila
El Conde
(Estur)
Holiday Inn
(Holiday Inns)

Residencias Anauco Hilton
(Hilton Hotels)

VIRGIN ISLANDS, BRITISH

Long Bay
Sugar Mill Estates
(Wolfe International)
Marina Cay
(American International)
Little Dix Bay
(Loews Reservations)

VIRGIN ISLANDS, U.S.A.

ST. CROIX
Cane Bay
Charter House
Pink Fancy
Tamarind
(Wolfe International)
Caribbean View
Club Comanche
Sprat Hall
(American International Hotels)
Reef Beach and Golf Resort
(ITR, Inc.)
St. Croix-by-the-Sea
(Utell International)

ST. THOMAS
Bali Hai
(Wolfe International)
Frenchman's Reef
(Holiday Inn)
Harbor View
Morning Star Beach Resort
(American International Hotels)
Virgin Isle Hilton
(Hilton Hotels)

WESTERN SAMOA

APIA
Aggie Grey's
(H.S.I. Reservations)

YUGOSLAVIA

BELGRADE
Hotel Yugoslavia
(SRS Hotels)
Hotel Metropol
Hotel Moskva
Hotel Slovia
(Centroturist)

YUGOSLAVIA
(continued)

ZAIRE

KINSHASA
Inter-Continental Kinshasa
(Inter-Continental Hotels)

DUBROVNIK
Dubrovnik Argosy
Hotel Excelsior
Grand Hotel Imperial
Hotel Leros
Hotel Tirena
Hotel Villa Dubrovnik
(Centroturist)

ZAMBIA

LUSAKA
Inter-Continental Lusaka
(Inter-Continental Hotels)

HOTEL REPRESENTATIVES
NATIONWIDE TOLL-FREE NUMBERS

Alexander Associates	800-221-6509	Marriott	800-228-9290
American International	800-223-5695	Melia Hotels (Except NYS)	800-221-2152
Americana Hotels	800-228-3278	Meridien Hotels	800-223-9918
Best Western Int'l	800-528-1234	NYS	800-442-5917
British Transport Hotels		Ray Morrow Assoc.	
(BTH) (Except NYS)	800-223-5748	(Except NYS)	800-223-9838
Scott Calder	800-223-5581	Penta Hotels	800-223-9868
Jane Condon Corp.	800-223-5608	Albert Pick Hotels	
CP Hotels	800-323-8811	(Except Illinois)	800-621-4404
Cunard	800-221-6800	Princess Hotels Int'l	
I. Oliver Engebretson, Inc.	800-223-7613	(Except Florida)	800-327-1313
Fairmont Hotels	800-527-4727	Ramada Inns	800-228-2828
First French Hotels	800-421-5917	Regent Int'l.	
Great Southern Hotels	800-225-9810	(Except California)	800-421-0530
Hawaii Hotel Marketing	800-421-0680	Robert Reid Assoc.	
Holiday Inns	800-223-6680	(Except Northeast)	800-621-6460
Hospitality House		Scanworld	800-423-2677
(Except NYS & Fla.)	800-238-5400	Sheraton Hotels &	
Hoteline (Except N.Y.		Motor Inns	800-325-3535
State)	800-223-7780	Sofitel Jacques Borel	800-223-5742
Hotel Representative, Inc.		Sonesta Hotels	800-225-1372
(Except NYS)	800-223-6800	SRS-Steingenberger Res.	800-225-5652
Hotels Unlimited	800-327-3384	Strand Hotels	800-223-5742
H.S.I.	800-421-6662	John A. Tetley	800-421-0001
Jack Hugen International		Calif.	800-252-0211
(Except Florida)	800-327-9471	Transportation Consultants	
Hyatt Hotels	800-228-9000	Int'l. Calif.	800-252-0063
Harry Jarvinen		Except Calif.	800-421-0652
(Except California)	800-421-0767	Travelodge	800-255-3050
Howard Johnson's	800-654-2000	Treadway Inns (Except NJ)	800-631-0182
InterIsland Resorts		Trust Houses Forte	
(Except California)	800-421-0811	(Except NYS)	800-223-5672
International Travel &		Utell International	800-223-9868
Resorts (Except NYS)	800-223-9815	Robert F. Warner, Inc.	800-225-6130
Maurice S. Kash & Assoc.	800-621-1010	Western International	
Knott Hotels (Except Fla.)	800-327-3384	Hotels	800-228-3000
Lex Hotels	800-223-5757	Wolfe International	800-223-5695
Lisland International			
(Except NYS)	800-221-5252		

Appendix I

MAJOR CRUISE SHIPS

BALTIC SHIPPING COMPANY

M. S. ALEXANDER PUSHKIN

Sails from New York, Leningrad, Bremerhaven, London, LeHavre and Montreal. Built/Rebuilt 1965/1975. Registry: U.S.S.R. Capacity: 700 Passengers; Normal Crew Size: 340 (U.S.S.R.).

Specifics: Gross Tonnage 19,860; Length - 580 ft., Width - 77 ft.; stabilizers; fully air conditioned; 3 elevators; inside and outside swimming pools; 9 passenger decks; gymnasium/sauna; gambling (slot machines); outside staterooms; inside staterooms; 350 dining room capacity; 125 theatre capacity.

Itinerary: Spring and Fall trans-Atlantic sailings from Montreal and New York to Europe. Summer cruising from Canada to Caribbean including Havana. Winter cruising in Europe (Mediterranean). Tenders some ports. Docks at most.

M.S. MIKHAIL LERMONTOV

From Leningrad, New York, Bremerhaven, London (Tilbury), LeHavre trans-Atlantic, Baltic countries and to Caribbean from New York and Montreal. Built 1971. Registry: U.S.S.R. Capacity: 700 Passengers; Normal Crew Size: 340 (U.S.S.R.).

Specifics: Gross Tonnage 19,860; Length - 580 ft.; Width - 77 ft.; stabilizers; fully air conditioned; 3 elevators; inside and outside swimming pools; 9 passenger decks; gymnasium/sauna; gambling (slot machines); outside staterooms; inside staterooms; 340 dining room capacity; 130 theatre capacity.

Itinerary: Trans-Atlantic from New York and Montreal to Leningrad, Bremerhaven, etc. during Summer and Fall. Winters from Montreal to Caribbean and West Indies, which include Havana.

CARNIVAL CRUISE LINES

TSS CARNIVALE

Sails Miami to Caribbean. Built/Rebuilt 1956/1976. Registry: Panama. Capacity: 950 Passengers; Normal Crew Size: 510 (Italian Officers with a mixed crew).

Specifics: Gross Tonnage 27,250; Length - 640 ft.; Width - 87 ft.; stabilizers; fully air conditioned; 4 elevators; 4 outside swimming pools and 1 inside pool; 9 passenger decks; gymnasium/sauna; gambling (full casinos: blackjack, craps, roulette); 575 dining room capacity; 180 theatre capacity.

Itinerary: Seven day cruises, leaving on Sunday and returning on Sunday. Stops Samana, San Juan (2 days), St. Croix. At sea three days. Air/Sea packages from most cities.

TSS FESTIVALE

From Miami to Caribbean. Built/Rebuilt 1961/1978. Registry: Panama. Capacity: 1,148 Passengers; Normal Crew Size: 570 (Italian Officers with a mixed crew).

Specifics: Gross Tonnage 38,175; Length - 760 ft.; Width - 90 ft., Stabilizers; fully air conditioned; 4 elevators; 3 outside pools; 9 passengers decks; gymnasium/sauna; gambling (full casinos: blackjack, craps, roulette); 700 dining room capacity; 202 theatre capacity.

Itinerary: Cruises for seven days; leaving on Saturdays. Ports visited - San Juan (2 days), St. Thomas, St. Maarten. At sea for 3 days. Air/Sea packages from most cities.

TSS MARDI GRAS

7-day Caribbean cruises from Miami. Built/Rebuilt 1961/1973. Registry Panama. Capacity: 906 Passengers; Normal Crew Size: 510 (Italian Officers with a mixed crew).

Specifics: Gross Tonnage 27,250; Length - 650 ft.; Width - 87 ft.; Stabilizers; fully air conditioned; 2 outside swimming pools, 1 inside pool; 9 passengers decks; 4 elevators; gymnasium/sauna; gambling (full casino: blackjack, craps, roulette); 550 dining room capacity; 200 theatre capacity.

Itinerary: Sunday departures to Nassau, San Juan and St. Thomas. Air/Sea package from most cities.

CARRIS CRUISES

MTS DANAE

Sails from New Orleans; Villefrance and Genoa or Piraeus. Built/Rebuilt 1956/1976. Registry: Greece. Capacity: 465 Passengers; Normal Crew Size: 250 (Greek).

Specifics: Gross Tonnage 15,560; Length - 532 ft.; Width - 74 ft.; stabilizers; individually controlled air conditioning; 2 elevators; 2 outside swimming pools; 5 passenger decks; gymnasium/sauna (sauna massage room); outside staterooms; inside staterooms; 468 dining room capacity; 245 theatre capacity.

Itinerary: Winters and Spring from New Orleans to Mexico and Aegean. From Villefrance, Genoa and Piraeus to Mediterranean and Red Sea; From June - September to Mediterranean and Black Sea.

MTS DAPHNE

From New Orleans; Villefrance and Genoa. Built/Rebuilt 1955/1975. Registry: Greece. Capacity: 465 Passengers; Normal Crew Size: 250 (Greek).

Specifics: Gross Tonnage 16,330; Length - 532 ft.; Width - 74 ft.; stabilizers; individually controlled air conditioning; 2 elevators; 2 outside swimming pools; gymnasium/sauna (sauna massage room); outside staterooms; inside staterooms; 468 dining room capacity; 245 theatre capacity.

Itinerary: Spring and Winter months from New Orleans to Montego Bay, Puerto Cortes, Santo Tomas. Summer from New York to LeHavre and from Amsterdam to North Sea countries.

CHANDRIS, INC.

S. S. AMERIKANIS

Leaves Charleston and San Juan. Built/Rebuilt 1952/1971. Registry: Greece. Capacity 650 Passengers; Normal Crew Size: 250 (Greek).

Specifics: Gross Tonnage 19,377; Length - 576 ft., Width - 74 ft.; air conditioning throughout; 2 elevators; gymnasium/sauna; gambling (small casino); outside staterooms; inside staterooms; 350 dining room capacity; 115 theatre capacity; 8 passenger decks.

Itinerary: 7-Day cruises departing Saturdays, May through October. Ports stopped at include Palma, Toulon, Tunis, Malta, etc.

S. S. ARIANE

Sails from Piraeus. Built/Rebuilt 1951/1974. Registry: Liberia. Capacity: 350 Passengers; Greek Crew.

Specifics: Gross Tonnage 6,644; Length - 454 ft.; Width - 58 ft.; air conditioned throughout; gambling (small casino); outside staterooms; inside staterooms; 1 outside swimming pool; 175 dining room capacity, 5 passenger decks.

Itinerary: 7-Day cruises departing on Monday from June through October. Leaving Piraeus some of the ports encountered are Hydra, Rhodes, Santorini, Corfu, other Greek Islands and Turkey.

S. S. BRITANIS

From Amsterdam or Genoa. Built/Rebuilt 1932/1970. Registry: Greece. Capacity: 1,600 Passengers on Trans-Atlantic cruise; Normal Crew Size: 420 (Greek).

Specifics: Gross Tonnage 24,351; Length - 642 ft.; Width - 79 ft.; fully air conditioned; 3 elevators; 1 outside swimming pool; gymnasium/sauna; gambling (small casino); outside staterooms; inside staterooms; 732 (2) dining room capacity; 155 theatre capacity; 9 passenger decks.

Itinerary: 14-Day cruise from Amsterdam to Northern Capitals - Holland, Sweden, Finland, etc., or to North Cape & Norwegian Fjords.

S. S. ELLINIS

Sails from Genoa. Built 1932. Registry: Greece. Capacity: 1,642 Trans-Atlantic Passengers; Normal Crew Size: 500 (Greek).

Specifics: Gross Tonnage 24,351; Length - 642 ft.; Width - 79 ft.; fully air conditioned; 2 elevators; 1 outside swimming pool; gymnasium/sauna; gambling (small casino); 9 passenger decks; outside staterooms; inside staterooms; 732 (2) dining room capacity; 155 theatre capacity.

Itinerary: 14-Day cruise departing on Saturdays. Departures May through October. Ports arrived at are Syracuse, Alexandria, Haifa, Kusadasi, Istanbul, Naples, etc.

S. S. ITALIS

Built/Rebuilt 1940/1965. Registry: Panama. Capacity: 2,258; Normal Crew Size: 600 (Greek).

Specifics: Gross Tonnage 34,449; Length - 723 ft.; Width - 93 ft.; fully air conditioned; 5 elevators; 8 passenger decks; gymnasium/sauna; 1 inside swimmming pool; gambling (mini casino); outside staterooms; inside staterooms; 1,132 (2) dining room capacity; 130 theatre capacity.

REGINA PRIMA

Leaves Venice. Built/Rebuilt 1939/1965. Registry: Panama. Capacity: 610 Passengers; Greek Crew.

Specifics: Gross Tonnage 10,618; Length - 493 ft.; Width - 64 ft.; fully air conditioned; 1 outside swimming pool; 7 passenger decks; gambling (small casino); outside staterooms; inside staterooms; 300 dining room capacity; 190 theatre capacity.

Itinerary: 12-Day cruise from Venice to the Greek Islands (Katakolon, Piraeus, Rhodes, etc.), Cyprus and Israel. Cruises April through October. Saturday departures.

M. V. ROMANZA

Leaves from Piraeus or Venice. Built/Rebuilt 1939/1971. Registry: Greece. Capacity: 630 Passengers; Normal Crew Size: 250 (Greek).

Specifics: Gross Tonnage 12,000; Length - 487 ft.; Width - 60 ft.; air conditioned throughout; 1 outside swimming pool; 7 passenger decks; gambling (small casino); outside staterooms; inside staterooms; 420 dining room capacity; 200 theatre capacity.

Itinerary: 21-Day Red Sea Cruise. Departure on Sundays in March. Stops made at Port Said, Suez Canal, Port Sudan, etc. 8-Day Legendary Lands Cruise. Departure every Saturday: April through October. Depart from Venice, stopping at Corfu, Rhodes, Piraeus, Heraklion.

M/S VICTORIA

From Venice. Built/Rebuilt 1939/1959. Registry: Greece. Capacity: 450 Passengers; Normal Crew Size: 300 (Greek).

Specifics: Gross Tonnage 20,000; Length - 575 ft.; Width - 72 ft.; fully air conditioned; 3 elevators; 2 outside swimming pools; gymnasium/sauna; gambling (small casino); 5 passenger decks; outside staterooms; inside staterooms; 250 dining room capacity; 250 theatre capacity.

Itinerary: 4 different cruises of 14 nights each. All depart from Venice on Saturdays. April through September is the Eastern Mediterranean-Egypt Israel cruise; May is the Ecumenical Cruise-Eastern Mediterranean including Katakolon, Heraklion, Haifa, etc.; June and September offer the Black Sea & Russia Cruise; and the final cruise is offered in October to Greece, Turkey, Israel and Egypt.

COMMODORE CRUISE LINE, LTD.

M/S BOHEME

Sails from Miami to the Caribbean. Built/Rebuilt 1968/1977. Registry: West Germany. Capcity: 500 Passengers; Normal Crew Size: 220 (International).

Specifics: Gross Tonnage 11,000; Length - 450 ft.; Width - 65 ft.; stabilizers; 2 elevators; 1 outside swimming pool; 7 passenger decks; gymnasium/sauna; gambling (blackjack, slot machines); outside staterooms; inside staterooms; 250 dining room capacity; 100 theatre capacity.

Itinerary: Departs every Saturday from Miami docking at Puerto Plata, St. Thomas, San Juan, Cape Haitien.

CARIBE

From Miami. Built/Rebuilt 1968/1976. Registry: West Germany. Capacity: 480 Passengers; Normal Crew Size: 200 (Mixed).

Specifics: Gross Tonnage 11,000; Length - 441 ft.; Width - 70 ft.; stabilizers; fully air conditioned; 1 outside swimming pool; 3 elevators; 7 passenger decks; gambling (blackjack, slot machines, roulette); outside staterooms; inside staterooms; 250 dining room capacity; 150 theatre capacity.

Itinerary: Saturday departures from Miami throughout the entire year. Docks at Freeport, St. Thomas, San Juan, Puerto Rico, Puerto Plata.

COSTA CRUISES

S. S. AMERIKANIS

Charter from Chandris, Inc. Sails from Charleston and San Juan. Built/Rebuilt 1952/1971. Registry: Greece. Capacity: 650 Passengers; Normal Crew Size: 250 (Greek).

Specifics: Gross Tonnage 19,377; Length - 576 ft.; Width - 74 ft.; air conditioning throughout; 2 elevators; gymnasium/sauna; gambling (small casino); outside staterooms; inside staterooms; 350 dining room capacity; 115 theatre capacity; 8 passenger decks.

Itinerary: 7-Day Caribbean Cruises. Sailing Saturdays to St. Maarten, St. Lucia, Martinique, Antigua, Barbados, St. Thomas.

M/S ANDREA C.

Leaves Venice. Built/Rebuilt 1942/1976. Registry: Italy. Capacity: 400 Passengers; Normal Crew Size: 180 (Italian).

Specifics: Gross Tonnage 8,600; Length - 467 ft.; Width - 57 ft.; fully air conditioned; 5 passenger decks; 2 outside swimming pools; 242 dining room capacity; 120 theatre capacity; outside staterooms; inside staterooms.

Itinerary: 12-Day cruises from Venice stopping at Piraeus, Delos, Mykonos, Istanbul, Corfu, etc.

M/S ANGELINA *

From San Juan. Built/Rebuilt 1939/1972. Registry: Italy. Capacity: 800 Passengers, Normal Crew Size: 350 (Italian).

Specifics: Gross Tonnage 24,400; Length - 672 ft. 4 in.; Width - 83 ft., 6 in.; stabilizers; 5 elevators; fully air conditioned; 8 passenger decks; gymnasium/sauna; gambling; 2 outside swimming pools; 1 inside swimming pool; outside staterooms; inside staterooms; 541 dining room capacity; 197 theatre capacity.

*Sank on 31 March, 1979, St. Thomas, V. I.

Itinerary: 7-Day Caribbean and South American Cruises, departing Saturdays to St. Maarten, Guadeloupe, Grenada, Caracas, St. Thomas.

M/S CARLA C.

Sails from San Juan. Built/Rebuilt 1952/1976. Registry: Italy. Capacity: 748 Passengers; Normal Crew Size: 370 (Italian).

Specifics: Gross Tonnage 20,477; Length - 600 ft.; Width - 80 ft.; stabilizers; fully air conditioned; 8 passenger decks; 2 outside swimming pools; 5 elevators; gambling; outside staterooms; inside staterooms; 244 & 384 dining room capacity; 145 theatre capacity.

Itinerary: 7-Day Caribbean and South American Cruises, sailing Saturdays to Curacao, Caracas, Trinidad, Martinique, St. Thomas.

T/S ENRICO C.

Leaves Genoa. Built/Rebuilt 1950/1976. Registry: Italy. Capacity: 700 Passengers; Normal Crew Size: 300 (Italian).

Specifics: Gross Tonnage 16,000; Length - 579 ft.; Width - 73 ft.; fully air conditioned; elevators; 7 passenger decks; 3 outside swimming pools; outside staterooms; inside staterooms; 657 dining room capacity; 150 theatre capacity.

Itinerary: 7-Day Cruises from Genoa to Cannes, Barcelona, Palma De Mallorca, Naples, etc.

M/S EUGENIO C.

24 Ports, 26,940 miles around the world cruise. Built/Rebuilt 1966/1976. Registry: Italy. Capacity: 1,637 Trans-Atlantic Cruise; Normal Crew Size: 475 (Italian).

Specifics: Gross Tonnage 30,000; Length - 713 ft.; Width - 96 ft.; stabilizers; fully air conditioned; 9 passenger decks; 3 outside swimming pools; gymnasium/sauna; outside staterooms; inside staterooms; 205, 220 & 622 dining room capacity; 230 theatre capacity.

Itinerary: October to December Around the World Cruise, some ports of call Genoa, Suez, Madras, Singapore, Kobe, Honolulu, Los Angeles, Acapulco, Sunchal, Cannes. Sails from Genoa.

S/S FEDERICO C.

From Genoa and Miami. Built/Rebuilt 1958/1976. Registry: Italy. Capacity:
800 Passengers; Normal Crew Size: 350 (Italian).

Specifics: Gross Tonnage 20,416; Length – 606 ft.; Width – 74 ft.; stabilizers;
4 elevators; 3 outside swimming pools; fully air conditioned; 8 passenger decks; gym;
gambling (when in Caribbean); outside staterooms; inside staterooms; 380, 218 & 135
dining room capacity; 170 theatre capacity.

Itinerary: 10-Day cruise from Miami to Caribbean and South America. Ports of call
are Montego Bay, Aruba, Cozumel, etc.

S/S FLAVIA

Sails from Venice. Built/Rebuilt 1947/1976. Registry: Italy. Capacity: 850
Passengers; Normal Crew Size: 240 (Italian).

Specifics: Gross Tonnage 15,465; Length – 531 ft.; Width – 70 ft.; stabilizers;
fully air conditioned; 2 elevators; 8 passenger decks; 2 + 1 children outside swimming
pools; gambling; outside staterooms; inside staterooms; 301/142 dining room capacity;
250 theatre capacity.

Itinerary: 7-Day cruises from Venice to Dubrovnik, Corfu, Piraeus, Rhodes.

M/S ITALIA

Built 1967. Registry: Italy. Capacity: 514 Passengers; Normal Crew Size: 240
(Italian).

Specifics: Gross Tonnage 12,200; Length – 488 ft.; Width – 70 ft.; stabilizers;
6 elevators; 8 passenger decks; 1 outside swimming pool; outside staterooms; inside
staterooms; 267 dining room capacity; 186 theatre capacity.

M/S WORLD RENAISSANCE

From Miami. Built 1966. Registry: Greece. Capacity: 528 Passengers; Greek Crew.

Specifics: Gross Tonnage 12,000; Length – 492 ft.; Width – 69 ft.; stabilizers;
fully air conditioned; 8 passenger decks; 2 outside swimming pools; gymnasium/sauna;
gambling; outside staterooms; inside staterooms; 400 dining room capacity; 115 theatre
capacity.

Itinerary: 10-Day Cruises from Miami docking at Port Antonio, Cartagena, Panama,
San Andres, Cozumel. Departure on Fridays. Air/Sea Package available from all major
U.S. cities.

CUNARD LINE LIMITED

CUNARD COUNTESS

Sails from San Juan. Built 1976. Registry: Britain. Capacity: 750 Passengers; Normal Crew Size: 350 (British, except for dining room).

Specifics: Gross Tonnage 17,495; Length - 536 ft. 10 in.; Width - 74 ft. 10 in.; stabilizers; fully air conditioned; 8 passenger decks; 1 outside swimming pool; 2 elevators; gambling (slots, blackjack); outside staterooms; inside staterooms; 500 dining room capacity; 135 theatre capacity.

Itinerary: 7-Day Caribbean Cruises every Saturday from June through October. Port of Call: Caracas (Venezuela), Grenada, Barbados, St. Lucia, St. Thomas.

CUNARD PRINCESS

Leaves Fort Lauderdale. Built 1977. Registry: Britain. Capacity: 750 Passengers; Normal Crew Size 350 (British, except for dining room).

Specifics: Gross Tonnage 17,495; Length - 536 ft. 10 in.; Width - 74 ft. 10 in.; stabilizers; fully air conditioned; 8 passenger decks; 1 outside swimming pool; 2 elevators; gambling (slots, blackjack); outside staterooms; inside staterooms; 500 dining room capacity; 135 theatre capacity.

Itinerary: 7-Day Cruises every Saturday June through October. Port of Call: Puerto Plata, San Juan, St. Thomas, Nassau.

QUEEN ELIZABETH 2

Sails from New York, Boston, Norfolk, Port Everglades. Built 1969. Registry: Britain. Capacity: 1,815 Trans-Atlantic; Normal Crew Size: 1,000 (British).

Specifics: Gross Tonnage 67,139; Length - 963 ft.; Width - 105 ft.; stabilizers; fully air conditioned; 13 passenger decks; 2 outside and 2 inside swimming pools; 13 elevators; gymnasium/sauna; gambling (casino w. slot machines, blackjack, and roulette); outside staterooms; inside staterooms; 834, 610, 102, 188 dining room capacity; 531 theatre capacity.

Itinerary: Cruises vary in length from New York to the Caribbean. Some Ports of Call are St. Thomas, San Juan, Nassau, Martinque, etc.

THE DELTA QUEEN STEAMBOAT CO.

DELTA QUEEN

From New Orleans, Cincinnati, St. Louis, St. Paul and Pittsburgh. Built/Rebuilt 1926/1974. Registry: United States. Capacity: 188 Passengers; Normal Crew Size: 77 (American).

Specifics: Gross Tonnage 1,650; Length - 285 ft.; Width - 58 ft.; air cooled; 3 passenger decks; outside staterooms; 188 dining room capacity.

Itinerary: Cruises ranging from 2-19 days up the Ohio and Mississippi Rivers.

MISSISSIPPI QUEEN

Sails from New Orleans, Cincinnati, and St. Louis. Built 1976. Registry: United States. Capacity: 377 Passengers; Normal Crew Size: 142 (American).

Specifics: Gross Tonnage 4,500; Length - 382 ft.; Width - 68 ft.; air conditioned; 7 passenger decks; 1 outside swimming pool; 2 elevators; gymnasium/sauna; outside staterooms; inside staterooms; 258 dining room capacity; 125 theatre capacity.

Itinerary: 7-Day trip from New Orleans to Natchez and Vicksburg with stops at St. Francisville and Baton Rouge. Departures every Saturday except during July. During July there are three different cruises available.

SANTA MAGDALENA

Built/Rebuilt 1964/1974-75. Registry: United States. Capacity: 100 Passengers; Normal Crew Size: 100 (American). Leaves from San Francisco.

Specifics: Gross Tonnage 16,329; Length - 546 ft.; Width - 79 ft.; stabilizers; air conditioned; 5 passenger decks; 1 elevator; 1 outside swimming pool; outside staterooms; inside staterooms; 106 dining room capacity; 100 theatre capacity.

SANTA MARIA

Built/Rebuilt 1965/1974-75. Registry: United States. Capacity: 100 Passengers; Normal Crew Size: 100 (American). From San Francisco.

Specifics: Gross Tonnage 16,329; Length - 546 ft.; Width - 79 ft.; stabilizers; air conditioned; 1 elevator; 5 passenger decks; 1 outside swimming pool; outside staterooms; inside staterooms; 100 dining room capacity; 100 theatre capacity.

SANTA MARIANA

Built/Rebuilt 1964/1974-75. Registry: United States. Capacity: 100 Passengers; Normal Crew Size: 100 (American). Sails San Francisco.

Specifics: Gross Tonnage 16,329; Length - 546 ft.; Width - 79 ft.; stabilizers; air conditioned; 5 passenger decks; 1 outside swimming pool; 1 elevator; outside staterooms; inside staterooms; 100 dining room capacity; 100 theatre capacity.

SANTA MERCEDES

Built/Rebuilt 1965/1974-75. Registry: United States. Capacity: 100 Passengers;
Normal Crew Size: 100 (American). From San Francisco.

Specifics: Gross Tonnage 16,329; Length - 546 ft.; Width - 79 ft.; stabilizers;
air conditioned; 5 passenger decks; 1 outside swimming pool; 1 elevator; outside
staterooms; inside staterooms; 100 dining room capacity; 100 theatre capacity.

EASTERN STEAMSHIP LINES

SS EMERALD SEAS

Leaves Miami. Built/Rebuilt 1944/1977. Registry: Panama; Capacity: 800 Passengers;
Normal Crew Size: 400 (International).

Specifics: Gross Tonnage 24,458; Length - 622 ft.; Width - 75 ft.; 4 elevators;
7 passenger decks; 1 outside swimming pool; air conditioned; outside staterooms;
inside staterooms; 465 dining room capacity; 158 theatre capacity.

Itinerary: Leaves every Monday for 4 night cruises to Nassau/Freeport. Also 3 night
cruises every Friday to Nassau.

EPIROTIKI LINES

APOLLO XI

From Piraeus. Built/Rebuilt 1948/1970. Registry: Greece. Capacity: 300 Passengers;
Normal Crew Size: 139 (Greek).

Specifics: Gross Tonnage 6,000; Length - 353 ft.; stabilizers; air conditioned;
1 elevator; 6 passenger decks; 1 outside swimming pool; outside staterooms; inside
staterooms; 200 dining room capacity.

Itinerary: 7-Day cruises every Friday from April to November. Ports of Call Istanbul,
Izmir, Ephesus, Delos, Rhodes, etc.

ARGONAUT

Leaves from Piraeus. Built/Rebuilt 1929/1965. Registry: Greece. Capacity: 200
Passengers; Normal Crew Size: 102 (Greek).

Specifics: Gross Tonnage 4,500; Length - 340 ft.; Width - 47 ft.; air conditioned;
4 passenger decks; 1 outside swimming pool; outside staterooms; 200 dining room
capacity.

ATLAS

Leaves Piraeus. Built/Rebuilt 1951/1973. Registry: Greece. Capacity: 675-700 Passengers; Normal Crew Size: 297 (Greek).

Specifics: Gross Tonnage 16,000; Length - 510 ft. 5 in.; Width - 70 ft. 3 in.; stabilizers; air conditioned; 9 passenger decks; 2 outside and 1 inside swimming pool; 2 elevators; gymnasium/sauna; outside staterooms; inside staterooms; 360 dining room capacity; 300 theatre capacity.

Itinerary: 7-Day cruises every other Saturday from April to November. Ports of Call Istanbul, Izmir, Delos, Mykonos, Rhodes, Herakleion, Santorini.

JASON

Sails from Piraeus. Built 1965. Registry: Greece. Capacity: 275 Passengers; Normal Crew Size: 112 (Greek).

Specifics: Gross Tonnage 5,200; Length - 346 ft.; stabilizers; 1 elevator; air conditioned; 7 passenger decks; 1 outside swimming pool; outside staterooms; inside staterooms; 300 dining room capacity.

Itinerary: 7-Day cruises every other Saturday from April to November. Ports of Call include Alexandria, Rhodes, Santorini, Patmos, Mykonos, Delos.

JUPITER

Built/Rebuilt 1961/1971. Registry: Greece. Capacity: 450 Passengers; Normal Crew Size: 212 (Greek).

Specifics: Gross Tonnage 9,000; Length - 415 ft. 5 in.; Width - 65 ft. 3 in.; stabilizers; air conditioned; 1 elevator; gymnasium/sauna; 7 passenger decks; 1 outside swimming pool; outside staterooms; inside staterooms; 330 dining room capacity; 110 theatre capacity.

NEPTUNE

Built/Rebuilt 1955/1972. Registry: Greece. Capacity: 190 Passengers; Normal Crew Size: 97 (Greek).

Specifics: Gross Tonnage 4,000; Length - 300 ft.; Width - 45 ft. 1 in.; air conditioned; 6 passenger decks; 1 outside swimming pool; outside staterooms; inside staterooms; 200 dining room capacity.

ORPHEUS

Built/Rebuilt 1952/1969. Registry: Greece. Capacity: 330 Passengers; Normal Crew Size: 139 (Greek).

Specifics: Gross Tonnage 6,000; Length – 353 ft.; Width – 51 ft.; stabilizers; air conditioned; 6 passenger decks; 1 outside swimming pool; outside staterooms; inside staterooms; 170 dining room capacity.

HELLENIC MEDITERRANEAN LINE

M/S AQUARIUS

From Piraeus. Built 1972. Registry: Greece. Capacity: 297 Passengers; Normal Crew Size: 125 (Greek).

Specifics: Gross Tonnage 4,800; Length – 340 ft.; Width – 45 ft.; stabilizers; fully air conditioned; 6 passenger decks; 1 outside swimming pool; 1 elevator; outside staterooms; inside staterooms; 180 dining room capacity.

Itinerary: 7-Day cruises leaving every Friday to the Greek Islands and Istanbul, Turkey.

M/S CASTALIA

Sails from Piraeus. Built 1975. Registry: Greece. Capacity: 380 Passengers; Normal Crew Size: 140 (Greek).

Specifics: Gross Tonnage 9,000; Length – 442 ft.; Width – 72 ft.; stabilizers; fully air conditioned; 6 passenger decks; 1 outside swimming pool; 1 elevator; outside staterooms; inside staterooms; 200 dining room capacity.

Itinerary: Daily departures from March to October.

HOLLAND AMERICA CRUISES

M. S. PRINSENDAM

Leaves Singapore. Built 1973. Registry: Neth. Antilles. Capacity: 388 Passengers; Normal Crew Size: 154 (Dutch/Indonesian).

Specifics: Gross Tonnage 9,000; Length – 427 ft.; Width – 62 ft.; stabilizers; 2 elevators; 6 passenger decks; 1 outside swimming pool; outside staterooms; inside staterooms; 200 dining room capacity; 104 theatre capacity.

Itinerary: 14-Day Indonesia Adventure Cruises October through April.

S. S. ROTTERDAM

From New York and Port Everglades. Built/Rebuilt 1959/1969. Registry: Neth. Antilles.
Capacity: 1,050 Passengers; Normal Crew Size: 560 (Dutch/Indonesian).

Specifics: Gross Tonnage 38,000; Length – 748 ft.; Width – 94 ft.; stabilizers;
fully air conditioned; 11 passenger decks; 8 elevators; gymnasium/sauna; 1 outside
and 1 inside swimming pool; outside staterooms; inside staterooms; 510 & 260 dining
room capacity; 620 (Incl. Balcony) theatre capacity.

Itinerary: 7-Day Cruises to Nassau and Bermuda from June to August.

S. S. STATENDAM

Sails New York and Port Everglades. Built/Rebuilt 1957/1972. Registry: Neth. Antilles.
Capacity: 800 Passengers; Normal Crew Size: 416 (Dutch/Indonesian).

Specifics: Gross Tonnage 24,500; Length – 642 ft.; Width – 79 ft.; stabilizers;
fully air conditioned; 9 passenger decks; 3 elevators; 1 outside and 1 inside swimming
pool; gymnasium/sauna; outside staterooms; inside staterooms; 438 dining room
capacity; 330 theatre capacity.

Itinerary: 7-Day Bermuda Cruises from June through August. Also Grand Caribbean
Cruises from New York or Port Everglades.

VEENDAM

Leaves Miami. Built/Rebuilt 1958/1972-73. Registry: Panama. Capacity: 666
Passengers; Normal Crew Size: 340 (International).

Specifics: Gross Tonnage 23,500; Length – 617 ft.; Width – 88 ft.; stabilizers;
fully air conditioned; 7 passenger decks; 3 elevators; 1 outside and 1 inside swimming
pool; gymnasium/sauna; outside staterooms; inside staterooms; 350 dining room
capacity; 200 theatre capacity.

Itinerary: 14-Day Caribbean Cruises, Port of Calls Port-au-Prince, Montego Bay, Aruba,
La Guaira, St. Thomas, etc. Departures every other Sunday.

VOLENDAM

Sails from New York and Miami. Built/Rebuilt 1958/1972-73. Registry: Panama.
Capacity: 679 Passengers; Normal Crew Size: 340 (International).

Specifics: Gross Tonnage 23,500; Length – 617 ft.; Width – 88 ft.; stabilizers;
7 passenger decks; 3 elevators; fully air conditioned; 1 outside swimming pool;
gymnasium/sauna; outside staterooms; inside staterooms; 350 dining room capacity;
200 theatre capacity.

Itinerary: 7-Day Cruises every Sunday to the Caribbean; 7-Day Cruises every Sunday
to Bermuda.

HOME LINE CRUISES

DORIC

Sails from New York. Built/Rebuilt 1964/1976. Registry: Panama. Capacity: 720 Passengers; Normal Crew Size: 425 (Italian).

Specifics: Gross Tonnage 25,300; Length – 629 ft.; Width – 82 ft.; stabilizers; air conditioned; 10 passenger decks; 5 elevators; 2 outside and 1 inside swimming pools; gymnasium/sauna; outside staterooms; inside staterooms; 375 dining room capacity; 273 theatre capacity.

Itinerary: Weekly trips to Nassau and Bermuda leaving every Saturday. April to November. Winter Cruises to the West Indies.

OCEANIC

From New York. Built/Rebuilt 1965/1976. Registry: Panama. Capacity: 1,034 Passengers; Normal Crew Size: 600 (Italian).

Specifics: Gross Tonnage 39,241; Length – 774 ft.; Width – 97 ft.; stabilizers; air conditioned; 10 passenger decks; 4 elevators; 2 outside swimming pools; gymnasium/ sauna; outside staterooms; inside staterooms; 575 dining room capacity; 420 theatre capacity.

Itinerary: Late Autumn and Early Winter Cruises to the West Indies; Weekly Cruises to Nassau and Bermuda.

ITALIAN LINE CRUISES INT'L

GALILEO GALILEI

Leaves Genoa. Built/Rebuilt 1963/1979. Registry: Italy. Capacity: 900 Passengers; Normal Crew Size: 450 (Italian).

Specifics: Gross Tonnage 27,905; Length – 700 ft.; Width – 90 ft.; stabilizers; air conditioned; 8 passenger decks; 3 elevators; 2 outside swimming pools plus 1 for children; gymnasium/sauna (massages); outside staterooms; inside staterooms; 700 (two sittings) dining room capacity; 220 (two levels) theatre capacity.

Itinerary: 7-Days docking at Cannes, Barcelona, Palma de Mallorca, Bizerte (Tunis), Malta, Catania, Naples.

GUGLIELMO MARCONI

Built/Rebuilt 1963/1978. Registry: Italy. Capacity: 900 Passengers; Normal Crew Size: 450 (Italian).

Specifics: Gross Tonnage 27,905; Length – 700 ft.; Width – 90 ft.; stabilizers; air conditioned; 8 passenger decks; 3 elevators; 2 outside swimming pools plus one for children; sauna – massages; outside staterooms; inside staterooms; 700 (two sittings) dining room capacity; 220 (two levels) theatre capacity.

K LINES-HELLENIC CRUISES

MTS ATLANTIS

Sails from Piraeus and Athens. Built/Rebuilt 1965/1976/78. Registry: Greece.
Capacity: 296 Passengers; Normal Crew Size: 125 (Greek).

Specifics: Gross Tonnage 5,500; Length – 350 ft.; Width – 53 ft.; stabilizers;
air conditioned; 6 passenger decks, 1 outside swimming pool; gambling (slot machines);
outside staterooms; inside staterooms; 196 dining room capacity.

Itinerary: 3 and 4 day cruises to the Greek Islands and winter cruise programs to
the Eastern Mediterranean/Red Sea. Ports of Call Haifa, Israel, Limassol, Cyprus,
Safaga, Egypt, etc.

MS CONSTELLATION

Built/Rebuilt 1962/1979. Registry: Greece. Capacity: 402 Passengers; Normal Crew
Size: 200 (Greek).

Specifics: Gross Tonnage 12,500; Length – 450 ft.; Width – 62 ft.; stabilizers;
air conditioned; 8 passenger decks; elevators; gambling (slot machines/casino);
gymnasium/sauna; 2 outside swimming pools; outside staterooms; 290 dining room
capacity; 125 theatre capacity.

MTS GALAXY

From Piraeus, Agadir, and Athens. Built/Rebuilt 1957/1971. Registry: Greece.
Capacity: 286 Passengers; Normal Crew Size: 125 (Greek).

Specifics: Gross Tonnage 5,500; Length – 342 ft.; Width – 52 ft.; air conditioned;
6 passenger decks; stabilizers; 1 outside swimming pool; gambling (slot machines);
outside staterooms; inside staterooms; 210 dining room capacity.

Itinerary: Cruises to the Greek Islands and Turkey for 3 and 4 days. Some Ports of
Call Ephessos, Rhodes, Crete, Santorini, etc. 7-Day Atlantic Islands Cruises every
Wednesday, December through March. Some Ports of Call Santa Cruz, Las Palmas,
Puerto del Rosario, etc.

MTS KENTAVROS

Sails from Salonica. Rebuilt 1964/68. Registry: Greece. Capacity: 212 Passengers;
Normal Crew Size: 125 (Greek).

Specifics: Gross Tonnage 2,500; Length – 311 ft.; Width – 41 ft.; air conditioned;
5 passenger decks; outside swimming pool; gambling (slot machines); outside staterooms;
196 dining room capacity.

Itinerary: 7-Day Cruises every Saturday. Ports of Call Skopelos, Chios, Istanbul,
Lesbos, Lemnos, Mt. Athos.

MTS ORION

Built/Rebuilt 1952/1969/1978. Registry: Greece. Capacity: 243 Passengers; Normal Crew Size: 125 (Greek).

Specifics: Gross Tonnage 6,200; Length - 414 ft.; Width - 55 ft.; stabilizers; air conditioned; elevators; 6 passenger decks; 1 outside swimming pool; gymnasium/sauna; gambling (slot machines); outside staterooms; 212 dining room capacity.

NORWEGIAN AMERICA LINE

SAGAFJORD

From New York, Port Everglades, Tilbury (London) and Genoa on trans-Atlantic, South Africa, Mediterranean and Around-the-World voyages. Built/Rebuilt 1965/1977. Registry: Norway. Capacity: 475 Passengers; Normal Crew Size: 300 (Norwegian & Northern European).

Specifics: Gross Tonnage 24,000; Length - 620 ft.; Width - 82 ft.; stabilizers; air conditioned; 9 passenger decks; 4 elevators; 1 outside and 1 inside swimming pool; gymnasium/sauna; gambling; outside staterooms; inside staterooms; 500 dining room capacity; 240 theatre capacity.

Itinerary: North Cape, Egypt, Adriatic, Scandinavia, Baltic and Eastern Europe, etc.

VISTAFJORD

Leaves New York, Port Everglades, London. Built 1973. Registry: Norway. Capacity: 660 Passengers; Normal Crew Size: 370 (Norwegian & European).

Specifics: Gross Tonnage 25,000; Length - 628 ft.; Width - 82 ft.; stabilizers; air conditioned; 9 passenger decks; 6 elevators; 1 outside and 1 inside swimming pool; gymnasium/sauna; gambling; outside staterooms; inside staterooms; 700 dining room capacity; 240 theatre capacity.

Itinerary: Winter season 7 to 14-day cruises to Aruba, Colombia, Haiti, Jamaica, San Juan, St. Thomas, etc.

M/S SKYWARD

From Miami. Built 1970. Registry: Norway. Capacity: 724 Passengers; Normal Crew Size: 300 (Mixed Crew, Norwegian Officers).

Specifics: Gross Tonnage 16,250; Length - 525 ft.; Width - 75 ft.; stabilizers; fully air conditioned; 8 passenger decks; 4 elevators; health club and sauna; 1 outside swimming pool; gambling (slot machines only); outside staterooms; inside staterooms; 452 dining room capacity; 190 theatre capacity.

Itinerary: Every Saturday 7-day cruises to Cape Haitien, San Juan, St. Thomas, Puerto Rico.

M/S SOUTHWARD

Sails from Miami. Built 1970. Registry: Norway. Capacity: 738 Passengers; Normal Crew Size: 302 (Mixed Crew, Norwegian Officers).

Specifics: Gross Tonnage 16,607; Length – 536 ft.; Width – 75 ft.; stabilizers; fully air conditioned; 9 passenger decks; 4 elevators; 1 outside and 1 splash pool; health center and sauna; gambling (slot machines); outside staterooms; inside staterooms; 404 dining room capacity; 200 theatre capacity.

Itinerary: 7-Day cruises every Saturday to Cancun/Cozumel, Mexico; Grand Cayman Island; Ocho Rios and the Berry Islands.

M/S STARWARD

Leaves Miami. Built 1968. Registry: Norway. Capacity: 742 Passengers; Normal Crew Size: 250 (Mixed Crew; Norwegian Officers).

Specifics: Gross Tonnage 16,000; Length – 525 ft.; Width – 75 ft.; stabilizers; fully air conditioned; 8 passenger decks; 4 elevators; health club and sauna; 2 outside swimming pools; gambling (slot machines only); outside staterooms; inside staterooms; 450 dining room capacity; 200 theatre capacity.

Itinerary: 7-Days: Port Antonio, Ocho Rios, Port-au-Prince, Nassau and the Berry Islands.

PAQUET FRENCH CRUISES

MS AZUR

From Toulon and Piraeus. Built/Rebuilt 1971/1976. Registry: France. Capacity: 600 Passengers; Normal Crew Size: 210 (French).

Specifics: Gross Tonnage 11,600; Length – 465 ft.; Width – 72 ft.; stabilizers; fully air conditioned; 8 passenger decks; 3 elevators; 1 outside swimming pool; gymnasium; volleyball court and sauna; outside staterooms; inside staterooms; 258 plus 110 in Grill dining room capacity; 260 theatre capacity.

Itinerary: 13-Day Mediterranean Cruise to Katacolon, Piraeus, Kusadasi, Rhodes, Alexandria, Haifa, Messina and Capri.

DOLPHIN (PAQUET/ULYSSES CRUISE)

Built/Rebuilt 1956/1973. Registry: Panama. Capacity: 683 Passengers; Normal Crew Size: 280 (International).

Specifics: Gross Tonnage 12,500; Length – 501 ft.; Width – 65 ft.; stabilizers; fully air conditioned; 7 passenger decks; 1 elevator; 1 outside swimming pool; gambling (full casino); outside staterooms; inside staterooms; 380 dining room capacity.

MASSALIA

Sails from Marseille. Built 1971. Registry: France. Capacity: 650 Passengers;
French Crew.

Specifics: Gross Tonnage 10,513; Length - 465 ft.; Width - 71 ft.; stabilizers;
fully air conditioned; 6 passenger decks; 2 elevators; 1 outside swimming pool; outside staterooms; inside staterooms; 272 dining room capacity (68 - Grill; 158 Cafeteria).

Itinerary: Weekly sailings between Marseille and Malaga, Tangier, Casablanca.

MERMOZ

From Toulon, Calais, Marseille, Miami. Built/Rebuilt 1957/1970. Registry: France.
Capacity: 550 Passengers; Normal Crew Size: 230 (French).

Specifics: Gross Tonnage 13,800; Length - 530 ft.; Width - 66 ft.; stabilizers;
fully air conditioned; 5 passenger decks; 2 elevators; 2 outside swimming pools;
gymnasium/sauna; outside staterooms; inside staterooms; 470 (plus 180 Grill) dining
room capacity; 260 theatre capacity.

Itinerary: 7-16 Day cruises to Caribbean Islands, South America/Africa, Middle East
in the Autumn; Turkey, Iceland/Ireland/Spain.

M. S. RENAISSANCE

Sails Port Everglades. Built 1966. Registry: France. Capacity: 350 Passengers;
Normal Crew Size: 215 (French).

Specifics: Gross Tonnage 11,724; Length - 492 ft.; Width - 69 ft.; stabilizers;
fully air conditioned; 1 elevator; 2 outside swimming pools; gymnasium/sauna; 8 passenger decks.

Itinerary: 12 and 14 day cruises to San Juan, Guadeloupe, St. Thomas, Santo Domingo,
San Blas Islands, etc.

PRINCESS CRUISES

ISLAND PRINCESS

Leaves Los Angeles, San Francisco, Vancouver. Built 1972. Registry: Great Britain.
Capacity: 622 Passengers; Normal Crew Size: 300 (British & Italian).

Specifics: Gross Tonnage 20,000; Length - 550 ft.; Width - 80 ft.; stabilizers;
fully air conditioned; 7 passenger decks; 4 elevators; 2 outside swimming pools;
outside staterooms; inside staterooms; 342 dining room capacity; 280 theatre capacity.

Itinerary: Varied cruises to Acapulco, Caribbean, South America, Mexico, Transcanal;
summer offers cruises to Alaska/Canada; and fall has South Pacific cruises.

PACIFIC PRINCESS

Los Angeles, San Francisco, San Juan, Vancouver. Built 1971. Registry: Great
Britain. Capacity: 622 Passengers; Normal Crew Size: 300 (British & Italian).

Specifics: Gross Tonnage 20,000; Length – 550 ft.; Width – 80 ft.; stabilizers;
fully air conditioned; 7 passenger decks; 4 elevators; 2 outside swimming pools;
gymnasium/sauna; outside staterooms; inside staterooms; 342 dining room capacity;
280 theatre capacity.

Itinerary: Cruises to Mexico, Caribbean, South America, Alaska/Canada – Ports of Call
Victoria, Juneau, Ketchikan, Glacier, etc.

SUN PRINCESS

Los Angeles, San Juan, Vancouver. Built/Rebuilt 1972/1974. Registry: Great Britain.
Capacity: 700 Passengers; Normal Crew Size: 324 (British).

Specifics: Gross Tonnage 17,000; Length – 535 ft.; Width – 75 ft.; stabilizers;
fully air conditioned; 7 passenger decks; 4 elevators; 1 outside swimming pool;
gymnasium/sauna; outside staterooms; inside staterooms; 400 dining room capacity;
186 theatre capacity.

Itinerary: Winter and Spring 7-Day Caribbean Cruise with Ports of Call: Curacao,
Caracas, etc.; Summer-Fall Alaska/Canada Cruise; varied lengths with Ports of Call:
Victoria, Juneau, Ketchikan, Glacier Bay, Sitka, etc.

ROYAL CARIBBEAN CRUISE LINE

M/S NORDIC PRINCE

Sails Miami. Built 1971. Registry: Norway. Capacity: 750 Passengers; Normal Crew
Size: 320 (Norwegian Officers; Multinational Hotel Staff).

Specifics: Gross Tonnage 18,500; Length – 550 ft.; Width – 80 ft.; stabilizers;
air conditioned; 8 passenger decks; 4 elevators; 1 outside swimming pool; sauna/
massage center; outside staterooms; inside staterooms; 450 dining room capacity; 500
theatre capacity.

Itinerary: 14-Day cruise to the Caribbean with some Ports of Call: San Juan, St.
Thomas, Guadeloupe, Aruba, Port-au-Prince, etc.

M/S SONG OF NORWAY

From Miami. Built/Rebuilt 1970/1978. Registry: Norway. Capacity: 1,040 Passengers;
Normal Crew Size: 400 (Norwegian Officers, Multinational Hotel Staff).

Specifics: Gross Tonnage 23,005; Length – 635 ft.; Width – 80 ft.; stabilizers;
fully air conditioned; 8 passenger decks; 4 elevators; 1 outside swimming pool;
outside staterooms; inside staterooms; 610 dining room capacity; 500 theatre capacity.

Itinerary: 7-Day Caribbean Cruises every Saturday, docking at Puerto Plata, San Juan, St. Thomas.

M/S SUN VIKING

From Miami. Built 1972. Registry: Norway. Capacity: 750 Passengers; Normal Crew Size: 320 (Norwegian Officers, Multinational Hotel Staff).

Specifics: Gross Tonnage 18,500; Length - 550 ft.; Width - 80 ft.; stabilizers; air conditioned; 8 passenger decks; 4 elevators; 1 outside swimming pool; outside staterooms; inside staterooms; 450 dining room capacity; 500 theatre capacity.

Itinerary: 14-Day Cruises on Saturdays. Ports of Call: San Juan, St. Thomas, Martinique, Caracas, Aruba, Curacao, Port Antonio, Port-au-Prince.

ROYAL CRUISES LINE, INC.

M. S. GOLDEN ODYSSEY

Leaves Piraeus. Built 1974. Registry: Greece. Capacity: 460 Passengers; Normal Crew Size: 200 (Greek).

Specifics: Gross Tonnage 10,500; Length - 427 ft.; Width - 63 ft.; stabilizers; air conditioned; 4 passenger decks; elevators; gymnasium/sauna; outside swimming pool; outside staterooms; inside staterooms; 252 dining room capacity; 170 theatre capacity.

Itinerary: Varied two-week cruises. Eastern Mediterranean: to Kusadasi and Istanbul, etc.; Seas of Ulysses to Hydra, Mykonos Rhodes, etc.; and Black Sea & Greek Isles to Rhodes, Izmir, Constantza, etc.

ROYAL VIKING LINE

ROYAL VIKING SEA

Leaves San Francisco and Port Everglades. Built 1973. Registry: Norway. Capacity: 500 Passengers; Normal Crew Size: 300 (Norwegian & Mixed European).

Specifics: Gross Tonnage 22,000; Length - 583 ft.; Width - 83 ft.; stabilizers; fully air conditioned; 6 passenger decks; 5 elevators; 1 outside swimming pool, plus one dipping pool; gymnasium/sauna; outside staterooms; inside staterooms; 500 dining room capacity; 156 theatre capacity.

Itinerary: Most cruises between 10 and 39 days. Cruise Alaska/Canada; Around the World; British Isles/Norwegian Fjords; Caribbean; Mediterranean, etc.

ROYAL VIKING SKY

From San Francisco and Port Everglades. Built 1973. Registry: Norway. Capacity: 500 Passengers; Normal Crew Size: 300 (Norwegian & Mixed European).

Specifics: Gross Tonnage 22,000; Length - 583 ft.; Width - 83 ft.; stabilizers; 6 passenger decks; 5 elevators; fully air conditioned; 1 outside swimming pool with a dipping pool; gymnasium/sauna; outside staterooms; inside staterooms; 500 dining room capacity; 156 theatre capacity.

Itinerary: Varied length cruises. Cruises of Alaska/Canada; Around the World; Mediterranean, British Isles/Norwegian Fjords; Caribbean, etc.

ROYAL VIKING STAR

Sails from San Francisco and Port Everglades. Built 1972. Registry: Norway. Capacity: 500 Passengers; Normal Crew Size: 300 (Norwegian & Mixed European).

Specifics: Gross Tonnage 22,000; Length - 581 ft.; Width - 83 ft.; stabilizers; fully air conditioned; 6 passenger decks; 1 outside swimming pool; 5 elevators; outside staterooms; inside staterooms; 500 dining room capacity; 156 theatre capacity.

Itinerary: Worldwide cruising. Varied lengths of time. Cruises to Mediterranean, British Isles/Norwegian Fjords; Alaska/Canada; Around the World, etc.

SITMAR CRUISES

T.S.S. FAIRSEA

Leaves Los Angeles and San Francisco. Built/Rebuilt 1955/1971. Registry: Liberia. Capacity: 830 Passengers; Normal Crew Size: 500 (Italian).

Specifics: Gross Tonnage 25,000; Length - 608 ft.; Width - 80 ft.; stabilizers; fully air conditioned; 11 passenger decks; 3 elevators; 3 outside (1 for children) swimming pools; gymnasium/sauna; gambling (slot machines); outside staterooms; inside staterooms; 590 (two sittings) dining room capacity; 330 theatre capacity.

Itinerary: Cruises range from 7 to 14 days. Cruises to Mexico docking at some ports: Acapulco, Puerto Vallarta, Mazatlan, etc. Also cruises to Canada and Alaska: Vancouver, Juneau, Sitka, Glacier Bay, etc.

T.S.S. FAIRWIND

From Los Angeles, Port Everglades, and Fort Lauderdale. Built/Rebuilt 1956/1972. Registry: Liberia. Capacity: 830 Passengers; Normal Crew Size: 500 (Italian).

Specifics: Gross Tonnage 25,000; Length - 608 ft.; Width - 80 ft.; stabilizers; fully air conditioned; 11 passenger decks; 3 elevators; 3 (1 for children) outside swimming pools; gymnasium/sauna; gambling (slot machines); outside staterooms; inside staterooms; 590 (two sittings) dining room capacity; 330 theatre capacity.

Itinerary: 7-11 day cruises to Nassau, Cape Haitien, San Juan, St. Thomas, St. Maarten, Martinique, St. Lucia, ect. Also cruises to West Indies, South America, Mexico.

SUN LINE CRUISES

STELLA MARIS

Leave Venice and Nice. Registry: Greece. Built/Rebuilt 1960/1966. Capacity: 212 Passengers; Normal Crew Size: 100 (Greek).

Specifics: Gross Tonnage 4,000; Length - 300 ft.; Width - 45 ft.; stabilizers; air conditioned; 4 passenger decks; 1 outside swimming pool; outside staterooms; inside staterooms; 164 dining room capacity; 50 theatre capacity.

Itinerary: 7-Day Cruises in the spring and summer to the Aegean and Mediterranean. Some Ports of Call: Dubrovnik, Corfu, Elba, Costa, etc. and Tunix, Katakolon, Malta, etc.

STELLA OCEANIS

From Piraeus. Built/Rebuilt 1965/1967. Registry: Greece. Capacity: 318 Passengers; Normal Crew Size: 140 (Greek).

Specifics: Gross Tonnage 6,000; Length - 350 ft.; Width - 53 ft.; stabilizers; air conditioned; 6 passenger decks; 1 elevator; 1 outside swimming pool; Monte Carlo Room; outside staterooms; inside staterooms; 200 dining room capacity; 75 theatre capacity.

Itinerary: 4-Day cruise every Monday from April to September. Ports of Call: Hydra, Santorini, Heraklion, Rhodes, Ephessos, Mykonos.

STELLA SOLARIS

Sails Piraeus. Built/Rebuilt 1953/1973. Registry: Greece. Capacity: 650 Passengers; Normal Crew Size: 310 (Greek).

Specifics: Gross Tonnage 18,000; Length - 550 ft.; Width - 72 ft.; stabilizers; air conditioned; 8 passenger decks; 3 elevators; 2 outside swimming pools; gymnasium/ sauna; Monte Carlo Room; outside staterooms; inside staterooms; 420 dining room capacity; 275 theatre capacity.

Itinerary: 7-Day cruises leaving every Monday from April to September. Ports of Call: Heraklion, Santorini, Rhodes, Ephessos, Istanbul, Delos, Mykonos.